A New World in a Small Place

A New World in a Small Place

Church and Religion in the Diocese of Rieti, 1188–1378

Robert Brentano

With an appendix on the frescoes in the choir
of San Francesco, by Julian Gardner

UNIVERSITY OF CALIFORNIA PRESS

Berkeley / Los Angeles / London

4431

University of California Press
Berkeley and Los Angeles, California

University of California Press, Ltd.
London, England

©1994 by
The Regents of the University of California

Library of Congress Cataloging-in-Publication Data

Brentano, Robert, 1926–
    A new world in a small place : church and religion in the Diocese of
Rieti, 1188–1378 / Robert Brentano.
        p.   cm.
    "A Centennial book"—P.
    Includes bibliographical references and index.
    ISBN 0-520-08076-9
    1. Catholic Church.   Diocese of Rieti (Italy)—History   2. Rieti
Region (Italy)—Church history.   I. Title.
BX1547.R46B74   1994
282'.45624'09022—dc20   92-35862
                                                                              CIP

Printed in the United States of America
9 8 7 6 5 4 3 2 1

For Carroll

*For the sake of the good reputation of the
people of Rieti and the honor of the city
the man should not be tortured.*

Giacomo Leoparducci
18 July 1334

Contents

Illustrations

FIGURE

MAPS

Acknowledgments

The name of my friend Alberto Sestili should appear first in any list of people whom I thank for their help to me in my study of the diocese of Rieti. He has been in various ways my guide and host for many years; it was for example through him that I met the nuns of Santa Filippa Mareri, through him that I found the *cavèdano*. He made me feel at home in the Cicolano. He cannot be separated in my mind from three generations of the Colangeli family who were also hosts to me and my family at Rieti's Quattro Stagioni at the site of Giovanni Petrignani's San Giovanni Evangelista. To the convent of Santa Filippa itself I was first introduced, after being introduced to her by Alberto Sestili, by Suor Clotilda, my oldest friend in the convent; through her I met the archivist, Suor Gemma, and the abbess mother Margherita Pascalizi. They and the other nuns of their convent adopted me, fed me, chauffeured me about, talked to me and showed me their documents, and even let me talk about their saint at her shrine. I cannot ever thank them enough, but I hope that their redwood will grow very large as a sign of my thanks.

To Don Emidio De Sanctis who was canon archivist of the Archivio Capitolare when I first went to Rieti to check a document in the San Salvatore Maggiore dispute, to his memory, I owe very special thanks. Into the often closed archives he welcomed me, for many days in many years. When I came to Rieti with one or more of my children when they were small, Don Emidio welcomed them too and let them play in the archive room and draw at the table at which I worked, draw the views (now unfortunately much less beautiful) that they saw from the tower windows. To Don Emidio's brother Don Lino, who was, until he died, priest at San Francesco, I am also grateful. The actual doorkeeper of Don Emidio's archives was the cathedral sacristan, my friend Franco Strivati, who became my protector and, for example, continually worried that I would be locked all night in the archive tower above the sacristy after the finish of evening service. These are, or were, old friends from my earliest days at Rieti. To theirs many other names should be joined; one which must appear is that of Cesare Verani, a wise and learned local art historian, who particularly connects my first with my last days of Rieti work, and thus with the new world of serious young Reatine research historians. Among them Vincenzo Di Flavio first helped me with information and advice and early modern material from the episcopal archives, material of the sort increasingly visible in his own published work. To his name should be joined that of Andrea Di Nicola; the quality of the research of the two men is suggested by their joint publication, the excellent *Il Monastero di S. Lucia*. I should also thank Henny Romanin for his kindness, and very specially Roberto and Claudia Marinelli, for their help both in Rieti and Borgo San Pietro, and for the particular delight of Roberto's mind and eye as they appear in his various kinds of history, for example in his *Il Terminillo, Storia di una montagna*. Roberto and his colleagues in Rieti's Archivio di stato have given the face of Reatine local history a new expression. Roberto Messina has helped me in the Rieti Biblioteca Comunale. Don Giovanni Maceroni and Suor Anna Maria Tassi, now keepers of the capitular as well as the episcopal archives at Rieti, have shown me many kindnesses.

I should like to thank Rita Di Vito and the families of the Case Galloni, and Barbara Bini, who not only carted me around the countryside as she took handsome photographs for me but also lent us her house between Contigliano and San Pastore, with its views across the *conca* to Terminillo, during one perfect Eastertide. The sindaco, Augusto Mari, took me on a tour of the mountain communities and uplands above Petrella Salto. The learned local historian Evandro Ricci advised me about Secinaro history and took beautiful photographs of the town for me. Don Antonino Chiaverini sat me down in his parlor in Sulmona and brought me the cathedral's records of the visitation of 1356 and of the canonization of Peter of Morrone. In Penne, the archivist of the cathedral archives of Penne-Pescara, Don Giuseppe Di Bartolomeo, heroically arranged for me to use those archives, from his hospital bed, immediately after a serious motorcycle accident incurred during that priest's vigorous pursuit of the pastoral care of his wide-spread flock. The Marchesa Luigina Canali de Rossi, who made Rieti more resonant during my whole time there, talked to me about the Rieti that existed before it had had implanted on it its current road system and its post–World War I values. I should thank Canon Pietro Bedeschi for his help at Ìmola and Don Giorgio Fedalto for his help with Olema, Dottoressa Anna Maria Lombardo for her guidance among the notarial archives in the Archivio di stato at Rome and Richard Mather for showing me the archives of Vèroli.

Daniel Waley sent me encouragement and a valuable document from Siena. Arnold and Doris Esch made me sharpen my interest in the diocesan landscape. Charles McClendon took me back to Farfa. The art historians Gary Radke, Julian Gardner, and Luisa Mortari made me look better at the artistic relics of the thirteenth and fourteenth centuries at Rieti. Anthony Luttrell helped me in many ways and particularly in his insistence upon the importance of the Paris Rieti manuscript. Here I continue to be indebted, as I was in earlier work, to those major historians of Italy, my friends Charles Till Davis, Gene Brucker, Lester Little, Peter Herde, Edith Pasztor, Eve Borsook, Agostino Paravicini Bagliani, Stephan Kuttner, and Fra Leonard Boyle. But in this book I am also indebted to newer friends, mostly of Padua, whose example has much affected me and should have made me a much better historian than I am, first of all, Paolo Sambin, and men and women like Giorgio Cracco, Antonio Rigon, Fernanda Sorelli, Sante Bortolami, and, perhaps honorary Padovani, Giovanna Casagrande, and Mario Sensi. I very much wish that this long, long-awaited, and eccentric book could be a more decent reward for their efforts.

I want to thank Kaspar Elm for having lighted up Franciscan studies for us all, even when he is not being used directly, and David Burr for "showing" Franciscanism. And I particularly want to thank the young English evangelical Protestant missionary whom I met one dark Rieti afternoon as I waited for the archives to open and who told me of bringing Christ, now, to the thirsty hill villages.

I must thank William Bowsky, Duane Osheim, Randolph and Frances Starn, and Margaret Brentano for their very careful and generous reading of the long text, and for their many suggestions. I wish that I could have used their suggestions better. I also want to thank Gerry Caspary, Irv and Betsey Scheiner, Beth Berry, James Clark, Miriam Brokaw, Joanna Hitchcock, Jane Taylorson, Tony Hicks, and very specially Edith Gladstone, for their advice and help. Many of my colleagues in history at Berkeley have, with their warmth and tolerance, made it possible for me as for others to be, each of us, our own kind of historian (and use our own kind of grammar). Arnold Leiman has made me much more sophisticated in my thought about memory, and Steve Justice has in my thought about narrative, although neither may be overwhelmed by the level of sophistication I have actually achieved.

I thank the John Simon Guggenheim Memorial Foundation, the National Endowment for the Humanities, and the American Council of Learned Societies for the support they have given me, and for their patience.

This book is very much a family book. My children have grown up (and, two of them, become parents themselves) living with it. But it has been an extended family, including particularly the Toesca-Bertelli and the Weyer Davis—the wise and richly subtle parents have advised me, and the children have joined mine: Frank and Bernie, early experts on Saint Francis and Saint Anthony, as well as bats; Pierino, on the central Italian countryside and its artifacts, as well as trains. All of them became Reatines. My children, James, Margaret, and Robert, have made everything in life to which they were or are attached a joy—and that includes Rieti.

Note

In the period of this book the year in Rieti began on Christmas day, so that for example a date recorded as 27 December 1298 would be, according to modern reckoning, 27 December 1297. (Modern reckoning is used in this book.) By the late fourteenth century the church of Rieti's fiscal year began on 1 July, and elections of officers were set, at least in some recorded cases, for 15 June, Saint Vitus's day. The calendar of the church of Rieti was dominated by feasts of Christ-God and the Virgin, but the local importance of Saint Barbara (supposedly of Scandriglia) was again apparent by the later fourteenth century.

The unit of land measurement normal in preserved Rieti documents was the Reatine *giunta*; the modern Reatine giunta is 1,617.32 square meters, and the modern *coppa* of the area of Poggio Moiano is about 2,000 square meters. Although careful measuring of land areas is apparent in the area of Rieti by the mid-thirteenth century, there is no necessity or reason to believe that the giunta in the period of this book had a fixed measure; still, it was a recognizable description of surface area, and for arable flatland it was probably thought of as a space which would now be between 1,500 and 2,000 square meters.

The surface of the diocese has been changed by the adjustment of its river systems and the creation of lakes, like the Salto, as well as by the drying of the land in the *conca*. The area is subject to earthquakes; the highest part of the mountainous areas which surround the conca of Rieti is Terminillo, which at its highest peak is 2,213 meters above sea level.

A clause in the first Reatine statutes says that in Rieti and its district all kinds of money were current—*current omnia genera monetarum*— and in fact diversity of currencies (at least in describing value and price) is apparent from the beginning to the end of the period of the book: in an early text *denari provisini* (of Rome) and *denari papienses* (of Pavia) appear together (and see Spufford, *Handbook of Medieval Exchange,* 67, 104). But there were usual currencies: in 1337 *soldi provisini* are referred to as *olim usualis monete,* once usual, in a text that needs the explanation of memory, and by the turn of the century, around the year 1300, the money of Ravenna, *ravennantes* (plural), had become the usual money, and it had then a varying rate of about 35 of its soldi to a florin (Spufford, *Handbook,* 72), at a time when the provisini were moving uneasily between 30 and 34 soldi to the florin (Spufford, *Handbook,* 67–68). (All visible lira currencies followed the convention of 12 denari to the soldo and 20 soldi to the lira.)

The florin itself was very much present in Rieti, as this book should make clear, particularly in its discussion of wills. Complexity at Rieti was increased by the proximity of the kingdom of Naples with its *augustali, tareni* (*tari*), *uncie,* and *carlini.* Just after 1300 the uncia (at Naples) was worth slightly less than 5 florins and the augustale slightly more than a florin; the florin was worth slightly over 6 tareni, and was worth 13 carlini (Spufford, *Handbook,* 59, 62–63).

From the 1350s on, the chapter account books give exact prices for a number of commodities, articles, and kinds of labor which were bought or sold by the chapter. It is thus possible to examine fluctuations within years, over time, and in various locations and climates, of grains—wheat, spelt, barley, rye—and sometimes legumes—*fave, ceci*—as well as oil, wine, and must. From the end of the thirteenth century and the beginning of the fourteenth, wills give real or estimated prices and values for specific items. It is difficult to establish equivalence from these values, but a list of some of them may help anyone reading this book: in 1363, 8 quarters of wheat brought 4 lire, and one quarter 20 soldi, and 4 quarters of spelt brought 14 soldi 7 denari; in the same year the painter Jani got 8 soldi 6 denari for a *pictura* of the king, and Cola Andrea got 1 florin for the *pictura* of Saint John and Saint Mary by the crucifix, a dove and a cock (*palomba, gallo*) cost 5 soldi 3 denari, and a key for the campanile cost 7 soldi; in 1364 the supplies and work for a door for the campanile next to the bell cost 18 soldi; in 1358 the pay for the singers at the feast of the Purification was 2 soldi 10 denari, and the pay for Antonio who carried the cross for the Rogation procession was 3 soldi.

In 1318 and 1319, 10 giunte of arable and 3 giunte of vineyard or 100 florins seemed an appropriate endowment for a private chapel. In 1301 silver chalices were valued at 15 florins, and through the first half of the fourteenth century tunics as gifts for the poor or worthy ran from 20 soldi down to 10 soldi or less. In 1297 a breviary or missal could be valued at 26 florins, and in 1348 a country pig was worth a florin.

Previously published lists of Reatine bishops have been inexact. I hope that the revised list published here will be helpful to the reader. Previous maps of the thirteenth-century diocese of Rieti have, I think, been unjustified in their exactness. I hope that the map published here will at least warn the reader of that.

I have, here, used the title *dompno* as a quasi translation of *dompnus* and most frequently for ordained priests whose offices were not sufficiently high to demand a *dominus*, so, generally, for example, for prebendaries but not canons. I have quasi-translated the word *castrum*, when it refers to a town or community, as *castro*, in part because I think the evidently alluring, generally accepted concept of *incastellamento* is misleading.

I have kept Latin and Italian in the text, when I have kept it, because I wanted to retain sound or tone, or because I wanted the reader to see the word which I had seen, because I wanted that precision for him or her or because I wanted him or her to translate the word or phrase for him or herself in terms of its specific usage. I have tried to make all retained Latin or Italian clear in paraphrase or explanation.

I have repeatedly retained varying spellings, because I wanted readers to see that variation as part of the reality I was trying to recover and as something important to the way these Reatines thought and read and heard. I wanted the reader to know, also, that I did not really know whether Reatines heard *Mertones* or *Mercones*, for example.

Finally I must warn the reader that a book about this material, done from these sources, under the archival circumstances that prevailed, by me, virtually must contain errors; the seeming precision of my approach should not hide that. And I must say that a foreigner doing local history, which is headbreakingly broadly demanding in any case, is foolhardy— I would suspect that no non-Ohio Valleyan could ever capture the sound, smell, shade, taste of the Ohio Valley—but an American medievalist, who believes that real history is local history, is caught.

Revised List of the Bishops of Rieti, 1188–1378

Note: The works cited in brackets refer to nonexistent bishops of Rieti.

Adenolfo de Lavareta "electus" March 1188 (predecessor Benedetto, still active 1185), still "electus" 9 November 1194; "episcopus" 4 February 1195, still "episcopus" September 1212; retired to Tre Fontane

Gentile de Pretorio (canon of Capua) unconsecrated elect, active 3 March 1214

Rainaldo de Labro active 26 May 1215 – 25 July 1233, almost surely alive on 21 February 1234, dead by 25 January 1236

    [*Odo:* Ughelli, Eubel]

    [*Rainerio:* Ughelli, Michaeli, Register of Gregory IX (edited), Eubel]

Giovanni de Nempha active 8 August 1236 – 2 September 1240

Rainaldo Bennecelli active 9 May 1244 – 11 March 1246

Rainaldo da Arezzo, OFM active 17 April 1249 – 9 March 1250, resigned before 3 February 1252

Tommaso (corrector) 3 February 1252 – active 23 July 1262, pope writes to a bishop 23 May 1263, dead before 23 August 1265

Gottifredo (bishop of Tivoli) 23 August 1265 – active 1275/6, dead before 10 January 1276

    [Disputed election, 1276–1278; Capitular candidates: Giacomo Sarraceno (canon of Rieti); Benvenuto, OFM]

Pietro da Ferentino (Romano, Egiptius, bishop of Sora) 2 August 1278 – 22 July 1286, translated to Monreale

Andrea (Rainaldi, or Rainerii, bishop of Sora) 27 July 1286 – active 1292

Nicola, O. Cist. active 26 November 1294 – resigned after 24 December 1295

Berardo (bishop of Ancona) 4 February 1296 – active 24 May 1298, dead before 26 August 1299

Jacopo Pagani (canon of Toul) 26 August 1299 – active 4 April 1302, relieved for cause before 8 June 1302

Angelo da Rieti, OFM (bishop of Nepi) 8 June 1302 – thought to be alive 14 June 1302, dead before 3 August 1302

Giovanni Papazurri (bishop of Ìmola) 3 August 1302 – alive 26 June 1335, dead by 12 June 1336

    [*Raimondo:* Ughelli, Michaeli]

    [*Giovanni:* Ughelli, Michaeli]

Tommaso Secinari (canon of Rieti) elected before 3 August 1338, confirmed 7 December 1339, died 5 September 1341

    [*Nicola Rainoni* (canon of Lateran), elected 30 September 1341, not confirmed]

Raimond de Chameyrac (canon of Amiens) 5 August 1342 – active 17 December 1345, translated to Orvieto by 1 July 1346

Biagio da Leonessa, OFM (bishop of Vicenza) 24 October 1347 – died 30 April 1378

Introduction

Ignazio Silone's *Pane e vino* begins with the picture of old Don Benedetto as he sits, with his sister behind him, on the low wall of his
garden, in the shade of a cypress, with the black of his habit absorbed
and enlarged by the shade, as the two, brother and sister, look and listen
and wait for the small world of young men whom Don Benedetto has
touched to return to him.[1] It must be difficult for anyone writing about
central Italy not to try to kidnap Silone's Abruzzese place, topography
and people, his mixture of sacred and secular, and to enrich with it his,
the writer's, own work. Here there is an excuse.

This is a book about the diocese of Rieti (see maps 1 and 2), where
the provinces and ideas and speech of Umbria, Lazio, and Silone's
Abruzzi join one another, and where the papal states and the Neapolitan
Regno—and their currencies—once met (and, when they were joined,
resisted the joining with a blur of brigandage).[2] The book deals with
the period between 1188 and 1378, from the first known notice of one
bishop-elect, Adenolfo, to the death of another bishop, Biagio. It is a
book about religion in society, about that aspect of society (of the lives
of men living in groups) which finds its focus in religion and the church,
or perhaps more exactly about society as it can be seen in the shapes of
church and religion, as they look out and observe what of it they need
or can use. In this sense the book imitates the collecting gesture of Don
Benedetto. And if it seemed necessary to choose one part of the Reatine
church more physically to represent the old priest, it would be the chapter of the cathedral church of Rieti, the canons of the church of Santa

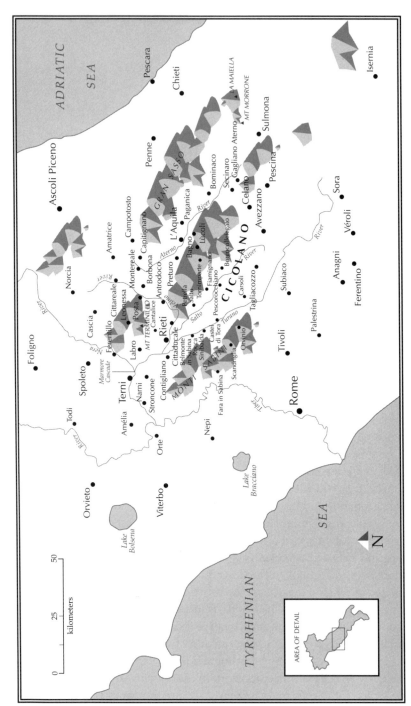

1. Central Italy.

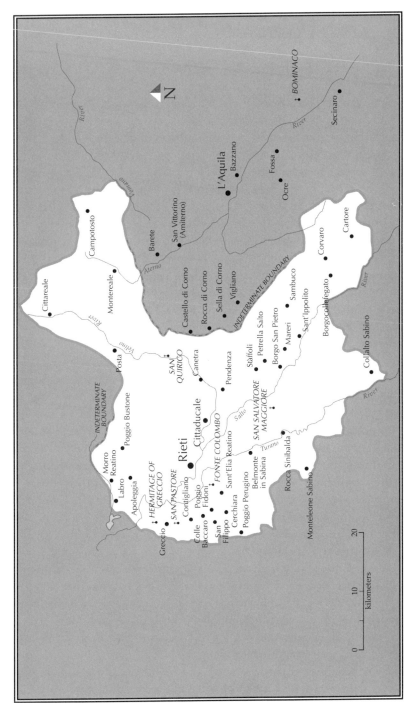

2. The thirteenth-century diocese of Rieti.

Maria, on the hill which dominates the city of Rieti at the diocese's center.

It is important for the purposes of this book to make clear that church and society are here not treated as, or believed to be, two different or separate entities, even ones seen as intricately interlocked. A more Scotist imagination is required. But, insofar as a formal separation is imaginable, the material here will show, abundantly and unsurprisingly, that ecclesiastical and secular, spiritual and material, body and soul, are very fully absorbed in each other. The most audibly spiritual bishop of Rieti from the period of this book, the Franciscan Rainaldo da Arezzo (who was active at Rieti in 1249 and 1250 and who had resigned the see before 3 February 1252), has left, or there have been left about him, the archival records of only two events during his short episcopate. One of these two is the bishop's dispute with the podestà of Rieti over who got the horse on which the podestà, or his servant, had led the bishop (echoing in the little distance emperor and pope) as he first came as bishop from the gate of the city to the church of Santa Maria.[3] Rainaldo did not long suffer a prelacy with this interpretation; but by the time of his resignation he had been forced to realize that being bishop of Rieti in 1249 involved riding on and litigating about a horse. Rainaldo and the horse show the uniting of spiritual and corporal at a high level, in high relief; but more regularly and more significantly the border between the two quietly shades into nonexistence, into the complexity of life lived by physical beings susceptible to spiritual aspirations and to the different complexity of spiritual acts performed with physical furniture: year after year during the last three decades of this book's time, the chapter's chamberlain, the (by then) canon Ballovino, made record in his accounts of the feast of the Assumption in August, but the memory recorded is the cost of the laurel bought for the feast, and of twine to bind the laurel into a form—in August 1364, for example, 10 soldi and 3 soldi 6 denari, respectively.[4]

Although this book is about a society as it is formed into a church, society is here interpreted as much as possible as a collection of, admittedly limitedly visible, individual men and women, at least in the first instance. Those moments when individual thirteenth- and fourteenth-century Reatines turn their minds' eyes toward the central religious problems of their lives, as when dying they make their wills, are particularly sought here. Many years ago my friend the historian Caecilia Weyer Davis asked me what I wanted to find out in doing the work for this book. Without thinking, I answered, "the color of men's souls." I may have succeeded in no cases, and in fact the phrase may be clear to no one else, but when I try to scratch at the evidence to see what is in the memory or mind of a farmer from the Cicolano come to give evidence before representatives of an ecclesiastical court, that is what I would most like to see.

Professor Weyer Davis's question was particularly pertinent because of the way the work for this book has proceeded. It began when I first came to Rieti in the 1960s to check the transcription of an edited document that I wanted to use for another book. I was immediately fascinated by the essentially unused thirteenth-century material of the Archivio Capitolare, then stored in a tower above the sacristy of the cathedral, into which the keeper of the archives, the canon Don Emidio De Sanctis, kindly admitted me. At first the city and diocese did not seem to me very striking; but their mild, persuasive attractiveness gained over the years such possession of me that I have found it hard to finish with them and go on to other work. From the beginning, and more so in the beginning, they suggested a place of which the history, or at least the ecclesiastical and religious history for a century or so, might be controlled by one person, who could observe all the surviving documents and monuments and topography.

That is what I wanted to do: to observe everything, and to decide after observation what questions could be, by me, most revealingly asked. I wanted the material to form the questions. I wanted to approach the existing remains like the kind of extreme physical archaeologist who would come to a site with no questions, which he could recognize as questions, formed in his mind. I realized, but of course insufficiently, the difficulties of the approach, but I had not realized that the questions formed by this kind of observation, questions to be used in going back through the material, might seem on their surface so disturbingly bland and obvious. In fact, that which I found most compelling was change over time, which would surely seem the most basic and obvious thing that every historian observes; although I generally have been more caught by the fascination of the other twin of the historian's constant pair, continuity. But this has come to be a book about how the church and religion changed over a period of almost two centuries in a specific place. That I have called an area as large as the diocese of Rieti "a small place" may seem odd; but there were not many people scattered over its difficult topography, and in spite of the repeated presence of the papal court in the city of Rieti, and even of Francis of Assisi, who was visibly present there, it was not in any normal sense, and certainly not more than episodically, an "important" place, or a rich one.

I have most frequently worked on the thirteenth century, and I had intended to study Rieti from the beginning of the papacy of Innocent III, in 1198, to the end of that of Boniface VIII, in 1303. The irresistibility of the fourteenth-century documents in the chapter archives changed my mind; and the interest, for me, of the men, three of them, who were the chapter's most important keepers of records between the 1260s and the 1370s, drew me into, and almost through, the fourteenth century—without, of course, endowing me with the knowledge and talents natural to real fourteenth-century historians.

Ballovino's account books in particular were the documents that drew me (with Bishop Biagio da Leonessa) across the Black Death and the changes it produced, or signaled, toward the end of the fourteenth century, as Matteo Barnabei's notarial cartulary, filled with a miscellany of church business, had drawn me into the fourteenth century. But the classes of individual documents which first drew me to Rieti—records of witnesses' testimony in litigations—and which have most held me there—wills and testaments—still seem to me most sharply, and at the same time resonantly, but not easily, revealing of what church and religion, and a lot else besides, meant there. They talk (in the heavily intrusive presence of the letter *u*) of envisaged space and remembered sensation. They give things names. And they give people names. And sometimes the names themselves are surprising in the memories they suggest, like the name of the rustic farmer Roland, who testified in a dispute over San Leopardo in Borgocollefegato in the Cicolano around the year 1210.[5]

The San Leopardo case, from almost the beginning of this book's period, is particularly pungent, with its remembered keys and bells, lunches and dinners, stories told and places stood, selected sacraments and clerical actions, and the relationships in which people were held and which other people remembered—Berardo, a knight, a blood relative of Bishop Dodone, remembering his own youth; Gisone, a member of the *familia* of the church of San Leopardo. Testimony in this case early indicates kinds of groupings that existed in society, that existed in people's memories, but also the kind of cross-hatching of the same individuals caught in various guises within different groups, which was characteristic of the recorded, remembered church in the diocese, this church with its intricate pluralism of benefices.

The talk, the conversation, within records of litigation and wills, however, is not free and open, not without rules and forms. The speech in these documents, and others, is shaped by questions asked, answers recorded, laws written, and presumably conventions understood. Aron Gurevich, with his translators (in his essay "The 'Divine Comedy' before Dante" from *Medieval Popular Culture*), talking of more clearly literary sources, has given us the helpful phrases of a formula: "A medieval author broke up a psychic experience, his own or someone else's, into semantic units meaningful for him, in accordance with an a priori scheme appropriate to the genre."[6] Both the record of witnesses' testimony and clauses recording bequests in wills break up the experience of memory, and also of expectation, and the sensation of piety, into semantic units with a priori schemes appropriate to their genres. They are elaborately shaped by forms. But, in spite of this, and in fact partly because of it, they break open the past and let its internal treasure spill out before the observer's eyes.

The language implied by the nature of the information found in wills and litigation documents is connected with the more generally accepted structure of language, of communication, for many kinds of (at least nonacademic) statement for essentially the entire period of this book, in central Italy (and many elsewheres).[7] Within the cage of formality, reality is described in the witness's or testator's memory's narrative and in the testator's more limited narrative of action predicted after his death. The *Scripta Leonis*, the collection of stories about Francis meant to show what he was like, recorded in the 1240s from the memories of his old companions at the hermitage of Greccio, within the diocese and a few miles from Rieti, offers a model of reality. Truth is description. Description is stories. Truth is stories. And it begins with *et*:

Et sedens cum illo fratre iuxta uitem cepit de uuis comedere ut non uerecundaretur solus comedere; et manducantibus illis laudauit Dominum Deum frater ille . . .

[And] Sitting with the friar by the vine, he began to eat grapes so that he should not be embarrassed at eating alone. As they ate the grapes, the friar praised God . . . [8]

Francis is the sitting, the eating, the inducing without embarrassment, the praising, the vernacular caught within the transparent skein of the Latin. In the contemporary sources used in this book one hears in smaller fragment the syntax shaped by the generally unstated assumption that this is a likely way to think or talk if you want to arrive at truth or knowledge (although this smaller fragment of syntax is not infrequently caught between the heavy binding, stated or presumed, of protocol and eschatocol, flourished invocation and validating seal). This antique assumption is also in large part the assumption of this book— the truth about the Reatine church, its description with any kind of exactness, could come only from a recapturing of its exact narrative syntax and a maintaining of the exact patterning of its images. (Thus there may seem a kind of irony in my citing Gurevich's stimulating book, so wrongly, I think, dedicated to the general and the collective.)

Even the soundest-seeming generalizations about change (for example: by the middle of the thirteenth century what had once been experimental religious experience was more and more channeled into institutions by then formed) are not crisply descriptive in a way that the specific statement of expenses from the Chapter Account Book written by a new chamberlain in the year after this book closes, for 1379–80, are.[9] They seem to sum up the church of this book, what it has become:

Item pro palmis   xx s

Item dedi dominus Agabitus de Columpna de pecunia Camere   flor xxvii s xiii d vi

Item pro una Crux pro altari magno   xii s

Item dedi Lucia pro aqua pro mensibus Octubris Nouembris Dicembris viiii s

Item pro una Ocha pro Sancta Barbara   v s

But even these items are chosen selectively, climbing up folio 62r of Don Agostino's account: the palms, the big money (in florins) for a Colonna (in his maintained nominative), the cross (also nominative) for the high altar, the money for Lucia (also undeclined) for water, the goose for Saint Barbara's day.

Seeing everything unadjusted, all together, the impossible, would be most desirable, so that one could find what Paolo Costantini, in the catalog for *L'insistenza dello sguardo*, has suggested photography can do: "La fotografia ha il potere di suggerire altre indicibili realtà celate sotto una minuziosa descrizione superficiale."[10] The depth of reality and interrelationship is strongly suggested by a meticulous description of surface, including light seen on the surface within the photograph, as again and again the photographs of *L'insistenza dello sguardo* demonstrate. The "minuziosa descrizione superficiale" is also, though, a potential tool for the description of change. In fact the most effective model for me for understanding change, in classes, in thinking about this book, has been a pair of photographs, taken fifteen years apart by

Italo Zannier, one of the composers of *L'insistenza dello sguardo*. He presents to his viewer the same woman, in the same pose, in the same room, in the same Friuli village house, in Claut, younger and older, in the presence of changed and rearranged furniture (plate 1).

To the Scotist one would like to add an Occamist imagination, reticent about anything but the particular. And reading the account books year after year, one can get the impression that one has done this. Sometimes, moreover, like the headlights in a photograph, individual entries suggest, in their emphasis, movement within the books' own flat surfaces. This happens on folio 61v of Don Agostino's 1379 account, a book that in general has few days and no hours:

Item: on the 17th day of the month of September, Saturday, at noon was broken the *naticchiam* [metal guard bar] of the mill of Santa Lucia; and the same day it was repaired.[11]

However, my attempt to capture the sort of change that occurs in the room at Claut is of quite a different kind, and is in, or is meant to be in, the tradition of Frederic William Maitland. The "rooms" to which this book will most carefully attend are words, big central defining words, like *bishop, diocese, boundary, testament,* and even bigger ones like *death* and by inference at least the biggest of all, *Christ* and *God.* The book will try to watch and show the changes that occur within the walls of these words.

Fortunately for the sake of this image, or for movement within it, walls change too. Within the period in which the definition of *bishop/episcopus/ vescovo* is swelling, significant churches become large. Two major monuments from the diocese of the period of this book are the small, relic-holding country church of Santa Vittoria in Monteleone Sabina (plates 2 and 3) and the great preaching church of Sant'Agostino in Rieti (plates 4 and 5). The full length of the boxlike structures assembled into Santa Vittoria is less than 30 meters; the open length of Sant'Agostino without its apse chapels is over 50 meters. The breadth of Santa Vittoria's facade is about 9 meters and Sant'Agostino's about 16; the main entry door of Santa Vittoria is 155 centimeters wide, Sant'Agostino's 275 centimeters. Santa Vittoria and Sant'Agostino represent different periods, different uses, and different notions about church—it is not just as C. N. Brooke once wrote, rather lightly, that "the sentiment for worshiping in tiny boxes as well as in enormous cathedrals can be paralleled everywhere." And the clearest change in the definition of the biggest words may in fact be pictorial or plastic, as in the quite startling differences between two public Christs, now both preserved in the Museo del Duomo at Rieti, the earlier a thirteenth-century fresco from an external wall of a church in Canetra (plate 6), the other a fourteenth-century piece of sculpture in wood, polychrome, until quite recently used for processions in the village of Sambuco (plate 7).[12]

A New World in a Small Place is divided into eight chapters. Chapter 1 is meant to be an introduction to the syntax, the vocabulary, the terms of the problems of the book: what is the church, and the religion, that is being considered here? what is change? what is the place, the diocese of Rieti, in which it is occurring? Chapter 2 is meant to be a lens through which "church" can be seen: two senses of *church* defined by the roughly contemporary actions, words, and memories (or reconstructions of memory) of two sets of actors on roughly adjacent, and sometimes identical, physical parts of the diocese. These chapters are meant to supplement each other and introduce the rest. Chapters 3 and 4 try in a number of very different ways to define "diocese" and "diocesan boundary"; they mean to describe change. The governmental and record-keeping change described in these chapters is probably the most obvious event of this book's narrative. Insofar as a world can be expressed by governmental self-consciousness, the Reatine diocesan world of the mid-fourteenth century is new and clearly different from that of the early thirteenth century. Its newness, moreover, is connected with newness in many other places. I have tried, however, in chapters 3 and 4, the concluding and beginning dates of which do not quite meet, to show, in dividing, a change in the nature of change, in its pace and material, and in the sources which reveal it. (And certainly a reader might have thought 1254, the date of Bishop Tommaso's verbal map, a more appropriate first ending than 1266, a point in the continuing removal of Amiterno to L'Aquila.)

Chapter 5 considers variety in the persons of bishops, the counterpoint of man against institution. Chapter 6 examines the stability of the cathedral chapter, whose members were more long-lasting and conservatively local than were the bishops, and compares the chapter with other ecclesiastical institutional groups like monasteries and houses of friars. Chapter 6 is meant to restate the descriptive argument of chapter 1, at a different level, with different intensity and depth, guided by the nature of the book's dominant institution, the cathedral chapter; chapter 6 means, in the rather plain imagery of institutions, to push hard to reveal the way in which forces for conservation and change worked against and with each other.

Chapter 7 deals directly with sanctity and heresy, twin expressions of relatively extravagant religiosity, particularly through the examination of one woman saint and one man heretic, and reactions to them. The heretic produces more talk; there is more sound around him; and, although it is almost entirely Latin talk, that does not entirely obscure the Italian sound beneath it. The heretic in his parody of sanctity and others' reaction to this parody offers a kind of diagram of what sanctity or at least piety have become, a century after Francis's death; the reaction to reaction offers, too, a new diagram of Reatine society in which the doors of city dwellings are hooked together by spreading gossip and begging friars, who go among them *hostiatim*. The heretic's world is both denser and more mobile than the saint's. The saint and the heretic are meant to suggest what, in a way, has become of the contrasting pair of participants in chapter 2, and to state again, in a different way, the counterpoint of chapter 5.

Finally, chapter 8, with at its center the examination of men's and women's wills, tries to bring together, around the examination of these articulate documents, what has been happening in this place during these centuries. I have chosen to describe here those wills, out of the larger group of wills, that seem most effectively to display what is new, and I think significant, so that they may stir to life this place, by now established, I hope, and do that particularly by showing what has become of the imitation of Christ. More generally I have tried to recall in specific person and image the themes and counterthemes of the book, to talk of religion, and to return the narrative, its themes and counterthemes, to the reality of specific place.

This outline has not suggested that the book will include a specific examination of lay or popular piety. I hope that by the time he or she has finished the book, the reader will realize why I think such considerations are generally mistaken and destructive. The outline does not refer to comparisons with other places, other times. This is a book about Rieti in the thirteenth and fourteenth centuries; it is local. Making it just that has been a hard choice, particularly for a historian constantly tempted to comparison. It can be seen formally as the third part of an informal trilogy: the first book was about one part of the English church; the second compared the English and Italian churches in general; the present book is about one part of the Italian church. But more choice is involved than this implies.

There are very important elements of church and religion that are almost, if not entirely, invisible in Rieti documents: confraternities, for example, hardly appear at all, although their existence is clear. It is tempting to talk of what they must have been like, with evidence from other places—a normal thing to do, particularly in an age of anthropological history. But I have decided, as much as I can, except for that comparison necessary for definition, to stay within my own evidence, even when it is meager. The value of local history is, I think, to show what its historian thinks he knows happened, knows existed, in its one place—to offer that pure to other historians—not to fill in what must have happened, what reasonably would have happened. But this is a pattern that is very hard to follow, like pure nominalism, perhaps impossible—and what historian of the canons of Rieti could keep his eyes from wandering to the documents about the canons of Narni? Who can think of Filippa Mareri and Paolo Zoppo and not have in his mind Margherita Colonna and Peter of Morrone? And frescoes are not bound by diocesan borders.

Finally, I would like to protect whoever reads this book before he or she reads it, by putting in the reader's mind two kinds of confusion, which may help to keep him or her from finding evidence of religious activity too direct, from thinking time and memory are too straightforward, from accepting answers that are too solid and clear.

In his parchment cartulary, under the date 7 May 1315, Matteo Barnabei recorded that, in the *proaulo* (portico) of the papal palace at Rieti, Nevecta Gentiloni Petri Johannis once of Labro gave in perpetuity to the bishop (then Giovanni Papazurri), for the church of Rieti, a house and lot in the Porta Cintia de sopra, in the parish of San Donato, on the hill, but that she reserved for herself and her two nieces Johandecta and Nicolutia Petroni Nicolai once of Greccio, habitation in the house for the span of their lives that they might live there as in a hermitage or anchorage (*in carcere*), and that she did this out of love of the church of Rieti and for her soul and for the remission of her sins. She with bended knee begged the bishop to accept the house and grant the anchorage; he in turn accepted and granted with the provision that the women should accept no other person to the place, with, among other witnesses witnessing, the nieces' father, Petrono Nicolai once of Greccio. It seems a moving enough little story—three women with their small-town heritages (Labro, Greccio) struck by the desire to live holy lives apart, closed within their own house, or the aunt's house, in the city parish of San Donato.[13]

But a few folios later Matteo recorded another action. On 16 August, still in 1315, Janductio the painter, formerly of the city of Rome, but then a resident of Rieti, received the house back in Nevecta's name. The bishop, in the presence of sixteen canons of whom one, Ventura "Raynerii," objected to the act, gave back the house for two stated reasons: because the house was obliged to another for debt; and because the house and contrada were not appropriate (*decens*) for an anchorage.[14] What exactly is hidden behind the words of obligation for debts and of inappropriate place, and behind Ventura's objection, cannot be surely known. But one thing is certain: the action in August casts in doubt and complicates our understanding of the simple-seeming act of piety in May.

In 1224 the religious house of San Quirico near Antrodoco within the diocese of Rieti was engaged with the bishop of Penne in a struggle about jurisdiction over a group of churches locally within the diocese of Penne.[15] Among these was the twelfth-century collegiate church of Santa Maria di Ronzano near Castel Castagna, which with many of its twelfth-century frescoes still survives. One of these frescoes, from the Old Testament cycle, the creation of the world (plate 8), offers a last opportunity for warning the reader about the complexity of memory and time, the inventiveness to which both of these concepts, both continually important to this book, are susceptible. The God who creates the world of the fresco is Christ, the Redeemer, with the wounds from the nails clearly apparent in His hands and feet. The world He creates is a disc within a circling firmament decorated with heavenly bodies. The disc itself is cut as if by the letter X into four parts, of which the top three represent aspects of earthly nature. In the fourth a man brandishing an axe, as if to clear for planting, stands behind a pair of oxen pulling a plow: that is, a representation of the labor to which humankind was driven after the Fall.[16] No one who recalls the close connection between Incarnation and Crucifixion will be completely surprised by this kind of juxtaposition. But it serves, I think, as a cautionary exemplum. The memories, or reconstructed memories, of the people of this book, which recall the past of their own and earlier lives, sensible and generally trustworthy as they usually seem, live in a world of higher memory, the sequences of which are not always measured by succeeding days and hours.

1. The same woman in the same room in the Valcellina village of Claut in the Friuli (a) in 1962 and (b) in 1976. Photographs by Italo Zannier. Reproduced by permission.

2. Facade and north flank of the rural church of Santa Vittoria near Monteleone Sabina reconstructed under Bishop Dodone in the mid-twelfth century. Photograph by Barbara Bini.

3. The early country apse of Santa Vittoria near Monteleone Sabina with surrounding olive trees and landscape. Photograph by Corrado Fanti, reprinted from Marina Righetti Tosti-Croce, ed., *La sabina medievale* (Milan, 1985), by permission of the Cassa di Risparmio di Rieti.

4. Facade and south flank of the late thirteenth- and early fourteenth-century urban Augustinian Hermit's (friar's) church of Sant'Agostino, Rieti, with its campanile. Photograph by Barbara Bini.

5. The late city apse of Sant'Agostino within the thirteenth-century walls of Rieti. Photograph by Corrado Fanti, reprinted from Marina Righetti Tosti-Croce, ed., *La sabina medievale* (Milan, 1985), by permission of the Cassa di Risparmio di Rieti.

6. Fresco of Christ blessing, removed from the external wall of the small church of San Sebastiano in Canetra, thought to be thirteenth-century, now in the museum of the cathedral of Rieti. Photograph by Luisa Mortari, reprinted from Luisa Mortari, *Il tesoro del duomo di Rieti* (Rome, 1974), courtesy of the Istituto Centrale per il Catalogo e la Documentazione, Rome.

7. Madonna and Child, portable statue (130 cm in height) in wood polychrome, from the parish church of Santa Maria di Sambuco near Fiamignano in the Cicolano, removed for restoration after heavy and prolonged resistance by the parishioners, and now in the museum of the cathedral of Rieti. Photograph by Corrado Fanti, reprinted from Marina Righetti Tosti-Croce, ed., *La sabina medievale* (Milan, 1985), by permission of the Cassa di Risparmio di Rieti.

8. Creation of the World, twelfth-century fresco from Santa Maria di Ronzano near Castel Castagna. Photograph reprinted from Guglielmo Matthiae, *Pittura medioevale abruzzese* (Milan: Electa, n.d.).

CHAPTER ONE

The Nature of Change, of Place, of Religion

In the very last years of the thirteenth and the first decades of the fourteenth centuries, in Rieti, three men made wills, specific and worrying and personal, which still reveal something of the quality of that part of each of their minds which can reasonably be called "soul." The first of these men was Nicola Cece, a citizen of Rieti but formerly of neighboring Apoleggia, who made a will in 1297, added to it a codicil in 1300, and wrote a new will in 1301; and he made the two wills in the refectory and chapter house of Sant'Agostino, Rieti.[1] The second was Giovanni di don Pandulfo Secinari, or de Secinaro, who made his will in the house of his dead father's sons (one of whom would become bishop) in Rieti, in 1311, but who placed in that will memories of his family's place of origin, Secinaro, across the border of the kingdom of Naples in the diocese of Sulmona.[2] The third was Don Giovanni di magistro Andrea, a canon of Rieti, who made his will in his own house in Rieti in 1319.[3] These wills form an articulate centerpiece in an arc of religious and ecclesiastical history which stretches from Pope Innocent III's heroic pronouncing and defining Fourth Lateran Council in 1215 to the beginning of the papal schism in 1378, and which stretches, with different emphasis and slightly different dating, from Francis of Assisi's brilliant (and, like the Lateran, remembered) presence in the diocese of Rieti in the years before his death in 1226 to the death of the third, and seemingly conventionally successful, Franciscan bishop of Rieti in an earlier part of 1378.

In spite of the sense of decline that one must get from seeing the

Schism and a conventional Franciscan bishop put next to, or rather following at a distance, the Fourth Lateran and Francis of Assisi, this arc or line of almost two hundred years was in a number of ways, some of which were very important, a line of, to use a word generally disliked by medievalists, progress. In 1227 in a precisely, but in a rather clumsily decoratedly formal, imperfect document, vertical, in an almost too careful curial hand, the Reatine citizen and scribe (*scriniario*), Magister Matteo, wrote that in his presence Abassa Crescentii had given a letter sealed with the seal of the bishop of Narni to Bertuldo the son of the by then dead Corrado once duke of Spoleto. And Bertuldo had asked, "What is this letter?" And Abassa had answered that it was a letter which pertained to the case between Bertuldo and the church of Santa Maria of Rieti. Bertuldo had not wanted to take the letter, and he had said to Abassa, "Go and stick the letter up the *culo* of an ass."[4]

In contrast with this blunt command and the document in which it is preserved, one finds the epistolary elegance of formal and verbal content in letters to the church of Rieti from two neighboring territorial noble houses, the Mareri and the Brancaleone di Romagnia, who dominated the southeastern and the southern parts of the diocese in the mid-fourteenth century. These letters, about clerical livings, were written by baronial chancellors of humane accomplishment. They are small and beautiful and sealed with small and beautiful seals; and in them graceful phrase succeeds to graceful phrase. Most elegantly perfect of all perhaps is a paper letter of 1346 (but itself too elegant to bear a year date, only the indiction and the month and day), small (29 × 18 cm), horizontal, with a tiny (1.8 cm in diameter) black seal *en placard*, from Nicola de Romagnia, in Belmonte, exercising his right of patronage over the church of Santa Rufina in Belmonte and presenting to the chapter (*uenerabilibus hominibus*) for that living, dompno Francesco di Sebastiano of Belmonte, and in this matter, *reuerendam et uenerabilem paternitatem et amicitiam uestram affectuose rogantes*.[5]

The contrast between *Uade et mitte* (go and stick) and *affectuose rogantes* (affectionately asking), which seems starkly to juxtapose a bear-like Germanic baron, old style, just stumbling out of his cave, and the Angevin elegance, almost perfumed, of a lord of Romagnia sitting in his airy view-filled palace on the pleasant heights of Belmonte, exaggerates. The Urslingen Bertuldo and the Brancaleone Nicola were both in their ways trying to maintain and protect their rights in property, including ecclesiastical property, and to ensure, presumably, the continued inheritance and prestige of their clans. It should be remembered that during the period of mid-fourteenth-century central Italian raids and wars, physical savagery was not dead, and that it would be hard to make a case for its declining, and that the first bishop of Rieti actually to be *freddato*, murdered or assassinated, would be Ludovico Alfani in 1397 in a reaction against the growing tyranny of his, the Alfani, family.[6] Nevertheless the difference between "affectuose rogantes" and "uade et mitte" does signal a real change in Reatine communal and ecclesiastical behavior, a normalization, perhaps even civilization, certainly bureaucratization, which occurred between the early thirteenth and the late fourteenth centuries.

When the first at all complete surviving official records of Reatine communal discussion and action, the Riformanze of 1377, appear, they are productions of accustomed professionalism, elegant, beautifully written and composed by a communal chancellor, Giacomo di fu Rondo, of Amelia, a writer of considerable accomplishment, able exactly to describe the four horses assigned to him by the podestà.[7] In the presence of serious threats and dangers, like the lurking and threatening *societas italicorum* in Leonessa, the faulty state of fortifications, the lacerations left from recent violent disputes between Guelfs and Ghibellines (and the distinction between these parties, like that between noble and non-noble, is apparent and assumed when the Riformanze commence), and in spite of the expressed worry that since Pope Gregory would be returning into Italy reform would undoubtedly (*absque dubio*) be demanded of the city and citizens of Rieti, the chancellor Giacomo, or he who dictated to Giacomo, was not only capable of phrases like "quod omnes tangit ab omnibus approbetur," but also of finding that the greatest fortification that any city can have is concord, and stating the belief that great concord can naturally follow great discord, as after the tempest comes the calm and "post nubilem dat serenum."[8] All this, including the elaborate governmental structure which the Riformanze record, is unthinkable of the primitive communal government established under Innocent III, when Berardo Sprangone (or Sprangono), a local scriniario and judge, almost omnipresent in the documents of the church of Rieti in various guises but chiefly as authenticating scribe, seems to have become the first podestà.[9]

The development that the first Riformanze indicate, which is a development of surface, but not only of surface, is one which occurs, or is parallel to one which occurs, not only in ecclesiastical structure—in the actual organization and in the recording of church government—but in religion itself, in the pattern and space of religious exhilaration.

This is most obviously connected with the kind of pastoral reform which was pressed forward by the Fourth Lateran Council and by the coming, the influence, and the changing nature of the orders of friars—in Rieti most particularly the Franciscans, but also the Dominicans and the Augustinian Hermits. Inseparable from the friar's presence and pastoral reform was the changing interpretation of Christ's message, particularly through Matthew, and the changing understanding of Christ's self— even, again, in the way He looked, in image, out upon His people, and the way His earthly houses changed as they became in a new way His houses. They, these houses, changed physically and noticeably, particularly at Rieti in the creation of the great open, internal spaces of the churches of San Francesco, San Domenico, and Sant'Agostino, which were placed at three points on the periphery of the growing city, in the area between the old walls and the new thirteenth-century walls, as those walls were being built.[10]

This development is present in wills. From 1371 one finds a record of part of the execution of the will of Pietro Berardi Thomaxicti Bocchapeca, *alias* Pietro Jannis Cecis, of the city of Rieti, in which will, the document says, *multa fecit legata*, he made many legacies; and one was for the dowries of orphans, or the dowry of an orphan, or of a poor woman. Pietro's executors, among whom the presence of his wife, Colaxia, is emphasized, in order quickly and well to execute his will, searched vigorously through the city of Rieti, *pluries et pluries*, for poor orphans, and they found Stefania, daughter of the by then dead Gianni di Andrea Herigi; she was a poor, wretched, orphaned person, lacking a father, and a person of good reputation (*personam pauperem, miserabilem, orfanam, et patre carente et personam honestam*). The executors settled upon her for her dowry a piece of vineyard in the Contrada Coll'Arcangeli.[11] This testamentary action is, in its way, fully expressed Christian charity of the new sort.

Pietro's, and Colaxia's, is a kind of charity, of interpretation of Christ, much more specific and extended than that suggested by the first relatively long and fully stated will which survives from after the coming of Adenolfo to the bishopric and Innocent III to the papacy, the will of Fragulino, written and authenticated by Berardo Sprangone in 1203. This Fragulino, a man of considerable property, was certainly the same Fragulino who is recorded as having been a consul of the city in 1188 and 1193, and so a man who connected the new governmental world of Berardo Sprangone with that which existed before Innocent III's reforms—a figure who shows continuity, a continuity extended by the appearance of Fragulino's son, Berardo Fragulini, who gave gifts inter vivos for the sake of his father's soul and his own in 1206.[12]

Fragulino thought of his soul. He left the church of San Ruffo in Rieti 20 soldi for his soul. Without specifying purpose he left 20 soldi to the relatively aristocratic San Basilio of the Hospitallers, and one soldo to San Salvatore, presumably to the great Benedictine monastery south of Rieti and physically within the diocese. For what ought to come to him from the will of his brother Pietro Zote he made the church of Santa Maria his heir for his brother's soul and his own. He left more actual and residual money to Santa Maria and its clergy, 40 soldi (provisini) for the clergy and 14 lire (provisini) for the rebuilding (*refectionem*) of the church. To the hospital *capitis Arci* he left 5 soldi. An uncertain but suggestive spiritual profile is drawn: family; attachment to the parish of San Ruffo, and perhaps to its neighborhood extending to San Basilio, with its tone of caste; a nod to a great old Benedictine monastery; and serious money for the cathedral church of Santa Maria particularly for building at what was probably a crucial point in the church's long building campaign. To this is added the 5 soldi for the hospital. These 5 soldi are in the line of the interpretation of Christ which will send Colaxia again and again through the city of Rieti searching for a poor orphan girl. But in the Fragulino will the interpretation of Christ remains relatively mute. One must imply the Christ of corporal acts of mercy, the Christ of Cana, who directly or indirectly provoked the soldi's giving.

The development from Fragulino to Pietro and Colaxia, however, is not so simply one of opening and blossoming as it at first may seem. Pietro's charity, or at least Colaxia's and her colleagues', is caught in a specifically institutional container. Stefania's vineyard dowry is to be hers only if, within two years time, she enters a monastery of nuns within, or in the immediate neighborhood of, Rieti, and takes her vineyard dowry to that monastery, and if she then dwells in habit there like the other nuns. If Stefania fails in this, the vineyard in Coll'Arcangeli is to go instead to a house of Dominican nuns, Sant'Agnese near Rieti.

Between the making of Fragulino's will and the execution of Pietro's, the great majority of religious thoughts, of those spasms of momentary piety, devotion and charity, which, within the diocese of Rieti, affected men's and women's minds and behavior, are of course untraceable. It might seem impossible with so much lost to try to sketch a line of development in this gauzy material; it is tempting to let it rest and to look only at the relatively solid lines of developing government and institution. But these latter things are inextricably connected with personal piety, and they lose their meaning if they are detached from its more nebulous material. Besides, much does remain, and much that is poignant and moving as well as puzzling.

This pious and testamentary development took place in and around the small urban capital, Rieti, of a big rustic diocese which stretched to different distances in all directions from the city. In its specific Reatine form the development is inseparable from the place in which and the people among whom it took place. Even in thinking as narrowly as one could about Reatine religion one would have to think about, try to sense and see in some detail, what kind of physical place, or places, the city and diocese were, what kind of and how many people lived there, in what patterns of human settlement and tenure and in what kind of geography (mountains, rivers, plants, animals), with what patterns of speech, image, and behavior, and to know something of what they produced besides prayers and churches, wills and heirs. Moving from city to country, and to town or village, from the rules of a great barony to the many speaking voices of a rural inquest and to the amplified voice of a single reacting bishop perhaps will create, at least, a sounding board for the Reatine sermon.

The city itself, for all the surrounding rusticity, was (and is) in the center of Italy and only about eighty kilometers, on the Via Salaria, north and slightly east of Rome.[13] The early thirteenth-century city (plate 9) stretched from west to east in an extended and uneven oval for 1,200 meters (which was at its widest point about 450 meters from north to south) on an outcropping (402 meters above sea level), a ridge above, and north of, the river Velino, where the river was met by the Via Salaria coming from Rome, and where parts of the Roman bridge remain. At the westernmost end and highest part of the ridge stood the cathedral complex with its piazza; close by to the east and slightly to the north developed the building and the area of the palazzo comunale on the site of the Roman forum (see map 3).[14] By the end of the thirteenth century the walled city had been extended in all directions (plate 10) but particularly to the east toward what became the *porta d'arce*, so that the city's total length from east to west had grown to slightly more than three kilometers. It was extended into the flat land to the north and down the hill to the Velino in the south (plate 11) so that at points it measured a kilometer, or slightly more, from north to south; and it was joined across the Velino, where the river was met by the Via Roma coming down the hill, by a *borgo*, a suburb, in the neighborhood of the

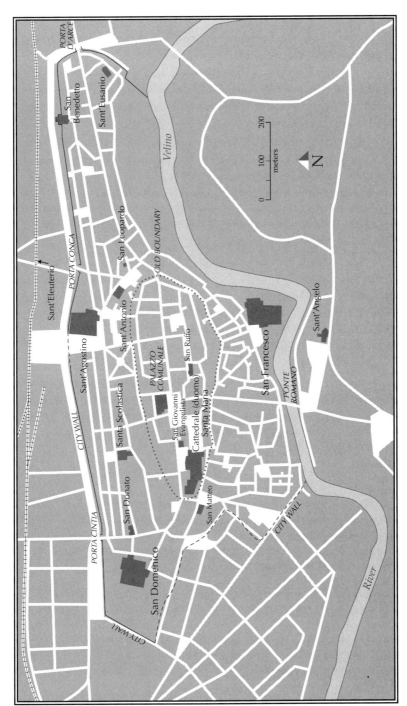

3. The city of Rieti.

church of Sant'Angelo. The new walls enclosed the recently established complexes of the Augustinian Hermits to the north (within the wall west of the *porta conca*), of the Dominicans to the northwest (in the corner of the city beneath the cathedral and to the west of the *porta cintia*) and the Franciscans to the south (actually bound by the Velino not the wall, east of the Via Roma); but they also enclosed another important communal complex, close to and southwest of the Augustinians, the Piazza del Leone, where in the early fourteenth century would be erected the palazzo del podestà.

By the end of the thirteenth century the walls enclosed not only the entire new cathedral dedicated to Santa Maria, which had been consecrated by Pope Honorius III in September 1225, and significant portions of all three of the friars' complexes, but also the new cathedral campanile, which says that it was constructed in or after his first year by Bishop Tommaso (1252–1263/5), and the new episcopal-papal palace which Bishop Pietro da Ferentino (1278–1286) made to be constructed (at the time of the podestà Guglielmo da Orvieto) in 1283, with a loggia added in 1288, under Bishop Andrea (1286–1292/4)—(from the time, as it says, of the podestà, Accoramboni da Tolentino)—and, from just before the turn of the century, the Arco del Vescovo, which bears Pope Boniface VIII's family arms.[15] A list from Bishop Tommaso's time, which does not here include Santa Maria or the friars' churches, does include twenty-nine functioning, or at least census-owing, churches under the rubric: *ecclesie de ciuitate*.[16] It was to this newly enlarged and monumental complex on its ridge above the Velino (plate 12), that members of the Secinari family, one of whom would become bishop, would come, around 1300, returning from their name-giving Abruzzese village, Secinaro (plate 13), to their Rieti house, perhaps already located in the position of their later palazzo on the Via Roma.[17] The contrast must sometimes have shocked them, but so too, except for scale and monumentality, must sometimes the similarity of the two, Rieti and Secinaro, have been assumed by them, human communities, on their ridges, of normal sorts in the rough pitted terrain in this central part of Italy, in spite of, in Rieti's case, the vastness of the great drying basin to its north.

About the actual population of Rieti, before and after the Black Death, it is only possible to guess. By the end of the sixteenth century, when it is possible to do more than guess, Rieti had a population of around six thousand people.[18] With this figure in mind, and with in mind the comparison of Sulmona, which in the late fourteenth century reached a similar figure, it certainly seems possible to say that, late in the thirteenth century, at least, Rieti's population could well have reached a figure around four thousand.[19] But this is speculation.

Rieti, once a Sabine center, had, under the Romans, become a Roman city; it was the home of the Flavians and appropriately of the agricultural expert Varro. Under the Lombards it had become part of the duchy of Spoleto. It had been the name-giving center of a gastaldate and then a county, which it remained into the twelfth century. Rieti was the victim of memorable and remembered destruction by Roger of Sicily in 1149. Its recovery and rebuilding were accompanied by the growth of communal government under the local direction of consuls. By the end of the century it had come under papal control.

Rieti's continued existence as a governmental center, if this is not too grand a term, was reinforced by its position as an episcopal see. Its traditions connected it with the blood of martyrs, and a fleeting reference to its church is found in the letters of Gregory the Great. Its episcopal position, and memories, were strengthened by the long and seemingly relatively effective episcopate of the twelfth-century bishop Dodone, at least from 1137 to 1179. Still Rieti remained essentially a secondary market and trading center at the heart of an agricultural and pastoral area dedicated particularly to the production of wine and grains, as well as garden and animal products and fish.[20]

From Pope Innocent III (1198–1216) Rieti received two important but not disinterested gifts. Rieti became a free commune, although not free of an annual census, with its own government organized under a podestà. It also became an intermittent papal residence. The city thus entered the thirteenth century, a period of almost universal demographic growth, the period of the growth of its own walled space, with two shaping advantages. Its communal government was able to survive and develop through two periods of violent disorder in central Italy: the wars between the papacy and the emperor in the second quarter of the thirteenth century and the period of seeming chaos and continuous partisan disruption, warring of private armies, and Neapolitan royal infiltration, from the time of the papal retreat from Italy in 1305 particularly until the coming of the legate Cardinal Albornoz in 1353 and the Reatine agreement with him in 1354.[21] There is considerable evidence, especially from the (in many ways more distracting) latter of the two periods, for the continued ability of communal institutions to focus elements of power, both shifting and continuing, within the city, to allow it, the city, to resist, although certainly with mixed effectiveness,

potentially intrusive external forces, royal and baronial. It could be argued that the efforts of the early Angevin kings of Naples, in the late
thirteenth and early fourteenth century, to strengthen their Abruzzese
borderlands with new income- and defense-regulating, relatively urban,
planned and gridded communities, like Cittaducale (plate 14) and Leonessa, not only threatened Rieti but helped it, by placing it within a
better ordered general neighborhood, and so in some ways echoed the
helpful papal organization of territory and border under Innocent III.
Certainly in the absence of the papacy, in spite of the presence of papal
governors, Rieti was drawn much more heavily into the ambit of the
kings of Naples; and it might have been helpful to Rieti if they in fact
had been stronger kings.

But Rieti, with its own constitution developed and intact, and visible
within its first statutes and its earliest existing Riformanze, survived;
and, in the end, it itself, its urban center, survived outside the borders
of the kingdom of Naples.[22] Both the army of Rieti, the *exercitus Reat'*,
camped in siege outside the gate of Lugnano in June 1251, and the
(particularly nonclerical) counselors from Rieti, asked to help decide
whether or not the heretic Paolo Zoppo should be submitted to torture
in 1334, suggest the continual existence of a body of responsible and
relatively weighty Reatines, of diverse background, substance, and experience, who in their different ways could represent with their strength
and wisdom the more general community—a thing which itself existed,
was thought to exist, and which could survive partisan fragmentation.[23]
In surprisingly similar terms could be described the composite chapter
of Rieti, of the cathedral of Santa Maria, representing its church and
community.[24]

Innocent III himself came to Rieti. There in 1198, we are told, he
consecrated the church of San Giovanni Evangelista (in Statua).[25] One
hundred years later in 1298, Innocent's distant successor Boniface VIII
came to Rieti and there, it is reported, threatened by the violent earthquakes of November, he took himself from celebrating Mass to the
relative physical safety of the cloister of San Domenico.[26] Five thirteenth-century popes, including Innocent and Boniface, the first and
the last, together, spent, with their courts, 1,226 days in Rieti: Innocent
III, 28 days; Honorius III, 239 days; Gregory IX, 547 days; Nicholas IV,
302 days; and Boniface VIII, 110 days.[27] Popes came to Rieti eleven times
for periods ranging from 28 to 547 days; in terms of time spent there,
it was the fifth most popular of thirteenth- (and very late twelfth- and
early fourteenth-) century central Italian papal residences outside of

Rome: after Viterbo, Anagni, Orvieto, and Perugia.[28] And the popes did not come alone. They came with hundreds of followers (some of whom preceded them to make arrangements), of whom five hundred or six hundred were direct dependents of the papal curia.[29] They packed or bloated the cities at which they arrived. They drastically altered the cities' demands on housing and public services and provisioning. They pushed rents up to as much as four times their normal figure. Some of them demanded hospitality and in what seemed unreasonably spacious quarters.[30] They caused expensive damage and they required protection.[31] They brought many problems and obvious discomforts to the host community; they threatened its fabric. But on the whole they (and the real or presumed economic benefits of their presence) seem to have been much desired, courted, built for; their potential and actual presence seems generally to have improved the facilities and increased the monumentality of the host city, to which they themselves came for various reasons: to strengthen papal presence in the area, to avoid the danger posed by Roman or Rome-threatening enemies, to escape the pain and illness of a Roman summer in a place as seemingly fresh and cool as Rieti—Cardinal Jacopo Stefaneschi's sweet Rieti (*amena Reate*), beneath its mountains and above its waters.[32]

The exact effects of the curia's presence on Rieti and the negotiations leading to that presence are not visible as they are at Viterbo and Perugia, but clearly the monumental center of Rieti, the papal-episcopal palace (built under curial bishops) and the arch of Boniface VIII are connected with attempts to attract the court to, and/or to keep and please it at, Rieti. So may have been, for example, the important fountain in the Piazza del Leone.[33] The late thirteenth century, between the battle of Tagliacozzo (1268) and the popes' departure from Italy, was a time of relative peace and of monumental building and decorating for central Italy; into this pattern the Rieti palace fits naturally, but its specific reason is surely papal presence.[34]

The papal curia brought the world and the world's events to Rieti. In 1288 and 1289, Pope Nicholas IV spent the summer, from mid-May until mid-October, in Rieti. In Nicholas's second year there, Charles II, the new king of Naples, recently freed from the imprisonment in which he had been held hostage, came, with a great following, to Rieti, and on Pentecost, in the cathedral, was crowned king. In memory of this event Charles promised the church of Rieti an annual gift of 20 *uncie* of gold from the royal treasury, and so an additional financial benefit came to the city, or at least to its church, from the presence of the papal curia there; but it was not a benefit without eventual problems or one the installments of which would always come free, as is clear from Bishop Giovanni Papazurri's excommunication, in 1311, of any canon who did not pay his share of the money required in order to get the 20 uncie from King Robert, and also in 1332, from the making of proctors by Bishop Giovanni's vicar and the canons of Rieti to appear before the king and dissuade him from any reduction of the sum. In the papal-royal summer of 1289 Rieti was further swollen by the presence there of the thirteenth chapter general of the Franciscan friars minor, men from all over.[35]

The chapter general calls attention to the provenance of the friars resident in the local houses of Franciscans, Dominicans, and Augustinian Hermits.[36] They were not from the whole world, and they were not all strangers, but the majority of those who can be identified did not come from Rieti or nearby villages but rather from other Italian places. In the early fourteenth century, after the second of the two periods of papal sojourns, and after many Reatines had themselves become members or followers of the papal curia, Rieti, with its Roman Papazurri bishop, was certainly not a place sealed against the outside world. Witnesses and actors who appear, for example, in the parchment cartulary of Matteo Barnabei, for the five-year period 1315–1319, suggest a generous presence of resident strangers.[37] There were signal figures with specific skills: Janductio the painter from Rome, and Magister Jacques, the physician from the diocese of Le Puy-en-Velay (Pandecoste), who had become a resident and *medico* of Rieti; but there were plenty of others, of course, from neighboring places like Labro, Morro, Greccio, Monteleone, Montereale, Poggio Bustone, but also from more distant and distinct places like Viterbo, Norcia, and Siena, and a sizable number from Rome.

Not all Reatines were Christians. There were Jews in Rieti in 1341, and the nature of their appearance makes it clear that they had been there for some time, if not in great number.[38] On 1 April 1341 in the house of Vanni di Don Tommaso Cimini (or de Ciminis), with as a witness Matteo di don Filippo Pasinelli, "Manuelis Consilii Judeus" came forward to act for himself and a group of some ten named associates, from a somewhat smaller group of families, men with names like those of the brothers (in the genitive) *Abrammi* and *Salomoni alias Bonaventure*, sons of the now dead Magister *Bengiamini*—a high proportion of *magistri*. Manuelis was present to come to an agreement, to end discord and litigation, with the brothers Musictus and Gagius, sons

and heirs of the by then dead Magister Elya Muse, who had formerly
formed a part of the association or shop (*apotheca*) which Manuelis
represented. The two brothers received, in addition to anything they
had received from the association in the past, 110 florins of gold, accepting an Aquilian stipulation (the conversion into a single stipulation
of a variety of obligations); and in return they gave up any share in
current actions or debts being pursued against or from the city of Rieti
or any person within it. They promised not to stay in future in the city
or county of Rieti more than two days a month and not to have there
a shop or *mercantiam* without the express license of Manuelis and his
associates. Juxta, the wife of Gagius, consented to this transaction and
waived all privileges and remedies at law protecting wives, including
privileges guaranteed by the city of Rieti. This document establishes the
existence of a self-controlled, in some ways at least, corporation of
money-lending Jews in Rieti in 1341, which seems to have operated
within perfectly recognizable community procedures, and which was
able to act with a witness from one of Rieti's most prominent patrician
families in the house of a member of another of those families. The
document suggests that these men with their families were the only
Jews in Rieti, that there was only one such consortium; and that suggestion would seem to be supported by a legacy in the will of Don
Berardo de Colle from the same year 1341: *Item dixit se debere dare
Judeis qui habitant Reate. v flor. aur. quos eis reliquid* (He said that he
ought to give the Jews who live in Rieti five florins of gold, which he
leaves to them).[39] Whether or not this formula was sufficient to remove
the florins from a category of immediately payable debt (as it presumably was intended to do), it certainly seems to imply a single recognizable receiving body.

The community of Rieti, the city, divided into its three double *porte*,
its six *sestieri*, in which Jews, foreigners, painters, doctors, notaries, patricians, women from Labro and Greccio, friars, and priests lived, was,
by the end of the Middle Ages, or was meant to be, regulated by a
composite body of communal statutes. Some of its contents come from
the time of Bishop Biagio da Leonessa (1347–1378): a compact between
bishop and commune arrived at in September 1353 clearly does.[40] But
some are, or at least one is, clearly considerably later; the section *de
feriis*, which refers to the feast of San Bernardino, is.[41]

The statutes present a city preoccupied with the problems common
to late medieval communes, from the organization of government and
the restrictions on governmental office to public hygiene: the faith and

the honor of the Roman church are to be preserved and the podestà is to be elected, communal notaries and communal bells are regulated; the expenses of construction for the fountain in the Piazza del Leone are apportioned to neighbors and neighbors defined; guilds are numbered and named; testaments and torture are regulated; the salary of the city's master of grammar is fixed at 40 lire for the year; the trimming of the limbs of fruit- and nut-bearing trees (olives, figs, almonds, filberts, walnuts, others) is regulated; Rieti with a mile-wide belt of land around it, is protected from the playing of dice—and the continued use, of a sort, of the statute book is indicated by a drawing in the margin of three dice (with a 2, a 3, and a 6 facing the reader); people in Rieti are forbidden to keep pigs in the city—and in the margin a belled pig suggests its filthiness; women of ill fame are forbidden to hang around any monastery or religious place in the city or borgo or any place in the city except next to the city walls and the road that runs by it—and an ambiguous, perhaps suggestive, drawing appears in the margin; the maintenance of fortifications and bridges is regulated. The use of injurious words is forbidden; and there is an attempt to keep housewives from being raped in mills.[42] The city declares its special rights over the "valley of the Canera" and indicates some of the places that are meant, in this sense, to be included in the valley: Santa Croce, Greccio, Rocca Alatri, Contigliano, Collebaccaro, Cerchiara, Poggio Perugino, and Poggio Fidoni.[43]

The statutes regulate the public behavior of mourners and the course of the palium to be run on the feast of Saint Mary in August (the Assumption, 15 August).[44] And with these last regulations one observes an aspect of this set of statutes which should have been suggested by its pious and ecclesiastical beginning: it is not simply secular; it involves itself with pious act and religion. Alms from the *gabella* are to go to San Francesco, San Domenico, Sant'Agostino and suburban, Cistercian San Pastore.[45] On the feast of Saint James in May (Saints Philip and James, 1 May) the podestà is personally to go to the church of San Giovanni Evangelista (in which *vox populi firmata fuit*) and there to offer, to the praise and honor of God and the honor of the people of Rieti, a ten-pound candle or torch to be lighted when the Corpus Christi is elevated; and then, that offering made, he, the podestà, and the captain of the people and the *priori* are to proceed to the church of San Giacomo and make a similar offering.[46] The local presence and miracles of Saint Francis are recalled, as the presence of Greccio, Fonte Colombo, and Poggio Bustone (plate 15) still testified, and the friars of

Rieti, and the monastery of San Fabiano, of the order of Saint Clare, or, as the statutes also say, the second order of Saint Francis—all to be borne in affection by the Reatines.[47] The church of Saint Francis in fact performed functions, physical ones of housing, for the operation of Reatine government, but the relations of the city with the great abbey of San Salvatore Maggiore seem to have been more complicatedly possessive; and the statutes insist that no one commit an offense in the lands of the abbey.[48] Hospitals, too, were protected.[49] But so were the city's rights of clerical patronage at Monte Calvo.[50]

It should be clear and unsurprising that at Rieti there was in the thirteenth and fourteenth centuries, through 1378, a continuous convergence of secular-civil and ecclesiastical institutions; the city in its various aspects came from (or produced) the same mold. Except, of course, for the imported and transient major figures of podestà and captain, the same men and, more, the same families (and the same external forces) appear in the recorded workings of both secular and ecclesiastical institutions. But secular Rieti was not a tightly controlled unitary thing; it was various, rather loosely organized, and, in its way, popular. One would not expect, and one could not find, in the Rieti of the period before 1378, the kind of structured secular-ecclesiastical coherence, with secular domination, that has recently been shown to have existed, for example, in the Verona ruled by the Scaligeri between 1277 and 1387.[51]

At the figurative center of the Rieti complex the *palazzo comunale* and the *palazzo episcopale* sat in very close physical proximity, the extended governmental center, insofar as it was local, and concentrated, of the whole place. But it could reasonably be argued that the real center of the community was not in palazzo but in *chiesa*, the high altar of the cathedral church and that church's sacristy where its treasure was stored. Of that treasure, of the goods which were found in the sacristy of Rieti on 15 January 1353, the chamberlain canon Ballovino di magistro Giovanni and his two sacristans, dompno Nutio di Pandulfictio and dompno Francesco di Pietro, have left us a list beginning with four chalices all of silver, all gilded, and three also enameled, all with patens.[52] The list includes miters and crosses (one little one of silver which the bishop wore around his neck when he was celebrant), an episcopal ring, sandals, vestments of various colors, fifty silk altar and/or other cloths and *duo palia que portauit ser Petrus Zutri de Florentia*, boxes, candelabra, documents and privileges of various sorts (like Pope Nicholas IV's grant of an indulgence of a year and forty days for the church of Rieti— the first listed), and books.

There is a list of ninety-eight books, with some suggestion of their order.[53] There is some talk of their size, their lettering, their binding and condition, their glosses, the signs (like call numbers) which distinguish a few of them. There are missals, antiphonals, an evangelary, an epistolary, a hymnal, responsories, legendaries, passionals, breviaries, office books of various sorts, psalters, Bibles, books of the Bible from both testaments, Paul, books of prayer, scholarly books (some) and books of devotion, books of medicine (a number, including one specified as Constantine on fevers translated from the Arabic), books of laws or canons (not many or modern), Isidore, histories (including one specified as a history of the Franks and the Lombards), lives of the saints, classics (Cicero on rhetoric, fifty homilies of Augustine, Josephus, Gregory on Job or a book commenting on Gregory's *Moralia*). There is a "de mirabilis mundi," a treatise on the eight deadly sins, a "vite patrum" (desert fathers lying in wait to snare a soul), a "librum tabulatum de vita beati Thome" (unidentified, but probably Becket of Canterbury). There is in closing a librarian's or a bibliographer's plaint "Item sex quaterni dissoluti de diuersibus rebus." There is also a short list of recent gifts by canons which suggests modern or personal taste, miracles of the Virgin, *legende* of the saints, sermons for Sundays:

Item librum miraculorum Sancte Marie nouum quem fecit fieri dominus Johannes de Ponticillis, canonicus Reatinus

Item simile alius antiquum

Item librum de legendis sanctorum per totum annum quem fecit fieri dominus Raynallus de Plagis, canonicus Reatinus

Item librum de sermonibus dominicalibus quem fecit fieri dominus Bartholomeus Bontempi canonicus Reatinus

and elsewhere in the list is a new psalter which Bartolomeo Alfani had had made:

Item aliud psalterium tabulatum quem fecit fieri seu dimisit dominus Bartholomeus Alfani.[54]

We are shown a rather old-fashioned country library of reasonable size, unprofessional, except for the profession of praying and perhaps home medicine.

These books and these chalices, the episcopal ring and the life of Thomas were at the center of the community, and the diocese, and occupied the mind of the canon chamberlain Ballovino in 1353. The property which the church and chapter held and which, in part, supported them, moves the observer's eye back out into the community. An inquest of holdings, in one example, from 1225 and the years just after that, was copied in the early fourteenth century, presumably in 1315, onto surviving paper gatherings of eight folios each. The inquest is divided into three parts, one for each of the double *porte*, the paired *sestieri*, of the city: Porta Carceraria, Porta Romana, and Porta Cintia— of which the first once contained 87 entries, the second 42, and the last (the Cintia) 225. The entries of the first gathering of the paper copy move through property over which the church claimed rights across the city to the east in, again, the Porta Carceraria, particularly in the parishes of San Giovenale and San Giorgio; of the 69 items in the first gathering 10 refer to properties in the parish of San Giovenale and 16 to properties in San Giorgio.[55] But other parts of then eastern Rieti are marked out, the parish of San Leopardo, or, in the case of the property of Matteo Allecerati, property in the *porta nova* in the parish of San Paolo, and other property an *actigale* (? a hut ? a straw hut) outside the *porta sancti pauli*, bordered by the *tanus*, a public street, and the *carbonaria*. And one is told of the *tiniosus flaianus* (a memory), of a tower "Bertesce," of the river, the city wall (at the edge of a property in San Giovenale), the Arce.[56]

But although the initial part of the inquest certainly seems to be an inquest of the area of the Carceraria, it is of the area in this sense: it asks responses of people denizened there who hold property of Santa Maria, or over whose property Santa Maria has or claims rights. So in some ways the inquest is very much about people, about property hold-ers; they are listed on its left margins. On specific days before specific witnesses they speak, and sometimes still in the first person. Oderiscio Raynerii, speaking of land he had bought from Senebaldo Gerardo says "ipse mihi dixit quod unus pasus est Ecclesie quando mihi vendidit (he told *me* one piece was the church's when he sold it to *me*)"; and Andrea Rustici says "et viam per quam vado ad vineam est ecclesie (the road or path on which *I go* to the vineyard is the church's)" and for it he gives the church each year one *sarcinam* of wine.[57] But in another sense, and more seriously perhaps, the inquest is about property, arable land and vineyards, as well as lots, and some garden and huts, and this land is not at all restricted to the city: there are references to five vineyards and a piece of arable at, or on, Monte Marone, southeast of the city, but also three references to pieces of land at Terria, northwest of the city; there are vineyards and land in Conca Maiu in the Campo Reatino, in Padula (northeast of the city), in Casamascara and Saletto to the west,

in Valle Racula, in Pratu Moro or Mori, in Vango, in Trivio San Giovanni—in those areas stretching out from the city in which the church
and its tenants could grow grain or vines. The majority of the tenants
held property in the country as well as, one assumes, in the city. Much
of the property was held jointly: over forty joint tenancies are recorded
in these eight folios, mostly by members of extended families with specifically stated relationships ("with my brother and my nephew"). A
man answers for his wife, two widows for their sons.[58] Some of the
names are specifically interesting. One tenant has the locally important
name (or patronymic) Carsidonei. One is identified as "Thomas Scriniarius," and one as "Raynutius Molenarius"; and there is a reference
to "Magister Petrus Conpange." A tenant is called Crescentio Macca-
bei, which could possibly suggest that he was Jewish.[59] Some of these
men have the remembered importance of three patronymics, or two
and a surname: "Bartholomeus Petri Johannis Theotonici," "Thomas
Palmerii Berardi Aliverii"; but the lack of need for any patronymic
might argue equal prominence: "Nicolaus Terradanus." There is reference to property held by a man identified as being from as far away
as Valle Antrodoco, and by one from Apoleggia.[60] On the other hand,
repeated patronymics suggest a less open and extended group than mere
numbers might, a kind of closing in, particularly in the case of the
Tedemarii (if this name has not in fact started at least turning itself into
a surname, which would not alter the point).

Although they are in various places, the lands attached to Santa Maria
surround each other in those places: the vineyard of Teodino Tasconis
in Conca Maiu is surrounded *ab omnibus lateribus* (by land held of)
Sancta Maria; the land of Rubeus Stracti at *portum cecorum* in the
parish of San Giorgio is bordered on one side by a public street and *a
tribus lateribus Sancta Maria*; the lot of Nicola Terradanus in the parish
of San Giorgio in the *portu Pellipariorum* (? of the tanners) has before
it the public street, behind it the river, and on the other side Santa
Maria; and the lot of Andrea Severi Travasacti has *ab uno latere flumen
ab aliis lateribus Sancta Maria*: the devil, one feels, in this little world,
and the deep blue sea.[61] But can one say of this devil that it has lots of
land? Whose is the land, Andrea's or Santa Maria's? Although there is
some talk, very rare, of how land is held (*emphiteotectico jure*), there is
no talk of specific returns, or very, very little, such as the *sarcina* of
wine.[62] These may be stories of memories of larger tracts once held by
Santa Maria and later divided: memories already in the time of Bishop
Rainaldo de Labro, grown more distant but of renewed interest in the

time of Bishop Giovanni Papazurri—not major sources of income in the time of Bishop Biagio da Leonessa.

The chapter's inquest, like the city statutes' securing of the adherence of the towns in the valley of the Canera and their talk of San Salvatore, San Pastore, and the Franciscan hermitages, takes one outside the city walls to the near country, not in these cases generally to identical places, but to places with the same sorts of closeness to the city, forming the same kinds of neighborhood in the nearest reaches of the big diocese of Rieti. At its most distant from its episcopal city the diocese stretched away to the northeast past Campotosto (if one measures simply by drawing a straight line) for more than forty-seven kilometers, and to the southeastern past Corvaro and Cartore for more than fifty-two; although its boundary to the east past Contigliano was hardly more than ten kilometers from Rieti. The physical size of the diocese changed drastically in the mid-thirteenth century, when in 1256 and 1257 Pope Alexander IV constituted the new diocese of L'Aquila and removed (or began to remove) from Rieti much of the large territory of Amiterno to the east of Rieti and to the west of the new city of L'Aquila, and reduced the surface of the diocese from an area of about thirty-five hundred square kilometers to one of about three thousand.[63]

As in the case of the city of Rieti, it is impossible to know the actual population of the thirteenth- or fourteenth-century diocese. When population is relatively knowable, because of visitation records, at the end of the sixteenth and beginning of the seventeenth century, it has been estimated by the historian Vincenzo Di Flavio to have been between 30,000 and 35,000 (between five and six times the size of the population of the city of Rieti) and to have been scattered in about 220 settlements ("villaggi, castelli, o terre"), with a median population of between 150 and 300, with only a few, like Antrodoco or Campotosto, actually reaching a figure of 1,000 or more.[64] Elsewhere Di Flavio has described the early modern diocese as being mountainous, and particularly sharply so in its Abruzzese parts, with a kind of settlement characteristic of central Italy (plate 16): lots of small villages at short distances from each other ("molti piccoli villaggi a breve distanza fra loro").[65] Between the beginning of the thirteenth century and Di Flavio's observed time there certainly had been specific changes in the arrangement of population centers, most sharply noticeable in the creation of the new towns of the Regno, the Angevin kingdom of Naples, like Cittaducale and Posta, and there almost surely had been growth, irregular growth and in actual numbers unmeasurable, after the demographic recession of the fourteenth century; but the general pattern which he suggests does not conflict with, but rather coincides with, the evidence for the thirteenth and fourteenth centuries.

The political, in the grand sense, situation of the diocese, before, during, and after the period of this study, was extraordinary. As Di Flavio says of his time, and it seems generally to have been true, with minor variations (as during the period of Angevin encroachment in the fourteenth century), from the end of the twelfth century until Unification, roughly two-thirds of the diocese was within the kingdom of Naples and one-third was within the states of the Church.[66] At the time of the compilation, in the twelfth century, of the *Catalogus baronum* of the old Norman kingdom, Cantalice (about eight kilometers, in a straight line) northeast of Rieti was within the Regno, but its immediate neighbor Poggio Bustone was not (nor were the other Franciscan hermitage sites). Rieti's western neighbors Lugnano, Canetra, Pendenza, and slightly farther south, Caprodossa, Stàffoli and Petrella, were all within the Regno; the border was close to, but not identical with, the River Salto as the border followed the river up, from its confluence with the Velino, into the Cicolano; the border seems to have crossed the river at least twice.[67] Thus, to use (of course importantly inappropriate) modern parlance, the diocese was in two countries: the border's path did not find its reason, in any obvious way, in physical geography or what would have seemed the more general social connection or rather lack of connection between neighboring communities, but instead probably, at this stage, the "national" border found its reason in the early pattern of military tenements held of the kings of Sicily.

The physical geography of the diocese was not totally incoherent and became somewhat more coherent after the removal to L'Aquila of Amiterno. At the diocese's administrative and population center was the relatively vast alluvial plain, the conca di Rieti (plate 17), once the site of a large lake fed by the river Velino. The conca is, in fact, similar to other large fertile plains or basins inserted in the Abruzzese mountainous areas of central Italy: L'Aquila, Sulmona, Fucino, Leonessa. Around Rieti's alluvial center, and its high terraces of sandy clay, rise sharply the limestone highlands and mountains, the Monti Sabini, the Monti Reatini (rising at their greatest height, at Terminillo, to 2,213 meters), and the northwestern rim of the Monti Carseolani.[68] The Reatini and the Sabini enclose the conca to the north and mark the northwestern boundaries of the diocese. South of Rieti, itself raised above the southeastern edge of the alluvial flatlands, the valleys of the rivers Turano and

Salto make approximately parallel cuts into the southern terraces (as one follows the rivers upstream), and the Velino valley goes off to the east. This area—alluvial flatlands, surrounded by high terraces cut by river valleys, and they in turn surrounded by mountains (or high limestone hills)—forms the rational geographical center of the diocese. To this part of the diocese was joined the upper valley of the Velino, from its sharp turn north at Antrodoco (as one follows it upstream) to its source beyond Cittareale, and the parallel valley of that part of the Aterna which remained in the diocese, after the departure of Amiterno, from south of Marana to the river's source beyond Aringo. This northeastern part of the diocese, the two valleys, with the area between them (with centers as important as Borbona) and areas farther east including Capitignano and Campotosto, was clearly that part of the diocese least closely tied to its center, a point made particularly clear by the existence for it of a separate vicar general at Montereale in the mid-fourteenth century. It was an area of mixed agrarian value, mixed topography, but it included areas of at least great agricultural potential.[69]

Pierre Toubert, in a lyric moment, has talked of the Sabina's, including the Reatine Sabina's, smiling heights and beautiful landscape where orchards and vineyards and fields of grain are mixed together: "ridenti paesi d'altura ed il suo bel paesaggio, dove l'arboricultura si unisce alla coltura della vite e dei cereali."[70] In another place, in what may be the most memorable section of his major book on medieval Lazio, Toubert, with his constant interest in words, has brought into focus with the blossoming of modern Sabina, including again the Reatine Sabina, the blossoming and leaving botany of its medieval past (where blossoming and leaving were not forbidden by bare, or almost bare, limestone or great height). Place names make that vegetable past visible. Greccio is heather. Sambuco is elder. Ginestra is broom. Dogwood, red cane, fennel, laurel, hawthorn, oaks (*quercus* and *robur*), fern, willows are as alive in the names on the land as olives and chestnuts are in the documents.[71] Toubert's Rieti had the "climat de colline," and around it stretching out into the Abruzzi mountains, in the nature-filled environment, the plains, scattered, seeded through the mountains, had the determining role in the occupation of the soil, in, obviously, the raising of cereal grains (wheat, spelt, barley, rye, millet, panic, sorghum [*sagina*], but not apparently oats, or not many oats), and more tangentially in the placing of rows of vines, and the gathering of chestnuts.[72] Olives had an extra dimension; their line of possible growth passes through the diocese of Rieti. Where men were in the diocese

there were gardens, fruit, the pear, the apple, the cultivated nut, and
noticeably the leek—remembered still in repeated luscious physicality,
on the dinner table of the Last Supper in the late thirteenth-century
frescoes at Fossa, in the diocese of L'Aquila, on, or off, the road between
Rieti and Secinaro (plate 19).[73]

The diocese was also not only a land of *castri* or walled settlements
on hills, but of castles, with barons in them. The city of Rieti itself may
be seen as having been more disturbed by the rivalries, or impertinences,
of neighboring towns, particularly those within the Regno, but the local
barons (who, or many among them, would eventually be replaced by
the great barons of Rome) were of vital importance to the area of the
diocese, to its rule and organization, and to the structure and peopling
of its church. Although it is not easy to examine them individually, these
barons give no sign of having been identical with one another, cut from
the same pattern. The lords of Labro in the mountains just to the north
of the conca, with their castle or castles in the papal states, do not seem
in all ways like the lords of Mareri to the south, with some of their block
of territory in the papal states, but essentially men of the Regno. The
lords of Labro, who fought against the lords of Luco, and who seem
to have been closely connected with the lords of neighboring Morro,
were very important to Santa Maria Rieti as neighbors but also as participants in its most important functions, as canons, as bishop.[74] In spite,
however, of their relatively easy identification with the family Nobili by
some more recent historians, they are hard to identify, to separate, to
pin down; some contemporary records suggest that they participated in
a kind of consortium, a kind of barons' cooperative, in which the relations of the members one to another are no longer visible. And of course
it is not always possible to say when a man is identified as "de Labro"
whether he was a lord of Labro or simply someone who came from the
castro; the presence or absence of *dominus* is not always decisive, and
the use of grander titles for local barons is sparing in the records of the
Reatine.[75] In the fourteenth century, as the walls of San Giacomo degli
Incurabili in Rome tell us, a Labro had found attachment to a Colonna;
in the thirteenth century another Labro was in the household of Cardinal Ottaviano Ubaldini, perhaps related to him, and later became
archdeacon of Bologna. In July 1296 the Sienese chose the *nobili viro*
Tommaso de Labro, *ciui reatino* (in the dative), as their podestà.[76] The
Labro were locally important landowners who were able to fight. They
were not without good connections. They commanded an imposing
castle-*castro* still very striking on its height.[77] But there is no suggestion

that they by themselves controlled in almost every way the massive domain of an almost royal substate.

Quite the opposite was true of the Mareri in the southern part of the diocese. By the time of the compilation of their late fourteenth-century "statutes," if the "statutes" are (and there is no reason to believe that they are not) a statement of conditions which then pretty much existed, the Mareri ruled a state which extended itself for considerable distance on both sides of the river Salto and, at one point at least, west across the intervening hills and high terraces (hospitable at least at times to transhumants) to the east bank of the river Turano, although this statement in a way distorts the "statutes'" own system of mapping, castro by castro. But, in any case, the Mareri were locally very *gran' signori*.

The surviving "statutes" list, in varying detail, the Mareri lords' rights, and the obligations of the denizens of each castro, for Petrella Salto, Castel di Tora (Castelvecchio), Rigatti, Marcetelli, Mareri, "Vallebona" (? at Colle di Sponga), Stàffoli, Poggio Poponesco (Fiamignano), Gamagna, Sambuco, Poggio Viano, Radicaro, and Castro Rocca Alberici or Alberti. Mareri control was very broadly imagined and realized. It was deep and heavy. The Mareri seem to have regulated almost every area of castro life: mills, justice, the bearing of arms, the selling of wine, the selling of meat, of dairy products and fish, of cloth, of oil and honey. They demanded hospitality for their messengers and familiars. The lord had rights over the piazza and fixed tolls for whoever crossed it, depending upon what he or she took across it: a horse or a mule, a cow or an ass, a goat or a sheep, wine, grain, cloth, wax, honey, leather, "spices," whatever the mind of the Cicolano could think of someone's profitably carrying.[78] Of every head of cattle raised in Petrella, when it was butchered, the lord should receive a haunch; from everyone the lord should receive a lamb, a *cordiscum*, and *cordisci* are defined as all lambs born between 1 March and 15 August ("videlicet omnes agnos qui nascuntur a kalendis martij usque ad sanctam Mariam de mense agusti").[79]

The lord had fortifications and houses. He had the watercourses; he had mountains and pastures. He fixed the time of the vintage. The lord had rights of hunting; and when he went to hunt the hare in any wood in his barony the men of that castro who had snares or hounds were bound to go with him, and when he went for the wild boar, men were to come with arms and dogs. The men of the place could not trap without license; what, licensed, they took, lost its head and a fourth part to the lord. Of partridges and other birds, hedgehogs, and hares, the lord got a half. No real property could be alienated without license, and an entry fee was to be fixed for anyone coming into property. "Nobles" found in the castro owed aid, suit of court, service. Weights and measures were regulated. Rents, dues, and services were fixed in several castri with men, women, and heirs listed next to that which they must pay (including lots of chickens and eggs).

The Mareri laid a heavy hand on the men they controlled. They seem absolute lords. But of course the very recording suggests a limit to their absolutism, to their depredation. And the significance of this written limitation, of writing things down, is suggested by the recorded presence of notaries in the area, and by the very real prominence of one notary, who appears, and whose wealth and importance appear, repeatedly: Giovanni de Lutta. Still the lords' control is great and clearly expressed. Of his half of Castel di Tora, the lord Lippo Mareri claims for himself and his heirs quite complete banal jurisdiction over present and future inhabitants "merum et mistum imperium cum gladii potestate et potest regere ibi curiam per se et vicarium eius et exercere iudicium ordinarium in civilibus et criminalibus et homines dicte medietatis corregere et punire ad eius voluntatem et arbitrium"; and also it is claimed, "Et homines ipsius castri [should acknowledge] nullum alium dominum et superiorem nisi solum Deum et dominos de Marerio"— only God and the lords of Mareri.[80] Naturally the lords of Mareri concerned themselves with churches.

In the small castro of Stàffoli, now so spare and reduced that its few stone houses seem to be returning to the limestone mountainside on which they lie and from which they came, the northernmost of the places of the surviving statutes, where the Mareri lords had their eyes on littering sows, so that from each litter, after it had been cared for at least for its first three weeks, a piglet must go to the lord's *curia*; this was to happen as was said "in the vernacular *quando la scrofa latanta*." As elsewhere, the Mareri lord dealt with the church. "He has the church of San Giovanni, which is *archipresbiteratus* [an archpriest's church, a *pieve*, baptismal and presumably collegiate], and is outside the castro. He has the church of Sant'Angelo, which is inside the castro. He has the church of San Nicola, which is outside the castro. He has the church of Santa Maria Sconzie, which the abbot of San Salvatore confirms [? accepts there provided benefice holders]. Of these churches the Lord Lippo is lord and patron."[81]

For larger Petrella, there is, as one would expect, more to say; including the restriction that no one could found or endow churches or chapels there without the lord's license. But in fact in Petrella there are two patrons who are not Mareri: of San Silvestro, the heirs of dompno Giovanni Protempze; and of the chapel of San Nicola in the church of Santa Maria di Petrella, the notary Giovanni de Lutta and his heirs—they are patrons of this chapel, founded and endowed by them, by the license of Lord Lippo and the bishop of Rieti. But the lord has the patronage of Santa Maria itself, whose parishioners all the men of Petrella are, and other existing churches and chapels, and the statute continues: "Et omnium ecclesiarum et capellarum que in postero hedificabuntur ipse dominus debet esse verus patronus et dominus et representare in eis clericos et rectores (he is the patron of all churches yet unbuilt; the church of Petrella shall always be his)."[82] But, the historian Andrea Di Nicola has noted, in only one church properly within the diocese, does a statute seem to withhold from the bishop what would normally be his: of the chapel of San Giovanni, in the *rocca* Castel Mareri, it is said "et est ipsa capella libera ab omni servitio papali et episcopali."[83]

As the statement about Santa Maria di Petrella shows, the Mareri fief (with its additions) is divided into parishes full of parishioners. A large number of the people in the castri, moreover, present themselves, with their names, to be counted; some of these places offer more information for estimating population than anyplace else in the fourteenth-century diocese. For "Villa de Illicis" a *frazione* of Marcetelli are listed twenty-one *homines dicti castri*, men and women, including the last named "mastro Angelutius," held, presumably as heads of households, to services; Marcetello itself, with perhaps less pretense to complete inclusiveness has fifty. Rigatti lists sixty-one names, presumably representing households (a number of them listed as *heredes*), besides fourteen *forenses*, people from Marcetelli, Vallececa, Varco, and Poggio (? Vittiano) including a notary from there.[84] These people are listed merely as people who owe rents and services, but in their enumeration they press forward a strong sense of their individual and group existence. And it is perhaps not too much to say that a strong and penetrating government always produces a group of governed with the potential of reacting in group to that government.

The formidable Mareri, in the early thirteenth century, gave the church of Rieti a very visible, at least at one point, canon, and they gave the diocese its most effectively remembered "saint." But their statutes come from (or just after) the end of the period of this study. From near its beginning, and from farther up the course of the Salto, and actually from a place on a tributary of one of the Salto's tributaries, fourteen and one-half kilometers (in a straight line) southeast of Castel Mareri, come a set of documents, a set of witnesses' testimonies, that reveal the diocese as a place in a more directly ecclesiastical way. They come from, or are about, the church of San Leopardo near Borgocollefegato. It, like the Mareri places, is in the Cicolano, the most distinctive region of the diocese, most internally connected and self-conscious, which stretches itself along the valley of the Salto southeast in the direction of the Montagne della Duchessa and Monte Velino.

Some time around the year 1210, when Transarico was abbot of Ferentillo, and his nephew Transarico was already a monk there, as was Jericho, and when Adenolfo de Lavareta seems surely still to have been bishop of Rieti, but equally certainly no longer an unconsecrated "elect," the Benedictine abbey of San Pietro di Ferentillo, locally within the diocese of Spoleto, and the bishop and church of Rieti were involved in a dispute about jurisdiction over San Leopardo and its clerks.[85] In itself it was not an unusual kind of dispute. It was not very unlike the closely contemporary dispute between the monastery of San Quirico in Rieti diocese and the bishop of Penne, over churches and clerks in the diocese of Penne. In cases like these, distant and recent history combined to make unclear and debatable the jurisdictional boundary between the rights of two claimants, both of whom had some reason to believe that jurisdiction was or should be theirs. At the moment of the actual disputes, frequently, some local disposition—like a temporary period of relative peace and order—or something more general—like the expansion of the accepted notion of episcopal jurisdiction of the sort encouraged by Innocent III, or even an extended sense of parish reality—pushed the parties into the need to define, to establish control, and so to litigate.

In the San Leopardo dispute, the witnesses interrogated (men who had traveled with or observed bishops of Rieti and men local to the place in dispute, at least those witness from whom testimony is preserved) were asked questions about things that they had seen or heard or in some way knew. And in answering these questions they, in various ways, described part of the diocese of Rieti in the early thirteenth century, and also in fact quite deep back into the twelfth century. They produced this depth because some of their memories, and among them some extended by the memories of others, were very long, or at least they thought or said that they were very long.

One witness said that he was almost one hundred years old and that for his whole life, except for one year, he had made continuous residence at San Leopardo and so he knew what had and had not happened there. Another witness, the farmer named Rollando, said that he had often heard, from the old men of the *paese*, to whom the church belonged (*pertinebat*), and it was to San Pietro Ferentillo.[86] He also said that the clerks of San Leopardo got their *crisma, oleum sanctum,* and *oleum infirmorum* from the church of Santo Stefano of Corvaro, which *est ecclesie Reat'*. Another farmer (*agricola*), Andrea, said that he saw the messenger of Gentile de Amiterno, who was called Giovanni Castelli, come to the church, close the gates (*ianuas*), extract the keys, and give them to a monk called Transerico; he gave them to Bartolomeo the *prelato* of the church. And how did he know he was a monk of Ferentillo? Because everyone said so, and besides he had seen him coming to the church with the abbot. Giovanni Bonihominis, another farmer, had seen Bishop Benedetto of Rieti dining on the vigil of Saint Leopardo's feast in the church, but he had not been at the church the next morning although he had heard the bells. Another farmer, Giovanni Franconi, had seen monks coming from Ferentillo and being received as if they were in their own home, *sicut in domo propria*, when San Leopardo was presided over by Pietro his uncle, his mother's brother. When the land of Teodino de Amiterno was under interdict, the interdict was observed by the church of San Leopardo until a monk from Ferentillo (whose name he did not know, but it was said that he was from Ferentillo) came and celebrated service publicly with bells ringing, but the clerks of San Leopardo themselves did not take part in the services. He had seen Bishop Dodone received at the church with bells ringing when he visited the parish. And he said too that the holy oils came from Santo Stefano, and that before the dispute arose the clerks of San Leopardo had been ordained by the bishops of Rieti. Another farmer, Giovanni Alkerii, who was of the *villa* of the church of San Leopardo, agreed about the oil and said that the children of local farmers (*pueri rustico-rum*) were baptized at Santo Stefano, and that he had three times seen a bishop of Rieti whose name he did not know given hospitality in the church (and he knew he was bishop of Rieti because everybody said so: *dicebatur ab omnibus*), but he had not seen a bishop for the last five years.

Oderisio Bonihominis, whose occupation is not specifically identi-fied, saw the abbot of Ferentillo "who now is" and who is called Tran-serico come to the church and be received with bells and procession and be as if he were in his own home; and he had seen three monks similarly at home, and they were called Dom Angelo, Dom Transerico, and Jericho.[87] Of an exchange of keys he had been a witness but he had not, as had an earlier witness, been in the church when Mass was sung, but he was against the wall of the church (*iuxta muros ecclesie*) and heard what was said. Nicola Jordani said that when the bishop came and was received he was given *cena* but not *pranzo* or *pranzo* but not *cena*—he was not given both (and another witness spoke of a visitor's not eating *cena* because he was fasting). Nicola said that he saw the abbot of Ferentillo coming to the church but that he did not know whether he was received in procession or not because he was sometimes in the fields and sometimes in his own house, which was next to (or very near to [*vicina*]) the church—but he heard the bells. And he said further that he had seen Pietro di Giovanni Gisonis (presumably the farmer Giovanni Franconi's uncle) having an argument with the old Lord Gentile de Amiterno during which argument Pietro had said that he did not hold the church from Gentile but from the abbot of Ferentillo. He said that everyone said that the abbot was as at home at San Leopardo and that it had been given to the abbey by the ancient emperors (*ab antiquis imperatoribus*).

Pietro Pelliparius (or Pietro the tanner), who said he came from the castro near the church (*et oriundus erat de castro vicino ipsius ecclesie*), had seen forty years earlier a clerk called donnus Annisio whom they had said was an oblate of Ferentillo but he did not wear a monastic habit; and he said that when Pietro had held San Leopardo he had held two other churches from the abbot of Ferentillo in the diocese of Marsi (*in episcopatu Marsican'*). The farmer Benedetto said that Teodino had received letters from the lord pope which returned the church to Ferentillo; he saw them, but he did not read them or hear them read, but it was said that they were the pope's letters. The farmer Simeone saw the letters, and the farmer Rainaldo Oderisii heard them read. The farmer Gualterio Petri said that he used to hear his father saying that the church belonged to Ferentillo, and Giovanni Petri said that his father (perhaps the same Pietro-father) spoke badly of (or cursed) the clerks of Ferentillo because of their acceptance of the bishop because he said the church belonged to the monks of Ferentillo.

These provoked memories of the farmer Rollando and his associates build an inconsistent but coherent oral church (remembered days in the field, by the wall, bells ringing, old emperors) for the southeastern corner of the diocese in the early thirteenth century. They are joined by more professional memories and socially more elevated ones. Most professional and professionally interested is the archpriest of Corvaro who offers straight and detailed evidence about past episcopal behavior and receptions and also offers an explanation of current difficulties. He says that a certain abbot of Ferentillo came to the church in question and sent to the witness and demanded that the witness receive him and give him procurations. He refused and said that he was a *vassallum ecclesie Reatine*. The abbot, whose name he did not know, then sent to the *ballivo* of the place, whose name was Rayn' de Latusco, who ordered the witness to receive the abbot "without prejudice" and give him hospitality and the necessary food for not more than one day.[88] And the witness heard nothing more of the matter until the current dispute arose, after the bishop placed San Leopardo under interdict for refusing proper procurations, which offered an opportunity to Teodino de Amiterno and the abbot of Ferentillo. Letters were got from Rome which allowed Teodino to give or restore the church to the abbot of Ferentillo, who then moved in and relaxed the interdict. The archpriest's partisan memory recalls a church under the normal control of the bishops of Rieti from the time of bishop Benedetto, through the time of this present bishop, Adenolfo, when he was elect. The archpriest evokes with particular clarity the time when Adenolfo was still elect because during that time since Adenolfo was not a bishop he could not perform episcopal functions and so ordinands had to be sent to other bishops.[89] He also remembers the custom that when patrons presented clerks to vacant churches the archpriests of Santo Stefano were accustomed in the bishop's name to institute and invest them in churches within the district, including San Leopardo. The archpriest's institutionally ordered mind gives a kind of sense to his testimony different from that of the farmer witnesses, but it does not, quite noticeably, give him a better memory for names, nor does it provoke him to a greater use of sensory detail.

The archpriest's memory is countered by that of Giovanni de Fonte, clerk of San Paolo di Spedino, who, since he had been a clerk of San Leopardo, had seen Dodone, Benedetto, and Adenolfo all come to San Leopardo, but he recalls the exact nature of the reception only vaguely.[90] He remembers that when the bishop demanded procurations that seemed inappropriate because of the church's pertaining to Ferentillo, and when, upon their being refused, the bishop imposed an interdict, it fell to the witness himself to go to Rome to appeal. The *episcopus respondit dure super interdicto*, and the witness knew that the *dominum terre* [was] *turbatum contra episcopum*: Giovanni provokes to emotion Adenolfo (the bishop) and Teodino (the lord of the place), scions of neighboring baronial houses.

The knight Lord Gomino remembered another interdict sixty years before when the land of Gentile de Amiterno was put under interdict because Gentile had put aside the daughter of the count of Albe. The church of San Leopardo, he recalled, had not observed the interdict because—as the prelate of that church, dompno Pietro, whose father had founded the church, often said—the church itself pertained to the church of Ferentillo.[91] When he was asked how he, Gomino, knew the other churches of the Amiterno lands observed the interdict and San Leopardo did not, he said because they did not ring their bells or even open their doors and the church of San Leopardo rang its bells and celebrated divine services.

For the Rieti side two canons testified: Pietro Cifredi and Rainaldo da Pendenza. The abbot of Sant'Eleuterio testified, and the episcopal cook who, professionally, remembered that the bishop was served both night and day. The clerk Berardo, a familiar of Bishop Benedetto, saw that bishop visit as he visited other parishes, and one year when he did not go he sent two canons of Rieti, Adinulfo d'Ascenso and Pietro Cifredi. And the witness himself had gone too.[92]

A knight named Berardo said that when he was young (*cum esset iuvenis*) he had gone with Bishop Dodone through the bishopric (*episcopatum*) because he was the bishop's blood relative (*quia consanguineus eius erat*) and that they had visited San Leopardo as they had the other parishes and that members of the *familia* had been given denari (a crucial point)—and he himself had received six or eight denari.[93] And another knight, Matteo Sinibaldi Dodonis, gave similar testimony, and Dodone was his uncle, his *patruus*. And Barbazano went with Dodone when he consecrated San Leopardo, because he often went with Dodone, but he can't remember who else was there.

Jacopo or Giacomo Sarraceno, having been asked the whole list of questions posed in order, said that he himself knew nothing.[94] But for the other side the deacon Oderisio Gerardi, the man almost a hundred, remembered a lot, some seeming confused, some of it hazy, some very exact: what happened when Bishop Dodone consecrated the chapel of Saint Martin at San Leopardo at the mandate of Gentile de Amiterno; that the bishop's boys were not given the bread they demanded in the morning; about the letter of Pope Innocent which Jericho had given to Gentile de Amiterno in the church of San Leopardo, restoring it to the abbot of Ferentillo—he had not read the letter but had heard it read by someone whose name he could not remember; and although there had been some clamor about the letter's being false, he, Oderisio, knew it was not, because he had put his hand on it (them) and "they were true (*vere erant*)."[95] It is old Oderisio who remembers to say that the monk Transerico was a nephew of the abbot.

Oderisio's long, trailing memory puts a kind of collecting net over all these voices talking, reanimating the local spaces and relationships of the distant southeastern diocese and its visitors in about the year 1210. They bring to light the power, but in the matters dealt with, rather indecisive power, of a potent long-remembered baronial family, the succeeding lords of Amiterno. These acknowledged patrons must, or do, use the pope, they seem to be used by an abbot of Ferentillo; and one of them is recalled to have argued with the local "prelate," a farmer's uncle. A series of bishops and bishops-elect are remembered moving through their *episcopatu*, actually visiting the parishes of their diocese, even though perhaps visiting mostly in search of procurations; particularly clear is the memory of Bishop Dodone moving with that overlapping mixture of *familia* and family. Remembered lunches and dinners are eaten or not eaten; and bells persistently ring. And that crucial segment of diocese, the *pieve*, the archpresbytery, is, in terms of Santo Stefano, Corvaro, defined in terms of holy oils, baptism of children, and accepted delegation of episcopal function. Papal letters are looked at and touched. Farmers are in fields and beside walls. Knights ride with bishops. Cathedral canons act for bishops. Mass is sung. And Bishop Adenolfo of Lavareta, as bishop, carries his potent family background into the lands of the lay lords of Amiterno, of not dissimilar background, as he, the bishop, follows the course of his late twelfth- and early thirteenth-century life from baronial youth, through bishop-elect of the local diocese, to bishop, to former bishop retired into the prayer-filled seclusion of a Cistercian monastery in the wet lands south of Rome.[96]

In contrast to the multiple Cicolano voices illuminating a single distant part of the diocese and a kind of rather normal working church-religion, a single piercing voice animates in a quite different way, from the center, the whole diocese and its connection with religion in the mid-thirteenth century. This is the voice of Bishop Rainaldo da Arezzo, the first Franciscan bishop of Rieti, the man who had to fight the podestà for a horse. In fact it is not quite a single voice one hears, because although the voice of Bishop Rainaldo does, in a documentary way, exist outside the chronicle by his Franciscan contemporary and acquaintance, perhaps friend, Salimbene di Adam, it is Rainaldo's voice as it is reproduced by Salimbene that we most effectively, and very effectively, hear. In finishing his talk of Rainaldo, just before going on to talk very briefly of Rainaldo's brother, the abbot of the Vallambrosan house of Bertinoro in the Romagna ("holy, learned, and good, and a dear friend of the friars minor"), Salimbene, after talking of Rainaldo's death says of him:

He was a liberally educated, very learned man, a great *lector* in theology, a seriously religious and also a popular preacher both with the clergy and the people, having an extremely elegant way of speaking (*linguam*), never stumbling: a man of magnificent heart. For two years I lived with him in the convent at Siena, and in Lyons and Genoa I saw him often. . . . I could not have believed, if I had not seen it with my own eyes, that Tuscany could produce such a man.[97]

Salimbene's telling and arranging voice is very noticeably speaking, as it is through the whole of his presentation of the year 1249, in which all of Rainaldo's story, even events that go beyond that year, is pocketed, or, better, around which year the whole story is strung. The arranging, connecting voice is very clearly Salimbene's own, specifically his, and yet very much of his time, in part because this thirteenth-century voice is characteristically specific, of the author, about the subject, both of whom must be made to seem, although to each other intimately connected, distinct and identifiable, recognizable selves. Of this voice Salimbene is a master, perhaps the great master. He rattles and sparkles and grabs his reader, ties his eyes to exact, peculiar detail: in early 1249 he went from Genoa into Provence: "When I left Genoa the almond next to the sacristy was in flower; in Provence I found the fruit of the tree big, with green husks. I also found big beans (*fave*) though just recently formed in the pods." And in Vienne he found another Franciscan friar Salimbene (*et dicebatur frater Salimbene sicut et ego*) who was Greek, with one Greek parent and one Latin parent.[98]

And at Lyons, much to the good fortune of all Rieti historians, Salimbene found his old convent-mate, Rainaldo of Arezzo. Rainaldo, however, was not, like the almonds, the beans, and the Greek Salimbene, the subject of passing bright observation. One could say of another kind of historian that he used Rainaldo to illustrate or exemplify one of the major problems of life as it was being lived in the world around him, the problem of the Franciscan in the mid-thirteenth-century world, the difficulty of in fact living the Franciscan life of Christ. But that description would distort, deny, Salimbene's way of speaking, writing, and presumably thinking. Salimbene presents Rainaldo. And Rainaldo is trapped or torn, or both, by the problems of being a responsible and serious and talented Franciscan, trying to live the life of

Francis or Christ twenty years after Francis's death. And the actual specific trap, the tar baby on which Rainaldo is caught, is the diocese of Rieti.

"At that time at Lyons was Fra Rainaldo of Arezzo of the province of Tuscany who came to the pope that he might be absolved from being bishop." When, Salimbene says, Rainaldo had been *lector* at Rieti, the bishop there had died. Rainaldo had been so appreciated that the canons of Rieti had *concorditer* elected him bishop. The pope, Innocent IV, hearing of Rainaldo's learning and holiness, did not want to absolve him; and having taken counsel with his brethren, the cardinals (*immo de consilio fratrum suorum, scilicet cardinalium*), he ordered him to be a bishop, and he did him the honor of personally consecrating him (with "me," Salimbene, there in Lyons).[99] Then Salimbene was off to Vienne, but by late spring he was in Genoa; and shortly there came, on his way back from Lyons, Fra Rainaldo the bishop. And on the feast of the Ascension, Rainaldo preached to the people and celebrated Mass, with his miter, in the convent church of the friars of Genoa (and I, *ego* [Salimbene], who was by then a priest [*et ego iam eram sacerdos*], served him at that Mass). And Rainaldo gave the friars an *optimum prandium*, *pranzo*, a really excellent lunch, of fish from the sea and other things, and in the refectory he ate familiarly with 'us.' But the following night, after matins, Fra Stephen the Englishman preached to the friars with the bishop, Rainaldo, listening; and he told a short exemplum to the confusion of the bishop. Stephen had known a lay friar in England, a holy man, who had talked about the paschal candle, which when it was lighted in church, burned and shone and illuminated, but when the horn of the extinguisher was put on it, went out and stank. And so it was with a certain friar minor. In the order he had burned with love and illuminated with example (with a more extended echoing of verbs). I, Stephen preached, have thought about what happened yesterday at lunch, when the friars genuflected before him when they served him a dish—and it came to me that what the English friar had said of the paschal candle fit this case.

And, Salimbene continues, when the sermon was finished, Rainaldo asked Fra Bertolino, the *custode* (who was a sweet man and later became *minister*) permission to speak, because the provincial was not present. And he defended himself saying indeed he had burned in the order and given good example, "as Fra Salimbene, who lived with me for two years in the convent of Siena, knows (*sicut scit frater Salimbene, qui duobus annis mecum habitavit in conventu Senensi, et vere cognoscit, qualem habent fratres de Tuscia de preterita vita mea*). And also the friars of that convent, who are old, know *meam conversationem*, my way of behaving, my style, because I was sent for that convent to study at Paris. If the friars did me the honor of bending their knees at lunch, it was not because I in any way suggested it or forced it (*nec erat meum cum baculo percutere eos*)." Finally, when he had finished speaking, on bended knees (*me* [Salimbene] *vidente et audiente*), he begged pardon if he had given bad example, and he promised that as soon as he possibly could he would rip from himself those horns that had been forced upon him. And the friars, honoring him, took him off to a house of white monks, of Cistercians, near Genoa, where there was an old man who had voluntarily resigned the bishopric of Torino, so that he, the old man, could more freely give himself to God in the cloister. And the old resigned bishop also preached to Rainaldo, "I wonder that a wise man could stoop to such folly as to accept a bishopric, you who were in the noblest of orders, that of Saint Francis, of the friars minor." The old man moved through multiple citations of scripture and cited the example of Benedict and other monks. Rainaldo did not answer. Salimbene understood why, because he knew Rainaldo was very learned and bright (*argutus*); he did not answer because he was hearing what he wanted to hear and because he knew that what the old man said was true. So Salimbene answered for him with apt, brief citations from Zechariah and Jeremiah, "Where is the flock that was given to you?" and a long quoted letter from Innocent III, with which Innocent had responded to a bishop, as Salimbene says, who asked to resign (and Salimbene gives the citation: *Decretalium libro I, de renuntiatione rubrica*, which begins "Do not think that Martha chose a bad part").[100]

Fra Rainaldo said nothing. He appeared not to like being bishop. In his mind he had decided to rid himself of the episcopal burden as soon as he possibly could. But he went off to Rieti: *ivit igitur ad episcopatum suum*.

When he got to Rieti, Salimbene continues, the canons of Rieti came to see him. And they said that one of their co-canons was *iuvene et lascivo* (in the ablative), and more lay than cleric. He wore his hair down to his shoulders and he did not wear a tonsure. And the new bishop pulled him by his hair and gave him a slap (*alapam*), and he summoned his relatives and those close to the sloppy canon, who were noble, rich, and powerful; and he said to them, the young man's own parents particularly, presumably, "That son of yours (*iste filius vester*) ought either to choose the lay life or to dress and comport himself so that he is clearly recognizable as a clerk, because the way he goes about now I cannot put up with at all (*penitus*)." And the parents, or relatives, said, "We want him to be a cleric and you do with him whatever seems good to you." Then the bishop himself cut the canon's hair and gave him a big round tonsure so that where he had sinned he should make amends. The canon was contrite, and his co-canons were pleased. But Fra Rainaldo was not able in good conscience to conceal from himself the fact that his clergy did not really want to turn to a correct way of life, so he went to Genoa to meet Pope Innocent IV and intended there to resign to the pope the episcopal dignity that the pope had forced upon him at Lyons.[101]

For something of Rainaldo's life at Rieti, we can step out of Salimbene's "1249." There survive at Rieti witnesses' attestations, essentially of memory and history, about the horse. There also survives, from 9 March 1250, sealed with the white or plain wax seal of Rainaldo as bishop, a set of capitular constitutions issued by Rainaldo, to which is added, or which includes, a compromise about which contenders shall succeed to the next vacant chapter prebends, and how. The document, of which the first letter is an enlarged *F*, begins thus:

Frater Rainaldus permissione diuina Reatinus episcopus Venerabilibus fratribus. . . . Capitulo Reatin', salutem et pacem in domino. Hec sunt que inter uos duximus statuenda uolentes et mandantes ut semper uiuatis pacifice unanimes et concordes. Siquis canonicorum alteri suo concanonico uerba iniuriosa dixerit.[102]

And from this hope of peace and capitular concord, supported by penalties for first injurious words, before the bishop or in cloister or chapter, or before lay people outside, follow penalties for insults, then for angry but light blows, then for blows that lead to breaking or bleeding. There follow ordinances against shady or shaded dealings in church property and against favoring canons' relatives with church property, and then specific problems with succession to canonical prebends and the division of commons and then the resulting arbitration. The arbiters—the bishop and two canons, Rainaldo Fatucli and Angelo Mathei, chosen by the two sides—give their arbitration to the two sides, of which one is the chapter itself and the other a group composed of the archpriest of San Ruffo, Magister Pietro Reatin', Filippo prior of Terni, Berardo de Guardiola canon of San Giovanni, and Giacomo Berardi canon of San Ruffo. They give an arbitration fairly intricate but generally clear, to which the parties are bound under penalty, an arbitration offered *pro bono pacis*.

His Rieti interlude over, Rainaldo found the pope at Genoa in order to resign to him the bishopric, *dicens quod penitus decetero non esset episcopus.* The pope, according to Salimbene, when he saw the straitness (*angustiam*) of his mind, his intention, (*animi sui*), promised to absolve him, but not on the spot, rather when he, the pope, would come into Tuscany. Because the pope still hoped, says Salimbene (watching or imagining the workings of these two minds), that Rainaldo would change his mind, his will (*voluntatem suam mutaret*). Then Rainaldo went to Bologna and waited for days, hoping that he would catch the pope on his way into Tuscany. In fact Rainaldo did not catch him until he got to Perugia, and there before the consistory of cardinals, Rainaldo resigned office and benefice, and he put the *pontificalia*, staff, miter, and ring (enumerated) at the pope's feet. Cardinals and pope were disturbed, and the pope especially because he had personally consecrated this man and because he had thought him perfectly suited to the see of Rieti (*virum ydoneum*)—and here Salimbene adds: *sicut ab omnibus credebatur et erat.* (The cardinals further argued, quoting Acts, "What if an angel had spoken to you?" or, they said, if God had revealed to you that you should be bishop?) And they argued, cardinals and pope, that for the love of God, and in their honor, for the good, utility, of the church and for the safety of souls, he should not resign; and he answered that, asking that, they labored *in cassum de materia.*

The pope, then, seeing the obstinacy of his mind (*obstinatum animum eius*), said a remarkable thing: "If it's the worry and care of pastoral rule that you don't want, why not at least keep the *pontificalia*, and the dignity and authority you have of ordaining, so that you will be in this of use to your order?" And Rainaldo replied, "I will have nothing at all (*Penitus nichil habebo*)." Absolved he went to the friars of Perugia and, taking a sack or bag or wallet (*saculum sive peram vel sportam*: Salimbene uses all three words), Rainaldo went begging that very day. And, going begging through the city of Perugia, he came upon a cardinal, whom he knew well, coming from consistory, and among other things the cardinal said to Rainaldo, "Don't you know that the Lord said that it is more blessed to give than to receive?" And a little war of tossed citations, back and forth, occurred on the streets of Perugia, but in the end the cardinal wavered because he knew that God had spoken in his saint.[103]

Rainaldo asked the Franciscan minister general John of Parma to send him where he would. He was sent back to the house of Siena, where he was known by many and where, according to Salimbene, he stayed from the feast of All Saints until the following Christmas and then died and went to God. The death was marked by miracle. A canon who had lain in his bed paralyzed for six years and had recommended himself to Rainaldo, heard in his sleep a voice say, "Know that Fra Rainaldo has gone from this world to the Father, and through his merits God grants you back your health." Waking, feeling cured, he called his boy and asked for his clothes, and went to the room of a co-canon and friend and told news of the miracle. They both rushed to the friars, and as they went out the gate, they heard the friars singing as they carried a body to the church. There was funeral and rejoicing. Says Salimbene: "Hic fuit frater Rainaldus de Aretio ex ordine fratrum Minorum, epis-copus Reatinus."[104]

For Rainaldo this *ydoneus*, this saint through whom God spoke, Rieti, the diocese, or at least being bishop of it, was the opposite of nothing, or of the nothing he would have, as opposed to the nothing he would give up, as he put the three symbols, or tools, of that second nothing, the staff, the miter, the ring, at Innocent IV's feet and rushed to get the beggar's wallet, the symbol or tool of the other, first and better nothing, to which tool Salimbene gave three names. For this intense man of the new order, the diocese seems to have been primarily the chapter. In his straitness, this repeater, at least in Salimbene, of the adverb *penitus*, he who would shine, as he himself said he had shone, an example, was able to resist all images of Martha and all talk of the salvation of (diocesan) souls. And Innocent IV, sometimes ambiguous (in dealing with pluralism) in his attitude toward pastoral care, but in general its firm proponent, was able to bring his practical self to lure Rainaldo to the bishopric by suggesting he retain its symbols and or-daining power but give up the burden of its pastoral care. And the nothing that Rainaldo chose to return to was a defined nothing; he was no simple rustic follower of Francis mutely acting out patterns of love and devotion. He had attracted the (presumably not generally very in-tellectual) canons of Rieti when he was *lector* to the Franciscans of Rieti, learned Parisian, whom he himself said with obvious pride had been chosen for Paris by his co-friars at Siena (who knew his *conversationem*). When he is not silent, he cites. He is full of learned words, and of pride in himself, as he clearly shows when he reacts in anger to Stephen the Englishman's unbearable sermon. As bishop he had time to have the matrix of his seal, with name, title, and standing bishop, cast. Although his stated goals were peace and order, what one can see of his behavior as bishop is neither particularly ordered nor restrained. Francis could act anger, but it is grotesque to think of one of his bleeding hands raised to slap an erring canon.

The problem of this trapped man is resolved in Salimbene with death and a miracle of healing (a canon), perhaps the only possible resolution. His, Rainaldo's, noisy descent upon Rieti makes his observer sharply aware of kinds of religious problems, and their words and images, that pierced mid-thirteenth-century minds. These problems are here tied to a place, to Rieti; but the diocese as far as we can see does not extend itself for Rainaldo. Had Salimbene, who cannot resist the taste of wine, the sight of beans, followed Rainaldo to Rieti, we might well have heard of leeks and crayfish. But, in the chronicle that exists, the diocese of Rieti, seen only in its chapter, is a place for the "saint" to fight with his spiritual problems.

The sharp narrowness of this diocese of Rieti's first Franciscan bishop is more striking if his visible acts there, during his short episcopate, are seen against a few quickly selected acts at Rieti of its third Franciscan bishop, Biagio da Leonessa, during his long episcopate (1347–1378). Biagio lives in the communal statute book because his sensible 1353 compromise with the commune over jurisdictional-judicial problems worked well enough in keeping order in the community and between two aspects of government that it survived. Biagio with his great wax vesica seal, carrying the impression of Virgin and Child, approved the only confraternity statutes for this period preserved at Rieti, with its meetings, its Masses, its Pater Nosters before the crucifix, its discipline, its whippings, its regulations against entering taverns and playing at dice, and for fraternal aid to the sick and burial of the dead, and then prayer for them.[105] Biagio had to face the problems of the Death. Some of them were rather surprising. The quick death of males in the house of Cimini leaving testaments which had not predicted the pace of death that the plague imposed, or in this case its gender selectiveness, left the Cimini ladies impoverished. On 1 May 1349 Biagio, acting on the basis of a constitution of the church of Rieti, which regulated gifts to the poor of Christ, was able imaginatively in this case to define the Cimini ladies as poor of Christ and thus to save them from penury.[106] Biagio accepted a broader interpretation of the imitation of Christ than had Rainaldo, and one much more generally tied to the place of his diocese.

But both bishops suggest the seriousness of religious preoccupations in their time and place. These preoccupations have many directions. Just after Rainaldo's *rifiuto*, in March 1252, an important Rieti widow, Risabella who had been married to Giovanni Impernatore, infirm and moved by her devotion to God and the Virgin, and for the sake of her own and her relatives' souls, left all of her immovable property to two Reatine convents for women, Santa Lucia of the Franciscans and Sant'Agnese of the Dominicans; she brings to sight the religion of the nuns and her own related religion.[107] In 1231 in the newly built Mareri church at Borgo San Pietro the relics in altars are named, those in the Virgin's altar to the east remembering holy women and Francis, those in Saint Peter's altar to the west holy men, apostles, relics (wood of the true cross, part of the stone where the Lord put His feet when He talked to Moses), Sebastian, Eleutherio, the Seven Sleepers, the Innocents— an essentially male assemblage, but miscellaneous, and including Francis. In the late fourteenth century officials of the city of Rieti occupy themselves with ensuring that proper honor is paid to Saint Barbara, a saint whose cult as patron visibly increases in that century.[108]

Again, the seriousness and pervasiveness of religion is suggested by acts of two of Rieti's major record keepers, Ballovino di maestro Gianni (see plate 20) and Giovanni di Pietro (see plate 22). Ballovino was, or became, a man central to the institution most central to the formal religion of the diocese. He was a canon of the cathedral church by January 1349 and had probably been one in November 1348. Before the Black Death he had been a prebendary of the church, a member of the community's second rank of clerics, people apparently normally appointed for their usefulness (and Ballovino's promotion from one rank to the other seems to have been unprecedented, but so was the plague). Ballovino had been active in the church's business since the early 1330s. In the last thirty years of his visible life, until 1382, he seems to have been the most active member of the cathedral clergy in doing its work, repeatedly acting as the chapter's chamberlain. More than any other single person he supervised, and recorded in careful account books, the income and expenses of the community's piety—the yearly purchase of laurel and cord, the expenses for anniversaries, the income from offerings at altars on feasts, from mourners of the recent dead. He paid painters and builders and bought stone and nails. More than anyone else he was the keeper of the church's furniture; better than anyone else, except perhaps his subordinate sacristans, he knew, in a humdrum way, the condition of all the church's crucifixes. In March 1372, however, when a new cross was made for the church at a cost of 90 florins, 10 florins came from a *giunta*, or approximately a giunta (in modern Rieti 1,617.32 square meters) of land sold by the bishop and chapter, 30 florins came from money offered for anniversaries by the bishop of Lucca who had been in Rieti as *riformatore* of the city, and 50 florins were given by Ballovino from his own money, "de sua pecunia pro anima sua et remissione suorum peccaminum ac suorum benefactorum"—after a year in which Ballovino's salary as chamberlain (but not his entire income) had been only 12 lire.[109]

In October 1338 Verardesca or Berardesca, the widow of Giovanni di Pietro Teodemarii, was dead; the house that she had been living in since Giovanni's death in 1314 was sold for 20 florins and the money given to the cathedral church.[110] Earlier, by 21 August 1318, the bulk of Giovanni's inheritance (of which the church was the universal heir) had been sold to a prebendary of the church acting for the bishop (Giovanni Papazurri) for 100 florins. With the properties bought the bishop endowed his own new chapel within the church, the chapel of San Salvatore. The sale money received by Giovanni's executors was applied to the building of the new tribune, the new shelter for the church's most sacred part.[111] Giovanni di Pietro had been active in the church's business from the early 1260s until the year of his death; and in fact, at least by pleasant coincidence, among the privileges in Ballovino's 1353 list of those he found in the church sacristy, important things like Nicholas IV's concession of a year and forty days indulgence to the church, is, unique in its category: "Item priuilegium pape Vrbani quarti [1261–1264] super concessione auctoritatis apostolice pro notario Janne Petri dudum scriba Reatine Ecclesie" (Giovanni's license as notary by apostolic authority).[112] By the mid-1260s Giovanni was the church's notary and scribe, and from 1293 a lay prebendary of the church. For fifty years Giovanni had observed and recorded the church of Rieti's everyday transactions in property. After he died, at his will, his financial substance was transferred to the physical structure of the church.

The institutional piety of Giovanni and Ballovino has a special tone. They were provoked in life, and Giovanni also in dying, to major gifts to an ecclesiastical institution of whose least spiritual acts they were for decades daily, working witnesses. No one knew the furniture to which he was contributing better than Ballovino; he clearly believed in its importance. And no one knew the physical property of the church better than Giovanni, and he must have believed in its importance. The seriousness of these men, their knowing what they were doing, cannot be doubted.

The pieces of Rieti history and Rieti description which have been presented in this chapter are meant to give the reader some sense of the place, some notion of the kind of religion that was expressed there in

the thirteenth and fourteenth centuries, and of its at least occasional
intensity, and some suggestion of those elements within church and
religion which could prove vulnerable to change over this period. The
reader has been presented with as much geographically and chronologically local image and sound as possible. A purpose of the voice and
sound, and the place, is to restore to the institutions, like diocese,
bishop, and cathedral chapter, which will be presented in later chapters,
their particular shape. A purpose of the fragments of religion and change
is to tempt the reader to want to know what kind of religion the inhabitants of the institutions expressed and how that changed. It is with
the background of these fragments that the institutions are to be examined. But not only with it; the next chapter is also an introduction
to place and church, but one of a different kind. In it will appear two
sets of voices and memories—one Franciscan like Salimbene's and Rainaldo's; the other much in the mouths or hands of scribes and recorders
like Giovanni and Ballovino—both from the same half-century, the first
of this study, before even Rainaldo and Giovanni; and both from more
or less the same place, the area close to Rieti, stretching west and north
from the city toward Montecchio, Terria, and Greccio. These comple-
mentary sets, relatively extended, and stitched to actual fields, swamps,
and villages, are offered so that the reality of the place and its specific
nature, as well as the nature and complexity of "church-religion," can
grow in the reader's mind.

   But, before that, there is one more fragment, one last document, to
be shown, to suggest the interdependence of what could seem the parts,
including the religious and ecclesiastical parts, of the society. It is a
sealed parchment document of thirteen lines, from 1317, written in a
beautiful and elegant (early) modern hand. Its elegance suggests that,
although it itself says that it was written in the church of San Francesco
Rieti, it comes from the hand of a clerk of the chancery of the lords of
Romagnia under whose names and over whose seals it was issued.[113] In
the document the lords Fortisbrachia, Ceccho, and Butio (Brancaleone), lords of Romagnia, promise their protection and that of their
familiars and vassals to Bongiovanni, abbot of San Salvatore of Rieti;
they promise perpetual peace, benevolence, and security for the persons,
properties, and goods of the abbot, monks, monastery, and their vassals.
The promise is made out of reverence, the document says, and honor
for the commune and people of Rieti, and is made to the podestà, the
knight Armanno "de Guelfonibus" of Gubbio, and the captain, Mocate
Piccolomini of Siena, and to the seven governing consuls of the guilds

of the people and to the whole council of the city of Rieti. It is to be observed, the lords say, "per nos, nostrosque familiares et vassallos cuiuscumque livoris" without revoking a *scyntillula*. There, on 26 July 1317 (a bad year), in the Franciscan church at the southern edge of the little city, a major baronial power from south of the city, presumably at the behest of the city, made formal a promise not to harass, and in words at least more than that, the great old Benedictine monastery also to the south of the city. The three lords' three seals in green wax were applied directly to the face of the parchment, with pieces of it cut out beneath them to hold them more firmly. The seals were small. Of one of them, the third (that to the right) a little lettering and design remain; if its parts were extended to form a rectangle, its sides would be about 3.5 cm in height and 3 in breadth. But it is not a rectangle. It is a little green wax heart.

CHAPTER TWO

'na Rosa mmist^ech^e

Between 1244 and 1246, at the hermitage of Greccio, about fifteen kilo-meters northwest of the cathedral city of Rieti, and within the diocese of Rieti, the Franciscan friars Leo, Rufino, and Angelo collected and wrote and then, as they had been asked, sent off to the minister general, Crescentius of Jesi, "striking examples" of Francis's "discourse."[1] The three men had, they wrote, "lived long in his company (*secum . . . fui-mus diutius conuersati*)." They knew Francis well; but they did not, they wrote, intend to write a new *legenda* but only, if the Minister General saw fit, to add to earlier narratives, stories which surely the venerable composers of those narratives would have included had they known them.[2] The companions produced a string of clustered, concen-trated points of didactic words free, for the most part, of the narrative of successive years of institutional development. The new stories are very personal, homely, full of convincing-sounding quotation, and also full of recreated localities and identified places. Among these places, not unexpectedly, Rieti, the nearby hermitage of Fonte Colombo (four kilo-meters to the southwest), and both the hermitage and castro of Greccio (plate 18) are prominent.[3]

Francis's Reatine activities, particularly as they reveal themselves in these Greccio stories, enchant the local places, give them something of the quality of the forests through which Lancelot moved, a quality ap-propriate enough for the new "round table." To choose perhaps the most obvious example, when Francis, on account of the disease of his eyes and his need for a good doctor, was staying in Rieti in the chamber

57

of the canon Teballo Sarraceno, he wanted one of the friars, who had
played the guitar when he was in the world (Pacifico perhaps), to borrow a guitar and play for him a song in God's praise. The friar was
ashamed to borrow a guitar particularly because the men of the city
knew that he had been accustomed to play one and so would suspect
his motives. To his objection Francis replied, "Ergo, frater, dimitta-
mus," and dropped the matter. During the following night, however,
when no one was in the streets, after the third ringing of the bell for
curfew, and Francis lay awake, for a full hour "around the house where
he lay he heard a sweeter guitar making music more delightful than he
had ever heard in his life." It was the air over the city of Rieti that the
music of this heavenly guitar, playing close and then moving away until
it could barely be heard and then coming back again, filled.[4]

Among the stories which exposed the "holy will and pleasure" of
Francis in Greccio, one, particularly and graphically local, displays a
realization about religious enthusiasm, important because it is Franciscan, realized by these friars. Because the story also offers a general and
true model of the normally transient nature of enthusiasm, it helps to
explain to modern observers, or illuminate for them, the pious behavior,
sometimes seemingly quixotic, sometimes unbearably intense, of the
men and women who lived in the diocese of Rieti (and other places)
during the thirteenth and fourteenth centuries.[5] Francis often stayed at
the hermitage of Greccio, or actually at a poor little cell connected with
it but removed from it (*cella una paupercula, que erat ualde remota*).
He was particularly fond of the hermitage, the *locus*, of Greccio, because
it was *honestus* and *pauper*, and because the men of the neighboring
castro of Greccio (two kilometers to the south along the same eastward
facing slope of the Monti Sabini) were *pauperculi* and *simplices*. Francis
liked these people better than others *de illa prouincia*. Because of Francis's example and that of his friars, many men from the *paese* became
religious, and many women although they stayed at home remained
virgins and dressed in the clothes of religion.[6] Even those who did stay
at home lived in common a life of fasting and prayer. "It seemed to
men and to the friars that their life was not among laymen and their
kindred but among the saintly and religious who had served God for a
long time."[7] Francis himself used to repeat, "De una magna ciuitate
non sunt conuersi tot ad penitentiam quot de Gretio, quid est ita pa-
ruum castrum (not from a great city have so many been converted to
penance as from Greccio, which is just a little castro)."[8] In the evening
when the friars prayed, the people of the castro (*homines illius castri,*

parui et magni) would come out on the road before the castro (*in via ante castrum*) and shout their responses to the friars' prayers: "Laudatus sit Dominus Deus"; and even little children, too young to talk properly, praised God, as well as they could, when they met the friars.[9] Because of all this, once when Francis was preaching to the people of Greccio, who had been suffering from a double disaster—huge wolves which ate people and destructive hail which devastated fields and vines—he promised them that if they made amends for their sins and turned to God with their whole hearts, the wolves and hail would cease to bother them. But if they "returned to their vomit," the wolves and hail would return and bring with them even greater tribulations.[10]

From that time, even when hail ruined the crops of Greccio's neighbors (presumably those of the canons of Rieti and the Cistercians of San Matteo as well as those of the people of Contigliano) it left the fields of Greccio unharmed. And this blessed state of virtue so rewarded continued in Greccio for "sixteen or twenty years." But afterwards wealth made the people of Greccio proud; they began to hate, to fight with swords, and even to kill one another, to rob by night, and secretly to kill animals (*occidere animalia occulte*). The wolves and the hail returned; moreover, the whole castro was burned.[11] The covenant was broken. The holy place on the side of the hill, the little Paradise of the third age, had become ordinary, or almost ordinary, again, as Francis's covenant itself makes clear that Francis knew it might.

The impermanence of conversion to penitence is illustrated a second time by the companions of Francis in a story of events which occurred within the diocese of Rieti, but this time at the very center of the diocese.[12] The act of conversion took place within the episcopal palace next to the cathedral church; and the convert was not an entire castro but a single man, Gidion, a cleric and perhaps a canon of the church of Rieti. Francis was staying in the bishop's palace because of the disease of his eyes; meanwhile Gidion was horribly ill with a disease of the kidneys or loins. Gidion was unable to get up or walk by himself, and even when he was carried his body was contorted by pain. Gidion was known to be a worldly man, although at least some part of his reputation may have come from his job as *yconomo*, steward and syndic in property management, for the church of Rieti, a position he can be seen to have been occupying, for example, in both 1213 and 1216; but in his pain Gidion asked that he be carried to Francis's presence, and there he prostrated himself before Francis and, in tears, asked Francis to make the sign of the cross over him. Francis was not predisposed in Gidion's

favor as he had been in favor of the people of Greccio.[13] He said to
Gidion, "Quomodo te signabo, cum olim vixeris semper secundum
desideria carnis, non considerans et timens iudicia Dei? (why should I
make the sign over you who have lived a life of carnal desire, never
thinking about and never fearing the judgement of God?)"[14] But Gidion's pain moved Francis. He made the sign of the cross over him, but
at the same time he warned him, "But if the Lord pleases to free you,
beware lest you return to your vomit, since I tell you in truth that if
you return to your vomit, your last state will be worse than your first."[15]
Cured (with a crackling noise) Gidion did, in the recurring biblical
phrase, later return to his vomit. As Thomas of Celano continues the
story, after having eaten one night at the house of one of his fellow
(according to Celano) canons, Gidion spent the night at the house; and
when, during the night, the roof fell, Gidion alone of the house's inhabitants died.[16]

Seen across and through the fields of Greccio and the person of
Gidion, as they appear in this major, lonely literary monument from the
thirteenth-century diocese of Rieti, those Christians of the diocese who
are more briefly visible suggest their own complexity. They seem less
simply frozen in their single moments of speech or action. They and
their institutions become less incomprehensible. They are enlivened by
the motion of potential change. Greccio and Gidion also make contrast
with the permanent conversion of Francis and so help define sainthood.
But, although the conversions of Greccio and Gidion were imperma-
nent, there is no evidence that forces one to doubt their temporary
intensity.

Greccio and Gidion make a particular set of points, and for the understanding of the church and religion in the diocese, a particularly
valuable set of points, but they are surrounded by other stories which
try in different ways to tell what Francis and his effect were like. When,
in the fall of 1225, both Francis and Honorius III's curia were staying
in Rieti, Francis was lodged with the poor secular priest of San Fabiano
outside the walls.[17] There many of the cardinals and great clerks came
to visit Francis nearly every day. By the house in which Francis actually
lived was a small vineyard, through which Francis's visitors had to pass
to get to the single door of the house. As they passed, they ate or
gathered or trampled the grapes and almost stripped the vines, and
ruined, as the poor priest said, his little harvest. Francis said to him,
"Do not be sad about it any more, speak no harsh words to anyone
over it." And he promised the priest that if he trusted in the Lord he

would have at least his usual 13 *salme* of wine from the vineyard. In fact he had 20 *salme*.[18]

Again, during the same period of treatment for his eyes, Francis was staying at the hermitage of Fonte Colombo. One day when Francis's doctor, who was very rich, had been with Francis for about an hour and was about to leave, Francis asked one of the friars to give the doctor a good meal. The friar excused himself by saying that the house was so poor that they were unable to give the doctor even a decent meal. Francis scoffed at the friar's lack of faith, and the doctor expressed his preference for eating with the poor. As they sat and began to eat, they heard a knock at the door. There stood a woman (*mulier*) sent by a lady (*domina*) from a castro some miles away. She carried a large basket full of beautiful bread, fishes, pots of crayfish (*mastillis gymarorum*), honey, and fresh grapes.[19]

Again, when a woman from Machilone (now Posta) came to Francis's doctor in Rieti, the doctor found that she was so poor that he would have to treat her out of charity. Francis was moved by the story and said to a friend, "Take this coat, and twelve loaves as well, and go and say to that poor sick woman, whom the doctor who is treating her will point out to you: 'A poor man to whom you lent this coat thanks you for the loan of the coat which you made him: take what is yours.' "[20] Although the woman was eventually very pleased, her immediate reaction (because she was presumably less aware of Saint Matthew and Saint Martin than were the Franciscans) was, "*Dimitte me in pace*; I don't know what you are talking about."[21]

The hermitage of Greccio, "the new Bethlehem," where these stories and many like them were composed (and to which, after 1262, the Joachimite, spiritually rigorous, "resigned" Minister General John of Parma would "retire" and be visited by Ubertino da Casale) was within a fast half-day's walking time from Rieti.[22] Leo, Rufino, and Angelo make this clear in the story of a good and spiritual friar who was staying at the Franciscan house in Rieti, and who walked to the hermitage of Greccio in the hope of seeing Francis and getting his blessing. Unfortunately Francis had eaten and gone back to his cell where, because it was Lent, he remained the rest of the day. The friar had to return to Rieti, although through a gentle miracle he was able to see Francis and receive his blessing in the distance. The companions' story is not specific about the length of time the walk took, but it suggests that the friar from Rieti left for Greccio as soon as he could after rising in the morning and that he, who had to be back in Rieti the same day, left the hermitage quickly after getting there.²³ That day's walk lay through, across, or around wet and marshy, but at least in places drying, land which was, in the first half of the thirteenth century, the site of a dispute between the canons of the cathedral church of Rieti and the Cistercian monks of San Matteo in Montecchio (or "on the island").²⁴ The stories of that conflict in the flat land make strange contrast with the companions' hillside stories of Francis's contemporary acts.

The convent of San Matteo requires some introduction. It was placed on a raised piece of land, then at least sometimes still an island, perhaps 100 meters above the surrounding marshy flatlands, about halfway, on a fairly straight line, between Rieti and the hermitage of Greccio. Believed to be a twelfth-century foundation, San Matteo was given new communal land and had a new church built early in the thirteenth century. It was a daughter of the house of Casa Nova in the diocese of Penne and a granddaughter of Santi Vincenzo e Anastasio at Tre Fontane just outside Rome, the dominant Cistercian house in this part of central Italy. Like other Italian Cistercian houses, San Matteo was thus of the family of Clairvaux.²⁵

San Matteo's connection with Clairvaux was in fact more personal, or so it has generally been believed, than this genealogy suggests. From 1130 to 1140, it is said, Balduino, son of Bernardo count of Marsi and friend of Saint Bernard of Clairvaux, was abbot of San Matteo. To him was written Bernard's well-known letter "number 201" of which the effective message is: *officium ergo tuum attende.* This injunction was a response to the Cistercian *contesino* abbot who had apparently been lamenting his exile in the marshes and had written sadly to Bernard: "epistola quam misisti," Bernard wrote, "affectum tuum redolet movet meum." Bernard's responding affection encased his injunction to office within a characteristic torrent of emotional phrases; as a mother loves her only child, thus Bernard loved Balduino when he was clinging to his side, dear to his heart; thus also he loved him absent: "Sicut mater unicum amat filium, ita te diligebam, haerentem lateri meo, placentem cordi meo. Diligam et absentem."²⁶ So Balduino stayed at his monastery and came, dead, to be revered as a saint. He is remembered in the name of a hill, Colle San Balduino, another raised piece of land four kilometers to the north of Montecchio. Balduino's head, in an encasing silver shell, is preserved in the treasury of the Duomo of Rieti. At least by 1674, when a correspondent of the Bollandist Daniel van Papenbroeck wrote to tell him what friends at Rieti had been able to find out about the cult, Balduino's body was being revered in a chapel in the Duomo; his feast, a double, was celebrated on 21 August.²⁷

Balduino is often, in a way mistakenly, called Balduino of San Pastore. This identification is easily explained. In the mid-thirteenth century (when the bad "air" of San Matteo's location had become too oppressive) the Cistercians moved their house from their island up the slope of the Monti Sabini to the site of their subject church of San Pastore, in the *tenimento* of Rocca Alatri, about seven kilometers to the west of Montecchio and three kilometers to the south of the castro of Greccio but lower on the slope than Greccio. The church of San Pastore had come to, and been kept by, the Cistercians of San Matteo in a rather odd way.

By an act of Pope Gregory IX, dated 5 October 1232, the Benedictine monastery of San Benedetto de Fundis, in the diocese of Narni, had, at its own wish, been made Cistercian and also been made subject to San Matteo. Recompense to the bishop of Narni for his loss of the monastery to an exempt order was made by the grant to him, from the patrimony of Saint Peter, of San Vittore, Otricoli. "The spirit breatheth where it will," Gregory IX, or his chancery, later wrote, quoting John (3:8). On 26 April 1233 the Abbot of Tre Fontane was sent to San Benedetto to induct the monastery and monks into the order. The bishop of Narni, however, was reluctant. More important, the enthusiasm of the monks of San Benedetto, like that of Gidion and Greccio, weakened. By 18 February 1234 Gregory IX's chancery was forced to add Numbers to John, and to compare the monks of San Benedetto to the children of Israel "sighing for the melons and garlic of Egypt" (11:5). The pope revoked the union, but he sent the bishop of Rieti and a canon of Rieti, Berardo Moysi, to correct and reform the monastery of San Benedetto and to see that the monks who had actually promised to follow the statutes of the Cistercian order did follow them.[28] This movement by a house of monks into and out of the Cistercian order was certainly not unique. It was, however, unusually quick; and it threatened to deprive the house of San Matteo of the opportunely acquired neighboring high lands of San Benedetto's subject church of San Pastore.[29] Fortunately for San Matteo, by October 1236 a trade had been arranged which would allow it to keep San Pastore; and by 1255 it was building, or rebuilding, there.[30]

On 11 March 1244, when they were involved in a dispute with the Hospitallers of San Basilio in Rome, the Cistercians of Rieti were still identified by the curia of Pope Innocent IV as "of San Matteo Rieti."[31] On 13 January 1251 Innocent addressed the Cistercians' abbot as "of San Pastore."[32] The house had moved to a healthier place and to what must

have seemed in the thirteenth century an even more appropriate dedication for communal lovers of the desert.[33] San Matteo itself became a
grange of San Pastore and was, over the centuries, reduced to ruin; but
another San Matteo (now San Pietro Martire), a church with a hospice,
in the city of Rieti, was attached to San Pastore.[34]

Just before the time of their move up the hill on 1 July 1235, there
were twenty-nine, or at least twenty-nine, of these Cistercians: an abbot,
a prior, a cellarer, eleven other professed monks, and fifteen *conversi* or
lay brothers.[35] A century later, on 6 March 1342, there would still be an
abbot, a prior and a cellarer, at least six other monks, and eleven conversi. In 1342 most of the Cistercians were identified by place names, in
this context almost surely indicative of their place of origin. Of the
monks one (the cellarer) was from Narni; one from Rieti; one from
Monte San Giovanni (in Sabina); three from Greccio; and one, named
Pastore, from Terni. Of the conversi five were from Rieti; two (of whom
one was named Francis) from Greccio; three from Contigliano; one
from Rocca Alatri. They were very local.[36]

Beneath the hill on which the monks would rebuild San Pastore,
near San Matteo, in the watery flatlands through, or by which, the friar
from Rieti walked (or perhaps over some of which he was rowed) to
and from Greccio, the Cistercians of San Matteo are to be seen in conflict with the canons of the cathedral church of Santa Maria, Rieti. Cistercians and canons were not, however, to remain habitual enemies. In
1251 the abbot of San Pastore was considered by Innocent IV's curia,
and presumably by the bishop and chapter of Rieti, to be a figure neutral
enough to protect the Reatine clergy from the harassment of two local
clerics who had Hohenstaufen connections.[37] In 1268 Clement IV considered the abbot an appropriate executor of his mandate to protect the
rights in Amiterno of the bishop and chapter of Rieti against the bishop
of L'Aquila; and in 1261 Urban IV, prodded, the evidence suggests, by
a canon representing the chapter, had entrusted to the abbot of San
Pastore the supervision of the renewed division of the bishop's and
chapter's *mense*.[38] In 1280 Bishop Pietro of Rieti, with the chapter consenting, gave the decayed church of Sant'Egidio in Vallonina(?) to the
abbot and convent of San Pastore for them to reform, and he retained
for the church of Rieti only an annual procuration of 4 lire provisini (of
the Senate of Rome) to be paid each year by the Cistercians at Christmas.[39] More affectingly, at the time of the Chapter General at Citeaux
in 1319, the abbot of Citeaux, at the petition of the abbot of San Pastore,
conceded to Bartolomeo da Rocca, canon of Rieti, in life and death, all

the spiritual benefits of the order.[40] Such confraternity was possible and could seem desirable, as late as 1319, between the Cistercians and an important old canon of Rieti. In 1294 and 1295 the bishop of Rieti himself had been the Cistercian Nicola, possibly elected by the canons from among the monks of San Pastore.[41]

These connections between the cathedral church and the neighboring Cistercians suggest an eventual and lengthily continued harmony between the two institutions. That they should have fought over the drying lands of the marshes, however, is unsurprising. The probably fifteenth-century inventory of San Pastore properties in Rocca Alatri and Terria, extracted from "certain instruments and the *Registrum* of the monastery," is dominated by holdings within and on the borders of the old marshland; and the 1307 reassignment of prebendal properties to the canons of Rieti is full of pieces of property from the marshland tenements of Fiume Morto, Collevaze (Collevasca), and Lacu Maggiore.[42] When it was wet, we know from a 1241 witness, the marsh provided fish, *gamberi*, and birds; when it was dry it produced wheat, beans, millet, spelt, hemp, and sorghum (*saggina*).[43] Teams of oxen were brought in to work it quickly as it dried, but its value increased, surely, as the land grew less heavy and as it was able to be worked more easily. It was desirable and desired land: on 7 September 1257 Bishop Tommaso and Pietro, archpriest of San Ruffo and canon and syndic of the church of Rieti, were invested by the commune of Rieti with a large new tract of this swampland for a price of 400 lire provisini of the senate. The land was sold for the utility or good of the commune. This utility, or good, is explained in a document which records the discussion of the proposed action at a meeting of the *consilium generale et speciale* and the *popolo* of Rieti in the cathedral church earlier in the same year: the commune had been pressed by debts, particularly to the *militibus Reatin' pro equuorum redditis ipsorum* (to the knights of Rieti, money for their horses), and thus could pay them.

The parchment on which the 1257 sale of land is recorded strongly suggests the land's inherent difficulty as well as its value. To the account of sale and investiture, without explicit explanation, is added a transcription of the commune's pious gift of land in Montecchio to San Matteo in May 1205.[44] Complexity is further underlined by the documents recorded on the piece of parchment stitched to the bottom of the 1257–1205 parchment. The second parchment records the creation and findings, in 1240, of counselors for measuring and establishing the boundaries of the church of Rieti's properties in Fiume Morto, Terria, and Portu Folicu, defining the boundaries between the properties of the church of San Matteo, and of others including certain *specialium* and *consortium*. On the same piece of parchment is appended a document which records the commune's 1209 investiture of San Matteo with its lands. To these two stitched-together pieces of parchment is stitched a third. The third is a 1222 document written by the prominent Rieti judge and scribe, and one-time podestà, Berardo Sprangone; it records the arbitration over marshland boundaries by arbiters (the priest Paolo and Berardo Assalonis, both canons of Rieti, and Giovanni de Ponte and Matteo Reat' de Necto) chosen by *Rainallus* bishop of Rieti and the canons and church of Rieti, on one side, and the monks of San Matteo *de Monticulo* (called *de Insula* elsewhere in the document), with the consent of Bartolomeo, abbot of Casa Nova, on the other. According to the arbiters' decision the properties were divided by a canal.

The difficulties of establishing and maintaining boundaries and divisions between the possessions of different groups of property holders in these drying marshlands is further emphasized by three other pieces of parchment, again stitched together, which are preserved in the capitular archives at Rieti.[45] The bottom of these pieces of parchment contains a 1304 copy of the record of a public reading on 2 September 1285 *in platea leonis in publica arenga Comunis ciuitatis Reat'* (in the Piazza del Leone where public announcements are made) after the Reatines had been summoned to hear it by the communal bell and the crier. What was read was a written statement by Giovanni Colonna, *Romanorum proconsul, Reatin' ciuitatis capitaneus et potestas* (proconsul of the Romans, captain and podestà of Rieti), which begins with the invocation: *In nomine patris et filii et Spiritus Sancti et Virginis Benedicte Marie, Amen*. The document had been written, at the mandate of Raynaldo da Palombara, Giovanni Colonna's vicar in the city of Rieti, and of Don Pietro de Oderisciis, Giovanni Colonna's judge, by Giovanni Egidii, *ciuis Romanus dei gracia Sancte Romane Ecclesie notarium et nunc notarium dicti domini capitanei* (citizen of Rome, notary of the holy Roman church and now notary of the lord captain); and the document was read by the same notary before the assembled city, but also before specific, named witnesses, including Don Filippo Pasinelli. (The 1304 copy has among its three literate witnesses two monks of San Pastore, dompno Saluato and dompno Angelo.) What Giovanni Colonna's document has to say, after an impressive harangue about the duties of his office, which include the recuperating of unjustly lost communal rights and which duties he hopes properly to perform, is that he intends to divide, distinguish, determine, and record the boundaries of communal possessions in marshland tenements, which he then proceeds to do.

This 1304/1285 document is stitched to the bottom of two pieces of parchment themselves held together, as they probably were in the thirteenth century, by a parchment strip woven through slits cut in their surfaces. These pieces of parchment contain a group of documents transcribed and notarized on 1 September 1284 by Giovanni Dati *dei gratia sacri imperii auctoritate et Reatin' ciuitatis scriniarius*. Among these documents is the record of the election of communal officials for the following year in the church of San Francesco on 28 May 1253. The elected councillors went, according to the form of the statutes, *ad brisulos*, and the *brisulus* for electing the syndic of the commune fell to the lot of the councillor Berardo di Nicola who immediately elected as syndic Berardo di Lorenzo, a man from his own *porta* or *sestiere*. This record, which Giovanni Dati copied from the records of Bonaventura once communal scriniario *super maleficiis*, is immediately followed by the account of the syndic Berardo di Lorenzo's being put in possession of extensive communal lands in the marshlands near Terria in 1253. The investiture was made by and at the decision of the communal judge Berardo Berardi, who was forced to deal with the problem of the possessions of Sinibaldo di domino Raynaldo Sinibaldi and his brothers; their lands bordered the possessions of the lords of Labro and ought not to be molested, as was clear from the sentence that the communal judge Gentile issued on 28 May 1241. Giovanni Dati, the 1284 notary, had copied not only this sentence protecting the rights of the sons of Don Rainaldo Sinibaldi but also the witnesses' testimony which allowed the 1241 judge, having taken counsel, to arrive at his verdict. These witnesses, the testimony of thirteen of whom survives intact, turn their readers' attention back again to the actual nature of the possessions which provoked this communal concern throughout the thirteenth century.

A 1241 witness, Ratino Taliatanus, who testified that for thirty years he had seen Don Rainaldo di Synibaldo di Raynaldo and his sons receive the profits of their marshland possessions, both when these were wet and when they had dried, when asked "quanta est terra et quanta aqua" (how much is land and how much water), said that he did not know. Giovanni di Giovanni Dati said that when he was a boy, he had gone to Grummulo, and a *vassallus* of Don Raynaldo's named Ugolino had said to him, "Jannuccio, rogo te ut uenias mecum quia uolo quod deferas hoc ensenium domino Raynaldo domino meo (Jannuccio, I want you to come with me because I want you to carry this *ensenium* to Lord Rainaldo, my lord)"; Giovanni said that he often carried fish and *gamberi* to Lord Raynaldo. The voices of the 1241 witnesses for the sons of Lord Rainaldo are joined by those of eleven witnesses who testified in 1229 in the interest of the holdings of the cathedral church in the marshlands.[46] They make clear (as does Giovanni di Giovanni Dati who carried things in his boat) that the marsh waters, besides providing fish and *gamberi*, had to be crossed.

Talking of Collevaze (or Collevasce), Giovanni Mercone (or Mertone), a significant witness, said that for the past ten years he had seen collectors gathering *pedagium* for the cathedral church. Rainaldo di Giovanni Romani had often seen collectors gathering *pedagium* for the cathedral church. Rainaldo di Giovanni Romani had often seen his own guests paying tolls, or he had paid for them, to be taken across the water from Collevasce (or Collevaze). Rainaldo had once given his own cloak to the canon Berardo Assalonis as a pledge for toll. The witness Pietro Rainerii said that he had watched collections being made for fifty years and had seen his own father, Rainerio, collecting for the cathedral church tolls of money, salt, and figs, and other things without any litigation, and he himself in his time had collected the church's major tolls. Other witnesses had seen merchants pay tolls in Portu Collevaze, and collectors collect tolls of money, salt, pepper, wax, cloth, leeks, and other goods. The witness Famulus had seen and heard when the major church, in the time of Bishop Dodone, bought the Collevaze (? Collevasce, here "Collevascorum") property from Rainaldo de "Lavareto" for one hundred pounds. The church had given Rainaldo fifty pounds of millet, which the witness himself had measured out for the greater part, and fifty lire provisini of the senate. And *de illa hora* to the present, the church had held and collected.[47]

In this wet and troublingly indecipherable place there ran two customs of Rieti, witnesses testified, which were sensible enough but which, like many sensible customs regulating the holding of property, also and quite naturally provoked dispute. The custom when swampland dried was for it to become the property of whoever had held its bank when it was wet; this custom must have derived from the belief that swamps dried slowly and that the new land formed would obviously be attached to a single identifiable shore.[48] The second of these troublesome customs was that if anyone built pens and sheds on property which was not his own, and if the true proprietor of the land wanted to show that he refused to accept and acknowledge the intrusion, the proprietor destroyed the intruder's pens and sheds.[49]

About one of the fights between canons and monks in this water and land the voices of sixty witnesses can still be heard.[50] Although the witnesses are explicit and various in the things they have to say, their own statements are not dated. It has been assumed that they come from the 1240s, from approximately the time in which the *Scripta Leonis* was being written, but it seems much more likely that they come from the 1220s, approximately the time in which Francis himself was in the neighborhood.[51] Although the preserved depositions or attestations are in a fond which includes a 1244 copy of a 1209 document, their hand does not preclude a date earlier than 1244. One of the witnesses speaks of the action of 1209 as ten years and more before his giving testimony.[52] Of the sixteen conversi of San Matteo of whom testimony survives, and of whom some clearly remember the incidents of 1209, only eight appear in the list of conversi preserved from 1235.[53] The protagonist monk does not appear in 1235; nor probably does the other monk witness.[54] Six canons of Rieti appear either as witnesses or as contemporary actors in testimony: Sinibaldo Mareri, Berardo Rainaldi Sinibaldi Dodonis, Berardo Salonis, Henrico, Berardo Moysi, and Rainaldo da Pendenza. Their other known active dates do not make them very helpful in dating the San Matteo dispute. Sinibaldo or Senibaldo Mareri, the most visibly active of the case's canons, is recorded as a canon in actions dating as early as 1218 (acting as syndic for the bishop and chapter) and as late as 1253, but a Siniballo Mar', who is probably he, is active as early as 1202.[55] Berardo Rainaldi Sinibaldi Dodonis is visibly active from 1225 (acting as an obedientiary of the church) to 1252.[56] Henrico (or a Henrico) is visible from 1201 to 1223.[57] Berardo Moysi is visible from 1230 to 1240.[58] If Rainaldo da Pendenza is the same as the priest Rainaldo, he is visible from 1230, or perhaps even from 1202, to 1240.[59] Berardo Salonis is visible from 1233 to 1261, but he is quoted as saying in 1246 that he had been a canon for twenty-four years, and in 1250 he remembers back thirty-eight years.[60] None of these bracketing dates excludes the existence of any canon at an earlier or later date. Certainly the named canons do not exclude for the dispute the 1220s date that the communal witnesses, the actual testimony, and the list of Cistercians suggest. The possibility of a date about 1225 would seem to be strengthened by the statement of one witness in the case, whose evidence probably should not be interpreted too precisely. Jai de Dodo seems to equate "before the church of San Matteo was built here" with "fourteen years ago."

If this church was built soon after the induction of 1209, then the date of the testimony should be about 1225.[61]

The document of 1209, which was copied in 1244 and which in this copy now accompanies the testimony of the collected witnesses, was in fact important to the case, and two of the men who had acted for the commune in 1205 and 1209 are among the collected witnesses.[62] One of these, Don Matteo Sarracenus (or Sarraceno), was, he said, a consul of Rieti, with the other consuls, and also the consuls "de consilio multorum bonorum hominum de Reate" when they for the commune gave to Fra Balduino, for San Matteo, the commune's swamplands between Casamascara and Monticchiolo (or Montecchio) and within its other borders, including the lands of the lords of Labro, gave them, that is, conventionally saving the rights of third parties. He was also present and saw Matteo Reatino de Necto induct the monk Tedemario for his monastery, into possession of the property, at Fiume Morto, by mandate of Don Matteo Sinibaldi Dodonis, then podestà of Rieti.[63] Another witness who recalls the induction is Matteo Reatino de Necto (here "Nepto") himself.[64] The 1244 copy is of Don Matteo Sinibaldi's mandate to Matteo Reatino de Necto to put the church of San Matteo "de Insula" in perpetual possession of the marshland, once of the city, which had been given "per concexionem et donationem nostrorum antecessorum in regimine nostre ciuitatis residentium" and by precept of Pope Innocent III; the mandate was written on 17 May 1209 in the presence of the canon priest Raynallo and other witnesses.

These witnesses who were interrogated in the 1220s(?) certainly answered a series of questions more formally fixed and rigidly arranged than the implied questions which were answered by the companions' stories about Francis. The witnesses were able, however, to include a great deal of miscellaneous circumstantial evidence in their answers. Master Guglielmo, for example, said that he had seen Rainallo *Merconis* carrying a tub of fish, and he had asked him, "Why are you carrying that?" Rainallo answered, "I am carrying these fish to Santa Maria di Rieti for the rent (*pro redditu*) which I have to pay for what I hold in the Fiume Morto from that church." And he said that he paid the rent three times a year. And at the church of Santa Maria he, either Guglielmo or Rainallo, often ate fish from that rent. And Master Guglielmo saw this in the time of Bishop Adenolfo.[65] Nicola Pectenal' (?the breeder, the tanner), who was a shepherd *unius boni hominis* of Rieti, said he had often seen many fishermen fishing in the water of Fiume Morto as he went to the shed where he kept his animals; he had asked

the fishermen for whom they fished in that water. They had said they
fished there for the church of Santa Maria di Rieti.[66] Berardo Amabilis
said that before the church of San Matteo was built he saw that the
Mercones held the property of Fiume Morto; he wanted to go cut wood
there, but the Mercones said that he could not and that they held the
property for the church of Santa Maria Rieti. He said he did not know
about "now" because he did not go there any more.[67] Pietro Deodati
had seen that the Mercones had held the place for forty years, but now
"those" of Santa Maria sent their *boues* there.[68] Gianni Petri said that
when the place was water the Mercones held it, and that they had had
a gate there; and once when he had been standing there they had come
and opened it and cut some trees down, and afterwards had closed the
gate. The Mercones themselves had told him they held the place of
Santa Maria.[69]

More witnesses talked of the time before San Matteo was built; and
one saw Adenolfo who had been bishop of Rieti come to Fiume Morto,
but he could not remember whether he then was *episcopus* or *electus*.[70]
Repeatedly, over and over again, the witnesses talk of the old days when
Fiume Morto was water and a source of rent in fish and *gamberi* and
then talk of more recent times since it had dried. A witness called Vo-
neczo said that by the will of the *Merconum* he once, forty years before,
had made a trap (*vergagam*) in the swamps that were then at Fiume
Morto and taken crayfish, and that for twelve years he himself had fished
in those swamps; but that for this he had not himself done service to
the church of Santa Maria di Rieti.[71] Vetulo Morici could testify that
the Mercones had held the place before and after its drying, for forty
years, from the church of Santa Maria di Rieti, and that while it was
water he had seen the Mercones do service to the church *de piscibus et
gamaris et de personis et aliis rebus*.[72] Reatino de Cenzo, a *familiaris* of
the church of Santa Maria had over forty years' time seen the Mercones
do service to the church, and when the place had been water he himself
had very often received the fish and the *gamberi*.[73] Another *familiaris*,
Andrea Petri, whose memory stretched back thirty years, had seen the
services in fish and *gamberi*, but also services of the Mercones' boats
and persons.[74] Rainucius Petri had heard from the Mercones themselves
(*a Merconibus*) that they held the woods and swamps from the church
of Santa Maria di Rieti; he had heard from the fishermen themselves
that they fished for Santa Maria there, in Fiume Morto and Cespa, but
of the exact boundaries of the place he was ignorant.[75] Girardo Nicolai,
a fisherman, thinking back thirty-six years and more, remembered see-

ing the services in fish and *gamberi*; and the witness Zaccaro also re-membered the fish and the *gamberi*.[76] A witness named Aristante, re-membering back as far as thirty years, knew of the services in fish and *gamberi*; he was there and saw it when the fish was taken out of the house of the Mercones for the church, but he himself had not followed along and seen what the messenger who carried them away had done.[77]

The evidence of these witnesses, who are busy establishing the old tenure of Santa Maria, is filled with fish and *gamberi* and also with the Mercones. Some of these Mercones, who according to other witnesses held Fiume Morto as a *feudum* (or in Fiume Morto held a *feudum*), speak for themselves.[78] Pietro Merconis, whose father and paternal un-cle and cousins (*fratres consobrini*) and brother with himself held the property in Fiume Morto which was in dispute, said that they had held it when it was water and when it had dried and to the present time *in beneficium* from the church of Santa Maria in Rieti; and they returned to the church *seruitium de piscibus, gammaris, et nauigiis*. He said that they had given some of the property to other persons to work it, but that they themselves held the property except for the part which the church of San Matteo had occupied in this dispute, which had now lasted two years.[79] Jai de Mercone said that his father and, after his father's death, he himself, held *in feudum* from the church of Rieti property in dispute, and for it they had returned service to the church of Santa Maria, but that for the last three years those of San Matteo (*illi de Sancto Matheo*) had opposed their working the land. He testified that the property was in Fiume Morto and next to the property of San Matteo, of Vetulo Morici and of Angelo de Iai de Lotheri. He said that when it was water they had held water and when it had dried he held land.[80] The neighbor Angelo (called here more conventionally Angelus Iohannis Lotherii, so Angelo di Giovanni di Lotherio) said that he had worked a piece of land for two seasons for the Mercones (*per Mercones*), and to the same Mercones (*ipsis Merconibus*) he had returned part of his labor (*partem laboritii*), which they received for the church of Santa Maria; later he had stopped working for them and in fact held his own inheritance.[81]

Dominant as the Mercones are in the testimony, the sharpest physical dispute between Santa Maria and San Matteo seems to have occurred on another tenement, that of Pietro di Rainaldo Montanagi (*Rainaldi Montanagi*). As a witness Pietro said that his father, his grandfather, and he himself (and they appear in that order) had held and still held from the church of Santa Maria, lands *de pede Monticuli de Terria usque in paludem* (from the foot of the hill to the marsh), and had held them without dispute.[82] But another witness Benencasa, *familiaris* of the church of Santa Maria, said that he had gone with the canons Sinibaldo Mareri (*Siniballo Marerii*) and Berardo Rainaldi Senebaldi Dodonis, and "the son of Rainaldo Montanagi" to the land which that "son" had held, and held, *in feudum* from the church of Santa Maria di Rieti. They had begun there to make a bank or ditch (*fossatum*) and mark boundaries.

At that point the son of Montanagi said that the Cistercians were coming, and in fact the priest and monk Filippo and a group of *conversi* from San Matteo advanced upon the canons. Filippo and Sinibaldo faced each other and both appealed against the depredations of the other side. Sinibaldo ordered Filippo to leave, but he came forward.[83] The resulting skirmish, which was described by several witnesses including one of its two principal protagonists, obviously startled and confused its observers and participants. Benencasa *conversus* of San Matteo saw the monk Filippo pull out a boundary stake (*passillum*) which the canons had put in and then saw the canon Sinibaldo Mareri hit or push Filippo hard, as Filippo objected to his act and appealed against it; Sinibaldo himself put the stake back in the ground and began to hoe, holding the hoe in his own hands.[84] Another *conversus* (Rain') said that when Filippo told the canons to stop putting in the stakes, Sinibaldo Mareri pushed him so hard that he almost fell into the river.[85] The Reatine *familiaris* Benencasa said that Filippo pulled out the wood with such force that it drove Sinibaldo's knees into the bank—or ditch (or forced him to put them against the bank or possibly forced him into the canal up to his knees).[86]

Sinibaldo Mareri's own testimony is somewhat extended. He thought it had been three years since he and some other canons had come to their territory now in dispute and there had begun to work it, with oxen, for the church of Santa Maria di Rieti and since they had forbidden the people of San Matteo to work there; at the same time they had appealed for its protection to the pope. But the people of San Matteo had later made sheds and worked the place. Then "this year" after Easter, Sinibaldo himself had come with his co-canon Berardo Rainaldi Dodonis and certain *familiares* of the church of Santa Maria and had worked there, also putting in stakes. Sinibaldo, "ipse testis, stabat appodiatus ad unam salicem quam fixerat ibi"; he had stood by a willow tree that he had just planted, or more probably beside a willow stake or branch, *una sargia*, in the current dialect around San Pastore, which he had fixed. Dom Filippo, the monk, with some conversi, had come angrily, or so he believed, toward him. Sinibaldo had appealed to the pope and put the church of Rieti under his protection so that neither the abbot nor the prior nor anyone else from the monastery would molest Santa Maria's property; but, instead of going away after this appeal had been made, Dom Filippo had seized the *salicem* (*sargiam*) and pulled Sinibaldo by the cloak, and Sinibaldo would have fallen if he had not had strong legs. More generally, Sinibaldo went on to say that they, from Santa Maria, had done no violence to San Matteo or pulled down sheds on San Matteo's property, on its side of the canal (although he himself did not know all the boundaries of the disputed properties). Sinibaldo said, too, that in the past he had eaten the fish and the *gamberi* taken from Fiume Morto and sent to Santa Maria by those who held it from the church *in beneficium*. The custom of Rieti, he then said, was that whoever held the land next to a swamp held the adjoining swampland when it dried.[87]

The sheds which appear in Sinibaldo's testimony are again referred to in the testimony of his co-canon and co-witness Berardo Salonis. Berardo had heard, both before and after he became a canon, *per famam publicam* in Rieti, that water and dry land and swamp in Fiume Morto were held by the Mercones from the church of Santa Maria di Rieti and that the Mercones did service for it in fish, *gamberi*, and *nauigiis* (services in tolls and portage). Three years before the time of the dispute, Berardo said, he had gone to the church's holding in Fiume Morto with other canons, Enrico, Berardo Moysi, and Rainaldo da Pendenza, and that then there were no animal pens or sheds in the place. The canons had forbidden the people from San Matteo to build any sheds on the place, and they had appealed to the pope and put their church's interest in it under papal protection. After that San Matteo had built the pens.[88]

It is these pens, and other buildings and works of San Matteo, and the custom they invoke, which are the subject of the other arm of violence—other than that of Sinibaldo Mareri standing by the willow, which is repeatedly talked about by the witnesses in the case. The priest Dom Filippo, the protagonist of the action against Sinibaldo Mareri, is first in the list of San Matteo witnesses. He testified that he was present, and observed, when, by mandate of the podestà, Matteo "Reatini de Nepto Reatinus ciuis" put the monk Tedemario and the witness Filippo himself in possession of the lands and water cultivated and uncultivated that lay between the holdings of the sons of the deceased Rain' Leonis and the swamps of Casamascara and between them and the holdings of the lords of Labro. He said that he himself had seen the letter from the lord pope to the podestà which directed him to give the property to San Matteo. He said that more than ten years had elapsed before the time when the canons "Sen' Marerii" and "Ber' Rain' Dodonis," in April of the year in which he testified, occupied the possessions of San Matteo and forcefully expelled the people of San Matteo, themselves objecting and appealing and saying that the monastery had held the land peacefully and that the bishop and canons had not objected before. And after a few days Filippo had seen the sheepfolds dismantled and the land being plowed and hoed by men who said that they did it for the church of Rieti. He heard, moreover, that the *familiares* of the church of Rieti had begun to destroy the sheds and cut down the trees, to use the pastures, and to break down the hedges. Then Filippo with Fra Berardo, at the mandate of the prior and brothers, went to the bishop and chapter because, Filippo said, they had doubted that these things had really been done by them. In fact, Filippo also said, he had seen that beyond the canal the church of Rieti held a strip (*lexcem*) of land.[89]

The *conversus*, Fra Rain', said that the monastery had been in quiet possession of the disputed land for six years and on it had had sheds, gardens, hedges, and pastures just as the monastery did on its other lands. Then Sinibaldo Mareri, Berardo Rain' Dodonis, Henrico, Berardo Salonis and some *familiares* of the church of Rieti had come and dismantled the sheepfolds and begun to destroy the pens; they had broken down the hedges, laid waste the pastures, cut down some of the trees, and plowed the *areas*.[90] Ratino de Cenzo, *familiaris* of Santa Maria di Rieti, told the same story of devastation, including that of the *bladum*, perhaps standing grain in the field. Ratino made clear the reason for the devastation; it was to demonstrate the fact that Santa Maria did not accept San Matteo's right to cultivate Santa Maria's land.[91] The *familiaris* Famulus, who gave bread and wine to the canons when they came, said that they had said that they came not to do violence but to defend the possessions of the church of Santa Maria. The *familiaris* Andrea Petri said he saw the other *familiares* of Santa Maria break the sheds of San Matteo to protect the property of Santa Maria because "illi de Sancto Matheo" said it was theirs.[92] The two monks, Filippo and Giovanni da San Giorgio, and the *conversus* Giovanni Martini remembered events in April.[93] The *conversus* Pietro could not remember in what month he had seen the destroyed pens and the broken hedges.[94]

Rainucelle Petri saw the destroyed sheds "this year" in the month of May, or the month of June; Henrico Oderisici, a *familiaris* of Santa Maria similarly remembered the month as "May or June," although he could be much more precise about boundaries: the "mountain," the lands of Vetulo Morici and Angelo di Giovanni Lotherii, and "mons ubi est ecclesia."[95] Pietro Merconis talked of the people of San Matteo insulting those of Santa Maria, and those of Santa Maria destroying a pen and climbing on top of a shed.[96]

The testimony may be confused and confusing but what happened is, in a general way, clear enough. Both Santa Maria and San Matteo had property in the marshland. As the swamp dried additional land became usable. Exact boundaries became necessary where none had been possible before. Each institution, aware of, and suspicious of, the acquisitiveness of the other, struck; and there resulted those sordid little scenes of petty violence which the witnesses remembered. The witnesses, or many of them, were asked to think to a more distant past. Although the subjects about which their memories were exact differed, the simple length of their memories is impressive. Aristante, Jai de Bonomo, and Famulus remember the behavior of the Mercones for thirty years and more: Ratino de Cenzo and Pietro Dodati for forty years.[97] Pietro Merconis remembers the way lands were worked for thirty-six years and more.[98] Although Benencasa had only been a *conversus* for three years, Giovanni Berardi for four, Rain' for six, and Rustico and Rainaldo for eight, another Giovanni had been a *conversus* for ten years, Pietro for twelve, and Girardo for sixteen.[99]

These memories stretching back, many of them to the crayfish caught in the swamps near Casamascara and Montecchio, and even more of them to the struggle over animal pens and boundary stakes, make sharp contrast with the memories of the companions of Saint Francis on the hills above. Sometimes the memories of the two groups of rememberers touch each other with almost explosive effect. Once when Francis, the companions recall, was staying at the *palazzo vescovile* in Assisi, he did not, in spite of the other friars' coaxing, want to eat. He said, though, that perhaps if he could have some of the fish, *qui dicitur squalus* (almost surely a *cavèdano*, in present Cicolano dialect *squau*), he might be able to eat it. And suddenly someone appeared who had been sent by Gyrardo, the minister of the friars of Rieti and who carried a basket in which there were three large and well prepared *squali* with *gamberi*, things which were not available in Assisi then, in wintertime.[100] These *gamberi* perhaps knew in life those whom the Mercones guarded.

The sharpness of the contrast is seen in full relief if the story of the surprised woman of Machilone "getting back" her coat is put next to the scene of the Cistercian priest Filippo struggling with the canon Sinibaldo Mareri by the willow and the dike or ditch. In the two scenes very different things are being done to and with property, although one could argue that property itself was being similarly observed and appreciated. One must be struck, however, by the ease with which the contrast can be made and seen. The little boxes of recaptured time in the witnesses' depositions look oddly like those of the stories about the saint. They represent a commonly shared group of assumptions about how one tells a story, how one proves, how one creates verisimilitude.

These storytellers and answerers of questions have relatives in many times and places but they also behave in a way particularly characteristic of the early thirteenth century. Their way of thinking and proving has perhaps been best examined in its most important place, in the process of canonization, during the period from 1200 to 1240, and within that process, in the growing rigor concerning rules of evidence and in the preference for "the simple unvarnished speech of the witnesses."[101] This way of thinking obviously echoes, or is echoed by, the Parisian emphasis, particularly that of Peter the Chanter and his circle and successors, upon the confessor's necessary concern with "pertinent circumstance."[102] The anecdote of sermon, inquest, saint's life, and confession are closely related. Sometimes the sermon has been thought to be the cause, at least in the final sense of cause, of this way of thinking and writing; but that explanation is too simple, and in its simplicity wrong. The use of these anecdotal containers of carefully reproduced evidence offered to lots of serious people in the early thirteenth century the most compelling way of establishing truth and of seeing reality.

This fortunately apparent similarity of techniques of seeing and telling in seemingly diverse places, at Greccio and in the depositions of the San Matteo and Santa Maria witnesses, is a lens through which should be viewed the Reatine church in the thirteenth century. Through that similarity should be seen the very striking dissimilarity of what people are doing in the two sets of stories, of the actions that the two sets of witnesses witness. The similarity of the frame helps the viewer to realize that both sets of actions were integral parts of the Reatine church in the thirteenth century, both were at home in it, and any definition of it should include both.

Within the two sets of actions there is further complexity and further contrast. This is of course obvious in the dispute over property because a significant part of its action is seen from two opposing points of view. The complexity within the companions' group of stories is, however, more obviously interesting. One sees it quickly in a story they tell about Francis when he was staying at the Reatine hermitage of Fonte Colombo. Fonte Colombo is near the road from Rieti to Sant'Elia Reatino. Sant'Elia is about two kilometers farther from Rieti than Fonte Colombo, but it is the village nearest Fonte Colombo. While Francis was staying at Fonte Colombo a particularly virulent disease of cattle, which was called *basaboue*, spread to Sant'Elia. At the time when the disease was beginning to kill the cattle of Sant'Elia a pious man in the village had a dream in which he was told to go to the hermitage and to get some of the water in which Francis had washed his hands and feet and then to throw it on the cattle—thus they would be cured. The man in fact did get up early and go to the hermitage to tell Francis's *sociis* what had happened. The *socii* saved *in quodam uase* the water in which Francis had washed his hands when he ate. Then in the evening, without telling Francis why, they asked him to let them wash his feet. The *socii*, the companions of Francis, gave the water in which Francis's hands and feet had been washed to the man from Sant'Elia. He sprinkled it on the cattle. The cattle were cured. This box of story ends with the final clause: "'in illo tempore habebat beatus Franciscus cicatrices in manibus et pedibus et latere (at that time Saint Francis had scars in hands and feet and side)."[103] Perhaps the most primitive of all the early stories of Francis's wonder working is concluded with a brief, and here very pertinent, reference to the most startlingly exalted wonder of his whole life, his reception of the stigmata, his becoming almost frighteningly like Christ.

Clearly the story of the stigmata itself is not told in the *Scripta Leonis* because it had been fully told in the *Vita prima* of Thomas of Celano, although no telling of it seems more effective than the companions' passing reference. Similarly, although the companions are writing at Greccio, they do not again tell the story of the Greccio *presepio*, with which Francis set before the eyes of the people there a real manger with a real ox and a real ass, so that they could more physically partake in the birth of Christ and in the meaning of Incarnation and so that Greccio would become the "new Bethlehem"[104] (see plate 32). The Greccio Christmas story that the companions tell has a very different tone. In it too Francis is staying at Greccio. A minister of friars has come to see him. In order to celebrate Christmas with their special guests the friars at Greccio have set the table (raised on some sort of dais) particularly carefully with beautiful white table cloths that they had gotten (*de pul-*

cris et albis toalleis quas aquisiuerant) and with drinking glasses (*uasis uitreis ad bibendum*). Francis comes down from his cell and sees the table raised and elaborately set (*ita curiose paratam*). He goes secretly and takes the hood (*capellum*) and staff of a *pauper* who has come that day. He then acts the part of a poor pilgrim who comes and knocks at this "rich" house and begs food and sits upon the ground to eat what he is given.[105] He thus performs a rebuke to his brothers in order to teach them again the importance of physical poverty. They respond with shame and tears. It is a bitter little Christmas story. It rips apart the sense of quick, blessed agreement produced by the *presepio* story. But in didactic method the two stories are similar.

These compounded complexities and similarities are brought together here to make something like that kind of mirrored kaleidoscope through which the seen shapes and colors of nature are rearranged into other patterns, and the potential revolutions within what have seemed immutable natural forms are revealed. This is done not just "to reveal unknown depths of strangeness," but to encourage a viewer to discard in part all preconceptions about what things do and what things do not go together, particularly within the church, and thus to look more freely and perhaps creatively, at what is present. One who looks should expect, if anything, strange mixtures, strange contingencies and appearances, and accept the fact that they are not in reality strange.

In an unexpected letter of 1312 Gregorio, the abbot of the enfeebled abbey of Farfa, writes to Nicola son of the *discreto* man Francesco da Greccio to present Nicola with one-fourth of Sant'Angelo and all of San Casciano of Greccio, churches within the diocese of Rieti vacant through the death of Pietro, Nicola's paternal uncle.[106] The churches pertained to Farfa, and the abbot wished to reward a family to which it was, for various reasons, obligated. The presentation occurs in an area tense with Cistercians and Franciscans, to the son of a man named Francesco da Greccio. Its record is preserved in the archives of the church of Rieti, and the action occurs some time after one might expect the Benedictines of Farfa to have retired from the area. The land around Greccio was oddly *macchiata*. The observer should not be surprised to find similarly but spiritually *macchiati*, as well as incompletely revealed, the characters of Reatine bishops, like Adenolfo and Tommaso Secinari, and the attitudes of the body of Rieti canons and of the other visible Christians of the diocese of Rieti.

In the later nineteenth century a man named Lorenzo Mascetta Caracci went about the countryside of the Abruzzi east of Rieti collecting examples of the peculiar uses of Church Latin in everyday speech. He discovered a generally unknown language, but a common one, which brought to his ear and mind strange associations of ideas and a new understanding of how the idiom of the liturgy penetrated and was penetrated by the matters of ordinary physical life. His work revealed the strange mixture of concepts surrounding the church and its language and so uncovered the strange mixed substance that the church, the actual church in real life, was. He found, for example, that when people wanted to say "to make a soup (*fare un minestrone*)," they sometimes said "*fa' 'na Rosa mmist^ech^e.*"[107]

CHAPTER THREE

The Definition of Diocesan Boundaries (1): to 1266

The thirteenth century was a world of dioceses. Clerks writing in the papal chancery had no serious maps but were not on this account discommoded. They wrote to a Christian world securely embraced and divided. Diocese met diocese everywhere. Nothing was excluded. Where was a place? It was at least locally, not always jurisdictionally, within a diocese. Curial letters and formularies make clear that this is what the clerks thought or assumed; and theirs was the assuming mind and idiom of formal Christendom.[1] Of course the real meaning and importance of diocesan boundaries, like any others, depended upon what they contained and what they divided; and these whats were, in the early thirteenth century, about to undergo significant, and really quite drastic, change.

In 1182 Pope Lucius III granted to Benedetto bishop of Rieti and his successors a confirmation of their rights and privileges, which included a description of the diocese's geographical boundaries, imagined as starting from and returning to the Tancia on the borders of the diocese of Sabina and passing through or near some still seemingly recognizable places, like Marmore, Stàffoli, Lago di Fucino, Collalto, Vallebuono, Canemorto (Orvinio), Pietrasecca, the torrente Farfa, and through other places less easily identifiable. The original privilege does not seem to have survived at Rieti, and, in fact, its wording suggests that it is copying the words of other earlier privileges which do not survive.

The copied, probably copying, privilege's description is, nevertheless, an affirmation of the idea of territoriality, a legacy, but also an idea related to that distant one, for example, which was changing the kings of England from *reges anglorum* to *reges anglie*, an idea which was neither clear nor locally limited. But it was, in the limiting sense of the word, an idea, although one with a potential for development and physical extension. Had a contemporary been able to describe the boundaries of the relatively large and complex diocese of Rieti in terms that a modern cartographer could follow, it would have been surprising. It is not clear that the composers of the Lucius privilege thought that they were describing actual and exact boundaries. They did not need to be exact because they were describing a general area in which they then proceeded to name the enclosed *plebes, pievi* (the baptismal churches). The privilege names seventy-five *pievi* and then some sixty "oratoria quae monasteria dicuntur (places called monasteries)" and some twenty more "infra ciuitatem in suburbiis eiusdem ciuitatis (within the city in the suburbs of the city)"; but these names, although they removed the burden of exactness from the boundary description, should not be thought all necessarily to represent places existing in 1182, or existing as *plebes* or *monasteria*. The rather indistinct category with which the privilege concludes its list of *plebes* and *monasteria* is followed by a list of seven *castra*, a *roccha*, and a *turris*.[2]

The surviving Anastasius IV confirmation of privileges from 1153 contains a similar but not identical list of *plebes* and *monasteria*, and it concludes with nine *castra*.[3] Although both privileges are essentially lists of the internal units of the diocese in which the bishop and cathedral church had jurisdictional and other rights, neither was probably meant to be seriously descriptive even in this sense. The privileges need not suggest that the popes themselves or any of their, particularly curial, contemporaries examined those rights in any rigorous way in connection with these confirmations. The evidence surviving from the time of the long-episcopated Bishop Dodone, Anastasius's bishop, however, suggests that Dodone was, at least in his time's terms, an unusually active diocesan; and the evidence surviving from Bishop Benedetto reveals activity.[4]

In the mountainous wastes along parts of the border of the diocese of Rieti, exact geographical boundaries would have been useless. In the broad high wastes behind San Pastore, for example, unless there had been measurable and returnable tithes in cyclamen and *fiori di pasqua* (or more realistically, perhaps, in hay or wood or animal droppings), who need have cared about diocesan or *pieve* boundaries?[5] The geographical boundaries that did matter, one must assume, were defined by local long custom. The diocese of Rieti shared boundaries with the dioceses of Sabina, Narni, Terni (after its reconstitution), Spoleto, Ascoli, Teramo, L'Aquila (and before it, Forcone), and the Marsi; it seems to have touched a corner of the diocese of Tivoli. Although there may have been some hostility between Rieti and Spoleto in the thirteenth and fourteenth centuries, and perhaps some problem with Narni and Terni, the only clear and sharply visible dispute over diocesan boundaries was with the diocese and diocesan of L'Aquila.[6]

L'Aquila was in various ways a special case. The city itself was an early member of a series of creations of centralized agglomerations of castri and castelli in the northernmost parts of the Regno, the reformed kingdom of Naples—places like Leonessa (an earlier Hohenstaufen foundation), Cittareale, Cittaducale, Borgo Velino, and Posta—places which were meant to offer amenities to their inhabitants and to make defense, administration, taxation, and the control of trade more effective, places which recall similar creations in northern Italy, southwestern "France" and elsewhere, places which also made the mountainous Abruzzi a more conventional part of urban Italy.[7] In 1256 and 1257 the episcopal see of Forcone was transferred to, or renewed in, this "new city" of L'Aquila. Bishop Berardo de Padula, who may already have been residing in L'Aquila as bishop of Forcone, was made its first bishop.[8] The sense of continuity which this implies, however, is misleading. The new bishopric was more vigorous than the old, attached as it now was to a real city, in a relatively toughly governed kingdom, at a time of generally increased diocesan activity.

Pope Alexander IV's privilege of translation seems to have granted to the new bishop jurisdiction over all the inhabitants of Forcone and Amiterno and to have named, roughly, a geographical outline of the diocese.[9] The vigor of the new see seems quickly to have been applied to Amiterno and thus to have provoked a dispute with the church of Rieti. A mandate of Pope Clement IV addressed to the Cistercian abbot of San Pastore and dated 2 April 1266 was obtained for the bishop and chapter of Rieti, perhaps through the intervention of Cardinal Giordano of Terracina. The mandate says that the bishop of L'Aquila *suis finibus et iuribus non contentus*, not content with his borders and rights, was forcing the rectors and clerks of Amiterno (the ecclesiastical area on the eastern border of the diocese of Rieti and to the north and west of L'Aquila) in the diocese of Rieti to come to his synods and that he was in various ways keeping the bishop of Rieti from exercising his appropriate jurisdiction in his own diocese; piling injury on injury, the man-

date continues, the bishop of L'Aquila had ordered, within a term fixed
at the bishop's own pleasure, that rectors and clerks of Reatine Amiterno, having destroyed their churches, should transfer themselves to
L'Aquila, where new churches should be constructed and where they
themselves should live—this on pain of excommunication and interdict.
The pope's mandate says that he, who did not wish calmly to tolerate
the bishop of L'Aquila's behavior, orders the abbot of San Pastore to
warn the bishop to cease his injurious behavior toward the church of
Rieti without delay. Should the bishop refuse, the abbot should cite
him to appear before the pope with documents which would establish
his rights and privileges, *cum priuilegiis, iuribus et munimentis*, within
an appropriate term, and the abbot should notify the curia of his action.
Another papal mandate, similarly dated, was addressed to the royal governor (*capitaneo regni*), a mandate procured for the bishop and chapter
of Rieti, again possibly through the intervention of Cardinal Giordano.
The mandate states that certain inhabitants of the city of L'Aquila, putting aside fear of the Lord and concern for their own safety, had repeatedly inflicted grave injuries and damages on the persons and goods
of rectors and clerks of churches in the diocese of Rieti; it orders the
governor to use his authority to see that such acts cease.[10]

Certainly in the early 1230s major parts of the old diocese of Amiterno
had been considered, without dispute, part of the diocese of Rieti.
Equally certainly, in the early fourteenth century the compilers of the
rationes decimarum (who admittedly need not have had much local
knowledge and who perhaps need not always have been really forced to
know in what diocese places actually were) put a number of these old
Amiterno places in the diocese of L'Aquila, where—at least topographically, because of the connecting valley of the Aterno—they made better
sense.[11] As late as 1282 the bishop of Rieti, Pietro da Ferentino, with the
force he had as a papal collector behind him, was able to treat the
churches of San Paolo and San Giuliano of Barete and San Pietro of
Popleto (or Poppleto) as if their *pievi* and churches still lay within the
diocese of Rieti, and to exact, or try to exact, an oath of loyalty from the
wayward rector of Poppleto through his, the bishop's, representatives,
the archpriests of the two Barete churches with the assistance of a canon
of Santa Maria di Bagno.[12] The eastern boundary of the diocese of Rieti,
close as it was to the troublesome boundary between the Regno, the
kingdom of Naples, and the papal states, was unstable in the thirteenth
century. It was changing and forming itself at the same time that the
nature of diocesan government was changing and reforming itself.

Tension between Rieti and L'Aquila is unsurprising. Rather more surprising is the selection by Pope Clement V in 1311 of Bishop Giovanni Papazurri of Rieti, presumably for reasons of propinquity, to be a member of a commission appointed to investigate the alleged crimes of the then bishop of L'Aquila, Bartolomeo. The accusations against the bishop of L'Aquila were, in the style of the early fourteenth century, sufficiently rich to satisfy the taste of any possible enemy. The palest but perhaps most significant of the complaints was that the bishop, without the knowledge or permission of the Holy See, extracted procurations from his diocese but did not give them to the Holy See. It was also complained that the bishop showed no reverence for God and that when he celebrated Mass he did not take off his miter but irreverently kept his head covered even at the Consecration. It was said that his cupidity was so great that for a sum of money which he had received he allowed certain homicidal priests from Guasto (Vasto) and Rocca San Silvestro, identified as being within the diocese of Rieti, publicly to celebrate Mass.[13] Liveliest of the complaints, however, was that which accused him of taking a monthly pension from publicly acknowledged prostitutes in the city of L'Aquila. If Giovanni Papazurri did not have some part in the instigation of these complaints, at least if he felt any diocesan campanilismo, he must have found some pleasure in them.

Rieti's neighbor to the west was Sabina, an old diocese with a cardinal bishop and a remarkably clearly defined Rieti border, at least by the mid-fourteenth century, in spite of wasteland. In 1343 when the *Registrum iurisdictionis episcopatus Sabinensis* was composed, after the careful, inventorying visit of the cardinal bishop's vicar general, the structure of the diocese was as palpably realized and described, although without actual geographical boundaries, as any diocese could be expected to be.[14] The contrast between fourteenth-century Sabina and thirteenth-century L'Aquila is very sharp. An Amiterno sort of dispute between mid-fourteenth-century Sabina and Rieti is inconceivable. Geography and chronology together made it impossible.

On 3 February 1252 Pope Innocent IV provided a new bishop to the see of Rieti, a man from his own curia, a corrector of papal letters, Tommaso. Tommaso replaced the Franciscan Rainaldo da Arezzo with whom, Salimbene shows, Innocent had tried to give the diocese inspired spiritual leadership. Having failed with his friar saint, Innocent chose as his successor an experienced administrator. The sermons on the active life with which Innocent and his curia had regaled Rainaldo were replaced by helpful papal letters and administrative powers, with which Tommaso could find the force to reconstitute the diocese in a mid-thirteenth-century pattern at an opportune moment, in 1250, after the death of the Emperor Frederick II, a ruler who both in the order and disorder he created had made ideal diocesan government, from an ecclesiastical point of view, impossible.

Tommaso's efforts to deal with the diocese are most immediately visible in the cathedral church's campanile, which extends in front of the church's facade into the piazza. Tommaso's responsibility for the new campanile is proclaimed on a stone placed within one of its sides. The campanile called the canons to their hours of liturgical prayer, and it thus echoes Rainaldo's struggle with his chapter; but it is also a sign of good and solid and planned order at the center of the diocese. The inscription includes the statement that Tommaso in his first year held a *concilium*, a synod, and visited the churches in his care. The new bishop's first year, the messages of and on the campanile suggest, was a year of new structure and of organization.[15]

That organization included the compilation of a new list which described the diocese: a *summa omnium ecclesiarum tam ciuitatis quam dyocesis*, a compendium (or an attempted compendium) of all the churches of the city and the diocese of Rieti and their customary payments to the Reatine church.[16] The summa begins: "Nos Thomas permissione diuina Reatinus episcopus uolentes scire iures et facultates ecclesie Reatine ad utilitatem nostram et subditorum curam facilius subportandam successorum nostrorum perpetuam memoriam omnes ecclesias que fuerunt et sunt in ordine congruo duximus adnotandas infra diocesem Reatinam"; and so the bishop wanting to know the rights of his church for future use and perpetual memory caused (or tried to cause) to be written down all the churches which were and had been in the diocese of Rieti. The list, as it is preserved in the Paris manuscript, begins with the churches of the city itself, written in sequence in lines extending across the folio; and then moving out of the city and to Labro first and Piediluco second, in the most northwesterly part of the diocese (if and when Piediluco was in the diocese at all), it proceeds, from its second folio with some regard for geography, folio by folio in two columns divided into groups of churches, each group signaled by a paragraph notation and each group beginning with the name of an important, presumably mother, church or the name of an order, monastery, or hospital with its members, chapels, or attached churches beneath it. There are 163 of these groups. The localities fully extend into the area of Amiterno.

Tommaso's list does not follow the pattern of the earlier papal privileges; it is not based upon them. It is in some ways simpler than they are: it does not talk, beyond customary income, about rights and jurisdiction, except to notice problems of exemption. It does not talk, as does the Lucius III privilege, about "plebes omnes cum cappellis," not about *plebes* or *parochie* at all, but about *ecclesie*; but it talks, as they do not, about religious orders, including new orders, and about churches attached to external bodies, like San Pietro, San Paolo, and San Giovanni Laterano in Rome and like Ferentillo and Farfa.[17] It is not a revolutionary document, but it is a newly imagined, a fresh one.

Tommaso's list can be seen as a *scheda*, as program notes for reorganizing the diocese, recollecting its parts. And that, surviving documents from Tommaso's episcopate suggest, was, with papal support, his program. Tommaso's personality is not revealed to us; but there is every suggestion that he was, as the papal document providing him to the see perhaps formulaically reveals, an upright person of good reputation, a man to be trusted, not only an orderly man.[18] He was a man chosen as arbiter. A dispute over properties in the area of Rieti between the church of Rieti and Pietro Bosi and then his heirs (particularly represented by Boso di Pietro Bosi, for example, from the years 1256 to 1260) was brought to court before a papal delegate, the pievano of Cascia in Spoleto diocese, and, by common consent, was moved to arbitration with Tommaso as arbiter.[19] In another example from 1254 Tommaso, who had been chosen as arbiter by the representatives of the cathedral chapter and of the Cistercian monastery of San Pastore, settled a dispute between those bodies about two pieces of land, one in Terria and the other in Greccio.[20] Tommaso continued to work not only with bringing its property back to the chapter but also with bringing order to the chapter itself.[21]

The diocese of Rieti to which Tommaso came, and in which and with which he began to work, was not an undefined geographical space, but rather an ill and unevenly defined one. Tommaso himself, or someone working for him, created in 1254 the sharpest and most revealing drawing, verbal drawing, or diagram of how that space could be seen from within the diocese in Tommaso's time by someone with his energy and imagination, and his evident desire to understand and control that space. Tommaso produced a pragmatic map in words.[22]

The map comes from a dispute between the bishop and his church, on one side, and, on the other, the old Benedictine monastery of San Salvatore Maggiore, the heavy ruins of which remain, about fifteen kilometers southeast of the city of Rieti in the uplands between the valleys of the Turano and the Salto. This case, together with others earlier than itself, like those between the church of Rieti and neighboring Cistercians over drying marshlands and between the church of Rieti and the abbey of San Pietro, Ferentillo, over San Leopardo in Borgocollefegato, is able to expose the early thirteenth-century diocese, its contents and so in a different sense its boundaries, and particularly contested boundaries, at a, at least in some ways, more convincing level of reality than do privileges and lists.[23] These cases can, that is, expose this reality to a reader who is able to muster the patience to watch with reasonable attention the composition and movement of their courts, the structure and angle of the questions put to their witnesses, and the attitudes caught in those answers—and even more than attitudes the flickering quick images, half-repetitive, half-changing, of which the answers are composed.

The San Salvatore case, the case with the map, was the result of, and part of, Tommaso's program of collecting again for the church of Rieti the rights and possessions which he thought it had lost or failed to exercise during the first half of the thirteenth century. The bishop's positions, which were meant to support the reestablishment of the rights that he claimed the church of Rieti should exercise over the monastery of San Salvatore and over its subject churches within the diocese, were presented in March and April 1254 before two canons of Rieti collegiate churches, Filippo canon of San Ruffo and Bartolomeo canon of San Giovanni Evangelista. These two auditors had been delegated by Pietro Capocci, cardinal deacon of San Giorgio in Velabro, himself the papal auditor in the case.

One aspect of the bishop's case was geographical and concerned boundaries. The bishop wanted to establish the fact that the subject church of Santa Cecilia was within the city of Rieti and that the abbey and its other subject churches were physically within the diocese of Rieti: *sunt site in diocesi* and *consistunt intra fines diocesis.* He thus had to deal with the diocese's extent. He did this by proposing a series of lines extending from the city of Rieti. He proposed that the diocese of Rieti extended from Rieti to Collalto, from Rieti to Monteleone, from Rieti to Antuni and beyond, from Rieti to Castelvecchio di Toro (Castel di Tora) and beyond, from Rieti to Rocca Sinibalda and beyond, from Rieti to Santa Maria del Monte and beyond, from Rieti to Poggio Perugino and beyond, from Rieti to Greccio and beyond, from Rieti to Labro and beyond, from Rieti to Sala (Santa Maria, which is now in the diocese of Spoleto), from Rieti to Capitignano ("Capinniano de Nouer' "), from Rieti to Sant'Angelo in Vigio (later in the diocese of L'Aquila), from Rieti to San Vittorino (later in the diocese of L'Aquila) and beyond, from Rieti to Cartore in the Marsi and beyond, from Rieti to Roccaberardi ("Roccam Vellardi") and beyond, from Rieti to Mareri and beyond, from Rieti to Petrella and beyond, from Rieti to Pendenza and beyond, and from Rieti to Valviano and beyond.[24]

The bishop of Rieti described (and the abbot of San Salvatore denied) his diocesan map in which Rieti was the hub from which spokes extended (or arrows pointed) to or through diocesan (or so claimed) towns and churches. In the map which the bishop projected to catch these churches, the spokes of his wheel or the directed arrows which he drew from Rieti into the diocese sometimes overlap (for example, those to Antuni and Castel di Tora); sometimes they seem out of order (for example, that to Monteleone). Rocca Sinibalda, except for its topographical obviousness and closeness to San Salvatore, seems an odd place to choose in establishing boundaries. The device itself, compared with that of the privileges and list, can seem primitive, only in the process of being worked out—but that of course is its strength, what makes it compelling. Tommaso's description seems particularly effective if it is thought of as being formed in the bishop's mind, and his advisers' minds, as they sat in Rieti at the top of the hill on which the Duomo is built and which dominates the *conca*, the basin, of Rieti, and from there looked out in all directions toward the farthest limits of the diocese.

To his radiating spokes the bishop added another, netting, element to catch the abbey and its subject churches. Similarly, he said, making a smaller, but not close, pattern of cross-weaving within the established lines, the monastery *est situm*, is sited, and the churches *site sunt infra*, are sited within the city of Rieti, Rocca Sinibalda, Castel di Tora, Posta, Paganica, Licetto (Ricetto), Roccaberardi, Mareri, Petrella, Pendenza, and Valviano. The priest of one of the subject churches made specific objection to some of the direction points and tried to bring the northeastern boundary closer to Rieti, and to dispute part of the southern boundary.

One of the bishop's positions connects his interest in geography with his curial background. He, former corrector of papal letters, said, and the abbot of San Salvatore agreed, that popes wrote to the abbot and convent as the abbot and convent of San Salvatore Reatino or of Rieti, and that under that name the abbot and convent impetrated letters from the Holy See. The bishop further asserted that the abbey was called

Reatino or of Rieti in common speech. Tommaso, the former corrector, could not possibly have thought that this terminology proved the sub-jection of the monastery to the local bishop. He could, however, seal with the acceptance of this terminology his argument that the abbey was locally within a place which was called Reatine; and he could try to tie the abbey more firmly to the place with his arguments that San Salvatore and its vassals went to arms at the command of the podestà and council of Rieti, formed part of the *hostem* and *parliamentum* of Rieti, and shared responsibility for city walls. With this as background Tommaso could try to prove that the bishop's episcopal authority should be recognized in San Salvatore's part of this Reatine space.

As well as being a geographer, Tommaso, or his adviser, was a his-torian; and in that art he was more conventional and sufficiently suc-cessful so that his case-supporting history of the early thirteenth-century bishops of Rieti is the most accurate, I think, that exists. Tommaso dealt directly with general history in attempting to establish San Salvatore's involvement with the imperial Hohenstaufen, antipapal cause, but his most exacting and extended job was local diocesan history. To prove his case the bishop had to establish the rather tricky claim that in spite of many events, particularly wars, which had impeded the performance by his predecessors of their rights and duties, enough had been per-formed clearly to show that bishops of Rieti had exercised their rights over San Salvatore and its subject churches. The bishop claimed that his predecessors had visited the churches and received procurations and *cathedratica*, that they had celebrated divine services and preached in one of the churches (Santa Cecilia in Rieti) and received a *census* from it, that they had heard marriage cases in the abbey's territory and or-dained abbey clerks. The bishop claimed that his predecessors had con-secrated churches, chalices, altars, and ornaments for the churches.

Thus, just before the creation of the diocese of L'Aquila, which would remove physical territory from the diocese of Rieti, Bishop Tom-maso tried to change and stiffen the actual consistency of diocese at Rieti. In doing it he tried to observe, control, manipulate, and finally change the course of history. The course of history to which he looked back included the episcopate of Bishop Rainaldo de Labro (active at least from May 1215 to July 1233 and almost surely in February 1234). Tommaso summed up Rainaldo's episcopal activity in this way: "Rai-naldo de Labro was unable fully to exercise episcopal jurisdiction for ten years and more because of the malice of the times and because of wars"—and about wars he specifies those involving the Emperor Frederick and also those of Count Rinaldo and his brother Bertuldo, who were the sons of old Count Corrado who had been duke of Spoleto—undoubtedly true, in its way, but interested, history.[25] Rainaldo can, at least, be seen acting very much as Tommaso would act in his disputes with two resisting ecclesiastical complexes within the diocese. The documents remaining from the ensuing cases at law expose a notion of diocese consonant with that exposed in the earlier San Leopardo and the later San Salvatore cases, but each of Rainaldo's cases offers its own kind of resonance to the definition of diocesan boundary and of diocese.

Twenty-five documents and fragments of documents, copies and drafts which were written between 1220 and 1234, are preserved from a dispute between Bishop Rainaldo and the clerks of the collegiate church of San Silvestro "de Petrabattuta."[26] The actions of the case bounce around the periphery of the diocese. They, in connection with the provenance of some of the judges who are involved, allow one to see the diocese of Rieti in an enlarged neighborhood. In following these actions and observing these judges one must make one's mind a map. One must see a map. That map will not have exactly the same principles and contours as would the participants' maps; but quite clearly they were thinking in their maps' terms.

Although the documents from the San Silvestro case are variously articulate, they leave their reader in ignorance, as do the documents preserved from many similar cases, about a number of crucial elements in the case itself. One cannot know exactly when the San Silvestro case began or when and how it ended, if in fact it had a distinct ending. One can be fairly sure of what sort of institution San Silvestro was in the early thirteenth century; it was a collegiate church of secular clergy which maintained for itself some of the terminology of an abbey. One cannot, it seems, be sure where San Silvestro was; its name, "de Petrabattuta," is spelled in fourteen different but closely related ways in the surviving documents.[27] There is more certainty about the location of its four subject churches which are mentioned in the documents: San Pietro de Cornu; San Tommaso de Viliano; Sant'Ippolito de Ciculis; San Nicola de Rivotorto.[28] Corno, and actually Rocca di Corno, where San Pietro was, and Vigliano are relatively close neighbors on the Via Sabina between Antrodoco and L'Aquila. Sant'Ippolito in the Cicolano, on the right bank of the river Salto just as it now swells into the artificial Lago di Salto, is some twenty-two kilometers south and slightly west of both Corno and Vigliano. San Nicola de Rivortorto, which still existed in 1907, took its name from the river which empties into the Salto about four kilometers upstream from Sant'Ippolito after flowing south through the Catena di Monte Velino from near the borders of Tornimparte, south and a little east of Vigliano.[29]

All four of the subject churches, and slightly less frequently San Silvestro itself, are repeatedly said by documents from the Rieti side of the case to have been physically within the diocese of Rieti. No surviving document from the San Silvestro side of the case denies this local description, although Corno and Vigliano were later within the diocese of L'Aquila, and although such a denial, if legitimate, would have been decisively helpful to San Silvestro. Pretty clearly all the churches were in or near the rough country which would become the boundary between the dioceses of Rieti and L'Aquila.

The matter in dispute in the San Silvestro case is stated, in slightly different terms, in several of the surviving documents. In dispute were the bishop's episcopal rights over the four subject churches and, perhaps even from the beginning, over San Silvestro itself; most specifically it concerned the collection of papal procurations, but also, at least by 1234, the Rieti side sought from the abbot and chapter of San Silvestro a fourth of the tithes, oblations, and mortuaries in the church of San Silvestro, *de iure communi*, especially (*maxime*) because the bishop was, it was claimed, in possession, *uel quasi*, of all other episcopal rights in the church.[30]

The opposing clerics of San Silvestro not only claimed that the demanded procurations were uncustomary but also claimed in 1231 that the bishop was seeking a further procuration for the episcopal see. They sought to have restored to them their subject churches, the named four, which they said had been despoiled by the bishop.[31]

All the dated documents in the case, except one (and a quoted papal mandate), come from the years between 1231 and 1234. The exception is from 12 May 1220. On that day at San Martino di Pile, Bishop Teodino of Forcone sat as a delegate of the cardinal deacon of Santi Sergio e Bacco (Ottaviano Conti, called *Dominus Ottavianus Cardinalis Sancti Sergii*) and listened to the bishop of Rieti and the abbot of San Silvestro.[32] The bishop was prepared to present his case, but the abbot said that he could not plead without his advocate or his clerks, "who were the cause of this dispute," and he added that he himself "had never wanted the dispute because hitherto there had been a composition with the church of Rieti concerning procurations and other things and that in the time of Pope Innocent and Bishop Adenolfo there had never been any discord between them." The bishop of Rieti asked that this confession be committed to the judge's memory; and he said that he had accumulated considerable expenses in coming to the place of judgment. The bishop of Forcone consulted his "assessors" and set a future term at which time the abbot could plead and give just compensation to the bishop for his expenses.

On 1 September 1231 at Bazzano, which is just east of L'Aquila and again in the Abruzzi, the dispute between Bishop Rainaldo and the clerks of San Silvestro once more comes into view. In Bazzano the papal delegate Ber*ardo*, abbot of the Benedictine monastery of Santa Maria Bominaco, was active, acting under the authority of a mandate from Pope Gregory IX, which was dated from Perugia on 2 July 1228.[33] The abbot of Bominaco caused his own action and sentence to be recorded, *ad maiorem cautelam et futuram memoriam*, by his notary Gualt*iero*, and *ad maiorem cautelam*, the abbot affixed to the instrument his own seal. In this instrument the abbot had the notary record the abbot's version of the events of the case after his receipt of the papal mandate. The abbot had summoned both parties in the dispute to Paganica, which is about two kilometers north and slightly east of Bazzano. Although San Silvestro had appeared through its proctor, the priest Alberto, the bishop of Rieti had not appeared at all. Wishing, he said, to deal gently with the contumacious bishop, the abbot had again summoned him, to Bazzano. Again Alberto appeared, but no one from Rieti did. Alberto immediately asked that the abbot inhibit the bishop and also the chapter of Rieti from further molesting San Silvestro in the matter of the unwonted papal procurations and the other procuration for the episcopal see, and that he order the restitution to San Silvestro of the four subject churches, and that he grant San Silvestro legitimate expenses.

The abbot consulted his "assessors," of whom one was *domno Petro fratre nostro* and also *aliis prudentibus uiris nobiscum residentibus,* they wanted to reassure themselves about the bishop's actual receipt of the abbot's citations. Alberto established, through the testimony of named witnesses, that the bishop had received both letters *apud Sanctam Mariam de Reat'.* Then the abbot, again after, he says, careful deliberation with his assessors and "aliis presentibus quorum consilio habito nobiscum residentibus in ecclesia Sancte Juste de Baczano (the others present and residing with us at the church of Santa Giusta di Bazzano whose counsel we had)," judged the bishop contumacious and granted possession of the things sought to San Silvestro. The witnesses to this act included Gualt*iero* di Gualt*iero* Oderici *canonicus Sancte Juste et nota-*

rius publicus, assessor et testis (that is, the document's own notary), Theodino di Gualt*iero* canon of San Massimo *assessor et testis,* and Miles (or, more probably, the knight) Oder*icus frater eius,* a cluster of brothers around the abbot. The abbot was then in residence, with his circle, at a place some forty kilometers northwest of his own abbey in the diocese of Valva Sulmona (the diocese southeast of Forcone), at Santa Giusta Bazzano, which was in that decade engaged on an ambitious campaign of reconstruction from which came its imposing church and remarkable painting. One of the canons of Santa Giusta acted as the abbot's notary, and as one of his assessors and witnesses.

On Saturday 18 September 1232, Luca, archpriest of Vigliano, acting as proctor of the bishop of Rieti (and very possibly in the interest of himself and the rights of his own church) appeared before the abbot of Bominaco in Sinizzo, a place near San Demetrio ne' Vestini, east of the Ocre villages, Fossa, and Sant'Eusanio Forconese, and about halfway between Bazzano and the abbot's own abbey; Sinizzo itself, according to the fourteenth-century *rationes decimarum,* was just within the boundaries of the diocese of Valva-Sulmona. The archpriest of Vigliano asked the abbot to revoke the sentence of contumacy against the bishop of Rieti because the bishop had not, he said, been cited to appear before the abbot. Since the abbot would not revoke it, the archpriest formally appealed the sentence to the pope. This action occurred before a group of named witnesses including dompno Passavanti canon of San Pietro di Sinizzo and the local *judex* Pietro da Sinizzo who redacted the instrument recording the appeal.[34]

On 1 January 1233 Bishop Rainaldo made Jacobus Sarraceno, canon of Rieti, his proctor to act before the abbot in the San Silvestro affair; and two days later the canon-proctor can be seen and heard acting. On 3 January 1233 the canon, representing the bishop and wishing, he said, to obey the abbot's mandate, arrived at Bominaco. But the abbot had, within the term fixed for the case according to the bishop's proctor, withdrawn himself to the imperial court, and had, as was apparent from his sealed letters, left as his proctor and representative (*uicem suam . . . procurauit*), his companion the monk Bartolomeo. Before this monk representative of the abbot, the proctor canon, who had brought with him as *fideiussores* the archpriests of San Vittorino and Santa Maria de Civitàte (Città di Bagno), *uiros diuites, nobiles et discretos* (rich, respectable, and responsible) offered *cautionem sufficientem exibere.* The monk utterly rejected *cautionem* and *fideiussores,* any surety at all. But, although he said he could not go beyond the abbot's mandate to him, he sought six uncie of gold as pledge for expenses and judgment. The proctor refused the pledge and appealed to the apostolic see. Witnesses to the appeal were Passavanti the canon of San Pietro Sinizzo, the priest Teodino and dompno Egidio clerics of San Salvatore Sinizzo, a man called Matteo Dodonis, and the two archpriests of San Vittorino and Città di Bagno.[35]

The next day, the proctor canon Jacobus Sarraceno went to the palazzo of San Silvestro Petrabattuta (here called Petravactita) itself. There he delivered to Alberto, a canon of San Silvestro, letters from Pietro, the prior of Santa Maria Terni, which informed the clerks of San Silvestro (*prudentibus uiris clericis de Petrauactita*, or in copy *Pretauactita*) that the case had been committed to him, the prior, by the pope, and that they should appear before him, or their proctor should, within thirty days of their receipt of his letters. At this point the Rieti canon proctor who had followed the case deeper and deeper into the Abruzzi, and followed the abbot of Bominaco to Bominaco only to find that he had removed himself to the court of the Abruzzi's Hohenstaufen king-emperor, transferred the case across the diocese of Rieti to the northwest, to the refounded Umbrian see of Terni, and into the hands of a man himself involved in that refoundation.[36]

On 2 January 1233, acting before the church of San Tommaso di Città di Bagno (south of Bazzano and just north of the Ocre villages), four clerks of San Silvestro (here called "de Petra Bacteta" [?] and "Petrabat"), including the priest Alberto and two men called "Rain'l" and "Rainal'," *cum uniuerso capitulo eiusdem ecclesie* (the whole chapter of the church) had made the priest Paolo their proctor in the case, and they had the procuration written for them by Guitto (?) de Saxa, *imperialis aule scriniarius*.[37] On 7 February Egidio the *scutifer* of the bishop of Rieti was at Petrabattuta ("Petravaccita") acting as a nuncio for the prior of Terni; he assigned to the priests Alberto and Paolo, the proctor, sealed letters citing them to appear before the prior at Terni on 17 February. The prior informed the San Silvestro clerks that a day after their proctor had left his court the proctor of the bishop of Rieti had come saying that the term had not yet elapsed and saying that all that the San Silvestro proctor had proposed before the prior was false. On 16 February Bishop Rainaldo made dompno Giovanni Arlocco, clerk of San Giovenale Rieti, his proctor in the case. On 18 February the priest Paolo, as proctor of San Silvestro, appeared in the palazzo of the prior at Terni and appealed from the prior to the pope. The prior tried to mollify him:

Frater [he said to the proctor], non est necesse te appellare cum nec te nec conuentum nec ecclesiam Sancti Siluestri de Petra Vactuta in aliquo grauerim uel grauare uelim. Sed ducas coram me aliquem sapientem et quicquid peterit ostendere tam de loco securo dando quam de longinquitate loci quam de alia suspicione et de litteris que fuerint per mendacium impetrate et omnibus aliis obiectionibus et exceptionibus que mihi rationabiliter ostense fuerint tibi de iure facere sum paratus.

In four preserved copies the words of the prior of Terni's statement vary slightly: a mood changes; *Frater* becomes *Amice*; a *tecum* is inserted; or an *illud libenter audiam*, which presumably had been omitted, is replaced. But essentially the copies agree: the prior tried to seem friendly and open to the San Silvestrini and their proposed objections; he said that he did not want to do harm to them or their church; he would gladly listen if they brought before him an expert who could substantiate their grievances about time or distance and mendaciously procured letters; it was not necessary for them to appeal because he was prepared to listen fairly. The copies also agree that the San Silvestro proctor was unsatisfied and went away.

On 21 February the prior of Terni sat again, this time in the palazzo of Guidone Machabei in Terni, before witnesses: Palmerio canon of the major church of Terni and Tommaso canon of San Lorenzo Terni, as well as Guidone Machabei himself, Nicola Elpizi and Merlino, citizens of Rieti. Prior Pietro found the appeal of the clerks of San Silvestro invalid. He declared the proceedings before the abbot of Bominaco null and void, and he granted possession of rights in the churches, and expenses, to the bishop of Rieti. He made the archpriest of Sant'Antimo di Valviano, within the diocese of Rieti, his *nuntius* and executor in the case.[38]

From Terni the case went to Rome and the Lateran. The auditor given in the case was the repeatedly active papal chaplain and subdeacon, Giovanni Spata.[39] Before him the priest Paolo presented a brief narrative from a San Silvestro point of view, of the progress of the case before the abbot of Bominaco and the prior of Terni. San Silvestro's proctor, he said, had appeared properly before the prior and asked for a copy of the papal letters giving the prior jurisdiction in the case, and the prior had refused to exhibit the letters. The proctor had asked for, and been refused, a place for hearing the case which would be safe for the San Silvestro side. The proctor further said that the court in Terni was beyond the statutory two-day limit of distance from San Silvestro.

On those bases he appealed, asked that the actions of the prior be declared invalid, and those of the abbot confirmed.

The Rieti side, which had had at least two of the documents from
the Terni phase of the case copied by a Reatine *scriniarius* on 2 November (before the archpriest Salvo, of the collegiate church of San
Giovanni Rieti and one of its canons, Eleutherio), was prepared to answer the San Silvestro objections to the Terni court before the papal
auditor. The Rieti proctor was prepared to argue from *de dilationibus,*
cap. 2, that it was not necessary for the judge to give both sides copies
of the original rescript, but that it was enough for him to read the
rescript before them; and the Rieti proctor was prepared to show three
instruments which would prove that the prior had read the papal letters
and had transmitted to the San Silvestro side the tenor of the letters
word for word, checked against and compared with the rescripts themselves. As for safety, the Rieti proctor claimed, certainly the war of Bertuldo (the man with the salty mouth) could not have kept the San
Silvestro side from coming to Terni, especially since in those days Bertuldo, besieged by the imperial army in Antrodoco, could not have hurt
anyone, nor was anyone hurt on the road to Terni: it was a frivolous
objection. Finally to the third objection—the Rieti answer was that it
could of course be decided by arbiters, but that it certainly was not true
that Terni was more than two days from San Silvestro, *maxime* because
it was not more than a one-day trip.[40] Like the San Silvestro side, the
Rieti side sought expenses, which it estimated at twenty-one lire.

Evidently the papal auditor was unsympathetic to the Rieti proctor's
rebuttal because, on 21 February 1234 in the palace of the Lateran, before
witnesses (Tebaldo the papal chaplain and the scribes Nicola Spina and
Jacobus Villani from Spoleto), an imperial *scriniarius,* Aimo called Ypo-
cras, recorded and redacted the viva voce appeal made by Rainaldo,
proctor of the bishop of Rieti, against the sentence handed down by
Giovanni Spata.[41] The case then moved a step higher, in Rome itself;
and both sides prepared to be heard by Sinibaldo Fieschi, cardinal priest
of San Lorenzo in Lucina (and later Pope Innocent IV). The clerks of
San Silvestro made their *scriniarius,* Nochero, their proctor to appear
before the cardinal; and they sealed their *procuratorium* with the chapter seal. Rainaldo appealed the Spata sentence before the cardinal and
presented to him the Rieti case, with its request for a fourth of San
Silvestro tithes, oblations, and mortuaries "according to the common
law of the church," and also with a request for expenses now estimated
at fifty lire of the senate.[42]

A half-century later in November 1282 an abbot (*angelus abas*) and
five or six canons of San Silvestro again present themselves at San Silvestro, next to the church, in order to make their *syndicum siue yconimum, actorem et nuntium* to appear before Pietro da Roma, the vicar
of the bishop of Rieti (Bishop Pietro da Ferentino), who had excommunicated the abbot and canons after they had, they say, appealed to
the pope.[43] Neither the abbot nor any of the six canons seem to have
survived from the 1230s dispute. The document, as its formal structure
makes clear, was written in the Regno, by a notary, by papal authority,
Gualtiero (da Preturo). The chosen syndic was Bartolomeo, archpriest
of San Tommaso Vigliano, whose church had been one of those in
dispute in the 1230s.

The San Silvestro case is a lesson in diocesan cultural geography. In
it the diocese of Rieti is placed within a larger area, a kind of triangle
with its points in Bominaco, Terni, and Rome; the center of the whole
triangle is the capitular-episcopal complex in Rieti. It is geography because thickets of clerks gathered cannot be considered less geography
than thickets of heather or broom, or their placement less geographically significant than that of limestone or oak (*quercus* or *robur*). About
diocesan boundaries the case is variously revealing. It focuses on the
unstable boundary between Rieti and Forcone. It shows the pene-
trability of boundary, as it moves across boundaries; and in the same
movement it shows the significance of boundary, the advantage to San
Silvestro of Forcone and Valva-Sulmona, the dioceses of the Hohenstaufen kingdom, and the advantage to Rieti of Terni. But content and
boundary are again inseparable: immune, or wanting to be, clerks and
monks against the order of diocesan government, as at Sinizzo. And
always beneath those elements subject to category are the hidden persuasions, tastes, and animosities, the jealousies and ambitions of individuals, hidden beneath the surface of the text, but in some ways suggested by the clustering in the texts of blood brothers and brother
monks.

Overwhelmingly apparent in the case is the presence of clerical
groups meeting together, living together, talking together, deciding
together—the logical social and legal extension of the matrix church
with its collegiate body of canons. It would not seem absurd to say—
as one looks at the San Silvestro case—that diocesan boundaries are
what separate one set of clerical collegiate groups from another. At the
same time the nature of movement within and across boundaries is
striking: the abbot of Bominaco (and does it matter whether he is *quer-*

cus or *robur*?) changing his surrounding groups as his itinerary progresses; the men of Sinizzo following the Rieti proctor; the travelers'
dodging around besieged Bertuldo, with that action's questioning of
the nature of war's inhibition; the quick movement of the Rieti canon
proctor, and the accessibility of Rome, and important men there.

The suggestions of the other "Rainaldo" case, the case of Santa
Croce in Lugnano, and the questions it asks and answers—at least as it
is seen here—are quite different ones. The structure of its evidence is
different, too. It has left fewer documents, only fourteen of them.[44]
They deal with a much smaller geographical area, tighter, closer to the
center of the diocese; and the area which they offer is that of the area
that produced the case rather than that of its courts. Although almost
all of the documents which are of particular interest come from one not
quite datable moment in time, and are the recorded responses of witnesses to that time's questions, one of the case's distinctive values is the
presentation of a long, stretched out chronology. The case's matter as
well as its witnesses' attestations remind its observer of the San Leopardo case, to which it, in its central events, is very close in time: it
explores the powers of a lay patron in a changing world. But it adds to
San Leopardo's kind of information a revealing spray of violence.

From a Rieti point of view, the two cases had different results. Ferentillo, later evidence makes clear, won its case with Rieti over San
Leopardo. The ruined church outside of Borgocollefegato (Borgorose)
is called San Giovanni in Leopardo or San Giovanni Leopardi, because
when at the beginning of the fourteenth century Boniface VIII gave
the deformed house of San Pietro Ferentillo (locally within the diocese
of Spoleto), for "reformation," to the canons of San Giovanni in Laterano, San Pietro carried San Leopardo with it. This movement interprets rather surprisingly the suggestion of an Innocent III letter review-
ing the work of an auditor (Leone Brancaleone, the cardinal priest of
Santa Croce in Gerusalemme) in the case and dated 26 April 1213 (preserved in copy, but not in Rieti); the letter seems to place San Leopardo
pretty clearly "infra limites dyocesis" of Rieti, but it makes seem decisive
the placing of San Leopardo among Ferentillo's churches in Bishop
Tommaso's list (with the qualification of half procurations). Quite the
opposite is true of Santa Croce Lugnano: later evidence simply tucks it
neatly under Rieti control, and Bishop Tommaso's list does not give it
to the Hospitallers.[45]

Two documents, at fifteen years distance from each other, specifically
tie Bishop Rainaldo de Labro to the Santa Croce case. In May 1215 (plate

21) and again in August 1230 Rainaldo and his chapter (in the first Rainaldo *cum capitulo nostre ecclesie* and in the second Rainaldo *cum con-canonicis nostre ecclesie*) make for themselves a proctor (or in the second document an *yconimum*) in their dispute with the Hospitallers of San Basilio Rome over the church of Santa Croce in Lugnano—in the first case specifically over Santa Croce, and in the second specifically before the papal chaplain Magister Andrea da Velletri (*de Villitro*) who had been made auditor by the pope.[46] (The 1215 proctor is a canon, the priest Paolo; and the document's witnesses include the proctor's nephew as well as Berardo Dolcelli, the same man presumably as a clerk who had seen Bishop Benedetto visiting San Leopardo.) It is not certain, however, that Rainaldo was bishop at the time the witnesses' attestations were gathered. They were gathered at a time when Bishop Adenolfo had retired from the see but was still believed to be living, as a monk at the Cistercian house of Tre Fontane just south of Rome, that is, after 1212. The attestations talk of a bishop-elect, an *electus*, as if he were presiding over the church of Rieti: this could be either Rainaldo before his consecration or, following Bishop Tommaso's list, his predecessor Gentile de Pretorio, who remained an elect and who was active as late as 3 March 1214.[47]

Although the last abbot of Santa Croce cannot remember what practice was when Santa Croce had belonged to the monastery of Farfa, because he had not been born (*nescit quia non dum natus erat*), some of the memories evoked in the case are very long memories. Berardo de Vico (or Vito), who had been cellarer, had a memory that stretched back seventy years; and he had seen nine abbots inducted at Santa Croce. The priest Paolo himself said that he had been a canon in the church of Rieti for thirty years, and Jacobus for more than forty. The witness Tomeo de Rater' says that he had been with Bishop Dodone for twelve years and to the time of his death; and the witness Teodino remembers to a time before the destruction of the city of Rieti (in 1149 by the army of Roger of Sicily).[48] As the past is remembered, the future is penetrated. The most legally significant document which is preserved from the case, the *carta liberationis*, or charter of liberty, granted by the lay patron Rainaldo de Lavareta to the abbot Giovanni, was made, at Rainaldo's request, by the *scriniarius* Berardo Malabranca in March 1196; but an authentic copy of it was made by the *scriniarius* Tomeo in July 1255 (and of two witnessing canons of San Ruffo, Rieti, one bore the same name as the Rieti *yconimus* of 1230).[49] The documents preserved from the case thus stretch from the time of Bishop Adenolfo to that of Bishop Tommaso; and the memories penetrate deep back into the long reign of Bishop Dodone.

The pieces of past that the memories recall, of course, in some part differ from each other; but put together they present a reasonably comprehensible story. The grandfather, according to witness, of the Lord Rainaldo de Lavareta (who, Rainaldo, also according to witness, was the father of Bishop Adenolfo de Lavareta) had received the church of Santa Croce Lugnano in an exchange with the abbey of Farfa. In 1196, according to the authenticated copy of the original *carta donationis* or *liberationis*, Rainaldo, for the redemption of his soul and those of his relatives (*pro redemptione anime mee et meorum parentum*), had made a grant inter vivos to the Abbot Giovanni and his clerks and their successors of all the rights that he, Rainaldo, had had in the church during the occupancy of a previous abbot. He made the church free of himself, its patron. The abbot, Giovanni, in turn (with, according to him, the counsel of Bishop Adenolfo) gave the church to the Hospitallers of San Basilio in Rome. He and the clerks of Santa Croce were received as brother and oblates of San Basilio; and the transfer was made with earth and stones, with branches of fig and vines of grape from Santa Croce and from one of its dependencies, San Massimo. The prior of San Basilio took counsel so that the transfer was canonically correct and brought papal confirmation of transfer to Rieti, according to Giovanni. He also brought papal letters to the canons of Rieti ordering them not to molest San Basilio over the gift of Santa Croce.[50]

But molest they did. A group of clerks and servants from the cathedral church, a group which included canons—the priest Paolo, the priest Rainaldo, Master Enrico medico, and Siginulfo—took the keys to the house of the sons of Tedemario, where the abbot of Santa Croce resided when in Rieti and where Santa Croce had a storeroom. They entered the house, measured the grain in the *pozzo* (its container) with a stick, and opened the chest where bread and fish and victuals were, and ate the fish they found prepared there, and they took the priest Egidio, the abbot's companion and by then an oblate of San Basilio, as a captive to the cathedral church of Santa Maria, Rieti. The cathedral group also went to the Rieti church of San Giovenale where valuables of Santa Croce or its chapels were deposited (or the canons gave orders to the clerks of San Giovenale that they bring them those valuables) so that they might be carried away: a little library of seven common books, twenty-six vestments and cloths used in services (including three *pannos altaris cruciatos*, three crossed altar cloths), two pewter chalices, and one ox or bull or cow (*unum bouem*).[51] This violence was appealed by the preceptor and brothers of San Basilio who, their witnesses claim, had already appealed to the pope before the violence occurred.

The eating of the fixed fish, the sequestering of the ox (or bull or cow), the antiphonals, and the missals, the episode of violence could have been an uncontrolled flash of anger or it could have been a calculated expression of power. Either way, it was an explosive, relatively superficial (or perhaps, like the sheds, ritualistically legal) incident in a dispute over the definition of authority within the church, over the structure of diocese. A cardinal point in the Rieti position was that "Ecclesia Sancte Crucis . . . sita est in diocesi Reatina." That the church was physically within the diocese was not in dispute. Lugnano is only about eight kilometers northeast of Rieti, close to the diocesan center. Rieti wanted testimony which would establish that "the church of Rieti had had and held the church of Santa Croce, just as it did the other churches of the diocese (*de episcopatu Reatino*) in spiritualities and temporalities, for a long time." And a Rieti witness, Tomeo the companion of Bishop Dodone, testified to another aspect of the ordinariness of Santa Croce, "that the Lord Rainaldo de Lavareta had held the church of Santa Croce just as he held the other churches *de terra sua* and that he was patron of this church just as he was of the other churches *de terra sua.*"[52]

Rieti attempted to establish this ordinariness of Santa Croce much as it had attempted to establish the past ordinariness of San Leopardo, by showing that the bishop had acted as diocesan in and to Santa Croce and its three chapels. In the Santa Croce case witnesses testify that bishops were received, and with procession and holy water, at Santa Croce, and were received and were served at San Massimo, that they received imposts—*cathedraticum, capitulum*, tithes, procurations—and other services from Santa Croce, that *exenia* were given at Christmas, Easter, and Assumption, that clerks were ordained, and prelates invested, by the bishop, that the abbot and clerks were called to synods and they came, that interdicts were observed, and sacred oil received, that the clerks who offended the abbot or other clerks were called to the bishop's curia where justice was done (as when Giovanni Gentili struck abbot Giovanni with a knife), and that, in a word used repeatedly in this case, abbot and clerks were *vasalli* of the bishop and church of Rieti and pledged fealty to them.[53]

The pieces of memory that contribute to the Rieti party's overall claim are often limitedly specific and particular:

Pinzono swears that in the time of Bishop Benedetto when he was a sergeant (or servant: *seruiens*) he went to Santa Croce with a palfrey of the bishop's and stayed there for two weeks and the abbot gave him and the horse victuals and gave him a shirt out of respect for the bishop; and in the time of Bishop Adenolfo he was seneschal (*senescalcus*), and he saw that the bishop received *seruitia* from the church of Santa Croce just as he did from other churches—he himself saw it because he went with the bishop.[54]

Witnesses speaking for San Basilio spoke of the patron Rainaldo de Lavareta's control of Santa Croce. Berardo di Vico, the cellarer who had seen nine abbots in the church of Santa Croce, testified that Rainaldo sent them and, when he wanted to, removed them, without asking the bishop (*sine requisitione episcopi*). And, in fact, the testimony reveals the removal of Abbot Giovanni himself, either by Rainaldo and his son Bishop Adenolfo, or by Rainaldo's son Matteo, and Giovanni's reinstatement and finally the confirmation of Rainaldo's *carta liberationis* by Matteo.[55] Abbot Giovanni's own testimony about services performed and promises given is especially provocative. Giovanni admits that he swore an oath to the church of Rieti, but it was when he was ordained priest and not at Santa Croce; and he swore as a simple priest and not as rector of the church of Santa Croce (*tamquam presbiter simplex non tamquam rector ecclesie Sancte Crucis*). He said that thrice a year *seruiebat in exeniis* to Bishop Adenolfo for the church of Santa Croce, but he gave the *exenia* to Adenolfo not as bishop but because Adenolfo was the son of Rainaldo (*non tanquam episcopo sed quia filius erat eiusdem Ray*naldi).[56]

The Rieti party sums up this sort of testimony from San Basilio-Santa Croce witnesses by saying that they claim in general that Rainaldo presided over the church of Santa Croce—as does the witness Buonuomo specifically that he saw Lord Rainaldo preside over (*presidere*) the church for (in Buonuomo's case) thirty years. But this is impossible, the Reatines claim, because a layman (*laicus*) cannot preside over (*presidere*) a religious place (*locum religiosum*); and they cite Pope Alexander III in the titulus "de prescriptionibus."[57]

Rainaldo, the agent, dead, is mute. He cannot respond or add his voice to this case. That he had a voice of a certain timbre, one might guess; in fact it is still audible. He can be heard being quoted by the witness Oddone, archpriest of San Ruffo, Rieti, in a case from 1181—or rather in double quote because Oddone is repeating what he heard Gualtiero de Trozo say. Gualtiero said that Rainaldo came to him with a group of knights and said to him, "I have heard that you have given your goods to the church of Santa Maria. I want you to revoke that gift and give them to me—and I will do you much good and on top of that I will give you a fief (*feudum*)." And Gualtiero said that whatever he had done for Rainaldo he had done because of force or fear.[58]

Rainaldo's live voice, and Gualtiero's, heard together remind their listener of their, and Bishop Adenolfo's, common background; they recall the section of the Norman kings' *Catalogus baronum*, which begins: "Raynaldus de Lavareta tenet a domino Rege in Amiterno Lavaretam (Rainaldo de Lavareta holds of the lord King in Amiterno, Lavareta)," and which includes among the list of those who hold of Rainaldo, "Troz . . . de eodem Raynaldo tenet . . . Roccam de Cornum."[59] Descendants of *Catalogus* barons are speaking, men of Amiterno, the lord with his *caput* at Lavareta or Barete, from families who seem to dominate the diocese of Rieti in 1200, but whose central holdings will be removed from it when the diocese of L'Aquila has been successfully constructed. That Lugnano and Santa Croce themselves, although they were in the center of the reduced diocese of Rieti, were of the Regno, the kingdom of Naples, one is reminded by the former, perhaps accidental, preservation at Santa Croce (when it itself was still preserved) of the most Angevin-seeming (probably because of its being carved by a French master) work of thirteenth- or fourteenth-century art in the diocese, the ivory Madonna of Lugnano.[60]

The most quickly memorable remnants of the Santa Croce case's attestations are sharply physical: not only the ox and the little library and the prepared fish eaten in the house of the Tedemarii, but also the pewter chalices, the keys and the knife, branches of fig and vines of grape, horse fodder and a shirt. They seem to have flown to the memory of the witnesses, and they stick in our memories. They are not just convenient mnemonic devices, peripheral—" 'though of course I had on my trousers,' " as Schinkel said in *The Princess Casamassima*—they are what the story of Santa Croce is about; they tie its abstractions to a different kind of lived life, a specific one.

But the abstractions of the Santa Croce case, or, more pompously but perhaps better, the historical forces visible in it, are central and important ones. The potent lay patron, Rainaldo de Lavareta, displays in himself an antique figure. His son was bishop. He gave churches to themselves. And in his acts he did not seem to recognize, to think, that a diocese was a different sort of territory, jurisdictional territory, from his or other men's lands; or, if he did, he saw the difference as something frail and insubstantial, which ought not to interfere with a lord's patronage—perhaps particularly when that patronage was meant to save his soul.

Rainaldo's acts, however, joined by Abbot Giovanni's, provoked from the representatives of the church of Rieti, from its canons and bishop and their representatives, a further definition of diocese, a further overt realization of what jurisdictional diocese meant—this most specifically and consciously in their restraining and putting in place the rights of the lay patron, but also in their again of necessity recalling those touchstones of diocesan reality which demonstrated that a specific place or specific places were part of a diocese, within its real boundaries: so they talked of the reception with procurations of the visiting bishop, the source of sacred oils, the ordination of clerks by the bishop, the use and validity of the bishop's court, the giving and receiving of customary gifts and rents and fees, of *cathedratica*, *capitula*, tithes, and *exenia*, and the successful summoning of clerks to episcopal synods (as the canon Rainaldo said, "He saw Bishop Dodone call to synod the abbots and clerks of Santa Croce, and they came just as did the other clerks of the diocese").[61] The clerks of Santa Croce were, in a word that makes the Reatine clergy seem almost as antique as Rainaldo de Lavareta, the "vassals" of the church of Rieti.

The indecisiveness, the blurred boundaries, of some of the Santa Croce evidence (were things given to the bishop or to the patron's son? was the oath taken as priest or rector?) recalls, makes analogy to, the blurred indecisiveness of parts of the early thirteenth-century diocese's physical boundaries. The coherence and definition which that diocese could find for itself, or which witnesses living within it could look for and find in it, are not those which would develop in the century which followed the episcopate of Bishop Tommaso the Corrector, in the century which followed the loss of the Amiterno territories to L'Aquila.

Tommaso the Corrector, who came from that curia where dioceses were thought of, was an imaginative and effective bishop; and he was supported by the strong and serious pope from whose curia he had come. Tommaso marked the center of the diocese with a new campanile. He made an extended and orderly list of his diocese's churches. He drew a verbal map of the diocese with an impressively indecisive, because physical, appreciation of its geography; and he drew it with an almost portolan concept of map-making. He offered himself as an arbiter to disputants within the diocese. He gathered back strayed rights and incomes, and he questioned immunities. He can be seen to be laying, probably quite consciously, the foundations for a new and more stable kind of diocese and diocesan government appropriate to the lengthy period of relative peace which might perhaps have been predicted from the time of the death of Frederick II in 1250. But Tommaso's gathering of rights and incomes, impressive as it seems, particularly in the context of the evidence which exists for his actually trying to understand the geography of his whole diocese, does not seem in its style or in his understanding of diocesan rights very different from that of his predecessors, particularly from that of Rainaldo de Labro and his canons, whose work Tommaso was almost forced to minimize. Tommaso's definition of diocese echoes Rainaldo's.

Evidence from the San Leopardo, Santa Croce, and San Silvestro cases show that Bishop Adenolfo de Lavareta, Bishop Rainaldo de Labro, and canons of Rieti were actively interested in preserving diocesan structure and in exercising the rights of bishop and cathedral church. This interest did not exclude the sacramental and the sacred. It included rights of visitation and summoning to synod (and for both the pontificate of Bishop Dodone was recalled, and of both the exercise was proclaimed on Tommaso's campanile). But visitation, at least in the testimony, seems primarily a matter of ceremonial reception and procuration—natural perhaps in litigation evidence, but this is the evidence that survives. And no one thought to recall the content of any synod. (It is, of course, possible that at each diocesan synod after 1215 the decrees of Innocent III's Fourth Lateran Council were read aloud as an interpretation of that council's canon 6, *sicut olim*, in this diocese with no provincial metropolitan set above it.)[62]

Viewed from outside (and later) the early thirteenth-century Reatine concept of diocese seems very much one of pennies paid and formal rights demanded. It is not at all clear, at least from witnesses' testimony, what pastoral duties early thirteenth-century bishops of Rieti, in their peregrinations, thought they were performing. In spite of ordinations, baptisms, and sacred oils, and of the real and conscious participation in "church" of lay Christians, the early thirteenth-century diocese really does seem to find an image of itself, although perhaps an exaggerated and distorted one (and one that should not be interpreted as too sharply distinguishing between clergy and laity), in Oderisio di Buonuomo's standing by the outside wall of the church of San Leopardo while the Mass was being sung within. Clear as daylight is the fact that he was standing in a diocese, no matter how ill-defined its boundaries were, full of colleges of secular clergy, and of important family ties.

9. Rieti, urban curvilinear internal street assumed to have been formed before the middle of the thirteenth century. Photograph by Corrado Fanti, reprinted from Marina Righetti Tosti-Croce, ed., *La sabina medievale* (Milan, 1985), by permission of the Cassa di Risparmio di Rieti.

10. Rieti, the thirteenth-century wall by the Porta Conca and Sant'Agostino, the northern boundary of Rieti. Photograph by Corrado Fanti, reprinted from Marina Righetti Tosti-Croce, ed., *La sabina medievale* (Milan, 1985), by permission of the Cassa di Risparmio di Rieti.

11. Rieti, the river Velino and San Francesco, the southern boundary of Rieti. Photograph courtesy of the Istituto Centrale per il Catalogo e la Documentazione, Rome.

12. Rieti, looking toward the church of San Francesco from the south across the Velino. Photograph by Barbara Bini.

13. The village of Secinaro. Photograph by the author.

14. Aerial view of the new town of Cittaducale. Photograph by the Ente Provinciale per il Turismo, Rieti, reprinted from Marina Righetti Tosti-Croce, ed., *La sabina medievale* (Milan, 1985), by permission of the Cassa di Risparmio di Rieti.

15. The hermitage of San Giacomo, Poggio Bustone, near Rieti, one of the three early important Reatine Franciscan hermitages. Photograph by Corrado Fanti, reprinted from Marina Righetti Tosti-Croce, ed., *La sabina medievale* (Milan, 1985), by permission of the Cassa di Risparmio di Rieti.

16. Rocca Ranieri (Longone Sabino), a rural *castro*, formerly subject to the Benedictine monastery of San Silvestro Maggiore, seen through a gate. Photograph by Alessandro Iazeolla, reprinted from Anna Maria D'Achille, Antonella Ferri, and Tiziana Iazeolla, eds., *La sabina: Luoghi fortificati, monasteri e abbazie* (Milan, 1985), by permission of the Cassa di Risparmio di Rieti.

17. The conca of Rieti seen from the west, from beneath the ruins of the Cistercian monastery of San Pastore, looking toward the Monti Reatini, with a spur of San Matteo to the right of the photograph. Photograph by Barbara Bini.

18. The village or castro of Greccio seen from below and from the south, from near San Pastore. Photograph by Barbara Bini.

19, opposite. Late thirteenth-century fresco of the Last Supper in Santa Maria ad Cryptas at Fossa, detail, leek on table. Photograph reprinted from Guglielmo Matthiae, *Pittura medioevale abruzzese* (Milan: Electa, n.d.).

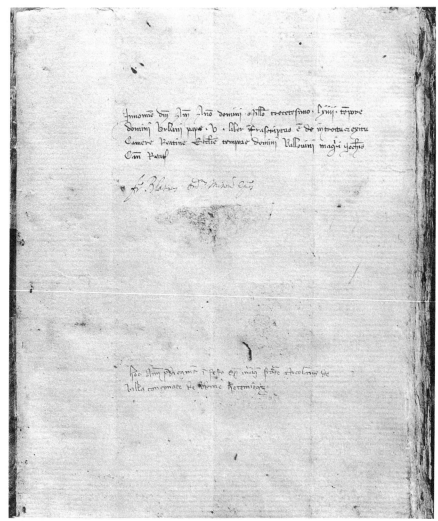

20. Rieti, Archivio Capitolare, first folio of the paper Liber Introitus et Exitus of 1364 (that is, 1 July through the following June), prepared by the canon Ballovino, with the record of that year's (presumably 1365) Saint Mark's day preacher, the Augustinian Hermit Nicola da Villa Conzonate. Photograph by Barbara Bini.

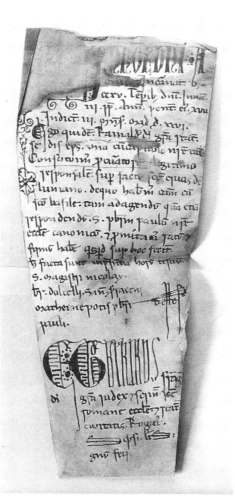

21. Rieti, Archivio Capitolare, IV.G.3, parchment document from 26 May 1215 in which Bishop Rainaldo (de Labro) and his chapter make the priest Paolo, one of the canons, their proctor in the case with San Basilio, with witnesses including Matteo the nephew of the priest Paolo. The document was redacted by the judge and *scriniario*, Berardo Sprangone. Photograph by Barbara Bini.

22. Rieti, Archivio Capitolare, VII.F.3, notarial act written by Giovanni di Pietro which records the reception of Bartolomeo de Rocca as canon by Bishop Andrea and the canons of Rieti, including three identified as "de Podio," on 5 August 1289. Photograph by Barbara Bini.

Iacobus miseratione divina Sancte Romane ecclesie diaconus cardinalis, dilecto sibi in Christo Bartholomeo de Rocca canonico Reatino cappellano suo salutem in Domino. Grata mentis fraterne ... et aliorum consanguineorum tuorum exigunt. et ad nos et dominum nostrum eorum continuata devotio promeretur ut te maiori gratia prosequentes personam tuam quanta cum Domino possumus honoremus. hic est quod nos tuis supplicationibus inclinati te in nostrum cappellanum recipimus et cappellanorum nostrorum consortio sociamus. Volentes ut decetero prerogativa potiaris etc. et ad nos recurras in tuis negotiis confidenter. In cuius rei testimonium presentes litteras ... fieri fecimus sigilli nostri appensione munitas. Data Rome in palatio Sancti Laurentii in Lucina. Sub anno Domini Millesimo Trecentesimo Octavo ... Indictione Pontificatus Sanctissimi patris domini Clementis pape Quinti Anno Tertio. Die xx mensis Octobris.

23. Rieti, Archivio Capitolare, VII.A.4, Cardinal Giacomo Colonna, out of gratitude for the service of Bartolomeo's family to the house of Colonna, receives Bartolomeo de Rocca, canon of Rieti, into his *consortium* of chaplains and records the act in a sealed letter of 20 October 1308. Photograph by Barbara Bini.

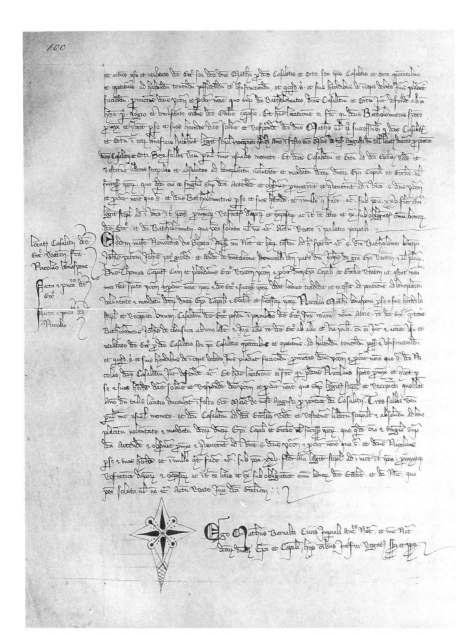

24. Parchment Book of Matteo Barnabei, page 100, record of acts from November 1317 with Matteo's notarial sign and subscript at end of gathering. Photograph by Barbara Bini.

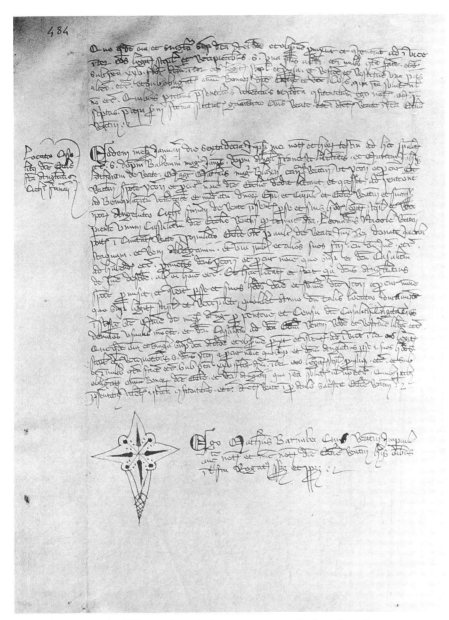

484

25. Parchment Book of Matteo Barnabei, page 484, record of act from January 1342 with Matteo's notarial sign and subscript at end of gathering. Photograph by Barbara Bini.

26. Rieti, Archivio Capitolare, III.C.3, the canons of the chapter of Rieti make two of themselves proctors, an act recorded in a document of 20 June 1280, sealed with the chapter seal. Photograph by Barbara Bini.

27. Chapter seal from 1280, Archivio
Capitolare, III.C.3. Photograph by Barbara
Bini.

28. Rieti, Archivio Capitolare, VII.G.10, sealed and notarized (by Nicola di Paolo of Rieti) letter from Bishop Biagio, instituting to the chapel of San Salvatore in the church of San Lorenzo, Rieti, Bartolomeo Cicchi, a priest of Rieti who had been presented by Giovanni de Canemorto, the chapel's patron, and ordering that the new chaplain be inducted by a canon of Rieti, 23 January 1356. Photograph by Barbara Bini.

29. Seal of Bishop Biagio, from 1356,
Archivio Capitolare, VII.G.10. Photograph
by Barbara Bini.

30. Tower in the ruins of the monastery of San Quirico.
Photograph by the author.

31. San Francesco, Posta (Machilone). From the Resource Collections of the Getty Center for the History of Art and the Humanities, Hutzel Archive.

32. San Francesco, Rieti, choir fresco, the presepio at Greccio. Foto Hutzel, Rome.

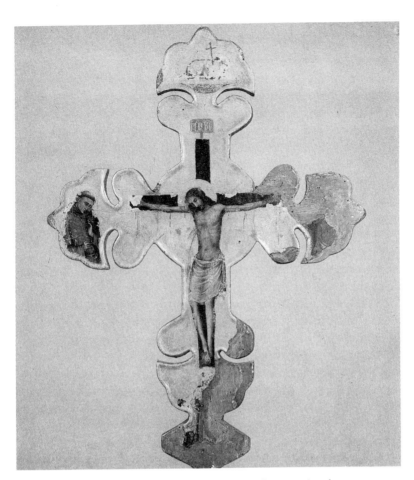

33. Fourteenth-century painted (gold background) processional cross from San Francesco, Posta, now in the Museo Civico of Rieti: reverse, on which Franciscan saints and a dead Christ replace Mary, John, and the live Christ of the front of the cross. Photograph by Corrado Fanti, reprinted from Marina Righetti Tosti-Croce, ed., *La sabina medievale* (Milan, 1985), by permission of the Cassa di Risparmio di Rieti.

34. The nuns of the monastery of Santa Filippa Mareri and the rising waters of the dammed Salto. Photograph by Barbara Bini, copy of photograph in the collection of the nuns of the monastery of Santa Filippa, by permission of Madre Margherita, the abbess.

35. Fossa, Santa Maria ad Cryptas, late thirteenth-century frescoes with heavenly and earthly witnesses to and mourners of the burial of Christ. From the Resource Collections of the Getty Center for the History of Art and the Humanities, Hutzel Archive.

36. Bominaco, San Pellegrino, late thirteenth-century frescoes on the entrance wall. From the Resource Collections of the Getty Center for the History of Art and the Humanities, Hutzel Archive.

37. Gagliano Aterno, Saint Martin, and the beggar, above the door of the parish church of San Martino. Photograph by the author.

38. Angel capital from the old *ciborio* of the cathedral of
Rieti, now in the Palazzo Cappelletti in Rieti, probably
carved before 1225, and removed from the cathedral in 1803.
Photograph courtesy of the Istituto per il Catalogo e la
Documentazione, Rome.

39. Angel capital which was, until stolen, in the crypt
of the ruined San Leopardo, Borgocollefegato.
Photograph by the author.

CHAPTER FOUR

The Definition of Diocesan Boundaries (2): from 1265

On the first day of Lent, 5 February, in 1315, during a papal vacancy, Giovanni Papazurri, "by the grace of God and the apostolic see," bishop of Rieti, sat in the choir of his cathedral church, in the presence of fifteen canons of his chapter and "all, or at least the greater part," of the clergy of Rieti (*Ciuitatis Reate*) and many other men (*aliis pulribus hominibus*), and read to them his constitutions on the rule and care of the parishes within his diocese.[1] It cannot have taken Giovanni long to read "the constitutions." They form a short, although dense, document, hardly more than a single elaborate statement, a condemnation of and remedies demanded for the presence of inadequate clergy, or the absence of clergy, in parishes. The improper appointment of inappropriate men to rule the parishes of his diocese, Giovanni said, left their churches widowed. The care of souls was neglected. The souls of parishioners were cheated. The parishes were deprived of divine services and teaching. The blood of the people of the parishes of his diocese should not be on his hands, Bishop Giovanni said. The concept of diocese, the definition of diocese, and so of diocesan boundary, that Giovanni expresses here, is stunningly different from the definition to be culled from Rieti litigation in the early thirteenth century. Bishop Giovanni's diocese is a collection of parishes full of men and women with souls to be ministered to; every soul counts. The diocese, like the parishes of which it is composed, fills out, is blown up, to extend fully to its borders.

Giovanni Papazurri (1302–1335/6) was a bishop who held synods and councils. Their constitutions and enactments, or at least some parts of them, were recorded and recalled. The constitutions of the council of Ash Wednesday 1315 were, at the bishop's orders, redacted by the Reatine citizen and notary, by imperial authority, Matteo Barnabei (or Matteo di Barnabeo), who then copied them into what would become his great parchment cartulary of copies of the Reatine church's documents, a cartulary eventually of twenty-four gatherings each of twelve folios which would cover the entire period from February 1315, the month of the constitutions' proclamation, to January 1348 (see plates 24 and 25, from 1317 and 1342). The constitutions were thus placed almost at the beginning of this, for Rieti, revolutionary piece of ordered record-keeping. Matteo Barnabei does not call the Ash Wednesday 1315 gathering a synod, as its recorder (quite possibly Matteo himself) does Bishop Giovanni's meeting in the "papal palace" at Rieti on 6 April (Easter Day) 1315 (but neither does he call Ash Wednesday Ash Wednesday, nor is Easter called Easter).[2]

It is said of the Easter 1315 meeting that its constitutions and sentences were read and promulgated by the lord bishop in the papal palace, in general synod (*in generali synodo*), with the chapter of Rieti present, today, 6 April, thirteenth indiction, before these witnesses (named) and many other prelates, canons, and clerics of the city and diocese of Rieti (*etiam magna multitudine alia prelatorum, canonicorum, et clericorum ciuitatis et diocesis Reatine*) in the year of our lord 1315, while the church of Rome was vacant, without a pastor. In his cartulary, in 1318, Matteo Barnabei refers specifically to the synod of 1 August 1311, from one of the statutes of which the addressee of a letter had been freed by license.[3] And in the Paris-Rieti manuscript an eschatocol of a synodal document, without naming its recording notary, talks of its constitutions and sentences having been read on 4 April (Holy Thursday) 1303 "in pleno synodo" in the papal palace, with canons, named witnesses, "et etiam magna alia multitudine prelatorum, canonicorum, et clericorum ciuitatis et diocesis Reat' ad ipsam synodum conuocatis (and a great many other prelates, canons, and clerks from the city and diocese of Rieti who had been called to this synod)."[4] The Holy Thursday and Easter synods proclaim their diocesan inclusiveness.

It is possible that in writing of the Ash Wednesday council Matteo Barnabei simply omitted the words *et diocesis* by accident and chose not to include the *multitudine alia* phrase—he was a writer (this creator of the word *pulribus*) sometimes rather careless with, or insensitive to, the formation of words, at least for a man who spent his life with them, a man, in memory at least, built of them. But, even so, it may seem odd here to break into Giovanni Papazurri's collection of synodal constitutions with the description of constitutions not from a council identified as a synod. There is a reason. Bishop Giovanni's other constitutions, those which are clearly synodal, are preserved in the Paris manuscript where they have been almost inextricably mixed with those of other Reatine bishops or at least those of Bishop Biagio da Leonessa (1347–1378).[5] The confusion seems complete. A section, which begins "In nomine Domini, amen. Nos frater Blaxius, miseratione diuina episcopus Reat' episcopus," ends three folios later with the Holy Thursday 1303 eschatocol. And this is followed in the hand of the Paris manuscript scribe by a rubric announcing "constitutions made in the second synod"; and there then follows a series of constitutions ending with the Easter 1315 eschatocol, which is itself written in a different (or at least cursive as opposed to normal book) hand and which completes the synodal constitution section of the manuscript. The hands suggest that the Paris manuscript scribe was writing at a time not very distant from Biagio's episcopate, but he was evidently sufficiently unaware of, or uninterested in, Rieti episcopal chronology not to have been productively disturbed by the order he created.[6]

Short injunctions following Biagio's "excommunicamus et anathematizamus" of heretics seem constructed to a single pattern which is almost surely Biagio's and seem very different in style from the constitution on the common goods of collegiate churches, which seems most securely, in part because of his name's being embedded within it, Giovanni's (but not all of the constitutions most likely to be Biagio's are in this easily identifiable quick style: *de pena clericorum excedentium in laicos*—very Biagio in subject and treatment and which has his name embedded in it—is not, although it does seem to share some of the simple lucidity of syntax of the short injunctions).[7] Close observation of or reference to a Lateran Council or to legislation of Boniface VIII suggests Giovanni; the use of *Virginis gloriose* perhaps suggests Biagio.[8] When Matteo Barnabei appears we are before 1349.[9] Admitting the possibility of eventual reasonable separation of at least some of the constitutions' attributions, their observer must for now hesitate before pointing to any Paris manuscript constitution and saying that it represents a position of 1315 or 1303.

This lack of separation, this creation of recorded copy of a group of constitutions and canons which cannot be separated and attributed to individual episcopal authors, or even scribes, is much to their point, to the point of fourteenth-century synodal legislation and proclamation, and to the point of Bishop Biagio da Leonessa as diocesan bishop. At Rieti Biagio seems to have been a diocesan of agreeable competence disinclined to emphasize revolutionary distinctness. A voice in the manuscript which is almost surely his repeatedly talks about his predecessors' constitutions *per predecessores nostros bone constitutiones.*[10] Biagio could have been expected sensibly to gather his predecessors, or at least Giovanni's, useful constitutions, to adjust them to his own purposes and add to them his own seemingly necessary or beneficial enactments: in its present form the Paris collection does not actually reveal this reasoned accommodation, but it admits of this reasoned accommodation's having been a step on the way to the surviving disorder.

The conflation of Giovanni and Biagio is part of a much greater scheme of borrowing and conflation which makes groups of synodal statutes from all over the peninsula, and much of Europe, part of a great family with a confused and complex genealogy, stemming at least from Innocent III's Fourth Lateran Council, and in a different but perhaps even more important way from Alexander III's Third Lateran Council of 1179, and the whole tree, at least in Italy, given, seemingly, new life by Clement V's Council of Vienne in 1312. The great initial period of Italian diocesan synodal legislation, of response to the stimulus offered by Innocent III in 1215, seems, in much of Italy, to have been the early fourteenth century. No one has as yet disentangled the Italian genealogy in brilliant exercise as has the great English historian of synods disentangled that of thirteenth-century England; but strong beginnings have been made from places as far apart as Novara and Amalfi.[11] Clearly Giovanni Papazurri's synodal legislation which cannot be isolated should not be isolated.

When Giovanni's constitutions of Ash Wednesday 1315 are seen as part of and in connection with the extended Reatine synodal activity of the Paris manuscript, their message about changed diocesan boundaries is not lessened, but rather it is confirmed and, much more, expanded into an almost embarrassingly articulate intelligibility. The Paris statutes begin with an *arenga*, an explanation of purpose: "quam periculosum sit et tremendum pastoralis officii dignitate fungentibus, quam sit onerosa cura regiminis gregis dominici (how dangerous and terrible it is to bear the dignity of the office of pastor, what a burden is the care of the rule of the Lord's flock)."[12] Theirs is a message in general statement and in detail of serious pastoral care, full of solemn echoes; twice we hear the ancient clause, which was heard also by listeners to the Fourth

Lateran, that the care of souls is the art of arts: "cum sit ars artium regimen animarum."[13] These are rules offered as part of the struggle for the salvation of the human race (*pro salute humani generis*).[14] They are rules directed to the *parochiani*, the parishioners of the diocese, through their to be made worthy and effective priests, and even more directly through what they themselves see at Mass.[15] Every priest when he celebrates Mass shall do it by the light of wax candle upon the altar and on that altar shall be a cross to remember there the passion of Christ (*ad memoriam passionis Christi*).[16] The Body of Christ in the Eucharist shall be conserved with honor in a clean pix or container, and when it is carried, properly covered, it shall be preceded by candle and bell; the Elevation of Mass is clearly regulated, so that at the words "Qui pridie" the priest holds the Host not too elevated but before his chest, and then when he says "Hoc est enim corpus meum" he raises the Host high so that all can see, and holds the Host firmly with both his hands.[17] The parishioners of the diocese are to see clearly God's body in the Eucharist.

The synodal constitutions are very much concerned with getting the faith as well as the sacraments to the people of the diocese—and the constitutions themselves must be read and explained throughout the diocese.[18] Priests must teach about the seven sacraments. They must teach parents to teach their children the Credo, the Pater Noster, the Ave Maria.[19] Confessions are to be frequent (*non tantum semel in anno, sed pluries*) and probing and instructive.[20] Heresy and usury, like abortion and arson, are faced, unsympathetically of course, but, although vicious, as elements within the community of the diocese.[21]

Not all of the injunctions can have been enthusiastically received even by the orthodox laity unengaged in major financial sins: even the simple farm worker busy among the sheep must have heard with restrained pleasure of the reminder that he should not have sexual relations with his wife from Advent until the octave of the Epiphany, from Septuagesima until the octave of Easter, and for three weeks before the feast of Saint John the Baptist.[22] But even this deflating admonition showed an episcopal awareness of the people, individuals with souls, in the bishops' diocese. This awareness, now apparent in Rieti, was not, it should be stressed again, peculiar to the diocese of Rieti; and certainly not all the injunctions connected with it were new, or even modern: the canon, for example, a sacramental canon, which instructs its reader or hearer what to do if a fly or a spider falls into a chalice of consecrated wine (no longer of course wine) is essentially that which Bishop Richard Poore

of Salisbury chose to exclude from canons which he copied and composed between 1217 and 1219, and for which exclusion of the old he has
been praised by the historian of English synodalia.[23]

It should be further noticed that the fourteenth-century emphasis
on sacraments offered by an instructing and orderly clergy is an emphasis also (and it can been seen as primarily this) on episcopal control
and on profitable diocesan order—the strong emphasis upon proper
reception of Holy Orders, upon sins for which absolution is reserved to
the bishop, which blend into the control of presentation and institution
to clerical livings and to the strong demand for episcopal fourths of
mortuaries and tithes.[24] And very surely there is an emphasis upon the
kind of order ensured by written record, from the constitutions themselves to the statute decreeing that every church shall have written down
at the end of a missal or breviary a list of all its possessions (or in another
statute the list is ordered to be written in a book or gathering kept in
the treasury or sacristy of the church).[25] And each parish priest shall
have a "manual" (with the order of baptism, catechism, extreme unc-
tion) and office books for day and night; and each priest is to be persuaded to have his missal and breviary according to the Roman rite.[26]

None of this obscures the fact that the diocese of the synodal statutes
is an enclosure of parishioners with their own parish priests all of whom
are or should be concerned with the salvation of each man's or woman's
soul.[27] The careful probing confessions and the Eucharist held up for
the people to view suggest something quite other than, different from,
the farmer's listening outside the church's wall at San Leopardo. These
fourteenth-century diocesan boundaries, seen by the bishops of Rieti
sitting in choir or palace, have very different dimensions from those that
Rainaldo de Labro or even Tommaso the Corrector were seen trying
to secure. To the fair objection that of course litigation documents and
synodal constitutions expose different attitudes toward diocese, the response must be that of course they do, but that the litigation documents
are the pertinent ones which survive from the episcopate of Rainaldo
de Labro and that the synodal ones only begin to survive from the
episcopate of Giovanni Papazurri—but further that the litigation documents seem to fit the period of Rainaldo (as in a different way does
his being host to Francis) and the synodal documents, Giovanni. Certainly there is a sense of a tremendous leaping when one compares
Giovanni's Ash Wednesday 1315 constitutions with the only at all comparable constitutions which survive from the thirteenth century, Bishop
Rainaldo da Arezzo's constitutions of 9 March 1250. Rainaldo's rather

disorderly compilation is concerned only with his chapter, and no doubt
it would be more fairly compared with Giovanni's various chapter regulations, one set of which is in fact the archival partner of Rainaldo's
(that is, it shares with Rainaldo's constitutions the same archival designation). Thus compared, the contrast does not seem so great, or
rather it has another color. But Rainaldo's chapter constitutions are all
that he, or really any of his thirteenth-century fellow bishops, has to
offer; Giovanni's chapter regulations are a specific, not necessarily pa-
cific, but relatively minor part of what he produced.[28] The distance from
Rainaldo to Giovanni is very great.

Giovanni Papazurri would not at first glance seem the obvious agent
for the production of the sacramental blossoming of a newly imagined
diocese. He came from a major Roman, of the city of Rome, family:
"one of the great Roman families (*le grandi famiglie romane*)," "a
family of ancient tradition" in the words of two very learned historians
of Rome.[29] His was not a family quite of the first order, but it was and
would continue to be intricately intermarried with other important families. Properties of the family's branches and family business were sewn
through the city's center from the neighborhood of Trevi and of the
church of Santi Apostoli to the Campo dei Fiori; and in some areas of
the countryside, as far away and south as Ferentino, Papazurri properties
lay thick and heavy on the ground. Papazurri women touched greatness,
in the mid and late fourteenth century, in two directions, by participating in the crowning of Petrarch, and by giving Bridget of Sweden a
house to live in. A man who has been identified as Giovanni's own father
was buried in Santi Apostoli: HIC IACET CORP(VS) / D(OM)INI NICOLAI
MUTI / DE PAHPAZVRIS'; and there remains a drawing of his tomb which
emphasizes, with his clothes, the importance of his position, and which
shows the family *stemma* (arms), the crescent moon, beneath his feet.[30]

Giovanni first appears in the register of Boniface VIII as one of the
pope's chaplains and as a canon of Santa Maria Rotunda, Metz, acting
for the pope as part of a commission which included Giacomo (or Jacopo) de Labro, canon of Rieti; the pertinent letters are dated 16 and
17 March 1296. His position and his title imply a university education.
Then in October and December 1297 he appears again, still a chaplain
but now a canon of the Lateran. He remained a chaplain and canon of
the Lateran until 9 March 1298, when he was provided by Pope Boniface
to the bishopric of Olema in Greece. On 6 February 1300 Boniface
released Giovanni from Olema and translated him to the see of Ìmola,
after he, Boniface, had refused to accept for that see its chapter's choice.

Then, on 5 August 1302, Boniface translated Bishop Giovanni again, this time to Rieti.[31]

When this Roman, provided and twice translated by Boniface VIII, former papal chaplain, had become bishop of Rieti, when he wrote letters in letter patent form, he always (in preserved letters) used, or his scribes did, a style then coming more generally into vogue, but not visible in the preserved letters of any earlier bishop of Rieti; he called himself bishop "dei et apostolice sedis gratia," that is, bishop by the grace of God and of the apostolic see.[32] Of Giovanni this was clearly an exact description, at least in its second half. But in spite of this papal patronage, Giovanni's translation to Rieti was not entirely smooth. He provoked from Boniface VIII, or from his chancery, an angry letter (if the letters in papal registers can speak anger); Giovanni had proceeded to Rieti without himself receiving, or sending a proctor to the curia to receive, his letters of translation—"spurning our letters," Boniface snaps—and the reader quickly has a sense of the touching of these two difficult men in a moment of tension.[33]

Giovanni Papazurri seems to have left no visible traces at either Olema or Ìmola.[34] It is possible that he did not reside in either place and that he came to Rieti, his third bishopric, with no practical experience of bishoping. But although Olema and Ìmola may have left no mark on him, his connection with the Lateran lasted a lifetime and he was, in the end, buried there. As bishop of Rieti Giovanni remained a Papazurri, and the connection is underlined by Matteo Barnabei's having occasionally noted the involvement of Bishop Giovanni in, or the importance to him of, an act recorded in Matteo's parchment cartulary by placing, as well as a miter, the Papazurri *stemma* in the margin of the folio on which he wrote the record of the act.[35] One of Bishop Giovanni's nephews, Francesco, became a canon of Rieti; and lists of witnesses to Giovanni's acts, the names of the people gathered round him, repeatedly recall his Papazurri, his Muti, and his Roman connections.[36]

When he was within the diocese of Rieti, Bishop Giovanni did not always stay in the city of Rieti. His predecessors had not, of course, been completely tied to the city: Bishop Gottifredo in 1276 was at the convent of Santa Filippa Mareri where he had perhaps gone to die, and his predecessor Tommaso the Corrector, who had supposedly visited his diocese, was, perhaps in the course of that visitation, at Collefegato thinking of Santa Filippa in 1253; and both Tommaso and Rainaldo de Labro have told us of their predecessors' formal procuration-gathering progressions through the diocese.[37] But—and in this he certainly seems typical of other thirteenth-century bishops when they were within the diocese at all—Tommaso's surviving dated acts place him, essentially always, in the city of Rieti itself. In another medium they tell again the story Salimbene would tell of Tommaso's predecessor's, Rainaldo da Arezzo's, interpretation of diocese.[38] Giovanni, the Papazurri Roman, extends diocese, in his constitutions, and in his habitation. As early as 1310 Giovanni was at Torano, in the extreme southeastern corner of the diocese, across the river Salto from the diocese of the Marsi, inducting a new rector in the church of San Martino.[39] More significantly in the late winter and spring of 1324 he was staying in Collalto, in the southernmost part of the diocese, near the point on the river Turano where the four dioceses of Rieti, Sabina, Tivoli, and the Marsi touched. From there his contact with the other center of diocesan government, the vicar general and chapter in Rieti city, was by messenger—so that a document issued by the bishop on 7 April might be officially read, copied, and dated by the others in Rieti only on 12 April.[40] From 1324 to 1331 Bishop Giovanni was in Montereale at the center of the distant northeastern segment of the diocese; it is quite possible that over those years he lived there continually.[41]

On 18 July 1334 Bishop Giovanni was corresponding with his vicar from Rome.[42] Giovanni's presence in Rome makes his observer face the reason for his absences from his cathedral city, the reason for the carefully copied and described episcopal letters with their described red seals. Rome was not a distant part of Giovanni's diocese. Some part of the motivation for Giovanni's exile may have been, in the grander sense, political. The second half of his episcopate was clearly a time of renewed disorder in central Italy. Even without being able to recreate the detail of local and regnal politics which would explain Giovanni's absence from his city and cathedral, Giovanni's observer can accept the serious possibility that it existed.[43]

But another, although not necessarily unrelated, kind of friction and animosity may have been the principal cause of Giovanni's removal, his inability to live happily with segments of the cathedral clergy and particularly his chapter. Although Giovanni was at times considered sympathetic enough even to act as arbiter for the local clergy, signs of tension clearly exist.[44] Giovanni's early capitular legislation, that which he issued in 1303 and which he had copied in 1306, might seem, were all the documents from everywhere before us, conventional, but it is certainly unpleasant—suspecting betrayal, the revelation of secrets, and fraud; demanding oaths; restricting absolution. And the beauty of the hand and elegance of the composition of a document written by the notary by royal authority Luca da Santa Rufina, with his notarial sign a kind of Byzantine cross hanging from its last line, does not hide the acerbity, almost brutality, of Bishop Giovanni's tone in his demand that each canon pay his share of the expense of sending Tommaso Capitaneo to Naples to get from King Robert money owed for the anniversary payment in memory of his father's coronation at Rieti.[45]

There is more direct, although not in detail unambiguous, evidence of hostility between Bishop Giovanni and his chapter which drove him from his see—finally to a Rome which in 1334 must have seemed wildly different from the Rome of 1302, the year of Giovanni's translation to Rieti. When Giovanni's successor was elected, some of the canons who elected him were under a kind of shadow. The matter or problem is revealed in a letter issued by an auditor of the papal chamber in Avignon and dated 3 August 1338; it was copied by Matteo Barnabei in his parchment book. The document records the absolution of a group of canons who had been accused of expelling and despoiling Bishop Giovanni and so had been cited by two rectors of the patrimony. The accused canons were said initially to have been contumacious. Yet later they were absolved by one of the rectors, the bishop of Orvieto, acting in Montefiascone on 3 December 1322, after one of the canons, Tommaso Cimini, had appeared for himself and the others before the rector. The canons who had been absolved and were specifically named were Tommaso Cimini, Giacomo di don Tommaso, Andrea the abbot of Sant'Eleuterio, Matteo di magistro Biagio, Matteo di don Angelo di Tufo, and Matteo di don Paolo.[46] Whatever the attitude of these canons had been toward Giovanni before their excommunication, it must have been chilled by the excommunication.

Again, Giovanni Papazurri, this repeated providee of Boniface VIII, this nepotist member of a rich and broadly connected Roman family, a man capable of annoying his provider through a casual, or perhaps arrogant, ignoring of proper form, this man who may have been an absentee bishop in his first two sees, and who certainly was long away from the cathedral city of his third, who could produce a remarkably antagonistic tone in pronouncing his demands to his seemingly alienated canons, this man seems an unlikely hero of the Eucharist, Confession, and the parishioner's soul. His figure is not, of course, really very visible. The lines with which one would draw him are not continuous. His episcopate is the first Reatine episcopate continuously described by a conscientious and, in copying, articulate recorder, Matteo Barnabei; but from that record in spite of the quite dazzling (in this little theater) acts of Giovanni's which are written into it, he himself, the bishop, is generally absent. The history of the church proceeds without him.

One must ask, is it simply an accident, coincidence, that his long episcopate coincided with such a lot of important change—in the definition of diocese, of church, in governing and in writing about government, in the moving of memory into continuous record, in ways of building church and burying? Was he just standing there, or really just standing in the distance, when it all happened?

I think that, in the end, particularly after one has thought about Giovanni and new chapels and the new tribune of the cathedral, and then remembered the synodal constitutions, that it is virtually impossible to reject the connection between Giovanni and change.[47] Not much can be known of the man; what can be known seems contradictory, contrapuntal, contrapostal. He is aggravated and aggravating. But he seems repeatedly even when he is not speaking originally to speak revealingly, tellingly. Though the words are conventional when he talks of his mind and soul in planning his chapel dedicated to the Savior, I at least believe that he is thinking of his mind and soul, in a world of minds and souls.[48] When, from Montereale in February 1328, he founded Santa Caterina, the new convent of cloistered Benedictine nuns in Cittaducale, in response to the supplication of Gentile da Foligno, the spiritually powerful Augustine Hermit and friend of Angelo Clareno, he could have acted without personal interest in nuns, Gentile, or Angelo; his response may have been merely formal and bureaucratic, but that seems unlikely.

When, in an *arenga* to the constitution most clearly his in the Paris manuscript, he says "tanto circa regimen et statum ecclesiarum nobis subiectarum tenemur amplius reuoluere intuitum nostre mentis, quanto in esamine stricti judicii tenebimur reddere rationem," I believe that this absentee (but not yet from Rieti) turns the problems of government and justice over in his mind, seriously, and seeks the right and apposite answers so that he may appropriately occupy his position as a responsible shepherd of the Reatine flock of souls. I think that we hear in him not, or not just, a formula from a formulary of *arenga*s but the echo of Charlemagne lamenting at the end of the Bodley Roland or of Joinville's Louis IX worrying about good governance, although in a geographically restricted and overtly spiritual sphere.[49] In this romance of Giovanni Papazurri's mind no reader need follow me.

In talking of Giovanni Papazurri, one talks of Matteo Barnabei. It is the notary, perhaps, whom we really see. One can, and must, argue that what we have watched is not a revolution in government and thought but rather a revolution in writing and recording. And then one must ask: is there a difference? how can one define the difference? can one separate the two pairs? does one pair push the other?

It would make sense to say that Matteo Barnabei, by himself, constructed the diocese of Rieti and gave it its real boundaries; it would make even more sense to say that he constructed the diocese that we can remember or find again. Either would be a statement more exact than the clichés of historical caution would tempt us to believe. Of course caution, common sense, and observation of the evidence force us to realize that he did not do it alone or begin the construction. Bishop Tommaso has made that clear. And, partly with Bishop Tommaso in mind, one must approach Matteo Barnabei from his past in order to appreciate his accomplishment. When one does appreciate it, one will appreciate the accomplishment, not the man. One cannot know the man, not even, not at all, in the way one can know Giovanni Papazurri, his partner, in a sense, in creation.

One can know that Matteo had a son, named Severio, who was old enough on 8 November 1346, when he acted with Matteo as a witness, to be a witness and probably a priest since he is called *dompnus*; and that, presumably, the Matteo notarii Matthei Barnabei, a witness on 12 July 1334, was another son.[50] One can know that Matteo was alive and working on 8 January 1348, and that he was not alive long after that date, and that he was active as a notary by imperial authority and working in the church of Rieti by 1308 and by 2 December 1314 he was already able to call himself "nunc scriba domini episcopi et capituli," and that by 12 February 1315 he had substituted the word *notarius* for *scriba*.[51] One can know that he was a citizen of Rieti, and know if not find the house and lands he was given as a *feudum* by the chapter on 23 June 1337.[52] One can know his itinerary between 1315 and 1348—a very Reatine itinerary. One can know very well his notarial sign, the capitals *E* and *M* of his notarial subscript, the way he decorated his grand initial *I* for *In nomine domini*, his mode of composition and dating and spelling (and so something of the way he heard sound). Best of all one can know his hand, his actual way of writing, and follow its progression, or in fact decline, year after year in his great book, from 1315 to 1348—and it was in its early years a very beautiful, a very perfect hand. So at the very center of the history of the diocese of Rieti, of its definition, is this man whom one cannot know as a man, unless one decides that knowing what we do know, not at all like what one knows of Rainaldo da Arezzo, but instead the shape of an *h* or of the abbreviation for *pro*, is also knowing a man (plates 24, 25).

There is very good reason to approach Matteo Barnabei through Bishop Tommaso the Corrector. Tommaso, although in his own way mute, was obviously a very strong and thoughtful administrator and diocesan who very definitely and distinctly did not do what, in their doing it, made Matteo and Giovanni, at Rieti, so remarkable. Tommaso came to Rieti from one of the two finest chanceries in Europe. He was a government man, a (if the word is used cautiously) bureaucrat. At Rieti he obviously did not govern alone. He used clerks and assistants. He wrote through notaries. But he did not create (or he seems not to have created) that system of what the chapter would later call obedientiaries, of people at least temporarily assigned to specific offices with specific responsibilities and a specific title.

So titled himself that he is known by his old title, Tommaso the Corrector, he did not give titles. He did not appoint an official bishop's scribe or notary. A number of scribes can be seen to have been working around the church of Rieti in the 1250s and early 1260s—Tommaso, Andrea Pasinelli, Rainerio, Rainaldo, Ambrogio, Magister Matteo.[53] Most prominent among them, in the surviving documents, is a papal notary and citizen of Perugia, Ranaldo, who worked repeatedly for Bishop Tommaso.[54] It is possible that Tommaso organized the episcopal-capitular writing office around Ranaldo, and that Ranaldo's neat but modest redactions, characteristically carefully and economically gathering a number of related documents into the panels of a single piece of parchment, a sort of proto-enrollment repeatedly noticeable in thirteenth-century Italian ecclesiastical writing offices, are connected with Tommaso's administrative interests and skills. But it seems clear that Tommaso did not appoint an official episcopal notary and that he did not develop a system of enrolling governmental acts in a codex register or cartulary.

If one moves back from Tommaso and Ranaldo one moves into a rather different scribal and diplomatic world, where things are relatively unsubdued and grand, and encounters scribes of documents for the church of Rieti who are called *scriniarii* of the holy Roman church and the city of Rieti: Giordano, Oddone, and Magister Bonofilio.[55] The earliest of these three, Bonofilio, produced in 1233 a square document (16.5 cm by 16.5 cm) elaborately prepared and written in a sort of Honorius III hand and also elaborately dated (incarnation, indiction, month, day, pontifical year: *temporibus domini Gregorii VIIIJ pape* . . .).[56] In 1225 a document of Matteo scriniario used the titulus to note abbreviations and added to its date "tempore domini Honorii IIJ pape" the statement that Frederick emperor of the Romans was then ruling, and the notation that the day was counted from the beginning of the month.[57] That document records a sentence of the then bishop Rainaldo de Labro and the judge Berardo Sprangone.

With these two, bishop and judge, the observable diplomatic, the scribal practice, of the church of Rieti in the thirteenth and fourteenth centuries begins. Berardo Sprangone "dei gratia judex et scriniarius sacre Romane ecclesie et Reatine ciuitatis," a Reatine of already observed importance, wrote documents during the pontificates of Innocent III and Honorius III (1198–1227) (plate 21).[58] Trapezoidal (the heads broader than the feet) but otherwise variously proportioned, sometimes decorated, carefully written in a hand that would have seemed respectable although perhaps a little archaic in Rome, produced by a major literate figure within the community, a judge in fact as well as a scribe, and a governor, these primitive elaborate documents argue both secretarial arrangements and a context very far from those of Bishop Tommaso and Ranaldo of Perugia and particularly from those which would noticeably begin to develop under Tommaso's obscure successor Bishop Gottifredo (1265–1275/6). In October 1265 a document is notarized by a man who describes himself as "Johannes Petri dei gratia Romane ecclesie et Reatine ciuitatis et dicti episcopi notarius."[59]

Giovanni di Pietro, whose physical substance we have seen being transferred after his death, in 1318, to the building of the new tribune of the cathedral church of Rieti, was an official titled employee of the church of Rieti, its bishop's notary.[60] Giovanni had been active in cathedral circles for several years before 1265; he acted as a notary for the chapter on 13 June 1263; he was a witness, in the choir, on 4 February 1261.[61] He was to remain active until at least 3 May 1314 when he wrote in his protocols the draft of a document (which he himself did not extend) in which he described himself as "dictorum dominorum episcopi et capituli scriba."[62] He thus spent more than fifty-three years as a professional man, a notary, involved in episcopal and capitular business. He was almost surely dead by 23 September 1314 when Simone Bonjohannis extended and redacted the 3 May 1314 document from "protocollis quondam notarii Johannis de Reate."[63] He had, one might reasonably assume, begun working for the church of Rieti when he was quite young; and the reasonable assumption is strengthened by the remaining record that his license to act as a notary by papal authority was issued by Pope Urban IV (1261–1264).[64]

Giovanni was probably a native Reatine; as an adult he was certainly a citizen of Rieti. He seems always to have been a layman, in the sense that lay prebendaries were laymen. His father's name was Petrus Johannis, of which name his own was a characteristic inversion. Almost surely Johannes Petri's, our Giovanni's, grandfather's name was also Giovanni. The notary Giovanni's name, fully extended, was Johannes Petri Johannis Tedemarii (or Teodemarii). The Tedemarii (or Teodemarii) would seem to have been fixed as a patronymic surname by Giovanni di Pietro's generation since his own name, at least once, includes the Teodemarii without the preceding Johannis.[65] Giovanni was married to a woman named Verardesca or Berardesca who survived Giovanni but was dead by, or in, October 1338.[66] He seems to have had no surviving children or other close personal heirs.

By 1294 Giovanni held property in the Porta Cintia region of Rieti (near San Domenico) and was acquiring more; in January of that year he promised 33 and ⅓ gold florins to Pandolfono Jacobi Accani of Apoleggia for a third of a house next to some of his own property there.[67] A property owner, lay, wived, Giovanni lived a citizen in Rieti, but his legacy, besides his part of the tribune, is a collection of great drifts of notarial instruments, which record a great variety of acts of the late thirteenth-century and early fourteenth-century bishops and chapter, and which form a very significant segment of the preserved individual loose documents in the chapter archives.

All of these documents are immediately recognizable because of the notarial sign which Giovanni used on all his subscribed work, an adaptation of sheath and ribbon, which, with a little imagination, can be seen as a *J*, because of its left-turning tail, with an efflorescent vegetable top, always placed by him (which was not true of all of his contemporaries) in the conventional notarial position before the subscript; his hand, too, in his subscribed work is recognizable, consistent and legible but without elegance. Although always recognizably his, Giovanni's notarial work is uneven. A document of some importance, an institution, which he wrote for Bishop Berardo in 1296, at the height presumably of his notarial powers, and which was once sealed with the bishop's seal, is a miserable job, owing in part to its badly dressed parchment, which looks like the sheep from lunch.[68] On the other hand Giovanni's document from 1289 and the episcopate of Bishop Andrea, with which he records the reception of a canon and in which he assigns himself no title, is a really handsome little piece of work (plate 22).[69]

In spite of the importance that should be assigned to Giovanni's having an official title, that title wavers, as in fact Giovanni's work does: "episcopi notarius" for Bishop Gottifredo; "episcopi scriba" for Bishop Andrea; "episcopi scriba" also for Bishops Berardo and Giovanni; but also "nostrum notarium" for Bishop Giovanni; and finally in 1314 "dictorum dominorum episcopi et capituli scriba" under Bishop Giovanni.[70] Giovanni di Pietro was not, when one can observe the phenomenon, the sole notary or even the always sole notary prebendary of the church; in some ways, and literally, he was one of a group. Conversely he was probably not solely occupied with the bishop's and chapter's business. In 1270 he redacted the record of a permutation between the friars of San Domenico and private persons; in 1292 he redacted a document concerning a Rieti prebend at the mandate of the beneficiary, not as the official notary of the church.[71] Although either of these acts could be disguised commissions of the great church, Giovanni's independent actions, since he seems to have kept no cartulary and his protocols seem not to have survived, would not be expected now to exist. In record keeping he seems not to have been particularly creative or imaginative. In fact his long tenure of the central position within his writing office may have retarded its development. And yet there are from his time of dominance, and from the episcopate of Pietro da Ferentino and his vicar general Pietro Romano, from 1278 and 1282, impressively preserved records of prebendal income, division and reassignment, which themselves make clear Giovanni di Pietro's initial involvement, although the handsome document in which they now survive would seem to come from a time close to that of Giovanni's death. Giovanni's 1278 and 1282 work may well have been reassumed, built up into this small codex record by his successors, but in this case he does at least seem to have helped form, with his lists, a sort of recording which would be developed into a serious instrument of government in the hands of Matteo Barnabei.[72]

Certainly as bishops came and went, and canons (or some of them) stayed, Giovanni di Pietro remained at the cathedral church of Rieti for more than fifty years, an official at the center of its writing office, providing it with memory in two ways, with his own retaining mind (retaining at the very least the memory of practiced form and behavior and of location), and with the retained defining documents which he wrote and which he, or his employers, kept in archive. To that diocese which extended from the cathedral church on its central hill and which was defined by the actions on and in connection with that church he gave a new kind of official and to-be-retained definition, so that one can surely say that a new kind of (perhaps potential) definition of diocesan boundary, a new kind of official writing that implies and describes boundary, begins with his assuming his official position in 1265, a year before the diocese's loss of Amiterno (or the serious beginning of that loss).

Giovanni di Pietro's employers appreciated him. On 8 October 1293, when both the see of Rome and that of Rieti were vacant, the chapter of Rieti, assembled, as they say, in their accustomed manner in the choir of the cathedral church, received Giovanni "Petri Johannis Theodemarii" long (*ex olim*) their notary as a lay prebendary of their church for as long as he should live and they ordered their chamberlain, *dompnus* Tommaso Capitaneo, to grant to Giovanni from treasury and cellar his share of daily distribution of commons, and they granted Giovanni as a prebend eight giunte (and again the modern Reatine giunta is 1,617.32 square meters) of land in Roscia or Vergaria Roscie of Colle Baccaro (and it is the name that is questioned, not the place because the boundaries are named), and they ordered two canons of Rieti, Rainaldo Alfani and Bartolomeo di don Oddone, to induct him and give him corporal possession of his tenement. And then on 26 November 1294, when the see of Rieti was no longer vacant, Bishop Nicola acting in his chamber, in a nest of Cistercians (Angelo abbot and Fra Simone da Foligno and Fra Giacomo da Butri, all monks of San Pastore), confirmed all that the canons had done.[73]

These documents are a monument to the appreciated value of written government. They are also, in their own forms, revealing. They combine notarial form with the form of the sealed letter. The chapter caused the notary Matteo Rayn' Tudini Cifredi to make a public instrument recording their grant, and the resulting document begins and ends conventionally for such an instrument; but it includes within it signs of the letter form; and the chapter had the instrument sealed with their seal. And Bishop Nicola, who rehearsed in his own letter-instrument both the grant and the induction by the chapter and had the whole thing notarized by the notary Pietro "Paczanelli," also had his document sealed with his seal. Rieti's was a church for which notaries wrote; its writing officers were notaries. But it was, not unconventionally, a writing office of mixed form. It knew the seal and the letter patent. It could not have not known them. Early and late in the thirteenth century

Reatine writers could watch papal spigurnels at work in their own Reatine palaces. Cardinals' sealed letters, Cistercian sealed letters, the sealed
letter of an archdeacon of Siena, the abbot of Bominaco's sealed document, and certainly the bishop of Narni's seal (which Bertuldo had
redirected) came before the eyes of Reatine writers.[74] And the bishop
and chapter of Rieti had their own seals and used them: Rainaldo da
Arezzo in 1250; Tommaso in 1261; the chapter of Rieti its own seal in
1280 (plates 26 and 27); Pietro in 1282; Nicola in 1295; Giovanni in 1324;
and the big (7.5 by 5 cm) pointed red wax seal of Bishop Biagio bearing
the image of Virgin and Child and hanging from the document by a
white and green cloth string that looks a little like a golf shoelace (plates
28 and 29).[75] Reatine writers (at least some of them) knew how to use
and adapt letter forms. But, again, theirs was a notarial office; they were
notaries. To the notary Giovanni di Pietro succeeded, essentially, the
notary Matteo Barnabei.

The speed with which Matteo Barnabei began his great parchment
cartulary after the death of Giovanni di Pietro (nine months almost to
the day after Giovanni's last preserved document) suggests, perhaps,
that he was waiting to take over. He had done some work for the church
as early as 1308 and was already a *scriba* of bishop and chapter by December 1314, as we have seen. The parchment book is reasonably described as a cartulary. It deals primarily with acts which concern property
rather than, insofar as these things are separable, acts which would be
described as governmental or administrative. It copies, essentially, previous notarial acts or extends notes from protocols, in which property
transfers are recorded, rents and incomes are fixed, holdings are divided
or exchanged. In its very first entry it records that, on 2 February 1315
in the church of Rieti before three witnesses, Tommaso Capitaneo as
proctor of the bishop and chapter had leased to a woman, Giovanna
Petri Celli, and her heirs, one-half a house lot with a small garden behind it, with specified boundaries including a public road, in the parish
of San Nicola, for an entrance fee of 18 soldi of Ravenna and a rent, to
be paid each year on 15 August, of 11 small denari of Ravenna, "now
the usual money."[76]

This action—the limited alienation of property by the bishop and
chapter through a representative to an individual or individuals—is the
base material of the book, its minimal matter. From this base material
the book moves into much more complicated proprietary actions, ones
which are much more closely connected with the distinguishing characteristics of the church of Rieti as an institution as well as its central

financial structure: it deals with the relations between bishop and canons, and among canons; it describes the structuring and restructuring
of prebends; it copies wills and codicils to wills; it records essential acts
of physical piety like the foundation of chapels. Miscellaneous in its
inclusions, it seems not to exclude. On its second page, it begins its
record of Giovanni Papazurri's parochial constitutions. Particularly in
its early years, the book is thick and dense.

It is a book primarily concerned with property, with the property of
the bishop and chapter. Matteo Barnabei, who can appear as the notary
for either bishop or chapter, is repeatedly the notary of bishop and
chapter together, of the vicar general, of either or both, and perhaps
most frequently of the church at Rieti, the undefined complex—in his
person and his work Matteo recalls a seal mentioned in 1287, but not
preserved: the seal in the singular of the bishop and chapter of Rieti.[77]
It should be noted that this is not a cartulary of the notary Matteo in
which he includes acts connected with the church of Rieti; and it is not
that one of a series of cartularies in which he places for convenience of
reference the acts of the church. It is the cartulary of the church of Rieti;
and in its existence it gives the church a new kind of existence. But in
its distinctness and inclusiveness it still remains sharply notarial: not only
is, for example, the record of the initial act, the grant to Giovanna Petri
Celli, the copy of an instrument notarized by Matteo Barnabei himself,
but also the whole book is a notarial act with Giovanni's sign and subscription appearing in gathering after gathering.

Matteo Barnabei's surviving individual notarial instruments are not
so unusual in their fineness as is his book, at least in its first two hundred
pages.[78] But they are clear and effective, the work of an accomplished
notary. They share with his parchment book that notarial characteristic
which gives the book much of its value as a source, the insistence upon
the exact notation and sometimes description of what could be considered peripheral detail. Truth to the notary is pertinent detail of time,
place, persons present, kind of action, type of currency.[79] So when Matteo Barnabei, quickly after Giovanni di Pietro's death, decided or agreed
to begin the composition of this planned and official book which would
detail and preserve the acts of the central, cathedral church of Rieti and
its officers, he in fact also decided to give that part of the diocese which
his acts would touch, its substance, a new kind of retained reality. The
cartulary is thick with detail and people; it gives flesh, and the memory
of flesh, to that which it touches. It is full of movement. Although it
interprets property broadly, it, perhaps inadvertently, argues the im-

portant reality of property in governmental and even pious act. The description is continuous: year follows year, and within each year month follows month; and the latter action, explicitly when that is appropriate, remembers the former. Continuity is description; or at least it moves description to a different depth.

I would argue that the creation of this book changes the diocese of Rieti. But it has, for purposes of diocesan description, clear limitations. The movement of which it is full, is restricted: it is generally movement from the choir of the great church of Rieti to the bishop's chamber, from the area at the foot of the campanile to the loggia of a Reatine citizen's house, from a canon's chapel to a canon's house. Occasionally its action moves to a distant piece of property, a church or chapel; and of course it almost begins with the parochial constitutions. But essentially the church of Rieti in Matteo's parchment book is the community, or closely tied to the community, on the hill in the city. This church often does not seem to be, but even in a way seems the opposite of, the new church, the newly defined diocese, of the synodal constitutions— and of course neither Matteo nor his book claimed for it new powers of definition.

As the book proceeds, moreover, from 1315 to 1336, through the period of its coverage of Giovanni Papazurri's episcopate, the bishop, who might be expected to represent a larger view of diocese than the chapter, seems to slip out of the book's pages as Giovanni himself slips into his years of provincial and then Roman exile, or at least distance. Further, as the book proceeds, its quality seems to decline. The strong beauty of Matteo's hand, as it appears for example in the year 1317, seems to be waning, or tiring, by, say, 1328. A reader who compares as a sampling the book's page 100, from 1317, with its page 484 from 1342, is aware of, in this sense, a sharply negative change (plates 24, 25): and he should note that the first one hundred pages have covered only three years, and that the next three hundred eighty-five pages have covered twenty-five years. The great book seems to be pulling itself in, minimizing itself.

It is thus rather stunning to find that in (or by) the 1340s, Matteo Barnabei has started a whole new career of collecting, recording, and defining, in paper. His most adventurous and in some ways important work is no longer confined to, or to be found in, his continuing parchment book. (And Matteo's own awareness of the distinction between his work on parchment and on paper and also the fact that the development of his work in the 1340s was already in preparation at least by 1334 are shown in a note in his parchment book for 5 February 1334 where he talks of "aliis actis meis qui scripti sunt in carta bammacina [other acts of mine which are written on paper].") Of Matteo's new books of paper (some of which paper at least was milled in Sulmona) there are two sets, of two books each, which deal with different matter and come from different (but overlapping) periods: 1340–1347; 1346–1347.[80] The earlier two books are continuous. They have sometimes been designated as different in matter: "Liber Collationum" and "Liber Contractuum"; but, although the earlier book in the beginning does quickly show its concern with *collationes*, presentations and institutions to clerical livings, both are concerned with a variety of actions as the generic *contractuum* suggests, and the distinction between the two is chronological. The later two books are court books, which, essentially, record the acts of the tribunal of the vicar general of the cathedral chapter, to whom or which jurisdiction *sede vacante* fell, from the vacancy of 1346–1347, after the translation from Rieti of Bishop Raimond de Chameyrac and before the translation to Rieti of Bishop Biagio da Leonessa. Although the first set of books is, essentially, entirely the work of Matteo Barnabei, and the second two are essentially his collections of material, none of the books proclaims itself his as flagrantly as does the parchment book (although four of the five gatherings of the 1340–1343 book do conclude with his sign and subscription). The parchment book emblazoned with his sign was the book of the church of Rieti, but these relatively depersonalized books show the diocese of Rieti in understood and seemingly accustomed administrative and judicial behavior; they are work books, connected with quick, pervasive action.

On the first seven folios of the 1340–1343 paper book are seven presentations and renunciations; one jumps quickly into what has seemed the book's business. An act of 3 March 1341 is a revealing example of that business: Leonardo Abbiamontis de Valviano di Cittaducale, patron for three parts of half of the church of San Nicola di Valviano in Rieti diocese, vacant through the death of Petrucio Henrici da Montereale, former clerk of the church, presents to Bishop Tommaso, for institution to the vacant church, his, the patron's, son Tuccio.[81] On 6 February 1342 Don Caputosto of Poggio Bustone as patron for an eighth part of the church of San Giovanni of Poggio Bustone, vacant through the resignation of Oddone Pasinelli, and the same Caputosto patron for an eighth part of Sant'Angelo of Poggio Bustone, vacant through the resignation of his own son Tommaso, presented to both churches: his own son Buccio to San Giovanni and Matteo di don Pandulfo of Poggio to Sant'Angelo; on 13 February Don Reche di don

Synibaldo of Rieti, patron of one-half of Santo Stefano di Catico, vacant
through the resignation of Syniballo his son, re-presented Syniballo
(and the presentation was confirmed).[82] On the last day of February,
three brothers, two of whom were canons of Rieti, Matteo, Angelo, and
Cola di don Paolo, patrons together of one-fourth part and one-twenty-
fourth part, respectively, of San Pietro and San Quirico de Plagis, presented to this complex a clerk native to the place of the two churches.[83]

This splintering of churches and livings seems to make nonsense of
the episcopal constitutions concerning good pastors properly presented.
In order that it should not make nonsense of the pastoral synods, obviously, very careful observation, control, and record keeping were necessary. The synods and the splintering together present problems of
dealing with patronage vastly different from and more pettily complicated than those involved with the attempted control of the great baronial patronage of the Amiterno lords at Ferentillo or the Lavareta
lords at Lugnano. Clearly, as these later cases show, the central diocesan
episcopal control of these relatively petty (in the individual instances)
patrons did not keep them from presenting, successfully, their own relatives (and in other cases friends and clerks) to these livings; and there
is no suggestion that it was meant to do so, if the presentees were
themselves technically suitable.

But the recording of these presentations in Matteo Barnabei's first
paper book, taken together with other actions there recorded—the regulation of licenses for absences to study at university, the imposing of
conditional controls when presentment arrangements seem to suggest
danger to parishioner welfare—show a serious concern for the implementation of the creative ideas about and definitions of diocese stated
in the synodal constitutions, show the necessity for that implementation
of records of the sort that Matteo Barnabei here created, and show the
integral connection between Matteo's kind of written government and
the expanded interpretation of diocese and, thus, of diocesan boundary.
An example of the sort of episcopal supervision which Matteo was able
to record is that of April 1342, actually during an episcopal vacancy when
diocesan administration was in the hands of the cathedral chapter, when
the chapter, acting as if it were bishop in this matter, issued a constitution regarding the churches of San Giovanni "de Castro Vetere"
(Castel di Tora) and Santa Maria de Illicis; it dealt with the fixed residence of priests and canons in the churches and care of souls, before it
accepted, with the provision of observing the constitution which protected the spiritual rights and needs of the church's parishioners, the

clerks presented for these churches by their potent patrons, the lords of Mareri.[84]

The two books which Matteo put together which deal with cases heard by the chapter's vicar general *sede vacante* or his representatives move into the diocese in a different and superficially more vivid way. They show the episcopal chapter's assumed competence in litigation in the diocese, its assumed interest in justice and in the control of diocesan crime. That they come from a period of episcopal vacancy is noteworthy, but not entirely surprising. Innovation, and unusually careful and visible control by an appointed official, seem not to have been unnatural or unreasonable corollaries of episcopal vacancies. Further, these books more than any of the others suggest that they may, but only may, be first survivals rather than that they were first occurrences; a chapter might naturally have in its, admittedly pretty random, archives, records of diocesan courts under its rather than a living bishop's control.

The division of matter in the two books as they survive is not completely rational, but it is essentially a separation into the two named categories. The normality of judicial administration is early set in the book of civil cases: the vicar sits for tribunal in Rieti in the papal palace *ad solitum bancum,* at the accustomed bench, and he sits *in hora causarum,* at the hour at which cases are heard.[85] A man named Cola di Giovanni Planetis is ordered on pain of excommunication to give over to his dead wife Lippa's executors the thirteen unpaid florins of the twenty-five she left to pious bequests.[86] The validity of marriages is repeatedly examined. Pietro Paolo di Giovanni Cicarelle of Rieti is claimed to have contracted marriage with Maxia or Massia di magistro Angelo da Rodio di Aquila but to have refused to accept her as his legitimate wife. Maxia's side claims both were of legal age at the time of the contract: Pietro Paolo was over fourteen and she over twelve; and this was commonly known *publica uox et fama* and particularly in the contrada Ponte. In the end Maxia's case could not be established.[87]

From the mind of the contrada Ponte, the vicar general must turn his attention in another case to the mind of the contrada Arce. Were Cola di Pietro Pauloni of Rieti and Margarita di Tommaso Nervi of Rieti within the fourth degree of kinship and should their marriage be annulled? Witness after witness from the contrada is called and asked to dig into his or her own and common knowledge of the genealogy of the two parties. Pietro di Matteo tells what he has heard from Pretiosa, his mother, and Matteo, his father, and other older people: Margarita Syniballi and Venuta Syniballi were sisters, and also sisters of his mother,

Pretiosa; Margarita was the mother of Pasquale who was the father of
Giovanna who was the wife of Tommaso Nervi and the mother of Margarita, the wife in the contested marriage; Venuta was the mother of
Gualterio who was the father of Petrutia who was the wife of Pietro
Pauloni and mother of Cola, the husband in the contested marriage—
so that husband and wife were indeed within the fourth degree and
were in fact (in modern terms) third cousins. Matteo Feste had seen
together Margarita and Venuta, the sisters, and Pasquale and Gualtiero,
the cousins. Matteo di Giovanni Berardi says Margarita had a sister
whose name he cannot remember, and Margarita had a son Pasquale,
and from the sister whose name he cannot remember came Gualterio.
The first action of the case had happened on the last day of July, when
Cola who had initiated the proceedings brought the case against Margarita; on 12 August Cola was himself present before the vicar, and
Tommaso appeared for his daughter and brought the vicar two letters
written on paper and sealed by Rainaldo former bishop of Rieti. By 17
October a nuntius declares that he has delivered a mandate to both
parties forbidding carnal intercourse until the case is decided; and this
mandate is rehearsed on 24 December 1347, more than a year later and
then final sentence delivered (and written by Matteo Barnabei) on 8
January 1348 by the vicar sitting under the loggia of the papal palace
with Cola present but Margarita absent, in which sentence the marriage
is definitively annulled and the two are free to marry other parties.[88]
The binding close together in the book of the actions in this long case
argues for its composition as a case book, not a list of daily actions.

The prominence of Rieti and its contrade in a book dealing in good
part with marriage and inheritance is unsurprising in various ways—
concentration of population, wealth, observation by people of one another, and understanding of legal technicalities and qualms of conscience, presumably went together with the availability of the vicar's
court. But quickly after the Arce case the book moves into the country
and two old women (*mulieres antique*) of the village of San Patrignano
de Plagis are being asked to stretch their memories back into village
genealogies.[89] And then on successive folios in the papal palace are heard
speaking themselves or through proctors: Don Giovanni Pantano abbot
of the church of San Lorenzo di Sambuco, men from Santa Rufina and
San Vittorino de Arpagano, Puccio Francisconi of the village of Colle
Secca of Leonessa (but diocese of Rieti), Roberto di don Angelo rector
of San Marco di Rocca Sinibalda, Magister Matteo di magistro Giacomo
di Piediluco.[90] And it is clear that country diocesan places should be

prominent too, although not in the same concentration as are affairs from Rieti, because the causes include definition of *feuda* and benefices and disputes over tithes—as, the latter, in the case of the church of San Valentino de Rocca Canetra.[91]

These five large gatherings of paper folios with interesting paper marks, this book has tucked into it sealed letters and *consilia*, by legists of local note like Giovanni di Canemorto and Don Casalle, judge of Rieti.[92] It includes material heard and initially decided by a subordinate vicar general, the chapter's vicar general for the area of Montereale, Pietro abbot of San Lorenzo di Montereale who acted in Montereale.[93] It also preserves on a paper letter from the vicar general in Rieti a partly surviving and partly legible wax seal (red, pointed oval, ca. 4.3 cm high) with a legend including "sigillum," "icariorum," and "cap," and figures including at center top a miter and beneath it where a figure of a man might be a crozier standing alone. The letter is said, by itself, to be issued "sub sigillo curie nostre."[94] This book loudly proclaims by the 1340s the regularity of functioning of an administrative diocese which stretches to its distant boundaries and for its most distant part supplies its own local vicar. Its seal, with miter over crozier but no human figure, proclaims the continuity of diocesan office not dependent on the presence of a specific human being.

Within the book of civil cases is at least one case of violent crime: that of Mathiutia di Nicola Massei, who is said to have laid her violent hands on Angelitto di Nicola Massei, her brother and an oblate at San Domenico Rieti, hit him on the face until she drew blood, and hit him a number of other times; she is excommunicated, but her proctor also represents her brother Petrucio and her sister Margarita.[95] Oddly, because of its placement, the case, like the crozier seal, gives a sharp sense of continuity of office and administrative function, because the case was presented before the vicar general of Bishop Rainaldo, Francesco archpriest of San Sebastiano Poggio Fidoni, who is further identified as Francesco di Giovanni de Bussata, and who in a later folio and case is called "Don Francesco di Giovanni Bussata in this office our predecessor" by the vicar general actually active in the cases of the book, Francesco archpriest of Santa Maria Antrodoco.[96]

The criminal act book (a book of criminous clerks) begins with a complaint of violence against a Rieti clerk, Antonio di Angelictio Petroni Oddonis, with an alias, Gauto, who had attacked another man of Rieti, Jannutio di Nicola Bartolomei, with knife and sword, and hit him two times in the head without, however, drawing blood. The clerk,

Gauto, had escaped from the chapter's jail—he broke jail ("fregit dictum carcerem")—a jail which was next to the church and palace and bishop's garden; and the fracas had occurred in Porta Carceraria fuori in the house of Rainaldo Molendinario (the miller) "in qua domo erat taberna et uinum in ea uendebat et predicta est publica uox et fama in dicta strada (in which house was a tavern and in it he sold wine and this was public knowledge in that street)." The chapter's vicar general had sat as a tribunal at the bench of justice in the papal palace in Rieti at the hour for hearing cases (*in ora* [or *hora*] *causarum*) and listened to pleading on 27 June, 28 June, and 4 July 1346 and had in the end fined Gauto 110 lire, of which 10 lire was for the insult he had offered and the blows he had given, and 100 lire for breaking jail.[97]

On the following 30 August the vicar general was forced to listen to the story of a different kind of violence, this time from a country village instead of the northern edge of the city. Filippa di Gentile of Verano claimed that she had been raped, in her father's garden (in Verano in the contrada Colle Stangtini next to the property of the heirs of Stangtino), by dompno Giovanni di Bartholomucio, the priest of San Vito di Verano. He, Filippa said, was diabolically inspired, and she unwilling and a woman of good reputation. The relationship was complicated and perhaps in some ways explained by her further statement that the priest had formerly kept Filippa's sister, Gerrantia, as his concubine.[98] In the same August the vicar listened to the case of a Rieti clerk who had entered by force and violence a house in the Porta Cintia di sopra in Rieti, in which house lived a man from Città di Castello and his Perugian wife, a woman of good reputation; the clerk had, against the Perugian wife's will, seized her body, thrown her to the floor, and raped her.[99]

In September the vicar dealt with two offenses committed, it was claimed, by the same foul-mouthed priest in the contrada "Unda." The priest, Pietro Britte of Rieti, had attacked his fellow-priest Pietro di Giovanni Turani of Rieti next to a widow's shop in the contrada and called him "Bisstone de merda"; and the same priest in the same month had attacked Lucto Saleztrum in the same contrada before the house of Rainaldo Cimini in which Lucto had a shop and called Lucto "Bisstone de merda."[100] In the same month and in October a man formerly of Spoleto who lived in Castro Butri—and again the hearing under the arcade of the papal palace in Rieti is about events which occurred, or didn't, outside the city in the diocese—complained that a priest of San Pietro di Butri, armed with a knife and angry, had assaulted him in the piazza before his own, the plaintiff's, house, and said "Bisstone stelgu de lu puctana, pro una manecare faciam te occidere"—and Matteo Barnabei notes that he, Matteo, recorded this hearing. The vicar general listened and made decisions which brought fines to chapter coffers; sometimes he found against both sides—as in the Butri case in which the defendant was fined for his language and the plaintiff for failing to make his case.[101]

With his *collationes* and his described cases which retain the recent memory of the piazza at Butri, sharp with the ugly half-translated vulgarity of an angry priest, and the longer memory of the contrada Arce, softer with the memory of dead aunts and of cousins seen together, Matteo Barnabei has written, and so created or recorded, a fully imagined and extended diocese, a governed place. In late 1347 full diocese and full record exist. Something of what is newly seen, any viewer would probably argue, is simply a new extension of writing, perhaps even of preserving; but could that viewer believe that the new writing is not the result of a new sensibility which sees a diocese as a more extended, more living, and more governable thing—and so is at least responsible for making it that? And could he or she believe that the newness was not created in collusion between Matteo the writer and the governors and administrators for whom he worked, and in collusion between them both and the society which formed them and which they governed?

Our understanding of this newness is extended by the survival at Rieti in the dean and chapter archives of three small parchment books: the first is identified as "III.B.1"; the second as Liber or Libro or Book VI; the third by the original date of one of its copied documents, "1212." The book called "1212" contains the parchment copy of the list of possessions of the cathedral church which was composed in and just after the year 1225 and which is essentially identical with the paper copy used here earlier in examining property and people in the Porta Carceraria. The parchment copy has not, however, lost its initial passages. In fact it begins, after an invocation, by saying that it is a copy of an old register found in the cathedral archives which lists land, vineyards, houses, and other possessions of the church as well as rents and incomes of various sorts derived from the church's possessions:

In nomine domini, Amen. Hec est copia siue renouatio cuiusdam Registri antiqui reperti in archiuio ecclesie Reatin' de terris, vineis, domibus et aliis possexionibus dicte ecclesie Reatine et de censu, pensione, decima et aliis redditibus qui debentur eidem ecclesie Reatin' de possexionibus supradictis.

It then continues to say that it was made at the time of and by the mandate of Bishop Giovanni, with Giovanni Papazurri's usual style, "by the grace of God and the apostolic see":

facta tempore et de mandato Reuerendi in Xristo patris et domini domini Johannis dei et apostolice sedis gratia episcopi Reatin'.

This copy, with its notarial-inscription beginning, was the copy of a document, an old register, which was found, in the time of Bishop Giovanni Papazurri, in the cathedral archives (which thus clearly then existed in some form) and was made at Bishop Giovanni's order. The inclusion within the document of the name of the presiding bishop (in the ablative) *dompno* [*sic*] *Raynaldo episcopo Reatin'* acting with three canon "obedientialibus" (and using an overlapping but not identical group of witnesses for each porta), ties together two very differently active bishops, Rainaldo de Labro and Giovanni Papazurri.[102] (And again two copies of the 1225 list survive, this one in parchment and the one in paper.)

The "1225" list is preceded by another list, which contains fifty-eight items, from 1212, a copy, "exemplum," it says in introducing itself, of a certain instrument written by the judge and "scriptuarius" Berardo Sprangon' and copied at the mandate of Bishop Giovanni (Papazurri) by the public notary Matteo Pandulfi.[103] The copied 1212 document speaks in Berardo's name and says that he made it "rogatus a domino Episcopo Adinulfo et Reatinis canonicis" so that various annual rents and incomes from houses, lots, and various properties given in various ways by Reatine citizens and others of the *comitatus* of Rieti would be recorded together, copied from various instruments which Berardo himself had written at various times. Berardo's document concludes with his subscript. There then follow five notarial subscriptions to the copy, which is dated 17 April 1315, of which subscriptions the last is Matteo Pandulfi's own in which he identifies himself as a citizen of Rieti and notary public by authority of the urban prefect. The third of these subscriptions is that of Pietro di notaio Giovanni de Clausura, a notary by royal and imperial authority and "nunc notarius et scriba dicti domini episcopi"; the second is Matteo Barnabei, "ciuis Reatinus, nunc notarius episcopi et capituli."[104] This copy ties together, then, the, in his own way, active Bishop Adenolfo and his scribe Berardo (who in fact appears as a cathedral tenant in the Porta Cintia in the "1225" list) with Bishop Giovanni and the, in this case, observing, and perhaps supervising, notary Matteo Barnabei—and the chapters of the early thirteenth and early fourteenth centuries.

The book identified as "III.B.1," which records the definition and adjustment of prebendal incomes in 1278 and 1282 during the episcopate of Bishop Pietro da Ferentino with the participation of the notary Giovanni di Pietro, includes part of Bishop Tommaso the Corrector's list of diocesan churches. Book VI, which lists prebendal incomes in and after 1307 from the episcopate of Bishop Giovanni Papazurri, records the work of the capitular chamberlain Tommaso Capitaneo.[105] Taken together the three parchment books help both to define and underline the newness of Matteo Barnabei in the time of Giovanni Papazurri. They show that in some matters even of recording, Bishop Giovanni could utilize the work of some of his predecessors and their scribes and notaries—and the predecessors' names are worthy of note: Adenolfo, Rainaldo de Labro, Tommaso the Corrector, Pietro da Ferentino. The three books show that Matteo Barnabei did not work alone, but they also show even more clearly the importance of his initial period of official activity.

Matteo Barnabei did not survive 1348, although he very surely did not die young. His successors, who did survive, conserved what he had created. They had it for a base; but they developed a different and more dispersed kind of record keeping. Of these successors three seem most significant: Bishop Biagio da Leonessa, the last bishop for whom, perhaps for as little as three months, Matteo worked; the notary Silvestro di don Giovanni; and the prebendary turned canon Ballovino di magistro Giovanni, who in 1372 gave fifty florins of his own money toward the cost of the new cross for the church of Rieti.

Silvestro di don Giovanni of Rieti was a notary by imperial authority, whose importance to the history of the church of Rieti is particularly connected with the survival in the chapter archives of his paper cartulary, very much the cartulary of him the notary, of his *contractus, protocolla, et acta*, described by him, and with his sign on its cover folio. The matter of the book stretches from 6 March 1336 through 17 June 1351. The cartulary (which is a very rich source) would seem on the surface to have no official connection with the church of Rieti but to be a perfectly ordinary notarial cartulary compiled by a notary who worked repeatedly for members of a group of rich and patrician local families, some of whose members held official positions in the church and/or left it significant bequests in their wills, families like the Pasinelli, the Cimini, and the Secinari.[106] The election to the bishopric of a member of one of these families, who had been a client of Silvestro's, Tommaso Secinari, in the late 1330s would seem to have brought Silvestro more firmly into the ambit of the cathedral church and its clergy. Certainly the connection was maintained or reestablished after the death of Tommaso. In the 1350s and 1360s Silvestro describes himself as "nunc notarius et scriba dictorum dominorum episcopi et capituli" and "nunc notarius et scriba dicti domini episcopi"—notary and scribe of the bishop and chapter but also notary and scribe of the bishop.[107] But Silvestro, and this seems particularly significant to the pattern of which he forms a part, not only does not work alone, as the only notary of Biagio and his church, but does not give clear evidence of having dominated a group as his predecessors Giovanni di Pietro and Matteo Barnabei did. In fact Bishop Biagio's style in employing official writers is suggested by an early document of his, once sealed, in letter form, dated on 14 July 1349 from his palazzo in Leonessa ("Dat' et act' Goness' in palatio nostro") and written by Francesco di Angelo of Leonessa, notary by imperial authority, and "nunc notarius, familiaris, et scriba dicti domini episcopi"—the bishop himself is very present (see plates 28, 29).[108]

The position and importance of Ballovino di magistro Giovanni are very different from those of Silvestro di don Giovanni. Ballovino was, like Silvestro, one of a group of recorders, but his recording was particularly innovative. He kept the church's, essentially the chapter's, new and carefully itemized account books from their first appearance, or surviving appearance, in 1355 until he was succeeded in this chore, his as chamberlain or *camerlengo*, by Don Agostino in 1379 (plate 20). He was alive still, and active, in 1382.[109] Since he had been repeatedly present acting as a witness to church business since the very early 1330s, present also for some part of the heresy trial of Paolo Zoppo in 1334, increasingly present in the late 1330s, and a prebendary and major actor for the church by 1337, his was a long connection, over fifty years, with the church of Rieti. On the eve of the Black Death he was still a prebendary; on its morrow, in 1349, he was a canon—a progression not earlier recorded in the church of Rieti. The actual progression is recorded in a document of 2 September 1348 which regrants Ballovino's old prebend which he had renounced to accept his canon's benefice.[110] As camerlengo and keeper of his books, he gave his church a new kind of thickness and continuity of memory and existence. He built on, extended, specialized part of what Matteo Barnabei had made.[111]

Even the most restrained observer who cannot allow himself to see that the remembering, copying, thinking, mapping, and defining of this string of senior clerks (in the writing, not necessarily the other clerical sense) created, moved to physical existence, and perpetuated a new kind of diocese with new kinds of boundaries, must see in them the development of a more professional chancery, the development of a central office in the government of the diocese. And the observer will have noticed during this development that of another central, nonchancery, official, who could find himself aptly represented by a miter over a crozier, without a human figure, on a seal. The development of the vicar general and his office is concurrent with the development of the new "chancery" and visible in its records. It also changes the nature of diocese and the position of the diocese's bishop particularly by offering a type of continuity of office, by allowing the development of a more professional bureaucracy (and being the central part of that development), and by freeing the bishop, if he chose to be free, from the trapping details of his increasingly elaborate job.[112]

One returns again to the administrator bishop, the organizer, Tommaso the Corrector, provided to the see from his own curia by Pope Innocent IV. Tommaso did not, obviously, do his important work alone. But when we can see him surrounded by his helpers, as we seem to be able to, for example at vespers on 26 April 1261 in the choir of the cathedral church with the chapter, those witnessing helpers are dompno Manuele, dompno Pietro Beralli, and Ugolino, his *familiares*, a little core of household clerks (in this case two-thirds priests) without specific continuing names for specific continuing jobs.[113] Certainly, at a time when continuing vicars (sometimes called vicars general) were beginning to become, or about to become, more common in Italian dioceses, Bishop Tommaso shows no sign of having had a vicar general.[114] In fact vicars general appear with the two successors of Gottifredo, Tommaso's own, not very well documented, successor.[115]

These two men were Bishop Pietro da Ferentino, translated by Pope Nicholas III from Sora in 1270, and Bishop Andrea Rainaldi, translated by Pope Honorius IV also from Sora in 1286.[116] Both, because of their backgrounds and careers, can reasonably be called curial bishops. Pietro da Ferentino is, and was, known by various names; one of the names used for him was Pietro Romano or "de Roma." At Rieti, this busily political bishop who had reason to appreciate a vicar, chose as vicar general a man called Pietro Romano or "de Roma," who was a canon of San Valentino, Ferentino.[117] Andrea, who succeeded Pietro both to Sora and to Rieti, had been a chaplain to Cardinal Giacomo Savelli (who became Honorius IV in 1285); his career before Rieti would have suggested to him the utility of vicars. Andrea, who had been a canon of Rieti before he was provided to Sora, chose as his vicar general at Rieti another canon of Rieti who had also been a chaplain of Giacomo Savelli; this man was Ventura Rainaldi, surely Andrea's own brother.[118] The third vicar general to be found at Rieti in the thirteenth century was Berardo, canon of Ancona. He, in 1298, acted as vicar general for his uncle Bishop Berardo, whom Boniface VIII had translated to Rieti from Ancona in 1296.[119] Three bishops of Rieti translated to Rieti from other sees employed at Rieti as vicars general their own relatives. The picture does not seem particularly edifying, but what at Rieti one can know of two of the bishops and one of the vicars—of neither Berardo can much be said—should cause the observer to be wary in making judgment. In any case, with these three, in the late thirteenth century, visible vicars general begin at Rieti.

Vicars general reappear at Rieti with Matteo Barnabei's newly full documentation and with Bishop Giovanni Papazurri. None of Giovanni's known vicars general was a Papazurri. Six of these vicars general, one specifically for the area around Montereale, are known to have existed. In 1323 two of them worked sometimes together and sometimes separately; twice they use their title in the plural (or it is used of them): *vicarii generales*. Of these two one, Giovanni, the secular abbot of the church of San Lorenzo di Fano in Montereale, had a chamber, a *camera* in the episcopal palace at Rieti; the other, Matteo Pandulfoni, was a prebendary of the cathedral church and extremely active, as Matteo Barnabei's parchment book shows, in its affairs.[120]

In June of 1325 appears Francesco archpriest of San Rustico di Valle Antrodoco, the figure most important in the development of the office of vicar general—at least he is if he is the same Francesco who appears as Francesco archpriest of Santa Maria di Canetra, vicar general, on 28 November 1332 (after Francesco of San Rustico's last act two days earlier on 26 November), and as Francesco vicar general and archpriest of Santa Maria di Antrodoco on 21 May 1338 (after Francesco of Santa Maria Canetra's last visible act on 14 March 1338), as I am convinced that he is. Even though he did not remain vicar general constantly, Francesco was active in the government of the church at least until 1347, and he was vicar general for the chapter *sede vacante* from 1337 to 1339 and from 1346 to 1347. Bishop Giovanni's absences from his cathedral city and Francesco's presence there during Francesco's long continuous first tour of duty from June 1325 to September 1334 must have made observers, and particularly the chapter with whom he worked daily, come to think of him as "the vicar general." Certainly members of the chapter knew his work well before they commissioned him as their own vicar general in 1337.[121] The bishop's absence from Rieti and the vicar's presence there threw the vicar, with particular force, into the events surrounding the heresy trial of Paolo Zoppo in the summer and fall of 1334. What the vicar counseled and some of the things he said are quoted in the account of the trial. What he thought and how his behavior was viewed is not knowable; nor is it possible to say whether or not there was a connection between the trial's "unsuccessful" conclusion (in the record) and Bishop Giovanni's removing Francesco from office—nor in fact is it possible to say whether or not there was a connection between Francesco's working so constantly and seemingly successfully with members of the cathedral chapter and other Reatines and his removal from office.

When a messenger from the inquisitor, then moved to Leonessa, who took letters to Francesco as vicar general in Rieti, reported back that Francesco had refused to accept the letters, he conventionally reinforced the verisimilitude of his account by being specific about the place where the refusal had occurred: in the house where Francesco lived, that is, in the episcopal palace, in the vescovado.[122] This act, the vicar's living in the vescovado, gives a physical extension to the office. Giovanni, abbot of San Lorenzo di Fano, had lived in the episcopal palace as vicar; so did Francesco's immediate successor, Andrea de "Postrotio," vicar from October 1334 to November 1335.[123] When Bishop Tommaso Secinari's second vicar general Filippo da Siena, prior of San Bartolomeo de Sanguineto in the diocese of Perugia, became vicar general in 1341, he moved from a room in a private house where he had been living to a room in the episcopal palace (*camera sua domorum palatii episcopi*).[124]

Bishop Giovanni Papazurri's first visible vicar, in 1315, had been a canon of Ancona, Ingraymo de Montelpro.[125] His vicar general local to Montereale, Nicola canon of San Flaviano di Montereale, acted in 1320, and connects this early period with Pietro, abbot of San Lorenzo di Montereale, vicar general at Montereale, subordinate to Francesco at Rieti during the vacancy of 1346–1347; and this division of diocese which already existed under Giovanni Papazurri is also apparent during the Leonessa phase of the heresy trial of Paolo Zoppo because of the repeated presence of dompno Giovanni Petri Berardi, archpriest of San Cristoforo di Posta Cornu, vicar (without the designation general) of the bishop of Rieti in the *terra* of Leonessa.[126] The cluster of vicars general from the first half of the fourteenth century includes other men: Bishop Tommaso Secinari's first vicar general, his co-canon, Giacomo di don Tommaso; Raymond's vicars general other than Filippo da Siena—Guillelmus Servientis, a bachelor in laws, and Francesco, or Cecco or Cicco, di Giovanni Bussato (the son of a man who had particularly enraged Paolo Zoppo's inquisitor); two vicars general of the chapter in 1341–1342—Nicola di don Nicola di Roio di Aquila, canon of L'Aquila, and Francesco di Ofagnano (Fagnano Alto), canon of Rieti.[127]

There seem to have been roughly a dozen of these men, some of them probably not connected with Rieti over a very long period of time, but rather particularly acceptable because of their special knowledge, skills, or connections with their employer or employers. But some of them, moving in and out of office, worked for the church concurrently, as did Francesco, archpriest of the Antrodoco and Canetra churches as vicar, and Matteo Pandulfoni, as chapter proctor.[128] During the episcopate of Tommaso Secinari, in August 1340, both of these men were present as witnesses as Filippo da Siena acted as vicar general.[129] Clearly they formed part of a small cadre, a little network, of professional administrators on whom the church of Rieti could count for normal administration. The most significant single office they could hold was that of vicar general, and because of that office the administration of the diocese could continue to function normally in the absence of the, or a, bishop. The vicar general could do those things a bishop could do which did not depend upon the bishop's sacred orders and which had been delegated to the vicar and not withheld from him—as *confirmationes et collationes* were specifically withheld from Nicola di don Nicola di Roio in the chapter's commission to him of 24 September 1341.[130]

When Bishop Biagio da Leonessa succeeded to the bishopric of Rieti in 1347 he found this administration in place. When, after the Black Death, he had reassembled the administration of his diocese, Biagio used vicars general; so in September 1363, in the episcopal palace at Rieti, Biagio's vicar, Giovanni da Montegambero, and Silvestro di don Giovanni his notary and scribe, can be observed together; and in September 1369, Biagio's vicar general, Pietro di Mascio de Labro, a canon of Rieti, joins other members of an impressive staff, assessor, official, and notary, in giving counsel in a difficult case being heard at the usual bench of law next to the "episcopal church."[131] In October 1293 when the chapter assembled, during an episcopal vacancy, to grant Giovanni di Pietro his prebend, they had their seal but they acted without any trace of the presence of a vicar general; their vicar general is the central character in the vacancy of 1346–1347.[132]

Although Lucius III's geographically descriptive privilege of 1182 could still seem worth copying in the later fourteenth century, the diocese that it had attempted to describe had found by the middle of the fourteenth century an unrecognizably fuller and more extended shape. A way of viewing, of thinking about, diocese, which gave form to and was formed by the writing of a kind of official chancery and the administration of a vicar general, allowed or demanded continuity of recorded geography and chronology. The diocese of Rieti was no longer a scattering of mountain tops and jurisdictional disputes. It was a place to which serious sacramental synodal constitutions could be projected and their results observed. The recording of what bells the farmers heard outside the church in Borgocollefegato, and the recording of what the people in the piazza of Castro Butri heard the priest say, "Bisstone stelgu de lu puctana," occurred in differently bound dioceses with differently extended ways of listening and remembering. Amiterno fell away from a diocese of a different kind from that to which Monteleone was bound.

When dompno Francesco di Giovanni Bussata, acting not as vicar general but as archpriest of the church of San Sebastiano in Poggio Fidoni for the church, in 1346, dealt with the old problem of tithing among parishioners, he did it with an exact sense and knowledge of boundaries of various sorts that made his discussion fit exactly into the new mapping of his newly observed and observable diocese.[133] Bishop Tommaso the Corrector's proto-portolan imagination as he sent his arrows out into the relatively unknown geography of his diocese did not in the hands of later bishops (insofar as we know) develop into a physical map of the place, but rather into a different and remarkably complete verbal mapping, which coincides in time, not surprisingly, with the geometric and planned new towns of the diocese, of which Cittaducale maintains the most striking presence (see plate 14).[134] Recollections not "valid for more than a kilometer" were brought together by careful administration and recording.[135] Bishop Biagio and his chapter were offered an administration in which the observer can notice close analogies to that essential quality of the new towns which provoked from their recent historian the statement: "In the new towns it was never necessary to straighten streets."[136]

CHAPTER FIVE

"Intricate Characters": The Bishops of Rieti

The cherry blossom pulls the daimyō down from his horse.

Haiku by Issa

To Adenolfo de Lavareta at the beginning of the thirteenth century and to Fra Biagio da Leonessa in the third quarter of the fourteenth century, being bishop of Rieti clearly meant different things. The definition of their office, in the sense that practice and act are definition, had changed. But the seventeen bishops of Rieti in the series which begins with Adenolfo and ends with Biagio (who are joined by two unconsecrated bishops-elect and at least two finally unsuccessful contestants for election) cannot be asked to link their arms in docile placidity to form a chain of progress or decline or any other consistent movement. The actions of these men and the evidence about them do not fit together to produce a smooth and predictable whole. In their resistant, and always incompletely visible, individuality, they make counterpoint to the progressive development of the concept of bishop and diocese.

These men, the bishops, were formally the successive rulers of the diocese, the local exemplars of "a universal governing institution throughout Christendom."[1] But there has been in the past not even a correct list of their names and the order of their succession. And, important as these men were to the diocese and are to its history, this absence of a list is in part the result of their having left inadequate, for us, evidence about themselves, and that in turn is in some part the result of a fairly universal difference between the formal principles of government particularly as they are seen by chronological outsiders and the way government seems actually to work. Bishops, because of their sacramental powers, because of the learned, intricate, observant, canon law of which they were a central focus, are and were better defined than most rulers.[2] But they show, at least in thirteenth- and fourteenth-century Rieti, remarkable tendencies to dissolve when they are placed in working, day-to-day, governmental documents like the parchment book of Matteo Barnabei.

They remain, however, among the major human figures in the history of their dioceses including Rieti; they are protagonists in diocesan stories. Accepting this, one moves to another set of problems for anyone who would describe or understand bishops, at least at Rieti; but these problems—as perhaps really does insufficient visibility—make the bishops seem more interesting, more worth the search. The evidence they do present about themselves—and of this Giovanni Papazurri is a clear, or sharply unclear, example—is sometimes contradictory. And one aspect of that contradiction is, what seems to us, their occasional, quite sudden and seemingly unpredictable change in behavior and values. They jump. Pietro da Ferentino is lured to the Franciscans by the Eucharist as Issa's daimyō is pulled by the cherry blossoms from his horse. The bishops of Rieti, only partially visible, must remain "spare, strange."[3]

Among these Reatine bishops it is thus pleasing enough to find the relatively fully developed figure of this bishop, Pietro da Ferentino (1278–1286), in his most readily visible guise, the upwardly mobile and impermanently attached prelate, with curial connections and assignments, who will end his life as a patriarch. But a different level of pleasure and a different kind of understanding come from observing those connections of Pietro's which are permanent, from observing his serious behavior (although observably serious in specific and limited ways) as bishop in Rieti, and from observing what is known of his death and his selection of place of burial. Pietro is an obvious example; and he can reasonably stand as a warning that, when these bishops are grouped and categorized, called members of baronial families or religious orders, electees or providees, local or foreign, pious or casual, their individual intractability should be kept in mind, as well as all that about them which remains hidden. At the same time, and in another direction, so should be kept in mind the indistinct and changing meanings and connotations of the words and phrases that define the categories, like "baronial," "member of a religious order," "foreign," and "pious."

The change in the value and tone of these category words is, to reverse again, clearly connected with the progress of time and with observable general changes, like the already observed change in the definition of diocese. The change in the connotation of category words offers another warning, a warning against an absorption in individual particularity so intense that it keeps the observer from discerning the very real changes that did occur, in a general way, in the types of men who became bishops of Rieti between the time of Bishop Adenolfo and that of Bishop Biagio. These two men, Adenolfo and Biagio, seem almost absurdly easy and effective models of two different kinds of bishops, who should have existed, and who did exist, at the two ends of a century and a half of change.

That evidence which remains for Biagio, and which is considerable although it is very uneven, clearly indicates that he was, at Rieti, a concerned and effective diocesan bishop, moderate, straightforward rather than unconventional. His abilities and interests are nicely suggested by his definitive treaty, of 1353, with the commune over the treatment of criminous clerks, a treaty included within the communal book of statutes. The tone and matter of this accommodating treaty are seen again, and in for them a more effective container, in the composite synods of the Paris manuscript. There Biagio (with his name still attached to the constitution), taught by experience of the multiple damage to the church of the seemingly inadequate punishments meted out to clerks who had attacked laymen—*sicut nos tam facti experientia quam frequens querela laicorum instruxit*—ordered, with appropriate reservations, that clerks be subject to the statutes of the commune of Rieti.

The force of the order, and the position of Biagio, is thrown into greater relief, when it is recalled that as recently as 24 August 1346, during the vacancy which preceded Biagio's translation to Rieti, the chapter's vicar general, Francesco archpriest of Santa Maria Antrodoco, sitting in the loggia of the papal palace, had absolved from guilt two clerics accused of consorting with exiles from the city. He then said that he and his court were not bound by municipal laws or the statutes of the city of Rieti, but by the sacred canons and the constitutions of the church of Rieti, and that since the statutes of the city of Rieti did not affect clerics, the two men were not guilty. Biagio's sensible use of experience is, again, suggested by the collection of conflated synodal constitutions itself. And in 1375, opposed by the Benedictine nuns of San

Benedetto Rieti who wanted the right to choose their own confessors, preachers, and celebrants of Masses, Biagio seems to have let them win.[4]

Biagio was a Franciscan friar from Leonessa, probably from that part of Leonessa within the diocese of Rieti on the border of the diocese of Spoleto, but also possibly from the diocese of Spoleto. About his family and social background nothing is known although his residing in 1348 and 1349 in "his palace" in Leonessa suggests that he, this Franciscan friar, came from a family of some local prominence and riches.[5] Biagio was translated to the see of Rieti from that of Vicenza by Pope Clement VI in 1347; Biagio was, thus, not only provided by the pope, he was translated from a distant Italian diocese in which he had already acted as bishop.[6]

Of Bishop Adenolfo's actual election, which occurred not earlier than 1185 and not later than March 1188, nothing definite can be said.[7] Adenolfo remained an unconsecrated *electus* until at least 9 November 1194, but he could call himself *episcopus* without qualification by 4 February 1195.[8] His surviving *acta* and contemporary references to him suggest that he was at least as active in his diocese before his confirmation as after it; in fact one of Bishop Tommaso the Corrector's positions in his case against San Salvatore Maggiore in 1254 argued that the war, disorder, and fear which eventually drove Adenolfo from his diocese kept him from exercising his power fully in the last ten years, and more, of his episcopate.[9] Whether, at a specific time, Bishop Adenolfo was still an *electus* or had become a consecrated *episcopus* was not clear, at least in memory, to all who observed him.[10]

Certainly there is nothing to suggest that this long-term *electus* was not elected locally and in local interests. There is nothing more striking about Adenolfo than his belonging to a local baronial family, the Lavareta of Barete, barons from at least the great Norman past. When Abbot Giovanni of Santa Croce, during his dispute with Bishop Rainaldo de Labro, was asked about the *exenia* he had paid Adenolfo when Adenolfo was bishop of Rieti, he said he had paid them, but to Adenolfo because he was the son of Rainaldo of Lavareta, not because he was bishop of Rieti. Bishop Tommaso of Rieti, calling on a longer and less personal memory, said that the war, of which the effects drove Adenolfo from his see, was a war between the citizens and commune of Rieti, on one side, and on the other the noble men, Abeamundo, Matteo, and Berardo de Lavareta, who were the bishop's brothers; and in whatever way Tommaso's evidence may have been skewed by the length of the memory or by his then current interest, he was certainly right in believing that at the turn of the century the bishop's brothers were very obvious barons within the diocese of Rieti.[11]

Adenolfo was a contemporary of Francis of Assisi. Biagio, a Franciscan, was translated to Rieti just over 120 years after Francis's death. Adenolfo's father was not a cloth merchant. He gave fiefs, and threats, and churches to themselves. (If he had been Francis's father, what would Francis have been?) One of Rainaldo of Lavareta's four known sons, our Adenolfo, went, was given (?) to the church. He got the local bishopric, but he was not consecrated bishop for at least six and one-half years after he got it. He had brought no episcopal experience to the job, but the evidence of later cases suggests that he worked at it in his way. He then retired to become a Cistercian, a not unbaronial thing to do, as Saint Bernard's family had advertised, but surely a personal choice.[12]

Adenolfo and Biagio offer sharp contrast; but if they are thought of in terms of their similarities to Francis, or dissimilarities from Francis, the contrast works oddly. So, too, does it if their observer asks what of their family homes. Biagio seems to have had this palazzo in the land of Leonessa. The Lavareta of Barete must have had places to sit, to lie, to eat; they cannot have moved only fighting and threatening through life. But of a domestic palazzo set in the Amiterno we know nothing. And Biagio the palaced Franciscan brought with himself to Rieti episcopal experience from a northern Italian see, and presumably some of the experience of an international and at the same time papally, and internally, domesticated order.

The more general change which the difference between Adenolfo and Biagio too sharply represents was both reflected and controlled by the ways in which the bishops were selected; and, in fact, nothing is more obvious in this general change than the manner of episcopal "election," and what the historian can know about "election." The first preserved letter of papal collation or provision to the see of Rieti is dated 5 February 1252. With it, Pope Innocent IV appointed the curial official, Tommaso, corrector of papal letters, to the bishopric.[13] There is no known evidence that Tommaso had had any significant previous connection with Rieti or that he was personally known by the members of the chapter. He was Innocent IV's choice for a diocese in which Innocent's interest had been forcibly maintained by the exotic behavior of Tommaso's predecessor.[14]

Clear and dated evidence of papal collation or provision exists for all but one of Tommaso's eight immediate successors as bishop, that is, for the bishops between his own episcopate and that of Tommaso II (1339–1341). The one exception is the Cistercian bishop, Nicola, who was bishop by 26 November 1294, was still bishop on 24 December 1295, but had resigned before 4 February 1296. There is no evidence that Nicola was not provided, although his local Cistercian connections may suggest that if he was provided he may have been postulated by the chapter of Rieti.[15] Of the other seven bishops, six were translated from other sees: Gottifredo by Pope Clement IV from Tivoli on 23 August 1265; Pietro da Ferentino by Pope Nicholas III from Sora on 2 August 1278; Andrea by Pope Honorius IV from Sora on 27 July 1286; Berardo by Pope Boniface VIII from Ancona on 4 February 1296; Fra Angelo by Boniface from Nepi on 8 June 1302; and Giovanni Papazurri by Boniface from Ìmola on 3 August 1302.[16] Between Berardo and Fra Angelo, on 26 August 1299, Jacopo Pagano, canon of Toul, Charles of Valois's vicar general in Romagna, was provided by Pope Boniface; but Jacopo was later, between 4 April and 14 June 1302, removed for cause, presumably political cause, by the same pope.[17]

Giovanni Papazurri was succeeded by Tommaso II who was elected by the canons of Rieti and whose election, after appeal, was confirmed by Pope Benedict XII on 7 December 1339. A further capitular election after Tommaso's death was not confirmed; and Raimondo (Raimond de Chameyrac), canon of Amiens, was provided by Pope Clement VI. From 1343 through the time of his translation to Orvieto this bishop acted as vicar general of spiritualities in the city of Rome for Clement; in this guise the bishop (whom the *Historie romane fragmenta* calls a "granne decretalista") participated in the pageantry and rule of (and protests against) Cola di Rienzo—climbed the Campidoglio with Cola in his early ascendancy, and later, stunned by Cola's excess, stood like a stick of dumb wood (*stava como leno idiota*) at the Lateran and then at a notorious banquet sat almost alone with Cola at a marble table in the old hall of the Lateran.[18]

All these translations and provisions can hardly help seeming, to the observer, as he first tries to see them through the eyes of succeeding providing popes (or papal governments), to be happening on that playing-board of movable, and not infrequently significantly politically allied, bishops, which the episcopal church seems to have become by the late thirteenth century. The qualities, both positive and negative, which the observer would expect these moving bishops themselves to bring to a local church like Rieti would naturally be different from those expected of their early thirteenth-century predecessors, who were indigenous or at least, one knows or presumes, locally selected as bishops, and bishops for the first time.

Before Tommaso's provision by Innocent IV in 1252 episcopal selection at Rieti had been different. The exact processes and actual dates of the elections of Tommaso's thirteenth-century predecessors are generally hidden; but, again, the surviving evidence argues strongly that these men were locally elected and elected in response to various local needs and interests. A significant piece of this evidence is the by now familiar short history of the difficulties and interruptions in the administration of the early thirteenth-century diocese which was written by or for Bishop Tommaso for use in his dispute with San Salvatore Maggiore. Tommaso's assuredly interested history, unlike all modern published lists of the bishops of Rieti, seems correctly to present the succession of his thirteenth-century predecessors.[19] There were six of these men:

1. Adenolfo de Lavareta (resigned between 12 September 1212 and 3 March 1214);[20]
2. Gentile de Pretorio (active as *electus* on 3 March 1214, identified as having been a canon of Capua by Bishop Tommaso, who says that Gentile, still unconsecrated, resigned his see two years after his election);[21]
3. Rainaldo de Labro (active as *episcopus* as early as 26 May 1215 and as late as 25 July 1233, surely alive on 21 February 1234, or a few days earlier, certainly dead by 8 August 1238 and almost surely dead by 25 January 1236; according to Bishop Tommaso, Rainaldo was elected a year after Gentile's resignation and died ten years after his own consecration (which is, of course, in error), during which time his jurisdiction was disturbed by the Urslingen and Hohenstaufen wars);[22]
4. Giovanni de Nempha (active as *episcopus* as early as 8 August 1236 and as late as 2 September 1240; the see vacant in March 1242; according to Bishop Tommaso, Giovanni was consecrated a year and one-half after Rainaldo's death and was bishop for three years, during which time he was unable to exercise his authority because of the wars and a dispute between bishop and chapter);[23]
5. Rainaldo Bennecelli (active as early as 9 May 1244 and as late as 11 March 1246; according to Bishop Tommaso, he was consecrated after a vacancy of four years and more following the death of Bishop Giovanni and, for the four years of his own episcopate, he

was unable to exercise episcopal jurisdiction because of the same wars that had disturbed Rainaldo de Labro and Giovanni);[24]

6. Fra Rainaldo da Arezzo (active as early as 17 April 1249 and as late as 9 March 1250; according to Bishop Tommaso, Rainaldo stayed in the see *per annum et parum* before he left it).[25]

Bishop Tommaso speaks of the "elections" of Gentile de Pretorio and Rainaldo de Labro; "election" is a slippery word, but, in the absence of other evidence, its casual unqualified use suggests actual local election. Of Rainaldo de Labro's specific early connection with the church of Rieti something more can be said. In a document of 18 September 1198 one of the witnesses of a gift to Bishop Adenolfo is "Dominus Rainaldus de Labro," who is identified as the archpriest of Barratina (? Varratina). On 16 December 1206 Rainaldo is archpriest of San Giovanni Barratina; and he still seems to be in July of 1212.[26] On 20 February 1204 Rainaldo gave to the church of Santa Maria of Rieti a major gift inter vivos "pro redemptione peccatorum meorum et pro anima mea." The gift was made to Berardo Tostoni for the church of Santa Maria, for Berardo's "brothers" and successors forever.[27] The instrument recording it was redacted by Berardo Sprangone. It was witnessed by Giovanni Pasinelli, Tommaso Capitaneo, and Rainaldo Oddonis. It brought pledges and properties in the Valreatina, Turano, and Vucagno, inheritances and Rainaldo's portion of lands which he shared with his brothers. Rainaldo stipulated that he should have the use of these Labro family properties for life but that after his death they should become a benefice of the church. At least eight years before he became the church's bishop (unless this is some other Rainaldo de Labro), Rainaldo, thus, in a very in-house church document, became the church of Rieti's benefactor and made family lands into church lands for the sake of prayer and redemption.

What can be said about the early connection of Rainaldo Bennecelli with the church of Rieti is somewhat less sure. The information that this Rainaldo was called Bennecelli comes from Bishop Tommaso's history; since Tommaso was provided to the see less than six years after Rainaldo's death, his information seems secure. As early as 1206 or 1207 a Rainaldo Benetelli or Benecelli can be seen acting for the church as yconomo alone or with another canon, Rainaldo Berardi Dodonis.[28] The coincidence of names is at least striking. Rainaldo acts as yconomo some thirty-five years before Rainaldo Bennecelli's episcopate—a long time, but not an impossible length of time for a Rieti canon. It is, furthermore, possible that Rainaldo Bennecelli is identical with the canon "Presbiter Rainaldus" who appears at Rieti between 1203 and 1240, and who in 1240 is called "prepositus."[29]

There is less suggestion of local connection about Gentile and Giovanni. Gentile's Capuan canonry shows influence and interest that extended beyond the narrow confines of the diocese of Rieti. Moreover, he did not establish binding enough ties with the church of Rieti itself to become its consecrated bishop or remain long in the see. More evidence of Giovanni's presence at Rieti is preserved. In September 1239 the chapter chose him as an arbiter; he had a nephew, Giovanni di Leone, present and active within the diocese—if he came from outside he did not come alone.[30] On the other hand, if the identifying name which Bishop Tommaso gave him means that he came from Ninfa (instead of, perhaps, Nepi), it would suggest connections with a family potent in Rome and the curia and argue that influences at least in part external to Rieti were important in his selection as bishop. In connection with the possible "foreign" origins of and power supporting these two bishops, the repeated presence of the papal court at Rieti during the papacies of Innocent III, Honorius III, and Gregory IX must be kept in mind. Still the fragmentary information that exists about these two bishops (or rather bishop and bishop-elect) does not at all compel the observing historian to believe that even they were imposed upon the diocese by people and interests external, or completely external, to it.

With the evidence for and visibility of these early thirteenth-century bishops, the evidence for and visibility of Bishop Tommaso's immediate predecessor, Fra Rainaldo da Arezzo, make sharp contrast. Fra Rainaldo was a Franciscan friar. He was from Arezzo. He was known and encouraged by Pope Innocent IV. Fra Rainaldo's life opens before the historian as does that of no other bishop of Rieti because that life touched the Franciscan chronicler Salimbene's life. Salimbene saw Rainaldo da Arezzo move. He watched his expressions change. He listened to his exact words and to the texts he cited. He tried to understand what Rainaldo was thinking and feeling, and what his motivations were, and how they were affected by other people's arguments. Although Salimbene principally observed a relatively short dramatic patch of Rainaldo's life, Salimbene was a man who had learned how to observe: he had listened to Giovanni da Pian di Carpina, that *magnus prolocutor*, talk of the Tartars from whom he had returned; Salimbene's own mind was shaped by stories of Francis.[31] From Salimbene, the historian can

know about Rainaldo of Arezzo levels of things (and perhaps particularly surfaces) that he cannot even guess about Rainaldo de Labro or
Rainaldo Bennecelli. To contemporary observers Rainaldo da Arezzo's
piety seemed powerful. The canons of Rieti, like Innocent IV, but before him, had thought that they needed this saintly seeming Franciscan
to reform them.[32] His, in a way unlikely, unanimous capitular election
is the only successful one of which we actually can be completely sure
at Rieti, before the election of Bishop Tommaso II in 1338.

The line between the election of Rainaldo da Arezzo and the provision of Tommaso the Corrector is in fact a very significant one pro-
cedurally. From 1252 bishops of Rieti were normally provided or translated to the see by the pope. The significance of this change is certainly
more than procedural. But the actual nature both of the selection and
episcopates of Rainaldo and Tommaso (and always the uneven quality
of the evidence) argue against too quick an assumption that there was
a general and predictable difference between the sorts of bishops who
existed on the two sides of the 1252 break.

On 2 August 1278 the pope, Nicholas III, translated Pietro da Ferentino, bishop of Sora, to the vacant see of Rieti.[33] At least on the
surface this translation seems a crucial turning point in the history of
the bishops of Rieti, more significant in terms of "real" change than
the procedure in 1252, and more decisive even in procedural change
(after the intervening episcopate of the "postulated" Gottifredo) than
1252: in 1278 both the kind of man who would become bishop at Rieti
and the way in which he would be "elected" seem actually and sym-
bolically to change in a way consonant with a change in the nature of
bishops and their selection throughout the dioceses of the Western
church. Pietro was a foreigner, a *magister*, educated, from Ferentino, a
papal curialist who by this time had already been connected with the
curia for at least fifteen years, and a man who would seem to Nicholas
III in 1279 an appropriate nuncio to lead an important and delicate, but
carefully directed, mission to the court of Castile (and so an appropriate
bishop to be absent from his diocese). Sora had been Pietro's first bishopric when Clement IV had provided him, a papal chaplain and canon
of Ferentino, to the see in 1267; but Sora was only the first of a number
of sees which Pietro would hold before his death in 1301: Sora, Rieti,
Monreale, Capua, Aquileia. Pietro seems a curial politician or diplomat
on the rise, one with no connection to Rieti and, as its bishop, able to

be absent from it, a transient member of the ecclesiastical establishment whom Nicholas III had deposited at Rieti temporarily so that he might be supported by an episcopal income.[34]

Nicholas explained his translation of Pietro to Rieti by saying that the provision was the resolution of a difficultly disputed election and that it would thus provide the church of Rieti with a pastor and prevent continued harm to the church's spiritual and temporal welfare. Nicholas's letter says that in the election following the death of Bishop Gottifredo, fourteen electing canons (still, obviously, believing that election was possible) had divided their votes between two major candidates. Seven canons had voted for their co-canon Giacomo Sarraceno. Six others voted for the Franciscan friar Benvenuto. Their lack of agreement, according to Nicholas's letter, had led the then pope, Gregory X (elected 1 September 1271, consecrated 27 March 1272, died 10 January 1276), to delegate the investigation of and hearings about the dispute to Ancher, cardinal priest of Santa Prassede. Litigation before Cardinal Ancher had dragged on "for years" (*annis pluribus*), and the business had not been settled by the beginning of Nicholas's papacy (elected 25 November 1277, consecrated 26 December 1277, after the short pontificates of Innocent V, Adrian V, and John XXI—Innocent elected 21 January 1276, John died 20 May 1277).[35]

Giacomo Sarraceno and Fra Benvenuto, the canons' two competing and rejected candidates, represent in a straightforward and obvious way two strong strains in the history of the early thirteenth-century church of Rieti. For this Franciscan diocese, for which its chapter had earlier selected as bishop a serious Franciscan religious enthusiast, and in which memories of Francis were strong and local, Benvenuto was a Franciscan. Giacomo Sarraceno was a canon of the church of Rieti and a member of a local patrician family. There had been continually a canon of Rieti called Giacomo Sarraceno since at least 1181, and there would be one at least until 1282. In 1220 there was also a canon Teballo Sarraceno. As early as 1152 Rainaldo Sarraceno had been a donor to the cathedral church of Rieti.[36] Giacomo seems as clear a representative as one could find, or for whom one could hope, of the local tradition, the patrician order, the cathedral church, and the electing canons themselves, of whom he was probably the oldest in office.

Against him stood Benvenuto, a member of that order whose founding members and initial ideals had most disturbed the spiritual and governing commonplaces of local churches and had connected them with a new and refreshing, sometimes almost intoxicating, view of primitive Christianity. The Franciscan disturbance, which was international, had unusually close Reatine ties and connections: Francis himself, who had actually at least once stayed with the bishop of Rieti as well as in the surrounding hermitages; but also the physical church and house of San Francesco, the *locus*, by the Velino at Rieti; and the actual, surviving physical hermitages in the hills, of which the most prominent was Greccio, where, at the time of this election, John of Parma was living his holy and withdrawn life—not, certainly, approved by all, but equally certainly approved by Salimbene, and connected by him with Greccio. John with his wonder-working virtue, as Salimbene shows us, packed into and exuding from his smallish but beautifully formed body, so that the thought of him forced from Salimbene a string of adjectives—"Largus, liberalis, curialis, caritativus, humilis, mansuetus, benignus et patiens. Homo deo devotus et magne orationis, pius, clemens et compassivus."[37] In the sense that Benvenuto was sought for this distinctly and continuingly Franciscan diocese, he too was local, or part of a local tradition.

Nicholas III removed these two differently local contenders and replaced them with Pietro da Ferentino, who still had a remembered locality, a localness of his own. But it was not Reatine. With the election of Pietro, Nicholas III would seem to have settled at Rieti the troublesome matter of episcopal elections, which have appeared to one modern historian "everywhere in the thirteenth century . . . a nightmare."[38] The Rieti local historian Francesco Palmegiani wrote that Pietro's predecessor Gottifredo "fu l'ultimo vescovo eletto dal capitolo."[39] In fact Palmegiani was wrong; Gottifredo was not the last, but although Gottifredo had been translated by Clement IV from Tivoli, he had, according to the papal letter, been postulated by the chapter, and his episcopate, of which little is known, suggests some attachment to Reatine diocesan things. More important, Palmegiani perceived, or at least suggested, a crucial turning point in Reatine episcopal history. Nicholas III had provided a man whom he must have judged a shrewd and capable, and valuable, outsider, with experience of the papal curia, in place of both the local canon from a local family and the Franciscan, quite possibly an outsider, in whom local electors could, because of his order, hope to find, if not a saint or holy man, at least a more than conventionally detached and virtuous man, a good man.

It might have been suspected that that localness which was Pietro da Ferentino's own was the papal curia itself. In fact he was called *Petrus dictus Romanus*, and he was introduced to the curia as were his broth-

ers, Giovanni Egiptius and Leonardo Egiptius, by their uncle Pietro
Egiptius da Ferentino, a papal subdeacon under Gregory IX and Innocent IV.[40] Pietro Romano, Rieti's Pietro, received livings in northern
France and Flanders, as well as central Italy, from Urban IV and Clement IV.[41] At least from the time of Giovanni da Ferentino, cardinal
deacon of Santa Maria in Via Lata, at the beginning of the century,
clerks from Ferentino had, unsurprisingly, been doing curial jobs and
receiving curial patronage in distant benefices.[42] Perhaps coincidentally,
perhaps more than that, some of these benefices and jobs touched men
important, in various ways, to Pietro's life: in 1272 Gregory X confirmed
to Cardinal Ancher possession of a prebend at York which had been
held by another Pietro Egiptius da Ferentino; Bartolomeo Egiptius da
Ferentino belonged to the circle of Gregory da Montelongo, a famous
predecessor, from 1251 to 1269, of Pietro's at Aquileia; Gregorio was also
from southern Lazio.[43]

By 1263 Pietro was establishing his own value to the curia as a papal
chaplain in missions concerned with Spoleto and Cagli. In 1267 Pietro
was given by Clement IV as bishop to the see of Sora, instead of the
abbot of the Cistercian house of Casamari whom the chapter had postulated. While Pietro was bishop of Sora, Gregory X, at the Council of
Lyons, named him collector of the crusading tenth for the peninsular
mainland of the Regno with the exception of Calabria. When in 1286,
while Pietro was at Rieti, Giovanni Boccamazza was made cardinal
bishop of Tusculum, Pietro succeeded him as archbishop of Monreale;
but since Monreale, after the Sicilian Vespers, was no longer available
to a papal candidate, Pietro was again given Sora, but this time as its
administrator rather than its bishop. Pietro kept Sora until 1295, when
for a short time he became Boniface VIII's rector of the Romagna, a
job at which he proved too conciliatory for Boniface; then, from 1296
to 1298, he was administrator of Nola. Meanwhile, in 1287 and 1288, he
had been a papal representative for those peace talks between the Ara-
gonese and the Angevins and French which were supervised by Edward
I of England. In 1298 Boniface VIII moved Pietro from being nominal
archbishop of Monreale to being actual archbishop of Capua. In 1299
Boniface translated him to the important and extraordinarily difficult
patriarchate of Aquileia, where in Ùdine, the castle town, which had in
the later thirteenth century become the capitol of the ancient, and pe-
culiarly secular and international, and disturbed patriarchate, Pietro
died.[44]

This man—had something not quite surely observable been different, had he perhaps come from a secular family less knightly and more baronial—might well have become a cardinal.[45] The pattern of his career draws very well, although perhaps a little extravagantly, the outline of an ideal career of one of the new civil servant bishops. Pietro could easily have seemed a hireling shepherd in those dioceses of which he was temporarily pastor (and in the Romagna he may even have been bought). Actually the image of the hireling shepherd came to Pietro's own mind, or to that of one of his chancery clerks.

A large but incomplete, elaborately but not perfectly written, Rieti document of Bishop Pietro's begins (under the one-line, abbreviated, superscription "[I]n nomine domini Ihu Xpi. Amen"): "[P]etrus permissione diuina Reatinus episcopus ad memoriam futurorum." The *arenga* of its text begins, with its initial capital *T* omitted, "Textus Sacre Pagine," which, it says, "in Nouo et Veteri Testamento" often appropriately speaks "de prelatorum officio" and beautifully compares to the inadequate pastor the hireling shepherd, *mercennarius*, who flees at the sight of the wolf. The text is elaborately fitted together and ornate, syntactically rather difficult, but its elaboration includes the insertion of clear explanation of the meaning both of wolf, "per quem designatur Ecclesie persecutor," the Church's persecutor, and sheep, "quibus figurantur subditi," the bishop's subjects. From these heavy phrases Pietro moves to thought, to remedy, to assembly: himself with his *sociis* the chapter of the major church of Rieti and the clergy of the churches of the city (*ciuitatis*) of Rieti, all gathered together. The beginning of this document reaches a level of intellectual explicitness and, again, elaborateness essentially unknown in earlier Rieti episcopal documents, and its text is decorated with equally novel rhetoric, like an "ex ergastulo proclamabat" in its thirteenth line.[46]

Another surviving Pietro document, addressed to the abbot and convent of Cistercian San Pastore, begins by explaining in general terms the responsibility of the bishops (*prelati*) and chapters of cathedral churches to keep in good order the religiòus places subject to them, and then proceeds to its reforming mission. This document, dated, and from 13 November 1280, with a seal flap and holes and white silk for three seals, and with a heightened and slightly decorated initial *P*, begins:

Petrus permissione diuina minister et . . capitulum Ecclesie Reatin', religiosis uiris amicis in Xpo dilectis . . abbati et conuentui monasterii Sancti Pastoris, Reatin' diocesis Cisterciensis ordinis. Salutem in domino. Inter sollicitudines uarias seu diuersas que prelatis et capitulis cathedralium ecclesiarum incumbunt prelati et capitula eadem pie tenentur considerationis oculo uigilare ut ecclesie aut quelibet pia loca eorum jurisdictioni subiecta nec in spiritualibus aut temporalibus collabantur collapsa quoque ad pristinum statum seu congruum reformentur. Sane cum ad aures nostras.[47]

The elaborate language of the universal church has burst into Rieti's notarial chancery, and the curial foreigner is bishop. But in both cases very clearly the foreigner says that he is acting in concert with his clergy (the chapter of the cathedral church and the clergy of the city in one case, the chapter and the neighboring Cistercian house of San Pastore in the other), and in both cases he is acting out of concern for the clergy and churches of his diocese. Bishop Pietro is loudly proclaiming that he is not a hireling shepherd. He is present, and he is guarding against the wolf.

The wolf is, admittedly, defined in a specific way, within a specific tradition, as the persecutor of the church. In the first case here he is the secular power of the commune of Rieti represented by Guelfone de Testis da Arezzo, the podestà, and Rainaldo da Castiglione Aretino, the *judex maleficiorum*, because of their arrest and imprisonment of *vassalli* of the church of Rieti for crimes allegedly committed by them and not denied by the clergy. Giacomo and Gianni, brothers and the sons of Berardo Jeroni, the church's *vassalli* in Venarossia (or Venarosscia), had been tried and convicted and sentenced by Guelfone, an act, according to Bishop Pietro, *contra generalem libertatem ecclesiasticam*. In fact, on 25 August 1284, at the mandate of Guelfone, the *consilium generale et speciale* of the commune was summoned to meet in the palazzo *in quo jura reduntur*, with Giovanni da Foligno, the *exgravator* of the commune, present; and to the council Angelo canon of Rieti presented the bishop and chapter's case for them. With the advice of the communal officers, the whole council, wishing to avoid discord between the bishop and chapter on the one side and the commune on the other, chose to elect a special council of twelve *buoni uomini*, two from the two halves of each of the *porte* of Rieti, to determine whether or not the men were true *vassalli* of the church, so that if they were they might be returned to its jurisdiction. The council so found; and on 1 September 1284 the podestà revoked his sentence. These acts and decisions were copied into the Riformanze of the commune, and from them transcribed, on 29 September 1284, by the notary Giovanni di Pietro, a transcription checked by the podestà's scribe, Pietro di fu Paganello Campigliano, citizen of Arezzo; and although the Riformanze for the year are lost, the copy remains in the chapter archives.[48]

This successful protest by Bishop Pietro and his chapter was not an isolated one even in its immediate period. On 17 March 1278, just before Pietro's translation to Rieti, before an assembly of the clergy of Rieti, including the chapter, in the choir of Santa Maria, Palmerio Berardi, canon and obedientiary of the church of Rieti, on the chapter's authority, excommunicated Don Paolo Lambertini, the constable of the Reatine militia. The constable had been properly warned of his danger by Ventura (Rainaldi), Palmerio's co-canon and the yconomo and proctor of the church. Palmerio, in the clerical assembly, proclaimed in formal language that, because the constable and his aiders and abetters had arrested and imprisoned *vassalli* of the church of Rieti, they should be punished as were Dathan and Abiron (and some biblical rhetoric certainly is seen to precede Pietro) whom the earth swallowed up. The excommunication was to be read on every Sunday and feast by every priest of the city of Rieti so that no one in the city could claim to be ignorant of it. This excommunication was exemplified in a notarial instrument by Giovanni di Pietro.[49]

On 5 June 1282 Giovanni di Pietro was again busy copying, from the *quaternis*, the parchment gatherings of the commune, a document connected with this continual source of discord. During the podestàship of Meo di don Guglielmo da Orvieto, on Saturday 11 April 1282, Donna Angela, the widow of Giacomo da Venarosscia, appeared before Don Buongiovanni, the *judex maleficiorum*; she pled that, while she was in her house in Villa San Filippo, Pietro di Giacomo of Venarosscia had assaulted her and struck her in the shoulder with a knife, drawn blood, and made a bad wound; she asked judgment against Pietro. On 14 April Pietro appeared and said that he was a *vassallus* of the church of Rieti and ought not to be summoned before a communal court. On 24 April the judge committed to the notary Tomeo the reception of witnesses for Pietro and his excuse. On Monday 11 May the judge pronounced the interlocutory decision that Pietro should not respond before his court because he was a *vassallus* and *subditus* of the church of Rieti and was thus subject to the court of bishop and church.[50]

Bishop Pietro, as he is seen acting his part, rather flamboyantly, in this continuing protection of the church's jurisdiction over criminous *vassalli*, is a very specific kind of good shepherd (specifically different from Biagio da Leonessa's later kind). Pietro's interpretation of his role as shepherd, here, seems a natural one for a man with his curial background. But he is acting in Rieti, and he is dealing with specific and definite Rieti problems. He has not fled or made himself absent.

Bishop Pietro can be seen again, in a composite document, supervising the collecting of the crusading tenth in the diocese of L'Aquila. Although he acts in this matter when he is bishop of Rieti, he is not acting specifically as diocesan bishop; but he uses the occasion to tie the diocese of Rieti more firmly together. Tommaso, archpriest of San Pietro Popleto, which is said in Pietro's documents to be within the diocese of Rieti, had proved to be a reluctant deputy for the bishop, and so the bishop had excommunicated him. Then with the aid of Rainerio, archpriest of San Giuliano di Lavareta, and Matteo, canon of Santa Maria de Balneo, his familiar, the bishop freed Tommaso from excommunication after Tommaso had sworn an oath of allegiance to Bishop Pietro and his successors as bishop, which included the archpriest's promise to come to Reatine synods. Thus, with the notarized copy of the oath as well as the oath itself, Bishop Pietro bound the archpresbytery into the diocese or tried so to bind it.[51]

Bishop Pietro, who was passing through the see of Rieti and whose absence from the see Pope Nicholas III contemplated as he planned the embassy to Castile, was in fact a resident bishop, even, as inscription records at the episcopal palace, a building bishop. Later archbishop of Capua for a very short time, nevertheless Pietro ("Nos Petrus permissione divina Capuanus archiepiscopus") was present and acting there.[52] Later still, although we are told on 19 March 1299 that Pietro had not yet come into his patriarchate of Aquileia and was acting through his vicar, Giovanni di Filippo, and although on 27 August the vicar, Giovanni canon of Ferentino, was still acting, on or about the feast of Saint Michael (29 September) Pietro (protected by Cremonese troops) entered Friuli, and on the feast of Saint Luke (18 October), he came *in Civitatem*[53]; and he died in the patriarchate. Moreover, even inaccessible Monreale had not completely escaped his attention: in June 1287 Pietro di Todino was his proctor general in Sicily; and in April 1291, Giacomo Bonaguri, canon of Sant'Agata, Ferentino, and Pietro's familiar, vicar, and proctor general in spiritualities and temporalities in the island of Sicily, was acting for Pietro in Palermo.[54]

Although Pietro seems very much a man of the curia and the international church, and although he clearly became involved in the dioceses of which he was bishop, as he moved and adjusted his local interests, he maintained his attachment to Ferentino and, almost inseparably from it, to his family. This maintained attachment is immediately ap-

parent from the names and ecclesiastical titles of some of Pietro's officials and household members in places far from Ferentino. At Rieti itself
Pietro certainly did not restrict himself to the use of Ferentine officers,
but he did have as his vicar general in both June and November 1282,
Pietro Romano (or *da* or *de Roma*), canon of the church of San Valentino, Ferentino. In 1284 when the Franciscan inquisitor presented
Pietro in his *camera* at Rieti with his church's portion of a heretic's
goods, among those present was Giacomo Bonaguri (here Boniagurii)
of Ferentino, who would be Pietro's vicar in Palermo. In September
1285 Bishop Pietro's proctor before the papal chamberlain in Terni was
Magister Andrea "de Verulis"—and Vèroli is hardly ten kilometers from
Ferentino, on the way to Sora.[55]

A striking physical relic of Pietro's maintained Ferentine attachment
survives in a cluster of *pergamene* within the Fondo Celestini in the
Vatican Archives. The *pergamene* concern a group of properties, including vineyards, in the area of Ferentino which Pietro was giving to
the local Celestinian house of Sant'Antonio out of reverence for God,
for the sake of his own soul, and for the remission of punishment due
for his and his family's sins. Some of the granted lands were obtained
in an exchange with a knight called Don Orlando of Zagarolo (and
Orlando's nephew), an exchange executed in 1296 by Pietro's nephew
Nicola Egiptius knight of Ferentino. The grants, complex with qualifications and warranties, were received by successive priors of
Sant'Antonio, Fra Sinibaldo in 1296 and Fra Roberto in 1299, for the
house. They include the names of neighbors of some interest, like that
of Pietro de Montelongo, and of witnesses of greater interest: Fra Tommaso "ordinis Sancte Marie de Canneta," who is identified in 1299 as
Pietro's cellarer and familiar; Pietro di don Pietro da Ferentino (in a
1296 document written by the notary "Petrus de Ferentino dictus
Torzianus").

Bishop-Archbishop-Patriarch Pietro (calling himself, or being called,
"Reuerendus pater dominus Petrus de Ferent' dei gratia archiepiscopus
Montisregalis" in 1296, and "Reuerendus Vir dominus Petrus de Ferent' [and also *Ferentino*] dei gratia Sancte Sedis Ecclesie Patriarcha
Acquilegen'" in 1299) was in Ferentino as late as 8 August 1299; and
he was still planning for the future in Ferentino. In the grant of land at
Fornelli, use for life is reserved for Pietro "in this manner, namely when
the Lord Pietro himself is present in the contrada and in those parts the
fruits of the said land are his, and he can do whatever he wants with
them." A further reservation states that although rights over the land

shall be consolidated in the monastery's hands when Pietro dies, still if, within two years of that death, Pietro's heirs should so desire, they may buy back the land from the monastery for 200 florins.[56]

Pietro made these grants, which ensured prayers and memory in his native place, during the pontificate of Boniface VIII, the pope who gave him both Capua and Aquileia as well as the rectorship of the Romagna. The recipient of the grants, however, was a house of Celestinians, Sant'Antonio, only a few kilometers from Fumone, "the prison" in which (under Boniface's rule) Peter Celestine himself died in 1298. At Sant'Antonio the body of the holy man had been deposited. The selection of the house, which seems natural in the 1300 will of the Celestinian cardinal Tommaso da Ocre, is in Pietro da Ferentino's gifts, admittedly in isolation, without the compendium of gifts which his will might show, suggestive of attachments not limitedly careerist and curial but rather spiritual and, again, local.[57]

These maintained local attachments of Pietro's are recalled in a sort of florid parable, with mistaken detail, which the historian of Sora, Crescenzo Marsella, wrote of him:

tanto amato e ripianto dal suo populo, chiuse la vita ad Aquileia. Di là Pietro Guerra con novello fremito di passione forse sussultò dalle ceneri il 27 Maggio 1915, quando, in mezzo alle armi italiane nuovamente apportatrici ad Aquileia del nome di Roma, vide anche i militi di Sora che egli aveva governata e retta come pastore di Cristo, forse sussultò e benedisse. . . . Benedisse all'immenso esercito dei fanti italici, che ripassò dopo l'oscuro abbandono della disfatta di Caporetto i piani di Aquileia con passo rapido come il volo, laggiù, nella chiesa madre, egli Pietro Guerra, dal sepolcro, vedeva finalmente la vittoria afferrare tremenda ed implacabile quella riva fu un'altra volta e per sempre italiana. . . . Era l'alba del 4 Novembre 1918.

[Marsella's Pietro], loved and mourned by his people, closed his life at Aquileia. But on 27 May 1915, roused by a new burst of passion, he perhaps rose from his ashes, surrounded as he was by Italian forces, brought again to Aquileia in the name of Rome, among whom he saw the soldiers of Sora which he had ruled as a pastor of Christ, saw them and perhaps rose and blessed them. . . . He blessed the huge army of Italian infantry, which again after the defeat of Caporetto passed over the plains of Aquileia so quickly it seemed to be flying; and there below in the mother church, that Pietro Guerra, from the grave, saw finally the tremendous victory that made that shore once more, and forever, Italian. . . . It was dawn, 4 November 1918.[58]

Mistaken, marvelous, bizarre, Marsella, like an incredible carnival medium rather eerily raises a figure whose outline suggests the reality of the "historical" Pietro of which we see traces in our collection of sources. The grotesque movement and misplacement are manageable. Marsella's D'Annunziesque placing of Pietro in the context of World War I emphasizes Pietro's adaptability. Almost surely, if Pietro's full will were available, it would testify to his having carried memories of Sora, as well as Ferentino and the other sees which had supported him, as well as his family, to the north. And what sepulchral eyes could see from Aquileia they could presumably see from Ùdine, particularly in the direction of Caporetto. And Marsella's Pietro's eyes, risen from the ashes, see.

Marsella does not, in the quoted passage, speak of Pietro's family, but he does call Pietro by the surname "Guerra." By that name Pietro has generally been known; but Norbert Kamp has shown his learned inability to find that surname in sources contemporary with Pietro's life.[59] It is hard to discard completely a traditional name so long and generally accepted. Pietro's relatives are, however, repeatedly called by the name "Egiptius" in contemporary sources. Pietro himself is called both "Romanus" and "de Ferentino." Together the three names describe, in a life whose transience is declared by changing ecclesiastical titles, the enclosing continuity of kin, curia, and place of origin.

The patriarch Pietro's August 1299 gifts to and induction of the Celestinian house of Sant'Antonio immediately preceded his trip north to his patriarchate, a place and job not always considered a nurse or nest of Christian sanctity in the thirteenth century. Salimbene, who seemed particularly to identify the patriarchate with Gregorio da Montelongo, in passages provoked by his remembering the words of Hugh of Digne, wrote, in talking of excesses of food and dress:

It is said, and it is true, and completely and mightily and utterly and at its heart excessive, that the patriarch of Aquileia on the first day of Lent has forty dishes, that is, of varieties and settings of food, and thus, descending to Holy Saturday, each day one dish is taken away. And it is said that the patriarch does this on account of the honor and glory of the patriarchate. Certainly those patriarchs of Aquileia do not in this take their example from Christ, who fasted in the desert forty days and forty nights.[60]

Just before the beginning of the Lent of 1301, on 12 February, Quinquagesima Sunday, the Patriarch Pietro, in his palazzo in Ùdine where he lay dying, made a codicil to his will (which is preserved in contemporary, or almost contemporary, copy). This codicil provided that, should Pietro die in Ùdine he should be buried at Santa Maria di Castello, and that there should be made for him a pretty sepulture in a church with remarkable thirteenth-century (or so they have been dated) frescoes, particularly of the Deposition.[61] According to the fourteenth-century chronicler "Julianus," Pietro died on 19 February and was buried in Santa Maria.[62]

On that day, however, 19 February, the first Sunday of Lent, the dead patriarch's body was being fought over. In the patriarchal palace, in the presence of Giovanni abbot of Rosazzo and Fra Asquino his chaplain, and a group of officially designated witnesses (including the recent patriarch's chamberlain, Don Pietro, and another member of his household, Fra Tommaso), Fra Bernardo, the *guardiano* of San Francesco di Udine, made appeal for his convent and order. Fra Bernardo claimed that the Patriarch Pietro, of his own free will, spontaneously and without inducement, had elected burial for himself at San Francesco di Udine amid the friars minor. The patriarch had selected San Francesco, according to Fra Bernardo, for the safety of his soul, out of the reverence that he had for the Franciscan order, and so that his spirit might more frequently observe the divine mystery of the Eucharist, *ut anima sua frequentiora sentiret misteria divinorum*—"and hear the blessed mutter of the Mass." According to Fra Bernardo, not only had Pietro made his selection with clear intent, but also he was persistent in his choice, so that when he was asked about it repeatedly, he always confirmed it.

In fact, record of the patriarch's repeated expression of his changed mind survives in late but reliable copy. On the day after the date of his codicil, on 13 February *circa horam nonam*, before a notary and summoned witnesses, including friars, in his room in the patriarchal palace in Udine, the patriarch said that should he die of the infirmity of which he then suffered his body should be buried *apud locum minorum de Utino*. And asked, he replied three times ordering that his body be buried there. And then again at the hour of Vespers in the presence of witnesses, the patriarch, infirm of body but sound of mind and spirit, stated and the notary copied his desire to be buried with the friars minor of Udine. In his appeal on 19 February Fra Bernardo said that Pietro had always had Franciscans in his household, and in their arms he had died, *in eorum manibus transmigravit*. Fra Bernardo said that his convent was ready to receive Pietro's body and to give it honorable burial. He applied to the Holy See for protection, for indemnity against the violation of the patriarch's intent, and for damages done to the convent and order by the priest Pietro rector of the church of Santa Maria di Castello di Udine, his clerks, or lay authorities.[63]

Perhaps it is not surprising that a successful careerist clerk, and book-

collecting *magister*, should die (or be said to die) in the arms of the
Franciscans of Ùdine thinking of the frequency with which the sepulchral eyes of his soul might look upon the Eucharist. Perhaps that is the
nature of normal man in the guise he has if he dies in 1301 in this part
of Christendom. But if this is true, it would be well to remember it in
the cases of men, including bishops of Rieti, of whom smaller pieces of
person survive, and who are thus more easily categorized. The relatively
full biography of Pietro, full particularly in the thirteenth-century biographical sense of his being datably at a relatively large number of places
and recognizably connected with a relatively large number of other people, must be kept in mind here because of that biography's obvious lack
of seeming consistency: the curial clerk always attached to Ferentino
and his natural family; the careerist favored by Boniface VIII who himself favors the Celestinians, and who hopes (it is said), dead, to watch
the Eucharist with the Franciscans; the transient bishop who, in Rieti,
as its pastor, guards the diocese of Rieti against the invading wolf, even
when that wolf is only the court of the *judex maleficiorum*.

Pietro changes color as one looks at him. But the two Reatine "local"
episcopal candidates whom this universal careerist replaced are themselves not so securely fixed and typical as they at first seem. Giacomo
Sarraceno (or Saraceno), representative of the local urban patriciate and
the body of canons, has another aspect. Asked who were the Sarraceno
of Rieti, a thirteenth-century historian might be expected to answer that
they were the Reatine family most closely connected with Francis himself because of the canon Teballo's having been Francis's host and
friend; the same historian, if he were a little more specifically learned,
when asked who was Rainaldo de Labro, could reasonably be expected
to answer that Rainaldo was the bishop of Rieti who must have received
Francis into his palazzo.[64] Perfectly possibly Giacomo Sarraceno was the
candidate of his electors as much because of remembered Franciscan
connections as because of his long tenure of a stall in the choir; Franciscan memories may have given him his specific distinction.

Benvenuto, by contrast, the Franciscan candidate, might have been
a Franciscan administrator, even, and perhaps more probably, a Franciscan inquisitor, with good connections—and even more specifically
Benvenuto da Orvieto, Franciscan inquisitor in the provincia romana
from 1266 to 1269. In the later thirteenth century Franciscans came to
fall quite naturally into bishoprics, and the ease and frequency of their
fall argue that their sharply distinguishing Franciscan characteristics had
become rather muted, that they were certainly not a pack of Rainaldo

da Arezzos.[65] The historian is forced again and again to realize that bishops tend to escape the types that he at first chooses for them, and that the progression of types, insofar as they do exist, is not always the one he would like because it would seem historically reasonable to him.

Bishop Pietro himself suggests another helpful facet to his career by the seeming connection between him and his successor both at Sora and Rieti, Bishop Andrea. Pope Honorius IV translated Andrea from Sora to Rieti on 27 July 1286, after Pietro had been translated to Monreale from Rieti; but it will be recalled that in fact Pietro became administrator of Sora, the see that Andrea, who was Pietro's successor there, was leaving.[66] When seven years before Andrea's translation, Pietro had left Sora for Rieti, and, according to a letter in Nicholas III's register, the chapter of Sora had compromised on two canon electors who chose Andrea, one of the canons of Sora mentioned in the description of the affair was Leonardo Egiptius, probably Pietro's brother.[67] Andrea thus seems entangled with the Egiptius family. Nicholas III's letter, however, offers other biographical detail about Andrea. He was, at the time of his election to Sora, a canon of Rieti and a chaplain of Giacomo Savelli, cardinal deacon of Santa Maria in Cosmedin, the cardinal who would in 1285 be elected pope and who would, as Honorius IV, translate Andrea to Rieti. From Nicholas's letter nothing can be said of Andrea's family, nor are Rieti historians helpful in this regard. (Unfortunately Bishop Tommaso the Corrector was long dead.) Ughelli enriched his meager biography of Andrea with two quotations.[68] The first of these is the inscription, from 1292, which Ughelli found on a bell in the tower of the Duomo:

> Virtutem largire Deus cum Virgine miram,
> Vrbem Reatinam pater Andreas cathedrabat,
> Qui decus Ecclesiae simul, uirtutis amabat.

In metallic compression Ughelli's bell celebrates Andrea's virtuous, decorating, God- and virgin-revering rule. Ughelli's second and very much longer quotation is of Nicholas III's confirmation of the grant by Charles II of Naples to the church, bishop, and chapter of Rieti, of twenty uncie a year (with regulations for its distribution) in commemoration of Charles's coronation by the pope in the cathedral of Rieti, on Pentecost, 29 May 1289.

One quite elegant and formal document issued by Bishop Andrea remains from the time during which he was bishop of Sora.[69] It was once sealed with Andrea's seal. Although the document comes from

Andrea's Sora period, it is not concerned with the diocese of Sora, but rather with the diocese of the Marsi, to the northeast of Sora and south of Rieti. The document begins, with a decorated initial: "Andreas miseratione diuina Sorianus Episcopus, procurator et amministrator Ecclesie Marsicane per Venerabilem G. Sabinensem Episcopum apostolice sedis legatum tam in spiritualibus quam in temporalibus." The document is a letter of indulgence, forty days, for the church of Santi Cosma e Damiano in Tagliacozzo. It proceeds through a rather unusual list of saints (with their bunched summer feasts), who are examples of those from whom comes the treasury of grace: after the Blessed Virgin, Peter, Paul, and Andrew, come Saint Sabina, virgin and martyr, Saint "Berardo," confessor, Cosmas and Damian, and Thomas, archbishop and martyr. The indulgence is for those, truly penitent and confessed, who devotedly come to the church on the feasts of the Annunciation, Nativity of the Blessed Virgin, and Assumption, through their octaves, and on the feasts and through the octaves of Cosmas and Damian and of Thomas Becket, on the feast of the consecration of the church, or on any Friday in Lent, and also to those who give aid to the work of bell and building "ad opus canpane, calcarie et cuiuslibet edificii dicte ecclesie." After its sealing clause, the letter is dated: "Data in Ciuitate Marsican', quarto Marcii, duodecima indictione, anno domini M° CC° lxxxiiii°."

This surviving act of Andrea's from the period of his Sora episcopate is a conventional sealed letter patent of indulgence, with certain peculiarities, rustic and particular, written locally for a local religious house— and, in fact, a particularly interesting and knowable house of canons and Benedictine nuns ruled by an abbess and subject to Montecassino; but all these peculiarities are local to Marsi, the diocese of which Andrea was the administrator acting for the legate cardinal bishop of Sabina, Gerardo Bianchi, not local to Andrea's own diocese of Sora. This job of Andrea's, his being a diocesan administrator while he was bishop of another diocese, shows him acting in the church which Pietro of Ferentino knew and acting in a way that Pietro also acted. Andrea is also seen acting in a part of Italy not distant from Ferentino. The diocese of Ferentino itself, throughout the period of both Andrea's and Pietro's local episcopal activity, was held by a bishop who was a member of the regular clergy.[70]

Two episcopal *acta* survive from the time of Andrea's Reatine episcopate.[71] Both are notarial, written by the notary Giovanni di Pietro; in the earlier of the documents Giovanni is identified as "dicti domini episcopi scriba." Both documents, one from 8 October 1286 and the other from 5 August 1289, are dated from the city of Rieti, the first from the episcopal palace, the second from the baptistery church of San Giovanni Battista. In both the bishop uses the style "Venerabilis Pater Dominus Andreas, dei gratia, Reatinus Episcopus," although in the second, in which the bishop acts with the chapter, the style, in the ablative, is extended: "Venerabili Patre Domino Andrea dei gratia Episcopo et Capitulo Reatin'." In the earlier document, the bishop makes the absent *Magister* Redita da Firenze his proctor to act in papal courts; the named witnesses are *Magistro* Raynerio Rayn', Syn' Rain', Giovanni Petri Rayn' Aymon', and Tommaso Beralli Impernat'. In the second document, before witnesses, Bishop Andrea and the named canons of the chapter of Rieti receive as a canon, with the customary kiss of peace, Bartolomeo domini Raynalli de Rocca, who had been provided by papal mandate. The witnesses include, besides the archpriest and a canon of the neighboring church of San Giovanni Evangelista and Giovanni di *Magistro* Andrea, Giovanni domini Rayn' de Bucco da Apoleggia; the canons include Ventura Rayn' (plate 22).

Since Bishop Andrea had been a canon of Rieti before his election to Sora, it would seem reasonable to hope to find some further identification of him in Rieti documents from the period before 9 June 1279, when he became bishop. The pattern of this evidence is complicated by the existence of two contemporary canons Andrea at Rieti. One of these canons, Andrea Pernatarum, Impernatoris, Impernatore, a canon of Sant'Eleuterio Rieti, with an important, although rather fluid, Rieti surname, had been provided to a canonry at Rieti and was being resisted by the chapter in 1252.[72] He became a canon, and he was active at Rieti at least from 1260 to 1271.[73] As early as June 1260 another Andrea was active at Rieti; by 4 February 1261 a canon Andrea, almost surely the Andrea of June 1260, was called *Magister* Andrea Rainaldi (and Raynaldi) and was acting for the chapter as proctor.[74] On 27 June 1263 he was acting at Orvieto in the palazzo of the papal chamberlain; he is again visible in December 1263 and in October 1265.[75] On September 1278, in a list of the canons' prebendal benefices, *Magister* Andrea's is the thirteenth; and on 10 October 1278 there is a conjecture "si magister Andreas esset absens."[76] He does not appear again as a canon; almost certainly he is the Andrea who became bishop of Sora. That man, the bishop, can thus with complete confidence be identified as *Magister* Andrea Rainaldi, canon of Rieti and chaplain of Giacomo Savelli, cardinal deacon of Santa Maria in Cosmedin.

The canon Ventura Rayn', who was one of the canons joined with Bishop Andrea in the reception of the new, provided canon, Bartolomeo domini Raynalli de Rocca, in 1289, can be seen, with his name extended to Ventura Raynaldi, acting, in 1292, as Bishop Andrea's vicar general in Rieti and receiving for him fealty and homage from *vassalli*.[77] This canon, often simply called Ventura, at times Ventura with an unextended Rayn', is sometimes, in 1303 and 1315, called Ventura Raynerii.[78] He can be observed as a canon from 1278 to 1315, for over thirty-seven years.[79] He had been provided by Pope John XXI to his canonry on 20 October 1276, with the proviso that if there were at the moment no vacancy in the chapter of Rieti, but there was one at San Nicola, Rieti, he might go there, if not, possibly to the archdeaconry with a prebend at Crotone[80]; in fact he came, probably although not surely, immediately to Santa Maria, the chapter, at Rieti. In his letter of provision from Pope John, he is called Ventura Raynaldi, canon of Rieti and chaplain of Giacomo, cardinal deacon of Santa Maria in Cosmedin.

Both Bishop Andrea and his vicar general seem clearly to have been called Rainaldi (Raynaldi)—although Ventura was not always so called; both had been chaplains of Cardinal Giacomo Savelli, and both had or formed lasting attachments to Rieti. The conclusion that they were brothers is irresistible, the more so because in March 1315 Ventura (at this significant point called Raynerii) can be seen acting as heir of "*olim Episcopi Andree olim Episcopi Reat'*." Whether or not they were also connected with *Magister* Rainerio Rayn', Syn' Rain', Giovanni Petri Rayn' Aymon', Bartolomeo domini Raynalli de Rocca, or Giovanni domini Rayn' de Bucco da Apoleggia is in each case an open question. Three unconnected Bishops Rainaldo of Rieti in the first half of the thirteenth century should make any historian cautious about this common name. An additional aid to caution is the fact that the bishop and vicar general do not seem ever to have been called "domini Rainalli." Still it is possible that other members of this presumably non-noble but educated family were around.[81]

That Andrea and Ventura were chaplains of Giacomo Savelli was undoubtedly important to their provisions, but it was not necessarily so important in the selection of Rieti as the place to which they were provided. Andrea's connection with Pietro da Ferentino probably began in the curia. All three men illustrate the balance of curial connections and lasting local attachments among prebend holders in central Italy and, in this sense, the division of official personality.

Pietro (with the extension of Andrea) forms the untidy center of the series of Rieti bishops between Adenolfo and Biagio. Pietro stands, in his variety and uneasy definition, at what would seem the moment of greatest change in the series. Defying easy definition as he does, poorly defined as he is, he could not have occurred much earlier. His position is central. Curial, translated, Pietro and Andrea undeniably mark a change in the nature of bishops and episcopal selection at Rieti.

Adenolfo and Biagio themselves are not without surprises and complexity. The same Adenolfo who was not consecrated for at least the first six and one-half years of his episcopate, who possibly was not a priest during that time, resigned his see to become a Cistercian at Tre Fontane. Baronial sons and brothers did become Cistercians, that is the twelfth-century story, told most notably by Bernard and his own family, but also by the not quite clearly historical Balduino of, or not of, San Matteo Rieti. It is not surprising that Cistercian piety could still impress, as it seems to have impressed the commune of Rieti, and as it certainly impressed contemporary popes.[82] But there is at least an added resonance to this baronial brother, caught in baronial wars and seemingly careless about consecration, when he is seen to have chosen for himself the Cistercian quiet and prayer of Tre Fontane. That Adenolfo's episcopate was not the waste that Bishop Tommaso suggests is clear from the evidence that Tommaso himself used against San Salvatore Maggiore, and in the evidence used against San Leopardo Collefegato and even against the Lavareta house of Santa Croce Lugnano; with mixed success Adenolfo tried to establish and maintain episcopal right in his diocese. This was not the spirituality of his contemporary Francis (nor, exactly, was Tre Fontane's); but it was the job of a governmentally conscientious bishop, and it had little enough positive to do, except perhaps in Adenolfo's having been taught to govern, and at Lugnano, with the family of Lavareta.

Biagio's surprises are more dramatic, but less internal. This sensibly compromising and ruling bishop of Rieti held the see from the year in which Cola di Rienzo became ruler of the city of Rome until the year after Gregory XI brought the papacy back to Rome, until, in fact, a month after Gregory's own death and through the month of Urban VI's election and consecration. Biagio was translated to the see in the second year after the murder of Andrew of Hungary (the unfortunate husband of Queen Joanna of Naples) and in the year before the Black Death struck central Italy. Biagio was translated to Rieti after the vacancy during which the chapter's vicar general refused to condemn clerics who had communicated with exiles from the divided city of Rieti.

Cardinal Gil Albornoz first entered Italy as legate in 1353, and he died at the end of his secularly brilliant but papally hampered career in 1367. Ferdinand Gregorovius wrote in his *History of the City of Rome in the Middle Ages*: "From the middle of the fourteenth century the errant soldiery constantly acquired greater preponderance."[83]

Through this tense and difficult, even uproarious, period of central Italian history, Biagio remained in his Reatine see.[84] He was there, acting in the sacristy of the church, in the palace and its loggia, and out in the extended diocese, in 1348, 1349, 1350, 1353, 1355, 1359, 1361, 1362, 1363, 1365, 1366, 1369, and 1375.[85] He was a resident bishop carrying on the normal pastoral jobs of a bishop, licensing chapels and hospitals, uniting poverty-stricken livings, supervising the execution of wills, instituting and inducting clergy, punishing criminous clerks, supporting local saints and feasts, presumably constantly administering sacraments, paying or trying to pay papal imposts and getting them reduced in time of famine (1377); he was occupied too with Albornoz and rulers of Naples.[86] Michaeli said that Biagio should be counted among the most distinguished (*insigni*) of the bishops of Rieti, and Ughelli said that he lived *santamente*.[87] Clement VI in his formal letter of translation wrote, through his chancery clerks, of the merits of Biagio's virtues and of his previous, useful pontificate at Vicenza.[88]

The Rieti historian thus turns to and reads with some shock the appraisal of Biagio in some of the more notable historians of the see of Vicenza. Battista Pagliarini (or Pagliarino), in his late fifteenth-century history, which was published in Italian translation in 1663, wrote:

In this year 1343 there sprang up in our city a greater plague than the Black Death, more cruel than the harsh tyranny of perfidious Ezzelino, because "Frate Biagio" of the order of friars minor, the bishop of Vicenza, a wild beast and more cruel than a tiger (*fiera bestia e più crudele di una tigre*) began like a starved wolf against the sheep (*a guisa di un affamato lupo verso le pecore*) with his jaws to inflict his cruelty upon the people committed to him by the apostolic see. *Deh, o dolore!*[89]

Tommaso Riccardi, in his *Storia dei vescovi vincentini*, published in 1786, rehearses Pagliarini's attack, talks of Biagio's suspension from office by Benedict XII and his translation to Rieti by Clement VI, and then says: "It came to my mind to see how this man behaved in his second bishopric, so I took up the first volume of Ughelli and looked at column 1208, which described to me a Fra Biagio full of zeal for his church of Rieti and leading a very holy life."

Ed ecco, io dico, se furono sempre equali gli uomini! pronti sempre a dire il male di alcuna persona, ed a tacerne il bene! Se F. Biagio pentito de' suoi falli in Vicenza commessi, diede saggio di pietà, di zelo, di costumi santi in Rieti, perchè nessuno l'ha mai scritto fuor dell'Ughelli?[90]

Riccardi, a Dominican, allows himself the luxury of musing on man's ever being willing to speak evil of another man and wondering, if Biagio had changed when he went to Rieti, why no one had bothered to mention it except Ughelli.

Two recent historians, Ugolino Lippens and Giovanni Mantese, have dealt with the problem of Biagio more successfully by considering his Vicentine behavior in context, particularly political context; they have rejected Pagliarini's partisan caricature. Mantese, moreover, has shown a Biagio who held a general synod of the clergy of the diocese as early as the first year of his episcopate, and, in this, his following the precept of his metropolitan, the patriarch of Aquileia, Blessed Bertrand of Saint Geniès, to whom, at Vicenza, Biagio seems to have been particularly closely tied. Mantese shows a Biagio in his early years, in 1335 and 1336, particularly concerned with the recovery of lost income and the reordering of local religious corporations, "too seriously engaged in the government of his diocese to be absent from Vicenza," a Biagio consistent with the Biagio of Rieti.

In September 1336, however, in the year in which the Florentine-Venetian-papal league against the Scaligeri of Verona had been formed (a league to which both the patriarch of Aquileia and the bishop of Vicenza adhered), Biagio was among those delegated by the patriarch to conduct an investigation of the election of Bartolomeo della Scala, bishop-elect of Verona. The treaty of January 1339 between the Scaligeri and their Florentine and Venetian enemies did not end the enmity between the Scaligeri and the bishops of the province of Aquileia; Biagio himself continued to live under the protection of the Carraresi of Padua in the recovered castle of Brendola (whose guard, Pagliarini seems to have thought, perpetrated robbery, arson, adultery, and the rape of many virgins, *quanti stupri di vergini*, for which Biagio was thus responsible). In April 1339 a provincial council of Aquileia, with Biagio present, attacked the Scaligeri "persecutions" of the bishops of Parma and Verona. From this council Biagio was not able to return to his diocese. He was settled instead in Padua, in the "palazzo episcopale vecchio," which had by then been abandoned by the bishops of Padua; he remained there, with some interruptions, until 1347. Between 1340 and 1345, Biagio was represented in Vicenza by a vicar general, Paolo da Trento. In 1346 Biagio was at the papal court in Avignon, presumably defending himself against attacks by Vicentine opponents. By 7 November 1345 Biagio had been suspended from the administration of Vicenza; and diocesan administration was in the hands of the chapter's vicar general, the archpriest Ugolino. On 25 October 1347 Clement VI translated Biagio to Rieti.[91]

In the hands of Mantese and Lippens, with the documentary evidence they use, the sharpness of Riccardi's question disappears, and the nature of the problem of the two Biagios changes. Still for Biagio, if not exactly in him, there was a real difference between Vicenza and Rieti. If not two diverse selves, he had two diverse episcopates. It was, moreover, not Biagio alone who changed sees; a household changed. At Vicenza, Biagio, who is there specifically identified as being from Leonessa, had about himself friars and relatives from Leonessa: his nephew Nicola da Leonessa (a doctor of both laws according to Riccardi), his nephew Matteo da Leonessa, the friar Andrea da Leonessa, the Bishop's familiar Gelucio da Leonessa, the Franciscan Alberto da Clampo, like Andrea an episcopal chaplain. Certainly not all the men around Biagio in the north were Franciscans or men from Leonessa, but those who were form a noticeable personal coterie. Embattled at Vicenza, accommodating at Rieti, did Biagio better understand politics close to his place of origin? or had he learned at Vicenza not only about synods but also about politics? or did he in politics at Rieti benefit from the absence of a powerful and persuasive metropolitan patriarch as well as the absence of the Scaligeri?

The outline of the moving figure of Fra Biagio acting, flexibly, as bishop of Rieti, among the complex currents that shaped his episcopate, is suggested by what can be seen of his behavior in the case between him and the nuns of San Benedetto in the early days of 1375. The abbess and nuns of San Benedetto had claimed that they, for ten, twenty, forty, fifty, sixty years, and for so long that no memory could contradict it, had, with the full knowledge of the bishops of Rieti, been in peaceful possession of the right to choose their confessors, those who officiated at their services, and their preachers, and particularly the Augustinian friars of Rieti, and that suddenly and without good reason the bishop had disturbed this ancient custom. The nuns had appealed and the case had come before Don Paolo "de Buccolis" of Perugia, abbot of Santa Maria di Valdiponte. But the nuns, they said, preferred concord to discord and they had arrived at an agreement with the bishop. The bishop, for his part, acting with the chapter, as the nuns' diocesan sought the safety of their souls and the avoidance of any appearance of scandal; he approved the continued coming of the Augustinian friars to San Benedetto to officiate, to preach, to hear confessions, but under specific conditions. The visiting Augustinian was to act under the mandate of bishop and chapter and to be, himself, chosen by bishop and chapter. The bishop and chapter then chose Fra Tommaso Jacobicti who was to go to San Benedetto accompanied by one *fraticello*, above suspicion, not a priest. These arrangements proclaimed in the nuns' cloister and the episcopal palace were approved by Nicholasia the abbess of San Benedetto and twenty of her nuns (of whom three had patronymics distinguished by the noble or patrician "domini") and by twelve canons of Rieti. One aspect of Biagio's behavior is involvement with his chapter, and that is seen in another way in his gift inter vivos, in 1364, of a large number of sacred and precious objects to Ballovino, canon and chamberlain, acting for the church. These were objects being brought out of pawn by the bishop's gift. Biagio, as bishop of Rieti, seems—in the pieces of him that can be seen—sensible, principled, and pragmatic.[92]

Among Fra Biagio's fourteenth-century predecessors at Rieti, Giovanni Papazurri (1302–1336), whose synodal statutes are conflated with Biagio's, makes nice contrast with Biagio because the conflicting strains of his official personality, or the conflicting pieces of evidence which are preserved about him, are not divided between his time in different sees, but rather they are at least in part contemporary with each other and in both, or all, directions visible at Rieti.[93] All four of Biagio's fourteenth-century predecessors, however, show, at different lengths, stimulatingly juxtaposed facets of themselves.

The Franciscan inquisitor Angelo was translated from Nepi to Rieti by Boniface VIII on 8 June 1302, after his predecessor Jacopo had been removed from the see. On 15 June he had promised to pay his common services of 300 florins, and two florins to 17 cardinals, and he was alive, or at least thought at the curia to be alive. By 3 August Angelo had been dead long enough to be replaced at Rieti, on that day, with Giovanni Papazurri, who was translated from Ìmola; although Angelo was not replaced at Nepi, with the Franciscan Paolo, until 31 August.[94] Nothing remains from Angelo's episcopate at Rieti. It is without visible consequence. His would seem the quintessence of the cliché of late medieval translation: a cosmopolitan (in the sense that he was both Franciscan and an inquisitor) bishop's being moved from one see to another to no local effect. But in fact, although for good or ill Angelo's episcopate was miserably abbreviated by his death, he was one of the most clearly Reatine of all the bishops of Rieti between Adenolfo and Biagio. He was known, perhaps even notorious, as Angelo da Rieti. Angelo da Rieti was one of those Franciscan inquisitors whose past work Pope Benedict XI questioned, in a letter of 1 March 1304, and whom he essentially accused of proceeding unjustly, "se," in the words of Fra Mariano d'Alatri, "col beneficio di uno sfumato condizionale (although with the clouding protection of the conditional mood)."[95]

Fra Mariano himself has unraveled the facts and significance of the *mastodontico processo*, which Benedict XI questioned and in which Angelo listed for inquisitorial consideration the names of five hundred men of Viterbo, a process in which Angelo used his inquisitorial office to political effect not by accusing the Viterbesi of actual heresy but by putting them on an inquisitorial blacklist and thus threatening them in order to break their resistance to an Orsini-Viterbo treaty which favored the Orsini.[96] Angelo's political behavior, including his preaching, with the authority of a papal letter of 30 December 1298, the crusade against the Colonna, a crusade in which the Viterbesi, like Angelo, participated, was rewarded and encouraged by Boniface's giving Angelo the diocese of Nepi on 1 June 1298.[97] Fra Mariano has found that Angelo emerges from the ample documentation of the Viterbo case as "a dynamic man, careless of the risks to which his office exposed him, undeniably capable in arranging and treating, but also willful (*prepotente*), stubborn (*puntiglioso*), hard, and not without ambition," that he remained "on the crest of the wave until his death," and that after Nepi "the indomitable friar, with one foot in the grave, obtained another promotion toward the middle of 1302, and succeeded in getting himself transferred to the see of his native city, where he died in July of the same year."[98]

The Orsini-Viterbo case was argued at Rome and Rieti before Cardinal Pietro Perregrosso between 1286 and 1290.[99] In his office of inquisitor of heretics in the Roman province, Angelo himself had come to Rieti. He can be seen acting, on 6 March 1282, in the presence of Fra Giacomo da Cerchiara in the Franciscan's cloister at Rieti, there disposing of confiscated land which had belonged to the convicted heretic Don Paolo di don Pietro (land confiscated by Angelo's predecessor inquisitor Fra Sinibaldo), granting it to Pietro da Rocca and his heirs for the price of eight lire provisini of the senate.[100] On 29 August (?) 1284 Angelo was acting, with his *socio* Fra Giacomo present, in the chamber of the bishop (Pietro da Ferentino) in the episcopal palace, giving to the bishop for the church his portion of a property which had once belonged to the condemned heretic Sydrac da San Liberato.[101]

If Fra Mariano is right (and one has no reason to doubt that he is), Angelo's loyalty and vigor bought for him from Boniface VIII his home see. In going back to it Angelo also went back to the neighborhood of the Franciscan house which probably had first attracted him to the order.[102] Angelo and his local associate had been, in Rieti, Franciscan inquisitors at home; and Angelo's becoming bishop of Rieti as well as his having become an inquisitor shows Rieti's position in the swell of the Roman sea. Although as bishop of Rieti Angelo is nothing that we can know or see, no one could better point out the way in which local attachments and papal service and patronage were intricately mixed.

Of Bishop Raimond (de Chameyrac), canon of Amiens, whom Clement VI provided to Rieti on 5 August 1342 and who was Biagio's predecessor, this certainly could not be said.[103] If he had had previous connections with Rieti they are unknown. Lippens wrote of him, "Since this bishop from the year 1343 exercised the office of vicar of the city of Rome, it can be deduced that the diocese of Rieti enjoyed little enough of the governance of this pastor."[104] It seems a reasonable deduction; and there is evidence enough of Raimond's occupation with his vicariate in Clement VI's registers.[105] Rieti, and Orvieto after it, seem convenient sources of income, close to Rome, for the papal vicar. Raimond probably knew Cola di Rienzo better and surely thought about him more than he did any Rieti notary; the Aracoeli was almost necessarily a more frequent picture in his mind than was San Francesco Rieti. Raimond employed vicars general at Rieti.[106]

Raimond himself was not, however, completely detached from his bishopric. On 27 December 1344 he had been staying in Rome; but on 18 February 1345 he can be seen acting "in giardino nostro post domus palatii episcopalis Reatin' " and calling himself "Raymundus miseratione diuina Episcopus Reatinus domini nostri pape in Urbe in spiritualibus vicarius generalis," and using the unusual, for Rieti earlier, salutation, "Salutem in filio Virginis gloriose."[107] Raimond was present in Rieti again on 20 October 1345, although said to be absent on 10 November 1345.[108] "Considering the goodness and merits of the worthy bishop" and "the services and gifts which the church of Rieti had received from him," the canons of the chapter of Rieti, gathered together in the sacristy of the church (before witnessing prebendaries some of whom like Filippo "de Senis" and Cicco di Giovanni were closely involved with Raimond's governing of his see) swore to celebrate each year an anniversary for Raimond's soul, both during his life and after his death. In 1363 the income from the eighteen days in the mill "antea de canalibus" which Bishop Raimond had given the church for his anniversary is specifically recorded in the church's book of accounts; and Raimond's anniversary is recorded in the church's list of anniversaries as occurring on 5 April.[109]

Among all the provided and translated bishops of Rieti in the fourteenth century, and, in fact, with the possible exception of the Cistercian bishop Nicola, among all those bishops from the time of the provision of Tommaso the Corrector and the postulated translation of Gottifredo, in 1252 and 1265, one bishop, Raimond's predecessor, who has been known as Tommaso II, was successfully elected by the chapter of Rieti, an election eventually approved by the papal curia. What has been known of Tommaso II can essentially be stated in the words of Ughelli's brief notice of him: "43. Tommaso, a former canon of the cathedral church, was elected by the chapter, in place of the dead Giovanni, and was confirmed by Benedict XII on the seventh day before the Ides of December (7 December) 1339 (Vatican registers). He died in 1342."[110] Ughelli's date, 7 December 1339, and his reference to Tommaso's election come from a letter recorded in Benedict XII's register, as Ughelli suggests.[111] Benedict's letter, from Avignon, is one of confirmation. It says that after the previous bishop of Rieti, Giovanni, had closed his eyes in death *in partibus illis,* the chapter had called all who should be called in that see, immediately subject to Rome, to an episcopal election; and those called had chosen to elect *per viam compromissi* and then had selected as elector the canon Giacomo di Tommaso, and that he in turn after consultation had chosen as bishop Tommaso, who was in priestly orders and of legitimate birth.

Tommaso himself and the chapter, through suitable proctors and nuncios, came to the papal curia for confirmation of election and elect. A certain clerk of the diocese, however, Giovanni "de Marterio" (but just possibly "Marrerio," which would be an important distinction), appealed the election and appeared before the pope in consistory to declare that Tommaso was unworthy of the episcopal dignity and that he had been elected improperly. In consistory, *viva voce,* the pope delegated the case to Peter cardinal priest of San Clemente. Giovanni "de Marterio" failed to prosecute his case; and a commission of cardinals (John cardinal bishop of Porto, Peter cardinal priest of San Clemente, and Galhardin cardinal deacon of Santa Lucia in Selcis) returned to the pope a certification of Tommaso's personal merits, laudable life, and learning in letters. The pope ordered John cardinal bishop of Ostia to proceed with Tommaso's consecration. And on the same day that he dated his letter of confirmation to Tommaso, he dated letters, as a matter of course, announcing his action and requiring obedience to Tommaso, to the chapter of Rieti, the clergy of the city and diocese of Rieti, and the people of the city and diocese.[112] The care of the church and the *gregem dominicam*, the Lord's local flock, were given to the former canon Tommaso.

Tommaso's election can be dated a little more closely and some of his supporters can be identified because the then still church notary Matteo Barnabei copied into his parchment book of documents the authenticated copy of a document issued by the auditor of the papal chamber in Avignon and dated 3 August 1338, in which Tommaso is called "elect." The document records the absolution of a group of canons, some of whom, at least, had supported Tommaso's election. These canons had in the past been accused of expelling and despoiling Bishop Giovanni and so had been cited by two rectors of the patrimony. The accused canons were said initially to have been contumacious; but later they were absolved by one of the rectors, the bishop of Orvieto, acting in Montefiascone on 3 December 1322, after one of the canons, Tommaso Cimini, had appeared for himself and his colleagues before the rector. The canons who had been absolved and were specifically named were Tommaso Cimini, Giacomo di Tommaso (here called *di don Tommaso*), Andrea the abbot of Sant'Eleuterio, Matteo di *magistro* Biagio, Matteo di don Angelo de Tufo, and Matteo di don Paolo.[113] Matteo Barnabei's book, which of course includes documents from the whole period of Tommaso's episcopate, also gives an approximate date for Tommaso's death. On 5 September 1341, Francesco archpriest of Santa Maria Antrodoco can be seen, in one of Matteo Barnabei's copied documents, acting for bishop and chapter; and on 15 September he can be seen acting for the chapter alone. On 2 October 1341 Matteo Barnabei says that the church is vacant through the death of Tommaso and that *Magister* Matteo di *magistro* Biagio is acting as *camerarius*, yconomo, and procurator of the chapter.[114]

Tommaso's death can be fixed with greater exactness by information contained in Matteo Barnabei's paper book of collations and contracts, which covers the period from 28 July 1340 to 3 September 1344. There it is stated that Tommaso died on 5 September 1341 and that he was buried on 7 September 1341. It is further stated that the chapter met at Mass on 28 September and set the following Sunday, 30 September, after the Mass of the Holy Ghost, for electing, or beginning the election of, their new bishop.

The chapter met and, electing by the method of scrutiny, chose as bishop a canon of the Lateran, Nicola Raynoni of Rome.[115] The canons' hope of two free elections in succession was, however, frustrated. There is no evidence that Nicola was confirmed; there is in fact secure evidence that he was not confirmed in Raimond's having been translated to Rieti in succession to Tommaso. It is possible that the peculiar circumstances, or the fluke, of Tommaso's singular free election were simply not repeated; it is also possible that Nicola was personally unacceptable. This possibility is somewhat strengthened by the repeated appearance during the year 1328 of a Nicola Rainoni in the abbreviated register of the antipope Nicholas V, the Franciscan from Corvaro in the diocese of Rieti. This Nicola Rainoni is identified in the register as a canon of Palermo, but he acts in Rome with other Roman clerics, including two canons of the Lateran, one of whom was a Cenci; and he acts in conferring a canonry and prebend in the Lateran, from which Giovanni de Fuscis de Berta had been deprived, on Nicola di Pietro di Nicola Thebaldi de Annibaldis, and on the same day conferring another, from which Omodeo Papazurri had been deprived for his inobedience to Pope Nicholas, on Nicola Annibaldi's brother Tebaldo.[116] In the account of the election of Nicola Raynoni at Rieti, the first canon listed is Tommaso Cimini, who in the month of October will be called "prior et antiquior" of the chapter.[117] Whatever Nicola Raynoni's past connections with the diocese or its Franciscan antipope or ancient enemies of the Papazurri, he did not become an active bishop of Rieti.

Of the bishop to whom the canons of Rieti chose Nicola as successor, much more than Ughelli wrote can now be said. Again, the entire period of Tommaso's episcopate is covered in the parchment book of Matteo Barnabei. Tommaso appears in Benedict XII's register and in the Rieti paper book of collations and contracts. From these three sources, however, it still would not seem possible to say who Tommaso was, except that he was a legitimately born, respectable-seeming canon priest, supported by canons, including Giacomo di don Tommaso, and that these canons included men who had opposed, or been thought to oppose, Giovanni Papazurri twenty years before Tommaso's election, and who were perhaps led by the long-in-office canon Tommaso Cimini. Bishop Tommaso seems pretty clearly to have been part of a, in some ways long-standing, capitular party.

A canon Tommaso who would naturally suggest himself is Tommaso de Labro, a canon evidently from a local baronial family and a connection of Cardinal Pietro Colonna's; Tommaso de Labro's help in establishing the Colonna hospital of San Giacomo degli Incurabili on the Corso in Rome is recorded on a damaged and in small part restored lapidary inscription in a cortile in the hospital. The early fourteenth century was a time in which major Roman families like the Colonna could be expected to express their power in the diocese of Rieti through the use of members of local baronial families with whom they had connections; Tommaso could have been elected in a seemingly free, although opposed, election because he was a surrogate Colonna and an early predecessor of the actual Colonna bishops who would rule Rieti from 1477 to 1555. But the lapidary inscription itself forces the reader to question this solution, particularly if the reader remembers that Tommaso was elected before the end of 1338: the San Giacomo stone calls Tommaso de Labro a canon of Rieti in 1339. In 1344, moreover, a prebend is described as vacant through the death of Tommaso de Labro, in a way that clearly suggests that he was a canon when he died. These pieces of evidence, particularly taken together, in themselves make the attractive conjecture that Bishop Tommaso was Tommaso de Labro seem unlikely.[118]

In fact Bishop Tommaso was not Tommaso de Labro; and it is rather surprising at this point in Rieti historiography to find that in the Archivio Capitolare itself a source exists which tells exactly who Tommaso was. That source is the notarial cartulary of Silvestro di don Giovanni.[119] Documents in Silvestro's cartulary answer not only the question of who Bishop Tommaso was, but also questions about his connections, his property, and even his piety.[120] In, for example, an instrument from 15 February 1341, which records an action in the bishop's hospice in Cittaducale before the bishop, the bishop is called "the reverend in Christ father and lord, Lord Tommaso 'de Secinali' by the grace of God bishop of Rieti."[121] The family of the bishop is here, and elsewhere in the cartulary, exposed; Tommaso was a Secinari, a brother and heir of that Giovanni di Pandulfo whose evocative will stretches across and ties together the diocese of Rieti and Sulmona, the life of the seignorial lord and the pious man. In Silvestro di don Giovanni's cartulary, written long after Giovanni di Pandulfo's 1311 will, the bishop (before and after his election) and other surviving members of the Secinari family from the bishop's and Giovanni's own and from the next generation spread out the business of their lives.

Silvestro di don Giovanni's cartulary also includes an early, and seemingly uncanceled, will of the bishop, before he was bishop, from 4 April 1336, in which Tommaso di don Pandulfo, then calling himself both a canon of Rieti and a canon of L'Aquila, planned his funeral, burial, and bequests. It is the only known will (as opposed to codicils) of a bishop of Rieti, or of a man who became bishop of Rieti, from the period between, and including, the episcopates of Adenolfo and Biagio. Tommaso chose burial in the chapel he had founded in the cathedral church of Rieti, the chapel of San Clerico (or San Quirico). Tommaso provided money, in his will, for the decoration of his chapel; and he left money for local churches. A maidservant, Festa, for whom Tommaso carefully provided, finds, with members of Tommaso's family, a prominent place in his will. Tommaso planned funeral services in Rieti, and also in L'Aquila if (some unidentified and curiosity-provoking) scandal should not make that impossible. Tommaso included among his executors both a brother, Berardo, and a fellow canon.[122]

Less interesting in terms of piety than the will of his brother Giovanni, Tommaso's will is tied to Giovanni's through the people who appear in both wills. Some of these people and some attachments of Tommaso's appear in other documents recorded in Silvestro di don Giovanni's cartulary. Tommaso can be seen borrowing from papal bankers, and as bishop using his palazzo, or having it used, as a temporary safe storage place for the treasure that had belonged to a non-Reatine bishop who had died. More interestingly, at least from a political point of view, Tommaso can be seen to have represented the commune of Rieti at the royal court at Naples.[123] This connection suggests that it was possibly a royal Neapolitan or Neapolitan curial connection of this family from the Regno that permitted the free election of one of its members to the bishopric in the 1330s—a different kind or at least a different area of politics from the Colonna connection that could have supported Tommaso de Labro.

Tommaso's late election and his identity indicate the sustained localness of the Rieti episcopate. But this should not be oversimplified; nor should the localness of the episcopate and the bishop's election by local electors be too tightly tied together. Still, one can say that as in other dioceses, like Padua, but not in all other dioceses, at Rieti bishops began regularly to be papally provided in the middle of the thirteenth century, but that at Rieti this did not mean that the bishops necessarily all stopped being local in origin or having local, but not solely local, interests. It certainly did not mean that they stopped being resident or that those who were generally not resident stopped being concerned with the government of their diocese. At Rieti, again as at Padua, the memory of election remained long after provision became regular; and at Rieti the memory was accompanied by actual late elections and probably by the belief that capitular election was the ordinary, normal way to select a bishop.[124]

Between Adenolfo and Biagio, what were Reatine bishops like?[125] It is hard to generalize. They were adult males in orders; perhaps nothing more can be said about the whole group, at least with any certainty. Of the categories into which they fall, more can, with caution, be said.

Most of these bishops of Rieti were secular clerics. Four men who actually ruled as bishops were, during their episcopates, in regular orders. One was a Cistercian, and three were Franciscans. Furthermore, one secular cleric retired from the bishopric to become a Cistercian, and another Franciscan was a serious candidate for the episcopate but was not confirmed. Thus two orders, and only two orders, were represented among the episcopal ranks: and they were the particularly obvious and popularly effective spiritual orders of the twelfth and thirteenth centuries. They were orders of general importance in the contemporary life of the diocese, but they were certainly not the only orders of spiritual importance to the contemporary diocese.

Bunching together the three Franciscan bishops, moreover, gives a false impression of their sameness. It is significant that the three were Franciscan, that each was a Franciscan, but they were very different from one another. Rainaldo da Arezzo could only with difficulty be persuaded to accept the bishopric, and he could not be persuaded to keep a bishop's horns. Angelo da Rieti, the inquisitor, seems to have been given his home bishopric, his second, as a reward. Biagio da Leonessa, sensible and methodical man, at least in his Reatine maturity, escaped to Rieti, his second bishopric. His being a Franciscan, however, was probably a major reason for the election or selection of each of them. The dominant tone of the order and the taste of electors changed together. But, of course, the Franciscanness of Angelo da Rieti was not the only kind available, important, or desired in the area of Rieti in the period during which his episcopate fell.

Of the learning of this whole series of bishops it is not possible to say a great deal. None seems in his lack of learning to have been a disgrace to his place and time. None seems to have been a scholar of long-remembered, clearly identified distinction, even though Rainaldo da Arezzo was a *magnus clericus* and *literatissimus*, according to Salimbene, and Raimond was called, by the anonymous author of the life of Cola, *un oltramontano granne decretalista* (a great decretalist from across the Alps); and Raimond's job, like those of a number of the other curialists, demanded real learning, although not necessarily much theology, and not all of it learning of exactly a university sort. Bishop Andrea, a curialist, a cardinal's chaplain, and a canon of Rieti, before he became bishop of Sora and then Rieti, was called *magister* when he was a canon. Bishop Pietro da Ferentino was called *magister* by clerks of the papal curia, and, as Carlo Polizzi has discovered, eventually had a library which included Avicenna as well as Thomas and Bonaventura.[126] The learning of the three Franciscans might be expected to have had a theological tone; and this is in fact not only suggested by Rainaldo's time in Paris, his lectorship, and his arguments concerning the burden of the episcopal office, but more somberly and in a way more seriously by Angelo's inquisitorial work. Bishop Giovanni Papazurri's thoughtfulness seems a learned thoughtfulness.

Besides members of religious orders and curialists, a third obvious category within the series of Rieti bishops is that composed of members of local baronial and patrician families. Two of the first three bishops in this period, Adenolfo de Lavareta and Rainaldo de Labro, were from baronial families established in the neighborhood of Rieti (if one accepts Rainaldo as of the family Labro). One of the last in this series of bishops, Tommaso Secinari, was a member of a family whose name came from holdings in the Regno but which by Tommaso's time had significant attachments and a family palazzo in the city of Rieti. The unsuccessful candidate Giacomo Sarraceno was a member of an important Reatine patrician family; Rainaldo Bennecelli's family may well have been quite similar to Giacomo's. Angelo da Rieti was Reatine, but of his family nothing can be said.

Patricians or members of baronial families from places other than Rieti are also present in the series: Giovanni Papazurri, Pietro da Ferentino, perhaps Jacopo if he was connected with the Pagani da Susinana (Forlì). Some of the stranger bishops came buttressed by satellite nephews (as Nicola seems to have been buttressed by satellite Cistercians): Giovanni Papazurri and Pietro da Ferentino again; Berardo, who came from the see of Ancona, with his nephew, another Berardo, canon of Ancona, who acted in Rieti as his uncle's vicar general[127]; Giovanni de Nempha. Biagio da Leonessa probably brought both Franciscans and at least one nephew, as well as men of Leonessa. Bishops without Reatine families could in a sense create them.

In spite of the local attachments of the bishops of Rieti and of their close connection with its chapter, only two successful candidates and one unsuccessful one were surely canons of Rieti before (and one not immediately before) their elections. Two more bishops, the two earlier Rainaldos, were quite possibly, and one at least quite probably, canons; and Ughelli, a very uneven witness even for Adenolfo, thought that he had been a canon of Rieti. Other bishops had, of course, been canons of other churches: the elect Gentile, of Capua; Jacopo of Toul; the unsuccessful Nicola Raynoni (like Giovanni Papazurri) of the Lateran.

Seven of these bishops of Rieti, however, had earlier been bishops of other sees: Gottifredo, Pietro, Andrea, Berardo, Angelo, Giovanni, and Biagio. The importance of the papal involvement of which they speak is amplified by the inclusion with them in a larger group of the bishops not translated but collated or provided and closely involved in papal and curial administration: Tommaso the Corrector, Jacopo, and Raimond. The period of the episcopates of these men, essentially the period from 1252 on, is clearly a period which is dominated by papal and curial bishops. That is the easiest and most obvious thing to see and say about the bishops of Rieti in the series from Adenolfo to Biagio.

It is perhaps more important to see and say that "papal and curial" is very far from being a totally or exclusively defining category and that the men who fall into this category are not all like one another. Saying that a man was a curial bishop does not tell you what he was like, nor does saying he was a baronial bishop or a Franciscan bishop. These are formal aspects of the man-bishop (as being a bishop is of the man); and the categories are not mutually exclusive: it would have been possible to have been a Franciscan baronial curial bishop, although none existed at Rieti; and baronial fits more easily with the other two categories than they fit with each other. Probably more important, and this is clear from the Rieti examples, it is quite possible to be both local and curial or both local and Franciscan.

No matter how the historian plays with categories, however, they remain, as categories, artificially secure in their defining of individual men. As imperfectly visible as are the bishops of Rieti in the period between Adenolfo and Biagio, they, at least the more visible of them, like Pietro da Ferentino, force their observer to confess that the things one can see about them are often, at least superficially, incompatible. What he can see may easily tempt him to misleading categorization.

Stanley Cavell wrote, "A statue, a stone, is something whose existence is fundamentally open to the ocular proof. A human being is not."[128] Certainly a thirteenth- or fourteenth-century bishop of Rieti is not.

CHAPTER SIX

The Chapter of Rieti

The bishops of Rieti were transients. Although many of them died in their see, and although some of them had long episcopates, continuity at Rieti, the maintenance of Reatine identity and tradition—at least before the episcopate of Biagio and the Black Death—did not depend upon them. Continuity at Rieti resided in the chapter. These men, twenty and later twenty-one of them, when their complement is visible, full, and not bloated, were as a group the continuing "church of Rieti."

The medieval chapter of Rieti is never so visible and never does it display such a strong sense of its own position and importance as in the vacancy of the see after the death of Bishop Tommaso Secinari on 5 September 1341. From that day until they became aware of the provision of Tommaso's successor, the official date of which provision was 5 August 1342, the canons as chapter ruled the diocese. They obviously felt powerful. They had, during the previous vacancy, succeeded in electing Tommaso one of their own number. Although Tommaso had clearly not proved a completely satisfactory bishop from their point of view, they intended to elect again.[1]

The chapter's sense of its own dignity is revealed in a group of impressive documents from 12 September 1341 which record its reception, approval, and acceptance of the oath of the elect of another body of collegiate canons, Santa Maria in Pantanis di Montereale, in the northeastern part of the diocese. Santa Maria in Pantanis was vacant through the death of its secular abbot, just as Santa Maria Rieti was vacant through the death of its bishop, and the canons of Santa Maria approved the new abbot who had been elected by the canons of Santa Maria in Pantanis, a clerk of Montereale named Nerio di Pietro, and had been presented in phrases similar to those which they themselves would use to proclaim the correctness and validity of their election of a succeeding bishop on 30 September.

After the proper burial of the dead abbot, the chapter of Santa Maria in Pantanis had been summoned by the canon who was *prior* and *antiquior, dompnus* Giovanni Tostani, who was in sacred orders; they had elected *sponte, communiter, et concorditer* Nerio and *unanimini uoluntate* sought his confirmation. No one having appeared to oppose the election, and the election having been found correct and canonical, and the elect of appropriate learning, age, of legitimate birth, laudable life, and *honeste conuersationis*, and in other ways *ydoneus*, this suitable man whom the chapter of Rieti, formally, hoped and firmly believed would govern his church well and defend its rights was confirmed as abbot; and the chapter ordered that he would be installed by a commission which included the chapter of Rieti's vicar in the *terra* of Montereale. This action occurred in the sacristy of the church of Rieti before witnesses including Filippo da Siena, who is identified as sometime vicar general of the bishop of Rieti.[2]

Upon receiving the chapter of Rieti's approval, the new secular abbot swore an oath on the Gospels promising reverence and due subjection to the bishop and chapter of Rieti, swore not to give aid to their enemies, promised to pay proper procurations and receive messengers of the bishop and chapter, and to come to synods called by the bishop or church of Rieti. Nerio further swore to defend the rights and property of his own church of Santa Maria in Pantanis. Then a few days later, on 17 September, *in Missis et ante Tertiam*, with witnesses including Filippo da Siena, the chapter granted Nerio a dispensation under the terms of Boniface VIII's constitution *cum ex eo*.[3] Nerio was permitted (notwithstanding any prohibiting canons) to go away to study. And for the period of his absence the chapter, under its ordinary authority, *sede vacante*, made as Nerio's vicars three priest canons of Santa Maria in Pantanis, dompno Giovanni Tostani, dompno Rizardo, and dompno Lorenzo, that they might serve the religious needs of the church.

In this affair each of the two properly functioning chapters seems to have done its job well. The ruling chapter of Rieti accepted the elect of Santa Maria in Pantanis, invested him in office, ordered his induction, extracted from him an oath of loyalty and office, and then gave him permission under the appropriate constitution *cum ex eo* to study for up to seven years so that his study might (when he came back finally its priest in orders) bring its fruits to the church of God, and presumably bring learning in the mind of a Montereale clerk back to the Montereale corner of the diocese of Rieti.

Here can be seen the same high seriousness in office and the same concern for the cure of souls as in the chapter's treatment of the lords of Mareri, when three of those powerful barons presented clerks to livings of which they were patrons, in the churches of San Giovanni di Castrovetere (Castel di Tora) and Santa Maria de Illicis. On 21 April 1342 the chapter instituted the presentees but only after, on the preceding day, preparing a new constitution for the two churches which insisted that there be one rector priest and one clerk to assist him in each of the two churches, so that the parishioners of the churches should not be defrauded of the divine offices or the administration of the sacraments.[4]

On Sunday 30 September 1341, after the Mass of the Holy Ghost had been solemnly celebrated and before terce, as they had prearranged, the chapter of Rieti met *ad electionem siue postulationem* of their future bishop.[5] In the process of the election the canons revealed their order and position more clearly than was usual for them. They had chosen to elect by scrutiny, and they chose three among themselves as *scrutatores*: Giacomo di don Tommaso, subdeacon; Magister Matteo di magistro Biagio, subdeacon; and Francesco de Ofangan' (Ofagnano) di Aquila, subdeacon. Each of the *scrutatores* swore to his two colleagues that he chose a nominee most suitable and useful to the church of Rieti and that he consented to and voted for the election of Don Nicola Raynoni "de Urbe" (of Rome), who was in sacred orders and of suitable age. Then after an appropriate interval the *scrutatores* summoned each of the other twelve canons present to take an oath of consent to the election of Nicola: Don Tommaso Cimini ("de Ciminis"), *prior dicti capituli*, archpriest of San Pietro di Cornu; Don Raynaldo da Piagge ("de Plagis"), priest; Don Giovanni da Ponticello ("de Ponticillis"); Don Giovanni of Rome ("de Urbe"), subdeacon; Don Berardo Secinari ("de Secenario"), subdeacon and secular abbot of the church of Santa Croce Lugnano; Don Angelo di don Paolo, subdeacon, and secular abbot of Sant'Eleuterio near Rieti; Don Matteo di don Paolo, priest and provost of Santa Cecilia, Rieti; Don Deodato da Terni, subdeacon; Don Giovanni di don Capo, subdeacon and archpriest of San Giovanni Evangelista, Rieti; Don Gentile Fuctii de Labro, subdeacon, who also swore as proctor for Don Giovanni de Thocca, deacon; Don Nicola di Pacicto, subdeacon; Don Neapuleone di don Paolo, subdeacon. This is the group of men then resident who in September 1341 bore the burden of Rieti tradition: two priests, a deacon, twelve subdeacons, and two men presumably not in major orders—seventeen men out of the possible twenty-one whom the established prebends could support. Members of the group included the provost of one, the secular abbots of two, and the archpriests of two other collegiate churches (all but one of these in the city of Rieti or its neighborhood). But only one of these dignitaries, the provost, was an ordained priest. Among the canons were a Cimini, a Secinari, and a Labro, as well as canons identified as being from L'Aquila, Terni, and Rome. They had no permanent obedientiaries or officers among them, no official structure within the group, only a *prior* and *antiquior*, the longest installed among them, and a diversity of order and external office.

The continuity that these men represent, that this body represents, is remarkable. The two senior among them, Tommaso Cimini and Giacomo di don Tommaso, had been canons in 1307; and although Tommaso Cimini would be dead and his prebend be competed for by 25 October 1344, Giacomo di don Tommaso would still be alive, after forty years as a member of the chapter, in August 1347.[6] *Magister* Matteo di magistro Biagio, Rainaldo de Piagge, and Giovanni da Ponticello had been members of the chapter, or at least presented to canonries, since 1313, 1319, and 1321.[7] Of these 1341 electors five would survive the Black Death and be recorded with unusually fully extended names in 1349: Giovanni Massarone de Urbe; Deodato di magistro Nicola da Terni; Giovanni di don Caputosti de Poggio (Bustone); Angelo di Paolo "de Urbe"; and Francesco da Ofanio.[8] They would have been joined before the plague by Liberato Beralluctii, who would, with Deodato (and Ballovino di magistro Giovanni), still be a canon in 1379; and Deodato would then have been a canon for at least forty years.[9]

Impressive as are these mid and late fourteenth-century stretches of time in office, they are matched and even in some cases surpassed by those of the thirteenth and early fourteenth centuries. Most striking is the case of Bartolomeo Alfani. On 20 December 1318 he, Bartolomeo di Oddone Alfani, made his will, in which he declared himself healthy of body and in which he left 25 florins for the fabric of the church of Rieti, his church, not far from the family palazzo which had been called, in his youth, the palazzo "filiorum Alfanorum." The first evidence of Bartolomeo Alfani as a canon is from 27 October 1249, in a list in which he joins another Alfani canon, Oddone, a canon since 1225. (And in his age he is joined by Rainaldo, Rainallo, Alfani, a canon from 1285, seemingly dead by December 1313, but whose 1307 prebend, unchanged, was listed as being held by Rainallo Alfani in 1349.) Bartolomeo is not visible in the early 1250s, but from the end of the decade he appears regularly.[10] The combination of evidence makes it seem likely that Bartolomeo was the long-haired clerk with whom Salimbene's Rainaldo da Arezzo had to deal, and that Bartolomeo may have been somewhat closeted during the reforms of the early 1250s. If this conjecture is correct, Bartolomeo in his person ties together the reforming capitular ordinances of Rainaldo da Arezzo and the reforming diocesan synodal statutes of Giovanni Papazurri. His tenure may have been interrupted, but, that aside, he would have been a canon for sixty-nine years. Bartolomeo Alfani's colleague, Bartolomeo Bontempi, who was favored as the son of a *familiaris* of Pope Innocent IV, was a canon of Rieti at least from 1261 to 1324, for sixty-three years.[11] Another canon from this period lived as canon fifty-one years, another for forty, another thirty-eight, three more for thirty, another twenty-seven, two more twenty-five, three more twenty-three, and another for twenty years.[12]

The case of Giacomo (or Jacopo [Jacobbus]) Sarraceno is peculiar. The name appears in a list from 10 July 1220 which also includes that of Teballo Sarraceno, familiar as Saint Francis's Reatine host. *Jacobbus* appears as early as 1181; *Jacobus* as late as 1280. In the 1280 list Jacobus's is the first name (as it had been in a 1261 list) which, because of a by then developing usage, reasonably suggests that he was the senior canon. In the 1270s seven of his co-canons had tried unsuccessfully to elect Jacobus their bishop.

There were surely two of these Jacobi-Jacobbi, although the change in spelling of their names should not, it will be clear, be taken too seriously. One was the disappointingly inarticulate witness in the San Leopardo case, the other the unsuccessful candidate for the bishopric; both bore a patrician surname important to the affairs of the church of Rieti at least since the mid twelfth century when, in 1152 for example, a Rainaldus Sarracenus had given his whole inheritance to the church, or to its Virgin, through the hands of Bishop Dodone. The new Jacobus may be he of the 1238 list, or of the 1246 list, or possibly only he who appears after the 1253 list when Jacobus is absent from chapter because *infirmus*. If the one hundred Jacobus Sarracenus years are rightly broken in two, the canon who represented Bishop Rainaldo as his proctor against San Silvestro in 1233 would have been the earlier of the two, a canon evidently since at least 1181.[13] However the breaks are made, the

Sarraceno canons like the Alfani canons establish family as well as personal continuity.

At least six of Jacobus's co-canons in 1238 had been canons since 1230. One of these co-canons, Berardo Salecti (Salectus), had been a canon since 1220; and the tenure of a second, the priest Rainaldo, stretches back into the indefinite past.[14] Another of these co-canons, Berardo Salonis, will testify in 1246 that he has been a canon for twenty-four years and more; and, in spite of the fact that one is naturally cautious about exact numbers of years remembered in testimony establishing long custom, and in spite of the fact that Berardo will still be a canon in 1261, in this company Berardo's testimony does not seem at all incredible.[15]

Their longevity gives an additional resonance to those canons repeatedly called to give witness in thirteenth-century Rieti cases at law. But their presence as witnesses and the acts they remember, as well as those actions of theirs which other witnesses remember, bespeak clearly the busy involvement of members of the chapter in the running of the church's business, their being of its, the church's, very essence. So speaks the witness canon the priest Paolo (a central figure in the history of the church in the early thirteenth century) in his memory of thirty years as canon in the church when he gives testimony in the Santa Croce case.[16] So speak others when they tell of his—and the priest Rainaldo's, and Magister Enrico medico's, and Siginulfo's—raid on Santa Croce property. So speak the actions of the canon Siniballo Mareri, fighting, physically, with a Cistercian *conversus* from San Matteo. These canons clearly thought of themselves as, or as of, the church of Rieti; and they thought of their long memories as its long memories.

The priest Paolo's position in the early thirteenth century is echoed by that of the canon Corrado de Murro (Morro) in the fourteenth century.[17] Canons acted as *camerlenghi*, or supervised the appointments of camerlenghi and *santesi* or sacristans. As temporary office holders they were *obedienciarii*. So in 1278 Palmerio Berardi, canon and obedientiary, is responsible for executing the bishop's and chapter's warning of excommunication to Paolo Lambertini, the constable of the Reatine militia, and he is aided in this difficult job by Ventura Rainaldi his co-canon, as yconomo and proctor ad hoc.[18] Rainaldo Beraldi is seen acting as obedientiary as well as yconomo and proctor of the church in 1253, dealing with a problem of provision which had taken a Rieti representative to Assisi, and the basilica of San Francesco, to present himself to a papal advocate, and which in Rieti brought together Bishop Tommaso and the whole chapter, except those specifically mentioned as absent, as on the last day of August were Jacobus Sarraceno, who was sick, and Magister Nicola, *quod non erat tunc Reate*.[19]

In 1246 in an examination of witnesses meant to establish that two men were *vassalli* of the church, an examination supervised by the canon Rainaldo Fatuclus, the canon Angelus Angeli Mathei recalled the time when "erat obediential' " of the church and had gone to Poggio and San Sebastiano on the church's business and had received *pro seruitiis* chickens and meat, bread and wine, as the *vicecomes* (the church's sheriff) had said; and it had happened often; and he then recalled the events of a certain year, *quodam anno cum esset obediential'*.[20] In another document, dealing with Cerchiara, witnesses recall the canon Berardo Moysi, in the presence of other canons in the cathedral sacristy, receiving, with Bishop Giovanni (so probably in the late 1230s) the oath of a *vassallus*, and the man's then placing his hands between those of the canons and of the bishop; and they recall, too, the church's *vicecomes*, Gregorio di Egidio, then, in the same week, investing the tenant in the tenement.[21] Or in a later and more routine action on 26 February 1337, in the vacancy following the death of Bishop Giovanni Papazurri, in the presence of Francesco, the chapter's vicar general, as a document of Matteo Barnabei records, the chapter elected as their chamberlain, camerlengo, and yconomo and proctor, for a term to last to the following first of July, their co-canon Berardo Secinari.[22] These canons worked for their church. They were its temporary officers, although they were not its only officers.[23] Their memories were furnished with their acts and observations from time in office.

Over the two centuries not all of the canons were present every day for Mass and vespers and chapter meetings. Not all of them were even always resident, although very few, if any, were never resident. But day after day, year after year, decade after decade, the majority of them sat together, prayed publicly together, and discussed business together. With their meetings, their memory, and their talk—always with some among them who remembered and carried forward the past—they form a tough, continuing, constantly renewed braid (of themselves, of lives, of memories) which connects 1181 to 1378. When in 1209 Girardo di Rainaldo da Canetra made a gift to Bishop Adenolfo "per te, ecclesie maiori Sancte Marie de Reate, et canonacis ipsius ecclesie" he was making a gift to an institution which would remain intact, particularly through the existence of these canons (with whom some of their bishops, at least early on, considered themselves co-canons) right down to the death of Bishop Biagio.[24]

The reason for the canons', for the chapter's, existence was the sacred cult, the prayers which they offered, at the great church at the diocese's center, for the living and the dead. Their primary activity was prayer, and their secondary but much absorbing activity was the management of property which would support them, and their clerical colleagues, and so make possible the continuance of that prayer. This connection is made unusually explicit and clear in a document prepared by Matteo Barnabei for, unsurprisingly, Bishop Giovanni Papazurri in 1315, which records Giovanni's diverting of the income from two rural chapels, San Pietro in Campo and San Marone, without cure of souls, people, or parish, to the camera (then insufficiently provided for) of the cathedral church, for commons, for distribution to the clergy who participated in the services of the canonical hours. To this arrangement Bartolomeo Bontempi swore his adherence for himself and the other fourteen canons present.[25]

Provisions for that distribution of property which supported the cult, and which with the cult formed the nexus that held the chapter together and gave it its shape, did not, as one would not have expected it to, always produce unanimous agreement. Individual canons at times made clear their disagreement, even at times when the point at issue was not, or not obviously, proprietary: "Arekabene, canon of Rieti, present at chapter, objected to the arrangement"[26]; "Deodato of Terni, canon of Rieti, present in chapter, expressly objected to this article"[27]; "Ventura Rainaldi objects to this division of benefices."[28] In the other direction, in 1320 the chapter appealed to three Anagni papal delegates that in a specific matter their colleague, Corrado de Murro and his associate's jurisdiction, ordinary or delegate, not be recognized.[29]

But unanimity was stressed. In their sealed document of 1280 the chapter, or its member canons, acted *unanimiter et concorditer*. The duality of their grammar expresses their indissolubility: "Nos capitulum Reatinum ad hoc specialiter congregati [then follow twelve names and the two adverbs and then] facimus, constituimus, et ordinamus." Then, "inter nos deliberatione prehabita diligenti, pro utilitate, bono statu et tranquillo ecclesie nostre seruando in posterum," they make two of their co-canons, Angelo Angeli and Berardo de Podio, one of whom is in the nominating list and one not, their proctors with very broad powers, but with the stipulation that if either should be away from Rieti for more than three months he should be replaced. And the document gives a kind of warranty by granting the canon priest Giovanni de Podio the right to excommunicate any canon not abiding by the agreement to which all had sworn on the Bible and on the holy relics placed on the altar. And to the document the chapter affixed its seal in white wax, which survives, with its seated Virgin with the Child on her left arm, and the device SIGILLUM CAPITULI REATINI (see plates 26, 27).[30] This document with its common seal, its union of singular and plural, its acceptance of common deliberation and common purpose, is a clear and self-conscious statement of institutional existence (but with an awareness of individuals within the institution).

The appearance of the common chapter seal in 1280 and the document which carries it suggest a natural, almost organic growth, an evolution of the chapter into cohesive awareness around their relatively unchanging cult, focused on Mass and vespers, in their church dedicated to the Virgin. In some major and real way this idea is not only compelling but probably exact. But it needs to be adjusted to include the awareness of a locally stunning, reactionary experiment into which, in the months between February 1259 and October 1261, the chapter had been forced, an experiment through which, or part of which, at least eight of the 1280 canons had lived as canons.[31] The reformation of 1259 was a response to and a reaction against an earlier reformation. As early as the pontificate of Honorius III an effort had been made to divide the chapter's *mensa* from the bishop's *mensa*.[32] Disagreements about the division of income between bishop and chapter, however, continued to be disturbing particularly, evidently, during the episcopate of Bishop Giovanni. In 1238 bishop and chapter were required to send to the papal curia suitably instructed persons prepared to make composition with the other party's representative to resolve recent disputes between the two over division of property; in the following month the chapter commissioned four proctors.[33] In June, in spite of some chapter objections to detail, Gregory IX supported a resolution to the difficulties which had been proposed by Rainerio cardinal bishop of Ostia, who had been commissioned to investigate and act in this matter. All of that part of the income of the church of Rieti which had previously been treated as common income was to be divided into four parts, three for the chapter, one for the bishop. The bishop's purely episcopal and jurisdictional rights were to remain intact. Procurations to papal legates and nuncios were to be shared equally by bishop and chapter. The composition was to be put into effect by the bishop of Terni.[34] The chapter continued to object, and the pope made some modifications in detail, but in August 1238 he wrote a letter to the by then executor, the bishop of Spoleto, which maintained the general principles of the composition.[35]

During Innocent IV's papacy the principles of the composition seem to have been in effect and working. They were the arrangements, invisible in the story, within which the drama of Salimbene's Rainaldo da Arezzo was played.[36] This very common separation of episcopal and capitular income seems at Rieti very late, but it was certainly not unique in its lateness. At Vèroli, close to Bishop Pietro's Ferentino, a similar separation occurred at approximately the same time as at Rieti. But at Vèroli the composition included clauses which demanded the maintenance of the old communal life of the canons, an idea that, clearly, still had living strength in central Italy. The Vèroli document emphasizes the importance for the cathedral canons of the common life. It says that the canons' goods should be held in common, that they should eat together, and that they should sleep together in a common dormitory—and the last injunction is underlined in the text.[37]

At Rieti, after twenty years, Gregory IX's division was reversed. In a letter dated 12 January 1259 Pope Alexander IV wrote to the papal scribe Master Bernardo of Penne lamenting (in whose words one does not know) the corrupting effect of Pope Gregory's division on a community which had once eaten together in the same refectory and slept together in the same dormitory, so that bodies and wills were joined *unanimiter*. Alexander's letter ordered Bernardo to return the church to its pristine state (*ad pristinum statum*). Bernardo, with the help of four of the canons, *quatuor de canonicis fide dignos* (probably Berardo Salonis, Angelo Mathei, Rainaldo Beraldi, and Matteo Laurentii—of whom only Angelo Mathei, quite surely one of the four, survived to be active in 1280), set up an elaborate program for recreating the common state. Under pain of excommunication he ordered the canons to eat and live together, as they had before, forever: "perpetuo comederent et conuersarentur insimul sicut prius." The plan was completed before the end of February.[38] In 1260, with Bishop Tommaso's at least superficial cooperation, the reform was being implemented; although the bishop appealed to Alexander and then to his successor Urban IV particularly against the sanction of excommunication against those who opposed Bernardo's injunctions.[39]

Less than two months pope, Urban wrote to the abbot of San Pastore and ordered him to quash Bernardo's sentence, which had caused trouble, provoked excommunications, and perhaps even endangered souls, and which had been instigated, "sicut creditur, quodam emulo Ciuitatis Reatin (it is believed by envy or hostility for the see of Rieti [or possibly, envy of the city])." Urban's letter to quash specifically rehearsed the common eating and living clause: "inter alia demandauit ut perpetuo simul comedere et conuersari deberent in contradictores excommunicationis sententiam promulgando." Urban instructed the abbot to return the church of Rieti and its *mensa* to its pristine state (*ad statum pristinum*), that is, to its state after Gregory IX's reform. This return, Urban's letter makes perfectly clear, was a response to the appeals, legitimate appeals, of the bishop and chapter. And on the letter's dorse where the procuring proctor's name appears is written the name of Magister Andreas, that curial canon, Andrea Rainaldi, who after having been bishop of Sora, would become his fellow Reatine canons' bishop in 1286.[40] In whatever way it was inflamed by Christian inspiration, this body of Reatine canons, that of 1260, was not inspired to follow Christ and his apostles to the common life. The early fourteenth-century noble canon Giacomo de Labro, for example, would be free, as he sat to make his codicil to his will, to sit in the cloister of his own house; he need not live in a dormitory or even have a chamber in a common palazzo (*in palatio canonicorum*) of the sort that clearly existed in 1224.[41] Late thirteenth-century canons, like those of the 1280 document, need not, like the Vèroli canons, sit together to eat the pork and cabbages of their rents (and when they can be seen eating together it is not pork and cabbages). And, moreover, the eight remembering 1280 canons, whatever they thought about the significance of their common seal with its Virgin, cannot have been drifting naively into an unimagined communal life.

The Rieti chapter of the mid thirteenth century attracted reform. It chose Rainaldo da Arezzo to reform itself. But it caught the reforming eyes of Innocent IV and Urban IV as well as of Alexander IV—or the eyes of their curias. Perhaps the chapter was particularly disturbed. Perhaps the new order that came into being when the wars ended made disturbed institutions visible, or visible as disturbed. Or perhaps in a more general growth of institutional orderliness, only in part dependent on the wars' ending, institutions like the chapter of Rieti in trying to find an order for themselves were observed to be struggling and, sometimes by request and sometimes rather officiously, helped by observing outsiders who considered reformation their business.

In any case the chapter of Rieti attracted some numerically remarkable papal letters. In March 1253, supposedly after investigation, Innocent IV wrote telling the cardinal bishop of Ostia to declare the election of a number of canons invalid because, it was said, the total number of canons at Rieti had grown to fifty.[42] In April 1249 (in a letter of grace which still carries its silk strings and *bulla*) Innocent had acceded to the request of the bishop and chapter of Rieti; he gave them permission not to receive as canons any more men provided by a pope or his legates who did not make specific reference to the indult itself, this because the financial resources of the chapter could only with difficulty sustain the canons already present.[43] (And by this time the bulk of supporting income had already been divided into twenty parcels, for twenty canons.) And a March 1253 Innocent letter of grace (still with its silk strings), which talks specifically of the statutory limitation of the number of canons at Rieti approved by the pope, offers similar protection.[44] Innocent's letters by themselves would suggest that papal monitions about numbers were shields obtained by the chapter against increasing incursions by providing popes like Innocent and his successor Alexander IV. But a September 1263 letter from Urban IV points to a more local problem and does it in a letter of justice with hemp strings.[45] Urban annuls sixteen—*et plures*—elections, when there were no prebends vacant, elections of "illiterates and boys, nephews and other relatives of the canons themselves."

The evidence that remains at Rieti from Rieti is less numerically dramatic than are the papal letters, which (a reader must feel, at any rate) a paying customer could get to say anything. Lists of canons and narratives of their activities do not suggest exaggerated numbers, although they clearly show concern about insufficient endowment and interest in resisting expectancies—the appointment of canons before prebends were vacant to receive them. Expectancies did exist, in spite of opposition, and a uniquely long list of canons from 7 July 1253, contains twenty-two names, including those of the absent Jacobus Sarracenus, the sick Oddone Alfani, and surprisingly, in concluding, "filius Bontempis," presumably Bartolomeo, eight years before he begins his regular presence as a canon which will endure for sixty-three years—a negative notation suggests that his tenure in 1253 was at best an expectancy, and also it is possible that this could have been another son of Bonfilius, although Bartolomeo's 1254 letter concerning Majorca income, in which he is identified as a canon Legionen', is at Rieti—eight extra years which would stretch Bartolomeo's presence at Rieti to a length of seventy-one years.[46]

The Rieti evidence fits Salimbene's description better than Urban IV's but it agrees with the direction in which Urban points. Family is very noticeable, as is, although not universal, identification by family and kinship. The twenty-second canon's name in the 1253 list is "filius

Bontempi"; among the other names are a Mareri, an Alfani, a Sarraceno, a Carsidonei, a Sinibaldi Dodonis, an Arcangeli, and two del Giudice. From about 1230 to about 1340 there is a heavy presence of patrician family names in the canon lists; they are particularly noticeable, of course, because they are recognizably significant. But the only occasional use for some patrician canons of surname or other family identifying device and the unsureness of identification when a patronymic alone is used mean, surely, that more patricians are contained in the lists than can be identified.

The use of a father's name preceded by a *domini* is sure identification of patrician status, but not of Reatine citizenship. A good example of both is Giovanni domini Capi, who is in fact Giovanni domini Caputosti de Poggio Bustone (but, also, the use of the external place name does not here, as it almost surely does in the names of contemporary friars, necessarily indicate place of personal origin). The use of a *magistri* before a father's name does not necessarily mean that the father was not patrician, but it suggests that being a patrician was not the significant thing about him. Of canons who are themselves called *magister* in the lists there are relatively few, men like Magister Salvus, Magister Andreas, Magister Nicolaus, Magister Andrea magistri Blaxii, Magister Tenetor.[47] They are strikingly apparent in the lists because they alone of the canons are not regularly called *dominus*.[48] This group, these *magistri*, sons and fathers, with the connections and skills that they brought the chapter, which on the surface seem distinct from those brought by Alfani and Pasinelli, form the second noticeable, coherent presence in succeeding lists of canons. The first group, the patricians, tied the chapter to local society; the second, the *magistri*, seems to have opened it to the outside world of papal court and university.

But one should be hesitant about drawing too sharp a line between *domini* and *magistri*, and perhaps be encouraged in this hesitance by the difficulty in drawing a line between two (or more) kinds of patrician *domini*, of placing these patricians. There would seem to be represented in the chapter of Rieti urban patrician families like the Alfani, the Pasinelli, the Sarraceno, the Carsidonei, and primarily nonurban seignorial families like the Mareri, the Secinari, the lords of Labro and Morro. It is possible even to imagine a shifting in balance and type of family representation as one moves from the late twelfth century to the middle of the fourteenth century. The Lavareta, from the greatest of the old families, disappear from lists before the lists have even taken on their regular form; and the Mareri, potent in the south diocese, do not appear after 1253. There would seem perhaps a shift away from really great baronial houses toward those of less grand stature; and at the same time there seems to be a disappearance of the names of accustomed patrician families, as if the patterns for expressing power or gaining wealth were changing in the fourteenth century.

But these are dangerous waters; identity is often uncertain. Petrus Mascii, a canon who appears as early as 1368 and at least as late as 1392, seems a stranger until one finds that his name can include a "de Labro." The "de Ponte" produced canons in the early thirteenth century and in the early fourteenth century; and would seem a normal Rieti urban patrician family.[49] But there is evidence that they are, or are connected with, the Ponte of Rome (whose name one would have thought came from Ponte Sant'Angelo where their Roman houses were), because why else would the best fourteenth-century description of the Roman Ponte's Roman houses be in the chapter archives at Rieti?[50]

To break the pattern again: the omnipresent Pasinelli seem completely Rieti urban patrician but in the fourteenth century in 1349 when the lady Buctia makes her will, she is described as the wife of Janni di don Gentile Pasinelli and the daughter of the by then dead Giacomo de Murro—those seemingly diverse families married.[51] How would one describe the Cimini? urban patricians in both Rieti and L'Aquila? merchants who sold animals in Rome? And the Secinari? arrivistes from the diocese of Sulmona growing rich on Rieti ecclesiastical incomes, very different from the Lavareta? But like the Lavareta they descend from a baron in the Norman Catalogue of barons, although a baron with a smaller holding and a step down on the ladder of vassalage.[52] This patriciate, heavily present in the chapter, cannot be too clearly defined and categorized. It existed. It corresponds with, seems of the same sort as, has names which very much overlap other patrician lists: the members of the consortium, condemned by Bishop Tommaso the Corrector in 1261, who held the castro of Colle Baccaro which was claimed by the church of Rieti; the lords of the army of Rieti in siege of Lugnano in June 1251.[53]

Among the members of the besieging army were not only Giacomo de Labro, Rainaldo de Montegambaro, a lord Rainaldo Beralli, a de Ponte, an Alfani, a Pasinelli, Tancredo de Roccha, but also Giovanni Tenitore.[54] The name Tenitore is worth noting because of its probable connection with the later Magister Tenetor, or Tenator Tenetore claimant of, external pretender to, a Rieti canonry in 1312, and a canon active at Rieti in 1315.[55] In 1308 Magister Tenator was a chaplain of Jacopo

Stefaneschi cardinal deacon of San Giorgio in Velabro, and the cardinal's notary, a notary by apostolic and imperial authority.[56] He would thus seem an outsider, with skills, favored by a powerful cardinal protector. But in 1308 he is called, at the curia, Magister Tenator of Rieti. This curial notary pressed into a seemingly resistant chapter (although he could be of obvious value to it) was actually a Reatine, and possibly one of important family.

Tenetor was one of many skilled Reatines who unsurprisingly found their way into the papal curia and the households of cardinals. Some of them came back to Rieti as canons. They belong, before the popes went to Avignon or had been long there, to a perfectly believable world in which the papal curia and papal Latian towns quite naturally meshed at a variety of levels from that of a Reatine cook in a cardinal's house to Pietro da Ferentino. When on 5 July 1289 the household of the papal chamberlain, Magister Nicola da Trevi, was temporarily in Rieti, there assembled together as witnesses in the houses where he was staying (*in domibus in quibus prefatus Dominus Camerarius morabatur*) the following men: Don Raynucio de Murro; Don Henrico de Labro, chaplain; Magister Paolo da Rieti, clerk of the papal chamberlain; Don Tommaso, knight, and Manfredo di don Pandulfo de Labro; Pietro Cimini da Rieti—they fit together, but who was who? Who was Reatine and who was curial?[57]

In October 1252 the chapter of Rieti was resisting the provision both of the papal scribe (*scriptor*) Nicola and of Andrea Pernatarum (Impernatoris, Impernatore), canon of Sant'Eleuterio, Rieti. In the same October Bishop Tommaso the Corrector, who had been accepted as arbiter by both sides in both cases, ordered the chapter, in separate decisions, to receive and induct both providees.[58] Nicola was a chaplain of Hugues de Saint-Cher, cardinal priest of Santa Sabina, a Dominican scholar who had taught both law and theology at Paris.[59] Nicola was a papal scribe and so in a position to help the church of Rieti at the curia; he certainly had already helped it by 1252.[60] A letter of 17 April 1249 from Innocent IV at Lyons to the Bishop of Todi, to reclaim for the bishop and church properties that had been appropriated by others after the death of the last bishop (Rainaldo Bennecelli), was not only written by Nicola but he acted as Rieti's proctor in obtaining it—or that is what the evidence of the exquisite little letter itself suggests: the *N* of the "Nos" of its third line, of the scribe's notation on the left flap, and of the proctorial dorse "N de Reat' " are identical.[61] Not only was he helpful but he was Reatine, and he would generally (it seems) be present in Rieti until 1278.[62] In helping he was, however, repeatedly absent from Rieti (*non erat tunc Reate*), but his absence at the curia could be a presence in many ways more important than would be his actual presence in chapter. His initial reception, that ordered by Tommaso, was of a stall without reception of daily commons in any case (and the rights of his particular position were protected by Alexander IV in 1257).[63] But the chapter's initial resistance to Nicola should be noted.

Andrea was clearly connected with Rieti before his provision. His surname, though of various spellings, was prominent in thirteenth-century Rieti. It was represented at the siege of Lugnano; and the pious bequests of Risabella Impernatore form one of the centers of thirteenth-century Reatine ecclesiastical history.[64] The dorse of Innocent IV's letter for Andrea suggests that Andrea was at Lyons and got it for himself; the dorse proctorial area reads (extended): *Andreas Pernatarum canonicus Reat'*.[65] Andrea was present as a canon of Rieti until at least 1271.[66] But he had been resisted.

The nature of provisions to the chapter of Rieti is made particularly clear, as is the curial-local complexity, by the cases of the Pasinelli canons. In 1252 the chapter was resisting the provision of Giacomo (or Jacopo [Jacobus]) Pasinelli. Not only was Giacomo from a prominent local family who had provided the chapter with a canon, Senebaldo, as early as 1181, but he himself was already a canon of Sant'Eleuterio Rieti.[67] After Bishop Tommaso the Corrector, again acting as arbiter, had ordered Giacomo's installation, he proved an active, resident, long-lived canon, present in chapter as late as 1280.[68] Within his very first year of office, Giacomo was already acting as a chapter official (of course temporary) in important business with his fellow and senior canon, Angelo Mattei, who had been a canon at least since 1238.[69] Neither before nor after Giacomo's provision does there seem anything even faintly foreign or non-Reatine about him except his election.

This impression is both intensified and questioned by the survival of a letter of 1290 from Matthew of Acquasparta, the Franciscan cardinal priest of San Lorenzo in Damaso, about a later Pasinelli canon, Oddone.[70] Oddone is called, in the genitive, "Oddonis nati Nobilis uiri Phylippi de Pasinellis de Reate militis, capellani Venerabilis patris domini M. Sancte Marie in Porticu diaconi Cardinalis." Cardinal Matthew of Acquasparta's letter written to the bishop (Andrea) and chapter of Rieti responds favorably to a petition read by the cardinal to Pope Nicholas IV and approved by him, a petition that requested that Oddone, who had been provided to a canonry, in expectation, of the church of

Rieti, and by apostolic authority admitted to the distribution of daily commons, like the other expectant canons in that church, be admitted to them in spite of the constitution newly published by the bishop and chapter and the oath then taken.

Matthew's letter exposes the papal breaking of the chapter's resistance to expectancies and to the dilution of the commons, but it also exposes the mechanism used to insert into the chapter a new canon from one of the most capitular of all Reatine patrician families, one at a high level, in Lazio, because *miles* was a significant title there. It also shows that which connected Oddone with the curia, his being a cardinal's chaplain, the chaplain, in fact, of the Dominican cardinal, Matteo Rosso Orsini. So again the papal provision (not fully effective by the time of the writing of the letter) had inserted a completely appropriate (in terms of family and caste) Reatine into the chapter. But that Reatine, Oddone, was in another sense an outsider, a cardinal's chaplain (and so could have been, or something similar, Giacomo). And how had he become a cardinal's chaplain? Perhaps because of family connections. A complicated, but not very complicated, little machine.

How much papal provision, by the second half of the thirteenth century, was the rule rather than the exception in appointments to the chapter of Rieti is difficult to say. We see essentially only provision, but perhaps only it need have produced documents that would leave traces. In these cases popes seem to have provided men who already had or came to have strong Reatine interests and connections. It seems not unreasonable to think that this had become the normal and accepted, although not invariable and although surely expensive, way for Reatines to gain admittance to their chapter.[71] It also would seem from the preserved cases that the chapter regularly resisted provision (although of course resistance leaves record) and that this was a second, also expensive, part of the mechanism. The curia had become a clearing house, capitular resistance a check point, but the appointments themselves were of perfectly acceptable, even obvious, people. The limited selection available (amplified to include among others the cases of Andrea and Ventura Rainaldi, if they were originally Reatine) also suggests that a good, if not the only, way to move into a position to be provided was to become a cardinal's chaplain (itself a check of quality—and position).[72] When the cardinal was a member of a family with growing local influence, an Orsini, a Colonna, a Savelli, it becomes difficult to tell whether the power of the providing thrust is more familial-seignorial or cardinal-collegial.[73]

The growth of Roman great family power in this part of Lazio seems to have been contemporary with this shift to curial provision in the making of canons; but the shift itself must in some part be, reasonably, assumed, because the evidence for early appointments to canonries is essentially nonexistent. But it is nevertheless also possible that the change in canon's surnames or identifying names in the later fourteenth century, if in fact a real change occurred, is complexly connected with both growing Roman family power in the country and the absence of the popes.[74]

Roman provisions were not always successful. The check could work (and the chapter could be glutted). In 1256 Pope Alexander IV provided to the chapter the clerk Benencasa di Nicola, the son of a citizen of Anagni, and in 1259 (in a letter written from Anagni) he provided his own relative, the clerk Tommaso di Giacomo de Pesclo. Neither provision seems to have been successful. Anagni was not Rieti.[75]

Men who came from curia to chapter could be unsuccessful in quite another way. A surprisingly undesirable man, or a man who came to seem (or who was made to seem) surprisingly undesirable, could be made a canon. Of this phenomenon one outstanding example comes from Rieti. This is the case of Magister Palmerio Leonardi, who in 1251 was a clerk of the papal camera (or chamber), but in 1252 a canon of Rieti, and in 1261 condemned as an adherent to heretics.[76] Palmerio's trip from camera to chapter might make him seem an outsider, but surviving documents make it clear that he was not.

In July 1251, when he was described as *domini pape camere clericus*, Palmerio, acting in his house or a house of his in Rieti, was buying up property that had belonged to his father, Leonardo Berardi Nicolai, and to his dead brother, Giovanni Leonardi. Palmerio's sister (Donna Berarducia, married to Berardo Reatin') and his nieces (Giovanni's daughters, Tanfelice and Alorita, married to Simone Bart' and Pietro Toston') with their husbands' consent sold to Palmerio for 50 lire provisini their shares of the house in the parochia of Santa Maria (the cathedral) which had been Leonardo's, Giovanni's, and Palmerio's, along with other goods and properties, giving to Palmerio the right to give the property to any heirs or assigns he chose in testament, or intestate, in any kind of disposition he chose. (Palmerio was perhaps preparing for his return to Rieti as a canon.)

In January 1261 Magister Palmerio, by then described as a canon of Rieti, before the podestà of Rieti, Don Nicola de Antiniano, in the legally established way gave all of his goods to his son Giovanni, who had been born of Rainallucia, then unmarried but by the time of this gift the wife of Giovanni Calantre. Palmerio reserved usufruct for life but gave warranty to defend Giovanni in his holding. Obviously by this date Palmerio knew that he was in danger of being condemned as a heretic, and his property was liable to confiscation, so he alienated it in the podestà's presence. The document extends the picture of his Reatine family.

In fact in April 1261 the Franciscan inquisitor for the Roman province condemned Palmerio. The inquisitor had, his document says, listened to many witnesses and had been assured that Palmerio had often received heretics (*paterenos*) in his house in the Porta Cintia facing the cathedral. They had stayed with him and he had talked with them, listened to their preachings, done reverence to them; and they had practiced heretical rites in the house. Palmerio had commended their way of life and their doctrine and he had frequently said heretical things to many people, attacking the *ecclesiastica sacramenta* and the very fundamentals of the faith. On oath Palmerio denied all this. But the inquisitor had consulted as he ought with the wise, including Bishop Tommaso the Corrector (like Palmerio from Innocent's curia), and he had condemned Palmerio as a receiver and aider of heretics, excommunicated him, deprived him of all ecclesiastical benefices, and confiscated all his property real and movable, two parts of which property should go to the Roman church, and the use of the inquisition, through the hands of three chosen receivers (including Nicola da Trevi, the future chamberlain), and one-third to the commune of Rieti. All alienations (meaning that to the son, Giovanni) were canceled and called void. The house in which the heretics were received, with all its outhouses, was, according to the law, to be completely destroyed, never to be rebuilt.

Within the same year, in November, the podestà of Rieti, Nicola de Antiniano, at the instance of Palmerio's son Giovanni, acting with his mother, here called Rainalda, as *curator*, annulled and revoked the confiscation of Giovanni's property. He thus provided, temporarily, the effect that Palmerio had hoped for. And he showed, in spite of the commune's third, the commune's ability to oppose the inquisition.

In May 1263 and January 1264 Urban IV and his chamberlain each wrote to the bishop and chapter from Orvieto. The pope, perhaps prompted from Rieti, said that he would prefer that the church of Rieti buy Palmerio's former properties than that they should go into lay hands; he suggested a price of around 1,000 lire of Lucca. In fact according to the chamberlain the sale was made for 1,000 lire of Siena, of which 900 went to the papal chamber and the other 100 went to the Dominicans of Rieti, the receipt of which Fra Lorenzo da Todi (?), proctor of the Reatine Dominicans, attested.

Between the writing of the two letters, in June 1263, the chapter of Rieti met, seventeen canons, and made two of them, Angelo Mattei and Giacomo Sarraceno, their proctors for proceeding with the acquisition of properties which had once been Palmerio's or his son's. The canons, present and acting, included, besides the two proctors: Rainaldo Beralli, Matteo Laurentii, Pandulfo Carsidonei, Rainaldo Sinibaldi, Bartolomeo Alfani, Tommaso del Giudice, Leonardo Arcangeli, Magister Salvus, Giacomo Pasinelli, Palmerio Berardi, Giacomo Berardi Odonis, Bartolomeo Bontempi, Berardo de Guardiola, Andrea Inpernatore, and Nicola de Rocca Sinibalda. Giovanni di Pietro wrote their document. They met together and acted together to procure the property of their expelled member. Their coherence survived the eruption, an eruption presumably caused by a kind of religious intensity that their public prayer did not satisfy.

Obviously not all canons were always able to fit into and to stay content within the unending routine of public prayer and capitular business. Berardo da Poggio Bustone, papal chaplain and rector of the Massa Trabaria in 1283, seems to have chosen, or been chosen for, a broader world (a world he may have dreamed of when he was in the household of Ottobuono Fieschi, a cardinal distinguished in diplomacy, destined for a brief papacy, and death, in the summer of 1276). He broke away. But he did serious and responsible work for the chapter, as canon, before he went north to Massa Trabaria; and after a mob assaulted him and his household, on 23 December 1283, in the house in which they were staying in Mercatello, he, at least eventually, came back home to Rieti.[77] Of the canon Berardo di Matteo Infantis's residency at Rieti less can be said, although he was sometimes at Rieti. But of all those benefices of his which spread across and decorate the folios of John XXII's register, his home benefice was his canonry at Rieti. He was Reatine.[78]

Into this hearth and cricket scene certainly some foreigners intrude, particularly foreigners from Leonessa and Rome. The Roman bishop Giovanni Papazurri brought Romans, including canons, to Rieti, but the connection between the two cities was old and natural. Leonessa is a place not unconnected with Rieti and part of the territory called Leonessa lay within the diocese, but its specific connection with bishopric and chapter seems to have come with Bishop Biagio da Leonessa and is most obvious in the career of Ser or Don Terio Lalli da Gonessa (Leonessa) who was a canon by late January 1349 and stayed one for more than twenty years.[79] The presence of strangers from these two specific places suggests the ability of fourteenth-century bishops to insert canons into the chapter, whatever mechanism they used. It is also possible that the less clearly identified canons of the later fourteenth century had become less heavily Reatine in origin.

The chapter was, however, an extremely conservative institution in its composition, a place of localism and longevity. Its members need not, for their office's sake, respond to any modern impulse except the election of bishops, insofar as elections existed, and were modern. The kind of prayer they were meant to offer required no special skills or ordination. They were expected to be clerks, to have received the tonsure. They needed presumably to read, and to be able to read aloud. They would wisely know how to keep books. Nothing about their office or institution would seem to suggest for them the necessity of sensibility to religious change.

Into this institution on 5 August 1289, when he was given the kiss of peace and welcomed to his canonry by Bishop Andrea, came Bartolomeo di don Rainaldo de Rocca.[80] Bartolomeo is more sharply visible than most canons, and his knowable biography emphasizes, questions, shades generalizations that seem to emerge from the group biography. In 1259, thirty years before the kiss of peace, Alexander IV had provided Bartolomeo, using his full name, to the collegiate church of Santa Cecilia, Rieti, and had ordered the provost and chapter to receive him; the pope had done this, he said, at the instance of his *ostiarius*, Marco.[81] At that time Bartolomeo was described as a student from Rieti. Bartolomeo was still a canon of Rieti in 1319, although in that year he was recorded as absent from chapter in both February and November.[82] In that same year Guillaume abbot of Citeaux, from Citeaux, sent a letter of *consortium* to Bartolomeo accepting him into confraternity with the Cistercians because, he said, of the pious devotion Bartolomeo was known to have for the order and because of Bartolomeo's request offered to Citeaux through the abbot of San Pastore near Rieti.[83] Bartolomeo was given a share in the spiritual benefits of the order in his life and after his death, and a promise that at his death his name would be pronounced in chapter general as it would be if he were a Cistercian, and at the prayers and masses during chapter general.

The ancient canon, who had been a student in the middle of the previous century, was through the good offices of the neighboring abbot accepted as a *consors*, presumably as he contemplated his death, in the by then old Cistercian order. (And perhaps coincidentally when in 1292 Bartolomeo, *nobilis uir*, had been granted the prebend in the church of Rieti vacated by the death of Radulfo de Labro, the executor of the provision, who acted through his deputy, a canon of Sant'Eleuterio, was the then abbot of San Pastore.)[84] Eleven years earlier than his Cistercian letter, on 20 October 1308, Bartolomeo had received a different kind of letter of consortium from Cardinal Giacomo Colonna written in the palazzo of San Lorenzo in Lucina, over which church Pope Clement V had given the once deposed (by Boniface VIII) cardinal deacon care. Giacomo, who was, or had been, a man of both political and spiritual intensity, and also a man of some learning, welcomed Bartolomeo into the *consorcio* of his chaplains. Giacomo had responded favorably to Bartolomeo's request, he wrote, moved by the continued devotion of Bartolomeo's brother and his other relatives to him, Giacomo, and his house, "domum nostram," the house of Colonna (see plate 23).[85]

Bartolomeo was, then, a noble Reatine. He had once been a scholar or at least a student. Before he became a canon of Rieti, he had been provided to a canonry in the local collegiate church of Sant'Eleuterio. He was long-lived. His family had supported the Colonna, and he was made the chaplain of a Colonna cardinal (after he was a canon of Rieti). In his great age he sought and obtained, through the mediation of the local Cistercian abbot, those shared spiritual benefits of the Cistercian order offered to a *consors*.

Although there are in this biography particulars specific to Bartolomeo's person and position, and to the time, the long time, of his life, they do not contradict the sense one gets from the group of canons of conservative continuity. Bartolomeo's localness and his long tenure of his stall, at least thirty years, emphasize continuity. Yet in the organization of the clergy of the cathedral church there were in fact significant changes. The disciplinary constitutions, conservative in expressed intent, through which succeeding bishops attempted to ensure or restore the good order and fiscal responsibility of the chapter and to restrain numbers (although an overpopulated chapter is seldom actually visible) could themselves announce change. In December 1313 Bishop Giovanni Papazurri with the consent of the chapter officially changed the number of canons' stalls and prebends from twenty to twenty-one. He explained the increase in a general way with an *arenga* that said that the affairs of men were disposed by the nature of the times so that as it changed they changed.

But the immediate reason for the increase was much more specific, and also explained. Because of certain increased possessions and growth of income it had been possible to create an entirely new prebend and to receive into it, *proprio motu* of bishop and chapter, a canon who was in excess of the statutory number which had created an irregular and potentially dangerous situation. This situation had been prolonged when the bishop and chapter had granted income from the prebend of a dead canon (Rainaldo Alfani), whose prebend had been instrumental in the increase, to Francesco Papazurri (the bishop's own nephew) without changing the official number of canons.

In the recorded act, bishop and chapter change the official number and receive Francesco fully into their body. But at the same time they demand new rigor in respecting the statutory number of canons and forbid themselves and their successors *proprio motu* (by their own action) to receive any canon who would cause the number to exceed twenty-one. Again this document regularizes the existence of the twenty-first prebend, which had certainly already been formed by 1307.[86]

A much more critical change seems unannounced in the documents and may have occurred gradually. In 1371, besides the list of seventeen canons, there is a list of eight prebendaries (*prebendarii*), and a list of seven chaplains. In 1371 the cathedral church exists in three tiers. And the lower two tiers presumably were composed in large part of priests (or in the case of the chaplains men who were becoming priests). But the division between prebendaries and chaplains was not, evidently, a clear one. Of seventeen prebendaries listed in 1379, at least four had been called chaplains in 1371.[87] In a letter written to the chapter from Orvieto in August 1344 Bishop Raimond spoke of sacred orders and of the regulations issued by his predecessor, Bishop Tommaso, with the chapter approving, that prebendaries with priestly obligations should be priests in accordance with the principle that a man should have the orders appropriate to the responsibilities of his position.[88] In the 1340s, then, the chapter remained essentially a body of nonpriests: in September 1341, two priests, a deacon, twelve subdeacons, and two men presumably not in major orders. They had been joined by a relatively formal corps of men in higher orders of whom the great majority, at least of those visible, seem to have been priests, with fixed benefices, prebends to which prebendaries succeeded when they were vacant as canons did to their larger prebends.[89] The old hard-working priest canons, like the priest Paolo of the early thirteenth century, had thus, in function, been essentially replaced.

A crucial figure in this change was a man from a prominent Reatine family, the priest prebendary Tommaso Capitaneo, who was at the center of much of the church's activity, up to the time of his making his own will on 10 March 1320, and from at least the time when he can be seen, in the years 1293 and 1294, acting as the church's camerlengo, being made responsible for Giovanni di Pietro's receiving, as lay prebendary, his daily commons (although it is not possible to say at what point in this span of years Tommaso became a prebendary).[90] Tommaso's unusual career, his unusual self, hinted at by his position in other men's wills, perhaps made unduly clear to his contemporaries the value of priestly prebendaries. (The value of priestly chaplains is obvious: their job was to say Mass in chapels, a function necessitated by the development of commemorative chapels.[91])

The notary Giovanni di Pietro had been specifically designated a lay prebendary, and in 1293 and 1294 Tommaso was ordered to see that he receive the *cotidianas distributiones que consueuerunt laycis prebendariis asignari*, the daily distributions customarily given to lay prebendaries.[92] He became part of what could then be considered a group with a history (who were "accustomed" to receive something). By the time of Ballovino's bookkeeping in the 1350s no such group, identified and receiving distributions of commons, seems to exist.

Whether or not Matteo Barnabei was often called or officially designated a lay prebendary, he certainly held, eventually, a *feudum* (which in the mid thirteenth-century rearrangements had been described as a word commonly used in Rieti for a *prebenda*). On 23 June 1337, with witnesses including the chapter's vicar general Francesco, the canon Berardo Secinari, acting as yconomo and proctor of the chapter, in his own house in Rieti, ordered that a list of holdings (*possessiones et bona feudalia*: a house in Villagralli, thirteen specified pieces of land, a garden, part of a mill, and some unspecified other *bona* with their *vassalli*) given "to me the notary Matteo" be written down and registered *ad futuram rei memoriam*. Prebendary or not, receiver of daily distribution of commons or not, Matteo, Giovanni di Pietro's successor, had the equivalent of a prebend. But it was not the group of holdings which had been bound together and held by a previous prebendary who had freed it by parting or dying, it was the *feudum* which *tenuit Jannonus Berardi Blanchilli uassalis ecclesie Reat'*; it had been a tenant's holding.[93]

When in 1348 the priest and prebendary Ballovino became a canon, he took his prebendary skills and tasks with him into the chapter. But as the elegantly writing camerlengo he received his salary of 12 lire and was aided by *santesi*. Not only had the established administration of the church been clericalized, it had been ordered and professionalized. When Ballovino was succeeded as a literal bookkeeper in 1379, his successor Agostino was also a canon, so that even the change based on Ballovino's personal career seems to have been institutionalized.[94]

In the period of Ballovino's bookkeeping, in the 1350s, 1360s, and 1370s, both canons and prebendaries are unusually visible because of the lists in Ballovino's books which describe, particularly, their share of commons, depending upon the number of times they had been present in the previous month or two months for the chapter's celebration, in the cathedral, of Mass and vespers. Both groups seem predominantly, overwhelmingly predominantly, resident, which relative poverty and commons may together have ensured. Some of the prebendaries of late century were long in their prebends, Domenico da Leonessa at least sixteen years, Nuctio at least twenty-one. But it seems impossible to trace prebendaries' careers in quite the way it is possible to trace canons' careers. Early in the century one can sometimes find collections of them acting as witnesses, like the eight of them gathered on 7 February 1317: Tommaso Capitaneo, Giacomo da San Liberato, Matteo Pandulfoni, Francesco di magistro Janni, Matteo Petroni Petri Raynaldi, Vanni and Petraca Ambrosicti, Angelo da Cornu—all men valuable to the administration of this property-holding institution, not yet all clearly designated as priests—and although Accurimbono does not find himself in this list he should probably be added to it.[95]

Canons and prebendaries alike were in part supported by prebends, carefully arranged bundles of income-producing property. It is in the arrangement and rearrangement of these bundles that the late thirteenth- and early fourteenth-century canons show their most impressive expression of community, not the kind of community that they had rejected in mid-thirteenth century when they refused to return to the common life, but not completely different from it either.[96] These documents should not be read coldly; they are powerful statements of the desire for equity and the belief that equity is at least among some people achievable—that which thirteenth-century English legal documents should have taught us, and the historian of Siena William Bowsky has tried to teach us. This ideal of equity among canons, and it is not a little ideal, did not presumably eliminate expressions of personal greed or selfish (or functional) defense of property. When in the mid-thirteenth century, however, Cardinal Pietro Capocci had written to the chapter approving the reform that divided the old common *mensa*, he had responded favorably to their request, he said, pressed by the duty of his office, to support a petition that was just and honest, as both the force of equity and the order of reason demanded (*tam uigor equitatis quam ordo exigit rationis*). He may have been speaking in formulas, but they were formulas which gave words to the dreams of the righteous.[97]

In 1278 three canons, Angelo Mattei, Berardo de Podio, and Giacomo Pasinelli, who had been elected by the chapter to level and adjust and add to benefices, to make them equal, announced, and had written, their adjustments.[98] The assessors were not dealing with the entire income of the canons. The commons distributions that the canons received were by definition equal for equal services. Their incomes from private or family sources, from external benefices, and from salaries and stipends were not considered (nor are they now ascertainable).

The assessors dealt with a body of properties which itself has at least negatively describable characteristics. Some thirteenth-century chapters can be thought of in some ways as the extensions of the olives, onions, pork and cabbages, or urban flats, which seem strikingly present in their lists of sources of income and rents received.[99] By 1278 at Rieti investments of individual prebends are, in contrast, balanced, mixed, and unexceptional; so is the investment of the commons when it becomes visible in the later fourteenth century. Each late thirteenth-century prebend was, it seems, largely composed of pieces of arable land, planted, when planted, in conventional grains, and to these were added parcels of vineyard, income from tithes and tenant rents, and from mills. A noticeable part of Rieti income in its late thirteenth- and fourteenth-century maturity was from mills both in prebends and commons, presumably because of the flow of rivers near the city. By the later fourteenth century income from urban rentals is important to the commons because of a few pieces of particularly valuable property which the chapter held in the city, valuable because of their location and their availability for mercantile use.[100] None of these sources of income are extraordinary or surprising. Chapter income in the early thirteenth century seems rather different, at least if the types of income exposed in the dispute between San Matteo and the chapter are a reasonable guide; in the early thirteenth century the chapter had received an income in crayfish from the drying swamps and at least some income in leeks.[101] Payments in kind had not disappeared by the late thirteenth century, but they were less locally specific: meat, chickens, wax, eggs, bread, and wine.

The income, then, with which the canon assessors had to deal was essentially conventional agricultural income. Insofar as it was measured by land area it was measured in Reatine giunte, and they could be taken from one parcel and added to another, as could rents and tithes from groups of tenants, or regular days' or parts of days' income from mills.[102] The work of 1278 begins (or seems to begin) three decades of complicated analysis of income and adjustment of segments by the canon assessors of 1278 and their successors, which was extremely complicated, and made more complicated in the reading by two distinct difficulties with similar results: the reader is unsure what portion of the negotiations is preserved and present; she is unsure what portion of total income, even really total prebendal income, is being considered.[103]

These difficulties make certainty impossible, but it seems that the small, basic, central core of each income's source in the early years of assessment is, in measured land, about 30 giunte (probably not much more than 15 acres); by the end of the period of assessment (or this group of assessments) the basic core in giunte seems considerably larger, increased as much as three times its original size; but it also seems that in later assessments the giunte measurements are being differently applied and include giunte from which the income is very partial. Besides different standards of measurement (which should be connected with the likelihood of increased farming of income)—and always taking into account the possibility of different or different-seeming modes of recording—two reasons for the necessity of enlarged prebends suggest themselves, reasons that could succeed in changing the size of prebends either because of the increased amount of land which the chapter had procured, or because of the movement of commons land to prebendal land, or both. Greater prebends were perhaps necessitated by the likely loss in productivity of the arable land assigned to prebends (and the records from the 1350s certainly show a lack of productivity, which seems not to be new, but the historical depth of which is difficult to measure in simply local terms). It also seems likely that the increased superstructure of administrative mechanism, particularly provision, which when paid for allowed the same men, in type, to go on, in a new papal-governmental world, to get and keep canonries, demanded of those men sufficiently greater expenses so that their prebendal holdings had, virtually, to be enlarged.

In 1307 the prebends of the twenty-one canons are listed, and there follow those of the existing nine prebend-holding prebendaries and then a division of commons between bishop and chapter. It is an elegant and definitive-looking job. But, even though the canons had promised to maintain the 1278–1282 divisions for twenty years, who would expect a process of adjusting and equalizing that had lasted three decades to come to a definitive end? And certainly there is evidence that individual prebends were adjusted after 1307 and that there was some more general although minor adjustment in 1317. But there is also evidence that 1307 was surprisingly, in fact, definitive.[104] To the names of the canons holding their prebends in 1307 are attached the names of later canons, the men who held the same prebends later: Arecabene's will be held by Liberato (who will still be present in 1379 but will be a canon by 1347); Magister Simone di Giacomo's by the rich and possessioned Berardo Infantis; Berardo di don Nepoleone's by Cola di don Giovanni de Canemorto—who is the son of the chapter's heavily used legal adviser and who will be a canon in 1349; Fuctio de Labro's by Terio da Leonessa (a perhaps symbolic transfer); Bartolomeo de Rocca's by Ballovino.

The canons' prebends could thus be seen as sufficiently defined so that a prebend of 1307 was recognizable in 1349. Rather more startling information comes from a list of prebendal properties in 1349. The twenty-one sets of holdings for 1349 are identical, or essentially identical, with those of 1307. The 1349 holdings are a copy of those of 1307, although the names of the canons, with the exception of "Raynallus Alfani" who holds the eleventh prebend in both cases, are different (and it should be noted that although the canons who hold the seventh prebendary—Don Simone and Giacobino Galiocti de Labro—are different, the name of a future holder, Bartolomeo Mariani, provost of Sant'Angelo, is written by both the 1307 and the 1349 canons' names). 1349 was, however, a peculiar year; and a quick conservatism, which might then have been thought helpful in preserving past income intact after the ravages of the Black Death, may not have been consistently maintained. As the canons' prebends were maintained so at least were some of the prebendaries' prebends. Tommaso Capitaneo's prebend, for example, would be held by dompno Giovanni Corradi (or di Corrado) who would still be a prebendary in 1379, and seemingly the senior prebendary (and who had already been active for the church in 1349). These parcels of income-producing property have thus, by 1307, found a relatively fixed state.

It could be argued that a man, a prebendary, or canon, is what supports him, the source of his income. With this in mind one can look at the prebend and sources of income of Tommaso Capitaneo in the early fourteenth century.[105] Tommaso held to his own use of the church's

land 31⅚ giunte, with the addition of an unmeasured piece of land held
in common with two canons. This land was scattered over ten locations
in parcels of two, three, or four giunte, for the most part, but with one
larger parcel of five giunte in Lacu Maior and one of ten in Sanguineto.
(And it will be recalled that the modern Reatine giunta is measured at
1,617.32 square meters.) All the pieces of land, like almost all of that held
by the chapter, were in the center of the diocese close to Rieti. Although
the land was presumably of different nature and quality, all of it is spoken of as if it were arable except one piece on the Via Salaria which was
divided between *terram* and *uineam*, that is, arable, presumably, and
vineyard, certainly.

It could be argued in a slightly different direction that a man, a
prebendary, is the property he works with. In that case the early
fourteenth-century Tommaso, as camerlengo responsible for the distribution of commons, had a more diversified substance. He was involved
with twelve mills of which the church had between thirteen days and
one-half day a month. He disposed of income from gardens and "waters," rents from houses, arable, and a cluster of *ensenia*. He was responsible for income from *vassalli*. Part, at least, of Tommaso's mind,
the mind of this priest, must have constantly been occupied by these
properties. Their manager was, at least, one of the *inquilini* within
him.[106] But he was always also a Capitaneo; his name seems never to
have been written without his surname. His propertied person must
have been in part formed by Capitaneo properties and memories of
Capitaneo properties.

With some sense of what sort of institution it was and what sort of
memories it had, the chapter of Rieti at the point of its most visible and
controlled self-consciousness, during the vacancy 1341–1342, can again
be approached. But first it must be seen across one more document,
with some thought about the irrecoverable conditions which produced
that document. The document, from 6 February 1319, was composed
with what seems to have been much force of purpose and with an active
but almost uncontrolled anger which shows itself in a repeated harshly
bombastic choice of words and also in an almost exaggeratedly careful
arrangement into topical paragraphs. This arrangement fails to conceal
the document's composers' inability to order the document's responses
to correspond exactly with the stimuli which provoked them.[107] The
document must have been produced at a time of intense animosity between the chapter, or almost every member of the chapter, and Bishop
Giovanni Papazurri.

The meeting in which the document's constitutions were read and accepted with a kiss of real peace (*osculo uere pacis*) in the choir of the church, with impressive and responsible witnesses—Tommaso Capitaneo, his brother dompno Giovanni, Giacomo di Petrucio da San Liberato—was a meeting in which participated eleven canons, including some by now very familiar: Bartolomeo Bontempi, Corrado de Murro, Giacomo di don Tommaso, Arecabene Nicolai, Giovanni di Egidio, Matteo di don Angelo, Tommaso de Labro, Magister Matteo di magistro Biagio, Giovanni di magistro Andrea. After the meeting the constitutions were taken to the room, *camera*, of the absent canon Andrea di don Sinibaldo Rainucii, read aloud to him, and approved by him; and Magister Matteo received his kiss of agreement. And the process was repeated for Giacomo de Labro and Bartolomeo de Rocca. The realized importance of the document is made clear by the fact that although it seems to survive in only one copy, that copy shows that the document was authoritatively reedited in 1320, 1322, and 1326, in one case under the supervision of a rector of the confraternity of the clergy of Rome.

The constitutions deal with major general points, the protection and administration of the commons, the election and confirmation of "prelates" in the diocese. They also deal with very specific and particular points, but ones which, although sometimes obliquely connected, are connected with the evidently enraging disorder and malfunctioning and the believed misappropriation with which the constitutions, in general, are trying to deal. The room (*camera*) which was once that of the canon Lionello shall always be conserved for the work and use of the church and canons—a nice regard for needed room. Each year on the feast of Saint Vitus (15 June) shall be elected two obedientiaries who shall have the power to summon the chapter whenever it seems expedient to them, and after the year is over their jurisdiction shall expire; and on the same day each year there shall be elected one sacristan (*santese*) and one cellarer who shall take an oath to perform their duties without deceit or fraud. There is talk of the canons' black habit, of the income from woods, and from *vassalli*, of the incomes and prebends of specific canons, of absent canons. There is the insistence, which is an often recurring theme of chapter organization and resistance, that collations and confirmations belong to both chapter and bishop, coupled here with the declaration that should the bishop fail to perform his part of the pertinent obligation and privilege, the chapter should do it for him. There is caution that the bishop not take for himself the chapter's part of oblations: caution to be taken *ut voracitas et indiscreta voluntas Epis-copi nostri iura nostra obsorbere non possit* (so that the greed and undiscriminating arbitrary will of our Bishop shall not be able to gulp down our rights).

The mixed order and disorder of this document, its understanding of the importance of time, room, office, combined with its apparent antiepiscopal fury, its memory of the past (*cum semper sic in ecclesia fuerit ab antiquis temporibus obseruatum*) and concern for the future (*canonici qui de nouo recipientur jurent observare omnia*) make it seem a step toward 1341. But the 1319 document was prepared when the see of Rieti was full, with bishop, not during a vacancy as were the documents of 1341. Moreover, oddly, almost ununderstandably without further information, Giovanni Papazurri, in his chamber in Rieti, on 7 April 1320, before witnesses including the notary Paolo di Nicolucio Papazurri de Urbe, listened to these constitutions as they were read to him and added to them the authority of his approval.

On 24 September 1341, on the Monday before the Sunday on which the seventeen canons met for the election of their new bishop, fourteen of them met, again before terce, to pronounce, accept, and swear on the Bible to adhere to a new set of constitutions meant, as they said, to improve and to conserve the state of the church of Rieti. They were summoned by Tommaso Cimini, "prior et antiquior," and among their witnesses was Cicco di Giovanni de Bussata. The tone of the constitutions is clearly procapitular and antiepiscopal. It is best expressed by the eleventh and final constitution, in which the chapter announced that it revoked, quashed, invalidated, and annulled each and every constitution made in any manner by the bishop of Rieti against the chapter and canons of Rieti or to their prejudice, and that from that moment all such constitutions were void and invalid. The sixth of the constitutions points even more specifically to a target: any canon who should become bishop of Rieti (as had the dead bishop Tommaso Secinari) was bound to obey each and every constitution written above (number six) and below (number six); and so does the ninth constitution, which says that when any canon of Rieti at any time should be persecuted by any bishop of Rieti he should be defended by all the canons at the expense of all and with funds drawn from the camera.[108]

The second and third of the constitutions pronounce a capitular constitutional principle of continuing importance: confirmation of each and every prelate in the city and diocese of Rieti shall be made by the bishop and chapter together (*communiter*) because according to right and an-

cient custom confirmations pertain to both; and each and every collation or provision or confirmation to each and every canonry or benefice
or rectory of a church in the city and diocese of Rieti or pertaining to
it shall, as it should by ancient right and custom, look to the bishop
and chapter in common (*communiter*); and any future bishop who
should not respect this right shall be opposed in every way. A series of
constitutions seek to protect the capitular funds in camera, and the
proper receipts in camera (like that from the city of Rieti when criminous clerks were condemned) or dispersals from camera (as on the day
of the new bishop's entry to the city). The tenth constitution deals with
expectancies: in future no one shall be received as a canon of the church
of Rieti *sub expectatione prebende* by order (*proprio motu*) of the bishop
and chapter—no one shall be received unless a canon's prebend (*prebenda canonicalis*) is vacant; nor shall a prebendary be otherwise received; neither canon nor prebendary should be, unless the canon or
prebendary is created by the apostolic see—and constitutions and ordinances made about these things, long ago, and sworn to be upheld
by bishop and chapter, shall in future be firmly upheld.

Remarkably, a sheet of paper which contains a rough working draft
for these constitutions survives stuck between the pages of a fourteenth-
century book in the archives.[109] It contains more constitutions less carefully and fully stated than the copy of the actual constitutions. On it
some draft constitutions are marked "fiat" and some "vac"—the former to be used, the latter to be discarded. Among the constitutions to
be discarded was one which limited the initiative of future vicars general
during vacancies to summon the chapter to elections, which suggests
that one of the reasons for emendation was political, in the very local
sense, an effort to win more general support (and it may also suggest
that the constitutions were revised with the advice of the vicar general).
Besides the search for consensus the revisers of the draft may have tried
to get rid of points which were too particular and specific and insufficiently general, although the constitution concerning the division of
the woods of Santa Maria, the second point of the draft, remains as the
first constitution in the final version. Above all the draft physically exposes the existence of forethought, planning, consultation in the preparation of the constitutions.

Dissatisfaction with the behavior of the dead bishop Tommaso Secinari is written all over draft and final version. From these documents
it becomes apparent that those clusters of Secinari which are so apparent
in records from Tommaso's episcopate, and which seem rather charm-

ing family groups to the casual observer, are probably indications of heavy family favoritism, nepotism, to which his canons objected and which to them seemed signs of episcopal tyranny.[110] The canons' triumph in successfully completing a free election of one of their colleague canons had turned sour, and although their constitutions talk of future bishops who might be elected from among the canons of Rieti, in 1341 they did not make that choice. They did not repeat the mistake of 1338.

When capitular opposition to Tommaso is recognized, evidence of it and the reasons for it become more obvious. On 1 December 1341 three of the dead bishop's nephews and his brother (Arlocto di don Matteo Secinari, Marcello di Paparia Secinari, Angeluccio di Andrea Secinari, and Don Berardo Secinari), as his heirs, were ordered to return income from churches (the major church of Rieti and two collegiate churches at Rieti) in which he had held benefices before he became bishop and which income rightly belonged to the papal treasury.[111] Alive, the bishop's voice is heard arguing with a canon proctor, Gentile de Fuctio de Labro, who said he represented Giovanni de Tocho of Rome, ill and unable to be present: Tommaso said he knew that illness well.[112] Suspicion is naturally aroused by gifts given by Bishop Tommaso to members of his own family: like the gift inter vivos in early 1341 by the bishop to Cichano di Janni Secinari, his nephew, of a house in the parish of San Giovanni Rieti "pro magno amore et dilectione quem et quam habet in eum et pro multis et gratis ac acceptis seruitiis ab eo receptis et que sperabat recipere in futurum"; but it comes to be aroused also by superficially innocent-looking actions like the consent of the canon of Rieti, Nicola Pacicti, to the sale by his brother of a house to Berardo Secinari.[113] The chapter seems to have been observing an unscrupulous bishop building the fortunes of his country baronial family, come to Rieti, from the incomes connected with the church; one seems to be watching a family growing to power at the episcopal court.

But, having pushed this far, one must turn back a little; it is not so simple. The December 1341 revocation of benefices granted by Tommaso without participation and consent of the chapter specifically excepts some grants including those to Vanni di Arlocto di don Matteo Secinari, the bishop's great-nephew (who had in October exchanged benefices with canon Berardo Secinari in another suspicious deal); and Vanni was probably still very young, and being managed, or at least his father's acting as his *administrator* and *curator* in December 1341 would make that seem to be true.[114] The complication of the situation is underlined by the fact that the canon Berardo Secinari was a participant in the making of the new capitular, antiepiscopal constitutions of September 1341. And through all this it must also be remembered that Tommaso Secinari was a man, an ex-canon, whom the chapter had known well and worked much with before they elected him.

What can be said is this. In the vacancy of 1341–1342 the chapter's articulate self-consciousness was in some good part built around an antiepiscopal position. That position was connected with the behavior of Bishop Tommaso, who disappointed his former colleagues by acting in matters that they felt pertained to them without their cooperation and consent. Bishop Tommaso is seen to have been very much surrounded by his family and is seen to have favored them. But the full mechanism of all this remains hidden, although, beneath the obscurity, the device that produced this seeming complication could be as simple as a deal between the chapter majority and the canon Berardo Secinari with a faction he represented, which traded support of capitular reform for retained Secinari properties—and yet that would not explain why Bishop Tommaso appeared to the electing canons something he turned out not to be.

Although the actions of 1341–1342 are striking, they do not stand alone. In June 1335 the chapter had been insisting that confirmations of *prelatorum* in the city and diocese pertained *communiter* to the bishop and chapter.[115] In April 1347, during the vacancy between the episcopates of Raimond and Biagio, summoned by their senior canons, the chapter again met and made constitutions. Again they firmly opposed expectancies. They regulated commons. They insisted upon the right number of canons and prebends. The number of canons remained at twenty-one. But they reduced the number of prebends from fourteen to twelve, and they stated the desired orders of those twelve: six should be priests, four might be deacons, and four more subdeacons. Clericalization is limited, tempered, perhaps, by circumstance.[116]

Nor in the vacancy of 1341–1342 itself was the chapter restricted to one session of constitution making. In September of 1341, after the preparation of the constitutions of 26 September, a further constitution was put forward which forbade the exchange and permutation of benefices by canons and prebends. The canon Deodato of Terni, there present in chapter, expressly opposed that constitution and protested that it could not de jure be made. He protested the forbidding of a process important to himself and to the Secinari traders. Deodato's interests and those of the Secinari seemed to conflict but evidently could be resolved. By trading, on 1 October 1341, benefices with Vanni di Arlocto di don Matteo

Secinari, a clerk of Sant'Angelo di Lugnano, who also held other benefices, Berardo Secinari, the canon, who was already in September abbot of Santa Croce Lugnano, seemed to ensure not only Vanni's successful entry into chapter but also the continuation of a Secinari voice there after his extended tenure should end. On 1 October in fact Vanni was inducted into his stall.[117]

On 10 May 1342 nine of the canons met in the sacristy for chapter, and three more were represented by those present: Giovanni di don Capu and Gentile di Fuctio de Labro by Tommaso Cimini and Angelo di don Paolo by his brother Matteo. They approved constitutions including one which insisted that daily distribution of commons go only to canons actually serving at the day's offices.[118] There is ample evidence that the canons met in chapter and acted officially repeatedly during this vacancy.

The actions of one of these meetings reveals dissension and again the recurring advance of clericalization. On 26 September in a chapter called by Tommaso Cimini, *prior et antiquior* of canons then resident in the chapter of Rieti, the canons Giacomo di don Tommaso, Magister Matteo di magistro Blaxii, and Deodato "for themselves and other canons" whom they said they represented (perhaps Berardo Secinari, who was not among the twelve present) protested, with Tommaso Cimini present and understanding, that Tommaso ought not to cite, convoke, receive the canons of Rieti to and in chapter, since by right and custom Tommaso could not because he himself was not in sacred orders; but Tommaso, whose right to cite and summon had been preserved in the earlier commission to the chapter's vicar general *sede vacante*, did successfully cite, including that very day, with the three subdeacons objecting.[119] To this sign of attempted change Matteo Barnabei's son Severio was a witness as was his father, the notary. The reaction of Tommaso who had been a canon then at least since 1307 must be imagined; but it should be remembered that his senior opponent, only less senior than he was in the chapter, had also been a canon at least since 1307. Long memories observed this action.

One knows enough about some of these men to want to know a lot more. The canon Giovanni di don Caputosti de Poggio Bustone and his father, Don Caputosti himself, like the canon Nicola di don Giovanni de Canemorto and his father, Don Giovanni de Canemorto, were active at Rieti at the same time; and the two fathers were at times together as they were on 17 January 1341 in Don Giovanni's house in Rieti.[120] Did, for example, contemporaries say of the canon Giovanni how much he looked like Don Caputosti, or did they not? Were they thought of as a pair? the Caputosti? the Poggio Bustone? Was canon Giovanni's normally used patronymic Capo, Capu, Capi because that was Don Caputosti's nickname? Were father and son thought of as Reatines and Poggio Bustone only as an identifying name, or were they, or was one of them, thought of as men, a man, from Poggio Bustone? (Don Caputosti was sometimes present in Rieti, but he still had a personal interest in Poggio Bustone benefices.) Was either of them at all involved with the Franciscan hermitage at Poggio Bustone? or did either talk of local legends of Francis? A thing we do know about canon Giovanni is that by 19 September 1340 he was not only a canon of Rieti but also archpriest of the collegiate church of San Giovanni Evangelista (or Statua) and that by 14 April 1349 he was canon and abbot of the collegiate church of Sant'Eleuterio instead.[121]

Repeatedly, frequently, canons of Rieti were canons or prelates of other Reatine collegiate churches. Canons of Rieti who were prelates of other churches are often, in lists of canons, identified only by their titles in those churches: abbas (of Sant'Eleuterio), prepositus (of Sant'Angelo or Santa Cecilia), archipresbiter (of San Giovanni). They can thus seduce casual readers of those lists into believing that there was, for example, a prepositus, provost, of the chapter itself—a chapter which did not have that kind of structure.

This phenomenon of canons of the church of Santa Maria Rieti who were canons of other local churches as well was recognized by Bishop Giovanni Papazurri in one of his synodal constitutions: "Canons of our church of Rieti who make their residence in it are not bound to reside in other churches as long as they can conveniently assist at divine services in the other churches."[122] This connection with two local institutions (and two sources of income) is a defining, although not necessary, characteristic of Reatine canons. Their essence seems plural. Like many of their contemporaries they can often be described better by the external institutions which are connected through them than by personal physical characteristics: they present more the image of spiderwebs than those of lead soldiers. It would be easy and natural to assume that this pluralism at Rieti came simply from the need or desire to supplement inadequate-seeming incomes. But I think that this particular Reatine pluralism is much more integrally connected with the whole structure of clerical presence in the diocese than the stipendiary motive alone would make clear.

The diocese was very noticeably a diocese of collegiate churches.

Again it would be easy to suggest that these were simply the heirs of a *pieve* system (a system of collegiate baptismal churches into which the diocese would have been divided as into deaneries) that was no longer fully functional, that these colleges of clerics were what was left at this point in the growth of parish-chapel independence. But actually when the churches are examined they seem to have almost no characteristics that would make that seem an exact analysis; they suggest rather that at least here at Rieti it would be easy to pay too much attention to a romantically imagined earlier *pieve*-dominated church. It seems wise at this point not to think of the organization of the clergy and its income in the diocese of Rieti in the thirteenth and fourteenth centuries as a stage in an evolution from an unclearly visible past but rather to see what sort of thing it was in its own time. Italian observers could be easily misled by coming to it with their minds fixed on the *pieve*-parish duality, English observers with their minds fixed by the neat dualities of what Grosseteste supported and opposed when he thought of pluralism and absentee rectors. Rieti's is an entirely different design from Grosseteste's and its emphasis seems completely different from that suggested by the expected tension between *pieve* and *parochia*.

The diocese of Rieti was not one in which one man had one living, every church had its own rector-pastor. It was instead a church in which benefices and livings were slivered into many pieces, in which one clerk could be connected with several churches, and several clerks with one church. The important thing for its idealists and reformers, its serious men, was to be sure that sacraments and sacred rites were decently available to the men and women of every church and parish, at least after the importance of the sacraments had become fully realized in the fourteenth century. The disorderly seeming (from an external point of view) settlement of clergy and livings at Rieti was susceptible to the realization of this ideal.[123]

It should be said that Bishop Tommaso the Corrector's list of the churches of the diocese, so articulate and so mute, can be read, and undoubtedly has been read, as a list (or as including a list) of *pievi* and their chapels; and certainly even in the fourteenth century some churches in the diocese were connected with other churches and in some ways dependent on them.[124] It should also be said that at the very beginning of the thirteenth century, in the testimony of witnesses in the dispute between Ferentillo and Rieti over San Leopardo in Borgocollefegato, one *pieve*, that of Santo Stefano in Corvaro, seemed to function, or to be expected to function, as would a classical *pieve*.[125]

Children were baptized in its church; sacred oils were dispensed from it; local clerks were presented for ordination by its archpriest.

Santo Stefano is one kind of collegiate church, one presumes: the position of its archpriest is defined by him, but there is no emphasis on a college of clergy. But it is only one example, and it is chronologically and geographically isolated. Another kind of college, or picture of one, is that of Santa Maria in Pantanis di Montereale bowing formally to Santa Maria Rieti and receiving a formal bow from it in return in September 1341 at the presentation of the Montereale college's new abbot.[126] Both in its reflecting in a smaller way the structure of the cathedral chapter and in its explicit concern for the care of souls Santa Maria in Pantanis di Montereale may represent quite well a significant proportion of the collegiate churches with which the diocese was filled. And although there were certainly churches within the diocese, functioning and of service, which were not collegiate, the most striking characteristic of the diocese's clerical demography is the heavy presence in it of these chapterlike churches, a presence underlined by Giovanni Papazurri's statute which attempted to preserve the integrity of their commons (fifty years after the division at Rieti).[127]

Montereale like Corvaro is in the distant diocese; the colleges in and very near Rieti could be expected to have a specific consistency. Sant'Eleuterio, of which Giovanni di don Capo was abbot in 1349, is repeatedly visible. On 24 November 1336 the abbot, Andrea domini Sinibaldi, canon of Rieti, through his vicar, Vanni Ambrosicti, prebendary of the church of Rieti, summoned (actually physically through his vicar, Pietro, the priest of the church of San Paolo, Rieti) the canons of the church of Sant'Eleuterio, who were Magister Matteo di magistro Biagio, canon of Rieti and in sacred orders, and his brother Claudio. The brothers were to come, as was the custom, to chapter that evening to the church of San Paolo in Rieti, a chapel of Sant'Eleuterio's. There they received, as canon and brother, Matteo di don Angelo Tufi, canon of Rieti.[128] They gave him the kiss of peace and admitted him to voice in chapter and stall in choir. They committed his induction to his benefice to the archpriest of San Sebastiano of Poggio Fidoni (presumably Matteo Pandulfoni, prebendary and former vicar general) and Petraca Ambrosicti, prebendary of the church of Rieti and Vanni's brother—a close family group, a cathedral family group.

In December 1305 Giovanni Egidii (di Egidio), canon of Rieti and canon of Sant'Eleuterio and proctor for its abbot and chapter, acted in Rieti in front of a Reatine private house; he granted for three genera-

tions a piece of land from his benefice in return for a yearly combination
of wine and money which included a denaro each year to be placed on
the altar on the feast of San "Loterio."[129] In May 1339 the then abbot
of Sant'Eleuterio, Angelo di don Paolo, canon of Rieti, was before the
chapter's vicar general Francesco, archpriest of Santa Maria Antrodoco,
acknowledging a debt to Tommaso Cimini, and among the witnesses
were Matteo Pandulfoni, the archpriest of San Sebastiano Poggio Fidoni, and Angelo's own brother, the canon of Rieti, Matteo di don
Paolo, who was the provost of Santa Cecilia, Rieti.[130] In truth,
Sant'Eleuterio seems a kind of extension of the chapter. Its location and
history may have inclined it to be that. Granted to the church of Rieti
by Conte Senebaldo di Gentile in 1122, its church consecrated by Innocent III in 1198, it lay outside the city to the north, suburban but not,
surely, in one of those bustling suburbs which were, theoretically, crying
for the services of more clergy.[131]

An election at Sant'Angelo in 1329 shows a different kind of local
college, and one with a different history because Sant'Angelo had once
been attached to Farfa.[132] The provost of Sant'Angelo, who had also
been a canon of Rieti, Berardo di Nepoleone, had died and been properly buried when on 6 March 1329 seven canons of the church were
summoned by the *antiquior* canon, Beraldo (or actually as customarily
at Rieti, "Berallo") di don Egidio. One of the seven canons held the
proxy for two others, and one, Corrado de Murro, had been summoned
but did not come (and the document contains a rather more inclusive
phrase, *omnibus aliis canonicis absentibus*). Before progressing to the
actual election, *forma scrutinii et compromissi*, canons in any way inhibited, excommunicated, or not in sacred orders were warned not to vote.

The canons then chose two canons as scrutators; and they with two
recording notaries retired behind the altar to ask each canon who should
be provost. Lorenzo Petri Nicolai, the first asked, after having taken an
oath to choose and speak truthfully, replied: "Ego credo dominum
Jacobum domini Thome, canonicum Reatin' et ipsius ecclesie Sancti
Angeli esse meliorem pro dicta ecclesia et per eum posse utilius jura
ipsius ecclesie defensari, et adeo in eum nomino in prepositum Ecclesie
memorate (I believe that Don Giacomo di don Tommaso, canon of
Rieti and of this church of Sant'Angelo, is the best man for this church
and by him the rights of the church will be most usefully defended, and
therefore I nominate him provost of the church)." Each other canon
so swore and stated, except Giacomo di don Tommaso himself, who in
the same words chose Lorenzo. Giacomo, who was said to be of good

life and proper behavior (*uite bone et honeste conuersationis*), competent in learning and of legitimate birth, and in sacred orders, was, to the honor of the Virgin and Michael Archangel, declared provost elect.

Then the document, in a passage unfortunately in large part illegible, talks of notifying the abbot of Farfa (but not it would seem because of Farfa's interest in Sant'Angelo but because of its abbot's role as representative of the Holy See), then of announcing the election to the people, ringing bells, singing the Te Deum in loud voices. The formal witnesses to this election included a chaplain of Sant'Angelo, three canons of Santa Cecilia, two (or perhaps three) of San Giovanni Evangelista, others with names, and also *aliorum fidelium multitudine copiosa*. Of the canons of Sant'Angelo one was Sinibaldo Secinari, one Tommaso de Labro, and one Rainaldo di Matteo de Montegambaro (men who bore familiar and powerful identifying names). Of one of these electing canons more should be said. On 21 February Tommaso de Labro had prepared a document giving his proxy to a co-canon. He acted in Castro Labro in the church of Santa Maria, and among those present was one of the Alfani. Tommaso said that he could not safely come to Rieti for the election because of the deadly enmity between Guelf and Ghibelline.[133]

It is not coincidental, probably, that a canon of Rieti who would be central to the fight for accepting the importance of sacred orders at the time of the episcopal election of 1341 should have listened, as Giacomo di don Tommaso did, to a warning about their importance to electors at the time of his own election to the provostship of Sant'Angelo in 1329. This aspect of clericalization was also important to Bishop Giovanni Papazurri (bishop, at the time of Giacomo's election, at Sant'Angelo), or to his successor, who composed the statute which follows and is connected with and seems contemporary with that statute most surely, and, surely, Giovanni's own in the Paris manuscript. The statute's exact pertinent words seem worth quoting:

Ut clerici in collegiatis ecclesiis constituti habeant causam et materiam faciendi se ad sacros ordines promoueri, presenti decreto statuimus ut cum in aliqua ecclesia collegiata ciuitatis uel diocesis Reatine de prelatio aliquo imminet electio seu postulatio aliqua facienda, quod illi tantummodo uacantis ecclesie canonici uocem habeant in electione seu postulatione prelati qui sunt uel erunt tempore electionis faciende in sacris ordinibus constituti.

So that clerks in collegiate churches should have a reason for proceeding to sacred orders we hereby decree that in any election of a prelate in any vacant collegiate church in the diocese of Rieti only canons in orders at the time of the election can have a voice.[134]

Giacomo's election seems to respond to the statute.

In the mid-thirteenth century, in October 1265, under the questioning of Bishop Gottifredo the consistency of the collegiate church of San Ruffo had been revealed; it was composed of nine or ten prebends, two of whom were assigned to the archpriest.[135] The archpriests of San Ruffo, San Giovanni Evangelista, and Santa Maria delle Valli, the provosts of Sant'Angelo and Santa Cecilia, the abbots of Sant'Eleuterio and at a rather greater distance of Santa Croce, Lugnano, after its definitive conquest by Rieti, joined by the canons of these places—all these clergy flood the ecclesiastical records of thirteenth and fourteenth-century Rieti.[136] They provided the city with a body of secular clergy, and their churches provided the secular clergy of the city with a body of prebends. The collegiate churches offered opportunities, on a smaller scale, similar to those of the cathedral church, and they were similarly subject to provisions, sometimes for men on their way to becoming cathedral canons—as notably in the case of Bartolomeo de Rocca, whom Alexander IV provided to Santa Cecilia in 1259.[137] And repeatedly provisions were made in violation of a restrictive constitutional number, by papal indulgence.

Occasionally the clergy of the city of Rieti, in which the often overlapping canons of the cathedral and collegiate churches formed a prominent part, met or acted together. So in 1312 in a prebendal dispute between Matteo di don Angelo Tufi and Magister Tenetor when the clergy of the city were ordered to announce publicly an excommunication on every Sunday and feast day, an excommunication that seemed illegitimate, a group of clerics came before Bishop Giovanni to record their appeal against the action; they acted, they said, for themselves and in the name of all the clergy of the whole city of Rieti ("nomine eorum et nomine omnium et singulorum canonicorum maioris et aliorum conuentualium ecclesiarum ciuitatis Reat' et omnium prelatorum, presbiterorum, rectorum, cappellanorum et aliorum omnium clericorum eiusdem ciuitatis"). They were Tommaso Capitaneo and two other priest prebendaries of the cathedral, a priest of Sant'Angelo, a priest chaplain of San Pietro de Porta, a priest chaplain of San Biagio, a priest chaplain of San Bartolomeo, the archpriest of San Giovanni in Statua (that is, Evangelista), a canon (Dompno Accurimbono) of San Giovanni, a canon of San Ruffo, a chaplain of San Donato, the archpriest of Santa Maria delle Valli and clerk of San Giovanni Baptista, a clerk of San Giorgio, a clerk of Sant'Andrea, and a clerk of San Nicola.[138]

Sometimes the clergy could be represented by a single proctor, as they were in 1285, by Magister Urso de Piscia, *procurator cleri et clericorum Reatin'*, in an appeal over the receipt of and procurations for papal *cursores*; and at that time the bishop, Pietro, was separately represented by Magister Andrea da Vèroli.[139] Although they were capable of acting together there seems no evidence that they were formed into a confraternity of clergy, although they presumably knew of such confraternities, like that at Rome, whose rector they used. Perhaps because the canons of the cathedral church remained so intricately and personally involved in the other lesser collegiate churches of the city, and because together major and minor colleges so dominated the small city, a confraternity did not, and did not need to, develop at Rieti. Certainly one would not say of Rieti, as Antonio Rigon has recently said of Padua: "già nel XIII secolo clero capitolare e clero parrocchiale procedono su strade diverse (already in the thirteenth century the capitular clergy and the parochial clergy were going down different roads)."[140] At Rieti arm in arm they seem to have stridden down the same road.

One should have an impression of a diocese as well as a cathedral city of a texture thick with collegiate churches, with all these colleges of canons, and all these holders of benefices in colleges and fragments of benefices outside of them, a web of men variously supported providing both administrative service and care of souls, and also sung prayers, to their interlocked places. But how into this web did monastic and religious groups and houses fit?

At the very beginning of the thirteenth century there were only three monastic houses of any significance within the diocese: two Benedictine houses, San Salvatore Maggiore, south of Rieti, and San Quirico, on the Velino north of Antrodoco; and one Cistercian house, San Matteo, raised above the swamps near Rieti.[141] When in the middle of the century Bishop Tommaso the Corrector made his list of the churches in the diocese he named many more houses. As a former corrector of papal letters Tommaso must have had a clear and sure sense of religious order. But the jurisdictional and fiscal purposes of the list, and perhaps his own way of thinking, kept him from a placement of the monastic and religious houses within it that would have distinguished them too carefully or isolated them too much from their more secular-clerical holdings— like Ferentillo's (itself of course external to the diocese) San Leopardo. To the old great houses, one of which had changed order and another name and location, Tommaso added—besides the local establishments of the Hospitallers, the order of Altopascio, and external monasteries—eighteen houses or cells of Franciscan men, seven of nuns (where identifiable, with Franciscan connections), and three of Augustinian Hermits.[142] When in his 1301 will Nicola Cece listed religious houses his purposes were further limited and specific and his interests confined, presumably, to central diocese, but his list includes four more Reatine houses of nuns (Sant'Agnese, San Tommaso, San Fabiano, and San Benedetto—one of which was Dominican, one Cistercian and one Benedictine) and San Domenico in Rieti; it made clear that Cistercian San Matteo Rieti was a distinct entity, and it singled out the Franciscan memory-laden hermitages of San Francesco Greccio, San Giacomo Poggio (Bustone), and San Francesco Fonte Colombo (called "Fronte Palonbe").[143]

According to Tommaso's list the Hospitallers had *loci* in the city and eight other places.[144] The Order of (the Hospital of San Jacopo of) Altopascio had *loci* in the city and at Santa Maria de Busseta.[145] Ferentillo had four places besides San Leopardo. San Benedetto in Fondi had two churches; Santa Maria de Valle, two churches; and San Clemente de Pescara, a chapel. San Paolo fuori le mura of Rome had at least four churches; and nonmonastic San Pietro Vaticano had one church, and San Giovanni Laterano one and part of another.

Farfa has twelve churches in Tommaso's list. They seem like fossils, disjoined parts of the skeleton of a great prehistoric mammoth stretched in part across the thirteenth- and fourteenth-century diocese of Rieti. But there are signs of life, although not very strong ones. A document of 4 April 1312, for example, shows brother Gregory, by the grace of God and the apostolic see, abbot of the monastery of Farfa, presenting Francesco da Greccio, clerk, to the rectorship of the fourth part of Sant'Angelo and all of San Casciano di Greccio, "our churches" vacant through the death of don Pietro, Francesco's uncle, clerk and rector. Preserved fourteenth-century registers at Farfa show a maintained interest in the abbey among Reatines: the presence of monks from Rieti, an Alfani will. Farfa's earlier historic importance to the diocese was of a different degree and quality from that of any other external monastery; but the early fourteenth-century presentation, or perhaps really provision, of Francesco da Greccio gives, probably, a fair indication of the business of these monasteries within the diocese, and also of why it was not foolish for Bishop Tommaso or his agent to list their churches, without too much distinguishing fuss, among the other clusters of churches within the diocese.[146]

Local to the diocese, San Quirico's (plate 30) list of dependent churches is impressive. There are eleven of them; and the last of the eleven, San Giovanni de Vena Mecla, is said to be at Camponesca in the northeastern diocese (an area that San Quirico's dispute with the bishop of Penne would suggest was one of San Quirico interest, as, to a certain extent, would its own valley position). The San Quirico group in the Tommaso list concludes: "quod monasterium est nunc premonstratensem set olim fuit ordinis Sancti Benedicti et plene respondet episcopo reatino (which monastery is now Premonstratensian, but was formerly Benedictine in order, and answers fully to the bishop of Rieti [that is, is in no way exempt])."[147] This rare historical note in the list is no doubt due to earlier discussions of San Quirico's Premonstratensian immunity as well as to the monastery's extraordinary thirteenth-century history.

The early thirteenth-century Benedictine monks of the monastery had called to papal attention the monastery's disordered state by murdering their abbot. Gervase abbot of Prémontré wrote after the death of Pope Innocent III to the emperor Frederick II to ask for his confirmation of the granting of San Quirico to the Premonstratensians; he wrote of its former Benedictine monks: "quod Abbatem suum necaverant et luxuriose viventes dissipaverant bona loci (they killed their abbot and living luxuriously they dissipated the property of the place)."[148] After Gervase had sent San Quirico a Premonstratensian abbot he found that problems did not cease; he was forced to send a visitor, and to ask Leone Brancaleone, cardinal priest of Santa Croce in Gerusalemme, for his help. From his great distance Gervase had to think of problems of Abruzzi tithes, of books in an Abruzzi library, of the possibility of new and expensive building projects in the Abruzzi. He had to warn Gerard, the Premonstratensian abbot of San Quirico, to be careful if anyone advised him to accept into his cloister Abruzzesi monks who wanted to profess themselves Premonstratensians: "for they are truly Lombards, shrewd (furbi) beyond measure and from ancient times practiced in deceitful fawning."[149] Gervase might have been wanting and in some ways might have failed, he wrote to Leone Brancaleone, whom he suspected of criticizing him; he had done his best, he thought, to send the canons to the Abruzzi well provided materially; and spiritually surely he had done well because he had sent appropriate visitors to correct the distant canons.[150] But Gervase had doubts about Gerard. He hoped that he would realize his inadequacy and come back to France. Gerard was, Gervase believed, a good man, and a pious enough one, but oh so simple. In putting him at San Quirico he had put in the ground a vine which did nothing; it did not extend its roots or its branches.[151]

The still Premonstratensian stick (although cannily still in its fight with Penne) could hardly make sharper contrast than it does with the orders of friars.[152] Planted, they were like kudzu. Bishop Tommaso's list tells us that Franciscan men alone had eighteen houses in the diocese by the time of the list's midcentury composition; although some of the houses, like those at Lavareta (Barete) and Popleto, were in places about to be taken by the diocese of L'Aquila, they reached the corners of the diocese: Antrodoco and Machilone (Posta; see plate 31), Monteleone, Corvaro.[153] They moved into the realms not only of San Quirico but of San Salvatore, at Longone. And in the friars' first century, when the geography of the city of Rieti would expand, expanded; that expansion, like the religious sentiments which accompanied it, was contemporary with, was expressed in good part by, and in some part surely was even caused by, the coming of the new religious orders of friars and the building of their churches. By the end of the thirteenth century three large spaces between the old walls and the new were occupied by the places of the Franciscans, the Augustinians, and the Dominicans.

In the middle of the thirteenth century the Franciscans had their place by the river near to the Roman bridge and to the suburb across the river. In 1245 and again in 1248 Innocent IV helped their building with a grant and then a renewed grant of indulgence.[154] As early as 1253 there was space at San Francesco which could be used for communal meetings. Franciscans had been at Rieti since before the death of Francis, presumably around the oratory of Santa Croce. In June 1263, Urban IV wrote to the podestà and consiglio ordering them to stop the construction of a new bridge which would flood the Franciscans especially in winter.[155] The Franciscan's city house (*domus*) was in Bishop Tommaso's list. So was the place (*locus*) of the Augustinian Hermits directly across the city from the Franciscans' on the inside of the new north wall and west of the Porta Conca; the actual building of the Augustinians' retained church seems to have stretched into the middle of the fourteenth century.[156] The place of Dominican men is not in Tommaso's list, and the Dominicans, whose methods of establishing themselves were more formal and regulated than those of their Franciscan and Augustinian colleagues, may have arrived in Rieti slightly later than the other two major new orders, but their presence is sure in the 1260s, as is the church, in the northwestern corner of the new city wall, in the 1270s.[157] In 1292, on 28 February, an elderly (*quasi senes*) couple had appeared in the church of San Domenico to assert their sterility and promise their chastity over "the altar of the church of San Domenico

of Rieti," so that she, Benvenuta, could be accepted by the Dominican
nuns of Rieti, and he, Pietro Giovanni, could freely give, for his soul
and his sins, four giunte of land in Lacu Maior, with the reservation of
usufruct for his life of two of the giunte, to the Dominican friars, who
received the giunte for their nuns.[158] By the early 1290s the three new
orders were well and extensively established in Rieti.

Their presence changed, went with or facilitated a change in, the
structure of the city of Rieti, it is believed, even more of a change than
their large presence, churches and piazzas, made necessary. Theirs was
the *città dei Mendicanti*. They, it has been written, brought straight
streets, from themselves to center city.[159] They also, all three, offered
large enclosed spaces. The friars thus, at Rieti as elsewhere, participated
significantly in moving the meetings of these urban Italians indoors,
within walls and a roof. People could, and did, then meet in large groups
inside, not just outside in piazza. They met in the places that had been
formed so that they could listen to sermons and, in large groups, together assist at sacred rites. The significance of this complex development in men's being together should not be avoided by the observer;
it is a major development in the expressed definition of self and other.
But, in observing, the observer should not jump too quickly to a pattern
of cause and effect. The causal position of the friars and their churches
is not easily defined. At Rieti that is pointed out by the almost immediately previous enlargement of the cathedral church. Santa Maria was
made more capacious before San Francesco, Sant'Agostino, and San
Domenico were built, although it was not made a hall church in quite
the way they were.

Together with the enlarged cathedral and the developing Piazza del
Leone and of course the new walls, the friars' three churches, stretching
away in three directions as if into corners from the center of cathedral
and commune, made a new pattern of the city of Rieti, a new kind of
place in which its people prayed and lived. In this Rieti is not unique;
this is a normal kind of new mid and late thirteenth-century patterning
of Italian cities, the arrival of the friars (among whom the Franciscans
had often been first settled in the country, outside the city) in the space
between old and new walls, often near important new gates.[160] It has
been repeatedly suggested that this was a strategy of the friars, to place
themselves in new areas of settlement devoid of old churches and to
reach through their gates out to new *borghi*, populous and insufficiently
served by clergy.

It is a tempting scheme, but not one appropriate to Rieti. Rieti was well stocked with clergy. There were churches between the walls. Its suburb near which the Franciscans settled had two functioning collegiate churches close together, from one of which the Franciscans obtained land.[161] Many of the Reatine clergy may not in fact have been priests, but the early Franciscans could hardly have been expected to remedy that problem. Their arrival and popularity at Rieti obviously had to do with religious taste and style. They probably placed themselves where they did because that was where there was land, and perhaps also, even that early, because it was considered appropriate, it was becoming customary for friars to settle on the periphery even in cities in which there was not in the periphery a crying need for new clergy.

In one very significant way that is connected, but not very obviously connected, with some of the more prominent elements of the mission of the friars, the professed inhabitants of the friaries were different from those both of the collegiate churches and of the old houses of Benedictines and Cistercians. The friars, when their places of origin can be first identified, were predominantly strangers, foreigners to Rieti; canons and monks were very local.[162] When Francis of Assisi said to the Perugian knights who were behaving badly as he preached in the piazza at Perugia, "Do not think of me as a man of Assisi," he of course underlined the city-boundedness of his society and himself, but he also announced his intention, which his friars would follow, to break those boundaries and bonds.[163]

A list of sixteen Dominicans at San Domenico from 14 February 1310 includes four friars from Spoleto, one from Orvieto, one from Cortona, one from Arezzo, one from Rome, and one from Gubbio, as well as three from Rieti and four from other towns in the Sabina.[164] The same friars remain on 14 February 1315, and in 1319 there are also friars from Viterbo and Vèroli.[165] A list of the Dominicans who had assembled in chapter on 14 February 1305 reveals a rather surprising fact. Not only was the same friar from Spoleto, Felciano, prior in the two lists, one drawn up exactly ten years after the other, but exactly the same sixteen friars are listed in exactly the same order, a striking testimony to stability. But the 1319 list is quite the opposite. The numbers have changed only slightly, an increase of one to seventeen. The distribution of places of origin is not very dissimilar although the actual places are different. But there is a new prior elect, Berardo de Plagis (Piagge), and a new noting of office and position: a subprior, a baccillarius, and a lector of the place. There are no men from Spoleto (? gone with their prior), although the new subprior's place of origin is not listed, and there is a different clustering: six from Sabina towns and one from Posta, two from Rieti, two from Viterbo, two from Cortona, two from Rome, one from Orvieto. And only four of the old sixteen friars remain.[166]

In contrast to the, perhaps decreasing, foreigners of the Dominicans, in 1342 the Cistercians at San Pastore, except for a major cellarer who was from Narni, were all, all who are identified, from the very immediate area—monks and conversi.[167] Two of the seven monks and two of the eleven conversi came from the immediately neighboring village or castro of Greccio: and one of the conversi was Fra Francesco of Greccio, a remarkable name for a Cistercian, and one that shows the local pull of the abbey. Other monks came from Contigliano, Monte San Giovanni, Rocca Alatri. One of the monks and five of the conversi are identified as being from Rieti.

At Farfa, locally over the border in the diocese of Sabina, in 1279, almost all of the monks listed came from places very close to the monastery: four including the prior were from most closely neighboring Fara in Sabina and one from Toffia.[168] Two were from Rocca Sinibalda, one from Scandriglia, one from Cerchiara, and two from Rieti. The Dominicans, in 1305, 1310, and 1315 particularly, were from the cities of central Italy led by Spoleto; the Benedictines and Cistercians were from the villages and towns around their houses and from Rieti.

Knowing as much as one can about the canons of colleges and particularly the canons of the cathedral, one would expect them, I think, to be conservative in religion, in piety, and in devotion (as in much else), as one would expect similarly local Benedictines and Cistercians to be conservative. Of the orders of friars one would expect, I think, the opposite; one would expect them to be less confined.

Certainly an observer of religious institutions in the city of Rieti in the year 1338 would have found it a bigger and more diverse place than would his predecessor in 1200, more open. It was a place that offered many more opportunities for institutional pious bequests to much more imaginative testators, and to their advisers in making their wills. And very noticeable among these new opportunities and attractions were convents of nuns.[169]

In April 1338 Vanni Nicole Pasinelli, heir to his brother Francesco, was going from place to place distributing bequests to representatives of institutions to whom Francesco had left them in his will.[170] On 13 April in the cloister of the Cistercians' church of San Matteo in Rieti (now San Pietro Martire), Vanni, before witnesses and with a recording notary, received an oral quitclaim for 20 soldi of Ravenna from Fra

Giovanni Sonantis, the chaplain of the church. On the same day Vanni received a similar statement of receipt for the monastery of San Benedetto's 15 soldi from Donna Nicolaxia, the abbess of San Benedetto, before the grille in the convent's church; and on the same day similarly for its 15 soldi from Suor Gemma abbess of Santa Scolastica in its church, and from Suor Mathia abbess of Sant'Agnese for its 15 soldi before the grille of its church. Again on the same day Vanni received a similar statement from Suor Stefania abbess of Santa Lucia for its greater bequest of 20 soldi before the grille in the church of Santa Lucia. And finally Vanni also received a statement from Suor Tommasia abbess of Santa Margarita for its 15 soldi before the grille of its church.

CHAPTER SEVEN

A Heretic and a Saint

lu ioco deli dadi
Translation of *Hec alea -lee* in the section
"De Ludo" of the fifteenth-century
"Glossario Latino-Reatino del Cantalicio:
Ordo vocabulorum sub cantalycio"[1]

Almost four years earlier, on 15 July 1334 (a Friday), quite different visitors with quite a different purpose were at Santa Scolastica, with its
abbess Suor Scolastica. The inquisitor of the Roman province, the Franciscan Fra Simone di don Filippo da Spoleto had come, with two Augustinian Hermits, Fra Andrea the lector at Sant'Agostino Rieti and Fra
Giovanni da Amelia, and with the inquisitor's notary, to interrogate one
of the nuns, Suor Ceccarella di Giovanni Retinecte, still young, about
twenty years old. Ceccarella was asked questions and she told a story,
and her abbess, Suor Scolastica, swore that she had heard the story and
that Ceccarella had told it.[2]

Ceccarella said that that Paolo who was being questioned by the
inquisition had said to her that he wanted to see if she was obedient to
him, and he told her to show her obedience by undressing. With some
difficulty he had made her strip to the skin and then he had done it too.
He had told her to lie on the ground naked and he had lain next to her
and taken her into his hands and tried to get her to sin with him. But
she had resisted and, by divine power she believed, had been able to

free herself from his grasp. Getting up she had redressed herself and then had sat totally stunned. Paolo had then come to her and asked, "Did you not want to obey me because you thought it was a sin?" And she had said, "Yes." But he had said that it was not a sin, that which he had done and wanted to do, and that he had had a revelation from the Holy Spirit, and that he would not have attempted it if he had not known that it was the will of God. And Paolo had said that Ceccarella should have obeyed him when he wanted to commit adultery with her. And she in her simplicity had not understood the word "adhulterij"; and she had said to him, "Quid est adhulterium (what is adultery)?" And Paolo had said that it was what he had wanted to do with her. And he had told her that his was the best way, better than any other, to mortify the flesh and that no woman in those parts no matter how saintly she was could be shamed by it.

Asked where all this had happened, Ceccarella said it was in a house that belonged to Contessa Jotii who was "now" in the third order of Saint Francis and for whom at the time Ceccarella had been a servant (*famula*) and that it was the house where Paolo had then lived. Asked if anyone else had been there, Ceccarella said no; and asked if the door to the house had been closed, she said yes. Asked when all this had happened, she said that it was the last Friday of the month of March in the year in which it had happened and she thought two years, or maybe one, before that Lent most recently past. She could not remember the year with certainty but she could remember, she said again, that it was the last Friday. Then Ceccarella's story went on. She remembered that in the same house, the one where Paolo lived, which was Contessa Jotii's, which was next to the house of Jacobutia di Zacharello the *macellaio* (butcher), Paolo had induced Contessa because of her obedience to him to undress herself. And he had said that there is no greater crown than that which a woman earns in this undressing and a lot of words like that. Then Paolo and Contessa went into a room (*camera*) in the house, he alone with her alone, Contessa consenting reluctantly but consenting, with Paolo saying to her the same things he had said to Ceccarella, and Contessa taking off her clothes until she was naked. Whether or not they had sinned sexually Ceccarella did not know.

And at another time when Paolo had insisted that Ceccarella take off her clothes, Contessa, whose maid Ceccarella then was, had said to her, "Daughter, you can do what he orders perfectly well, that is, undress yourself before him, because I did the same thing when he ordered it." Ceccarella could not remember exactly when this conversation hap-

pened but it was after Contessa had undressed herself and it was before
Ceccarella did. And Ceccarella further said that when she was disturbed
after the incidents Paolo told her not to be disturbed because he had
been told by God or by the Holy Spirit that he could not sin sins of the
flesh. And Contessa had told her that she could not be shamed because
she had done nothing that Contessa would not do. And on the same
day of inquisition Fra Simone the inquisitor asked Ceccarella how old
she had been when this all happened and she replied, always under oath,
that she believed that she had been over ten, because she believed in
fact that she had been eighteen and more.

On 15 July, the same day, in the house of the Franciscans at Rieti, in
the inquisitor's room, in the presence of Fra Giovanni di don Bartolino
da Spoleto, and Fra Matheutio da Poggio, and the Franciscan notary
Berardo, the inquisitor examined Paolo Angelecti Venuti da Rieti, of
the sestiere Porta Romana de sotto—that Paolo Zoppo alias Paolo de
Carcere whose notorious fame had come to the ears of the inquisitor,
he said, notoriety for having gathered with other men and women and,
forgetting his own safety and divine and ecclesiastical law, under the
pretense of mortification of the flesh and demonstration of special perfection and virtue, had made nude women lie with him and commit
improper and libidinous acts.[3]

Paolo, at the inquisition of 16 July, confessed that he had made Contessa the daughter of Jotio and widow of Paolo, who was "now" in the
third order of Saint Francis, undress in his presence and believe she was
doing a good thing. Asked where, he answered in Contessa's house in
the contrada of the Piazza Maggiore next to the house of Zaccarello
Accorsechti the butcher and to the street. He said that they were alone
in the room when he gave her the discipline. Asked how long ago it
had been, he replied that he could not really remember but that it was
a year and more. He confessed that another time in the house of Contessa that is the house of Tommaso di Cola next to the house of the
sons of Schaiacta in Rieti he had made Ceccarella di Giovanni Reti-
nechte lie nude on a bench telling her she was mortifying her flesh for
the love of Jesus Christ, and he had undressed himself and had lain next
to her; and then, frightened, she had gotten up.

Thus begins (for us) through day after day of recorded questioning
and answering a Reatine story which grows broader and deeper and in
various ways more frightening and sordid, but also more poignant, and
more puzzling, as it progresses. It is recorded in an exquisite paper
book, now in the Vatican library at Rome, written by the inquisitorial

notary (by imperial authority) Martino di magistro Aimone of Viterbo at the command of the inquisitor Simone, written in an elegant and careful hand, by a notary who was not always perfectly attentive (as when Paolo according to Ceccarella approached her, he *excesit ad eam* corrected—in another or altered hand—in the manuscript to *accesit*) and not always able perfectly to read the documents he copied (as when he mentions Contessa's dead husband for the first time and leaves blank his patronymic).[4]

The composite document of the paper book is an inquisitorial record and it shows many of those qualities for which inquisitorial records are notorious. Much of its questioning and answering may have come from the textbooks of inquisitorial manuals formed without interest in or knowledge of Reatine physical or spiritual topography.[5] The motives of the questioning it records are not disinterested: most particularly the questions are put by a conventional and conventual Franciscan who in the section in which he first describes Paolo's notoriety has extended the description of his responsibilities, as the representative of Pope John XXII, of searching out and extirpating heretics and those who favor them, specifically to include the "sect of the fraticelli of the poor life" condemned by the apostolic see.[6] Simone was a good Franciscan (good in the sense that John XXII was a good pope) out to get the bad Franciscans, and to tar them with bad connections, like Paolo Zoppo. It is, after the nature of inquisitorial processes, as we have been taught, drenched with sex.[7] It begins with sexual acts tied by the inquisitor, and probably also by Paolo, to the common heretical notion of perfection through courted and, in proper cases, resisted temptation. From this beginning it moves toward more disturbing gestures of sexual perversion.

What kind of historical truth can this record tell? It tells, as any historian now could answer, itself. But that self is not simple and it cannot be left at rest. A fresh and vigorous recent essay on inquisitors written by James Given helps one enter these documents, see things in them, uncertainly, beneath the surface of the text, and helps one, having accepted the fact that only the text exists, push toward those events, people, minds, external to it and prior to it, that one wants to see.[8] And one has at least the illusion of help from the fact that here in this Rieti case one is repeatedly dealing with people and piazzas whom and which one knows in other ways.

Given quotes, from a Paris manuscript, an extreme example of the early fourteenth-century stated consciousness that inquisitors could persuade their victims to say anything and to be seen in any way they, the inquisitors, wanted. The Franciscan Bernard Délicieux told Philip IV, Given tells us, that, had the inquisitors had before them Peter and Paul, these two could have been found heretics.[9] And the inquisitorial techniques that Given's essay suggests, the circling questioning, the isolation, the fluctuation of attitude, the bondage, exist to sweep the pathetic Reatine figures, Paolo and Contessa, into the pit. Franciscans and Dominicans with their trained attention to personal response, to preaching, to anecdote, to illustrated event, with their accustomed ways of explaining things personally, were of necessity experts in human psychology, and this is dreadfully apparent in the first questioning part of the work of the Franciscan inquisitor, Simone da Spoleto.[10]

Simone may have been unusually avid, driven; one cannot tell when one observes him in isolation. But he adds himself to the composite portrait of the penetrating, trapping Franciscan inquisitor. The observer of his victims cannot be sure what in the victims' confessions has not been created, not just abstracted but created, by the manipulation of the inquisitor. But he, the observer, also knows that the composite narrative that emerges in the record is one that could make enough sense, reason, to be said, heard, written down in 1334, that it is (insofar as it can be separated from our shaping reading) an early fourteenth-century artifact, created, with the patterns given them, by this Spoletan and these Reatines, at Santa Scolastica, at the Franciscan house by the river, in the cathedral, in Rieti. This document, difficult as it is as a piece of evidence, has tremendous potential value for the understanding of fourteenth-century Rieti, its religion, its people.

Perhaps one can experiment a bit with the (superficially, to the modern mind) most disgusting, or degrading, story at the dark center of Paolo Zoppo's confessions. For a time Paolo, who we are told was called Paolo de Carcere, had lived as an urban anchorite, in a *carcere*, a cell attached to the Reatine church of San Leopardo.[11] On the seventh day of recorded testimony, on 25 July, in the camera of the inquisitor at San Francesco, with Fra Francesco da Longone, Fra Matteo da Poggio, and "me" the Franciscan notary Berardo da Rieti present, Paolo confessed that while he was at the cell at San Leopardo (*existens ad carceres Sancti Leopardi*) he took (*accepit*) a female dog (*vnam canem*) and stuck his fingers into the vagina of the little dog (*canicule*) and manipulating the vagina of the dog he brought himself to ejaculation (*corrupit se ipsum*)—and in this inquisition ejaculation is as important, as focused on, as is the shedding of blood in inquisitions concerning assault, a kind of legal decisiveness probably encouraged by limited anatomical understanding.

Now we ask questions. Did the notary or the inquisitor simply lie about the dog, make her up? Was it a form of degradation which the inquisitor had been taught or had taught himself to elicit and present? Had the inquisitor been taught or taught himself, through the use of manuals or in some other fashion, that this practice, the digital sexual abuse of a dog, was an appropriate one to be suggested to the shaken minds of victims of low status, to disheveled witnesses, particularly those meant to be connected with the fraticelli? Did the inquisitor successfully suggest the incident to Paolo? Did the frightened Paolo seeking in some way to please the inquisitor search in the depths of his own mind for an image which would be sufficiently disgusting to satisfy the inquisitor, even to allow the inquisitor to stop probing Paolo's memory, his consciousness of himself and his past behavior? Was Paolo's use of the dog something that he had been brought to think he had remembered? Had Paolo in his enclosure, almost crazily, abused the dog? Had Paolo rebelling against the advertised holiness of living in a cell sought and found a debasement sordid enough to satisfy his distaste for his position or his hypocrisy? Questions of this sort can continue in our minds as the inquisitors' questions continue day after day in the account. But is this, here, entirely the wrong track? Was this kind of behavior with dogs common, in image and act, in relatively rural central Italy in the fourteenth century? Was it in its setting normal behavior?

As often, the historian must be guided by his own inner darkness. But the narrative, the incident, exploded by questions, reveals a variety of otherwise unknown Reatine sentiments and structures, as does the entire inquisitorial source with its involvement of canons, vicar general, families like the Alfani and the Secinari. In following the events of the source's narrative the reader's mind must be armed with critical questions, not entirely different from, perhaps only an exaggerated form of, the questions he must always be asking a historical source. But here, particularly in certain scenes, as when one deals with the helpfully significant account of Paolo's false miracles, one must be particularly sensitive, aware of a subsurface of various possibilities held together by the Latin surface of the text.[12]

In his first preserved interrogation, his first interrogation on 15 July, Paolo, asked, had said that he had gotten Contessa to undress at a time before he had gotten Ceccarella to do so, and that he had gotten Contessa to undress twice in the way he had confessed, in her own house, with no one watching.[13] Beyond that, in his first session, Paolo denied all allegations. On the same day he was again interrogated and then admitted having gotten Ceccarella to undress a second time in Contessa's house while he and Contessa were both present in the house, but he said that Ceccarella was inside a *camera* and he and Contessa were outside of it. Asked if he ever said that the act of fornication (*fornicationis*: genitive) was not a sin he said no. Asked if he believed that the women who undressed before him gained merit for doing it, he said that he had then believed it but that he now thought that the acts were mortal sins (*peccata mortalia*). Asked if he knew anyone else who shared his old opinion of that rite, he said no, not unless Contessa believed that about those heretical rites (*supradictis hereticalibus ritis*). Asked if he knew anything about what was going to happen between him and the inquisitor before he came before him, he said that "yesterday" Reccha of Rieti had said to him "You better get away because something has been said to the inquisition against you"; and asked if he had talked about it to anyone he said, yes, to Contessa: he had said, "It's us—*Sibi nos sumus, sibi tu et ego incusati Inquisitioni*," and she had replied, "It's caught up with us—*Male uadit factum nostrum.*" This interrogation occurred in the same place as the previous hearing and with the same witnesses, with Matheutio identified more fully as of Poggio Bustone (and one should notice the Franciscan witnesses from places which had had Franciscan establishments by the time of Bishop Tommaso's list).[14]

On the same day, presumably at another session, Paolo was told by the inquisitor that he had six days to defend himself.[15] He was told that he should stand ready to be summoned at any time, that he should not flee or go away from the place where he was put and that he should not talk about the affair with any person without special license to do so. Then on the following day, the sixteenth, this time in the sacristy of the cathedral church with the bishop's vicar general Francesco, archpriest of Santa Maria di Canetra present, Paolo's questioning began again: the scenes of undressing, the convincing of the women, the words said.[16] Paolo ended the session (as it is recorded) by quoting his definition to Ceccarella, "Adhulterium est illud quod ego uolui facere tecum," as if both would remember, as they might have remembered, this personal dictionary definition. The presence of Paolo in the cathedral sacristy with Francesco the vicar general is the first recorded notice of the entry into the case of the official diocesan church, a necessary entry for the case's legitimacy.

On 16 July Paolo was subjected to two more sessions of inquisition in the sacristy with the vicar general present, and then he was again warned by the inquisitor not to run away.[17] In the second session of the day Paolo's motivation for making the women undress was further explored. Paolo again said that Ceccarella had undressed completely and so had he, and that he naked lay next to her naked, and that he wished and intended to approach her as a husband does his wife (*sicut appropinquat maritus uxorem*), or as a nude man a nude woman but without orgasm (*sine corruptione*). Paolo admitted that a lewd intent, the malice of lust, led him to induce Ceccarella to undress. And he admitted that when he was with Contessa, and they two were in a camera together and Ceccarella was outside alone, he made her undress for the pleasure of seeing her naked, at a time when he talked of testing her obedience.

When Paolo was asked by the inquisitor to tell him from whom he had learned this rite of obedience, he said that he had learned it from Fra Rainaldo, a fraticello from Spoleto, who had then been staying in the place (*loco*) called Foresta at Rieti and San Marone or Maro near Rieti. Paolo said that Rainaldo was "now" dead and that he had died in the house of Lotorono Alfani of Rieti and that he was buried in the cemetery of the major church of Rieti. Asked what Rainaldo had taught him, Paolo replied that he had taught him that this behavior was practiced at Spoleto, that a nude man lay with a nude woman without intercourse. Asked whether Rainaldo had said that it was a good thing to do, Paolo said that Rainaldo had not said it was good or bad. Asked where this instruction by Rainaldo had taken place, Paolo replied in the city of Rieti but he could not remember where; asked about when it had happened, he said about ten or twelve years before. Asked if, when he had heard about these things from Fra Rainaldo, he had believed him and, more, had believed they were not sinful, Paolo answered yes.

At the third session in the sacristy on 16 July Paolo swore of his own free will, the record says, and without fear of any torture or other force that all the things he had confessed in the *loco* of the friars minor "yesterday (*heri*)" and all that he had confessed in the sacristy of the cathedral church with the vicar general present "today (*hodie*)" were true. And at this final session of the day other witnesses were present, including Don Angelo di don Paolo of Rieti, Giovanni Reatino, Ballovino di magistro Giovanni, Leonardo Angeli, and a man from Spoleto named Petronio Jannanucti—altogether seven witnesses besides the notary.

In further confessions which are dated 17 and 25 July and which took place in the camera of the inquisitor at San Francesco, Paolo added material to his story of his encounters with Contessa: a bed in the chamber; the undressed Contessa's making five genuflections in a cross on the floor; her saying "I put myself in your hands do with me what you will"; Paolo's holding her in his arms, holding her tight to him and kissing her on the mouth, and wanting to sin with her and have an orgasm within her; and their being thus alone many times, perhaps twenty; and her holding his head in her lap and Paolo's thus masturbating; and Contessa's undressing, or undressing to the waist in her dress with the large neck; and Paolo's talk of merit in the eyes of God. On 17 July Paolo also said that he had told these stories in confession to dompno Filippo de Cospiano who lived near San Giovanni Evangelista Rieti and to dompno Giovanni Petrignani, and that both of them had given him absolution.[18]

On 16 July at San Francesco in the camera of Fra Appollonio of Brescia, with Appollonio and Fra Giacomo the educated *baccellario* of the convent and the Franciscan notary present, Contessa herself faced the inquisitor; and here she is identified slightly more fully: Contessa filia Jotii uxor quondam Pauli Piscis de Reate de Porta Romana de super.[19] The inquisitor read her his charge and explained it in the vernacular, and she admitted knowing of Paolo's lying naked with Ceccarella in her own house and inducing her to sin with shameful words (*turpia uerba*); but then Contessa added a new scene to the narrative. Paolo had come to her, after his experience with Ceccarella, and had begged her out of compassion to come with him, and all three—Paolo, Contessa, and Ceccarella—had gone to the garden of dompno Giovanni priest at the church of San Giovanni within the walls of Rieti, and there in the garden before dompno Giovanni, and with another priest of San Giovanni, dompno Filippo, present and hearing, all of them hearing, Ceccarella had told everything that Paolo had done and attempted to do. And Paolo had said "Ego dico culpa mea de illis rebus (I say that the fault is mine in these things)"—but he did not specify. And after that Paolo began to engage Contessa herself in small talk and he was more frequently at her house. Then he began his seduction of obedience and merit and undressing. And then Contessa spoke of the five—here five or six—genuflections which he made her do (and so they may have thus found their way into Paolo's narrative). Contessa said that two years had since passed and that she had often since then confessed these things and been absolved by many priests (*pluries fuit confessa et absoluta pluribus Sacerdotibus*). On 18 July in the same place (now called the *cella* or camera of Fra Appollonio—a nice hesitance) before the same witnesses Contessa faced the inquisitor again. She spoke of Paolo's words and acts as he had her undress to the waist and totally, of his talk of merit, of his giving her the kiss of peace on the mouth.[20]

On 18 July, in the *foresteria* (the place for visitors) at San Francesco, the inquisitor asked the secret advice and consent of his board of local counselors: the bishop's vicar general (Francesco); two of the podestà's judges; Tommaso Cimini; Giovanni de Canemorto (who was repeatedly counselor to the chapter); the abbot of Sant'Eleuterio (who was Andrea di don Sinibaldo); Don Giacomo Leoparducii; Fra Bernardo de Bagnoregio, the *custos* of Rieti; Fra Francesco da Santa Rufina, the visitor of the pope; Fra Berardo da Rieti; Fra Giovanni di don Bartolino.[21] The inquisitor asked the counselors to answer three questions: first, were the things said and confessed against Paolo "Cioppo" heretical? second, should Paolo be condemned as a heretic? third, should he be put to the torture to make him confess fully?

Don Giovanni de Canemorto's responses are recorded first: yes it was heresy; no he should not be condemned as a heretic, because of some vacillation; yes he should be put to torture in order to arrive at and confirm the truth. A number of the counselors agreed with Don Giovanni: Tommaso Cimini; the three communal judges; Francesco, the vicar; the Franciscan visitor; and the Franciscan *custos*. Don Giacomo Leoparducii's counsel was different: he thought that the things confessed were heretical; he thought Paolo should not be condemned because of his wretched (or low) condition: "quia est uilis condictionis inspecta condictione persone"; Paolo should not be put to the torture in order to preserve, not to damage, the good reputation of the people of Rieti and the honor of the city: "non est torquendus propter famam conseruandam popularum Reatinarum et propter honorem Ciuitatis"— and he offered a fourth consiglio that Paolo should be put in prison or in some other way punished. The abbot (the canon Andrea di don Sinibaldo) agreed with Don Giacomo. The Franciscan notary, Fra Berardo da Rieti, counseled that the inquisitor should perform the duties of his office, but with mercy ("faciat debitum officij sui cum misericordia"). Fra Giovanni di don Bartolino counseled that the words were heretical but that the inquisitor should accommodate the city and citizens as much as he could ("condescenderet Ciuibus et Ciuitati quam posset"). Fra Nicola da Fossa, whose name was not in the list of counselors, said that Paolo should not be tortured and that the words he said were not heretical.[22]

On 20 July Francesco, the episcopal vicar, gave his consent to Fra Simone's proceeding to torture Paolo, to which, as the record says, presumably because Francesco had said it, the greater part of the coun-selors had agreed. Francesco said this before Don Corrado de Murro, Don Giacomo di don Sinibaldo, and the Franciscan notary Berardo, in the piazza of the major church and of San Giovanni Battista (the bap-tistry), in front of that church.[23] On the same day Paolo was again before the inquisitor, but in the camera of the podestà of Rieti, and in the presence of his two judges who were counselors to the inquisitors (Al-berico de Montegammara and Matteo de Fermo) and, of course, the Franciscan notary, and counselor, Berardo da Rieti. He was back to the story of obedience, undressing, lying together, without perhaps know-ing whether he should emphasize or conceal the belief that it brought merit in the sight of God. But in this room, presumably nearer to in-struments of torture than was the inquisitor's room at San Francesco, a new figure enters the recorded testimony, the *diavolo* whose involve-ment in the practice he had once but no longer believed was good, he now acknowledged.[24]

On 23 July Paolo was again before the inquisitor talking of people who had known of his behavior: dompno Giovanni Petrignani, Don Matteo Loderoni (di Ladorono), Angelicto de Palatio, and dompno Filippo (like Giovanni a priest of San Giovanni "de Statua," as San Giovanni Evangelista is here called); and all except Angelicto had re-proved him. This had happened in the house of Angelicto. And Paolo talked of frequent gatherings in the garden of the priest dompno Gio-vanni Petrignani. A group went to the garden to see dompno Giovanni, and there he read to them: Contessa Jotii and other women including Nicolutia who lived with (*prope*) Nicola but was never married (and any reader must feel the inquisitorial net closing around the priests of San Giovanni Evangelista and feel at the same time interest in and some surprise at this reading group, oddly seeming to predict early fifteenth-century Norfolk). This session of the inquisition occurred in the in-quisitor's camera, with as witnesses Berardo the notary and Fra Gio-vanni di don Bartolino of Spoleto, two *familiari* of the inquisitor—and before the name of one of these the Viterbese notary inserted the "me" which belonged to Berardo and had then to cancel it.[25]

Paolo's session of 24 July (a Sunday) took place in the loggia of the inquisitor's camera at San Francesco.[26] It demanded of Paolo an unac-customed, here, kind of memory, a very short one. And he told a story dramatic in a new way, the story of his escape from and return to im-prisonment. That day, Paolo said, he, kept in a house closed to make a jail (a *carcere*) and bound hand and foot by order of the inquisitor, fled,

escaped, hid himself. Asked how he managed to do it, Paolo answered
that he freed his hands with his teeth, and then his feet with his hands.
He went toward the gate, went up the steps to it, but the gate was
closed. He took it with his hands and lifted it from its frame and got
out. He ran to the piazza of the Cappellarii and then into a house of
Rainaldo di Pietro di don Giovanni (or Rainaldo Pietro di don Giovanni) which Rainaldo "had for living in," but Rainaldo was not home,
and Paolo hid in the house. When Rainaldo came home to his house
he found Paolo there. And he rebuked him for escaping, and he said
"You did a bad thing when you escaped." Then Paolo sent Rainaldo
to Petricono Cimini so that he would tell Don Tommaso Secinari (the
future bishop) that Paolo wanted to place himself in Tommaso's hands.
Rainaldo coming back to Paolo from Petricono brought him Petricono's message that he, Paolo, should return himself to the inquisitor. Then
Paolo sent Rainaldo to the inquisitor to say that he wanted to return
to captivity. Rainaldo came back and took Paolo to the inquisitor.

Paolo, asked by the inquisitor if he had any help in his flight, in the
opening of his house of detention, or untying his hands and feet, or
any kind of aid, help, counsel, or favor, said no. Asked if he met anyone
in his flight or when he escaped from the house of detention, Paolo said
that he met a lot of people but no one whom he knew.

On 25 July Paolo was before the inquisitor within his camera, again
with as witnesses Fra Francesco da Longone, Fra Matteo da Poggio,
and the notary Berardo. In this session he enriched his testimony.[27]
After Paolo had taken to wearing religious dress he once went for the
indulgence of the Portiuncula and on the trip he repeatedly kissed Cintia Rubei Petri di don Giovanni and they planned to have sexual relations with each other, but they did not find an opportunity to sin.
Afterwards they returned to Rieti and many many times (*multotiens et
multotiens*) they were together and kissed in her house and elsewhere
and she consented to have sexual intercourse with him but they did not
have an opportunity to sin. This all began, Paolo said, about twelve
years earlier. And Paolo confessed having spiritual conversations with
Maglietta Catalicii; and he was with her in her house and wanted to
hug and kiss her and have sexual intercourse with her, but she refused.
Then he told the story of the female dog in his anchorage. He said that
that happened at the time he was involved with Cintia (so presumably
he was not locked in his cell), and he said it was about the time in which
his (otherwise unmentioned) son was born—and he stopped being involved with Cintia about six years before the time of the inquisition.

In a second session on 25 July again in his camera at San Francesco the inquisitor returned Paolo to the old question of undressing women and lying naked with them naked; and a new woman was introduced into the cast, Giovanna the daughter of Giovanni di Giovanni de (?)Arono, citizen of Rieti (*ciuem Reat'* agrees with Giovanna, accusative, not Giovanni, genitive).[28] She was approached in the house of Contessa, who was present in the house, as "it seemed to Paolo (*uidetur sibi*)" was Ceccarella. It was a time more recent than the first Contessa incident. Did Giovanna believe Paolo's words? Paolo believed not. And, as with the question of Ceccarella's presence, the uncertainty of seeming and believing now appears in Paolo's words: "Interrogatus si illa Johanna credebat uerbis suis, respondit quod credit quod non ut credit."

After the Giovanna part of the inquisition Paolo's talk returned, or was returned, to the priests of San Giovanni Evangelista, and here Paolo gives dompno Giovanni Petrignani a different tone (a surprise in the reader in the garden) with a dangerous joke and a playful and unexpected way of addressing his colleague. Paolo swore that he told openly to dompno Giovanni Petrignani and dompno Matteo Loctheroni the story of his rite with Contessa and Ceccarella; and then dompno Giovanni said to dompno Matteo: "You should do it, what Paolo did, son of Loctarono (*Faceres tu hoc fili Loctaroni quod fecit Paulus*)." And dompno Matteo replied, "God save me from that (*Deus liberet me*)" and was (Paolo thought) displeased. This little piece of litany Paolo remembered as having taken place behind Sant'Agnese.

Then the inquisition turned to Paolo's supposed creation of false stories of miracle. Those "false" miracles identified by place happened at Greccio. One cannot help noticing the places and kinds of religious practice that combine themselves in Paolo's life or in the inquisitor's mind: the anchorite's cell; the Portiuncula; the fraticelli; the third order; San Marone and Foresta; the women listening to the priest reading in the garden; and finally Greccio and what happens there, including the idea of miracle and uncontrolled sanctity—artifacts of belief and piety connected with "extreme" Franciscanism, artifacts of belief and piety farthest from magisterial and curial control, and from the kind of Franciscanism that sits in loggias before cameras and deals with judges in defining orthodoxy.

But it is also a Greccio far from, connected with but far from, Francis's and the companions' Greccio, and part of that distance is defined by time. Paolo told the inquisitor that he had spread broadly (disseminauit inter multos) the story that once Paolo was at the Franciscans' (the *loco*) at Greccio with Fra Appollonio and there were there two young friars, novices. Because of an abundance of snow they lacked bread; and because of that the novices wanted to quit the order. Fra Appollonio said to them, "Wait three days and the Lord will provide." Then on the third day without bread, when the novices were wanting to leave, there was a knocking at the door; and when one of the novices ran to the door the only thing he found there was a canister of bread, nothing else was around; and after the table was set (*posita mensa* [? they were sitting at table]), there was another knocking at the door, and one of the novices ran to answer, and he found there a wolf knocking with his paw (actually *branca*). The wolf went away leaving a kid (*crapaiolum*). This was the story, but at the inquest Paolo said that it was all false and that he had made it up to try to praise Fra Appollonio into sainthood.

And Paolo said that he had spread falsely another miracle about a certain queen who gave Appollonio necessities and that Appollonio had found in his camera a chest of queenly bread brought by an angel (*Vnum Cassectum portatum ab angelo cum pannis reginalibus*). The mind or minds which composed these miracles used familiar props: the snow, the wolf, the bread, the angel. But the sets are oddly constructed: pushed by tiredness, torture, carelessness, the driving necessity to attack radical Franciscans? And this Greccio, wilder, more Abruzzese, than Francis's or the companions', still has camera, doors and tables, novices and an order.

On 26 July Paolo's inquest was again in session, again in the inquisitor's camera.[29] Paolo was brought back to the Cintia story: in a bed in her camera, in her vineyard, lying unclothed on top of her, with his member in her member, but not to orgasm (and the protagonist of Paolo's inquest may well seem the male orgasm); then repeatedly with orgasm (but the use of the word *corruptionem* not accidentally darkens the meaning of orgasm). Again on 27 July Paolo talked of Cintia in the inquisitor's camera; he talked of his fingers moving under the covers one night in the house of Tommasello Martini Mictenessi at a time when Tommasello himself was there sick in bed.[30] Then he talked again of Ceccarella and lying with her in the straw in a container (a *naui*), in the house of Contessa, and of not intending to come to orgasm with her. And in another session on the same day in the same place Paolo swore to the truth of all he had said.[31]

And again in the same place twice on the next day, 28 July, Paolo appeared before the inquisitor and talked of Contessa and Ceccarella and the *nauicella* or *nauicula* in the house with straw in it.[32] And he swore that all that he had confessed was true and stated of his own free will without fear or force. And again on the same day, but this time in the sacristy of the cathedral church, Paolo swore the same thing, and he said he had not been tortured by the inquisitor, that he had been treated mercifully by the inquisitor; and renouncing all further defense he put himself in the inquisitor's hands.[33] This he did before twenty-three witnesses; they included ten men who were or would be canons of Rieti and the father of another: Corrado de Murro, Tommaso Secinari, Tommaso Cimini, Berardo Secinari, Giacomo di don Tommaso, Matteo di don Paolo, Matteo di don Angelo, Rainaldo de Piagge, Matteo di magistro Biagio, Angelo di don Paolo, and Don Caputosto. Then on 3 August Paolo was back at the inquisitor's camera at San Francesco talking of the undressing of Contessa and Ceccarella in Contessa's house and of the three of them together in the garden of dompno Giovanni Petrignani telling and confessing their story to Giovanni and to dompno Filippo de Crispiano.[34]

But out of order in the document is talk of a different kind of event, the reuniting of the inquisitor's counselors on 30 July (a Saturday) in the foresteria of San Francesco (*in loco fratrum minorum de Reat' in domo que dicitur foresteria*). Only six of these sixteen counselors had also been counselors on 18 July; and they included none of the counselors of 18 July who had disagreed significantly with the majority consensus. Present in the foresteria on 30 July were the episcopal vicar Francesco, Tommaso Secinari, Corrado de Murro, Giovanni de Canemorto (here identified as *judex*, present with three other men identified by the title *judex*, including Francesco de Murro), also the two podestà's judges who had been present on 18 July, the Franciscan *custos* of Rome as well as again the *custos* of Rieti, and again the Franciscan papal visitor, the canon Rainaldo de Piagge, the Dominican Berardo de Piagge, and two Augustinian Hermits from Sant'Agostino (Amatucio, and Angelo da Accumoli).

On 30 July there was, we are told, consensus among those counselors who were not members of religious orders, that is, among those learned in the law (the *juris periti*), the clerks (*clerici*), and the vicar of the bishop, about three points (*super tribus puntis*): first that because of those things already confessed and discovered Paolo ought to be put to the final torture (*et gomitibus extensus*) before sentencing; second that, even without further confession, because of the perverse and heretical dogma he had confessed he should be punished as a heretic; third that he should be canonically punished as a heretic even if he renounced his heresy. The counselors who were members of religious orders agreed except that they said that Paolo should be tortured to reveal what he seemed still to conceal without the brutal and contorting torture described as *tormento flactionis bracciorum uel exibitionis calcis* or other similar tortures.[35]

Then on 3 August (a Wednesday) the inquisitor, in the loggia before his camera, with witnesses, including some "familiars" of his own household present, commissioned those familiars to take Paolo Zoppo to the podestà of Rieti and his vicar so that they should diligently guard him so that he should not escape or be moved without the inquisitor's express license, and so that he should talk to no one except his guard, and so that he should not receive embassies from anyone, and so that nothing should be carried to him. The familiars of the inquisitor with the Franciscan notary took Paolo to give him to the podestà and fulfill their commission. But since the podestà was not at the time in the city they handed him over to the podestà's son and knight who conveyed him to the podestà's vicar.[36]

From that point the inquisitor, driven, moved to the attack of his enemies, to those who opposed him, and most specifically to an attack on Giovanni de Bussatta (the father of the future vicar general) who had had, the inquisitor said, the audacity to make excuses for Paolo and his crimes of heresy and to say publicly that Paolo should not be detained and, out of love for Paolo, to say that he was innocent and without fault.[37]

The presentation of Paolo to the podestà's son on 3 August took place less than three weeks after Ceccarella's first recorded testimony at Santa Scolastica on 15 July. After these intense weeks the persons of the major actors, Paolo and Contessa, disappear. The action changes. In the middle of the inquisitor's attack on Paolo's sympathizers the inquisitorial record breaks and jumps folios and then begins again. But it begins days later, on 8 August, a Monday, with different notaries present, and in a different place, in the church of Santa Maria di Croce in the territory of Leonessa (*in terra Gonesse*, sometimes *Gonisse*) but still in the diocese of Rieti.

There and then the inquisitor sat and composed a citation for Contessa, fully and explicitly identified, and here called a confessed heretic. She should appear, within three days of the receipt of the citation, before the inquisitor at Santa Maria di Croce or, even with her absent, he would proceed to graver condemnations and penalties. The inquisitor prepared the citation with care. It was sealed with the seal of his office, it was registered, it was notarized by the notary Pietro Gualterucci of Leonessa; and Pietro's copy was read aloud and listened to in a group, with the Franciscan Matteo de Planitia also reading. The citation was then entrusted to the inquisitor's messenger, or nuncio, Petrono Giovanucci, to take to Contessa's house in Rieti and to make sure that she was aware of its contents.[38]

Two days later, on 5 August, Petrono was back at Leonessa, at Santa Maria di Croce, telling of the adventures of his trip. Carrying the citation and two other letters from the inquisitor, he had arrived at the Porta Conca, the gate in the middle of the north wall of Rieti. There he had found guards posted, by officials of the commune, specifically to prevent any person, citation, or letter sent from the inquisitor from entering the city. The guards, or one of them, had threatened Petrono with a raised plank. They had seized him and told him to undress: "Spolia te." They had put their hands under his clothes and harassed him; they had disarranged his clothes, even his breeches, and had undone his laces and removed his sword. This all had happened about noon with a lot of people whom Petrono did not know present, and then the notary Pietro di don Giacomo of Rieti had turned up. The guards, who had not found the inquisitor's citation and letters, then had taken Petrono off to those communal officials called "the six." And the six (*illi sex*) had interrogated him and asked if he carried letters from that inquisitor of whom he was the messenger, nuncio. Petrono, out of fear, had answered no; and the six had dismissed him.

Dismissed, Petrono had gone to the Franciscans' to give letters from the inquisitor to Fra Berardo who had been his notary in Rieti but, there, Fra Berardo had refused to take them. Moreover the guardiano of the Franciscans' at Rieti had told him that "that day [that is, yesterday (*heri*)]" the six had ordered that he, Petrono himself, should not be allowed to depart unless the letters were found. Because of the danger to their persons the guardiano had gone to a secret place to read the letters; and "today (*hodie*)" he had told Petrono that, again to avoid danger, he had burned the letters, after having taken off the seals, in the same secret place at the Franciscans'. And again to avoid danger, Petrono, who had heard that it was generally said that the six had posted guards at all the gates just as they had at the Porta Conca, had left Rieti not by any gate but by going across the river (by the Franciscans'); and he said that in leaving he had been accompanied for a mile by two friars minor and two other men. Finally Petrono said that he had heard from the guardiano and more generally from the friars and others at the Franciscans' and from other men in the city, that the six had ordered, in an order accompanied by heavy threats to the Franciscans, the Dominicans, the Augustinian Hermits and to the (secular) clergy, that no one should accept any letter from the inquisitor. The prominence, in the statement, of the orders of friars is noticeable.[39]

On 12 August, a Friday, Fra Simone da Spoleto, the inquisitor, was again active, reacting formally, but not seemingly without emotion, to the events surrounding Petrono's unsuccessful mission. In the weeks between 12 August and 8 October, a Saturday, Fra Simone repeatedly sat at his bench of justice in the church of Santa Maria di Croce and issued documents and initiated actions that involved a significant segment of the clergy of the Leonessa area within the diocese of Rieti. He, the inquisitor, made himself the center of a network of messengers and notaries and witnesses, some of whom came to his court to report what was happening and being said in Rieti, twenty-five kilometers to the southwest. On his first recorded Leonessa Friday Fra Simone wrote an open and public letter to the official community of Rieti: to the podestà, his vicar, the *capitaneo*, the six, other officials "however titled," counselors, and the commune of Rieti. He rehearsed in general terms difficulties he had found in executing his duties in Rieti, including those that had made necessary his removal to Leonessa, and warned that those difficulties, including inhibitions of and threats to his messengers, must stop on pain of excommunication, interdict, and heavy fines. He demanded that Paolo Zoppo, whom he had left in the podestà's custody, be presented to him or to his deputies, the Franciscan Fra Matteo da Leonessa and dompno Giovanni archpriest of San Cristoforo, to appear before his tribunal at Santa Maria di Croce, and that Contessa, should she continue to ignore the inquisitor's mandates, be jailed. The inquisitor demanded of the Reatine governors a formal response by public instrument and special nuncio and placed them and their territories under punishments of excommunication, interdict, and fine from the time of his issuing his letter should they fail to comply with his orders.[40]

At Mass on the great feast of the Assumption in the presence of the nobleman Ugucio de Corneto, royal vicar of Leonessa, and of Don Giovanni da Terni, the vicar's judge, of two priests of the church of Santa Maria di Croce, and of a multitude of clergy and laity, in the church of Santa Maria di Croce, the notary Brunacio de Cornalto (then a notary and clerk at the office of Riformanze in Leonessa) read the inquisitor's letter to the commune of Rieti in the vernacular and explained it clearly to his listeners. Similarly a group of clerics testified that they had presented the letter in various churches in the area, at Mass, on Sunday 14 August: Giovanni, archpriest of San Cristoforo de Posta Cornu in the diocese of Rieti, here identified as vicar of the bishop of Rieti in *terra Gonesse*, in the church of Santa Barbara in the territory of Leonessa; dompno Raynerio, parish priest (*sacerdos parroccialis*) of the church of Santa Maria di Croce itself in that church; dompno Giovanni da Leonessa, rector of Sant'Egidio of Leonessa in that church; dompno Francesco, rector of the church of San Savino in Rieti diocese in that church; dompno Tommaso da Leonessa, rector of the church of Santa Maria de Cerreto in Rieti diocese in that church. All gathered at Santa Maria di Croce formally to report their actions before the inquisitor and his then notary the Franciscan Fra Giovanni da Cascia and a group of witnesses including the pievano of San Massimo of Leonessa within the diocese of Spoleto.[41]

Then on 19 August, a Friday, again at Santa Maria di Croce, two men, one a priest of Santa Maria di Croce, testified that they, with a third companion, on the previous Tuesday, the day after the feast, had gone to Rieti and stayed there until "yesterday (*heri*)," and they talked of what was being said at Rieti and of the fact that the Reatines certainly knew of the inquisitor's acts. They heard Reatines discussing the inquisitor's processes in various places throughout the city, and they themselves talked to Reatines around the city about the inquisitor's processes against them which had been published in various churches in Leonessa, but the Reatines said that they did not care, and they disparaged the inquisitor, and some of them (whose names the priest did not know, he said) threatened the inquisitor and said, "If that inquisitor himself ever comes back we will do something [this and that (*hoc et illud*)] to him." And one of the priest's companions heard threatening Reatines say among other things that they would like to burn the inquisitor himself. The Reatines, the inquisitor was assured, knew of his actions.

Fra Simone, assured that the Reatine officials knew of his actions, proceeded to declare those officials contumacious, excommunicated, fined, and their territory under interdict. He further announced that he intended to make inquisition against them: to correct them as they should be corrected and to punish them as they should be punished. He announced this in front of a group of clerical witnesses from the area of Leonessa, which included the bishop of Rieti's vicar there, dompno Giovanni Petri, archpriest of San Cristoforo; and also an Augustinian Hermit, Agostino da Leonessa; as well as Giovanni da Terni, judge of Ugucio, the royal vicar of Leonessa. And at this point Fra Simone pronounced the individual names of his prey. They begin high with Abiamonte de Lecto "the captain of the castle or the royal vicar in the city of Rieti or the captain for war of the city." And one should note the division between the royal vicar of Leonessa acting as a witness to the inquisitor's pronouncement and the royal vicar of Rieti named as one of its targets—not only because the presence and description of the vicars shows a diocese caught within the Regno, but also because the division describes something of the real and complex geography of royal and political power in the Regno, as the alignment of the bishop of Rieti's vicar in Leonessa and his vicar general in Rieti describes that of ecclesiastical and political power.

The name of the royal vicar is followed by the title of the podestà and then the name of Don Salomone de Betton', elsewhere identified as captain of Rieti, and then the six priors of the guilds (later called consuls of the guilds) listed by name and sestiere, and then the title of their notary. Finally come the names of six men identified here simply as citizens of Rieti. The first four names arrest their reader's attention: Don Giacomo Leoparducii, Angelucio Jotii, Ceccho Jotii, and Giacomo Jotii—who one would guess, correctly, were Contessa's three brothers. And a party of her sympathizers forms in the document: Giacomo, who had defended Paolo because of his pathetic condition, and Contessa's family to which Giacomo may have been connected and whose interest in Contessa must have been in some part at least proprietary, and in her house, in which heretical acts were said to have occurred and which must have seemed vulnerable to the stone-by-stone destruction at times meted out to houses which had housed heresy.[42]

Through late September and early October the inquisitor continued to sit at his *banco* in the church of Santa Maria, to collect witnesses and grievances, to build his case and his networks, and incidentally to draw an increasingly detailed map of Rieti and the northern part of the diocese through the record of his actions entered, sometimes out of chronological order, in the neat paper folios of the Vatican codex. On 15 September, a Wednesday, in the presence of his continual companion, the Franciscan friar Petrucio di don Francesco da Spoleto, and of Fra Giovanni da Rieti of the order of Santo Spirito (who was actually staying or stationed in the hospital at Leonessa), the inquisitor issued a formal and public citation to Contessa and the named officials of the city of Rieti including the *gonfaloniere*, Nardo di notaio Pietro, in which the podestà of Rieti is also named, Don Razzante da Firenze, and the captain, Salomone, is given his patronymic "di Monaldo." The inquisitor caused the citation to be proclaimed with trumpet sounded by Vanni di Biagio, the *bannitore*, crier or herald, of Leonessa between the preface and the elevation of Mass.[43]

On 15 September, too, a man named Bernardo Ferrarii from Venice (or just possibly Benevento), who lived in Rieti, testified at Santa Maria about the guarding of the gates by the six and the gonfaloniere Nardo; he said he had heard of it often and from many people, specifically when he was in the communal jail of Rieti, and particularly from one of the podestà's men (*famulus*) called Sandro who said he had stood guard himself. On 16 September dompno Tommaso di Tommasone da Cumulata di Leonessa, a clerk of the diocese of Rieti, talked of the guarding and of Nardo, of a man named Jutio da Pendenza who brought a message from Rieti to Leonessa, and of someone who was offered a florin to take a message from Leonessa to Rieti.

On the same day, a Friday, dompno John Gilbertson from the city of "Sancte Floris de Ibernia," chaplain of the royal castle in Leonessa, testified that the Sunday before (11 September) he had taken letters from dompno Giovanni di Pietro, the vicar of the bishop of Rieti in the territory of Leonessa, to Don Francesco, the vicar of the bishop of Rieti, to the place where he lived, the episcopal palace, where Don Francesco had wanted not to accept them. He had said: "Iste sunt littere inquisitoris; nolo eas recipere (those are letters from the inquisitor; I don't want to receive them)." And he would not have taken them, John said, if he had not first seen the name of the vicar Giovanni (who was a listening witness to John's testimony) on the letters.[44]

On 17 September an Augustinian Hermit, Fra Stefano Petroni da Rieti, testified that he and his prior and other friars of their order had been forbidden to act as emissaries or messengers for the inquisitor. This witness knew things because he went from door to door (*hostiatim*) in Rieti collecting alms. He personally knew of the guarding of the gates because he went, repeatedly, in a normal way, out to collect the *elemosina canipe*; when he returned from the district of Lama he was stopped at the city gates and searched, as were other Augustinians. And to this testimony an Augustinian from Leonessa, Fra Martino di Oddone, joined two Franciscans as witnesses.[45]

On 19 September two Franciscans from Monteleone gave testimony. They had gone as an embassy from the commune of Monteleone to the captain general of Rieti, and when they got to the Franciscans' at Rieti, where they went to eat, the guardiano there said to one of them, who was in fact guardiano of his own house in Monteleone, that he had better watch out: "Caueas ne portes litteras inquisitoris." And in fact, as they ate, the notary of the six came to them, particularly suspicious, they said, because the lector of the Franciscans at Leonessa was himself a man who came from Monteleone (*oriundus de Monte Leone*), and he had been sent by the inquisitor to read his process in Rieti. The notary took the Franciscan ambassadors from Monteleone to a gate in the city wall and ejected them. They were not allowed back in, but they walked around along the outside of the city wall until they came to the gate leading out toward Leonessa where was the castle of the captain, the royal vicar, to whom they bore letters. He there received them and explained to them more of the hostility of the Reatines to the inquisitor and that they, the Reatines, intended to start an action which would establish the fact that the inquisitor's process was based on falsehood; and the captain then said, "And I know it's false (*et scio quod falsum est*)."[46]

On 20 September dompno Pietro Andreonis, formerly of Poggio Bustone, testified that he had brought the inquisitor letters from Don Francesco, the archpriest of Santa Maria di Canetra, vicar, and here called specifically vicar general, of the bishop of Rieti, "letters dated Tuesday"—that is, the same day in which he made it clear that he could not and would not receive letters from or execute orders sent by the inquisitor—saying "If you direct me to execute some order against the commune of Rieti I cannot do it without personal danger: [instead] I shall simply stay at home (*ad domum propriam remearem*)."

Then on 22 September the already mentioned Jutio di Nicola da Pendenza testified at the bench in Santa Maria. He said that in August he had been sent as messenger or ambassador by the officials of the commune of Rieti with letters telling the inquisitor to stop his actions against them and alleging the close, and so threatening, friendship between their commune and Leonessa. But on 22 September Jutio himself was confessing his fault, being and seeming contrite, and receiving absolution from the inquisitor so that he could again receive the sacraments. He was also telling the inquisitor news of Rieti and the opinions held there. The inquisitor's troubles in executing his office in Rieti had been brought about through actions of Contessa's brothers, Giacomo Leoparducii, and their allies. This was common belief and rumor in Rieti: *publica uox et fama*. And what, Jutio was asked, does *publica uox et fama* mean? And he answered, what is commonly said and by most of the people (*quod dicitur communiter et a maiore parte gentis*).[47]

On 24 September the inquisitor again cited Contessa and he also cited Giovanni Petrignani of Rieti to appear before him before terce on the following Monday (26 September). On that Monday he moved to a solemn and extended condemnation of the named officials of the city of Rieti, of Giacomo Leoparducii, of Contessa's brothers, and their named allies. They were contumacious and had ignored first, second, and third citations; they were aiders and abettors of heretics; and, contumacious and disobedient, they were now condemned to those punishments recited in the citations—they individually were fined 100 gold florins and excommunicated, and the city and district of Rieti were placed under interdict and fined 1,000 marks of silver. On 8 October the inquisitor's companion, from his own order and his own city, Fra Pietro (or Petrucio) di don Francesco da Spoleto, a man with a maintained patrician name which suggests familial devotion to Francis, testified before the inquisitor as did his companion, Fra Ludovico di Pietro da Monteleone. The two of them had been to Rieti to make sure that the officials of the city and the accused and condemned in the inquisitor's process were fully aware of what the inquisitor had done and of the nature and extent of their condemnation. They had presented themselves to the royal vicar, Abbiamonte (or Abiumonte), and read to him the communication from the inquisitor addressed to him. The two friars had presented themselves and read their documents on 30 September and on 1 and 2 October, and their presentation was witnessed not only by the vicar, but by Don Giacomo Leoparducii, and two of Contessa's brothers, in the chapel of the royal castle at Rieti.

The friars also went to the Franciscans' at Rieti and, in the garden there, they told the guardiano of the place of the interdict. The guardiano said that the inquisitor's process was not valid because it was not made in the *provincia romana* of the inquisition (where the inquisitor's charge ran). But the friars said that it was indeed made within the *provincia romana*, because it had been acted in the church of Santa Maria di Croce in Leonessa, which was within the diocese of Rieti and so, according to the division of inquisitorial provinces, within the *provincia romana*. The city and diocese of Rieti, the guardiano was told, were under interdict. The friars then returned to Leonessa to announce and swear to the successful completion of their mission.[48]

On 21 October when the record for Fra Simone's inquisition recommences, he has established himself in the church of San Francesco at Viterbo and has collected around himself men from religious orders and clergy, judges and a notary, from its neighborhood rather than that of Leonessa, thirty-five of them in the initial naming: Don Matteo, prior of Sant'Angelo and vicar of the bishop of Viterbo; the archpriest of San Lorenzo, the cathedral church of Viterbo; the priors of San Matteo in Sonza ("de Sunsa," and himself named Matteo), Santa Maria Nuova, and San Luca; two priest canons of San Sisto, two priest canons of Sant'Angelo, one priest canon of San Matteo, and one priest canon of Santa Maria Nuova; four Franciscans, two Dominicans, two Carmelites; two Premonstratensians (?) from Santa Maria della Verità, and four Benedictines (?) from San Pietro della Castagna (men who actually came from Orvieto, Florence, San Sepolcro, Gualdo, Sezze, Montefiascone, Tarquinia, Rome, and Vetralla, as well as—four of them—from Viterbo itself); six judges and doctors of law; a local notary. Present for the inquisitor's restatement of the case on 26 October was his old companion Fra Pietro (or Petrucio) di don Francesco da Spoleto, as well as a number of Viterbo priests, or priests living in Viterbo, like Nicola da Orte, chaplain of San Martino in Viterbo.[49]

On 28 October, still in Viterbo, the inquisitor chose a new direction. He sent messengers to Federico de Murro (Morro), a citizen of Rieti who was podestà of Orte, and to his judges, notaries, and familiars who were from Rieti, and to any Reatine who happened to be living in Orte, ordering them all to see to the solemn publication of his acts and condemnations in Orte. The inquisitor ordered that his acts and citations be posted outside of the cathedral church of Orte and in other places where it seemed best to affix them, and that those Reatines against whom the inquisition was proceeding be cited to appear before him within fifteen days at whatever place he should be within the diocese of Viterbo or of Orte or of Orvieto. On 2 November, the messengers, one of whom was actually, like the inquisitor, from Spoleto, swore that they had accomplished their assigned mission, in the communal palace of Orte, and that they had attached the inquisitor's letter patent, with his seal on its dorse, outside the cathedral church of Orte.[50]

From 2 November the inquisitor's record jumps to a February (but presumably back to February 1334) and to Tivoli, where the inquisitor's attention was focused directly on the fraticelli, who were quite surely the central target of his entire campaign. The first figure recorded testifying before him at Tivoli was the fraticello Fra Francesco da Assisi, more fully Francesco di Vanni da Assisi, who was staying in a place near Tivoli (*in territorio Cole Comitis*). Francesco was also identified as Francesco junior because he was one of two fraticelli called Francesco da Assisi whom the inquisitor was investigating. The other, Francesco da Assisi senior, was identified as, "was called," the guardiano of San Biagio di Castro Poli. The two men who bore their saint's name and who were under Fra Simone's inquisitorial scrutiny make clangingly evident the clash of values and models and action within the broader Franciscan community of 1334.[51]

From Fra Francesco, Fra Simone extracted the common stories of fraticelli diversity. Fra Simone made Fra Francesco answer whether or not he had heard notorious fraticelli statements, where, and by whom. Fra Simone pushed toward the star of which Paolo Zoppo was perhaps a crazy and defective and potentially damaging satellite. Did Fra Francesco know anything that smelled of heresy? Not anything unless it was that he had heard from the *fraticelli de paupere vita* talking among themselves in lots of places and saying that Pope John was not pope and calling him Giacomo from Cahors; and he said that he had heard the fraticelli saying that the pope had cut off the head of the life of Christ, because he abolished the fraticelli and because he had published a decretal that said that Christ had had property, and saying that there was a "prophecy" that the Roman church is made a whore and had crossed the mountains the better to fornicate, and that the so-called friars minor were not the true friars minor but that the fraticelli were. Asked if he had believed these things Francesco said yes. Asked how long he had believed, he answered that he had spent more than five years in various places among the fraticelli and then he had believed. Asked if he had made any profession, he answered that he had been received and inducted by the fraticelli, and he had promised to follow the rule and the testament of Saint Francis, and he had sworn this on the Bible and the rule and the altar and in the hands of Fra Paolo da Assisi who was called the minister provincial in "the province of Saint Francis." This had been perhaps four years before and at Santa Maria de Rapichiano (Rapicciano) in the territory of Spello in the diocese of Spoleto. And asked who was the general of the order, Fra Francesco said that it was Fra Angelo Clareno da Fossombrone. In a few folios Simone has pushed his diverse witnesses and his book's readers back from the fumbling nudity of Paolo Zoppo to the generalate of Angelo Clareno. And this movement was recorded in the year 1334, during which Angelo fled from central Italy to rest in the safety of Robert the Wise's south and to prepare, in his own words, his escape from the prison of the body and the exile of the world.

Fra Francesco gave Fra Simone the names of eleven friars, beginning with the senior Fra Francesco da Assisi, four of them from Spoleto, from whom he had heard these things. And Fra Simone, returning to the questioning on the same day, demanded to know where Fra Angelo Clareno had been staying and heard that it was at San Benedetto Subiaco. Fra Simone's big net in which Subiaco is caught with Angelo recalls (or predicts) his little Reatine net in which San Giovanni Evangelista was caught with Paolo.

But the Reatine connection becomes sharp and clear in the inquisitor's interrogation of 2 March. On that day Fra Simone's witness was the novice in the order of friars minor Fra Giovanni di Lodorono Alfani of Rieti—a son of Lodorono, like Giovanni Petrignani's companion in the garden of San Giovanni Evangelista, more specifically a son of Lodorono Alfani, in whose house had died Fra Rainaldo da Spoleto, who had, Paolo Zoppo said, taught Paolo how men and women lay naked together in Spoleto.[52]

Fra Giovanni di Lodorono testified in the chapter of the Minors at Tivoli with Fra Gerald of Man, or perhaps Wales (*Giraldo de Mananea*), acting as inquisitor's notary and recording his statements. Giovanni testified to hearing the sort of statements that Francesco da Assisi had heard; he had also heard it said that the established friars minor did not have the understanding or good conscience to observe the rule of Saint Francis to the letter and that they were not in a state of grace or salvation but rather of damnation. But among those badly spoken fraticelli who were servants to error, Fra Giovanni said, should not be included his brother, Fra Giovanuccio da Rieti, although the reported errors were common in the district of Rieti. When Giovanni was asked where he had been with these erring fraticelli, whose head was Fra Angelo, he answered, at Rome, and in Marino, and in places around Rieti.

On 18 March Francesco di Vanni da Assisi was again testifying before the inquisitor. He said that he had heard, near Tivoli, during the evening of the night between Christmas and the feast of Stephen, from Pietro da Lombardia the repeated bitter joke about Saint Anthony's and Saint Benedict's and Saint Francis's all having to be in hell not in heaven, or else they would have done something about the followers who bore their names, would have plunged them into the abyss. And in telling the story Fra Pietro had called the friars minor the fat friars (*fratres minores quos vocabat fratres grassos*).[53]

In the "fat" friars' attack on the "fraticelli of the poor life," the church and commune of Rieti were caught and, for us, exposed. Fra Simone's direct attack at Tivoli on the followers of Angelo Clareno displays the central purpose of his mission and thus reveals with contingent clarity the subsidiary nature of his attack on Paolo, Contessa, and the commune of Rieti. But the inquisitor's questions about Reatine matters and the testimony he provoked with them, at least coincidentally, raked into view many elements in the physical and mental structure of the place.

If the observer of the Vatican manuscript moves back through its recorded documents, if he or she starts with the Tivoli testimony (and reserves for special use the statements and person of Fra Giovanni di Lodorono Alfani), he or she comes next in this paper passage to the Viterbo and Leonessa processes in which Fra Simone through his minions tried to approach and penetrate Rieti from the outside. The observer then becomes sensibly aware of Rieti as a walled (and rivered) place set within a more open, or at least more easily penetrable, diocese, in which were established vicars of the king in Naples as well as episcopal vicars, and through which could move representatives of the "fat" Franciscan inquisition established by the Roman pope in Avignon.

Although the year 1334 lies within a period of considerable confusion about political boundaries in those areas of Italy where the kingdom of Naples and lands under direct papal control touched each other, the inquisitorial material, with its royal Neapolitan vicars in the royal Neapolitan castles or palaces or fortresses, gives strong evidence of the dominant presence of Robert the Wise's Naples in the area. But that evidence is immediately countered by evidence of local and communal strength and independence as, for example, in the case of the two royal vicars who seem to stand divided between support of or at least apparent adhesion to the inquisitor in Leonessa and the commune of Rieti; and within the commune there is the power of faction of the sort we see when we are told that the action from Rieti is controlled by "the six" and their officers, themselves prodded by the local party of Giacomo Leoparducii and the Jotii brothers. The division between the royal vicars is echoed by, or echoes, that between the two episcopal vicars, the vicar general in Rieti and the vicar of the territory of Leonessa, as one stands witness to the inquisitor's Leonessan acts and the other stays in his lodgings in the episcopal palace and refuses to receive the inquisitor's letters and adds to his refusal rather salty statements that must have seemed impertinent to the inquisitor's ears, particularly from a man who had (our evidence seems to show) given him his complete support when the inquisitor was actually present in Rieti. In fact all of formerly cooperating Rieti seemed to have turned against the inquisitor, as the guardiano of the fat Franciscans at Rieti argues about diocesan and provincial boundaries and as Reatine denizens argue that it is the inquisitor (and not his victims) who should be burned. The inquisitor's excommunications seem to have flown with less effect than his letters did (with exceptions, or at least one exception: Jutio sought to receive the sacraments again), this in spite of careful and broad publication and that in spite of closed gates.

The evidence for communal coherence and independence, and for penetration into and escape from small urban community, is abundant in the case, but its total message is as complex as is that, about the same matters, at an earlier stage, which can be gathered from the writings of Francis's immediate followers. The containing city of Orte was obviously a hospice for Reatines, including ruling Reatines; they were available to the inquisitor in Orte, and they offered him connection with the city, Rieti, from which they had come and to which in the inquisitorial mind they still, in a significant way, belonged—even the citizen podestà, pretty clearly from the noble family of the rustic hill castro of Morro. The Franciscans of Monteleone, ambassadors of their own commune, were suspect to the Reatines because the lector of the Franciscans at Leonessa, who had been given a charge by the inquisitor, had come from Monteleone (*oriundus de Monte Leone*).

Witness lists as well as behavior give evidence about the consistency of the clerical community. Certainly they show that a local clerical community was assumed to exist, and that within that general community there was also an assumed community not just among the members of individual orders of friars but among friars—Franciscans, Dominicans, and Augustinian Hermits, at least orthodox ones—more generally. The friars themselves, in this inquisition's towns, were by 1334 both local and foreign to the towns in which they lived. More settled, perhaps, than in the thirteenth century, they were still mobile. But their activities, or some of them, also tied together and made more communal the communities in which they lived, not just through their grand activities within their great churches but also, for example, through their begging, *hostiatim*, door-to-door, collecting and dispersing, as they moved, the *vox publica*, the rumors and gossip, which bound the community together or separated it into camps.

But there was also division among clergy and order and not just the flamboyant dispute between the "fat" and "poor" Franciscans. What, for instance, was the true position, what were the true attachments, of the guardiano of the Franciscans at Rieti in 1334? As interesting as any division within an order, moreover, was the connection among orders, most interestingly and most famously, that connection centered in the great old Benedictine complex at Subiaco, which seems to have been as alive as Farfa seems to have been dead, and most particularly alive with "poor" Franciscans and particularly their leader Angelo Clareno.[54] The Rieti tightly closed within its walls in the testimony of Petrono Giovanucci was placed within a Reatine territory clearly open to the influence of Franciscan Subiaco in the earlier testimony of Fra Giovanni di Lodorono Alfani. The inquisitorial record opens to view some part of the spiritual force of Angelo Clareno and again reminds its reader that Angelo's influence and attachments were not limited to men and women in the Franciscan order. In this connection one should recall that just a few years before the inquest, in 1328, it was Angelo's friend, the Augustinian Hermit Gentile da Foligno, to whose supplication the bishop of Rieti, Giovanni Papazurri, responded in founding Santa Caterina, the new convent of cloistered Benedictine nuns in Cittaducale.

Again pursuing the paper passage backward through the Vatican manuscript from those documents that record the inquisitor's activities in Viterbo and Leonessa to those that record his activities in Rieti itself, their reader is pushed into a display of Rieti structures, of the sets and props of inquisitorial and alleged heretical action: to clothes and doors and rooms, and furniture within rooms, benches and beds and containers of straw, to internal enclosures and loggias and gates, to external spaces and piazzas, to a jail (with gossip in it) and to a cemetery (with a "dangerous" friar buried in it), to where the butcher lived, to where the Franciscans lived, to where the bishop's vicar lived, to where the podestà lived. A physical, an intermittent physical, Rieti is set up before our eyes, the infrastructure, to make for a moment a false division of Reatine spirituality. And in the physical structure, on the stage, are placed individual figures connecting themselves with one another in expected and unexpected patterns and groups, agreeing and disagreeing, attracting and repelling one another, pretending to explain. In this little city they move through streets, or say they do, seeing people they do not recognize, and then at the other extreme they expose to us surprising, close connections.

In this setting appears the person of Giovanni Petrignani, priest of San Giovanni Evangelista. He is physically placed; he appears, listening to confession, in his garden near the center of Rieti, near the Duomo, reading there to a group of listeners noticeably including women. He jokes with a son of Loderono (or Eleutherio). The interest of this figure, of Giovanni Petrignani, increases when we recall that one of the correspondents and friends of Angelo Clareno, and of Fra Matteo da Rieti, the sympathetic guardiano of the Roman convent of San Giovanni in Porta Latina, and of Fra Andrea da Rieti, who served as messenger between Angelo Clareno and Gentile da Foligno, was called Giovanni Petrignani (who has been identified by the editor of Angelo's letters as a friend of Matteo da Rieti and probably a layman sympathetic to the Spiritual Franciscans).[55] Angelo Clareno's Giovanni Petrignani almost surely must be Rieti's priest of San Giovanni Evangelista, which gives a different, higher, and more serious tone both to his readings in the garden and to the inquisitor's poking into that garden. Seen by itself the inquisitor's record suggests that Giovanni Petrignani's position in Rieti was seriously threatened, but—and this is informative about Rieti, about local independence, and about the power of the inquisition—in 1350 Giovanni Petrignani will be both archpriest of San Giovanni Evangelista and a canon of the church of Rieti.

Actually from 1349 comes a full description of Giovanni Petrignani's prebend, the prebend which had been Tommaso Cimini's in 1307, with measured land of about 40 giunte, a noticeable part of which is in vineyard in Campo Ratino, San Pietro in Campo, and other places; and from land at Santa Rufina the holder of the prebend was to get each year five soldi and a chicken. Ten giunte were in Fiume Morto (on the road that went to the island hill [*collem insule*]) and four in Casamascara—in the area where the chapter had once fought the Cistercians for drying land and where the lords of Labro still held lands. One piece of the prebend's land had once been held by the notary Pietro de Clausura. Before Giovanni Petrignani held this prebend, before he was a canon of the cathedral church but two years after the inquisition of Paolo Zoppo, in April 1336, Giovanni Petrignani had been the first of the witnesses listed in the will of the future bishop Tommaso Secinari, another actor in the Zoppo story. In 1358 then canon Giovanni Petrignani was given two soldi for singing Mass (with a deacon and a subdeacon who were given 14 denari) in the cathedral on the feast of the Assumption. In 1358 Giovanni was receiving commons including grain. He was alive in April 1359, but presumably not in June 1360. Whether Giovanni Petrignani had joked his way through the Black Death to more conservative attitudes or had brought fraticelli attitudes to the cathedral chapter, it is not possible to say, but he had clearly survived his brush with the inquisition.[56]

Giovanni Petrignani teased his fellow-priest Matteo di Loctarono (or Lodorono or Eleuterio) whom he called, in his teasing, "fili Loctaroni," a way of naming which takes on a heightened significance read in the context of Angelo Clareno's correspondence in 1315 or 1316 with Francesco and Giovanni, nicknamed Citto and Vanne, "filiis Domini Lotaronis" of Rieti.[57] Angelo wrote to the young men to urge them not to let the tears of their parents persuade them to give up the life they had chosen in imitation of Christ; in harsh words and phrases Angelo attacked the dangers of that damaging and containing parental love which would take the brothers back from their life with the Spiritual Franciscans. He quoted the severe words of Christ in Luke (11:27–28), when he responded to the woman who had said "Blessed are the womb that bore thee and the breasts that gave thee suck" with "Rather blessed are those who hear the word of God and keep it." Further Angelo asked other friars to help Citto and Vanne, to take them to Pozzaglia, and to try to keep them from going home. It is complicated—people change. This Vanne has been thought to be the same Giovanni who (still or again a novice?) testified, cooperatively perhaps, before the inquisitor Fra Simone da Spoleto. Vanne's father is almost surely the same Lodorono or Lodoro in whose house in Rieti Paolo Zoppo's instructor Fra Rainaldo da Spoleto died. This branch of the Alfani family was clearly entangled with the Spiritual movement in the Reatine, and its entanglement gives the movement an enhanced local quality. The inquisition was clearly touching things and people at the respectable and powerful center of the city, people who were not in any contemporary conventional sense crazy or vile. The respectable and powerful connections of the inquisition's targets are seen again in the effectiveness of Contessa's brothers and in Paolo Zoppo's attempted flight to Tommaso Secinari, the future bishop whose seignorial family came from the Regno, then ruled by Robert the Wise, Angelo's protector.

Giovanni Petrignani's garden seems the center of spiritual intensity in the inquisitor's documents' narrative of Rieti, but the protagonist in the actual story, while it remains in Rieti, is Paolo Zoppo. This man of "vile condition," forced to confess, or say, that he had made a woman undress not really for pious reasons, but because he wanted to see her naked, forced to confess, or say, that he had polluted his anchorite's cell by libidinous activities with a dog, and forced to confess, or say, that there were women with whom he had had religious conversation with whom he had repeatedly and unsuccessfully tried to have sexual relations, this man was the figure whom the inquisitor Simone da Spoleto chose to make his Rieti heretic.

In choosing to make Paolo his heretic, Simone chose to make him, or to recognize in him, a kind of "holy man," a weak perversion of a "holy man" perhaps, but recognizably that person. He was an urban holy man, caught in the frenzy, if that is not too strong a word, of early fourteenth-century urban movement—to the Portiuncula, to bed in the house next to the butcher's, to a cell next to an urban church, to discussions in a garden next to another urban church, a holy man caught in a world of urban mistresses and maids, in which a mistress felt that she could advise a maid about spiritual propriety and in which the mistress could become a Franciscan tertiary and the maid a Benedictine nun in an urban convent. He was a holy man who kissed the kiss of peace on a woman's mouth. The enclosed space in which Paolo's figure was created was fixed not just by its geography but also by its chronology; his story is a story of the 1320s and 1330s, in terms of Franciscan development, papal attitude, Neapolitan presence, the power of the six, the position of Alfani and Secinari in Rieti, the closing years of the episcopate of Giovanni Papazurri, the physical, social, and psychological structure of the city (including the Franciscan buildings, including loggia and foresteria, by the river).

The creation of the figure of the heretic suggests in shadow the creation of a figure of a saint. Moreover, one of the aspects of Paolo's supposed heresy was, it was claimed, that he in lying tried to help create a saint, presumably a fraticello saint. The story of his lies, which Paolo is led to confess, is an absurd one, disjointed and silly; but the distorted description of the props of sanctity, although surely deliberately foolish, suggests the kind of props which could be more wisely and resonantly used to establish the sanctity of a worthy figure. So Paolo Zoppo offers two false holy men to the viewer, himself, the perverter of the kiss of peace, and his "saint" Fra Appollonio of, or at, Greccio. And in the latter at least the reader recognizes something of the climate of the great and famous, and in all senses neighboring, saint, Pietro of the Morrone (Celestine V) as he is seen in his "autobiografia."[58] They share the disjointed world of snowy mystery and hard mountain fact.

In Paolo's story a wolf, a beast repeatedly and naturally sensitive to Franciscan persuasions, returned to the area from which Francis had once driven wolves, knocks on a door where hungry novices eat, or do not eat, but in an almost suburban mountain hermitage. The wolf brings bread and then, the table set, presumably, returns with a second course, of meat—after God has perhaps been tempted: three days and no more without bread or the novices would leave, then at the last minute comes the, otherwise quiet, knocking friend. And this story is followed by another of the lies, again about bread, this time brought by a queenly person. Bread is a natural substance for miracles, particularly Christian miracles. Cuthbert's bread and Anselm's bread indirectly evoke the Eucharist.[59] Fra Appollonio's bread seems to evoke nothing. There seems a deliberate poverty in the stories' presentation; the events are made to appear simple wonders, signs of nothing.

The empty interstices that emphasize the isolation of the images of wonder in Greccio's domesticated snowy wildness are, no doubt, in large part the result of harshly diminishing inquisitorial animosity. But the broken emptiness is not entirely inappropriate for a group dedicated to intense voluntary poverty. These images without resonance can, moreover, seem like limbs broken off the eccentrically controlled structure of the masterpiece of a strange, but again appropriate, genre, the "autobiografia" of Peter of Morrone, in which particles of blunt naturalism are suspended in a magically supernatural atmosphere and tied together by ringing bells and flying birds, a realm dominated by the Holy Ghost.[60] The autobiografia's hungry world is a world not only of mountains and castri but also of snow: *et erat nix magna, et tunc ningebat* (there was much snow, and then it snowed). The snow of the autobiografia also appears in stories of Peter's miracles; it dominates one of Paolo Zoppo's lies about miracles. But snow had not seemed important in the stories of Francis's companions; even in their Greccio, the place of Paolo's snowy miracle, it was *grando*, hail, not *nix*, snow, which devastated.[61] Perhaps the companions' perception and sensibility remained Umbrian, and Paolo's have become Abruzzese. The two localities seem appropriate for the two spiritualities at a century's distance from each other.

But snow also enters the stories of miracles told about Filippa Mareri, the uncanonized but recognized saint of the Cicolano and its great family, who died on 16 February 1236. For the three days before her death "nubecula quaedam spissa et alba, sicut nix et quasi glomerata, stetit in claustro monasterii, videntibus cunctis et admirantibus (a little cloud, dense and white, like snow and shaped into a ball, rested in the cloister of the monastery, and was seen, and wondered at, by everyone)."[62] The snowball cloud departed when the white-clad soul of the saint was carried by the Holy Spirit into heaven—and, the tale of the wonder continues, there were at the time no other clouds around the monastery. The story is recorded as one of the particles pretty obviously gathered for the saint-making of Filippa, a precursor of the process mocked by Paolo's inquisitor when he extracts from Paolo his "lying" stories of Fra Appollonio's miracles.

It was a process, this interested promotion of sanctity, sufficiently common to be joked about in a period well before the telling of Paolo's stories, and for the jokes to be recorded by the saints' promoters—or at least this was true in the case of the holy Roman patrician Margherita Colonna who died in 1280. A scoffer in a Margherita miracle story, when he found that a physician he sought was off on a pilgrimage, with a Colonna, to places in a Colonna-dominated part of Lazio connected with Margherita's holy life, complained that her noble family was trying to shoot her into heaven.[63] These stories promoting sanctity formed a part of the developing rite and rule of papal canonization in which the exact details of miracles as well as of holy lives had increasingly to be produced in authenticated form and able to withstand the probing of inquisition or inquest. The peculiarity in Filippa's candidacy for official sanctity is that the case for her, at least as it now remains, seems to have been prepared so slackly.

Filippa's life, insofar as it can be reconstructed with any security, looks like this. She was born in about 1190 in the Cicolano, the third child of Filippo, baron of Mareri, and his wife, Imperatrice. From her early youth Filippa wanted to know more of God, and fortunately she was taught about God by a certain chaste man "learned in the Scriptures." Filippa began to despise "the world." She resisted and opposed her family's many plans for a noble marriage and sought instead to preserve her virginity. Since she had no other place to retire, she imprisoned herself in a room within a family palace and lived there as in hermitage or as a *monaca in casa*. But because of the tumultuous behavior of members of her family and its household, and particularly that of her brother Tommaso, she could not find sufficient quiet at home, and so in the society of other serious women she fled up the mountainside to a cave above Mareri, where she lived with her women in a simple community.

Filippa's brother, Tommaso, was, however, inspired by God and changed his attitude toward her. He begged her to come with her band of holy women to the church of San Pietro of which he held the patronage and which he offered to her for her to hold freely. San Pietro became the women's monastery, and they established in it a custom of life based on that of Saint Clare of Assisi at San Damiano. The monastery's freedom and exemption were guaranteed by a "public instrument" drawn up for Tommaso; and Filippa petitioned to have confirmation of his grant from the church of Rieti (*que est caput diocesis*) and the Roman curia. There, in the monastery, Filippa lived; and on the night that she died, it was later written, "a resounding voice rushed through the castles, castri, and villages [of the Mareri Cicolano] saying, 'Saint Filippa is dead.' " And in the morning a crowd—men, women, clerics—with lighted candles came to the monastery shouting, "Saint Filippa, Saint Filippa."[64]

Any account of Filippa's life must stay both tentative and spare because of the particular nature of the surviving evidence about her, evidence as difficult to use as is that about Paolo Zoppo but for very different reasons. The oldest, at all serious, biographical account of Filippa is her *legenda*. Its nine *lectiones* or readings do not now seem to exist in an edition earlier than that which was printed in 1545.[65] To tell when the *legenda* was actually written does not seem possible. Most of the quite vague detail with which it attempts to give tone and taste to Filippa's sanctity seems so generic and commonplace that, except for chronology, geography, family connection, gender, and very general type, it cannot be seen to describe the specific way of living of a specific person. Filippa is presented as a family saint who resists marriage, retires, attempts a rather experimental group life in a high-country cave, and then accepts the communal life of a convent which adopts Franciscan usages.

The outline of the life presented is in a number of ways similar to that of the later Margherita Colonna, who, however, came from a more cosmopolitan, urban, and powerful family, and whose two *vite* are full of evocative and exactly descriptive detail: this difference in detail can quickly be seen, for example, in a comparison of the ways in which the two saints show their love of God through charity to the poor.[66] Margherita's life and her miracles exemplify the style demanded by the evolving process of canonization or by the taste that made that process necessary. But Filippa's is an undeveloped example of a Margherita type of sanctity; and the specific connection between the two lives is made in one of the Margherita *vite* in the recording of a wonder which occurred after Margherita's death. The Franciscan Fra Bartolomeo da Gallicano was in Assisi on a vigil of Saint Clare. Bartolomeo, thinking of the sermon which he would preach on the feast, the next day, to the sisters, was walking, and then stopped and drowsed and dreamed in the cloister of the friars. He dreamed that he saw a group of blessed virgins walking. Among them were not only Clare and Margherita, but "a certain virgin, Filippa by name, distinguished because of her family but even more because of her sanctity"; and it was Filippa who explained the significance of the virginal group to Fra Bartolomeo.[67]

The Margherita life makes explicit the idea that both saintly women belonged to the same *caterva*, the same troop or company, of virgins. Possibly Filippa's life influenced Margherita's; possibly Margherita's written lives influenced Filippa's *legenda*. The sphere of Colonna political and spiritual influence and interest in the late thirteenth and early fourteenth centuries included the Reatine; transmission to and from the Colonna was possible. The Colonna presence was suggested not just by the presence of Giovanni Colonna in Rieti, and by Giacomo Colonna's patronage of the Reatine canon, Bartolomeo di don Rainaldo de Rocca, but also by the Colonna involvement with the locally persuasive Angelo Clareno. Angelo was tied to Subiaco and so was the cult of an earlier local cave saint which may have helped form Filippa, or legends about her. The saint, Chelidonia of the cave, was believed to have come from the Cicolano, and according to local tradition actually from Pescorocchiano, and to have lived and died (in 1152) and been buried in a cave at Morraferogna, a place between three and four kilometers from Subiaco and then locally within the diocese of Tivoli.

Filippa fits into a set of hagiographic conventions in a way that is related to, but obviously different from, Paolo Zoppo's historical figure's being formed, in significant part, by a series of inquisitorial questions and conventions. In the first *lectio* of the *legenda* Filippa's pregnant mother received a visit from a marvelous anonymous pilgrim bearing a significantly flowering palm. The *legenda* tells us that the young sacredly educated Filippa retreated to a cave, but that she, Martha as well as Mary, improved it so that it would be a more appropriate place to live, then with her sister, many nieces, and other noble women came down to her new monastery, that she was obedient to the church and to her spiritual father, the Franciscan Fra Ruggero, that she humbled herself and fasted, and that she was generous to Christ's poor and worked wonders.[68] But the *legenda* seems to be so generalized (except for its local names) and could, with its appended miracles, be so late that its reader might be tempted to believe that no Filippa had ever existed outside of its pages, if the physical evidence of her existence was not so palpable, so heavily apparent on the land.

The monastery itself and its village were moved up the hill from the banks of the Salto when the artificial Lago di Salto was created and the relic of the saint was carried from the old monastery to the new on 4 July 1940; when the convent was flooded (plate 34), the nuns left it and continued their lives on the hill.[69] They carried with them (or had had carried before them) the saint's heart and the saint's cup and their own sixteenth-century frescoes. They also carried their archives, which included, and include, among much else, a 1231 letter of grace from Gregory IX (while he was staying in Rieti) to Filippa and her nuns and a 1247 letter from Innocent IV to the abbess and nuns granting an indulgence of forty days on various feasts including that of Santa Filippa herself.[70] The archives also include Bishop Rainaldo de Labro's letter of 23 November 1231 describing his consecration of the new church of San Pietro di Molito on that day and a grant by Anfelice di Rainaldo de Turre of all of her goods to Filippa the second abbess of the convent on 1 September 1336.[71] With slight interruption and some change (including the grand change of the nuns' theater from cloister to world in 1929), the monastery and cult of Santa Filippa have continued from her own time to the present.[72] In the twentieth century, paper banners proclaim from their airy fluttering or their fixed positions pasted on local walls: LA SANTA BARONESSA and LA SANTA DEL CICOLANO.

The nature of Filippa's continued saintly presence is suggested by a comparison of the story of her heart with the story of the heart of another central Italian holy woman, Chiara da Montefalco, who died in 1308. By the light of dawn on the morning after her death the nuns of Chiara's convent discovered that her heart, opened, contained the cross of the crucifixion and the instruments of the passion. Chiara's heart contained, physically, the evidence of her having carried in life the death of Christ in her heart (although one male witness for her canonization inquest, who was a Franciscan as she was not, suspected a mechanical implant).[73] Filippa died in 1236. No details of the manner of her heart's conservation in the years following her death are available; but in 1706 it was found intact. It remains to give comfort to the afflicted.

To Filippa's *legenda* in its printed edition are appended three sets of miracles. Although the miracles are also relatively mute, they give, at least superficially, a stronger sense of closeness to the saint than does the *legenda*, because they are thick with the detail of personal name and specific place and because the record of them talks twice, in a truncated way, of how they were known and have been recorded. In this the miracles recall the parts of the *legenda* which seem to come closest to providing real evidence of something outside itself and its genre when it talks, in the eighth *lectio*, of Filippa's powers and, in the sixth and ninth *lectiones*, of Fra Ruggero, Filippa's spiritual adviser and a witness of her death. Fra Ruggero's position in the *legenda* suggests (perhaps was meant to suggest) that he might have written the *legenda* or written something from which the *legenda* was adapted or been the source of information and ideas included in the *legenda*.[74] He, like the nuns' having adopted a Damianite model, brings Filippa into a Franciscan net, and his presence helps interpret those words of the *legenda* that (in the third *lectio*) talk of Filippa's being formed, instructed, by Saint Francis and "other contemplatives"—words that have been taken to mean that Francis came to Mareri and talked to Filippa or in her hearing.[75] Two of the *legenda*'s wonders are specific: the daughter of the nobleman Bernardo da Valviano, Margherita by name, had an infirmity which distorted her mouth terribly and which with Filippa's intercession was cured; Filippa's niece, Imperatrice, daughter of Ruggero de Montana, had entered her monastery but Imperatrice's brothers and Tommaso de Mareri (Filippa's brother and the male protagonist of the *legenda*) quickly came to the monastery and demanded that Imperatrice, unwilling, return to them, but as she was being returned, and as the women prayed and lamented, the Holy Spirit fixed Imperatrice to the ground so the men could not move her.[76]

Most of the appended miracles are recorded in very brief narrative patches. They are not reinforced with the sort of verisimilitude of detail which historians have come to expect of stories from the thirteenth and fourteenth centuries that attempt to establish sanctity. The second and longest of the three clusters of miracle stories is introduced by a statement that says that the compiler will not attempt to list all of the holy woman's miracles but that he will write down some that are recorded by a notary (*manu publica sunt notata*) and attested by appropriate witnesses (*testibus idoneis approbata*).[77] This witnessing would of course heighten the stories' credibility and make it seem more probable that they were actually prepared for a formal canonization process. But no notary's name or subscript remains with the document, and there are no lists of witnesses except in the sense that each story's protagonist is a witness. The list itself suggests carelessness; of the twenty-three stories in the second group of miracles, two clearly refer to the same person and incident.[78] The stories seem to have led to no canonization process. Superficially the stories' carelessness may make them seem untrustworthy. But although the detail may seem inadequate, what later inventor would have done a job so badly, would have included believable names but almost no authenticating, and easily inventible, detail?

The three miracles of the first group, wonders really, are connected with the saint's death. They are the most detailed stories. One is the snowball story. Another tells of what happened to "a famous preacher in the order of friars minor," Tommaso da Civitella d'Abruzzo, on the night of Filippa's death. He was praying in the church of San Francesco in Assisi on the night of Filippa's death and he saw her soul traveling to heaven. On the following morning he told the story to the friars; and later it turned out that he had seen Filippa in the actual hour of her dying. The other story is of an Abruzzese baronial couple, Bernardo d'Ocre and his wife, people who had founded Santo Spirito and would found Sant'Angelo d'Ocre, and who were staying on the night of the saint's death at "Poggio Santa Maria." The baron saw a globe of fire lighting up the sky, particularly over San Pietro di Molito (of which the baron could be sure because of its closeness); and at the hour of the saint's death he saw it ascend to heaven. The baron understood and went back to tell his wife and household what he had seen and that Filippa was dead.[79]

Of the twenty-three miracles in the second cluster, actually (because of the repetition) twenty-two, twenty are specifically connected with the saint's tomb. A priest (with scabies almost to the point of having leprosy) is only said to have prayed to the saint, and a man with a contracted arm has relics held over him, but probably at the tomb. In one of the more extended little stories a certain girl from Rieti city (*puella quaedam de civitate Reatina*), named Altadonna, who had for three months had a contracted hand and foot and lost her speech and had set out for the saint's tomb, was cured before she actually got there.[80] The suggestion of movement caught in Altadonna's story is visible again in another of the slightly extended narratives (this one of thirty-nine words): Gemma the daughter of Accardo (presumably Azzardo) and wife of Pietro Rainaldi, but of place unspecified, went wandering about for five years and more, insane and without sense and practically naked (*ibat vaga et insana et quasi nuda ac sine sensu*).[81] But for the most part the sense of movement in the stories is restricted to the mention of the attracting tomb and the place of origin of the person healed (when place is mentioned). These points, however, do prick the outline of a neighborhood. One of the seekers, a Pietro Capocci, came from as far away as Vicovaro (in the diocese of Tivoli) and, healed, returned to his *patriam*.[82] Two came from Rieti. All the others, whose place of origin can be ascertained, came from the extended neighborhood of San Pietro where the convent was: three from Rigatti; one from Pescorocchiano; one from Oiano; one from Vallebona; one from Borgocollefegato; and one, a *famulus*, from the monastery itself.

The twelve postulant women, of whom two are called girls, and the ten men (of whom one is a *senex* and one a priest) bring sicknesses and deformities to the tomb: two cases of loss of sight; four cases of fever; two possessions by demons; a sickness in the throat; a "celsus" in the forehead with bleeding; a migraine severe enough to cause loss of speech; the five-month wanderer; an amnesiac epileptic; and eight cases of whole and partial paralysis (including Altadonna's pretty clear results of stroke), crippling pain, and growths.

The fourth group of miracles begins with four miracles connected with the wooden cup, still preserved, which, according to the eighth *lectio*, Filippa carried about with her when she prayed in church so that neither her tears nor her spit (because the force of nature sometimes made her spit) would dirty the floor of the church (a niceness that rather primitively recalls Francis's interest in the physical cleanliness of church).[83] The first two miracles in the group were worked for two Franciscans, Palmerio da Magliano and Paolo da Rieti; both had terrible abscesses, both drank water that had rinsed Filippa's cup, and both were cured. The second two cup miracles were worked for women of the Mareri family: Illuminata the daughter of Francesco, who could have been abbess Illuminata, and who suffered in the throat; Caterina the daughter of Giovanni, who is identified as an abbess and may have been that Caterina who was presiding over the monastery in 1295 and 1301, and who suffered in the lip.[84] The agent of these miracles was an object which had been closely connected with the live Filippa. Their beneficiaries were people close to her not necessarily in time but in order and family.

The three final miracle stories are connected with the four that precede them not through the agency of the cup but through their having been preserved by memory and speech, not by previous writing.[85] In one of these stories a man called Giacomo "de Marerio," who seems to have had epilepsy and for whom no medicine worked, fasted on the vigil of the *festa* of Santa Filippa and was cured. In a second story an unidentified man from Santa Rufina, who suffered from a similar affliction and for whom also no medicine worked, vowed to make an image of Santa Filippa and to fast on her vigil, and he too was cured. In the third story a woman called Rainaluttia from Fara, in the Sabina, near Farfa, who was crippled, visited Filippa's tomb and was cured.

The strange and uneven structure which is the record of the life of Filippa Mareri, the sturdy richness of relic, land, building, people, cult, archival document, combined with the fragility of *legenda* and miracle, can seem too unmanageable for generalization or interpretation. But in fact the complex does offer to its observer a figure, Filippa, in some significant ways describable. She was a baronial country woman who was, in life and death, surrounded by her own family: in life she lived in their places, traveling little, up and down a hill; and in her death she, "glittering with miracles (*corruscans miraculis*)," as the *legenda* hyperbolically states, scattered those miracles among her relatives and neighbors. To those neighbors should be added members of the Franciscan order, the order which captured this traditional cave virgin and domesticated her within itself.

The differences between the woman saint and the man heretic, although both were tied to the Franciscans and to the diocese of Rieti, are many and obvious. The factors which can help explain those differences are also many and obvious. To begin with, although sometimes a man or a woman may have become one or the other, heretic or saint, almost by chance, a shake of the dice, once his or her status was accepted, the mode of preserving his or her memories depended very much on that status. Heretics did not work miracles for the orthodox. Shrines and monasteries were not built above their bones, nor if they had been would they have received papal privileges, been joined to illustrious orders, or produced pious anecdote and hagiography. Paolo has only his hostile inquest; Filippa has a mass of paraphernalia.

Had Filippa, or rather the memory of her, been subjected to an expert inquisition-inquest for canonization, the things known about her would have balanced better with those known about Paolo. But Paolo was examined by a very professional inquisitor, and the material gathered to support Filippa's cult seems pretty clearly the work of amateurs, at least if one excepts the *legenda*. Filippa was a rural woman of high status, a female member of a very major family from the topographically rough southern, Neapolitan, part of the diocese. Paolo was a man of little status, vile, from the city, the, in principle, papal commune of Rieti. The two people had connections, very different connections, with the chapter of the cathedral of Rieti: Filippa through her Mareri family; Paolo through his unclear, and perhaps very distant, at least attempted, attachment to Secinari and Alfani and through the involvement of canons in his inquisition.

In spite of the necessity for being very cautious in discussing chronological cause, a reader must believe that a part of the difference between the two was chronological. The Franciscans to whom the two figures were, or became, tied were very different; the order was very different in the two periods. Filippa was involved in forming some sort of group of holy women which was eventually shaped into a house of the new order.[86] By Paolo's time the order was so developed, and fragmented, that its apparatus appeared even in the hermitage of Greccio.

City heretics certainly existed, and were sexually active or said to be, before the time of Filippa, but the change in location, in action, in status (or its description) from Filippa to Paolo is not uncharacteristic of the change in time—from the baroness moving up and down the family mountain and resisting marriage, to the denizen of Rieti scooting about its streets and onto pilgrimages in search of women to lay on beds and benches (and it may be worth noting sexual acts of which Paolo is not accused—nothing with another male—and a potentially vulnerable Rieti group not tarnished by connection with him—the Jews). The details of Filippa's and Paolo's recorded behavior, the behavior of these two protagonists, brackets a lot of the observable and thinkable behavior of the people of the diocese of Rieti in the thirteenth and fourteenth centuries. And one aspect of the bracketing is chronological.

It is instructive, or at least pleasing, to rehearse in one's mind the differences between the quiet that holds the hill and the frenzy that scratches the town, the differences between the ways in which they are described. Think of the two heroes sexually: Filippa with her essentially unimagined grave chastity; Paolo with his constantly provoked concern with orgasm. What they do with their love-expressing hands, the liquids that exude from them, the nature of their friendships, the places they go, and always the stages and sets through which they move and the props they hold, are different. And the greatest difference of all, surely, is in the detail that is reproduced around them.

Paolo's life of sin is intricately described. It is bursting not only with movement but also with objects—straw, doors, beds—and with words, quoted, and with names given, and with attitudes investigated. The religion that Paolo perverts is much more elaborate, much more intricately explored, than that which Filippa personifies. It is difficult to imagine Filippa or any of the other characters in her story sitting in the urban garden of a priest from a collegiate parish, with other women, listening to a man like Giovanni Petrignani read.

CHAPTER EIGHT

Last Wills and Testaments—
and the Apples of Secinaro

Most people who think of sin, at least literary sin, in a small city, in a town, probably think of Yonville and of Emma Bovary with her heart filled with greed, rage, and hatred. Most people who think of a cathedral chapter in a small city probably think of Trollope's Barchester. Both are surely instances of continuing existences set, in their cases, with a fierce or heavy sureness in their specific times and places. The Rieti of this book is related to both.

The reader who watched Paolo Zoppo escape through the removed gate into the Piazza Cappellarii may have sensed that Paolo was escaping into, among other things, the stifling closed stillness of the small market town which could offer a suitable stage for, even the necessity for, de-grading sin or the degrading imagination of sin. But the walled city was not continuously closed; the inquisitor Simone brought his instigating mind from Spoleto, from Avignon; the real or imagined stories of carnal temptation which came, supposedly, from the mouth of a dead Frati-cello buried in the cathedral cemetery, came from a Spoleto mouth. Paolo Zoppo and his inquisitor, local and foreign, break through, tear open, the placid administrative buying and selling, neighbor-next-to-neighbor surface of the cathedral city—as would, in a different way, the fear caused, in the following year, by the Sabine raids of "Ghibelline" Roman exiles under the leadership of Ottaviano Capocci and Jacopo Caracciolo. "Peace," Petrarch wrote from and of northern Lazio an-other year later, "is the one thing I have not found."[1]

But to the ordinary reader of ordinary Rieti documents the peace of ordinariness seems dominant. In this peace a kind of sin different from Paolo's presents itself to our eyes. Twenty-three years before Paolo's trial, on 1 September 1311, the sick Giovanni di don Pandulfo Secinari, the brother of that Tommaso who would become bishop of Rieti and of Berardo Secinari his canon brother, made his will; and Pacicto di Giovanni Carisie of Rieti, notary by imperial authority, notarized it.[2] In his will Giovanni remembered sin.

Giovanni's is a will with distinct characteristics. It was made in the house of the sons of the dead Don Pandulfo Secinari in the center of the city of Rieti and among its witnesses were two canons of Rieti, Pandulfo de Podio and Giacomo di don Tommaso.[3] But its provisions, its legacies, stretch out of that center, and back, to the places and, obviously, events of Giovanni's life, both in Rieti and in the family places around Secinaro in the diocese of Sulmona within the Neapolitan Regno. They reach across diocesan boundaries which were, at the time when Pacicto was writing, becoming the containers and limits of different kinds of substances.

Giovanni Secinari's will is thick with family. His heirs are his live brothers. Those of his possessions, movable and stable (or real), which have not been dispersed in bequests or legacies are to go equally to Don Matteo, Don Synaballo, Gualterio, Berardo, Don Tommasio, Francesco, and Andrea. He remembers the souls of his father and mother and dead brothers. He leaves any remnant of eighty florins, from which legacies were to be paid and some of which were reserved in his house, in part for the building of his brother Berardo's chapel in the church of San Clerico (or Quirico) in Secinaro. Giovanni leaves money to his sisters: a florin to that sister Cecha who is a nun at Franciscan Santa Lucia and another florin to that other sister also called Cecha at the Franciscan convent of San Fabiano. He leaves another florin to his sister Altarocha; and he repays a debt to his sister Oddorisia; and, in a rather elaborate negotiation, he provides that a piece of vineyard, once bought by the Secinari brothers, from the canon Raynaldo de Podio (a witness to the will), be transferred to Oddorisia and her son Matteo (elsewhere Matteucio) or to him, or if not, that the purchasing fifty florins be retained for her, or them. Giovanni remembers his niece Margarita and his uncle (*patruo*) Ruggero. And Giovanni chooses for burial the cathedral church of Rieti if the bishop and canons would assign him a place which pleased his brothers—otherwise he chooses the church of San Francesco, Rieti. Giovanni's is a very Secinari family will.

It is also a very Secinaro-place will. In its center there is a cluster of some ten legacies and restitutions to specific people in Secinaro and its neighborhood, like the two florins left to the heirs of the notary Benedetto of Gagliano or the gold *augustale* to the heirs of Luca di Gualterio of Secinaro or the five *tareni* (or *tari*) of gold to Giacomo di Vitale of Secinaro or the two tareni to Giovanni Farin' of Secinaro or the single tareno to Tascone Arrate of Secinaro.[4] There is a restitution of Giovanni's part of some money gotten from the sale of animals in L'Aquila. There are three florins to be given to Maria Angelica of Gagliano if she still lives and to be spent for her soul if she does not. To his vassals (*vaxallis*) in Secinaro Giovanni left ten florins to free them from imposts within the year. To the commune of Secinaro he left a florin for the buying of apple trees.[5] For *male acquesitis incertis* (unspecified misgotten gains) in the diocese of Valva-Sulmona, Giovanni left three uncie of gold to be spent within the diocese by his executors for the Regno. To Berardo Nati of Gagliano, or to his heirs, Giovanni left five florins which he had had from gaming if by right or law they ought to be given to him or his heirs. Giovanni left to the *loci* of the friars of San Francesco, San Domenico, and Sant'Agostino in Sulmona a florin each. He left two florins for Masses to be sung for his soul in the Regno. Should money be left from the eighty legacy-providing florins, that money which Giovanni's executors might, at least in part, divert to Berardo's chapel in San Clerico or Quirico in Secinaro, the executors might also choose to give money for the bell of San Giovanni in Gagliano.

But the geographical center for those provisions of Giovanni's will which looked to the future safety of his soul was the city of Rieti with its immediate neighborhood. And at the center of this center was the cathedral where he would be buried, if he could be at the proper place selected by his brothers, where the bulk of the wax to be used for his obsequies might most significantly blaze, there and perhaps at the Secinari palazzo, where would, presumably, be distributed the memorial meats and fish of his *septima*. To the bishop, Giovanni left twenty soldi of Ravenna, and to the church five florins of gold, and to the church of San Francesco, his alternate choice for burial, he left two florins (this against, for example, the twelve lire of Ravenna for *septima* meats).

On the parchment of the will, immediately after these funeral and burial arrangements come Giovanni's legacies to his confessors, twenty soldi of Ravenna to the friars of Sant'Agostino and ten to dompno Accurimbono. Then follow his bequests to the *loci* of San Francesco and San Domenico, twenty soldi, for each, and then to a list of churches ten soldi each: Sant'Agostino, San Matteo, San Benedetto, San Tommaso, San Fabiano, Sant'Agnese, and Santa Margarita—that is, male Augustinian friars, male Cistercian monks, female Benedictines, female Cistercians, female Franciscans, female Dominicans, and more female Benedictines.[6] There follow the bequests of forty soldi to the Franciscan nuns of Santa Lucia, four times as large as that to the other nuns, and then five soldi to each of three hospitals: San Leonardo, San Salvatore, and *extra pontem*. Then follows a bequest of two soldi to each priest of Rieti for singing Masses, then twelve denari for each religious not a priest, and the same amount for each recluse.[7] Slightly farther on, with the legacies to his two nun sisters, Giovanni leaves two and a half florins with which his brothers are to buy clothing (a *tunica*) for Clara, or Chiara, a nun at Santa Lucia.

In this personal-seeming will there are some clearly personal memories. Giovanni leaves four florins to Corradicto who had been the servant of the dead Raynaldo the Spicer (or Speciale), four florins he had of Corradicto from cheating him at gambling or from a forbidden game, *de ludo malitioso*. Preparing to die, Giovanni remembered the sin of gambling. When in 1311 as death approached him, or he it, and, probably prodded by one of his Augustinian confessors or the prebendary Accurimbono or one of his favored Franciscans or even his notary, he tried to remember, or could not help remembering, what had been wrong in his life, he thought of his past winning at gambling. And Giovanni's memory crosses a thousand years of Christian worrying with dice: "Flee the pursuing devil," the pseudo-Cyprian had said, "flee the dice." Everyone and everything were against dice: Aristotle and the Digest, biographers of Caligula, the ancient canons of Elvira, endless local councils and synods from Salisbury to Città di Castello, and the statutes of lots of Italian communes including Rieti, which forbade dicing any place within a mile of the city (and which statute in the Rieti manuscript is decorated with the later drawing of three dice with their pricks of two, three, and six facing the reader). The connection of dice with the lots cast for Christ's seamless robe (particularly from John 19:24–25) would be made pictorially sharp at Rieti in the Venetian Zanino di Pietro's Crucifixion with its ugly front-center-stage scene with three dice, a picture which was at Franciscan Fonte Colombo before 1450. It was a great horror, the sacred relic and the game of chance. Chance, *il gioco de la zara*, thus begins the sixth canto of the *Purgatorio*, and its temptation supposedly led the scholar Giovanni Bassiano, who had lost even his clothes, to remain nude at the dice. Raymond of Peñafort in the most influential of thirteenth-century penitentials, influential in fourteenth-century Italy, wrote of the sin of playing at or even watching the game of dice. He listed, in his neat didactic way, nine reasons for its being bad: it is cupidity, robbery, usury, multiple lying, blasphemy, corruption of neighbors, scandal to the good, contempt of the prohibition of mother church, a wasting of time. In Giovanni Secinari's will the reader can see what might have seemed only centuries of platitudinous propaganda penetrate the individual mind of a man whose thoughts were turned to dying. In this will full of friars, hospitals, Masses, dedicated women, and other protagonists of then modern piety, the testator's personally worrying sin is gambling (and perhaps also heavy exactions from tenants).[8]

The executors named in Giovanni's will are Don Tommaso (or Tommasio) Capitaneo and Eleuterio di don Gentile Alfani, that Tommaso who is at the very center of the church of Rieti's activity in the early fourteenth century and that Eleuterio who appears as a father in Angelo Clareno's correspondence and in whose house lodged the fraticello from Spoleto who was Paolo Zoppo's informant, the fraticello who by the time of Paolo's testimony was in the cathedral cemetery. Both of these men, Tommaso and Eleuterio, had been named executors, with Mathione Andrionis di donna Andrea, by Nicola Cece, a citizen of Rieti but once of the town or village of Apoleggia, in his will of 11 May 1301, a will made three months almost to the day, after Bishop, then Patriarch, Pietro da Ferentino had made his burial codicil in Ùdine and then the next day had chosen, the Franciscans of Ùdine claimed, to move his burial to San Francesco Ùdine in order that his soul might witness more frequently there the sacred mysteries of the Mass.

Nicola Cece begins, as would Giovanni Secinari, with twenty soldi (in this case described as of the "usual money" and "for his soul") for the bishop of Rieti.[9] He continues in a way that seems absolutely characteristic of him (of the testator Nicola Cece not the notary of this will, Matteo Pandolfonis, notary by authority of the urban prefect). Nicola leaves, for his soul's sake, thirty-six florins which his executors are to spend on some good book (*aliquo bono libro*) or some work (*opere*) or thing that will seem to his executors more useful for the church of Rieti, the church in which Nicola chooses burial; but Nicola then specifically states that he wants to be sure that the money does not come into the hands of either bishop or chapter but rather that it be spent quickly, in the way specified, by his executors themselves. In a kind of small and rustic echo of the relatively recent (opened at Rome 4 August 1292) will of Jean Cholet, cardinal priest of Santa Cecilia, who left one hundred gilt chalices and patens to be distributed in the dioceses of Rouen and Beauvais, Nicola left silver chalices, each worth fifteen florins, to selected churches and *loci*, San Matteo of the Cistercians, San Francesco, Sant'Agostino, and San Domenico (although San Domenico's chalice was to wait until the sale of Nicola's house after the death of Nicola's wife, Cara). And the executors were to make sure that in each church which got a chalice Nicola's name was to be written in the missal where the dead were remembered next to the canon of the Mass.

And for his soul's sake, and to help with vestments or perhaps clothing, Nicola left twenty soldi each to the convents of Santa Lucia (of Franciscan women), Sant'Agnese (of Dominican women), San Salvatore (of Benedictine men), San Tommaso (of Cistercian women), San Fabiano (of Franciscan women), San Benedetto (of Benedictine women), and a similar amount to the *loci* of San Francesco Greccio, San Giacomo of Poggio (Bustone), and San Francesco of Fonte Colombo (written "Fronte Palonbe"), the three Franciscan hermitages, for the friars staying in those places. To the church of Sant'Angelo of Apoleggia, Santa Maria de Bovilga, and Santa Maria of Canetra, he left, to each, thirty soldi for an altar cloth (and to each of the canons of Santa Maria of Canetra fifteen [?] denari). To Sant'Angelo Rieti, for the work or building (*opere*) of the church he left fifteen florins; and to the monastery of San Pastore of Rieti (Cistercian men) he left forty soldi for pittances. With the abbot and canons of the church of Sant'Eleuterio out his gate of the city of Rieti, that which opened toward Apoleggia north across the flat basin of the dried lake, with whom, the abbot and canons of Sant'Eleuterio, in the hills he shared the working of a vineyard, he left an elaboration of money and agreement which combined charity and the protection of his heirs, and also four soldi to the abbot and two to each of the canons who should be present at his burial. In the middle of these pious bequests Nicola's notary inserted a further cautionary statement, that all the chalices, books, and altar cloths should be given to the legatees in the things themselves, not in money, that the left objects and works should never be permitted to be alienated nor the legacies applied to human uses.

Nicola left thirty soldi and a torch to the fraternity of Santa Trinità. He left to every priest in Rieti, secular or in a religious order, twelve denari apiece; he left to every priest of Apoleggia twelve denari for singing Masses. He left to each recluse of Rieti twelve denari. He left to the hospital *extra pontem* his bed—mattress, pillow, cover, best *cultram*, everything; and to the hospital of San Leonardo twenty soldi. He left to the poor of Apoleggia, the most needy, twenty soldi. When his executors should have executed the provisions of his will (including granting forty soldi to each of themselves), what remained should be left to his universal heirs, the poor of Rieti, the most needy, in the judgment of his executors.

Nicola's legacies to members of his family were as carefully designed and as personal as his pious bequests. To the heirs of his mother, Raynalducia, Nicola left ten lire. To his niece Imilgucia, who was in the house of Tommaso Capitaneo, he left ten florins. To the heirs of his sister Finita, he left forty lire of "the usual money." To dompno Tommaso, his godfather, he left ten soldi. The legacies to his wife, Cara, expand and complicate themselves: clothes; household goods; thirteen *braccie* of burnet cloth (*blachia brunecte*) for tunic and mantel at thirteen soldi the *bracchia*; his silver belt (*scagalem*); his *suppedaneum* (chest, pie-safe) for baking, the *suppedaneum* he had bought from Donna Theodina; another *suppedaneum*; vats; the house—he wills that his wife, Cara, should keep his house (probably the earlier mentioned house he had bought in the Porta Cintia di sopra) in good state (*tam de tecto quam de terraco*) for the whole time of her life so that it does not deteriorate around her or in her hands (*ita quod ipsa domus non deterioretur apud eam*).

The house and land that he had bought from Oliverio and Clariello, by contrast, should be sold back to them for seventy-six florins if they want it for that price.[10] His fee (*feudum seu beneficium*) of Apoleggia he left to Marteno di Giacomo di Pietro Odonis and to the heirs of Marteno's brother Simonicto or their heirs if they themselves should not survive Nicola, and he willed that they should do service for the fee to Mathucio de Pulegia (Apoleggia) just as Nicola and his ancestors had done service—and to Margarita their sister and her heirs he left one hundred soldi. The money from the half-house which Nicola had bought from Leonardo di Tommaso Girardi, Nicola left from "now" for the welfare of his soul to the cathedral church of Santa Maria to go to it after Cara's death, or should she remarry, after it had been sold by his executors; but not the money itself, it should never come directly into the hands of bishop and chapter—it should be spent for the fabric or the wall of the church or for a use that should seem better to the executors.

The witnesses to this will of thoughtful or fussy detail and complexity—with its recording of the notarization of earlier acts of transfer of property by other notaries (Magistro Giacomo di donna Manuhula,

Mathiucio Cifredi), witnesses present in the chapter house of Sant'Agostino, were Fra Petrucio da Rieti, Fra Pietro de Valvo then vicar of the place, Fra Petrucio di Petrono di Giovanni di Giovenale, Fra Giovanni da Rieti who was the son of Menstecanse, Fra Giovanni da Catino, Fra Johanducio da Norcia, and Fra Giacomo da L'Aquila— an assemblage of Augustinian Hermits, local and from a little distance. They witnessed a will which said that it canceled all previous wills and codicils; and in Nicola's case this was not an idle formula.

Nicola had earlier written at least one other will and one codicil. They survive.[11] They are from the hands of notaries other than Matteo Pandolfonis; the codicil, which is now stitched to the earlier will, from 1297, and is itself from early (4 January) 1300, was notarized by Pacicto di Giovanni Carisie. The 1297 will shows most of the provisions and attitudes of the 1301 will already in place so that they cannot have been the work of the notary Matteo unless he had formed them in a still earlier and unfound will. There are, however, differences; and those differences can be seen forming in the 1300 codicil. In the 1297 will Nicola had left fifteen florins to the church of Sant'Angelo di Marmore for a chalice; but the codicil removes those fifteen florins and grants them instead to the church of Sant'Angelo of Rieti to be used for the construction of its walls with the money's use to be supervised by Nicola's executors; and if by the time of Nicola's death the walls' work should be finished, the executors should spend the fifteen florins for a silver chalice for the church, or a book, or some other use that seemed best to the executors. Here again is a church, in this case Sant'Angelo, which is a very passive partner, if partner at all, in the transaction of bequest—its clergy does not choose what would be of greatest use to it.

In the 1297 will Nicola's legacy to Sant'Eleuterio is intricate, as it is in the 1301 will; and it is connected, in both wills, with ten lire owed by the abbot and chapter of Sant'Eleuterio, a debt recorded in an instrument written by the familiar notary Giovanni di Pietro, as both wills say. In the 1297 will the executors are instructed to buy for Sant'Eleuterio a breviary or a missal or something else useful for twenty-six florins, with the addition of fifteen florins to the ten lire mentioned grown to be worth eleven florins, but with the provision that if the money is not spent within a year the ten lire should go to Nicola's heirs. As the 1301 will would be, the 1297 will was drawn up at Sant'Agostino, Rieti, but in the refectory rather than the chapter house and, as in 1301, with Augustinian Hermit witnesses, although different ones, including the prior, a friar from Cascia, and dompno Tommaso Capitaneo, who in this will is specifically identified as that Tommaso who was Nicola's godfather, and who in this will with the same colleagues is named an executor.

On 10 March 1320 Tommaso Capitaneo, identifying himself as a prebendary of the church of Rieti, made his own will, in the *proaulo* of the sacristy of the cathedral; and he named as his executors his co-prebendary Giacomo di San Liverato and his own brother Giovanni.[12] Tommaso's will is shorter, simpler, and more straightforward than the wills of Giovanni and Nicola. It deals as theirs do with family, Tommaso's two brothers and his sister, Giovanni, Symonicto, and Panfilia: Giovanni and Panfilia are to share one house and Symonicto to have another in places near properties of Corrado de Murro, Macino de Murro, and Giovanni Pasinelli. Panfilia was to have Tommaso's cloth, both linen and canvas.

Though simpler and more spare than theirs, Tommaso's will, with some variation, restates the pattern of piety of the wills of Giovanni and Nicola to which he was executor. Tommaso's will, made, it says, in health and, again, within the cathedral complex, has among its seven witnesses six canons of the cathedral, led off in the list by the venerable Bartolomeo Bontempi, a canon of Rieti for at least fifty-nine years by the time of the will's making; the others are Andrea di don Siniballo, Arecabene, Giovanni Egidii, Magister Andrea magistri Blaxii, and Matteo di don Angelo Tufi. Unsurprisingly perhaps, Tommaso, the priest prebendary, who chooses as Giovanni and Nicola do burial in the cathedral, is more generous than they to the bishop, leaving to him three lire of Ravenna, three times their twenty soldi, and also leaving to the church of his burial his own missal. To each cathedral canon who would be present at his obsequies, he leaves four soldi, to each prebendary, two. And for those obsequies he also leaves a more considerable sum, eight florins, for torches, for two nuns' churches, Santa Lucia and San Tommaso, and also for San Giovanni Battista, the baptistry church, a church to which, in personal selection, this godfather seems to pay particular attention, leaving it forty soldi, *pro opere*.

In light counterpoint Tommaso follows the charitable bequests of the other wills: to each secular priest of Rieti for singing Masses twelve denari; for each clerk beneficed in any church in Rieti, eight denari; to each recluse of Rieti, twelve denari; to the friars' churches, San Francesco, San Domenico, Sant'Agostino, ten soldi for each; to the churches of the convents of nuns, Santa Lucia, Sant'Agnese, Santa Margherita, San Benedetto, San Tommaso, and San Flaviano, five soldi for each; for three hospitals, in this case San Leonardo, Sant'Heranio, and *extra pontem*, four soldi; more personal bequests, few of them, for San Nicola de Paterno twenty soldi for the roof or some other work, twenty soldi for Giacomo da San Liverato for singing Masses, five soldi for dompno Giovanni Ratigoni, three soldi for dompno Francesco di magistro Gianni (the seventh witness) for singing Masses, and ten soldi to Suor Bartholotia da Rivodutri (a village very close to Apoleggia, and to Morro and Poggio Bustone), a nun at Santa Lucia. Tommaso orders that six tunics be made for the poor of Christ at fifteen soldi the tunic.

The particulars of Giovanni's and Nicola's wills give to each of them a separate distinguishing identity: Giovanni's apple trees for Secinaro, his bell for Gagliano, his taxed vassals, his gambling; Nicola's worrying about transfers of funds, his pittances for San Pastore, his bed for *extra pontem*, his book for the cathedral, his chalices. But Giovanni and Nicola share with many contemporary testators the attention they pay to that kind of expression of the corporal works of mercy that can continue after the testator's own death and thus make of death of the body a more transparent thing, a friendlier sister in Francis's term. Testators can continue to shorten their purgatories. Their funerals can lead to celebrations and Masses can be said, but also the religious and institutionalized poor of Christ can be supported: Franciscans, Dominicans, Augustinians, and Cistercians, still, and convents of nuns, Christ's sisters, or Himself. Testators choose tunics of different quality for differing numbers of the actual literal poor of Christ; they support hospitals; and they give money, in towns which contain them, to recluses. And repeated sums, like the twelve denari to each recluse, expose the self-consciousness of some of the repetition. This repetition suggests that the message of active corporal giving and identifying (by both the receiver and the giver) with Christ, Christianity has been absorbed and at the same time in some part institutionalized, as it has been in the new orders. But in these wills one constantly sees an active decision-making testator, following in chosen ways the mandates or person of Christ, the Christ who existed after Francis.

In Fragulino's will of 1203, written within the lifetime of Francis, this Christ and this decision-making are at least lightly foreshadowed. Fragulino does leave five soldi for the hospital *capitis Arci* and fourteen lire for the rebuilding of the cathedral.[13] But, for its time and place, early thirteenth-century Rieti, Fragulino's will is remarkably articulate; although, of course, hospitals were founded and endowed much earlier, and in this connection *pauperes Christi* were spoken of (in the foun-

dation of San Bartolomeo in the Reatine) as early as 1112.[14] Early gifts
were often large, in a way that would be essentially unknown in the late
thirteenth and early fourteenth centuries, as when in 1196 Rainaldo de
Lavareta "for the redemption of my soul and those of my parents [or
relatives]" gave Santa Croce to itself.[15] Sometimes the old cry identified
with Cluniac reform was voiced as in the 1171 gifts from a man "for the
remedio of his soul and that of his *parentum*" that they might receive
mercy on the day of future judgment and hear the voice of the Lord
saying, come you blessed with me into Paradise and receive what has
been prepared for you since the beginning of the world[16] (and thus
emphasizing rather than disguising, as the bequests for corporal works
of mercy do, the break at the testator's death, and suggesting a long
blind period of inaction between death and Last Judgment). But more
generally, early Reatine wills, before the period of their increased survival after the middle of the thirteenth century, are stubbornly mute.[17]
The increased survival itself is of course important, and it is clearly connected with those changes in recording legal and governmental actions
which marked the growth of diocesan government; Matteo Barnabei
and Silvestro di don Giovanni give us wills. But survival is the corollary
rather than the cause of the change in wills.

Even, of course, after the middle of the thirteenth century, some
testators are relatively mute, or hesitant to press into their wills evidence
of their personal preferences. In 1258 Bertollo di Pietro, an inhabitant
of Rieti, ill, left his goods to his son Paolo, whom he made his heir, but
he made some bequests for his soul: five soldi of the provisini of the
Senate of Rome for Santa Maria Rieti, twelve provisini for the church
of San Nicola de Prefectis for the use of the church and twelve more to
Andrea priest of that church for *scorarico* or *scoriarico* and twelve more
for the *camerariis* for the walls of the city—this may be simply the
reticence of an exile from Rome, from a Colonna part of Rome.[18] In
1293 Giovanna, the daughter of Don Synibaldo Rayn' and wife of Tosto,
ill, who uncharacteristically (in these wills) announces her emancipation
from her father and cites its recording document, puts her pious bequests completely in the hands of her brother Don Andrea, forty florins
from her dowry to be spent however he chooses (*expendos et distri-
buendos ad sensum et uoluntatem domini Andree fratris mei*).[19] This
woman who left one hundred florins to her husband made her daughter, Andriucia, her heir, unless she should die within her twelfth year,
and then she made her husband and her father each heir to half her
estate—the will of a manumitted but enclosed woman.

The 1305 will of the still healthy notary Manfredo di Benedetto May-
fredi, written by himself, is essentially a list of moneys, 189 and ½ florins
and 57 soldi of Ravenna, some few of which seem clearly to have been
left as personal legacies, but the bulk of which were repayment of loans
and deposits, the collection one suspects of a usurious notary.[20] If from
his money anything remains, Manfredo writes, these denari should be
spent for his soul as seems best to his executors, Bartolomea, his mother,
and Andrea di magistro Angelo, his brother—a brother who does not
share Manfredo's resoundingly Ghibelline name.

But involvement in lending and borrowing did not necessarily exclude testators from participation in personally selected modern testamentary piety, as the 1314 will of Giovanni Nicolocti of Rieti, ill, flamboyantly proclaims: I leave to each convent of nuns in the city of Rieti
five soldi of Ravenna *pro male oblatis* "for the souls of those from whom
I have extorted money but whose names I do not remember," to each
monasterio of Rieti, namely to San Francesco, San Domenico,
Sant'Agostino, and San Matteo twenty soldi of Ravenna *pro male oblatis*
"for those people from whom I have taken usury and whom I cannot
remember."[21] To every recluse of the city, Giovanni leaves twelve denari; to each of named hospitals—Monte, San Leonardo, Sant'Heramo,
and the Marmore—five soldi; to his godfather, dompno Accurimbono,
ten soldi; to the bishop twenty soldi; for his obsequies six florins for
wax from which the cathedral was to have one torch; one hundred soldi
to his wife for Masses to be sung by the priests of Rieti; to that wife,
Maria, twelve lire of Ravenna for funeral clothes—and his house—in a
will (written by the imperial notary Giovanni di Eleuterio of Rieti) in
which a postnuptial contract with Maria (written by the notary Pacicto
di Giovanni Carisie) is specifically canceled; lots of specific bequests,
returns of money, payments because of earlier usurious dealings; and a
house in the parish of San Giovanni Evangelista, next to, among other
things, the house of Don Bartolomeo de Rocca, to Donna Berarducia
for the love he had for her and in repayment of goods which he had
received from her.

Nor certainly did being a woman necessarily shelter the testator from
this selection. The still healthy Donna Oddorisia, a widow, once the
wife of Giovanni Reatino, one of the women attracted to the Dominicans of San Domenico who intended to be buried in their church, left
five florins for the *opera* of the church and three for wax and five for
her *septima* in her 1299 will; and she made her executors the prior of
San Domenico at the time of her death and her own brother Petrucio.[22]

She made the will in the church of San Domenico and her witnesses were five friars, two conversi, and one oblate of the place. She left twenty soldi to the cathedral. She made her niece, Margherita, Petrucio's daughter, her heir, and left money (five florins) to her own daughter, and more (another five) to another female descendant. She left twenty soldi to the cathedral and then picked recipients of other bequests: twenty soldi to San Giovanni Evangelista; ten each to San Francesco and Sant'Agostino; twenty to Sant'Agnese (Dominican nuns); ten to Santa Lucia; five each to San Fabiano, San Benedetto, and San Tommaso; three to each hospital of Rieti and to that at Marmore; twelve denari to each recluse of the city of Rieti; a florin for Masses to be sung; ten soldi for the prior of San Domenico at the time of her death; five soldi for the Dominican Pietro de Marcellano; four soldi for a pair of shoes for Fra Paolo—in general, this, an individual selection within conventional guidelines by a widow of Dominican devotion but with a special connection, parochial perhaps, perhaps devotional, to San Giovanni Evangelista, the church with the communicating priest in its garden.

In country villages there were different limitations. At Sant'Elia, the primitive rustic center near Fonte Colombo, the place of which the companions tell the most primitive miracle—the curing of cattle disease with the water stolen from the washing of Francis, that non-miraculous saint—and in the brutal summer of 1348 Filippa, widow of Nicola di Giovanni, ill, who made her daughter her heir and chose burial in the church of Sant'Elia and left it a florin for candles and other funeral matters and ten soldi for singing Masses, planned her funereal feasts, her *septima*, her *consolu*, for her soul's sake by leaving five *quarti* of grain and a pig worth a florin.[23] Although Fonte Colombo was very close, the normal spectrum of attractive pious targets did not evidently spread itself before Filippa's eyes.

But a man from Pendenza, a place east of Sant'Elia in the Regno, and admittedly less small and insignificant than Sant'Elia, made in 1318 a will which showed that the testator need not be restrained by the limited objects for pious bequest within his own village.[24] Giacomo di Rainallo di Gualterio da Pendenza, using a judge and notary from Cittaducale, made, at his own house, a will which thought of his family, which left to his wife among other things a black pig, and to his daughter, who was married to another man from Pendenza, two *pedes* of olive trees in a dependency of Pendenza called "vineales," and in a place called Cerreto a piece of land with ten *pedes* of oak, another black pig, two hens, and a *trapellum* of linen cloth, and more olives and a stand of chestnuts. Giacomo chose burial at San Silvestro di Pendenza and, for his soul, left it ten soldi for the improvement of the church; he also left eight soldi to both San Cipriano and Santa Maria di Pendenza and seven soldi to both San Giovanni and San Nicola di Pendenza for the fabric of these churches. He left five soldi for his godfather, dompno Nicola di Andrea di Pendenza; and he left four pounds of wax for the churches of Pendenza to be used to light the Corpus Christi. He left money for buying tithes. But he, awaiting death near Pendenza, also left money, ten soldi, for the great hospital of Santo Spirito in Rome and money, twenty soldi, for San'Agostino in Cittaducale. Giacomo shows his reader that the testator deprived of an alms-receiving hospital and an alms-receiving church and house of friars in his own small town or village could reach out to other places. He also shows his readers that one of the functions of the recently created Cittaducale was to offer to men and women in the Regno portion of the diocese of Rieti a relatively urban center which could contain urban pious places that could be recipients of rustic pious bequests.

In 1347, the year before Filippa the widow made her will in Sant'Elia, a widow named Mathiutia, also ill, also thought of her *septima*, which should be celebrated by the people on both sides of the way from her own house and that of a man named Lucco de Piciolura (?), with twelve denari to be given to each household (*pro quolibet foculari*); but she also thought of the poor to whom her executors should give eight tunics at a price of twenty soldi each, and of the recluses of Rieti who were to receive twelve denari each, and of the three friars' churches and also the convent of Santa Scolastica (Benedictine nuns) each to receive twenty soldi, with five soldi to go to all the other convents of nuns in Rieti.[25] She chose burial at the cathedral, which she left a florin, and another five soldi for the "frabrica." She left six florins for wax for the funeral and three for singing Masses. But she also left the church of San Donato a florin for its "frabrica," and a florin to San Donato's chaplain, dompno Giovanni da Cascia, and also a florin to dompno Ballovino. These tunics for the poor, and other things, are in a will rich with servants, furs, and expensive clothes.

In January 1349, ill in the house of her husband, the lady Bucia, the wife of Janni di don Gentile Pasinelli and the daughter of the no longer living Don Giacomo de Murro—an important connection—a woman who intended burial at San Francesco, left twenty soldi provisini to each house of religious men in Rieti and ten to each house of religious women, and left twenty soldi to the church of Santa Marina and also

to the hospital of Santo Spirito of Rieti and twelve denari to each recluse, and a florin to Belladama the daughter of Gentile Pasinelli (her
sister-in-law), a nun at San "Flabiano."[26] In a will rich in silk and linen,
Bucia ordered that ten tunics be made for *pauperes Christi* at a value of
twenty soldi each.

In a little gathering of wills from 1348 within the paper notarial cartulary of Silvestro di don Giovanni is the will of Bucio Lucarelli made
as he lay ill in his own house, on 5 February of that mortal year, in the
presence of Bucio's brother Cola, a doctor named Magister (or Magistro) Luca di Egidio Macapede, the priest dompno Bono rector of
San Giovenale and Don Bertullo di Pietro the provost of Sant'Angelo
(one of whom was Bucio's godfather), the Augustinian Hermits Matteo
da Amelia (a legatee) and Nicola de Podio, and a member of the Carsidonei family.[27] One might not have suspected that Bucio would have
then applied himself to the discriminating selection of Christian pious
bequests. Although Bucio's two sons were named Francesco and Antonio, the will has an Augustinian hue; and, in spite of that, Bucio chose
burial in the baptismal church of San Giovanni Battista, to which he
left a florin. He left a hundred pounds of wax for his funeral. He left
the cathedral a florin, the bishop twenty soldi, and twelve denari to each
recluse in Rieti. He left the Augustinian Fra Matteo da Amelia five
florins for a dalmatic and three florins to the church of Sant'Agostino
for its fabric (actually "frabrica" in "Frebruario"). He left a florin each
to San Francesco and San Domenico. He left ten florins for tunics for
pauperes Christi. Each *petente* seeking satisfaction from the testator
should, on his own oath, receive up to ten soldi and, with a witness, up
to forty. Bucio left ten lire for the singing of Masses. But it is among
the convents of nuns that he most nicely distinguishes: San Tommaso,
ten soldi; Santa Scolastica, one florin; San Benedetto and Sant'Agnese,
twenty soldi each; Santa Margarita, Santa Lucia, and San Fabiano, five
soldi each. For the church of San Giovenale for buying tithes for money
to be used for fixing the church three florins (and the use was not to
be diverted) and for dompno Bono, priest of the church twenty-two
soldi; a florin to Santo Spirito Rieti and one to Sant'Antonio (both with
hospitals), again restricted to use for the fabric. To the Augustinian Fra
Vanni Angelucii (Angelutii) he left a florin. He made four men his
executors: the guardiano of San Francesco, the priors of Sant'Agostino
and San Domenico, and Fra Matteo da Amelia (who seems his most
likely adviser). He left as his potential reversionary heirs the hospital of
Santo Spirito di Rieti and the churches of San Francesco, San Dome-

nico, Sant'Agostino, and Sant'Antonio. Beyond all this he left three lire to each of three churches, San Francesco, San Domenico, and Sant'Agostino, for buying candles to be lighted during the Mass.

Another of this group of 1348 wills shows, perhaps coincidentally, more of the physical stress of the year. The will of Antonio di (fu) don Petruccio Thomaselli, ill on 29 August 1348, is written in a singular and shaky hand, almost as if it had been written in bed; and thus it remains in the cartulary although with a subscript written in a steady professional hand.[28] The testator, whose father's shop is mentioned in the will, chose burial at the cathedral, to which he left a florin. He left twenty soldi for wax; and he left ten soldi for singing Masses to Sant'Agostino (and one of his executors was to be the prior of San Domenico). He left a florin to Colaxia di Egidio, a nun at Santa Scolastica, and, worthy of note, ten soldi to the church of San Giovanni de Statua (Evangelista) and ten soldi to its priest, quite probably to Giovanni Petrignani of the garden. But Antonio's distinguishing rose of pious bequests is a set of dowries, or endowments for poor women, or lands from which the monies can be drawn: four giunte of land with which should be endowed some wretched (*miserabiles*) widowed women to be chosen by his brother-in-law and two other men; another piece of land, in a different location, for two other wretched widows; and his vineyard in "Valle Mayna" for two other wretched women so that they would be able to enter the convent of Santa Margarita. With the memory in his mind of his father's Rieti shop, Antonio, pressed by the plague, still managed to select his method of following, after his death, the footsteps of Christ.

In circumstances heavy, like that of August 1348, and less heavy (although the thought of death, even the new Franciscan-Christian Sister Death of the Body, may never be really light), testators, although often and in many ways both conventional and institutional, chose their own paths. In 1310 Gemma, the ill wife of Angelicto Reatino, who remembered her godfather, Dompno Berardo, left twenty soldi for a pilgrimage overseas.[29] And in 1341 a seemingly rich and well connected knight (*nobilis miles*) from L'Aquila, Mathiula de Aquila, well, made his will in Rieti at the Hospitallers' San Basilio.[30] Among his witnesses were two Augustinian Hermits from the Regno, Fra Giovanni da Leonessa (Gonessa) and Fra Pietro da Popleto di Aquila, and also Vanni di Nicola Pasinelli and Angeluccio Thomaselli of Rieti; and Mathiula made Fra Pietro one of his executors. Mathiula chose burial at San Biagio di Aquila unless he died in Rieti, in which case he chose the cathedral. He left half a florin to King Robert. He wished the funeral and anniversary rites

of his house to be observed: "uoluit quod tempore sui funeris fiat officium sicut consuetum est fieri aliis de domo sua predecessis . . . voluit
quod eidem testatori fiat septima et anuale prout consuetum est fieri
aliis defunctis in domo sua." Mathiula was able to find in the by then
century-old city of L'Aquila and its neighborhood a sufficient supply of
appropriate recipients for his pious bequests of uncie, *tareni, carlini,
gigliati* (as well as some florins and denari)—L'Aquila had become in
that important sense, important to the expression of religion, a city.
Mathiula could and did leave money for the works and building of
L'Aquila's San Domenico, San Francesco, Sant'Agostino, and also its
Santa Maria di Collemaggio, a major church of the order of the Celestinians, the order of Pietro da Morrone (Celestine V), an order of great
importance to the dioceses of L'Aquila and Sulmona but not to that of
Rieti. L'Aquila was a city with recluses, and Mathiula was able to leave
each of them within the city's walls four denari. It was also a city of
poor (*pauperes*) in hospitals, and Mathiula left them tunics: six white
tunics to the poor of the hospital of Santo Spirito L'Aquila, two to the
poor of San Matteo, and three to those of Sant'Antonio.

As he made his will in Rieti, Mathiula did not need to turn to its
institutions to find a home for his bequests; and he remained a stranger
in his piety as Giovanni Secinari and Nicola Cece had not, although
they retained memories of Secinaro and Apoleggia. Mathiula's foreign-
ness may explain his inclusion in his will of a kind of bequest familiar
in late medieval wills but not in fourteenth-century Rieti wills: he not
only left each of the priests of San Vittorino one *carlino* for singing
Masses, he requested that a hundred Masses be said, by unspecified
priests, for his soul's sake. Mathiula's knightliness, as well as his for-
eignness, is apparent in his will, and the fact that the given name Cam-
ponesco (like Caracosa) appears repeatedly in the will, together with his
request for a San Biagio burial, certainly suggests that Mathiula (whose
identifying or surname is left blank in Silvestro di don Giovanni's cartulary) was a Camponeschi of L'Aquila. Mathiula left San Biagio a banner to be made into a chasuble or cope for the church's use. Similarly
he left another banner to Santa Maria di Civitate—"quas banderias scit
dompnus Franciscus ubi sunt et quis eas habet (which banners, dompno
Francesco knows where they are and who has them)." Like the women
of the Pescheria in Rome turning their tablecloths into altarcloths,
Mathiula turns his banners into chasubles, as he personally, with Francesco, breaks into his will.[31]

Lorenzo Castellano's relatively simple will of 1297 leaves sums of the "usual" (Ravenna) money for funeral and feast, and money for the church of his burial; twenty soldi each to San Francesco, San Domenico, and Sant'Agostino and ten to San Matteo; ten soldi to his godfather; twenty for the fabric of San Nicola; five soldi to each of the *obstipuli* of Rieti and also five to that of the Marmore; and twelve denari to each Rieti recluse.[32] Francesco di Nicola di don Filippo Pasinelli's 1337 will is much more elaborate, and much richer. But it too leaves money for San Francesco, San Domenico, and Sant'Agostino, forty soldi, and half that sum to San Matteo.[33] It remembers, in a differentiated way, the convents of nuns: five soldi each for San Tommaso, San Benedetto, Santa Scolastica, Santa Margherita, and Sant'Agnese, twenty soldi for San "Flabiano" and Santa Lucia, and ten lire (all still money of Ravenna) for Santa Caterina's fabric. He left money to his mother, Nicolaxia, to his executors the guardiano of San Francesco and the prior of San Domenico. To "Fra" Arecabene priest of San Ruffo he left his coat with a wolf-fur collar. To the church of Santa Marina money for buying tithes, and to Santo Spirito Rieti he left a fully furnished bed. He left money for his Franciscan confessors: Fra Pietro and Fra Francesco da Longone (one florin each). He left money to a specific recluse, the recluse at Sant'Angelo, and to a specific hermit, Nicola da Foresta. Both wills display parts, Francesco's a larger and more specifically designated part, of that garden of local appropriate recipients, who and which could help the testator after his death continue good works of the sort Christ sought, a selection among the least of Christ's brethren, and who and which could also temper the testator's purgatory. The development and establishment, the definition, of these recipients form a major part of the history of the development of piety, of religion, in thirteenth- and fourteenth-century Rieti. The development, in this sense, from the reticent little wills of the early thirteenth century is a remarkable one.[34]

A related but more striking change in these wills is more general. They become much more articulate. Early thirteenth-century wills are very still. Early fourteenth-century wills, at Rieti, not only talk, they gesticulate. And they gesticulate more expressively, more comfortably, in an urban setting—but with an eye toward reclusion. The difference between these early thirteenth- and early fourteenth-century wills recalls the difference between Filippa Mareri and Paolo Zoppo. The later testator seems to be writing something like an autobiography; or perhaps an autobiography seems to be trying to emerge from, to get out of, the written will. He or she, the testator seems like those chroniclers from, for example, Salimbene to Francesco da Fabriano who cannot resist exposing pieces of their own lives—"and in the year following [1251], on the second day of the month of September, that is, on the feast of Saint Antonio, I was born, and she herself [my mother] told me that," the Blessed Francesco insists upon telling us.[35] It is a point in time, in central Italy, when, as the autobiografia of Pietro da Morrone, whoever wrote it, shows us, the impulse to autobiography was very strong. And in the later wills it is the individual soul encumbered with remembered gambling or harsh exactions from tenants or usury that must be guided through death's open door as the soul remains involved in the performance of corporal works of mercy, as it continues to imitate Christ and attempts to be close to him.

In October 1319, in the decade after Giovanni Secinari had composed his will and only shortly before Tommaso Capitaneo would compose his, two canons of Rieti tried, one in a will and one in a codicil, to continue their closeness to Christ, in a special and, in Rieti, very recently invented way. The canons, Giacomo de Labro and Giovanni di magistro Andrea, established, or formally marked the establishment of, commemorative chapels in the cathedral. At Rieti the first surviving, and found, testamentary selection of a specific church for burial comes from 1297; it is in Nicola Cece's first will. In 1299 Oddorisia chose San Domenico; and in 1304 Suor Angeluccia, another of the women who seem to have formed a group clustered around San Domenico, also chose it.[36] In 1311 Giovanni Secinari chose the cathedral with San Francesco as an alternate choice. In 1320 Tommaso Capitaneo chose the cathedral. From about 1300 the inclusion of a selected place of burial within Rieti wills becomes normal. Of thirty-two places chosen for burial (of which two are second choices) among a sample of fourteenth-century Rieti documents, excluding Don Mathiula's essentially L'Aquila will, only three were for places outside Rieti and its borgo: Pendenza, Sant'Elia, and Apoleggia (and, in the case of Apoleggia, only should the testator native, who lived in Rieti, happen to die back in Apoleggia).[37] Besides the two testators who chose Rieti's San Giovanni Evangelista and San Giovanni Battista, one, a canon of Sant'Angelo, chose Sant'Angelo.[38] Three testators chose San Domenico, and five of them chose San Francesco. Half of the selectors of friars' churches were women. No one in the sample group chose Sant'Agostino, although bequests to Sant'Agostino, legatee, witness, and confessor Augustinians, and even a reference to a Sant'Agostino burial are evident. The other eighteen burial requests in the sample are for the cathedral church of Santa Maria.

This preponderance will not seem surprising because the documents are almost all from the cathedral archives. But this is a less compelling reason for the skewed selection than would at first seem likely because copies of late medieval central Italian testaments seem to have been kept by all or many of the ecclesiastical institutions which received even minor or residual legacies from them. Sometimes preserved fourteenth-century testaments come from quite surprising archives: the only known surviving Reatine sepulchral monument from the period which can be connected with a testamentary disposition is the displaced San Francesco slab of Caterina di Giacomo di don Berardo de Podio (Poiani); Caterina's will, from 11 September 1365, seeks burial at San Francesco to which she leaves twenty-five florins but all else to her sister, Smiralla, whom she makes an executor along with Giovanni de Canemorto and the prior of San Domenico and the guardiano of San Francesco.[39] It is not immediately apparent why Caterina's will, which does not mention the cathedral church, should be preserved in its archives. And those archives also hold the will of Giovanni Nicolocti of Rieti who elected burial at (now destroyed) San Giovanni Evangelista, in the *sepultura, quam fecit Motius de Florentia*—Moccio da Firenze.

On 7 October 1319, in the cloister of his own house in Rieti, the noble canon Giacomo de Labro composed a codicil to an earlier will, of which the notary but not the date is recorded; in the codicil's transcription in the parchment book of Matteo Barnabei, Giacomo's nobility is specifically indicated by a *stemma*, presumably the arms of the house of Labro. There is no talk in the codicil of Giacomo's intended place of burial, but following the transcription of the codicil in Matteo's cartulary is the note that Giacomo the testator died in the year 1320 (third indiction, time of Pope John XXII), and that he was buried on 14 December next to the altar of Santa Maria Maddalena, which is in the cathedral church and which was endowed by Giacomo, and that Giacomo's anniversary will be celebrated on 14 December.[40] Giacomo's codicil begins with a short *arenga* declaration that in the healthy body the mind is better able to collect itself and, with reason, better able to provide from the testator's goods, in life as in death, for his soul; the codicil continues to say that Giacomo had decided to add and subtract things from his previously made testament. The bulk of the addition is concerned with the endowment of the altar of Maria Maddalena and the provision for its chaplain, who would, with his successors, throughout the future celebrate Mass there. The chaplain should celebrate these Masses every day, Masses of the Virgin and other saints, for the soul of the testator and his *parentum* (surely in this case parents), his brothers,

sisters, nephews and nieces and his benefactors, and he should com-
mend the testator's soul to God, to Saint John the Baptist, and to the
Magdalen. The chaplain should be a priest at the time of his appointment, and he should maintain residence, not being absent, ever, for
more than eight days without license of the bishop or chapter. When
the chaplaincy should fall vacant the bishop and chapter should select
a new chaplain within two months, but if the bishop, because of neg-
ligence or discord with the chapter, should fail to present, the power
should devolve to the chapter alone; and if within eight days after the
two months the chapter too should have failed to act, the selection
should devolve to Giacomo's heirs, who should be permitted to move
the endowment to another church in the city or diocese of Rieti. Giacomo specified lands to support his endowment and bequests, and he
provided for their reversion should the provisions of the codicil not be
carried out. He carefully specified that the endowment should be in his
own hands, controlled by him, until his death. The cancellations of the
codicil make it clear that Giacomo had already provided some endowment for the altar of the Magdalen in his will.

His total pattern of bequests of course need not appear in the codicil,
but some provisions beyond the chapel's endowment do appear. Giacomo instructed his heirs to give the friars minor of Rieti for their sus-
tenance a *rugghio* of grain or twenty-five soldi each year for ten years
after his death on the anniversary of his burial, and the friars on their
part were to be bound to an anniversary vigil and conventual Mass for
the soul of the testator. And the heirs should also provide a florin each
year in perpetuity to the chamberlain of the chapter on condition that
an anniversary vigil and Mass be sung each year on his anniversary for
Giacomo by the canons and prebendaries of the church of Rieti; the
florin should be divided so that each participating canon would receive
eighteen denari and each prebendary nine, and that the celebrant should
receive as much as a canon. Again Giacomo was careful: if the heir did
not provide the money the chapter could take it; if the chapter failed in
the observance for two years the heirs might move the devotion to the
Franciscans. The two executors named in the codicil are Tommaso the
nephew of Giacomo and Don Corrado de Murro.

On 28 October 1319, in his own house in Rieti, but with as witnesses
not only Tommaso Capitaneo, but also eight Dominicans including the
prior of San Domenico, the canon Giovanni di magistro Andrea, ill,
made a will with rich and articulate spiritual bequests, and he named as
his executors the guardiano of the Franciscans, the prior of the Domin-

icans, Eleutherio (Lotherio) di don Gentile Alfani, and Giovanni's own father, Magistro Andrea, whom he also named his heir—and the formal emancipation from whom Giovanni cites in his will.[41] Giovanni's will helps to explain the significance of Giacomo's codicil and suggests the connection of both of them with Nicola Cece's bequests of silver chalices, with talk of candles for the Corpus Christi, with Pietro da Ferentino's dying wish for burial at the Franciscans', and with Bishop Giovanni Papazurri's legislation about the Eucharist.

Giovanni's is a family will. Ten of his relatives (including his rather mysteriously named sister, Francesco di Pietro Rossi, in a family that admitted and corrected illegitimacy) besides his father, Andrea, appear in the will; they include an Andreuccio and a Giovanuccia. Giovanni worried about the future housing of some of them. Giovanni thought of Dominicans, and made it possible for one of them to buy his copy of the Summa. Giovanni received money from benefices at Sant'Eutizio di Marano and San Giovanni Evangelista, and he left money for the fabric of San Giovanni Evangelista. He left a reversion, should the provisions of his will fail, half an inheritance to the great hospital Santo Spirito of Rome, and half divided between San Francesco and San Domenico Rieti. But Giovanni's chapel dominates his will as Giacomo's does his codicil.

Giovanni left ten giunte of arable and three of vineyard to endow his chapel of Sant'Andrea, next to the tribune and within the walls of the cathedral church, in which he chose to buried. He left the chapel his missal (*missale meum mangnum*) and breviary (*breuiarium meum mangnum*) and a gilt silver chalice and all his vestments, all of which were to be kept and listed in the sacristy of the cathedral and never sold, or pawned, or lent, or in any way alienated from the chapel's use; and he wished that a chasuble be bought for the chapel with the three florins which the prior and convent of San Domenico owed him. Giovanni instituted as chaplain a poor scholar, Giovanni di Biagio Romano, who was not yet of an age to be priested, but, following a constitution of Bishop Giovanni Papazurri, he reserved the income from the endowment to support Giovanni di Biagio at his studies, while a curate, dompno Giovanni di Luca, should receive ten lire of Ravenna from the endowment's income until Giovanni di Biagio could finish his study and become a priest. (And in fact on 6 November 1319 Giovanni di Biagio was declared to be of appropriate maturity and status actually to reside and celebrate in the chapel which "the former canon Giovanni di magistro Andrea had had constructed for the praise of the divine name and that of Saint Andrew," as appeared in the will of the canon *constructor et dotator*, and Giovanni di Biagio was taken to the chapel and inducted with its altar linens by the canon Corrado de Murro. And a recording public instrument was notarized and sealed with the chapter seal.)[42]

Giovanni di magistro Andrea had planned the rotation of daily Masses which should be celebrated each week in his chapel: Monday a Mass for the dead; Tuesday the Mass of Saint Andrew with commemoration of the Virgin; Wednesday and Thursday Masses for the dead; Friday Mass of the cross with commemoration of the Virgin and the apostle; Saturday for the Virgin and commemoration of cross and apostle; Sunday the cross, the apostle, the Virgin. Giovanni's chaplain would say the matutinal hours in the cathedral's choir with the other prebendaries. But the chaplain appointed must never be a prebendary of the cathedral.

Giovanni's is a will that shows specific concern for the Eucharist and its provisions, and not unconnectedly for the priesthood. In those future morning and evening sacred memorial celebrations which he plans in his chapel Giovanni distinguishes, in terms of money paid to each, between priest prebendaries (twelve denari) and prebendaries who were not priests (eight denari). In a reversionary clause Giovanni reserves five giunte of land from which the harvested grain should be given to the cathedral sacristan, enough to suffice for making hosts for all the sacrifices of the Mass at the cathedral of Rieti. In another bequest Giovanni left money for the fabric of the new tribune of the church, that new shell for the sacrifice at the high altar, next to which he placed his own chapel of Sant'Andrea—and should the building of the tribune be finished, the money should go to the poorer orphans among his relatives or some other use chosen by his executors.

Giovanni ordered that each year on the feast of Saint Andrew bread from a number (eight?) of *rugghi* of grain and a quarter of beans (*leguminum*) should be distributed by his heirs to the poor out of reverence for that glorious apostle and that a like amount should be distributed on the feast of Saint John the Evangelist. If Giovanni's heirs should prove negligent in this distribution, Giovanni's executors would have the power to take all the produce of a specifically designated piece of land which Giovanni owned, and had himself bought, in order that they might execute the provision, which served the poor and honored the two apostle saints. The heirs who were meant to execute this bequest were, until his death, Giovanni's father, Andrea, and, then after his death, Giovanni's brother Ratino, his nephew Andreuccio son of Pe-truccio (who, Andreuccio, had been born illegitimate but who had been legitimized by the count palatine and the legitimization preserved in notarial instrument), and Vanduccio son of that Andreuccio, the three to succeed to equal portions.

Giovanni binds together, enmeshes, as well as he can, family saints and family names, charity to Christ's poor, the observed and continuing celebration of Mass and the Eucharist, and his own chapel of Saint Andrew. The will of Giovanni di Andrea presents a vision of the family assembled comfortably in the presence of Christ in the Eucharist in the chapel and on the edge of the space of the more public presence of Christ in the tribune, that reassembly of family which Dante, in canto XIV of the *Inferno*, shows the soul of the dead craving.[43]

The new tribune of the cathedral church of Rieti, to which Giovanni di Andrea left a bequest and next to which he built his chapel, was being constructed during the episcopate of Giovanni Papazurri, bishop, it will be recalled, from 1302 to 1336, the bishop from whose time come the first surviving Reatine episcopal synodal constitutions, which are con-cerned with the cure of souls, the sacraments, and specifically the Eu-charist. To the new tribune Bishop Giovanni in 1318 contributed one hundred florins. But his donation was part of a more elaborate pious transaction. The florins were the price of goods left to the church by its long-term notary and lay prebendary Giovanni di Pietro, a man, it will be recalled, who had worked for the church as early as 1263 and who had died before 23 September 1314, after having made the church and its fabric his heir, and fully that after the death of his wife would end her life tenancies. In 1318, during the fairly elaborate negotiations conducted by Giovanni di Pietro's executors and particularly by Tom-maso Capitaneo, Giovanni the bishop bought for his own new chapel in the cathedral church its actual property of endowment, which was the property left to the church by Giovanni di Pietro. For this property Bishop Giovanni paid one hundred florins, and these were the florins that the bishop gave to support the tribune's building campaign.[44]

The bishop dedicated his chapel to San Salvatore, a reasonable ded-ication for a canon of the Lateran and a dedication not strange to the diocese of Rieti; but it is a clearly Christocentric dedication. The bishop may have intended to be buried in his chapel. He may in 1318 have already hoped to return to Rome and the Lateran for burial. The bish-op's San Salvatore is in any case the first commemorative chapel of its sort of which there is any notice in the cathedral church or city of Rieti.

In the year before the bishop bought Giovanni di Pietro's bequeathed property for the endowment of San Salvatore, in September 1317, he published a constitution on the endowment of chapels. The bishop acted in his chamber in his palazzo, and he had gathered around him eleven consenting canons. Among the prebendaries who were also present was Tommaso Capitaneo. The bishop's constitution, it says, was for the benefit and protection of Giovanni and his successors as bishop, for the canons of the church, and for other clerical and lay, "uolentes cappellas in nostra maiori ecclesia in honorem diuine maiestatis cos-truere, ut ministrentur in ibi pro remissione peccatorum diuina officia et ecclesiastica sacramenta"; as the constitution protected, it induced—causing chapels in the cathedral to be built and ministered to, the sacred mysteries to be celebrated for the remission of the punishment due for sins.[45] So in 1317 this active and relatively articulate, but in many ways opaque, bishop from a Roman family, himself once familiar with the Rome of Boniface VIII (a place of chapels), this bishop who was a producer of sacramental synodal constitutions brought, or at least signaled the bringing of, new commemorative chapels to the cathedral of Rieti, chapels fit to receive, in burial, bishops, canons and their families, the rich and noble and their families. In these chapels the spirits of their buried inmates might reassemble in adoration of the Christ of the Eucharist, in attendance at Mass, while they again enjoyed family unity and sentiment, and, if appropriate, proclaimed the honor attached to the family *stemma*.

Through the remaining years of the fourteenth century chapels at Rieti accumulate or become visible.[46] Presumably as they became more usual the sharp impulse and awareness of the purpose of the original foundations became blurred. By 1430 when a member of the Cimini family asked to be buried where his ancestors were, in a chapel of San Francesco, the two institutions, the chapel and the friars' place, had aged into a related kind of convention.[47] The fitting of family members into family chapels is characteristic of the later fourteenth century. Bartolomeo de Rocca seems to have been joined in his chapel of Santo Stefano in the cathedral (from 1334) by the noble Riccardo di don Corrado de Murro and his family; the chapel of the Apoleggia family, Amico and his son Gentile, is visible in 1348 and 1363. In 1366 the canon Guillelmo di Giovanni de Ponticello asked for burial in the cathedral at the place where his father, Giovanni, was (and he left the cathedral vestments and land, and he made bequests to the hospital of Santo Spirito in Rieti and a reversionary bequest to the Lateran for its rebuilding and to the basilica of Saint Peter's in Rome).[48]

But even as these chapels grow more familial and formal they record a moment of significant Eucharistic devotion, an appreciation of the real presence of Christ in the Eucharist, the vision of Bishop Pietro da Ferentino (turned patriarch of Aquileia) of what would happen at the Franciscans' of Ùdine, the worrying care of episcopal visitors in visiting the diocese of Sulmona in 1356 (in Canzano: "ut faciant in muro ecclesie parrochialis fenestram clausam pro conseuanda Eucharistia"), the exalted promise of half a town and castle to God made by the Magnifica Margherita Colonna (daughter of the Magnifico Stefano Colonna and widow of the Magnifico Giovanni Conti) which she made "long before" her will of 1355, as she stood at Mass in the church of the Augustinian Hermits San Trifone in Rome and observed the elevation of Christ's Body.[49]

The accumulation of deaths in 1348 brought new administrative responsibilities to the bishop, the new Franciscan bishop Biagio, and, presumably under gruesome circumstances, offered him the opportunity to define better an aspect of his office, that aspect connected with the supervision of the probation of wills, particularly those parts of wills designating pious bequests, and also assuring the collection of the bishop's "fourth." It is not entirely paradoxical, although it may at first glance seem to be, that the plague which generally destroyed order should have contributed to this kind of episcopal order.

The plague also allowed the bishop to express a specific kind of Christian charity, one at the same time both affectingly moving and formalizing in its definition of *pauperes Christi*, the poor of Christ. At Rieti the house of Cimini was very hard struck by the plague. Petracha di Tommaso Cimini, Petrucio, his son, and Tommaso, his father, all died in quick succession. And there also died four ladies of the house of Cimini—*dominarum*, in the genitive, *de dicta domo Ciminorum*—Tommasia, Imiglia, Vanna, and Margarita. The executors of the seven who attempted to pay from their inheritances the bishop's fourth found themselves without funds, without the 160 florins that they should pay him. They gave to the bishop instead a house which had belonged to Petrucio di Petracha, in Cittaducale next to the town piazza, and a garden which had belonged to Petracha with public roads on three sides of it and the enclosing wall of Cittaducale on the other; and in the loggia of the episcopal palace the notary Silvestro di don Giovanni observed and notarized gift and receipt on 11 November 1348. On 1 May 1349 two live women of this beplagued extended family of the Cimini, the noble Donna Cecilia, mother of the deceased Petricono di Cono

Cimini, and Donna Brunella, his widow, appeared as supplicants before the bishop and claimed that they were paupers. In his will Petricono (without, presumably, thought of a quick series of male deaths) had made his two sons his heirs, with the stipulation that if either died without legitimate masculine heirs, he should be succeeded by his brother, but if both died without legitimate masculine heirs, as in fact had happened, that half of his inheritance should go to the sons of Tommasello Cimini and those of Venturella Cimini, and the other half should be offered for Petricono's soul and for that of his family (*parentum*). Because to him, the bishop said, looked the distribution of the half inheritance left for Cimini souls, according to the regulations of the synodal constitutions of the church of Rieti, he had the right to choose the *pauperes* to whom he would give the money for Cimini souls. He, finding the suppliant Cimini women in fact needy, *pauperes*, unable to live and maintain their state, chose them as his receiving *pauperes*.[50]

No one could fail to notice the presence of women among the recipients of pious bequests. The convents of nuns, as well as individual nuns, and the recluses appear again and again; and there are *miserabiles* widows and orphans without dowries. The repeated patterns of the wills press upon their reader's mind a sense that the poor and undefended or pious woman is the most needy, perhaps even the most representative, poor of Christ—that in some sense this Christ after Francis is more present in his sisters than in his brothers. An early fourteenth-century Latian Martin would have given his cloak to a woman beggar (although the woman Donna Bucia left bequests to convents of men twice as large as those to convents of women). Moreover, as the great abbeys can be seen to drift away from the center of donor attention, particularly urban donor attention, as San Quirico remains an ungrowing stick in the ground, as Farfa and San Salvatore seem distant, and San Pastore represents itself through San Matteo, as they recede into rustic distance, the convents of nuns crowd into Rieti and its close neighborhood as they crowd into the wills. They join the houses of friars.

The most striking and familiar of donations to female convents is that to Santa Lucia and Sant'Agnese by Donna Risabella Veglianocte, the wife of Giovanni Impernatore. Hers was a significant gift of property from a major inheritance. From it sprang (or with it were much increased) the first known Reatine houses of Franciscan and, perhaps, Dominican nuns. Risabella's will which leaves her property to Santa Lucia–Sant'Agnese is dated 7 March 1252. Negotiations about the legacy occurred in 1253. Although Risabella's grant did not establish convents in the center of the city, Santa Lucia and Sant'Agnese became the center of Reatine female monachism of the new orders.[51]

In the southern part of the diocese Santa Filippa's monastery continued to attract gifts but unsurprisingly they seem to have been local gifts. In 1258 Andrea di Giovanni da Veccareccia left money to the convent. In 1263 Matteo da Poggio Aviano made Abbess Giovanni his heir and left her his real and movable property. Gemma Burelli da Offeio, who made her will at the monastery in 1273, left it a miscellany of goods, furniture, cloth, grain, nuts (*nuces*).[52] In the northwest Giovanni Papazurri's foundation of Santa Caterina in Cittaducale could, naturally, attract bequests—like the two *barili* of wine a year left in 1380 by Cecilia di Angelone Sarraceni, wife of Cecco di Pietro Mastroni of Cittaducale—from Cittaducale. At Santa Caterina there were at least thirteen nuns in 1350 and at least twenty-one in 1361, of whom at least two were from L'Aquila and one from Rieti.[53] In 1343 in the cloister of San Felice at Posta at the election for a year of Abbess Caterina Celli, in the presence of Augustinian friars, there were nine electing nuns.[54] The outer diocese was not deprived of convents.

The nuns of San Felice do not declare their order. In 1338 the nuns of Volta in or near Rocca Sinibalda are declared not to have an order.[55] Their abbess is said not to be an abbess; they are told they may not call themselves a convent or say they have a chapter. They do not have an approved rule. Their anomalous position seems less anomalous because of the historian Giovanna Casagrande's recent clarification of the position of assembled religious women in central Italy.[56] The nuns of Volta seem part of the same spectrum as the sister anchoresses at San Leopardo Rieti in whom the historian Andrea Di Nicola has recently found, or so it seems, the originating group of dedicated women who were the nucleus from which was formed Santa Caterina Cittaducale.[57] Recluses and anchoresses, groups of them together, houses of nuns who do not state their orders, houses of nuns with specific orders but who choose, for example, confessors from other orders, as the nuns of San Benedetto Rieti had chosen Augustinian Hermits, seem together to offer themselves as targets of pious benefactions.[58] They perhaps offered an escape from the increasingly institutionalized, clarified, clericalized fourteenth-century Reatine church. (But one ought not to forget, for example, the repeated evidence for perhaps quite ancient hermits' caves in Bishop Tommaso's list of diocesan churches, like the *speco* of San Nicola of Stàffoli.)

Certainly the hardening of ecclesiastical boundaries seems connected with the sometimes very enthusiastic performances of male anchorites as well as female recluses; and it is very probably connected with their attraction to testators and other members of the Reatine community. Most visibly flamboyant of anchorites is Paolo Zoppo, whose own experiences are amplified by the visions of Greccio in his mind, or at least on his tongue, or the inquisitor's. In 1315 Nevecta, Johandecta, and Nicolutia tried to close themselves in their house in the parish of San Donato. In 1321 the three sisters Andreuccia, Giovanuccia, and Floretta, recluses "in carceribus Sancti Leopardi de Reate in porta carceraria de foris," granted to Matteo di Giovanni Sbare, canon of San Leopardo, the structures of their anchorages placed around the church of San Leopardo and next to it (*positis in circuitu dicte ecclesie et positis iuxta ecclesiam*) and to the public street.[59] These three women at San Leopardo not only seem to echo (probably in a different key) the three women of San Donato, but they make San Leopardo, where Paolo had lived with his dog, seem a rather specific point of reclusion and one probably protected by the canon Matteo. In 1351 Fra Bartolomeo da Monteleone, "nunc habitator ciuitatis Reat' et spiritu reclusus in quadam cella seu domo ecclesie Sancti Eusaney de Reate prope domos et plateam dicte ecclesie posita (now a denizen of the city of Rieti, a recluse in a certain cell or house of the church of Sant'Eusanio, Rieti, located next to the houses and piazza of that church)," sold a house in the parish of San Leopardo and next to its property to another neighbor, a house left to Fra Bartolomeo in a will for the soul of its testator.[60]

In his 1337 will Francesco Pasinelli had left a bequest to the recluse Nicola da Foresta. The need of testators, of their consciences, as they attempted to follow Christ, coincided with the creation of institutions and the emplacement of individuals who were appropriate and available to receive their bequests. Fra Nicola da Foresta, who was also called Fra Nicola da San Gemino, can be followed in slightly greater detail. In September 1319 Fra Nicola can be seen receiving for himself and for Fra Giovanni di Nicola Cordischi of Rieti, both of whom are described as (in the dative) *religiosis et seruis Dei in heremis habitantibus* (religious men and servants of God who live in hermitages), a piece of land, woods and desert, in Valle Rovarie, with a spring or fountain, with the rights to its water, and on the land a church dedicated to the blessed and glorious virgin Mary. The two hermits are to hold church and hermitage in perpetuity for themselves and for other *seruos Dei* who come to stay in the same place for the purpose of serving God and of praying, and to have the right to enlarge the buildings on the land. The servants of

God are not to be permitted, however, to alienate the land to any ecclesiastical or religious person, or to any secular prelate or any chapter
or college, or to concede to them any jurisdiction. The grant was made
by the lady Filippa, the widow of Lucarello di Tommaso di Nicola, and
by Vanni, the couple's son, and for Cola and Jacobuccio, Lucarello's
sons and heirs, in the house of the sons of Lucarello, in praise of and
out of reverence for almighty God and the Blessed Virgin and all saints
and for the remission of the sins of the donors and Lucarello.

In December 1336 Donna Filippa, by this time remarried to Recho
di don Siniballo, was, again with Vanni and for the others, acting (under
the arco of the house of don Giovanni and don Angelo di don Bartolomeo). She renewed her contract with Fra Nicola and his successors
after freeing Nicola from responsibility for the expenses Donna Filippa
had incurred in opposing and remedying the judicial eviction of Fra
Nicola by Donna Bartolomitia, widow of Citio Bonummandi; Filippa
freed Fra Nicola of obligations but insisted that he not alienate his gift
until no descendant of Bucio Lucarello lived.[61] In February 1346, however, for his own soul's sake, Fra Nicola, acting in the camera of the
episcopal palace at Rieti and in the presence of Don Neapoleone di don
Paolo canon of Rieti, dompno Riccardo di Giovanni Calcelle de Montereale canon of Santa Maria in Pantanis and others, granted to Bishop
Raimond, for himself, the chapter and church of Rieti, the church of
Santa Maria de Foresta sited in Reatine territory, with all its buildings,
woods, and rights.[62] For more than thirty-five years Santa Maria de
Foresta had been, although not undisturbed, an institutionalized home
for hermit servants of God.

In the city itself, besides the recluses like those at San Leopardo, and
the formal and institutionalized poor, the friars and the nuns, were the
actual poor, the "poor of Christ," the receivers of tunics and dowries
(and the Cimini). Here too the need of the conscience seeking to follow
Christ coincided with an appropriate external institution, in this case
the city itself, the pattern of modern human settlement, the urban place
with its attendant aggregate poor people, collected conveniently for the
reception of alms. Some of these poor people were also able to be collected more efficiently for the reception of alms, and presumably for
their care, with the sick and disabled, in hospitals, although these hospitals were themselves not in fact restricted to the city: *extra pontem*
was presumably in the borgo but Marmore was, again presumably, in
the countryside to the north, and its inmates were quite probably re-
cruited from the northern villages and countryside and from the diocese

of Terni. (But the presence in Bishop Tommaso's mid-thirteenth-century list of a number of country hospitals, some of which are specifically joined to *leprosaria*, makes it seem possible that Marmore was a *leprosarium*.) Hospitals are prominent in wills, and they were exactly appropriate legatees for followers in the footsteps of Christ.

Hospitals existed before the thirteenth century but their names multiply in the period of increasingly articulate wills, and the foundation of at least one hospital, Sant'Antonio, is visible. On 28 July 1337, in the presence of Don Francesco archpriest of Santa Maria di Canetra, vicar general of the chapter *sede vacante* after the death of bishop Giovanni, and of Ballovino di magistro Gianni, both prebendaries of the cathedral church, in the sacristy of the cathedral church, the chapter of Rieti (as ordinary during the vacancy) granted a license to construct to Fra Nicola da Pescia, Lucca diocese, brother of the hospital of Saint Anthony of Vienne.[63] Fra Nicola, who had it seems already obtained a papal license, was granted by the chapter the right to build a hospital with an altar, a chapel, a bell, and a cemetery in which could be buried the brothers and servants, the sick and the poor of the hospital, a hospital to be called Sant'Antonio and to be located in the parish of San Leopardo in Rieti. Fra Nicola promised for himself and his successors the payment of a pound of wax every year at Christmas. The agreement was notarized by Matteo Barnabei and sealed with the chapter seal. With Sant'Antonio established, testators like Bucio Lucarelli could leave, as he did, bequests to it or its fabric or its poor. (And Sant'Antonio lasted; its sixteenth-century church remains in beautiful ruin in Rieti.)

In his wills Nicola Cece remembered the confraternity of Santa Trinità. Confraternities are, however, not frequently visible in Rieti wills, although they would seem to have been, as they were in many places, suitable recipients for pious bequests. The foundation, or approval, of one Reatine confraternity is, however, still visible in a surviving document. The document is Bishop Biagio's undated (so between 1347 and 1378) sealed (with Biagio's big, 7.5 cm by 5 cm, red vesica Virgin and Child seal, embedded in a white wax skippet hanging, now, from a white and green cloth string) approval of confraternity statutes or regulations—in fact the document is composed of the regulations with Biagio's subscribed approval.[64] The document's first words are "To the honor and praise and glory of almighty God and our lord Jesus Christ and the blessed Virgin Mary and all saints and the whole celestial court (*curia*) and also to the honor of holy mother church and of the reverend in Christ father and lord, lord brother Biagio by the grace of God bishop of Rieti."

One of the statutes states that each member of the fraternity is bound each morning to go to church and to say before the image of the crucifix five Pater Nosters, unless the member is prevented by some grave impediment, in which case he is to say twice as many of the prayers not in the church. The statutes demand more daily Pater Nosters. They demand fasting on specific days of the week and the hearing of the Mass of the Virgin on the first Sunday of every month. They demand that the brothers assemble for flagellation four times a year: Good Friday, the Saturday before Pentecost, the vigils of the Assumption and the Annunciation. The brothers are forbidden to enter taverns and if they enter to sit down. They are forbidden *ludat ad taxillos*—the dice that decorate the contemporary statutes, the gambling to which contemporary clergy in the diocese of Sulmona fell victim, and which darkened earlier the memory of Giovanni Secinari.[65] The brothers are enjoined to obey the prior, who has the right to expel any member not living justly and well. The bishop, finding nothing in the statutes which did not do honor to God, the Virgin, and the saints, approved. Among the approved statutes were those that underlined not only the confraternity members' suffering with Christ but their following him and his injunctions in corporal works: when a brother died the others were bound to say a Mass and fifty Pater Nosters for him; when a brother was ill they were bound to keep watch over him, to visit him when he was sick, and to bury him when he died.

From the episcopate of Adenolfo to that of Biagio, visible religion at Rieti was Christocentric, and Christocentric in a way that had been suggested by Francis and for which a remembered Francis formed a model. The shape of this Christocentricity changed and so did the various memories of Francis. The central importance of the Eucharist, pure Christ, grew—a concentration on essence but also a step, perhaps, in the direction of the later overwhelming devotion to the name of Jesus. The confraternity statutes which Biagio approved suggest a formalization, a counting, a bringing inside, particularly inside the church, of the following of and devotion to Christ. But the corporal works of mercy, somewhat circumscribed, remained. The Franciscan Christ penetrated its future. In 1334, at San Lazzaro del Valoncello, a leprosarium on the Nera near Norcia, a witness who said that he had been seventy years at the hospital, said that he had heard it said that Francis often came to the hospital to wash the feet of lepers and to visit them. This Francis, exemplum of exempla, was not forgotten. At Rieti in the first half of the fourteenth century men and women visibly moved to religion tried like Ubertino da Casale, at different distances, to follow Christ. They did not follow relics. No relic appears in a will or in talk of founding a chapel in the cathedral. In this period, as at other times, relics were needed for altars, for dedications and consecrations, but notice of them is very rare. Filippa Mareri's cup, her altars, and her body stand, in preserved documents, essentially alone. She is singular. She was a modern, a local, and a family saint, who needed relics in her new altars and women saints near her, and who was attached by name and feast to Saint Philip the apostle. Saints' names, although not noticeably their relics, followed families, as in the dedication of the canon Giovanni's chapel to Andrew, the name of his father, and his own identifying patronymic. Just before canon Giovanni, however, bishop Giovanni dedicated his chapel to the Savior. The Virgin's position is of course different, and closely, familially, connected with Christ's.

The cathedral of Rieti was dedicated to the Virgin. Its feast of consecration was the Nativity of the Virgin (8 September). The cathedral's connection with Mary was reasserted on 11 October 1289 by Pope Nicholas IV, a man from Ascoli and a very institutional Franciscan, a pope with Marian connections as well as close ties to the Colonna.[66] Pope Nicholas, who was then in Rieti, granted a year and forty days indulgence to penitents who each year on one of the feasts of the Virgin or its octave, or on the anniversary of the dedication, visited the cathedral church of Rieti "que est in honore ipsius Virginis dedicata." Throughout the diocese Marian dedications, which had not arrived there in the thirteenth century, were heavy on the ground. They are a plurality in Bishop Tommaso's mid-thirteenth-century list, easily leading all competitors; there are more than eighty of them, more than twice as many than there are dedications to Sant'Angelo, San Nicola, San Pietro, or San Lorenzo, the nearest, in order of frequency, who are themselves followed at a little distance by Andrea, Stefano, Martino, Tommaso, Croce, Vittorino, and Giovanni. Few of the dedications that exist in any number are particularly local, although some of them are noticeable— San Quirico, San Giovenale, Sant'Eleuterio—because of the importance either of an institution bearing the name, or a person (like Eleuterio Alfani) who carried it.[67]

Few of the names are, again, particularly local and few except Maria are women's names. Even so the absence of Barbara who would become the recognized protectress of Rieti and be considered particularly local (supposed birth in nearby Scandriglia, relics in Rieti) is noteworthy.[68] Her arrival at importance to Rieti, or her return, may coincide with a more general return of "little saints" in the late fourteenth century, by which time the concentration on Christ himself may have become too intense to bear or may have come to seem too empty of attractive hagiographic narrative and wonder, although in fact Marian devotion itself seems to have had a source of new support in the foreign Bishop Raimond who used the salutation "Salutem in filio Virginis gloriose" and had with him at Rieti, at least on occasion, a Carmelite (and so particularly Marian) friar, and also in Bishop Biagio with his big Virgin seal (see plate 29).[69]

Barbara was honored, and honor was demanded for her, by the joined action of bishop and chapter and communal council, in 1365, from which year's Riformanze pronouncements were copied into the church's "Book IV." They ordered an augmentation of the yearly accustomed offering of wax on her feast, "on the feast of the most holy virgin and martyr Saint Barbara, whose body lies under the altar of the major church of Rieti, to honor which [relic] men come from the farthest ends of the earth (*de ultimis finibus terre*) . . . so that this blessed virgin by whose merits the city of Rieti has been saved from many tribulations and dangers, will maintain the city and its people and preserve them in a peaceful, prosperous, and tranquil state."[70] In 1390 the leaders of the commune promised each year on the feast of Saint Barbara to offer on her altar a silver lamp worth eight florins—never to be alienated.[71] In the communal statutes of 1489 Barbara is called "Santa Barbara advocata et protectrice de quista nostra Magnifica Cita."[72] In Ballovino's list of oblations received in the cathedral on various important feasts, the feast of Santa Barbara appears regularly. On her day in the account for 1363 twelve soldi were offered—more than the eight soldi on the feast of the Purification of the Virgin, or the seven soldi on the feast of All Saints, or the ten soldi on Sant'Egidio, or the twenty-two denari on the feast of the Conception of the Virgin; but Santa Barbara does not rank near the top of this list: thirty-one soldi (and three pounds of wax) on Sant'Andrea; thirty-seven soldi on Christmas and Santo Stefano; forty-five soldi on the Assumption; and three lire eighteen soldi on the church's great feast, the Nativity of the Virgin.

The sums themselves are moderate; eight of the church's twelve mills brought more income to the church than did the offerings on the Nativity of the Virgin, one mill more than four times as much. But clearly in terms of these oblations the Nativity of the Virgin was a more compelling feast than was Santa Barbara. In the accounts for 1364 "on the feast of Santa Maria and the consecration" four lire and six soldi were received, on the Assumption three lire and two soldi, on Christmas and Santo Stefano thirty-nine soldi, and on Santa Barbara only sixteen soldi. In the accounts for 1374 three lire were received on the Nativity of the Virgin and only sixteen soldi on Santa Barbara. In the accounts for 1392 four lire were received on the Nativity of the Virgin and eleven soldi on Santa Barbara; in 1358 it had been three lire and four soldi on the Nativity of the Virgin, twelve soldi six denari on Santa Barbara.[73] In the fourteenth century, these figures argue, it was the Virgin's church. But perhaps it is more important to note that Santa Barbara, a saint of obvious importance to the commune, was also the patron of a major cathedral feast. In the list of feasts on which the commune donated wax, in equal amounts, to the cathedral, for example in the accounts for 1374, Santa Barbara is one of the six feasts, and the other five are all feasts of the Virgin: Assumption, Nativity of the Virgin, Conception, Purification, Annunciation. By the second half of the fourteenth century Rieti's local saint was already prominent but not, certainly, in every area dominant.

Bishop Tommaso's mid-thirteenth-century list carries the names of more than one hundred recipients of dedications; and a scattering of specific diverse dedications has here been observed, dedications occurring at perhaps a slower pace in the later thirteenth and fourteenth centuries, dedications of institutions, of churches, of chapels, of hermitages, of altars. On 23 November 1231 (using the mode of dating of the classical Roman calendar) Bishop Rainaldo de Labro dedicated Filippa Mareri's newly built church of San Pietro de Molito, and in his formal recording document he listed the internal dedications and relics: on the east side, in the altar dedicated to the honor of the Virgin Mary, relics of saints Mary Magdalen, Margherita, Caterina, Constantia, Agnese, Agatha, Antia, and Francis; on the west, in the altar dedicated to the Apostle Peter, relics of saints Peter, Andrew, Paul, Bartholomew, Philip, the Forty Martyrs, the four Crowned Saints (Quattro Coronati), the Seven Sleepers, Francis, the Holy Innocents, Sebastian, Denis, Eleuterio, Hypolitus, Cornelius, Pope Felix, the wood of the cross, and the stone where the Lord (*dominus*) put his feet when he appeared to Moses. Bishop Rainaldo granted an indulgence for those who visited the church on the feast of Saints Philip and James, 1 May.[74] Rainaldo and San Pietro offer a nice and patterned bed of appropriate sanctity.

The really significant additions to dedications in the thirteenth century, however, were San Francesco, San Domenico, and Sant'Agostino; and they emphasize the new dedication to the evangelical life, the direct following of Christ. A similar shaping might be expected in the devel-

opment of "given" names. To the sometimes observable and not surprising miscellany of the early thirteenth-century neighborhood names—
local, Germanic, common saints, all sometimes obscurely spelled—one
would expect to be added the new saints of the friars, and from the old
names one would expect to be dropped some old Germanic and not
recognizably Christian local names and local spellings. And certainly
one would not be entirely disappointed.

Still, when in the 1220s a man from the Porta Romana talks of property that he and his brothers hold in fee, and says that his name is Andrea
di Berardo di Reatino di Nicola and that his brothers' names are Berardo, Pietro, Odone, Nicola, Tommaso, and Angelo, he surely does
not suggest that he precedes some revolution in Christian naming. Nor
do the list of tithe-payers to Tommaso del Giudice and Giacomo Sarraceno in the 1280s with their perfectly conventional saints' names—
Pietro, Giovanni, Giacomo, Paolo, Nicola, Matteo, Andrea, Simeone,
and Angelo—suggest much of a revolution. Yet a broader selection of
tenants' names from the same source, which shows much the same
pattern, can be stretched to include a Francesco and an Antonio. An
impressionistic observation, a sampling, of the evidence preserved suggests a more regular use of recognizable saints' names in the later than
in the earlier thirteenth century, but they are, overwhelmingly, old, old
saints' names. The transformation is complicated in another, and enlightening, way. The reader of names is transferred from the archaic
unknown, insofar as that exists, with remarkable rapidity, to the vernacular nickname preserved within the Latin text. Close on the heels of
Francesco arrives, among the Vannis and Colas, Cecco, Ceccho; there
is hardly time to savor the presence of the saints.

Francesco does appear; the visible actors in this book make that clear.
By 1445 the number of Domenicos in Contigliano is startling. Among
the prebendaries in Ballovino's lists for 1368 are a Francesco, two Domenicos, and two Antonios; and in Rieti Antonio tends perhaps to
usurp somewhat the position of Francesco.[75] But the significance even
of the full and clear name (perhaps like that of dedications) is not really
obvious. Francesco da Greccio did not name himself—give himself his
name; but Bucio Lucarelli, the man whose mother patronized Fra Nicola of Foresta, did presumably name his sons Antonio and Francesco,
although in his preserved will he seems particularly attracted to the
spirituality of Sant'Agostino.

These doubts about personal names make one approach again, from
another angle, that problem to which every observer of this church must

always return, the actual significance of the coming of the friars and of Francis. Anyone who looks at the painted fourteenth-century processional cross from San Francesco Posta and sees there Christ's red blood (plate 33), and the communicating sorrow of Mary and John, and the great Franciscan saints, Francis and Anthony, sees a very major religious development tied to a clearly Franciscan public artifact which rested, when it was still, in a Franciscan place. But what really is the meaning, beyond expressiveness, of the arrival of this object? What kind of religious change does it actually represent? And did the Franciscans bring this change or did they merely express it particularly effectively? At Rieti itself no physical change at all connected with religion is so obvious as the swelling of the city around the establishments of the three sets of friars and their big churches. The friars, these followers of Christ, came to Rieti where Francis had been, and they built these big auditoriums in which they could preach to the Reatine people the word of Christ; and, at least in the fourteenth century, one order after another sent a yearly preacher on Saint Mark's day to preach to the cathedral chapter in or near the cathedral which itself had swollen to auditorium size, slowly, before their churches were built. The friars sent confessors, or offered them, to visible testators.[76] They obviously taught (even perhaps in their own interests) the corporal works of mercy. They made the city a visible instrument for satisfying donors' charitable needs. They changed the world—or at the very least they most noticeably proclaimed its changing.

But as donors softened, the friars hardened. The inquisitorial scenes at San Francesco, in a camera, in a loggia, in a foresteria, seem to be erasing the scenes of Francis himself at Greccio. Does the succession of the three Franciscan bishops of Rieti not seem to be saying the same thing as the Damianites painted in the Francis cycle at Assisi, quickly dressed and costumed and made into an order? Both seem related to the repeated panels of the Dominican attitudes of prayer and to be telling of a freezing into convention, valuable and even necessary convention perhaps, but convention and a kind of more easily bearable normalcy. The raw perception of the companions, the surface of whose panels seems all exposed nerve, has been replaced by the fresco cycle at San Francesco Rieti, copied, in which (within the bit of narrative framed) Greccio is not Greccio on the neighboring hill but Greccio from the cycle at Assisi.[77] And Greccio itself, the Greccio of Francis and of the companions, has changed into the place of Paolo Zoppo's or Simone da Spoleto's fantasies, a wild snowy place but a Franciscan *locus*, a place with the order's accouterments, novices, rooms with doors. But the progression is not simple, or not simple in just this way. Greccio continues. The old man at San Lazzaro near Norcia recalls the Francis who himself washed lepers' feet. Rieti did not return after a hundred years to the Rieti that had existed before Francis heard music and clothed a poor woman there.

The institutional, and so closed, quality of the later friars, of the Franciscans, seems, at least in style, related to the closed quality of some parts of the better ordered, more fully expressed, diocesan church, to the clericalized canons (with their fixed prebends). This closedness makes more understandable (at least at our distance) not only the attraction of the Fraticelli and the continued escape to individual or un-ruled seclusion, but also the formation of a group of spiritual leaders, of spiritual advisers in a small city like Rieti, not unconnected with the orders of friars but not at all bound by them. At Rieti the combined fragments of document argue that there was such a group, or at least that there were three men, who appear, more than accident would de-mand, at crucial moments of spiritual intensity or whose names appear repeatedly in documents of spiritual significance: Giovanni Petrignani, priest at San Giovanni Evangelista, the man in the garden; Eleuterio or Lotherio Alfani, executor of important pious wills, protector of a du-bious Spoletan Fraticello, father of Fraticelli sons who, like Giovanni Petrignani, turn up in the letters of Angelo Clareno, the father, presum-ably of Giovanni's friend, Matteo di Loterio; and Tommaso Capitaneo, co-executor with Eleuterio of important pious wills, a figure centrally present for significant Reatine ecclesiastical change.[78]

But they do not emerge, these men, entirely in reaction to or against the closing of boundaries, the formalizing of institutions, the institu-tionalizing, the clericalization that is apparent in the diocese of Rieti, its church and chapter, in the thirteenth and fourteenth centuries. Tom-maso Capitaneo was much involved with the building of institution. He connects the world of the articulate will with the world of priestly preb-endaries. He forces his observer to realize that it is possible that the closing of diocesan boundaries, the forming of the office of vicar gen-eral, the recording of documents by an official scribe, and the freedom to live a life of imaginative Christ-like charity may actually be integrally connected—the discipline and the freedom—not just opposed to each other. Tommaso Capitaneo can be seen as a representative of advanced definition in both directions; and, close to lay enthusiasm, he is quin-tessentially clerical.

Eleuterio Alfani's name recalls Fraticelli (and also a father's weeping for wayward Fraticelli sons); but no family name is more capitular than his, and, although a layman, he is noticeably present in the church of Rieti. Giovanni Petrignani, in spite of the heresy with which Simone of Spoleto wanted to connect him and his seemingly advanced open-air instruction of the laity, in spite of his harsh humor, emerged from the Black Death to become not only archpriest of his church of San Giovanni but a canon of the church of Rieti. He was given Tommaso Cimini's old prebend, a prebend which included land in the dried area near the old hill of San Matteo where in the early thirteenth century the canon Sinibaldo Mareri had fought physically against Cistercians to preserve, or gain, property for the cathedral church. It would be hard to think of a more telling symbol of adherence to the central institution of the institutional church.

That central institution, the chapter, need not, to fulfill its formal definition, have participated in the spiritual changes of the thirteenth and early fourteenth centuries. Its conventional functions, the localness and longevity of its members, would suggest for it an essential conservatism. Protected by its prebends, absorbed in the shadow of its choir it need not, one would think, have looked and listened and waited for any external spiritual stimulus. But the chapter, its member canons, and its prebendaries did participate in the more general religious sentiment and in some ways, at least as encouraged by their advisers, were even among its leaders, as the will of Giovanni di magistro Andrea shows. That will emphasizes the Eucharist and the testator's participation in its mysteries even after the testator's death. This element of the new piety, with its expression in chapels within the cathedral (and in the cathedral's new tribune), seems to have been the chapter's most particular contribution. With it the cathedral clergy reinforced in testators' minds the continuing importance, even dominance, of the cathedral church in the age of the friars' great churches, an importance changed but further strengthened in the later fourteenth century by the cult of Barbara and her relics underneath the altar.

In the thirteenth and fourteenth centuries the diocese of Rieti changed. One cannot imagine really how a fourteenth-century Romagnia lord of Belmonte would react to the early thirteenth-century canons of Rieti struggling with the Cistercians in the drying marsh over which they fought; one cannot imagine how his chancellor or secretary could have described the struggle. The marsh dried. The crayfish of the place (and of Francis) seem to have disappeared. Leeks no longer enter recorded conversation. But crime does—in regularly administered diocesan courts. Memory is not leaning against the church wall; it is a record in a notarial cartulary.

Giovanni Papazurri and Biagio of Leonessa issue synodal statutes that imagine a pastoral diocese and parishioners observing and receiving the Eucharist. The old thirteenth-century rather frightening, stiff God-Christ, Savior blessing, in the fresco on the external wall of Canetra (plate 6) is replaced by the charming child with his mother, carved wood, polychrome, fourteenth-century (plate 7), prepared, almost surely outside the diocese, to spend a long future blessing people lined along the village streets of Sambuco—like the Madonna and Child of San Domenico (with donors) trying, it would seem, affably and sweetly to extend themselves to the aroused community. The tiny relic-box of a church of Santa Vittoria Monteleone (plates 2 and 3) continued to exist in the countryside, and to bring forward the twelfth century's kind of blessing, but it was joined by big, urban, open and relatively empty (except for people) Sant'Agostino inside the new walls of Rieti (plate 4). The conca of Rieti remained the center of interest for the chapter of Rieti on its hill, but it was a center from which the chapter spread out, for example, in its *sede vacante* diocesan courts into the whole territorial and governed diocese.

That diocese had a kind of reality which can now be only sensed; it was a box at least in part filled and painted. The Montecassino Passion, a play on its way from Montecassino to Sulmona, presumably moved through or near a diocese similarly interested in the dramatic death it showed and spoke. It was a place for drama, of that sort that centuries later, in a countryside in which it could be believed that Sallust, the repeatedly popularly referred to Sallust, had been an ancient archpriest of San Vittorino, where children would in popular Christmas plays say "Beh, beh" to make themselves, on whatever stage they had, seem the sheep that had surrounded Christ's birth.[79] The friars' Christmasy hands had helped make of the diocese a future sounding-box for the lightly sweet Christ-remembering "Beh, beh."

Thirteenth- and fourteenth-century pictures remain in the diocese, particularly collected now in the museum that covers the space that was once San Giovanni Battista, actually at the diocese's center in the extended Duomo. Among the most impressive are thirteenth- and fourteenth-century paintings from San Domenico, Rieti. Not many frescoes from the two centuries remain on the walls of country churches in the diocese, but their absence is in some part compensated for by those which do remain in nearby parts of the Abruzzi at Bominaco and Fossa, in an area that can be thought of as lying between the two homes of the family Secinari. These frescoes open the pictorial mind of the late thirteenth century, and some of them show to remarkable effect that close tying of the life of Christ and his family to the actual life of late thirteenth-century families living and eating and praying and dying in the rough Abruzzi countryside. So on the wall of Santa Maria ad Cryptas in Fossa leeks appear on the dinner table, but the dinner table is that of the Last Supper (plate 19). On the wall of the same church appears a deeply moving Crucifixion with Mary and John, and also a tragic Entombment, and beneath the small but extended family of the Entombment is, in half-echo, hopeful echo, the knight and his lady, the men and women, of the donor family (plate 35). At Bominaco whoever was in the church was reminded of the continuing world outside by an effective but conventional calendar painted on the wall, and reminded of the dangers that inhabited that world by one of the huge Saint Christophers who rather startlingly offered themselves to those who departed from Christian churches (plate 36). There was also here from the later thirteenth century a Saint Martin on his horse offering half his cloak to a beggar, as there would be in sculpture in the fourteenth century on facades of churches in Sulmona and in that Gagliano which is one of the places of Giovanni Secinari's will (plate 37).

In Secinari country Francis's model remains after Francis's coming, to question again the exact nature of Francis's part in the change he brought, as well as to show in another way the dominance of Franciscan Christianity, and perhaps at least to raise the questions: is it possible that Martin survived in the knightly countryside as Francis dominated more completely the city with its spending merchants and its urban poor? Is this another sign of the kind of division between city and country which was marked by the distinction between places which did and did not have institutions and groups appropriate to the ready reception of bequests from testators anxious adequately to satisfy the new demands of posthumous charity? How much more difference was there between city and country than the kind of simplification of text and style that one sees, or saw, in the beautifully severe angel capital (now stolen) in the crypt of San Leopardo, Borgocollefegato (plate 38), drawn from its presumed late twelfth-century model, the elegant angel capital from the old ciborium of the cathedral of Rieti (plate 39; now in the Palazzo Cappelletti)?[80]

The effect of the Fossa paintings, with their leeks, is related to that gotten from extended parts of Ballovino's account books, from their intermingling of what is generally considered religion with what is generally considered life. Money paid for bells (of which the survivors bear messages including ones about the freedom of the *patria*) marches with money paid for keys and wood and water carried. Income from anniversaries is separated in space from that depleted income from land unworked (still because of the plague?) or devastated by hordes of *grilli* (locusts, crickets, grasshoppers?) in the 1360s. Painters are paid repeatedly, as for the John and Mary of the Crucifix; money is spent for the wax consumed as the Corpus Christi was carried through the city. The props for feasts are bought, and the machines of mills are repaired. *Nebule* are bought for Pentecost. In his 1358 accounts Ballovino recorded that he paid 8 soldi for two quaterni of paper; 3 soldi 6 denari for keys for the campanile; 6 soldi for rope for the new bell; 3 soldi 5 denari for pepper; 4 denari for onions; 35 soldi for twelve partridges and a lamb; 13 soldi 6 denari, another time, for four partridges and a hare; 7 soldi 6 denari for Don Nicola and Don Therio for wine "when they made peace"; 10 soldi for laurel for the Assumption; 2 soldi for the bell-ringing (at the Assumption); and, for that feast, the 2 soldi for Don Giovanni Petrignani for singing the Mass. Ballovino's is in this sense a working, living Christianity, and one that he obviously took seriously and found essentially unobjectionably arranged. It was also, at the cathedral church, a carefully accounted Christianity. Ballovino's meticulous successor in the first year of his holding office could show a profit. When he had finished his accounts he had a surplus of 201 lire 12 soldi, which he divided among the bishop and canons.

The cathedral chapter's "Book IV" tells the story in slightly different terms in its catalog of anniversaries.[81] It is a sort of specialized Book of Life for a group of canons and Bishop Raimond. "Giacomo de Labro, once canon, left in his testament, written by Matteo Barnabei, once notary . . . each year, one florin to be distributed by the camerario . . . his anniversary 27 August." "Don Corrado di don Riccardo de Murro, once canon . . . his chapel of Saint Stephen next to the church of Rieti and the chapel of Saint John the Baptist . . . three anniversaries, 11 March, 22 July, 10 August . . . souls of Don Riccardo and his mother . . . to give wine and hosts . . . for all time, for the sacrifice of the Mass at the main altar of the cathedral and at the chapels of the church."

"Bartolomeo Bontempi, once canon . . . anniversary 5 August." "Don Andrea di don Syniballo de Tortolinis of Rieti, once canon and abbot of the secular church of Sant'Eleuterio near Rieti . . . hand of Matteo Barnabei . . . anniversary 3 December." "Don Berardo de Secinario, once canon of Rieti, and abbot of the church of Santa Croce Lugnano . . . anniversary 10 January." "Don Tommaso Cimini, canon of Rieti . . . two anniversaries, 16 February the day of his death, and 24 August for his soul and the souls of his people." "Bishop Raimond . . . anniversary 5 April." "Don Gentile Fuctii de Labro, once canon of Rieti . . . land in Fiume Morto . . . next to property of the lords of Labro (*dominorum de Labro*) . . . his brother Transarico . . . anniversary 19 June." They return to the church, these prelates of it, the mixture of their lives and goods to produce the singing and saying of the Mass through the calendar of its year, for this church which spent, in 1379, 6 soldi and 4 denari for a cock, 18 soldi and 8 denari for six doves (*tortore*), and on the feast of Pentecost 5 soldi for another kind of dove (*columba*)—to eat or to celebrate?

One returns to the will, from 16 October 1341, of the knight Don Berardo di don Raynaldo de Colle: his gifts to nuns; his worrying about his father's soul and the will of his mother, Elena; talk of tunics for the poor; the three friars' churches but burial in San Domenico; the hospital of Sant'Eramo (Erasmo), money, 8 florins, to buy beds, and the church of Sant'Eramo, money, 4 florins, for the fabric; and to the hospital 3 *vegetes* which Jotio of Rivodutri is keeping and one of which has a capacity of 3 *salme*, and one of 2 ½ *salme*, and one of 5 ½ *salme*; the sons of Herigono da Rivodutro his vassals; the garden by the river and Sant'Apostolo which he leaves to the chapel of Santa Maria Novella of Rivodutri, and giunte in Fiume Morto; and his chapels in San Domenico, the chapel of Sant'Andrea and that of Sant'Elena (his mother's name); the friars of San Francesco; and a silver chalice, which dompno Silvestro the priest of Sant'Angelo of Rivodutri holds, to that church for the performing of the sacred mysteries there forever; gold and silver and everything in a chest or cupboard at San Domenico; and property under the wall next to that of Giovanni Petrignani; and a silver chalice to Santa Maria Novella for celebrating the sacred mysteries forever; and clothes and cloths to be used as vestments at Santa Maria Novella; and to his daughter Imilutia 250 florins dowry unless she chooses to enter a convent, then only 50; to the church of San Domenico two banners for Berardo's soul's sake. All this and much more, this richly material but also richly spiritual integration of life and death, was to be supervised by Berardo's executors: Giovanna, his wife; the prior, whoever he should be, of San Domenico; and that central professional, Don Giovanni de Canemorto.[82]

Pilgrims to Rome and Gargano passed through Rieti.[83] In 1292 a couple vowed continence at the altar of San Domenico.[84] In 1376 the widow of a knight named Angelo sought burial where her husband was buried in the cathedral next to a newly built chapel.[85] Bishop Rainaldo de Labro (and Bishop Adenolfo of the house of Barete before him), Bishop Tommaso the Corrector, and Bishop Pietro da Ferentino had built a diocese. Giovanni Papazurri and Biagio da Leonessa legislated to it. But in religion's change what real importance did the bishops have? Were they rulers? Was there in religion rule? The diocese became an institution filled with institutions but also with related fugitives from institutions (seen as institutions): were the bishops institution or fugitive? Did the bishops speak the change that was occurring within permanence? How, in their incoherence, could they? But did not the inconsistency of individual bishops also have a kind of consistency of something that can, too easily, be called style or, to borrow from a great genre, modus operandi: Tommaso the Corrector, Pietro da Ferentino, Giovanni Papazurri, Biagio responding unsurprisingly to the confraternity, the nuns. The progression of these styles can be seen developing in a line parallel to other more manageable developments. And Giovanni Papazurri, at least, answers quite surprisingly: yes, there was rule; yes, a bishop could, in a way, rule.

In 1319 the canon Bartolomeo de Rocca (whose prebend would eventually become Ballovino's) in response to what must seem by then, at Rieti, a conservative request, received from the abbot of Citeaux at the petition of the abbot of San Pastore, the spiritual benefits in life and death offered by the Cistercian order.[86] The geographical confusion or conflation in the diocese, San Pastore and Greccio, Franciscans at San Salvatore's Longone, is accompanied by the kind of chronological retention caught in Bartolomeo's confraternity with the Cistercians. At Rieti the new church did not entirely displace the old. As the water in the conca dried, the conca itself and Terminillo above it remained. For the things of church, this is said best, I think, by Pier Paolo Pasolini in *Atti impuri* as he watches, through the smoke and intense cold of the Friuli sunset, modern villagers praying in the ancient little church of Viluta, and being watched, too, as they pray, by the antiquely shaped eyes of their church's frescoes: "Degli affreschi, giotteschi e tolmezzini, guardavano coi loro occhi di tedeschi la povera gente di Viluta che cantava le litanie."[87]

In the diocese of Rieti change was restricted by syntax, by topography, including the shaping topography of memory and perception, of what men call the human heart. And the predominant color of the souls of the visible men and women of "this populous village"—tinted in significant part by the active optimism of Christian hope—was green, various shades of green.

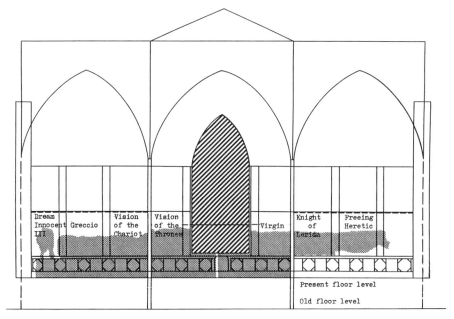

| Dream Innocent III | Greccio | Vision of the Chariot | Vision of the Thrones | | Virgin | | Knight of Lerida | Freeing Heretic |

Present floor level

Old floor level

1. Placement of the choir frescoes, San Francesco, Rieti. After D. Blume, *Wandmalerei als Ordenspropaganda* (Worms, 1983).

The Frescoes in the Choir of San Francesco

Julian Gardner

The frescoes of the legend of Saint Francis in the choir of San Francesco at Rieti have only recently attracted the sustained attention of art historians, although they have been known for a considerable period.[1] The fragmentary cycle now occupies a single register running round the choir chapel (plate 32 and figure 1). The aim of this discussion is to set out very briefly the problems posed by the Rieti frescoes rather than to propose definitive solutions.

According to tradition it was during his second visit to Rieti in 1210 that Saint Francis occupied the small oratory of Santa Croce.[2] The present church was begun toward the middle of the thirteenth century. On 15 September 1245 Innocent IV granted an indulgence of forty days to all who assisted the construction of a Franciscan convent at Rieti, which, it appears, had already been begun.[3] This indulgence was renewed three years later, on 20 May 1248.[4] In 1289 the friars bought a piece of land from the canons of Sant'Angelo.[5] The low-lying site beside the Velino was prone to flooding, and an inundation is recorded in 1263.[6] A particularly disastrous flood in 1634 prompted the raising of the church floor, damaging the frescoes in the process.[7] Although they must still have been visible in the fifteenth century, to judge from the sequence and placement of the Quattrocento frescoes in relation to the older stratum, the cycle of Franciscan scenes is not mentioned in the sources.[8] Even after the collapse of the vault during the severe earthquake of 1898 they do not seem to have come to light. Shortly before 1954 they were restored by the Soprintendenza ai Monumenti.[9]

The cycle is badly damaged, and the still recognizable scenes are the following: (1) the Dream of Pope Innocent III, (2) the Miracle at Greccio, (3) the Vision of the Chariot, (4) the Vision of the Throne. To the right of the east window the series is interrupted by a preexisting votive fresco of the Madonna and Saints Peter and Paul. The cycle continues on the south wall of the choir with (5) the Healing of the Knight of Lerida, (6) the Freeing of the Heretic. The last scene on this wall is lost. Apart from the Franciscan scenes a number of somewhat mediocre Quattrocento frescoes survives in the choir.

Beneath the cycle of Franciscan narratives is a *basamento* of fictive illusionistic mosaic pierced by hexagonal openings within which are set busts of angels. In the two central hexagons of the west wall the angels wear *pallia* and hold censers.[10] The raising of the choir floor in the seventeenth century has brought these angels unnaturally close to the ground, and this alteration has also minimized the calculated viewing point of the framing of the Franciscan scenes.[11] The scenes themselves begin approximately 130 cm above the present floor level. At least part of the damage done to the scenes appears to have been caused by the subsequent insertion of the choir stalls.

Architecturally the choir is a simple rectangular space, approximately 9.3 meters square. Parts of the original vault responds survive, cut back below capital level, presumably at the time of the insertion of the baroque vault.[12] A large gothic east window, its tracery now substantially restored, provides the only source of light. In their main lines both choir and transept very probably go back to the middle of the thirteenth century.

A considerable amount of reconstruction in the mind's eye is necessary for a proper understanding of the Franciscan scenes. The upper parts of all the surviving narratives are lost. It may be that we owe the preservation of the surviving fragments to the protection of the later choir stalls. Whether there was a second, upper register of scenes is uncertain and will be considered presently, but the basamento proves that the remaining scenes constituted the original bottom level. The plaster joins (*giornate*) of the basamento cornice molding overlap the borders of the scenes, demonstrating that the normal painting process in fresco of working from the top downwards was followed at Rieti.[13]

Some further technical observations may be made. On the north side of the choir (at least where plaster overlaps are visible), it is evident that the framing elements between the scenes were painted first and the intervening scenes thereafter. This painting sequence has been noted on the triumphal arch of the Scrovegni Chapel at Padua of circa 1305, and (at least partially) in the Saint Francis legend in the Upper Church at Assisi.[14] The bases of the fictive columns which frame the narratives are decorated with a strip of fictive Cosmati work. These columns, which differ in detail, are set against a dark blue "void": a pair of thin white lines separated by a broader band of red earth forms the borders of the scenes themselves. All the halos project slightly from the surface of the wall and their rays were indented with a stick, a common practice at the time. The basic measurements of the frescoes appear to have been calculated in *braccie*.[15] A good deal of the upper layer of paint has flaked away. Some minute fragments of siccative filling survive in the basamento. The votive fresco to the right of the window is earlier than the fresco layers at either side, as is proved by the sequence of plaster overlaps, and it would appear to have been purposely preserved by the designer of the cycle of Franciscan narratives, perhaps at the wish of the donor who kneels to the left of the Virgin. The east window is taken, not always consistently, as the source of light in the cycle, illuminating the forms from right to left on the north wall, and from left to right on the south. This convention had been found earlier in Giotto's frescoes in the Arena Chapel at Padua and was widely imitated thereafter.[16]

One of the most puzzling questions raised by the Rieti cycle is its narrative sequence. The upper, damaged, level of the scene is some 130 cm above the raised floor level and was originally some two meters higher. The subject of the first fresco on the north side of the choir, the Dream of Pope Innocent III, is certain. Even if there were originally an upper register of scenes in the choir at Rieti, the surviving group does not agree with the historical progress of Saint Francis's life as codified in the *Legenda Maior*, the textual sources for the model of the Rieti cycle, the legend in the Upper Church at Assisi.[17] At Assisi the Dream of Pope Innocent III, which at Rieti begins the sequence on the north wall of the choir, is the sixth in the cycle of twenty-eight narratives. The second Rieti scene, the Miracle at Greccio, is thirteenth in order at Assisi and so on. These elisions would be of no great moment in so greatly abridged a cycle but for the fact that the third scene at Rieti, the Vision of the Chariot, occurs eighth at Assisi, that is, preceding the Miracle at Greccio. Thus the abbreviated Rieti cycle not only omits scenes from its model but also rearranges their temporal sequence. That the Assisi cycle was in fact the model for the frescoes at San Francesco in Rieti is evident from the many compositional similarities and from repetitions of detail.[18] If, for example, we juxtapose the figures of the two soldiers in the Freeing of the Heretic or the kneeling

Francis in the church at Greccio, the filiation is evident. The compositions at Rieti lack the scale and spaciousness of Assisi despite the recurrence of many individual motifs.[19] Furthermore, the Rieti narratives are articulated less comprehendingly in space than had been the case at Assisi. It would appear that the designer of the Rieti cycle employed a combination of compositional sketches and motif books, a phenomenon noted elsewhere in early Trecento painting in Italy.[20] The designer's selection demonstrates too the canonicity of the Assisi legend as a whole.[21]

In contrast to its prototype the Rieti cycle is much simplified, both as regards the architectural framing of the cycle and its internal design. The "bay" system which forms so marked a feature of the overall design of the Assisi legend is lacking on the north wall of the Rieti choir, partly as a consequence of the reordering of the scenes, although the painted framing, and to a more limited extent the lighting, acknowledges the fall of the light from the east window.[22] There does not appear to be any parallelism in the Rieti scenes, although so little survives that its original existence cannot be excluded with certainty.[23]

It is difficult to judge the style of the Saint Francis scenes at Rieti. The votive fresco is quite evidently Roman in its formal idiom. Peter's coiffure can readily be compared with works from the circle of Pietro Cavallini, as can the color range and the curvilinear but rather sharp-edged drapery style of the composition.[24] The diffusion of Cavallini's stylistic influence from Rome was widespread, and it can be traced in the region at Santa Maria in Vescovio, the episcopal church of the cardinal bishopric of Sabina.[25] Nonetheless, even in this earlier stratum at Rieti, details like the monochrome angel in the niche of the throne side are comparable with details in the legend at Assisi, although the architecture of the throne itself is not dissimilar from that in the badly damaged *Annunciation* at Santa Cecilia in Trastevere of circa 1293.[26] The Franciscan scenes themselves are more difficult to date, and their sedulous imitation of a revered prototype exacerbates the problem. In their coloration and style they present some resemblances to Umbrian paintings of the 1320s, although they may not be quite so late as this.[27] In the present state of knowledge it is probably wiser to ascribe them to a minor local artist imitating a major, earlier model.

More interesting perhaps is the question, why was the decision taken to copy scenes from the Assisi legend?[28] Rieti was an important center of the order in an area specially dear to Francis himself. Yet there is nothing in the textual sources to suggest that, Greccio apart, the chosen scenes were particularly linked to the locality.[29] Such imitation of Assisi occurred in murals elsewhere. An important surviving instance is the series of Franciscan scenes at San Francesco at Pistoia where the setting is also transferred to the choir.[30] The Pistoiese cycle also reiterates the Assisi legend, although in a more accomplished manner than at Rieti: there they appear to have been complete by 1343.[31] At Pistoia, as at Rieti, the spatial relationships of the prototype are garbled, despite the accuracy of individual detail. The phenomenon of imitation in fourteenth-century Franciscan painting remains in need of further investigation.[32] At San Francesco in Rieti the original gothic high altar block may also have extended the range of reflections of the basilica at Assisi.[33]

Despite their modest artistic quality, the frescoes in the choir at San Francesco at Rieti yield valuable information about Franciscan artistic programs and contemporary patronage within churches of the order, besides shedding more light on a still imperfectly understood process, the accurate transference of monumental frescoed designs from one location to another.

Notes

Introduction

1. The sequence of editions and publications of this novel can be found, for example, in the introduction to the 1973 Oscar Mondadori edition of *Vino e pane*. For an introduction to the actual language of the area, see Baldelli, *Medioevo volgare*, 195–209.

2. For postunification *brigantaggio* along the old border in the area of the diocese of Rieti, see Montagner, "Reazione e brigantaggio nel Cicolano"; Maceroni, ed., *Il brigantaggio*. A strong sense of the problems which the boundary caused the early modern diocese and its bishops and their administrators can be got from Maceroni and Tassi, *Società religiosa e civile*.

3. Rieti, Archivio Capitolare (hereafter Arch. Cap.), VIII.C.4. For the almost exactly contemporary painting, probably three years earlier, of emperor and pope of the "officium stratoris," in the chapel of San Silvestro at the Quattro Coronati in Rome, see Mitchell, "St. Silvester and Constantine," 19 and fig. 14. This does not mean that there are no other archival records from Rainaldo's episcopate: Arch. Cap., IV.A.5 (in which Innocent IV supports the recovery of rights and property lost since the death of Rainaldo's predecessor, Rainaldo); IV.Q.10 (18 September 1249, in which a tenant promises a payment in pepper yearly at Christmas, Easter, and Assumption).

4. Rieti, Arch. Cap., Libri de Introitu et Exitu (hereafter Lib. Int. et Exit.), 1364. The notion of person which informs this book is obviously very different from that offered by Sabean in his *Power in the Blood*, 35: "There was as yet no notion of the person as a single, integrated center of awareness." I point this out because, in spite of difference in time and place, so many of the ideas and questions in Sabean's powerful work (to which I was introduced by my colleague

Randolph Starn) seem pertinent to, and helpful in considering, the matter of this book.

5. Rieti, Arch. Cap., IV.P.3. See Baldelli's suggestions of caution about *u* in substantives (*Medioevo volgare*, 204–205), but also note the Latin in these texts, and the names; see Baldelli, too, on ld-ll (206).

6. Gurevich, *Medieval Popular Culture*, 126. For a light but suggestive exploration of witness memory see Delumeau, "La mémoire des gens d'Arezzo et de Sienne"; in the same volume are other essays pertinent to the material of this book: Comet, "Le temps agricole"; Paul, "Expressions et perception du temps"; Berlioz, "La mémoire du prédicateur."

7. I think that there is a significant relationship between this kind of communication, of "truth," and much contemporary academic statement connected with new ideas of truth, but that the connection is with what lies beneath the verbal, syntactical surface of academic statement; and I think that the connection is most apparent if it is made through the bridge of belief and statement about proof at law. For an informative and provocative introduction to contemporary purely academic thought and statement see Marrone, *William of Auvergne and Robert Grosseteste: New Ideas of Truth in the Early Thirteenth Century.*

8. Brooke, ed. and trans., *Scripta Leonis*, 94–95, no. 5. It will be apparent here, and throughout, that I essentially follow Brooke's understanding and placing of the Perugia Fragment: Scripta Leonis. For Brooke's more recent consideration of sources for the life of Francis and the position of this text within them, as well as the work of other scholars, see her "Recent Work on St. Francis of Assisi"; and of that work see particularly Di Fonzo, "L'Anonimo Perugino."

9. Rieti, Arch. Cap., Lib. Int. et Exit., 1379. The unexceptionable generalization is adapted from De Sandre Gasparini, "Movimenti evangelici," 160.

10. Costantini et al., eds., *L'insistenza dello sguardo*, 11.

11. Rieti, Arch. Cap., Lib. Int. et Exit., 1379, fo. 61v.

12. I tried to put these changes together in a preliminary paper for the conference "Faire croire" held at the French School in Rome in 1979, published as "Correspondences at Rieti." For the two Christs see Mortari, *Il tesoro del duomo di Rieti*, 9, 17–18, plates I, XII; for the churches, see chapters in Tosti-Croce, ed., *La sabina medievale*: Ferri, "Monteleone," plates 89–104; Mortari, "Rieti," 130 and plates 133–137 for S. Agostino, also plate 145 for Canetra and plates 176–177 for Sambuco. The lifetime of work and perception of these and other Reatine monuments by the local art historian Cesare Verani is suggested in his work *La provincia*. The quotation is from C. N. Brooke, "The Ecclesiastical Geography of Medieval Towns," 22. The measurements are mine.

13. Rieti, Arch. Cap., parchment book of Matteo Barnabei (hereafter Lib. perg. di Matteo Barnabei), 26–27 (the Liber has modern pagination).

14. Rieti, Arch. Cap., Lib. perg. di Matteo Barnabei, 31–32.

15. The dispute of 1224 is recorded in a roll of witnesses' testimony now preserved in the diocesan archives at Penne. It was called to my attention by a reference in Pellegrini, *Abruzzo medioevale*, 38, 70; Pellegrini stated that the roll had been transcribed in a tese di laurea at Chieti, of which he was the relatore, by Renata Agostinone, and that the roll was in the archdiocesan archives of

Penne-Pescara, to which the archivist, Don Giuseppe Di Bartolomeo, kindly gave me access.

16. For Santa Maria di Ronzano, see particularly Guglielmo. Matthiae, *Pittura medioevale abruzzese*, 19, and plate 22.

Chapter 1

1. Rieti, Arch. Cap., IV.N.2, IV.N.3 (and of course there may have been others).

2. Rieti, Arch. Cap., IV.N.3 "3."

3. Rieti, Arch. Cap., V.E.1.

4. Rieti, Arch. Cap., III.D.1.

5. Rieti, Arch. Cap., "Liber Contractuum, 1344–1347," the letters, unbound, are inserted loose among the pages of the Liber. For an introduction to the Brancaleone family see Kamp on the thirteenth-century Andrea: *Dizionario biografico*, 13:809–810.

6. Michaeli, *Memorie*, 4:100.

7. Rieti, Archivio di stato (hereafter A.S.), Riformanze, I, fo. 4r. Giacomo di fu Rondo of Amelia was the notary of those portions of the Riformanze of 1365 that the chapter preserved (in copy) because of their importance to the cult of Saint Barbara (and chapter income); and one of Giacomo's witnesses in this instance was Nicola Jacobucii also of Amelia: Arch. Cap., Lib. IV, fos. 51r–54v.

8. Rieti, A.S., Riformanze, I, fo. 13v, and fos. 8v, 16v, 61v, 64r, and Riformanze, II, fo. 16v.

9. Michaeli, *Memorie*, 3:189. I suggest the aurally less compelling, I think, reading Sprangono because of the use of Sprangonus and Sprangoni by the notary Matteo Pandulfi in his 1315 copy of Berardo's collection of acts from 1212; Matteo, at his distance in time, may or may not have been copying Berardo's own spelling: Rieti, Arch. Cap., Parchment Book "1212" (now at least temporarily called Lib. Istr. 1 by Suor Anna Maria Tassi), fos. 1r, 5r, 6r (1, 9, 11).

10. See most conveniently, Guidoni, "L'espansione urbanistica," and also Mortari, "Rieti," in *La sabina medievale*, ed. Righetti Tosti-Croce, 156–187, 104–155; and see Brentano, "Early Franciscans."

11. Rieti, A.S., fondo San Domenico, 6. The significance and importance of the term miserable (including its use for orphans) is described with particular clarity by Trexler in his "Charity and the Defence of Urban Elites," 74.

12. Rieti, Arch. Cap., IV.M.1 "22" and "23." Michaeli, *Memorie*, 3:185–189.

13. For a general introduction to Rieti, particularly for the period before 1200, besides (and perhaps still most important) Michaeli, and *La sabina medievale*, one should use, with care, Palmegiani's work, which is at its most general in *Rieti*. But much of the most helpful Reatine work is scattered in a way that may seem odd to historians who have worked on places with different and better, or more thoroughly, organized historiographies; it is to be found not only in periodicals including the local, and in the first case transient, *Rieti* and *Il Territorio*, but also in occasional papers published under the auspices of local

financial institutions and in guide books. The Biblioteca Comunale in Rieti has a very useful catalog of this work, and its librarian, Roberto Messina, has done work in local history. I would, however, particularly like to call attention to two very learned local historians-art historians, whose learning has found its way not only into scholarly articles but into guide books: Sacchetti Sassetti has reduced the almost totally unmanageable political history of thirteenth- and particularly fourteenth-century Rieti into the few pages of his "Cenni storici" within his *Guida di Rieti*, and I am much indebted to his guidance; Verani, for whom there is a helpful, partial bibliography in *La sabina medievale* (234), and some of whose valuable work has actually found its way into a series of calendars, as well as his own helpful guide, *La provincia di Rieti*, and who is now the recipient of a festschrift ed. by Andrea Di Nicola. I think that the best and most effective description of a part of medieval Rieti is that by Di Nicola of the sestiere Porta Cintia di sotto in Di Flavio and Di Nicola, *Il monastero di S. Lucia*, 11–17. But see too the careful descriptions in Leggio, *Le fortificazioni di Rieti*, particularly 11, 67.

14. See Di Flavio, "Ombre e luci." Palmegiani, an erratic, emotional, and, in 1932, fascist observer, is at his most interesting and perhaps right-minded when (173–174) in *Rieti* he attacks the destruction of the proper framing of monumental medieval Rieti buildings, through the removal of surrounding buildings and the mindless creation of big piazzas—the "radicale modernizzamento della città," which would create "una Rieti . . . vestita all'Americana!"

15. See particularly Palmegiani, *Rieti*, 211–232, with very valuable photographs and drawings. Palmegiani himself was responsible for much of the restoration, which has seemed to me unconvincing and romantic, but Gary Radke of the University of Syracuse, who knows most about provincial thirteenth-century papal palaces, has told me that he is favorably impressed by its exactness. Palmegiani's title suggests the separability of episcopal and papal palaces; of this I am unconvinced. See Sacchetti Sassetti, *Guida*, 30–31; Mortari, "Rieti." Accoramboni should remind the reader of the fifth story of the eighth day of the *Decameron*.

16. Paris, Bibliothèque Nationale (hereafter B.N.) latin 1556, fos. 18r–26r, 18r–v.

17. See Palmegiani, *Rieti*, 262, for a photograph of a window in the palazzo Secinari, which Palmegiani dates "sec. xiv–xv"; I should like to thank the local historian and archeologist, Evandro Ricci, for his generosity in talking to me of Secinaro and its neighborhood: he himself has written much about the area, for example, *I Peligni Superequani; Elementi di civiltà;* and *Superaequum.*

18. Di Flavio, *Sinodo reatino.* Di Flavio's continued, careful, exhaustive work with early Reatine episcopal visitation records has given him unusual command of early modern Reatine demographic sources: see too his "Visite pastorali."

19. Mattiocco, *Struttura urbana*, 144–145; Sulmona's fourteenth-century catasto makes its population quantitatively visible in a very unusual way for this part of Italy.

20.The dates for Dodone come from documents within Rieti, Arch. Cap., IV.D.10; for his dedication dates at Santa Vittoria Monteleone, see Ferri, "Monteleone," 89 n.9. For the general development of Italian political geography in the early Middle Ages, see Wickham, *Early Medieval Italy*, for a remarkably crisp outline of the development of ecclesiastical institutions, see Violante, "Primo contributo."

21. See particularly, Michaeli, *Memorie*, 4:89–90.

22. Michaeli, *Memorie*, 4:62–86.

23. Rieti, A.S., Fondo Comunale, 8 (1251); Biblioteca Apostolica Vaticana (hereafter Bib. Apos. Vat.), Vat. Lat. 4029, fo. 367r (1334). A reader might reasonably object that the representativeness of the counselors of 1334 is very thin compared with that of the soldiers of 1251, and strikingly less Reatine. I mean to suggest a continuing summonable group who can represent the community; and I hope that the transition to the chapter clarifies this point.

24. See discussion in chapter 5, and Brentano, "Localism and Longevity."

25. Mortari, "Rieti," 112, 130.

26. Michaeli, *Memorie*, 4:59–60, 136–137.

27. The statistical material here and much valuable analysis, with, in notes, a comprehensive bibliography of studies pertinent to the mobile thirteenth-century court, is to be found in Paravicini Bagliani, "La mobilità"—for these days 164.

28. Paravicini Bagliani, "La mobilità," 163–165.

29. Paravicini Bagliani, "La mobilità," 174–178, 180–185.

30. Paravicini Bagliani, "La mobilità," 206–216.

31. Paravicini Bagliani, "La mobilità," 202, 208.

32. Stefaneschi is quoted in Michaeli, *Memorie*, 4:129. Certainly modern Rieti is ideal in summer, but its climate must have been significantly changed by the drying of the water in the basin; it does not seem immediately obvious that shallow, essentially stagnant waters would be overwhelmingly pleasant or healthy.

33. For later medieval regulation of the fountain, see Rieti, A.S., Statuti 1, fo. 30r. Compare the material in *Il duomo di Orvieto*, ed. Riccetti, particularly "Il duomo e l'attività edilizia" by Rossi Caponeri, 30–32.

34. Paravicini Bagliani underlines the productivity of the period ("La mobilità," 219), particularly basing his remarks on the work of the art historians Julian Gardner and Richard Krautheimer.

35. Michaeli, *Memorie*, 4:52–53; Paravicini Bagliani, "La mobilità," 242, 253. An entire fascicolo of the Rieti Arch. Cap., IV.C.1–14, is composed of documents (the last of which is from 1363) dealing with Charles II's promise of the annual offering of 20 uncie a year; for difficulties see particularly nos. 8 and 11. For the world at the curia see Brentano, *Two Churches*, 3–61.

36. For the provenance of the friars, see below chapter 5.

37. Rieti, Arch. Cap., Lib. perg. di Matteo Barnabei, 1–137. Because of the existence of chamberlains' accounts similar to Ballovino's (but in the vernacular) in Cortona, Bornstein has been able appropriately to attribute lost paintings in that city: "Pittori sconosciuti."

38. Rieti, Arch. Cap., Lib. Silvestri domini Johannis: "Liber III, 1336–1351," (modern pagination), 76–81. My caginess about numbers is due to my not being sure exactly where all these unusual names in the genitive divide and exactly which are patronymics.

39. Rieti, Arch. Cap., Lib. Silvestri domini Johannis, 112.

40. Rieti, A.S., Depos. Com., Statuti, I, fo. 126r.

41. Rieti, A.S., Statuti, I, fos. 76r–v.

42. Rieti, A.S., Statuti, I, fos. 9r, 13v–14v, 15v, 30r (and 44r), 39v–40r, 67r–67v, 83v, 39r, 46r, 99r, 115r, 30r, 85r–v, 114v. The continued use of the statute book is further indicated by its having later been printed.

43. Rieti, A.S., Statuti, I, fo. 33r.

44. Rieti, A.S., Statuti, I, fos. 115r, 34r.

45. Rieti, A.S., Statuti, I, fo. 36v.

46. Rieti, A.S., Statuti, I, fo. 42v.

47. Rieti, A.S., Statuti, I, fos. 51v–52r.

48. Rieti, A.S., Statuti, I, fos. 50v–51r; for San Francesco, see for example, fos. 20r–21v, 34r; and for the use of Sant'Agostino's refectory, Rieti, A.S., Riformanze, I, fo. 13v. For San Salvatore and the city, see Di Nicola, "Monasteri, laici," 220–221.

49. Rieti, A.S., Statuti, I, fo. 58r.

50. Rieti, A.S., Statuti, I, fos. 42r–42v. For Monte Calvo (Sabina dioc.), see Rieti, Arch. Cap., III.D.2.

51. Varanini, ed., *Gli Scaligeri*, particularly De Sandre Gasparini, "Istituzioni ecclesiastiche," 393–396; Varanini, "La chiesa veronese."

52. Rieti, Arch. Cap., Lib. IV perg., fos. 45r–48r. I use the "dompno" because local contemporary sources clearly distinguish between dominus and dompnus, the latter of which is appropriate, for example, for a priest prebendary.

53. The books are listed on fos. 46r–47v.

54. These listed gifts come from fos. 46r and 47r. I have left the listing of the old (*antiqum*) book of miracles not merely to maintain the order of the manuscript, its composer's or scribe's way of thinking, but to make it clear that Giovanni's text was not a new one, or one of which the chapter did not have a copy (although of course there may have been emendations).

55. The paper copy of the inventory, here identified as "Inquest 1225," is to be found in the bundle which holds and is identified as being the Lib. Int. et Exit. of 1358 (that is, of Ballovino) in Rieti, Arch. Cap. I am here using the first gathering, which (in the paper copy) begins in the middle of things. A fuller and better identified copy of the inquest exists at Rieti, in parchment, in the book in the Arch. Cap. identified as "1212," from fo. vii, r (p. 13) to fo. liv, v (88). It begins: "In nomine domini, Amen. Hec est copia siue renouatio cuiusdam registri antiqui reperti in archiuio ecclesie Reatin' de terris, vineis, domibus et aliis possexionibus dicte ecclesie Reatine et de censu, pensione, decima et aliis redditibus qui debentur eidem ecclesie Reatin' de possexionibus supradictis facta tempore et de mandato reuerendi in Xpo patris et domini domini Johannis dei et apostolice sedis gratia episcopi Reatin'."

This copy is attached to, included in the same volume, as the inventory of 1212, which was notarized by the copy's scribe, Matteo Pandulfi, on 17 April 1315. I use here a sample taken from the paper copy rather than the parchment one in spite of its lacking the first thirteen items, since it is a sample and since I think the thirteen would not change the impression I give (and certainly not more than would expanding the sample into the folios of either copy, particularly into the chapter's heavy claimed holdings in the Porta Cintia where the house-lots cluster); but I use the paper copy particularly so that I can point out one of the jokes of the archival life: during the period in which I was actually writing this chapter the parchment copy had disappeared; it was not moved from the old archives when the general move took place and was lost; it was re-found during repairs to the roof of the old archives. For a discussion of the importance of "1212" see chapter 4 below.

56. Rieti, Arch. Cap., Inquest 1225, particularly fos. 7v, 1r, 1v, 6r. See Brooke, *Scripta Leonis*, 115 n., for *carbonaria* as city ditch or boundary.

57. Rieti, Arch. Cap., Inquest 1225, fos. 6r, 4v.

58. Rieti, Arch. Cap., Inquest 1225, fos. 6r, 2r, 8r. Leggio, *Le fortificazioni di Rieti*, 11: "*Carceraria* derived its name from the *carceri* of urban hermits near San Leopardo."

59. Rieti, Arch. Cap., Inquest 1225, fos. 8r, 5v, 8v.

60. Rieti, Arch. Cap., Inquest 1225, fos. 5r, 6v, 3r, 7v.

61. Rieti, Arch. Cap., Inquest 1225, fos. 8r, 3v, 6v.

62. Rieti, Arch. Cap., Inquest 1225, fo. 4v. In the list of possessions of the church of Rieti in Lib. IV, fos. 18v–19r, divided by parish, time of Bishop Biagio, there are only eight items from San Giovenale and four from San Giorgio.

63. See below chapter 3 on the definition of boundaries, and see Maceroni, ed., *San Francesco*, 43–44.

64. Di Flavio, *Sinodo reatino*, 19. Fifteenth-century *catasti* do exist for some of the towns near Rieti, but I, at least, find it impossible to expand them into a convincing estimate of total population; certainly one can learn something, for example, about individuals and groups who held property in Contigliano in 1445, and for the same year in Poggio Fidoni; but these *catasti* would have to be read by a historian with much more contextual information and much broader experience with their kind of *catasto* for them to reveal a convincing estimate of population beyond a blank minimal number of households: Rieti, A.S., Catasti, 7, 8.

65. Di Flavio, "Le visite pastorali," 229. In this connection one should also consider an interestingly written fifteenth-century paper copy of a list of San Pastore properties in Rocca Alatri and Terria: Rieti, Arch. Cap., II.G.1: when the archives were in the sacristy tower there was a separate numbering for documents *spectantes ad communitatem Reatinam*: this is from that group. For an intense study of settlement in a neighboring, related area, for an earlier period, see Wickham, *Studi sulla società*. For a recent discussion of the new cities of the period, see Friedman, *Florentine New Towns*, 112 on Cittaducale.

66. Di Flavio, "Le visite pastorali," 229; see Maceroni and Tassi, *Società religiosa e civile*, passim.

67. This border is visible in the map included within Jamison, ed., *Catalogus baronum*. For the problem of boundaries, see below chapter 3, where it is dealt with extensively; for a particularly interesting consideration of the idea of boundary, with bibliography, see Sahlins, *Boundaries*.

68. "Le milieu naturel" is exhaustively treated in Toubert, *Les structures*, 1:135–149, and the included map "Les milieux naturels du Latium"; see too Verani, *La provincia*, 4; also see Pesce, "Aspetti geo-paleontologici." For a sparkling, wonderful book about Terminillo: Marinelli, *Il Terminillo*. See the

pertinent warning—"no two mountain valleys are the same"—in Wickham, *The Mountains and the City*, 3.

69. For the vicar general and his separateness see below chapter 3; for a sense of this part of the diocese, see D'Andreis, *Cittareale*. Antrodoco and Borbona are photographed in Verani, *La provincia*, foto 52, 53.

70. Toubert, introduction to *La sabina medievale*, 6. Verani's foto no. 3 in *La provincia* nicely illustrates Toubert's *ridente*.

71. Toubert, *Les structures*, 1:169–173, particularly, 169 n.2, 171 n.2, 173 n.1; one should not ignore Toubert's emphasis on transhumant pasturage, 196–197. References to it are almost nonexistent in the Rieti documents I know, but in Rieti, A.S., Fondo Comunale, no. 26, from 11 May 1295, Tommaso Cimini of Rieti receives in Rome for himself and his associates the price of 116 *li provisini* for 124 sheep and 13 goats (*castrati*). For a recent introduction to southern Italian transhumant pastorage, see Marino, *Pastoral Economics*. See too, for an understanding of what grows where, with the addition of fauna, Pratesi and Tassi, eds., *Guida alla natura*, particularly 102–103, 177–190. I should like to thank Doris and Arnold Esch for having brought this guide to my attention. See too Verani, *La provincia*, 6. For the diet of medieval Italy, what was grown, what was caught and picked, and what was slaughtered, see Montanari, *L'alimentazione contadina*, particularly: "Il maiale," 232–244; "Il piccolo allevamento domestico," 250–253; "I prodotti della caccia," 271–276; and "I prodotti della pesca," 292–295. For a more pictorial presentation by Montanari of pigs and pork, see *Porci e porcari*. For the memories preserved of traditional production and diet in an Abruzzi town I am indebted to a manuscript by Annino Saltarelli, "Pescasseroli: History of its People" (translated by Eliza R. Wareham, 1982), which is clearly informative about the raising and slaughtering of pigs.

72. Toubert, *Les structures*, 1:146, 135, 244–245.

73. See the reproduction of a leek from the Fossa Last Supper in Matthiae, *Pittura medioevale abruzzese*, plate 89.

74. Michaeli, *Memorie*, 4:57 for the Labro-Luco dispute of 1298; this volume of Michaeli is particularly rich, as are its appendixes, in exposing the baronial (and communal) composition of the Reatine, and the connections between Rieti and the valley of the Canera, Rieti and San Salvatore Maggiore, Rieti and Monte Calvo: see particularly 44–45, 48–49, 65–67, 99, 118–122, 152–153, and for the Labro and Mareri in close conjunction, see 42. The appearance of a major cosmopolitan political figure, or the threatened appearance of one, Frederick II, Manfred, one of the Angevins, Henry VII, Albornoz could stir these normally hidden components of the social structure into visible action.

75. Michaeli, *Memorie*, 4:51; Rieti, Biblioteca comunale (hereafter Bib. Com.), MS F.3.21: "Genealogia fere omnium familiarum huius civitatis . . . per D. Romualdum Peroctum de Caballis." See Wickham, *Early Medieval Italy*, 163, for the southern Italian *castello* in which "peasants lived . . . freely, with binding leases." Actually continued thought about the lords of Labro makes me hesitate about my hesitations. The *stemma* which Matteo Barnabei placed in the margin at the beginning of his copy of Giacomo de Labro's will (Lib. perg. di Matteo Barnabei, 149, see below chapter 8 note 40) of 1319 is not really legible, but very careful scrutiny suggests that it could be an eagle holding a fish in the

top half of the *stemma troncata* and waves beneath, which would not be inconsistent with later Nobili arms as for example Perotti Cavalli's Nobili Vitelleschi,
3, eagle above, fish below (and see his text: 26–28, alternative numeration 16–
18). The manuscript is not dated, but Perotti Cavalli talks of people still living
in 1666. The Labro seem worth studying in their own right, although it is not
clear to me, as I look at them as part of the Reatine, that the scattered notices
of them, assembled, would really be very thick; I feel that much about them
could be untangled from references like those in Arch. Cap. (commune side)
I.D.1, a document from 1299 which includes a document from 1237 setting out
certain Labro relationships (Giacomo and Pandalfo are sons of Tommaso); and
I.C.1 (same category) setting out others in 1298; or the reference to the anniversary of Don Gentile Fuctii de Labro who in the fourteenth century held land
in Fiume Morto in common with his brother Transarico (Lib. IV, fo. 20v),
which shows the continuity of the holdings of the lords of Labro in that area
from the time of the thirteenth-century capitular-Cistercian disputes described
in chapter 2 below.

   76. Paravicini Bagliani, *Cardinali di curia*, 297; Brentano, "Notarial Cartularies and Religious Personality," 179. For Siena: Siena, A.S., Consiglio Generale, 50, fos. 31v–32r; I would like to thank Daniel Waley for having called this
reference to my attention and having sent me a photocopy of it. See Digard et
al., eds., *Les registres de Boniface VIII*, index "Labro."

   77. Labro's is a photogenic strikingness, see *La sabina medievale*, plates 4–
7, and 8–9 for Morro, and Palmegiani, *Rieti*, 386–392 with the plates on those
pages, and Verani, *La provincia*, foto 48.

   78. Archivio Segreto Vaticano (hereafter A.S.V.), A. A. Arm. I–XVIII, 3660:
Sella, ed., "Statuti del Cicolano," 3:863–899; for the area to which the statutes
applied, and the family Mareri, see particularly *Storia e tradizioni popolari di
Petrella Salto e Cicolano*—the relations of Andrea Staffa, Henny Romanin, and
Andrea Di Nicola: the last is of particular value in dealing with the statutes, as
is Di Nicola's relation, "Monasteri, laici," particularly 221–223. The core of the
Mareri holdings, fief, is recorded, as that which Raynaldus Senebaldus held *in
capite* from the Norman king in the mid-twelfth century: *Catalogus baronum*,
no. 1133, 224; Jamison discusses clearly the dating of the list in her introduction,
xv–xviii. For the Mareri see also chapter 2 and especially chapter 6, below. Di
Nicola, 217 (citing Domenico Lugini, Jr.) emphasizes afresh the importance of
fortification and defense in the actual siting of the Mareri castri.

   79. Sella, "Statuti del Cicolano," 866: Vat MS, fo. 5v.

   80. Sella, "Statuti del Cicolano," 875: Vat MS, fos. 23v, 24r.

   81. Sella, "Statuti del Cicolano," 895: Vat MS, fos. 65v, 66r. I would like to
thank Don Giovanni Maceroni and Suor Anna Maria Tassi for an unforgettable
tour of Stàffoli.

   82. Sella, "Statuti del Cicolano," 867–868: Vat MS, fos. 6v–7r. I would like
to thank the mayor of Petrella Salto, Augusto Mari, for an equally unforgettable
tour through its "mountain" countryside, and to thank the historian Henny
Romanin for helping me to understand the place. One of the stimulating qualities of Cicolano historians is their particular attachment to and knowledge of
their places of origin: Romanin to and of Petrella; Maceroni to and of Corvaro.

83. Sella, "Statuti del Cicolano," 891: Vat MS, fo. 57r; Di Nicola, "Monasteri, laici," 221.

84. Sella, "Statuti del Cicolano," 887: Vat MS, fo. 49r; Sella, 887: Vat MS, fo. 48r; Sella, 887: Vat MS, fos. 45r–46v.

85. Rieti, Arch. Cap., IV.P.3 (in 3 parts); I have moved the testimony around out of order for the use to which I want to put it here; for an understanding of witnesses' testimony before ecclesiastical courts see the very clear description in Helmholz, *Marriage Litigation*, 19–20. The dating depends of course upon the dates of office or presence of those monks and officials named who are in fact datable. There are superficial elements of confusion about the bishop of Rieti "who now is," but I think it absolutely certain that that bishop is Adenolfo, after his consecration, and so the testimony must come from no earlier than late 1194 and no later than very early 1214 or really 1213; since Innocent III appears the date could not be before 1198. Sansi in his *Documenti storici inediti* gives (209–210, no. 8) a July 1190 Ferentillo document with Transerico as abbot (and a monk "Geronimo") and another (228–230, no. 19) from May 1217 with "T" abbot, an Angelo as provost and a Transarico as monk. Gentili, *L'abbazia di S. M. di Chiaravalle di Fiastra*, reproduces a document facing 279 from May 1206 in which Transarico is abbot, and the monks listed include Angelo as provost, Transarico, and Iericho; Rome, A.S., Pergamene, Fiastra, Cass. 142, no. 498 from July 1214 has Transarico and Angelo; and Cass. 144, no. 690 from November 1228 has Matteo as abbot and "Jeronimo" as provost. For Ferentillo and Fiastra see Brentano, *Two Churches*, 270–271. A later copy of Innocent III's approval of a compromise in the case arranged by the cardinal priest of Santa Croce (very interestingly, the local Leone Brancaleone) in 1213 makes almost inescapable the conclusion that the witnesses were heard before May of that year: Paris, B.N. latin 1556, fo. 28v.

86. I have repeatedly translated *pertinebat* as "belonged" so that the ordinariness of the expression would come through, but I very much do not want to simplify or distort thirteenth-century ideas of possession or to imply in these records a modern sense of ownership. Any reader who is acquainted with the History faculty at Berkeley will guess that my attention was particularly drawn to articulate peasants some years ago by Scheiner's essay, "The Mindful Peasant." It is provocative here to compare the statement of Sabean's Schultheiss who "suggested that people had given false information at various times because 'they did not know how to remember' ": *Power in the Blood*, 182.

87. I have maintained the wavering spelling Transarico/Transerico, to save for the reader the tone it gives the document. I hope the reader will notice in the talk about Santo Stefano the rather nice definition of *pieve* in action.

88. The reader will understand my hesitance in extending Rayn' or Rain' after observing the difficulties that that extension has caused past historians, see chapter 4 below. For the Amiterno fief see *Catalogus baronum*, 221 no. 1123: Gentilis Vetulus, because of his holdings, must be one of our Gentili, or a very immediate ancestor. For Latusco, Latusculo, see Di Flavio, *Sinodo reatino*, 73.

89. For the legal powers of bishops elect, see Benson, *The Bishop-Elect*, particularly 45–55.

90. For Spedino, see Maceroni and Tassi, *Società religiosa e civile*, 113, 215.

91. For the count of Albe, *Catalogus baronum*, 215–216, no. 1110.

92. Although he is identified as a canon, Pietro Cifredi is called *dompnus*.

93. The document, in its body, talks of both *denari provisini* and *denari papienses*. For (at the time of the statutes) "in civitate Rheat' et eius districtu currant omnia genera monetarum": Rieti, A.S., Statuti, I, fo. 30v.

94. For Sarraceno see chapter 5 below.

95. "Letter" in the document's Latin is, of course, normally in the plural, even if (as is sometimes clear) a single letter is meant; here I must shift back to the plural to give the Latin original.

96. In his visitation of the Cicolano in 1564 Cardinal Bishop Amulio visited the old Mareri lands, Santo Stefano Corvaro and San Leopardo; of the last he (or his registrar) says: "ecclesiam S. Leopardi, abbatiam vulgo nuncupatam . . . ecclesia est campestris et fere nunquam ibi celebratur quia deserta est excepto tam in die festivitatis dicti Sancti cui dicata est. Ecclesia est admodum antiqua et egregie constructa et habet cryptam pulcherrimam multis et variis columnis." Of Santo Stefano, the visitation record says, "it is a collegiate church and has six canons": Rieti, Archivio Vescovile (hereafter Arch. Vesc.), X–3, Vis. Amulio, 1563–70; there are two sets of foliation and I quote from old 62v–63r, new 99v–100r, and old 64v, new 101v. See Di Flavio, "Le visite pastorali," 232–233. For Amulio's attitude as bishop, see Maceroni and Tassi, *Società religiosa e civile*, index under "Amulio, Marco Antonio." When I began working on this study the crypt of the ruin of San Leopardo maintained its columns with their remarkable capitals; they have since been stolen. In 1300 Boniface VIII transferred the monastery of Ferentillo to the chapter of St. John, Lateran, because, in part, of disorders which included rebellions of the monastery's "vassalls," in which two abbots were killed, according to the letter of transfer; this transfer presumably explains the San Giovanni which becomes attached to San Leopardo's name: Sansi, *Documenti storici inediti*, 373–375, and 374 n., with Pius IX's transfer of spiritual jurisdiction over Ferentillo to the archbishop of Spoleto in 1852; see too Paris, B.N. latin 1556, fo. 25r, where, in Bishop Tommaso's mid-thirteenth-century list, San Leopardo is recorded as pertaining to Ferentillo; ironically the list of Ferentillo churches follows immediately after the list of the Lateran's churches in this document. For the Cicolano, in general, the standard older, and still useful, general history is Lugini, *Memorie storiche*.

97. *Cronica fratris Salimbene de Adam*, 329; for the "proliferation of Franciscan bishops and archbishops" see Thomson, *Friars in the Cathedral*, particularly 20. Translating Salimbene is, of course, delightful, but it has difficulties. In trying to preserve his exact meaning, including tone in one direction, one sometimes errs in another; this passage is more slack and extended than is the original Latin.

98. *Cronica fratris Salimbene*, 321.

99. *Cronica fratris Salimbene*, 322–323; I think it is worth noting Salimbene's use of *de consilio fratrum suorum*.

100. *Cronica fratris Salimbene*, 324–326. Salimbene calls Bertolino a *dulcis homo* (*dolce*), 324. The reader might note Rainaldo/Salimbene's use of *conversationem*, 325. The long citation of the decretal certainly does more than suggest that Salimbene refurbished this part of his reported discussion when he wrote.

338   NOTES TO PAGES 49–54

So the reader may question the validity of his many quoted statements from Rainaldo and other discussants. It is a common problem. I think that Salimbene had a good ear, a good memory, and was anxious to distinguish speakers one from another and have their conversation be representative of the men he was presenting—one should note his repeated giving of *penitus* to Rainaldo. All one can say surely is that Rainaldo's remarks are the remarks of the Rainaldo whom Salimbene has recreated (possibly as late as 1282), and that with them he has created a believable and surprisingly complicated person. I myself am in the rather peculiar position of having used these passages earlier to make what seemed to me important points in another book. I could not omit them here. I decided to use them as seemed appropriate now, and not to concern myself any more than I could help over whether the present treatment either repeated or contradicted that of twenty years ago: *Two Churches*, 184–189.

101. *Cronica fratris Salimbene*, 326–327; the reader will notice Rainaldo's concern with externals.

102. Rieti, Arch. Cap., II.B.1. This is one of a number of documents which at least temporarily disappeared from the old archives, without obvious explanation, when I thought that only I was working there. They seem to have been borrowed by one of the canons. I do not mean to say that there are no other documents in the archives (besides horse and constitutions) which survive from the time of Rainaldo's episcopate.

103. *Cronica fratris Salimbene*, 326–328. For my belief in Innocent's concern with pastoral care, see "Innocent IV and the Chapter of Rieti"; for a harsher view, recall Robert Grosseteste.

104. *Cronica fratris Salimbene*, 328.

105. Rieti, Arch. Cap., II.G.10.

106. Rieti, Arch. Cap., Lib. Silvestri domini Johannis, 241–242. This act of Biagio's would be consistent with a policy of defending the urban elite of Rieti: see Trexler, "Charity and the Defense of Urban Elites" and below chapter 8.

107. Rieti, Arch. Cap., III.D.2: see below chapters 5 and 7.

108. For Borgo San Pietro, see below chapter 6; Rieti, Arch. Cap. V.D.2, and Lib. IV perg., fo. 51, copy of Riform. of 1365: both communal material.

109. The 1372 notice is entered in Rieti, Arch. Cap., Lib. Int. et Exit., 1371, in a hand with a different appearance from the body of the book; it should be remembered that those accounts go from July to June, so that March 1372 is a natural part of 1371. For a sense of Ballovino see Rieti, Arch. Cap., Lib. Silvestri domini Johannis, 98–99, 193, 202, 209, 257; Lib. Collationum, fo. 65v; Lib. Int. et Exit., 1364 (fo. 57r), 1371, 1379, 1382; Lib. IV perg., fos. 45r–47r; IV.C.11; and see chapter 3 below. For Ballovino's change of status, see particularly Rieti, Arch. Cap., VII.G.14.

110. Rieti, Arch. Cap., Lib. perg. di Matteo Barnabei, 419.

111. Rieti, Arch. Cap., Lib. perg. di Matteo Barnabei, 129–130.

112. Rieti, Arch. Cap., Lib. IV perg., fo. 47r, for the recorded privilege; for Giovanni more generally: Rieti, Arch. Cap., IV.G.4, IV.A.3, III.D.10, II.D.10, IV.F.4, IV.Q.3, IV.N.3, VI.G.11, III.C.4, IV.G.8, IX.F.5, II.C.4; Rieti, A.S., San Domenico, 7 (old 92); Brentano, "Localism and Longevity," 300–301 and notes; see chapter 3 below.

113. Rieti, Arch. Cap., II.C.1 (communal side); for the particular political difficulties of these years: Michaeli, *Memorie*, 4:66–68: John XXII's absence, King Robert's encroachments, rebellions, exile of Ghibellines. Suor Anna Maria Tassi has shown me some extremely effective and, some, in fact, beautiful, representations of the physical diocese, and holdings of the church, from later times; some plates in Maceroni and Tassi's book illustrate them: plates XXV, XXVII, XXIX, XXX: Inventario dei beni del capitolo della cattedrale di Rieti, 1728; and XXXV, XXXVI: Leonessa illustrated in the argument over the confines of the dioceses of Rieti and Spoleto, 1757.

Chapter 2

1. *Scripta Leonis, Rufini et Angeli Sociorum S. Francisci: The Writings of Leo, Rufino and Angelo Companions of St. Francis*, 87: "striking examples of his discourse" is Brooke's translation but she is careful (n.2) to explain that the normal meaning of *conuersatio* is "manner of life"; she suggests that this passage may be one in which *conuersatio* carries both this normal meaning and the narrower one "conversation, discourse." My dependence upon Brooke's edition and translation should be obvious to any reader, but I would like explicitly to express my admiration of it and gratitude for it. This seems the more appropriate since I will occasionally suggest an alternate reading or identification; that the *Scripta* seems to me by far the most compelling of Franciscan sources, undoubtedly has a great deal to do with Brooke's beautiful English translation. For the composition of the *Scripta* I depend upon and accept Brooke's introduction; see 4ff. and in the text 86–89.

2. *Scripta Leonis*, 86–89.

3. See both *Scripta Leonis*, 24–25 and John R. H. Moorman, *The Sources for the Life of S. Francis*, particularly here 98–101, on both the quality of the companions' stories and on their emphasis on eye witnesses and specific places. Brooke surely misidentifies the hermitage of San Eleuterio in cap. 85, 234–237; Quintillianus, which it was "near," is the modern Contigliano and not at all in the same direction from Greccio, which Contigliano is quite near, as the (secular, when visible during the period of this study) abbey of San Eleuterio near Rieti "now swallowed up in the cemetery of Rieti" (234 n.1); Contigliano and this San Eleuterio are in different directions from Rieti. See too "ad fontem Sancti Eleutherii" near Contigliano in 1165: Rieti, Arch. Cap., IV.L.10. The companion Angelo is usually believed to have been "of Rieti"; it would not seem unlikely that Fra Illuminato de Arce (a quarter and gate of Rieti) an informant of the companions, and himself Francis's companion in the east, as we know from Bonaventura, was also Reatine, although Michaeli (*Memorie*, 3:12), following Wadding, thought him from Rocca Accarina (and see Waley, *The Papal State*, 53–55). I certainly do not mean to imply that all the valuable Franciscan Rieti stories are to be found in the *Scripta Leonis*, particularly since the companions explicitly avoided the use of stories already in Celano's *Vita prima* (*Analecta*

franciscana, vol. 10), and so, for example, the story of Francis's *presepio* at Greccio, for which see the end of this chapter.

4. *Scripta Leonis*, 130–133. Pacifico seems (as he does in Brooke's index) a probable friar because of the placing of this story after another Pacifico story, 126–131, and because Pacifico is elsewhere (164–167) identified as "the king of verses . . . who had been a really courtly doctor of singers." Although I have been told by experts in medieval musical instruments that guitar is an inexact translation of *cythara* I have maintained Brooke's "guitar" because I think its effect is exact. I think that the companions' (genitive) *Tabaldi Sarraceni* is almost surely the *Teballus Sarracenus* of Rieti, Arch. Cap., VI.G.7 who is, unlike the Tabaldus of the *Scripta*, identified as a canon; it seems important to call Teballus by his surname *Sarracenus* or *Sarraceno* (rather than to treat it as a patronymic as Brooke seems to do, by maintaining the genitive) because the Sarracenus family was an early user of its surname in Rieti (see chapters 4 and 5 below), although some thirteenth-century sources certainly do use, as Brooke does, *Sarraceni*: and also Sacchetti Sassetti, in his *Anecdota franciscana reatina*, 38–40, talks of Tebaldo *Sarraceni* and of the *Sarraceni* family's flourishing in Rieti between the mid-twelfth and late fourteenth centuries. For "these brothers of mine are knights of the round table": Brooke, 212–213. It is important not to translate *camera* as "house" (as Brooke does) because the idea of communal living was an accepted ideal for canons at Rieti even after this time (see chapter 5 below), although it seems clear from the story of Gidion, below, that canons in Francis's time did have houses. For the curfew in the fourteenth-century statutes of Rieti, see Rieti, A.S., Statuti, 1, fo. 15v.

5. *Scripta Leonis*, 146–151. The quotation about "holy will" is from 87. For the meaning of the name Greccio see Toubert, *Les structures*, 1:172 n.

6. *Scripta Leonis*, 146–149.

7. *Scripta Leonis*, 149.

8. *Scripta Leonis*, 148.

9. *Scripta Leonis*, 148–149. I believe that Brooke's translation of *pueri* as "little boys" is probably mistaken and that *pueri* here is the equivalent of *ragazzi* and so does not necessarily mean only male children. The record sources that refer to Greccio would not in general make one particularly aware of a great distance between *parui* and *magni*; but the Franciscan sources underline the distinction because of the appearance in them of "dominus Johannes de Greccio" who gave Francis the feather pillow in which Francis thought the devil was hidden; this Don Giovanni "loved the saint with great affection and showed his friendship for him in many ways the whole of his life": *Scripta Leonis*, 254–257, and especially 257. See also Celano's *Vita prima*, cap. 84 for Giovanni, whom Francis "loved with a special love," who "had trampled upon the nobility of his birth and pursued nobility of soul," and for whom Francis sent "as he often did" to help him with the preparation of the *presepio* at Greccio (in 1223): Habig, ed., *Writings*, 299–300—an extraordinarily helpful and convenient collection of Franciscan materials; *Analecta franciscana*, 10:63–65. The Quaracchi editors of *Analecta franciscana* remind their readers that Francis's literally reproduced animals do not appear in Luke or any Gospel but rather in fourth-century commentators.

10. *Scripta Leonis*, 148–149; neither wolves nor hail seem now to be considered particular problems in Greccio, but wolves still do exist in the diocese and until about fifty years ago occasionally invaded farmyards near Greccio, and hail is a danger for crops in fields near Greccio. The importance of covenant in Franciscan thought and writing will be discussed by Arthur L. Fisher in his forthcoming book, *The Franciscan Observants in Quattrocento Tuscany*. The reference to vomit is from Proverbs 26:11, a favorite text, which compares the dog's returning to his vomit with the fool's returning to his folly.

11. *Scripta Leonis*, 148–151. Brooke suggests (150 n.2), and in this follows the Quaracchi editors of *Analecta franciscana* (10:152 no. 20), who are using Riccardo da S. Germano, that the burning of Greccio may have taken place in 1242 when Frederick II is said to have been ravaging the Reatine countryside (see below chapter 3); this is possible but in some ways it seems to me unlikely that the burning of Greccio of which the companions write was the work of Frederick's forces: thirteenth-century towns seem to have burned easily without the help of hostile forces. The position of Greccio does not make it seem a very likely target for Frederick's troops; the companions, who were writing in 1244–46, do not mention Frederick's responsibility; a general ravaging of the countryside could not seem so easily to the companions a specific divine punishment of Greccio as could a limitedly local fire. None of this makes Brooke's date seriously wrong, because Greccio's peculiar prosperity lasted "16 or 20 years" from the time of Francis's blessing.

12. *Scripta Leonis*, 188–191.

13. I here use the spelling Gidion instead of *Scripta Leonis*'s Gideon because of the former spelling's prevalence in the available Rieti documents that mention him. Thomas of Celano used the story of Gidion in his second life, and there completed it. In Celano's *Vita secunda* no. 41 Gidion is specifically called a canon, although he is not called one in the *Scripta: Analecta franciscana*, 10:156–157 no. 41; Habig, *Writings*, 398, 591 n.43. No document I have seen at Rieti calls him a canon and, although the position of yconomo for the church, which Gidion repeatedly held, was certainly often given to a canon at the beginning of the thirteenth century; Gidion's appearance in witness lists with the designation priest but not canon would suggest that he was not one. The Quaracchi *Analecta* editors use Sacchetti Sassetti's search through Rieti documents for Gidion (*Anecdota franciscana reatina*, 44–47) and his use of Rieti, Arch. Cap., IV.G.3; IV.M.1–4; IV.O.1; IV.P.6; IV.Q.1,8; IX.F.1. From these documents Sacchetti Sassetti was able to give Gidion a spread of dates from January 1201 to August 1236. The Gidion documents I have been able to find within the slightly shifting *pergamene* in the Arch. Cap. are somewhat different: IV.M.1 from 1201; IV.M.1 from 1208 (as yconomo); IV.M.2 from 1212; IV.Q.8 from 1213 (as yconomo); IV.M.3 from 1214; IV.O.5 from 1216. The last three documents Sacchetti Sassetti used (which I cannot locate), two from 1222 and one from 1236, more than double the time of Gidion's connection with the church of Rieti; they seem to me also to make less likely his having been a canon because with them the argument from silence grows longer and longer.

14. *Scripta Leonis*, 188.

15. *Scripta Leonis*, 189.

16. Celano, *Vita secunda*, no. 41, 10:156–157; Habig, *Writings,* 398. Proverbs 26:11.

17. *Scripta Leonis*, 132–135; Potthast, *Regesta pontificum romanorum*, 1:640–648: Honorius III in Rieti from 23 June 1225 to 31 January 1226; he had been there earlier, 11 June 1219 to 1 October 1219 (532–537), during almost all of which time Francis was out of Italy.

18. *Scripta Leonis*, 134–135.

19. *Scripta Leonis*, 134–137; I agree with Father Placid Hermann's translation in Habig, *Writings,* 401, of this story as incorporated by Thomas of Celano, and not with Brooke's translation of *uuis quasi recentibus* (136–137) as "eggs seemingly straight from the nest" because I believe "fresh grapes" is a more natural translation. I also disagree with Brooke's translation of *mastillis gymarorum* as "crab patties": the actual word *gymarorum* together with the crustacean produce of the Rieti area demand Italian *gamberi*, that is, English crayfish, American colloquial crawdad; *mastillis* is, I believe, essentially Italian *mastelli*, here pails or pots. The Quaracchi *Analecta* editors (158 no. 9) gloss, I believe incorrectly: "id est pastilli e gammaris seu cammaris, i. e. cancris, contritis confecti." See Leo Sherley Price's translation of *Speculum perfectionis*, no. 111, Habig, *Writings,* 1249. The *Analecta* editors (158 no. 1) suggest the possibility of the doctor's being Magister Nicolaus, a point that Sacchetti Sassetti thought himself really to have proved in *Anecdota franciscana reatina*, 40–43. The distance of the place from which the food came perhaps suggests the castro of Monte San Giovanni.

20. *Scripta Leonis*, 180–183; in *Vita secunda* no. 92 Celano puts Francis in the palace of the bishop of Rieti for this story: Habig, *Writings,* 437–438; *Analecta franciscana*, 10:184 no. 11. Machilone, "Vico, uti conicimus, olim prope Reate exstante"; Verani, among others, has located Machilone more precisely, at the site of the present Posta.

21. *Scripta Leonis*, 180–181; Matthew 25:34–40; Sulpicius Severus, *Vita Sancti Martini*, cap. 3.

22. "Greccio was made a new Bethlehem: *et quasi nova Bethlehem de Graecio facta est*": Celano, *Vita prima*, no. 85, *Analecta franciscana*, 10:64; Habig, *Writings,* 300—from the story of the *presepio*, for which see below. To the chronicler Salimbene, Greccio connoted the *presepio* as is clear in the two references he makes to it and the "representationem pueri Bethleemite cum presepio et feno et puero" in connection with John of Parma's seclusion there: *Cronica fratris Salimbene*, 303–304, 510. For John, see Lambert, *Franciscan Poverty*, 103–123, and for Ubertino's visit, 159. For Angelo of Clareno's account see Ehrle, "Die Spiritualen," 286. Ubertino talks of himself in the *prologus primus* of the *Arbor vitae*, reprinted with an introduction by Davis; his life and works are concisely described by Godefroy, in *Dictionnaire de théologie catholique*, vol. 15, cols. 2021–2034, see particularly col. 2021. For John's 1248 visit to Italy, John R. H. Moorman, *A History of the Franciscan Order*, 191. Greccio, because of its position near the (drying) lake, was also reminiscent of Galilee. Since I read and listened to Steven Justice, the connection between these Franciscans and Joachimism has gained more meaning for me, as it will for readers of Justice's forthcoming book. My reading of the friar's trip to and from Rieti

depends upon my interpretation of two phrases "morabatur in loco" and "ad locum suum" (twice): I think, but I am not sure, that *locum suum* means the friary at Rieti.

23. *Scripta Leonis*, 142–143. From conversation with Marchesa Luigina Canali de Rossi, who well remembers the area around Rieti before it was reshaped by modern roads convenient to tourism, I have learned that in the early twentieth century Greccio did not seem a close neighbor to Rieti in the way that it now does; the roads, as well as the earlier drying of watery lands, have clearly changed the geography of the area.

24. For the places around Greccio, San Pastore, and Montecchio, see Istituto geografico militare, Carta d'Italia, fo. 138: particularly II N. O. "Greccio," but also II S. O. "Contigliano," and II S. E. "Rieti." I gauge the rough height of Montecchio above the alluvial plain from the first of these three, trying to take into account the difference in land level produced by fill and solidification. See, too, for a general history of the lake that has disappeared, Duprè Theseider, *Il lago Velino*; most recently, for a geological study of the area with bibliography, see Pesce, "Aspetti geo-paleontologici."

25. In fact the "isola" of Montecchio, with its Vecchiarelli villa, seems to dominate the Agro Reatino as one looks across it from the slopes of the Monti Sabini; it is an imposing wooded outcropping, looming over the fertile flatland, and something of its internal construction is immediately visible because of the cut made in it by the quarry on its southern flank. For San Matteo and San Pastore see Duprè Theseider, *L'abbazia di San Pastore*. As Duprè Theseider wrote, this was "mio primo lavoro" (3 n.2); his expressed gratitude to Sacchetti Sassetti and the inscription in the Rieti Biblioteca Comunale copy of the book, from the Palmegiani collection, "offre ai cari zii Palmegiani," make clear the local connections of this man who would become a medievalist known throughout and beyond Italy.

The work shows the charming avidity of a young historian looking at monuments and searching for records, and it is remarkably inclusive, for example in using material from episcopal visitations in 1566 and 1832 as well as a full range of medieval sources. The short work also shows some of the natural flaws of a first effort, not uncharming in themselves; for example, in interpreting a carefully transcribed 1255 inscription that remained at the abbey and gave the day and month date as *mense Madii die V intrante*, Duprè Theseider translated "al mattino del 5 Maggio." If the grand old historian, fifty years of experience later, ever noticed this error it must have amused him. Duprè Theseider used an earlier essay on San Pastore by "M. M." (Michele Michaeli), *Notizie dell'antico monastero*. This elegant little piece of research, interpretation, and writing justifies Michaeli's maintained high reputation; it is particularly impressive in its creative doubt about the twelfth-century history of the abbey, and it is in no way parochial. Duprè Theseider's continued attachment to Rieti is exposed in a recently published, moving letter (Vasina, "Ricordo di Eugenio Duprè Theseider," no. 5, to Muriella Lanzoni, 24 April 1969, 141–142): "In questi ultimi mesi ho dovuto superare una dolorosa prova. Nella mia cittadina di nascita, Rieti, avevo la vecchia casa, ormai quasi disabita e abbandonata . . . mi sono deciso a venderla ed e stata una ben dolorosa decisione, perche vi era connesso tutto un tesoro di ricordi. . . .Quante volte ho pensato alle parole del Signore: 'dimitte mortuos sepelire mortuos suos.' "

One should see too, for San Matteo-San Pastore, Janauschek, *Originum cisterciensium*, 222, no. 576; Cottineau, *Répertoire topo-bibliographique*, vol. 2, col. 2836; Canivez, *Statuta capitulorum*, 2:8, 19, 384, and particularly 17 where, in 1222, the abbot, called of San Martino, is among those condemned to three days of light punishment, including one day on bread and water, for not having carried back to the chapter general their *commissa*. The connection between San Matteo and its mother house, Santa Maria de Casa Nova, is underlined by the consent by Gentile, abbot of Casa Nova, to a San Matteo sale of land on 28 June 1235, as well as by Abbot Bartolomeo's involvement in the compromise of 6 December 1222: Rieti, Arch. Cap., IX.A.2 and IV.Q.11. See, too, Caraffa, ed., *Monasticon Italiae*, 1:138–139 no. 96: "Contigliano (RI) S. Pastore."

26. Bernard of Clairvaux, "Lettere," ed. Migne, vol. 182, no. 201, col. 369. The accepted version of this story, which I repeat here with some hesitation, is completely endorsed by Bedini in *Bibliotheca sanctorum*, vol. 2, cols. 729–730, and it seems also to be accepted by Toubert, *Les structures*, 2:902 n.3. My hesitation is based on the fragility of the documentary connection between the recipient of the letter and San Matteo; Michaeli did not believe that Balduino was at San Matteo, and certainly Duprè Theseider was very hesitant about the connection. And yet it seems likely to me that the petition of the abbot of San Pastore to the chapter general, in 1264, asking to celebrate in his house the feasts of the founders and of San Pastore, was talking of the feast of San Balduino: Canivez, *Statuta capitulorum*, 3:19. In the other direction the testimony from the dispute between San Matteo and the cathedral church discussed below could be seen to suggest a very short history for San Matteo, certainly not one stretching back to the mid-twelfth century.

27. *Acta sanctorum*, August, for 21 August, 451. For Balduino's head, see Mortari, *Il tesoro del duomo di Rieti*, 43–44, no. 34, and plate XLVII; the reliquary bust was made in 1496 by Bernardino da Foligno.

28. Auvray, ed., *Les registres de Grégoire IX*, nos. 1171, 1172 (the union of 5 October 1232), 1260–1261, 1820–1821 (John and Numbers), 2092, 2093 (. . . propter aeris intemperiem . . .), 3338–3339.

29. For a rather lengthy discussion of attachments of this sort to the Cistercian abbey of Fiastra in the Marche see my *Two Churches*, 261–281; *Grégoire IX*, nos. 2092–2093, 3338–3339. The San Pastore compromise seems, like much of this affair, to have been arranged, or at least supervised by Goffredo Castiglioni, cardinal priest of San Marco (1227–38), later (1238–41) cardinal bishop of Sabina.

30. The large and beautiful ruin of the Cistercian abbey of San Pastore remains on the slope of its hill, prey to time, the weather, and a rather startling vandalism. One hundred years ago Mass was being said and heard there (and still was heard, on feasts, by the parents of the senior generation now living in the neighborhood); the major bell is said still to have been there, and able to ring, thirty years ago; the two major thirteenth-century inscriptions (and much else that is now missing, like jambs) were there twenty years ago. The ruin is picturesque and can be seen, shrouded in ivy, from a great distance to the east. The nave and apse are full of ivy and wild cyclamen; the cloister and the close

are full of blackberries, wild anemones, and, again, cyclamen. The buildings were measured by Duprè Theseider (facing 48); the cloister is a square with sides 35 meters in length, the total length of nave and apse is about 47 meters; the transepts that extend about 7 meters from the nave are about 10 meters broad; the nave is about 28 meters wide. The best preserved of the medieval rooms around the cloister, the chapterhouse, is about 12 meters broad and 20 meters deep; it still contains, on the two sides of the external eastern door (originally a window), disintegrating fourteenth-century frescoes of St. John the Baptist and the Virgin and Child. Both Duprè Theseider and Michaeli transcribed the two thirteenth-century inscriptions, and a legible photograph of the longer one is preserved in the Biblioteca Hertziana in Rome, so that both can be reconstructed, copied, or extended: "Anno domini MCCLV, tempore Alexandri IIII pape, in / perio uacante, mense Madii, die v intrante / fundata fuit domus ista, sub abba/te Andrea et Ruberto priore et s / uppriore Palmerio, et domino Anselmo / magistro opere, qui primus cepit fundamenta / predicte domus. Anime quorum requiescant in pace"; and "Anno MCCLV frater Iohannes de Coruara cum discipulis suis, silicet fratre Berardo et fratre Iohanne, fecit hoc opus" (see particularly Duprè Theseider, *L'abbazia di San Pastore*, 19, 18).

Duprè Theseider also transcribed the inscription on the major bell: "† Ave Maria gratia plena Dominus tecum† mentem sanctam spontaneam honorem Deo et patrie liberationem† adde nouem decies sic et duo mille ducentis† tempore Natalis Domini tunc Angelus abbas Saluatus prior Dominicus Urbeuetanus fecit campanam de mille quater fore [*sic*] libris" (Michaeli, *Notizie dell'antico monastero,* 14 "ho letto"; Duprè Theseider records another of Domenico of Orvieto's bells, from 1288, at San Francesco, Rieti, that is, four years earlier than his 1292 bell here at San Pastore: see 29). For San Pastore, still somewhat active in 1829, see Rieti, Arch. Vesc., Visita Ferretti, 100.

31. Rome, Arch. Cap. (Vallicella), Archivio Orsini, II.A.I.26 (olim 25). The papal letter of 11 March 1244 imposes silence on San Basilio, which has appealed the recent investiture of San Matteo with, in and at San Damiano in Poggio "Arnulforum" in the duchy of Spoleto through Fra Synebaldo, abbot, and Riccardo, prior of San Matteo. The investiture followed a series of processes held at least in part (see also *Grégoire IX*, no. 456, 11 May 1230) before Pietro Capuano, cardinal deacon of San Giorgio in Velabro (died 1241 or 1242), and the papal subdeacon Giovanni Spata (for whom see below chapter 3), before whom the case was *diutius litigatum* and then referred to Rinaldo da Jenne, cardinal deacon of Sant'Eustachio (translated to Ostia in 1231), chamberlain and chaplain of the pope, who acted under a special papal mandate. The Hospitallers appealed his action, through the prior and a brother of San Basilio, because of the Grand Master's being overseas. On the dorse of the letter: "A." For Cardinal Rinaldo, see Paravicini Bagliani, *Cardinali di curia*, 1:41–53; and for Pietro Capuano, 1:16.

32. Rieti, Arch. Cap., VII.E.1. Innocent responds in this letter to a petition of the bishop and chapter who have asked for protection from the harassment of Donato and Benedetto clerks of the diocese. The procuring proctor, recorded on the dorse of the letter, was "N de Reat." In the Cistercian *Concilia* records of 1252 the monastery is called San Pastore: Canivez, *Statuta capitulorum*, 2:384.

33. San Pastore's is the first of the five lives of desert fathers in which, at the

end of the Golden Legend, Jacobus da Voragine exemplifies regular virtue. San Pastore is he who convinces his mother that she would as willingly next see her sons in another world and who preaches poverty and pain.

34. The fate of San Matteo has been traced by Duprè Theseider; see *L'abbazia di San Pastore*, particularly 48 and 71 (for the miserable condition of San Matteo di Montecchio recorded in the Ferretti visitation of 1832); see the work for references to San Matteo, Rieti, particularly 14 (1266), but also 81, where, in the sixteenth century, it is linked with the Cistercian nunnery of San Tommaso. From 29 March 1278 there is a record of the Cistercian Fra Filippo da Poggio from San Pastore then acting in the cloister of San Matteo, Rieti: Rieti, Arch. Cap., IX.A.2. Palmegiani discussed San Matteo in Rieti in *La cattedrale* and in *Rieti*, 310, in both cases under "S. Pietro Martire" and in both cases with helpful material, particularly in the latter book from the Ferretti visitation of 1827. The longer treatment in the earlier book is made difficult by Palmegiani's seeming to have confused the original San Matteo all'isola with San Matteo, the hospice in Rieti, and treating them as one. Their actual distinctness is perfectly clear, and recorded, as for example in Rieti, Arch. Cap., Lib. Int. et Exit., 1364, fo. 9r: "Cera recepta ab ecclesiis, inprimis: Recepi a frate Nicola de Sancta Rufina abati Sancti Pastoris pro Sancto Matheo de Reate et pro Sancto Matheo de lacu. . . . 2 li cere"; and see other years (e.g., 1360, 1363, 1368) on fo. 9r or, when a flyleaf has been added, fo. 10r (e.g., 1371).

35. Rieti, Arch. Cap., IX.A.2, 1 July 1235: Guilielmus, abbot; Robertus, prior; Munallus, cellarer; Dompni Benuenutus, Ber', Jacobus, Raynall', Petrus, Deodatus, Gratianus, Bartholomeus, another Bartholomeus (explicitly called *alius*), another Petrus (*alius*), another Raynall' (*alius*), monks; fratres Raynerius, Johannes Verlandi, Reatinus, Adenulfus, Benuenutus, Ber', Matheus Simeonis, Johannes Moranus(?), Johannes Jouanni, Maxeus', Petrus, Marinus, Andreas, Stefanus, Angelus, *conversi*. On 24 March 1283 Frater Paulus, a *conversus* of the monastery, acts, in buying, as proctor and yconomo of the monastery of San Pastore at the convent of San Tommaso: IX.A.2.

36. Rieti, Arch. Cap., VI.E.3: on 6 March 1342, summoned by bell to chapter in the accustomed place were: Frater Gentilis, abbot; Dominus Johannes Sonantis [genitive], prior; Dompnus Petrus de Narnia, major cellarer (listed before the prior); dompni Johannes Guidi, Nicholaus de Greccia, Johannes Thodinucii de Reate, Thomaxius de Monte S. Johannis, Vandis [genitive] de Greccia, Pastor de Interampne, Nicolaus Carluctii de Greccia (the last two of whom are being made proctors); fratres Nicolaus notarii (or possibly notarius) Berardi de Reate, Petrus Berardesche de Reate, Stefanus Raynallicti de Greccia, Nicolaus Bonagure de Reate, Matheus Marchoni de Reate, Johannes de Quintiliano, Petrus de Quintiliano, Franciscus de Greccia, Franciscus de Quintiliano, Andreas de Rocha Alatri, Jacobus de Reate, *fratres* (*conversi*): in some cases the reconstruction of these names is complicated by their being, for the most part, in the genitive. On 23 January 1339, the monk "Dompnus Gentilis" had acted as yconomo and proctor for the monastery in the granting away of a *casalinum* in the castro of Greccio: VI.E.2. See A.S.V., Obligationes et Solutiones (OS), 22, fo. 213r, 14 November 1357, for Master Paolo da Viterbo, *magister in medicina*, who promises in the name of the monastery of San Pastore and Fra Pietro, its (ob-

viously new) abbot, to pay the abbots "common service" of 36½ *flor. aur.* within term; for an explanation of Obligationes et Solutiones and their importance, see Boyle, *A Survey of the Vatican Archives,* 157–164. There exists in the capitular archives of Rieti (II.G.1, numbering for communal documents), on two folded sheets of paper, a list written, by the notary Giovanni "Hycremie," of the possessions of the monastery of San Pastore in the tenement and appurtenances of Rocca Alatri, "in uuto Alatrense," "de quibus instrumentis et registro dicti monasterii summatim extracta . . . pro breuiori informatione legentium"; the list seems, from the hand, to be fifteenth-century. It contains twenty-seven items, in which there is repeated talk of canals (or a canal) and of swamps; one item (fo. 1r, no. 9) describes the property's neighbors on two sides: "rem Sancte Marie de Reat' et rem Greccensium"; another item (fo. 2r, no. 24) "in Terria in Uto Alatrensi" speaks of "rem Gallonis," and so touches the present and the Case Galloni; another (fo. 2r, no. 21) talks of land "in contrata Terrie" next to "rem Johannis Ursini" and near the present land and house of the local family Orsini; another (fo. 1v, no. 13) has as a neighbor "rem Angeli Carsedonii." Most noticeable, however, is the concentration of adjacent monastery properties.

37. Rieti, Arch. Cap., VII.E.1.

38. Rieti, Arch. Cap., IV.A.3. Copies both of Clement's letter and of the closely related one (IV.A.2) dated the same day, which was sent to the *Capitaneo regni Sicilie* and which exhorted him to do everything in his power to prevent "nonnulli homines ciuitatis Aquilen' habitatores" from harassing bishop, chapter, rectors, and clerks of the churches in the diocese of Rieti, are preserved in the capitular archives. Both letters are in good condition; and on both the curial notations are particularly clearly visible. On the dorse of each, at the place where it becomes customary for curial proctors to place their names, is written: "Dns Jordanus Card": presumably the letters, and probably the action, had been procured for Rieti through the intercession or aid of Giordano da Terracina cardinal deacon of Santi Cosma e Damiano, although the vice-chancellorship of the former notary cardinal perhaps permits a more formal explanation. Both letters are included in the 1353 inventory that Bishop Biagio ordered to be made of the church's privileges (21 in all), books, and other possessions preserved in the cathedral sacristy: Rieti, Arch. Cap., Parchment Book IV, fo. 47r, nos. 16 and 20. Urban's letter is IV.D.6. It and its proctor, Master Andrea, are cited in my "Innocent IV and the Chapter of Rieti," 389.

39. Rieti, Arch. Cap., VI.E.1, for 13 November 1280. This document in letter form with a flap and holes for three seals, and with white silk string remaining, is 38.5 cm × 32.5 cm. It begins:

Petrus permissione diuina minister et .. capitulum Ecclesie Reatin', religiosis uiris amicis in Xpo dilectis .. abbati et conuentui monasterii Sancti Pastoris, Reatin' diocesis, Cisterciensis ordinis. Salutem in domino. Inter sollicitudines uarias seu diuersas que prelatis et capitulis cathedralium ecclesiarum incumbunt . . . [It concludes:] Insuper ad utriusque partis cautelam presencium litterarum chirographum nostro et capituli nostri et monasterii uestri sigillis munitum de communi concordia fecimus duplicari, ut unus penes nos in sacristia nostra remaneat, reliqus [*sic*] uero penes dictum monasterium conseruetur. Dat' in ecclesia Reatin' presentibus uolentibus et consentientibus episcopo et capitulo, abbate

ac Fratre Raynaldo de Arcestianula monacho et yconomo dicti monasterii ad hoc specialiter constituto. Anno domini Mo. CCo. lxxxo. mens' Novembr' die xiiio. apostolica
sede vacante.

40. Rieti, Arch. Cap., VII.C.6; the letter preserves its seal (of white or brown
wax) on a seal strip. An illuminating statement that helps explain the reasons
why monasteries admitted important people into confraternity is quoted in John
W. Elston's unpublished doctoral dissertation "William Curteys, Abbot of Bury
St. Edmunds, 1429–1446" (University of California, Berkeley, 1979), ch. 1 n.112:
"We make you one of us, not as with others, in order to put pressure on you
to be our friend," quoted with Mr. Elston's permission.

41. Rieti, A.S., San Domenico, 8 (ol. 47): 24 December 1295; and particularly
Arch. Cap., IV.G.4: 26 November 1294, in which Bishop Nicola acts in Rieti
"in camera domini Episcopi supradicti coram religioso uiro domino fratre Angelo Abbate Monasterii Sancti Pastoris de Reat', fratre Symone de Fulgineo,
Fratre Jacobo de Butro, monachis eiusdem monasterii." Finding a monk of San
Pastore from a place even as far away as Foligno is worth noting; "Butro," on
the other hand, was close to Rieti, southwest of the city walls. In both of these
documents the bishop is called "Frater Nicolaus miseratione diuina Reatinus [in
IV.G.4: Reatin'] episcopus," but in the once sealed letter form, San Domenico,
8, a grant of 40 days' indulgence to those who give aid to the *opere* of San
Domenico, or of the convent buildings, or help the friars in their other needs,
the capital "F" of *Frater* was never written. Perhaps Bishop Nicola resigned
before the letter received its final touches; Berardo was translated to Rieti from
Ancona to replace him on 4 February 1296. One should also know that Ughelli
wrote that Bishop Tommaso of Rieti (see below, chapter 4), who was bishop
in 1255, was a benefactor of San Matteo-San Pastore (Ughelli, *Italia sacra*, vol.
1, col. 1204) and that in 1292 a letter patent from Bishop Tommaso and the
chapter of Rieti, which freed San Tommaso, the local Cistercian convent of
nuns, from ordinary jurisdiction, and which had been dated Rieti, 3 May 1265,
seemed worth restating and having confirmed, so that it obviously seemed more
than a mere formality to the nuns (Langlois, ed., *Les registres de Nicholas IV*,
no. 6600). The Rieti letter is fully transcribed in Nicholas IV's register (A.S.V.,
Reg. Vat. 46, fo. 148r, no. 740). The letter that had been sealed with the seals
of the bishop and chapter spoke of the bishop's and chapter's laying the cor-
nerstone of the monastery that had been founded with the aid of the cardinal
bishop of Porto (John of Toledo). This suggested sense of general harmony
should not obscure the fact that any contested property or right would naturally
project Santa Maria and San Pastore into litigation again: see, for example, the
matter of the house in the parish of San Donato in 1371: Rieti, Arch. Cap., Lib.
Int. et Exit., 1371, in a list of chapter expenses, eight folios before the end of the
book, and just before a listed payment to Frater Stefano monk of the monastery
of San Pastore and Collector.

42. Rieti, Arch. Cap., II.G.1; see above note 36 for a fuller description of the
San Pastore inventory. Rieti, Arch. Cap., Parchment Book "7" contains the
redistribution of properties in 1307.

43. A witness who is particularly clear about the produce of this area is Ratino

Taliatanus in 1241: Rieti, Arch. Cap., VIII.A.2, first piece of parchment, second of fully recorded witnesses. Ratino saw the return of crayfish, fish, and money and talks also of receipt of fish, crayfish, and *cuppis*(?); from the dry land he notes "postea granum, fabas, milium, speltam, adque candavitium." Bartolomeo de Grumo, on the second piece of parchment, thirteenth of the fully recorded witnesses, says: "uidit eos percipere in blada uidelicet granum, milium et fabas et saginum." In the Lib. Int. et Exit. of 1364 a noticeable part of the land in the area is recorded as having been left, for the year, unworked (fo. 13r): for "terra monticuli," after itemizing the use of 11½ giunte, the book records, "residuum dicte terre non laborantur"; the following item is "de terra reliquid domini Gentilis Futii posita in contrada Fluminis Mortui que est xi junte nichil recepi quia non fuit laborata"; the next item, "de terra casamascara," is 15 giunte of land of which 12¼ are worked; land elsewhere is also not worked (for instance, 12 giunte left by Donna Margherita Corradi in nearby *pratu longu*: fo. 12v); and the land of Casamascara, at least, gave a good annual return to the church, 10 soldi per giunta.

44. Rieti, Arch. Cap., IV.Q.11. The twelve granting consuls of 8 May 1205 are named and include Matteo Synibaldi Dodonis, Matteo Sarracenus, and Beraldo Galganus; the land is "in ducatu Spoletan' in Monticulo Cervaliolo" near Casamascara and has as neighbors property of the church of Rieti, of the lords of Labro, of Rayn' Leonis, as well as the swamp. For Berardo Sprangone see chapter 4, below, but also Michaeli, *Memorie*, 2:189.

45. Rieti, Arch. Cap., VIII.A.2. For the notary Giovanni Egidii the indiction has changed by 2 September; but for the Rieti copying notary of 1304, it has not changed by 23 September, nor has it for Giovanni Dati on 1 September. The 1253 sentence is dated 3 *stante* July, and one of its witnesses is Matteo Infantis.

46. Rieti, Arch. Cap., IV.Q.1: 11 December 1229 (one of six parchments and documents stitched together, which group is only one of the members of IV.Q.1).

47. There is some inconsistency in naming and spelling with these records. The interchangeable "c" and "t" of "Mercones" (the former seemingly more frequent) is a particular problem.

48. Rieti, Arch. Cap., IV.P.5: "consuetudo est quod quicumque tenet iuxta paludes si dissicatur terra remanet sibi." This date answers a question asked by Waley in his biography of Giovanni Colonna in the *Dizionario biografico degli italiani*.

49. IV.P.5: "est consuetudo Reatin' quod siquis faceret mandrias uel cappannas in rebus alienis si uellet eas tenere per illum cuius est tenet, si uero tenere nollet ille cuius est eas deuastat."

50. Rieti, Arch. Cap., IV.P.5, which has seven pieces which have been numbered by a later hand. See Sayers, *Papal Judges Delegate*, 88–89, for numbers of witnesses and the attempt to limit them.

51. Duprè Theseider, *L'abbazia di San Pastore*, 47 and no. 4.

52. The monk and priest Filippo: IV.P.5. For an unusually clear definition and description of "depositions and attestations," see Helmholz, *Marriage Litigation*, 19–20.

53. The witness *conversi* are Stefano, Benencasa, Rainaldo, Pietro, Jai di Pie-

tro, Rain', Girardo, Giovanni, Giovanni Ber', Rustico, Ber', Giovanni Caputostu, Paolo, Caniato, Angelo, and Giovanni Martini: IV.P.5.

54. The protagonist priest is Filippo: IV.P.5; the monk witness is fr. Johannes de Sancto Giorgio.

55. Called in his own testimony "Sin' Mareri" but also elsewhere "Sen' ": Rieti, Arch. Cap., IV.P.5. For other references to him see Arch. Cap., Book IV (parchment), fo. 21; IV.O.5; IV.G.3; IV.D.1; IV.Q.2; IV.O.4; IV.Q.3 "14"; III.D.2; IV.O.1; IV.M.1 "16": *Sinibaldus, Siniballus, Syn', Senebaldus.*

56. Rieti, Arch. Cap., IV.Q.1; IV.G.3; IV.D.1; IV.Q.3 "14"; IV.I.1; II.D.3. Berardo's name does not always include the *Sinibaldi* (variously spelled); it does not in IV.P.5.

57. Rieti, Arch. Cap., IV.M.1 "11"; IV.Q.6 "1"; IV.G.5: in the last of these, from 1223, *Henricus* is called a priest.

58. Rieti, Arch. Cap., IV.G.3; IV.D.1; IV.Q.2; IV.O.1. *Grégoire IX*, nos. 1820–1821.

59. Rieti, Arch. Cap., IV.M.1 "17"; IV.G.3; IV.D.1; IV.O.1; IV.P.6 "1,2,7."

60. Rieti, Arch. Cap., IV.G.3; IV.D.1; IV.Q.2; IV.O.4; IV.O.1; IV.I.1; II.O.2; II.D.3; II.D.5; III.D.2; IV.O.5; IV.D.4. The statements of long memory are within IV.O.1.

61. These depositions are to be found in Rieti, Arch. Cap., IV.P.5, which is composed of seven parts, of which "2," "3," and "4" are the pertinent testimonies of witnesses; "1" is a single parchment, a 1244 copy of Berardo Sprangone's act of 17 May 1209, in which Matteo de Necto is ordered to invest the monks of San Matteo; "5," "6," and "7," are notations concerning the witnesses—"5" and "6" concern Santa Maria witnesses, and "7" concerns San Matteo witnesses; "2" is a roll of three parchments stitched together to form a whole about 112 cm long and contains *testes monasterii Sancti Mathei de Monticulo*, and its first witness is the monk Filippo. Essentially identical in content and contemporary in script, "3" and "4" are *testes Sancte Marie contra monasterium*; "3" is four pieces of stitched parchment about 168 cm in total length, and "4" is also four pieces of parchment and about 170 cm long; both begin with the witness Jai de Dodo. (In "4" the testimony of the witness Mgr. Guillielmus is written in a hand different from that of the testimony of the other witnesses.) For the sake of convenience, IV.P.5 "2," the roll of San Matteo witnesses, is called here IV.P.5:I (the first group of witnesses); and IV.P.5 "3" and "4" are, together, called IV.P.5:II (the second group of witnesses)—thus Jai de Dodo, the first Santa Maria witness, is IV.P.5:II, 1. The way in which the witnesses were divided into two groups was obviously dictated by the way in which the depositions were taken, not necessarily by the sympathies of the witnesses, so that the two testifying canons of Rieti fall within the first group. For an explanation of the process of taking depositions see Helmholz, *Marriage Litigation*, 19–20.

62. Rieti, Arch. Cap., IV.P.5 "1"; see also IV.Q.11, and, above, note 44.

63. Rieti, Arch. Cap., IV.P.5:I, 8.

64. Rieti, Arch. Cap., IV.P.5:I, 11.

65. Rieti, Arch. Cap., IV.P.5:II, 30.

66. Rieti, Arch. Cap., IV.P.5:II, 20.

67. Rieti, Arch. Cap., IV.P.5:II,32.

68. Rieti, Arch. Cap., IV.P.5:II, 33. Dodati in "3."

69. Rieti, Arch. Cap., IV.P.5:II, 14.

70. Rieti, Arch. Cap., IV.P.5:II, 16, 22, 21. Adinulfum in "4"; Adenulfum in "3."

71. Rieti, Arch. Cap., IV.P.5:II, 3. Vonezo in "4"; "uergagam" in "3," "uergarzam" in "4" I take to be a trap like *la nassa, le nasse* (*martaelli* in Cicolano dialect), or *il cogolo* (which is used for *gamberi*), or possibly *il parangal, la passelera*, or simply *la bilancia*.

72. Rieti, Arch. Cap., IV.P.5:II, 4. Morice in "4."

73. Rieti, Arch. Cap., IV.P.5:II, 5. Ratino in "3."

74. Rieti, Arch. Cap., IV.P.5:II, 6.

75. Rieti, Arch. Cap., IV.P.5:II, 12. Rainucellus in "4."

76. Rieti, Arch. Cap., IV.P.5:II, 13, 10.

77. Rieti, Arch. Cap., IV.P.5:II, 31.

78. Rieti, Arch. Cap., IV.P.5:II, 26, 4 (the Mercones' neighbor Vetulo Morici, presumably a well-informed witness). Jai de Mercone also uses *feudum*. For a concise and very enlightening discussion of the terms *feudum* and *vassallus* in Lazio, see Toubert, *Les structures*, 1:513 n.1. "Jai" does not seem now to be a nickname for Giovanni, as "Jua" and "Juanitu" are, in the area around San Pastore.

79. Rieti, Arch. Cap., IV.P.5:II, 18.

80. Rieti, Arch. Cap., IV.P.5:II, 9.

81. Rieti, Arch. Cap., IV.P.5:II, 15.

82. Rieti, Arch. Cap., IV.P.5:II, 25.

83. Rieti, Arch. Cap., IV.P.5:II, 27. Sin. in "4."

84. Rieti, Arch. Cap., IV.P.5:I, 3.

85. Rieti, Arch. Cap., IV.P.5:I, 7.

86. Rieti, Arch. Cap., IV.P.5:II, 27.

87. Rieti, Arch. Cap., IV.P.5:I, 15; *una sargia*, I gather, most commonly denotes the flexible willow branch used for tying, as vines to elms, but also the stakes used to hold together fodder piled on the ground. It is now sometimes the practice in Lazio and, for example, the Romagna near Ìmola to plant a willow at the end of a row of vines; it presumably adds stability to the bank of soil, and protection, as well as conveniently providing *sargie*. The actual struggle is hard for me to follow exactly but the "per capam" and "cecidisset nisi habuisset fortia crura" are quite clear.

88. Rieti, Arch. Cap., IV.P.5:I, 16.

89. Rieti, Arch. Cap., IV.P.5:I, 1. I have left the names in the form in which they appear in Filippo's testimony, to give some sense of the irregularity of the spelling of personal names.

90. Rieti, Arch. Cap., IV.P.5:I, 7.

91. Rieti, Arch. Cap., IV.P.5:II, 5.

92. Rieti, Arch. Cap., IV.P.5:II, 2, 6. Compare the testimony of the Santa Maria witness in 1229, note 47 above.

93. Rieti, Arch. Cap., IV.P.5:I, 1, 26, 27.

94. Rieti, Arch. Cap., IV.P.5:I, 5.

95. Rieti, Arch. Cap., IV.P.5:II, 12, 26.

96. Rieti, Arch. Cap., IV.P.5:II, 18.

97. Rieti, Arch. Cap., IV.P.5:II, 31, 11, 2, 5, 33. The notations about Santa Maria witnesses in IV.P.5 "5" make a particular point of listing lengths of memory: forty, thirty, thirty-two, twenty-four, twenty years.

98. Rieti, Arch. Cap., IV.P.5:II, 18.

99. Rieti, Arch. Cap., IV.P.5:I, 3, 19, 7, 20, 4, 18, 5, 17.

100. *Scripta Leonis*, 140–141. A freshwater *squalus* may seem inconceivable, but within living memory the *squau* (*cavèdano*, fam. Cyprinidae) were thick in the Salto and frequently eaten, although perhaps seldom, if ever, on restaurant menus or sold in urban *pescherie*. I owe my knowledge of the squau, like much else, to my friend Alberto Sestili of Sant'Ippolito and Rieti. More recently my Berkeley colleague Don C. Erman, professor of forestry and director of the Wildland Resources Center, has explained to me much more about the *cavèdano*, which he says is common in Italy and distributed widely in Europe. It is commonly called "chub" in English; and, although it is a member of the minnow family, it is capable of reaching weights of ten pounds or more. The generic name of the chub was once *squalius*. For the gamberi of the Rieti region see Truini Palomba, *La cucina sabina*, 111 "li ammari."

101. Lawrence, *St. Edmund of Abingdon*, 11; Lawrence's entire chapter, "The *Quadrilogus* and the Canonization Process," is extremely helpful and interesting in this connection.

102. Baldwin, *Masters, Princes, and Merchants*, 1:55; this chapter, "Theological Doctrine," is also very helpful and repeatedly suggestive, as it is in its penultimate sentence, 1:59: "What their theories lacked in consistency and unity, was compensated by richness of detail."

103. *Scripta Leonis*, 186–189. For the stigmata in the *Vita prima*, see nos. 94–96, 112–114: *Analecta franciscana*, 10:72–74. To describe, now, Fonte Colombo as on the road to Sant'Elia is somewhat misleading; the importance of the two places has clearly been reversed. The terrain of Sant'Elia suggests that it was never rich and was always, as the story suggests, pastoral.

104. *Vita prima*, nos. 84–87: *Analecta franciscana*, 10:63–65. No reader should fail to notice Francis's choosing to make real the New Testament birth of Christ by emphasizing the ass and the ox, which, although they were assumed to have been in the scene by the fourth century, were not, of course, in any New Testament account; this is a helpful clue to understanding Francis's sense of the literal interpretation that was so important to him. For the ox and the ass, see *Analecta franciscana*, 10:84 no. 9.

105. *Scripta Leonis*, 144–147.

106. Rieti, Arch. Cap., VI.F.5. The letter, the original of which survives, was dated from Farfa on 4 April 1312, with, in addition, indiction and papal year dates. It records the names of three witnesses, at least one of whom, "Fratre Jacobo de Putealea," was a monk of Farfa. The letter was once sealed with the abbot's seal, and it maintains its red silk string. San Michele Greccio is now served by the Franciscans of Greccio.

107. Mascetta Caracci, "Il latino della Chiesa," 273 but also 270. The word

minestrone itself, of course, is a figurative way of describing a miscellany of things.

Chapter 3

1. I think that the best introduction to thirteenth-century curial clerks and their work is to be found in the studies of them by Herde, particularly *Beiträge* and *Audientia litterarum contradictarum*. To the works of Herde, Paravicini Bagliani's *Cardinali di curia* is a very helpful addition concerning a specific category of clerks. The quickest way to get a sense of curial work is to peruse the published register of one of the thirteenth-century popes; in the register of Boniface VIII (Digard et al., eds., *Les registres de Boniface VIII*, 4:xxxiii–xxxviii) is Fawtier's excellent discussion of papal scribes. I wrote what I then thought of Italian dioceses in *Two Churches*, ch. 2.

2. Bib. Apos. Vat., Cod. Barb. Lat., no. 2406 (olim XXXII, 197), cap. 146–149 (seventeenth-century copy); Michaeli, *Memorie*, 2:268–272, no. iv. (The privilege, or a privilege, of Lucius's was in the sacristy in 1353: Rieti, Arch. Cap., Parchment Book IV, fos. 46v–47r, no. 9.) The Rieti evidence which Toubert found unusual in some ways, *Les structures*, 2:798 n.2, does not seem to me really to add much support to his belief in "la réalité territoriale du diocèse comme ensemble de castra" (2:797 n.2) and, in fact, leads me to suspect a certain circularity in his thesis of *incastellamento* when it is applied to *les structures religieuses*. Although some of Lucius's names are very hard (impossible for me) to locate or to place exactly, some of them particularly near Tanzia and Orvinio suggest a boundary that wanders into other dioceses. The thirteenth-century evidence certainly makes the reader believe that some of the *monasteria* and *oratoria* would have fit their category oddly even in the twelfth century. See Kehr, *Italia pontificia*, 4:23–24, no. 10; Jaffe and Loewenfeld, *Regesta pontificum*, 2:442, no. 14675. On the other hand it should be noted that for some reason the Lucius privilege was copied, I think in the 1370s, into what is now Paris B.N. latin 1556, fos. 27r–28r, and that at some time parts of that copy were, but not for immediately ascertainable reasons, underlined.

3. Rieti, Arch. Cap., II.A.1, which is printed in Michaeli, *Memorie*, 2:265–268, no. 3; see too Kehr, *Italia pontificia*, 4:23, no. 7, and Toubert, *Les structures*, 2:797 n.2, and 798 n.1; and Jaffe and Loewenfeld, *Regesta pontificum*, 2:95, no. 9821 (incorrectly placed as Kehr noted).

4. I should say that the Rieti historian, Cesare Verani, a man whose learning and understanding I very much respect, wrote to me that he did not think that the privileges' boundaries were in any way fictitious. The activity of Dodone and Benedetto is particularly clearly revealed in the San Leopardo, San Silvestro, and Santa Croce cases, but see too Ferri, "Monteleone," 76.

5. Actual tithing in this period and contemporary opinion about it have been studied carefully and explained lucidly by Boyd in *Tithes and Parishes*; her explanations reenforce, in my opinion, the lack of importance of exact Reatine boundaries. Tithe disputes are less noticeable in surviving early thirteenth-

century Reatine documents, I think, than an outside observer, particularly from northern Italy, might have expected.

6. In naming these dioceses I am, with some trepidation, following Sella's map "Umbria (sec. XIV)" from *Rationes decimarum ... Umbria*, except of course for the Forcone-L'Aquila border. The case of Paolo Zoppo, below, suggests problems with the Spoleto boundary near Leonessa, as do early modern disputes between the two dioceses, for which see particularly Maceroni and Tassi, *Società religiosa*, 206–213. Bishop Tommaso's placing of Piediluco suggests a further problem, see below. For the reconstruction of Terni, see Manassei, "Alcuni documenti," 414, nos. 5, 7, 8 (Honorius III in the years 1217–19). See too, Coste, "I confini occidentale della diocesi di Tivoli." The work of Di Flavio on early modern Reatine visitations and synods is constantly helpful in understanding the earlier extension of Rieti, see for example his *Sinodo reatino*.

7. See Guidoni, "L'espansione urbanistica," 163–187; Gizzi, "La città dell'Aquila" (a richly annotated article). See too Ludovisi, "L'organismo del comune," part 19, 1–41. For the new towns more generally and particularly Florentine ones, see Friedman, *Florentine New Towns*.

8. For an excellent bibliography of work on and sources for Forcone/Furcone-L'Aquila, see Kamp, *Kirche und Monarchie: Abruzzen und Kampanien*, 1:21. For the foundation of L'Aquila and the transfer of the see: De Stefano, "Le origini di Aquila," 7–26, and particularly 21; De Nino, "Nuove congetture sull'origine dell'Aquila," with the nice disclaimer, 83, "Ahimè! Congetture troviamo, e congetture lasciamo!"; Chiappini, "Intorno alla fondazione"; Alinari, "L'antica chiesa di S. Massimo"; Pansa, "Catalogo descrittivo e analitico"; Sabatini, "Saggio bibliografico"; de Bartholomaeis, "Federico II e l'Aquila"; Chiappini, "Fondazione, distruzione"; Palatini, "Cenni storici," and his "La signoria nell'Aquila," particularly 199: "l'Aquila guelfa e Rieti ghibellina" for conflict; and Ludovisi, "Corografia storica," particularly 7 (1917), 224, for a discussion of the quasi-episcopal rights of the archpriest of San Vittorino under the bishops of Rieti; and also his "Storia dei contadi di Amiterno." And see Ughelli, *Italia sacra*, cols. 373, 381–384. It seems to me that Duprè Theseider's use of the foundation of L'Aquila ("Vescovi e città," 64 and n.1), which Toubert seems to accept (*Les structures*, 2:802 n.1) is misleading in suggesting that L'Aquila's creation was an example of the movement of diocesan sees from depopulated places to city-like towns; the Forcone-L'Aquila move is surely a much more complicated motion than that, and, I think, essentially different from it. For the residence of the first bishop, Berardo de Padula, see Kamp, *Kirche und Monarchie: Abruzzen und Kampanien*, 1:23–25.

9. Bib. Apos. Vat., MS Barb. Lat. 4539, "Istoria sacra delle cose notibili della Città dell'Aquila scritta dal Sig. Gio. Gioseppe Alferi," a not disinterested work (fo. 3v: "O felici, et veri Aquilotti, / o voi felici, et Beati in vero, / . . ."), fo. 16v–17: "Il privilegio della translatione," of 20 February 1257; Alferi says that the actual *translatione* occurred in Alexander IV's first year (20 December 1254–19 December 1255). There is an informed, extended discussion of the transfer of Amiterno diocesan rights to and from Rieti in Maroni, *Commentarius de ecclesia*, 51–58. The Anastasius-Dodone 1153 privilege is thick with the names of Amiterno

pievi and towns, like: Amiterno, Corno, San Vito, San Vittorino, Popleto, Preturo, Collettara, San Marco, Foce, Cagnano, Cascina, Vigliano.

10. Rieti, Arch. Cap., IV.A.3., IV.A.2; see above chapter 2 note 38.

11. Sella, *Rationes decimarum ... Aprutium, Molisium.* Readers should know that the history of the Abruzzi is becoming much more readily accessible due to production of increasingly fine work at centers like the Istituto di storia medioevale e moderna at the Università degli studi "G. D'Annunzio" Chieti, for example, *Ricerche di storia abruzzese.* Place-name searches, among much else, are facilitated by, for example, Clementi and Berardi, eds., *Regesto delle fonti archivistiche.*

12. Rieti, Arch. Cap., II.E.3.

13. *Regestum Clementis Papae V*, no. 6925; the churches of the two homicidal priests will be found in the diocese of L'Aquila in the *Rationes* list. It is possible that "Rieti" is an error.

14. Rome, Vallicelliana, Archivio capitolino, Pergamene Orsini, II.A.IV no. 51 (olim 50): Tomassetti and Biasiotti, *La diocesi di Sabina*, 63–95. Kehr, *Italia pontificia*, 2:54 n.3; Toubert, *Les structures*, 2:798 n.2. The registrum is a piece of evidence which seems strongly to support Toubert's concept of the new diocese as a collection of *castra*/castri; but it should be read with two qualifications constantly in mind: (1) *castrum* has become the word used to describe a particle of the diocese, but the word does not necessarily control the nature and meaning of the diocesan particle/division; (2) the structure described within the particle is clearly more conventionally ecclesiastical than *castrum* might suggest to the casual reader.

15. Berger, ed., *Les registres d'Innocent IV*, no. 5614; Rieti, Arch. Cap., II.D.1 (two original copies of Innocent's letter to the chapter of Rieti announcing Tommaso's appointment); Herde, *Beiträge*, 19, 21–22. It should be noted that Innocent did not withhold helpful letters from Rainaldo da Arezzo; one survives at Rieti: Arch. Cap., IV.A.5 (procured by proctor "N de Reat" as the dorse of the letter shows). For the campanile, see Montari, "Rieti," 104–112 and plates 119–121; and Brentano, *Two Churches*, 108 and n.131. See Rieti, Arch. Cap., IV.A.6, 7, 8 for Innocent and Tommaso's job at Rieti; and also Brentano, "Innocent IV."

16. Paris, B.N. latin 1556, fos. 18r–26r. I want again to thank Pierre Toubert for first having informed me of the existence of this manuscript in connection with its synodal constitutions, see chapter 4 below, and again to thank Anthony Luttrell who looked at the manuscript for me and had it photographed and from the beginning insisted upon the unusual importance of Tommaso's list; there is a copy of its beginning parts preserved at Rieti: Rieti, Arch. Cap., III.B.1, 22.

17. See particularly, Paris, B.N. latin 1556, fos. 24v–25r.

18. *Innocent IV*, no. 5614.

19. Rieti, Arch. Cap., III.D.3.

20. Rieti, Arch. Cap., II.D.6.

21. See, for example, Rieti, Arch. Cap., IV.F.1 and II.D.4.

22. Rieti, Arch. Cap., IV.P.1 "3".

23. It was the use of documents from the San Salvatore case by Desanctis,

Notizie storiche, which I wanted to check, which, in writing an earlier book, first drew me to Rieti and its archives; the documents from the case (IV.P.1) obviously fascinate me still. IV.P.1 is a collection of five documents of which the most informative contains the bishop's positions and the responses of the abbot and clergy of the subject churches, and which was absent from the archivio for some years but then returned; the minor documents are particularly interesting because of their suggestions about the preparation of witnesses: Desanctis edited the major document: appendix, xv–xx. See, too, Schuster, "Il monastero imperiale," and "Il monastero del Salvatore." For Santa Cecilia in 1265, see Guirard and Clémencet, eds., *Les registres d'Urbain IV*, no. 1345: the pope with the assent of the abbot and convent of San Salvatore Maggiore provided to a canonry of Santa Cecilia a clerk and familiar of John of Toledo, cardinal bishop of Porto, a clerk named Pietro Jacobi or di Giacomo, which makes clear San Salvatore's continued interest in Santa Cecilia Rieti—for John of Toledo's *familia* see Paravicini Bagliani, *Cardinali di curia*, 1:228–255, where Pietro is no. 36. Records of San Salvatore Maggiore's partial patronage of the church of Santa Maria della Valle, Rieti diocese, are preserved from 1319 and 1337: Rieti, Arch. Cap., VI.F.6 and VI.F.8. On 26 July 1319 "venerabilis pater dominus frater Bonusjohannes permissione diuina abbas monasterii Sancti Saluatoris Maioris Reatin tamquam patronus ecclesie Sancte Marie de Vallibus pro ea parte que pertinuit ad dictum monasterium infra Reatin' dyoc'," at the time vacant through the death of *dompnum Oddonem* once archpriest and rector, made as his proctor, to appear before the bishop and chapter of the church of Rieti, the man of religion *fratrem Jannem Oddonis*, monk of the monastery, to present to the living Don Giacomo di Don Tommaso (*domini Thomasii*) canon of Rieti: and one should observe the buttressing of interests. On 15 June 1337 during the vacancy of the see of Rieti, the abbot Filippo, using the same style as Bongiovanni with the consent of the assembled monastery, chose his own brother the clerk Mattia, son of Filippo de Collibus, knight, to rule as rector of the church of Santa Maria de Vallibus, vacant through the death of the former archpriest and rector, Pietro di Transarico, through the right of patronage which the abbot and convent shared with certain noblemen and which the abbey had exercised within the prescribed term. The abbot's request to the chapter of Rieti and its vicar general canonically to institute his brother was made at the monastery in chapter before Giacomo da Sabina, Astallo da Urbe, and Farrato da Rocca Sinibalda, the abbot's *familiares*. The action and appeal were described and written by the abbot's *scriba et officialis*, the notary by imperial authority Pietro di don Gentile of Rieti. The relation of the abbey to the church of Rieti is suggested by the will, dated 25 March 1382 of Matteo *Jannis Georgii de Castro Purciglani districtus abacie Sancti Saluatoris maioris de Reate et reatine diocesis*. VI.F.9. The Reatine statutes make clear, what would be perhaps obvious in any case, the importance to the city of Rieti of San Salvatore's controlled and contributing loyalty; see Rieti, Arch. Stat., Statuti 1, fo. 41r. For the case with the Cistercians and drying marshlands see chapter 2 above, for San Leopardo see chapter 1 above.

24. For Capocci see Waley, *The Papal State*, particularly 149–150, 153–154,

and "Constitutions of the Cardinal-legate Peter Capocci," 660–664; and at greater length, Reh, *Kardinal Peter Capocci.*

25. Rieti, Arch. Cap., IV.P.1. The actions of the Rieti proctor at Rome in the case of San Silvestro, below, on 21 February 1234, certainly suggest that Rainaldo de Labro was alive, or believed to be alive—and so alive within the last few days: Rieti, Arch. Cap., II.C.1, h. For Corrado, Rainaldo and Bertuldo, and the Urslingen in general, see Sacchetti Sassetti, "Rieti e gli Urslingen," particularly 1–5, and also Waley, *The Papal State,* 126–127, 129–130, 132, and index. See too, below, note 40.

26. Rieti, Arch. Cap., II.C.1, a, b, d, e, f, g, h, i, k, l, m, p, r, s, t, u, x, y, z; II.C.2r; IV.P.4 (in five parts).

27. Petrabattuta, Petrauattuta, Petrauactuta, Petrauactita, Petrabacteta, Petrauaccita, Petrapattuta, Petra vattuta, Petra Vactuta, Petra Bacteta, Petra Vaccuta, Preta Bactita, Pretabatt', Petra cacc. The reader will be aware of the easy and normal exchange of *c* for *t* in thirteenth-century hands, although in a number of cases the scribe seems clearly to have one or the other in mind. Capital letters are unstable. The initial *pre,* when used, is generally not extended. Naturally these variations in spelling tell more about the practices of thirteenth-century scribes than about the specific place; but they do make physical the mystery of its location. It is worth noting, however, that the location of the abbey's subject churches make a location near Monte San Silvestro not unlikely. The fact that Lugini, the historian of the Cicolano, in his *Memorie storiche,* 152–153, in his discussion of Anastasius IV's privilege, did not mention San Silvestro suggests that he did not know where it was or had been. Anastasius IV has "Petra Battuta"; Lucius III has "petrabattida"; Sella, *Rationes decimarum . . . Aprutium, Molisium,* nos. 214, 238: Pretavactita.

28. San Tommaso and San Pietro are listed among the *pievi* in the Anastasius IV privilege, and next to each other; San Silvestro is listed among the *oratoria, que monasteria dicuntur.* They are similarly listed by Lucius III, but San Tommaso is called "in Villato." See Sella, *Rationes decimarum . . . Aprutium, Molisium,* nos. 163, 164, 235 (San Tommaso and San Pietro); Battelli, *Latium* (Sant'Ippolito).

29. Lugini, *Memorie storiche,* 159, said it then (1907) existed.

30. Rieti, Arch. Cap., II.C.1, h.

31. Rieti, Arch. Cap., II.C.1, p.

32. Rieti, Arch. Cap., II.C.2, r. See Sayers, *Papal Judges Delegate,* for the use of assessors (103–104) and for confessions (89–90, 237–238).

33. Rieti, Arch. Cap., II.C.1, p. Both Bazzano and Bominaco preserve major artistic treasures from the thirteenth century: for Santa Giusta, Bazzano see Matthiae, *Pittura medioevale abruzzese,* 28–29, 70, 77, plates 42, 43; for San Pellegrino, Bominaco (with references also to Santa Maria itself) see particularly, 31–44, but throughout, and plates IV–X, XII, 45–76.

34. Rieti, Arch. Cap., II.C.1, d. In 1328, San Pietro di Sinizzo had a provost: Sella, *Rationes decimarum . . . Aprutium, Molisium,* no. 1936 (in the diocese of Sulmona).

35. Rieti, Arch. Cap., II.C.1, e, x, y; see Sella, *Rationes decimarum . . . Aprutium, Molisium,* nos. 173, 174, 304, 310. This *cautionem* is pretty surely a surety,

but for the documents *cautiones*, see Sayers, *Papal Judges Delegate*, 58. For uncie and other currencies see below, chapter 8 note 4, and above, xx, xxi.

36. Rieti, Arch. Cap., II.C.1, x, y.

37. Rieti, Arch. Cap., II.C.1, z.

38. Rieti, Arch. Cap., II.C.1, l, g, i, s, b, m, a, and see II.D.6. See, too, for Pietro and the restoration of Terni, Pressutti, ed., *Regesta Honorii Papae III*, 1:171, no. 1004, 2:493, app. 2, no. 2208.

39. Rieti, Arch. Cap., IV.P.4; for papal chaplains in the period see Elze, "Die päpstliche Kapelle," particularly 147, 182–189.

40. Rieti, Arch. Cap., II.C.1, k. The wars in the Reatine for this period are covered with almost unbelievable smoothness, but with considerable conviction by Michaeli (*Memorie*, 3:5–106). His account is based largely on the chronicle of Riccardo da San Germano: Riccardo da San Germano, *Chronicon regni Siciliae*: for Bertuldo's withdrawal to Antrodoco in or after May 1231, 364; for the withdrawal of the imperial army from Antrodoco, still in 1231, 365; for the surrender of Antrodoco by Bertuldo to the imperial justiciar Enrico de Morro in July 1233, after Rainaldo duke of Spoleto, Bertuldo's brother, had been brought to Antrodoco to induce his brother to surrender, and for the withdrawal of the two brothers from the realm, 370; for the affairs that led to the brothers' alienation from Frederick II, 350, 357, 359, and particularly 364; finally, for the revolt of the lords of Popleto, the destruction of Popleto, and the siege of Capitignano by Duke Rainaldo and the imperial forces in 1228—an event which may have disturbed, or seemed to disturb, boundaries in the northeastern corner of the diocese, 350. For legal points at issue, in the Decretals of which Raymond of Penaforte was in the concluding phases of preparation when this part of this case occurred, see cap. 28, X.I.3 and cap. 2, X.II.8; the former of these which limits the distance to which a party may be summoned to two days beyond the boundaries of the diocese, and which is from canon 37 of the Fourth Lateran Council, could hardly be applicable here, since Terni is about 20 kilometers of relatively easy road from the border of the diocese of Rieti, fewer and certainly less arduous seeming kilometers than the way of the friar from Rieti to Greccio and back. Ironically, Rieti's claim to a fourth of tithes which would earlier have seemed reasonable enough, represents a position just then being overruled in the new law, see Boyd, *Tithes and Parishes*, 141–142.

41. Rieti, Arch. Cap., IV.P.4.

42. Rieti, Arch. Cap., II.C.1, f, v, h, t; IV.P.4.

43. Rieti, Arch. Cap., II.E.5. Counting precisely is difficult because of the indecisive endings of names.

44. Rieti, Arch. Cap., IV.P.6, 1–11 (which include copies and repetitions); VI.G.6; IV.G.3 (2 of its members).

45. *Boniface VIII*, no. 5325, and see Rome, Archivio di San Giovanni in Laterano, Q.5.A1 (indexed as containing this material); Lauer, *Le palais de Latran*, 557–558. The Lateran attachment followed an attempted reformation of Ferentillo by the Cistercian house at Fiastra for which see Brentano, *Two Churches*, 270–271 and Gentili, *L'abbazia di S.M. di Chiaravalle di Fiastra*, 100–103. In Tommaso's list (Paris, B.N. latin 1556) "S. Leopardus de Colle Fecato" is listed under "Mon de Florentill'" (fo. 25r) and not under Santo Stefano di Corvaro

(fo. 22v); under itself (fo. 23r) it is listed as owing a half procuration (and so rationalizing all the talk of its witnesses about *pranzo* or *cena*) and belonging to Ferentillo. In March 1574 a papal visitor found an abbot and six canons at San Giovanni Leopardi: Rieti, Arch. Vesc., Visitatio 1573–74 (for episcopal and related visitations at Rieti, see Di Flavio, "Le visite pastorali," particularly 232); and the later history of San Leopardo is surely properly made to seem less neat by the episcopal nephew and canon of Rieti, Hercules Pasquali, who in 1614 holds among his benefices a canonry at "S. Joannis Leopardi de Collefegato" (Di Flavio, *Sinodo reatino*, 59–60, 74). During the time I have been working at Rieti, the quite remarkable capitals of the supporting columns in the crypt at San Leopardo have disappeared, one of a continuing series of similar thefts in that part of Italy. Santa Croce is in Tommaso's list, by itself, immediately followed by San Massimo, which is preceded, as are independent churches, by an item/paragraph mark; San Massimo is followed by five other churches, of these churches two are identified as being in Lugnano (Paris, 1556, fo. 21v). The Hospitallers' list of churches does not include Santa Croce (fo. 25r). Neither is it included in the "Book" of all houses of the priorate of Rome in the 1330s (Bib. Apos. Vat., Vat. Lat., 10372—for which references I should like to thank Anthony Luttrell), although a section of the book is given to the "Status domorum sancti Baxilii de Reate, sancti Johannis de Ponte, et sancti Angeli de Vallibus" under the preceptor Enrico "de Murro," following fo. 22v. More conclusive is the fact that in September 1341 the canon of Rieti and subdeacon Berardo Secenari, was "abbas secularis" of the church of Santa Croce, Lugnano (Rieti, Arch. Cap., Liber Collationum "3", "1340–1343", list of electors, fos. 66v–67v); and also see the witnessing Abbot Giovanni at Rieti in August 1318 (Rieti, Arch. Cap., Lib. perg. di Matteo Barnabei, 129). For an introduction to the Hospitallers and their bibliography, see Luttrell, *The Hospitallers*, particularly valuable for the area near Rome is "Two Templar-Hospitaller Preceptories North of Tuscania"; see too Silvestrelli, "Le chiese e feudi" 174–176; Delaville Le Roulx, *Cartulaire général*; Brundage, "A Twelfth-Century Oxford Disputation." Santa Croce no longer exists; I have been shown a terrace of land beneath the town where, according to local tradition, Santa Croce was.

46. Both: Rieti, Arch. Cap., IV.G.3.

47. See particularly, Rieti, Arch. Cap., IV.P.6, 7, and for the bishops, chapter 5 below. All of the IV.P.6 documents are attestations.

48. Rieti, Arch. Cap., IV.P.6: 1, 2, 6 and 7, 9 and 10; for the destruction see, Michaeli, *Memorie*, 2:171.

49. Rieti, Arch. Cap., VI.G.6.

50. Particularly Rieti, Arch. Cap., IV.P.6, 3, 6, 7, 8.

51. Rieti, Arch. Cap., IV.P.6, 3, 6, 7, 11. (The books were two missals, two antiphonaries, a *flores evangelii*, a *collectaneum*, and a *Boccardum*.) San Giovenale is said by local historians then to have been in a part of Rieti close to San Basilio Rieti (and its tower), near what is now the corner of the Via Garibaldi and the Via Centuroni, to the northeast of that intersection in what became the garden of the family Blasetti. San Basilio Rieti, which is included in Bishop Tommaso's list (Paris, 1556, fos. 18r, 25r, and Rieti, Arch. Cap., III.B.1, 22), almost surely did not exist at the time of the action which the depositions rec-

ord—if it had, why would the food and treasure be stored elsewhere?—but the house of the Tedemarii may well have been near or on San Basilio's future site.

52. Rieti, Arch. Cap., IV.P.6, 1, 2, 4, 9, 10.

53. See particularly Rieti, Arch. Cap., IV.P.6, 1, but also 4, 6, 7, 9, 10. I am disinclined to give quick translations for the names of some imposts and think that the maintained original Latin names, as they are used in Rieti examples, will prove more helpful to readers than a conventional translation; my attitude has been encouraged by a thoughtful, defining passage in Trexler's powerful recent paper-essay, "Diocesan Synods," particularly 301–304.

54. Rieti, Arch. Cap., IV.P.6, 1.

55. Rieti, Arch. Cap., IV.P.6, 6, 7.

56. Rieti, Arch. Cap., IV.P.6, 6, 7; VI.G.6.

57. Rieti, Arch. Cap., IV.P.6, 10 (reference to what will become cap. 7, X.II.26 (as decretal of Alexander III)); the Rieti testimony makes repeated references to canon law: whether or not members of the cathedral clergy or their consultants were learned or trained in the law, they obviously thought that it was important to seem learned in and knowing of it.

58. Rieti, Arch. Cap., IV.N.1 (1381).

59. *Catalogus baronum*, nos. 1143, 1147. In the documents connected with the diocese of Rieti the reader is aware of repetition of person and group: a 1244 document in the Orsini archives in Rome at the Vallicelliana, Archivio storico capitolino, Archivio Orsini, II.A.I.26 (olim 25), is a papal letter of Innocent IV concerning a dispute between the Cistercians of San Matteo, Rieti, and the brothers of the Hospital of San Basilio, Rome, in which Giovanni Spata had been given as auditor and two monks from Tre Fontane had acted as witnesses at the papal chapel at the Lateran—members of a repertory cast seem reassembled.

60. D'Achille et al., eds., *La sabina*, 210; for a photograph see Verani, *La provincia*, 92.

61. Rieti, Arch. Cap., IV.P.6, 4.

62. I would suggest a now convenient and authoritative edition of the canons of the Fourth Lateran, which are of course widely available: García y García, ed., *Constitutiones concilii quarti Lateranensis, sicut olim* is on 53.

Chapter 4

1. Rieti, Arch. Cap., Lib. perg. di Matteo Barnabei, 2–4.

2. Paris, B.N. latin 1556, fo. 17v: Martène and Durand, eds., *Veterum scriptorum*, vol. 8 (hereafter Martène and Durand, 8), col. 1529. Our understanding of the nature of synods has been much enriched by Trexler's recent paper-essay "Diocesan Synods in Late Medieval Italy," see particularly, 298–300, 334.

3. Rieti, Arch. Cap., Lib. perg. di Matteo Barnabei, 122.

4. Paris, B.N. latin 1556, fo. 8v: Martène and Durand, 8, col. 1513—the editor in Martène and Durand silently corrects *pleno* to *plena*.

5. They are Paris, B.N. latin 1556, fos. 1r–17v (with fos. 11, 12 missing); Mar-

tène and Durand, 8, cols. 1494–1529, the missing fos. were already gone and are noted as missing, col. 1517.

6. Paris, B.N. latin 1556, fos. 5v, 8v, 9r, 17v: Martène and Durand, 8, cols. 1494, 1513, 1529. (It should be noted that the distortions of Reatine witnesses' names, "Tenibrale," "Capuano," are the editor's not the scribes: col. 1529, fo. 17v.)

7. Paris, B.N. latin 1556, fos. 7r–8r, 10r–10v, 5v–6r: Martène and Durand, 8, cols. 1509–1512, 1515–1517, 1505 (the Martène and Durand editor has, col. 1505, fo. 5v, changed *Blaxius* to *Blazius*).

8. Paris, B.N. latin 1556, fos. 6r, 4r, 1v: Martène and Durand, 8, cols. 1506, 1502, 1495 (in fact of course dating from reference to much earlier promulgations depends upon the sharpness of the reference).

9. Paris, B.N. latin 1556, fo. 15v: Martène and Durand, 8, col. 1524.

10. Paris, B.N. latin 1556, fos. 1r, 5r: Martène and Durand, 8, cols. 1494, 1504—the quotation is from the first reference.

11. See Brentano, "Vescovi e collocazione," 253–254 with nn.31–33, for exact references to Italian synods. See Cheney, *English Synodalia*, an exquisite description of synodal relations based on his own editorial work for which see the collection, Powicke and Cheney, eds., *Councils and Synods*: see in *English Synodalia* particularly "Introduction to the New Impression," (v–x), and for Durandus's important synodal instructions, see 40–41. The Italian edition most helpful here is, I think, Briacca, *Gli statuti sinodali novaresi*, for Papiniano's interests, methods, for influences on him and sources for him as well as for general structure, and for Durandus see his 73–78. (For Papiniano see also Herde, *Audientia litterarum contradictarum*, 171.) The Amalfi reference is to Caiazza, "Sinodi pre-tridentini," where Caiazza works delicately with extremely fragile and difficult materials. There is one very helpful edition with an English introduction and apparatus: Trexler, *Synodal Law*. The Rieti constitutions show close relations with constitutions from Ferrara, Perugia, Benevento, Aquileia, Fiesole, Padua, and Milan.

12. Paris, B.N. latin 1556, fo. 1r: Martène and Durand, 8, col. 1494.

13. Paris, B.N. latin 1556, fos. 4v, 9v: Martène and Durand, 8, cols. 1502, 1514; Fourth Lateran, canon 27, García y García, 72.

14. Paris, B.N. latin 1556, fo. 1r: Martène and Durand, 8, col. 1494.

15. Paris, B.N. latin 1556, fo. 3r: Martène and Durand, 8, col. 1498.

16. Paris, B.N. latin 1556, fo. 16r: Martène and Durand, 8, col. 1526.

17. Paris, B.N. latin 1556, fo. 13r: Martène and Durand, 8, cols. 1517–1518.

18. Paris, B.N. latin 1556, fos. 8v, 16v: Martène and Durand, 8, cols. 1512–1513, 1526.

19. Paris, B.N. latin 1556, fo. 14r: Martène and Durand, 8, col. 1521.

20. Paris, B.N. latin 1556, fos. 14v–15r: Martène and Durand, 8, col. 1522.

21. Paris, B.N. latin 1556, fos. 7r, 8r–8v, 7v: Martène and Durand, 8, cols. 1509, 1512, 1510.

22. Paris, B.N. latin 1556, fo. 16r: Martène and Durand, 8, col. 1525.

23. Paris, B.N. latin 1556, fo. 13v: Martène and Durand, 8, col. 1519; Cheney, *English Synodalia*, 52.

24. See particularly Paris, B.N. latin 1556, fos. 9r, 15v, 8r, 17r: Martène and Durand, 8, cols. 1513–1514, 1523–1524, 1511–1512, 1527–1528.

25. Paris, B.N. latin 1556, fos. 4v–5r, 17r: Martène and Durand, 8, cols. 1503, 1528.

26. Paris, B.N. latin 1556, fo. 14r: Martène and Durand, 8, col. 1520.

27. Unfortunately no visitation records seem to survive from fourteenth-century Rieti so that one cannot see, in the way that they could show us, the carrying of the message of the constitutions into the diocese's parishes, and the questioning there of the constitutions' application, although such evidence is available for the close and rather closely related diocese of Valva-Sulmona for 1356, and it certainly shows close attention being paid to some of the constitutions' preoccupations, like the decent care of the conserved Eucharist and basic teachable knowledge, in the clergy, of simple fundamentals of the faith: Celidonio, "Una visita pastorale": I should like to thank Vincenzo di Flavio for first having brought this visitation to my attention and Don Antonino Chiaverini for allowing me to sit in his house and read the manuscript record of the visitation which he had brought there for me. In it, see for example 172 (fo. 7r) Squintrono, which had an archpriest who (*domp'*) presumably was a priest, another priest (*domp'*) and a deacon, as well as two external "abbots" who held local churches; it was said that the archpriest did not know the articles of faith or the sacraments, nor it was said did the priest know them or the precepts of the law, and the deacon was ordered for an entire year to learn (*discat*) well and with understanding the divine office or lose his benefice. In Canzano 173 (fo. 8v) which had an archpriest and six (seeming) priests, one, Dompno Canzano, was said not to know how to explain the articles of faith and not completely to know the deadly sins; and it was said of Canzano, the place (Cansano), that the synodal constitutions were not published or proclaimed there once a month. The related evidence for regular preaching of instructional, or inspirational, sermons is sadly lacking in the diocese of Rieti (but see below, chapter 8); some preaching of sermons is visible; in the 1360s and 1370s on Saint Mark's day, 25 April, a friar preached a sermon, presumably particularly to the cathedral community, and the preacher's name or office was recorded by Canon Ballovino, when he was keeping books, on the fly-leaf of the year's book of accounts (which went from July to June), so for 1365 in Rieti, Arch. Cap., Lib. Int. et Exit., 1364: "Hoc anno predicauit in festo Sancti Marci Frater Nicolaus de Villa Conconate de ordine Heremitarum"; and similarly, for example, in 1369, the prior of San Domenico preached: Rieti, Arch. Cap., Lib. Int. et Exit., 1368 (unless, of course, in both years Ballovino is remembering the April sermon of that year as he begins preparing his first *quaternus* of the new year with its material for that year's July and August—in which case we have here the preachers for 1364 and 1368).

28. For Rainaldus: Rieti, Arch. Cap., II.B.1 and above chapter 1 note 102; Giovanni's act with the same archival identification, "warnings and sentences of excommunication" which attack subversion and disloyalty among the canons, was read by him before eleven of the canons, in his chamber in the episcopal palace on 8 January 1303 and written in the "protocol" of the notary, Nicola "de Palatio," then notary of the bishop; it was extended by Giovanni di Pietro, episcopal notary and scribe, at the bishop's order, 17 January 1306. (The notary

Nicola's name is more fully extended, Nicola di Pietro de Palatio, citizen of Rieti, notary by imperial authority, in a 1297 document: II.E.2.) For Bishop Giovanni's constitution restraining chapter members: Rieti, Arch. Cap., IV.F.4.

29. Paravicini Bagliani, *Cardinali di curia*, 300 (Paravicini modifies this description of his list of families with "di quell'epoca"); Lombardo, "Nobili, mercanti e popolo minuto," see particularly 300, but also 292 (for families not like the Orsini and Colonna but "che già da tempo avevano accumulato ingenti fortune") and 298.

30. Amayden, *La storia delle famiglie romane*, 2:128–130, where it is firmly stated of Giovanni (128 n.1) "Era figlio del Nicolo," and where there is talk of the *stemma* and of the crowning of Petrarch. For Nicola's tomb effigy at Santi Apostoli and other useful notes, see Garms, Juffinger, and Ward-Perkins, eds., *Die mittelalterlichen Grabmäler*, 1:72–73, and plate 35. See too Oliger, "Due musaici," 244. The property and business sewn through Rome is also sewn through the records of Rome's late fourteenth-century notaries, as Anna Maria Lombardo, who had charge of and was working with their documents at the A.S. in Rome, graciously informed and showed me particularly in the protocols of Francesco Stephani de Capudgalis nos. 475–477, so 475 fos. 60r–60v, 341r–341v, 343v–344r, 359r–360r, 362r–363r, 367r, 368r–369r, 453r–453v; 476, fos. 38v, 69r, 325r–325v, 327r–327v; 477, fos. 34v–35v, 37r, 38v, 39v, 48r, 127v–129v, 318r–320v, 358v–361v—and this is only a short and random (except for examples pointed out by Dr. Lombardo) selection. For the area of Ferentino, see for example, A.S.V., Fondo Celestini, 7, for a raft of Papazurri and Muti neighbors—the connection of Muti and Papazurri is suggested for example in Amayden-Bertini; Muti seems not to have been used normally by Giovanni. For the connection with Bridget, see for example Collijn, ed., *Acta et processus canonizacionis beate Birgitte*, particularly 436–447, 442; I am very grateful to Mary Ann Rossi, who has worked with Bridget, for her suggestions and citations in this regard and for her notes on Francesca Papazurri's donation of her house to Bridget in January 1383. For reference to the *regio Pappazuris* in Rome, see Hubert, *Espace urbain et habitat à Rome*, 291.

31. *Boniface VIII*, nos. 926, 2164, 2221, 2498, 3465, 4729. For papal chaplains again see Elze, "Die päpstliche Kapelle."

32. Rieti, Arch. Cap., II.B.2, VI.G.11, IV.G.8 (one member), III.C.4, IV.F.4, IV.K.13, IV.G.7, IV.G.8 (another member), IV.Q.3. Giovanni's predecessors, Pietro, Andrea, Nicola, and Berardo, in preserved letter forms, had used "permissione diuina," "dei gratia," and "miseratione diuina": Rieti, Arch. Cap., II.E.3, VIII.B.9, II.E.6, VII.F.3, IV.G.4, VII.F.5; Rieti, A.S., San Domenico, 8.

33. *Boniface VIII*, no. 5038.

34. My friend Don Giorgio Fedalto has found no traces of Giovanni in or from Olema; and I have found nothing in a search at Ìmola, where I was aided by Canon Pietro Bedeschi, the capitular archivist, whom I would like to thank, and also to thank Dottoressa Rosaria Campioni of the Archivio storico comunale for her advice.

35. Rieti, Arch. Cap., Lib. perg. di Matteo Barnabei, 95, 129 (for the Papazurri *stemma*); see 205 for an example of the miter alone. In introducing the codicil of canon Giacomo (or Jacopo) de Labro, for October 1319, Matteo also

uses a *stemma*, presumably that of the Labro; this suggests that the idea of *stemma* may have been in Matteo's mind when he was thinking of family chapels.

36. Papazurri, Muti, and men of the city (Rome) are very noticeable around Giovanni. Giovanni's nephew, Francesco, who was made a canon of Rieti, is the most visible, particularly in the parchment book of Matteo Barnabei, but see him as clerk of the church of San Pietro in Campo on 1 December 1313, where he is called in a letter from Bishop Giovanni, written in the third person, "Francisco de Papazurris de Urbe, nepoti suo," and where one of the witnesses is "Petro Herami de Urbe, domicello nostro": Rieti, Arch. Cap., VII.G.3. On two days in May 1306 two different sons of Pietro Muti de Urbe act as witnesses, and with one of them a man named Pietro di Nicola Egidii de Urbe: VI.G.10. Two other men, Papazurri of the city, are Giovanni di don Bartolomeo and Paolo Nicolutii: VII.G.4, III.B.4; see too VI.G.11. On 7 July 1326 when Bishop Giovanni was staying at Montereale, and living in the house of the notary Nicola Petroni, his witnesses included both Paolo Nicolutii de Pappazur' and a man identified as Lucio di Nicola Phylippi de Urbe; and in 1316 Paolo had been specifically identified as Giovanni's nephew: Lib. perg. di Matteo Barnabei, 205, 52–53.

37. Borgo San Pietro, Archivio del Monastero di Santa Filippa Mareri, nos. 34, 22: Chiappini, "Santa Filippa Mareri," 110 no. 34, 104–105 no. 22. For the episcopal progressions see above chapter 3.

38. For Tommaso see Rieti, Arch. Cap., II.D.1–10; III.D.3, 10; IV.D.4, 5; IV.H.4; IV.O.1, 4. For Salimbene's Rainaldo see above chapter 1.

39. Rieti, Arch. Cap., VII.G.1; for the roughly contemporary Madonna of Torano (now in Rieti) see Mortari, "Rieti," 142 and plate 175.

40. Rieti, Arch. Cap., Lib. perg. di Matteo Barnabei, 181; IV.G.7.

41. Rieti, Arch. Cap., Lib. perg. di Matteo Barnabei, 205; II.G.4.

42. Rieti, Arch. Cap., Lib. perg. di Matteo Barnabei, 345.

43. See the not very full coverage in Michaeli, *Memorie*, 3:62–84; see Bowsky, *Henry VII in Italy*, 159–177.

44. Rieti, Arch. Cap., Lib. perg. di Matteo Barnabei, 415; III.C.4.

45. Rieti, Arch. Cap., III.B.1; IV.G.8.

46. Rieti, Arch. Cap., Lib. perg. di Matteo Barnabei, 415, 454.

47. See the discussion of Giovanni and chapels, tribune, and burial below, chapter 8. For Giovanni in the diocese of Rieti outside of Matteo's book, see for example, Rieti, Arch. Cap., III.B.1, 4; III.D.5; IV.C.8; IV.F.4; IV.G.1, 3, 4, 5, 7, 8, 11; IV.K.13; IV.N.3 "1"; VI.G.11, 14; VII.G.1, 3, 4, 5.

48. For a suggestion of conventionality compare Giovanni's wording with that of Giacomo de Labro: Rieti, Arch. Cap., Lib. perg. di Matteo Barnabei, 133, 149—and consider the importance of the notary's mouth, mind, pen, and formulary.

49. Paris, B.N. latin 1556, fo. 10r: Martène and Durand, 8, col. 1515. For Santa Caterina, Van Heteren, "Due monasteri," particularly 67.

50. Rieti, Arch. Cap., III.B.8—and see "Liber contractuum et collationum" (hereafter Lib. con. et col.), I, fos. 40r, 43v, 79r, 133r (where Saverio appears as a witness in Matteo's documents in 1341 and 1342); Lib. perg. di Matteo Barnabei, 341.

51. Rieti, Arch. Cap., "Liber processuum causarum ciuilium, sede vacante, 1346–1347" (hereafter Lib. proc. civ.), fo. 26r (actually for 8 January 1348), and see the very end of Lib. perg., which grows quite illegible, but which goes through 27 January 1348, and also see VI.G.16 from 27 January 1349 when another notary, Mannus Angeli de Cornibus, imperial authority and Reatine citizen, redacts by mandate of the bishop and perhaps suggests that Matteo is dead (1348 is of course, in Rieti, an obvious death date); VI.B.4 (1308); IV.I.5 (1314); IV.M.6 (1315).

52. Rieti, Arch. Cap., Lib. perg. di Matteo Barnabei, 396–397 (*feudum*, in Villagralli etc.) granted in house of Berardo Secinari; citizen comes from its repetition in his subscript.

53. Rieti, Arch. Cap., II.D.6, 7, 9, 10; III.B.3, 6; IV.Q.3 "15," 6 "3."

54. See, for example, Rieti, Arch. Cap., II.D.2, 3, 4, 5; III.D.2.

55. Rieti, Arch. Cap., IV.Q.3 "14"; IV.D.1; IV.G.3 (1 of 6).

56. Rieti, Arch. Cap., IV.G.3 (1 of 6).

57. Rieti, Arch. Cap., II.C.4.

58. See, for example, Rieti, Arch. Cap., IV.G.3 (another of 6); IV.G.5.

59. Rieti, Arch. Cap., VI.A.3; but it should be noted that a 25 July 1233 document of Bishop Rainaldo de Labro, a bishop who repeatedly surprises, lists among its witnesses, in the genitive, "Alibrandi notarii episcopi": IV.G.3; and see below chapter 5 note 22.

60. See above chapter 1.

61. Rieti, Arch. Cap., III.D.10; II.D.10.

62. Rieti, Arch. Cap., IV.F.4.

63. Rieti, Arch. Cap., IV.F.4.

64. See above chapter 1 note 112. At least one original notarial license and record of investiture does survive at Rieti: Arch. Cap., Lib. Int. et Exit., 1368, binding, license 3 February 1312, from Albert de Allyate count palatine to Ypolito quondam Thome de Quarto Aymonis, investiture through *pennam, calamanum et cartam*; see Cheney, *Notaries Public*, 83 and n.1, 156–158, for the Allyate (Alliate) counts palatine and further references, and for Alberto as Albertino witnessing his father's grant (158); for a Rieti copy of a papal license for P. Stabile in 1207 see Rieti, Arch. Cap., VII.A.1; and for Pietro Stabile's work, in 1216 where he is called *scriniarius sacre romane ecclesie*, IV.O.5.

65. See Brentano, "Localism and Longevity," 300–301. Giovanni could have been related to the Tommaso Tedemarii who is recorded as selling for seven lire property in the borgo in 1217, or to Bartolomeo Tedemarii who is listed as a neighbor in the Porta Carceraria in 1226: Rieti, A.S., San Domenico, 7 (olim 92)—date on document is 1218 because it was written on 28 December after the beginning of the new year; Arch. Cap., II.C.4. But the status of the name in these cases is insecure as it is in the Inquest 1231, see above chapter 1 note 60.

66. Rieti, Arch. Cap., Lib. perg. di Matteo Barnabei, 419.

67. Rieti, Arch. Cap., IX.F.5 (1 of 19).

68. Rieti, Arch. Cap., VII.F.5.

69. Rieti, Arch. Cap., VII.F.3.

70. Rieti, Arch. Cap., II.E.6; VII.E.5; II.B.2; II.C.4; IV.F.4; Rome, A.S., Sant'Agostino di Terni, 5.

71. Rieti, A.S., San Domenico, 5 (olim 2); Rieti, Arch. Cap., VII.F.4. For two witnessing notarial prebendaries Mathiucio Pandulphoni and Berardo Mathei, IV.F.4 (1313), see too IV.G.8.

72. Rieti, Arch. Cap., III.B.1.

73. Rieti, Arch. Cap., IV.G.4 (two members). At this time the approximate normal nucleus of a canon's prebend seems to have been 30 giunte.

74. See for example Rieti, Arch. Cap., VII.B.4 (a beautiful little 1290 letter of Matthew of Aquasparta, cardinal priest of San Lorenzo in Damaso, red pointed oval (*vesica*) seal on green string); VII.C.6 (1314 letter from abbot of Citeaux with white/brown seal on strip) and IV.G.6 (transcription of letter of abbot of San Pastore, 1251, seal described); III.D.10 (1266 exact description of seal of archdeacon of Siena); for the abbot of Bominaco see above chapter 3 and for the bishop of Narni chapter 1.

75. Rieti, Arch. Cap., II.B.1 (Rainaldo da Arezzo, white wax, pointed oval, 5.2 × 3.2 cm, remnant of legend EATINI EPI RAINAL over and around bishop in pontificals standing; on tag 32 cm wide, 5.2 cm long); II.D.8 (Tommaso, seal lost; 1 cm fold carries seal tag, .4 cm wide); III.C.3 (chapter, pinkish white wax which seems to have left reddish stain, pointed oval-broken, ca. 5 × 3 cm, legend SIGILLUM CAPI / TULI REATINI in two parts on seal's face around a seated Virgin in gothic draperies holding a Child on her left arm and what would appear to be a lily or liliated scepter in her right hand; style of lettering and, with less sureness, image of Virgin suggest that the matrix cannot have been very old in 1280); III.C.3 (Pietro, actually acting as collector, seal described as green); VII.F.5 (Berardo, seal missing, flap, 3 cm, and slots .5 cm); IV.G.7 (Giovanni, description: red wax, image of bishop with crozier and legend: sigillum d. Johis dei gra Epi Reatin'); II.D.10 (Biagio). Rieti, A.S., San Domenico, 8 (olim 47) (Nicola, strip now torn away).

76. Rieti, Arch. Cap., Lib. perg. di Matteo Barnabei, 1.

77. Rieti, Arch. Cap., III.B.1, fo. 2v (the common seal).

78. For some of Matteo's work: Rieti, Arch. Cap., III.B.3, 5, 6, 7; IV.H.4; IV.I.2, 3, 7; IV.K.13; IV.Q.3, 10; VI.B.4; VI.D.5.

79. See Rieti, Arch. Cap., Lib. perg. di Matteo Barnabei, 399, for a reference in 1337 to "sol. provis.," money of the Roman senate, as "olim usualis monete."

80. Rieti, Arch. Cap., Lib. con. et col., I, to 1343 has five paper gatherings, and 261 numbered folios, but begins with fo. 2; Lib. con. et col., II, three gatherings and 308 pages; Lib. proc. civ., five thick gatherings which are not numbered, first has 52 fos.; "Liber processuum maleficiorum, sede vacante, 1346–1346" (hereafter Lib. proc. malef.), three large irregular gatherings of ca. 55, 23, and 58 fos. For Sulmona watermarks see Mattiocco, *Struttura urbana*, 131 fig. 11; for the 1334 note see Lib. perg., 333.

81. Rieti, Arch. Cap., Lib. con. et col., I, fos. 18v–19r.

82. Rieti, Arch. Cap., Lib. con. et col., I. fo. 113r.

83. Rieti, Arch. Cap., Lib. con. et col., I, fos. 116v–117.

84. Rieti, Arch. Cap., Lib. con. et col., I, fos. 132v–133v (and see for regulation of absences for study, fos. 47v–48r).

85. Rieti, Arch. Cap., Lib. proc. civ., first gathering, fos. 1r, 8v.

86. Rieti, Arch. Cap., Lib. proc. civ., first gathering, fo. 9v.

87. Rieti, Arch. Cap., Lib. proc. civ., first gathering, fos. 10r, 14r.

88. Rieti, Arch. Cap., Lib. proc. civ., first gathering, fos. 16r–20v, 25r–26r. The final date seems unlikely but the sequence of indiction dates seems to make it inescapable.

89. Rieti, Arch. Cap., Lib. proc. civ., first gathering, fo. 21v.

90. Rieti, Arch. Cap., Lib. proc. civ., first gathering, fos. 27r, 32r, 34r, 38r, 41r, 47r.

91. Rieti, Arch. Cap., Lib. proc. civ., second gathering, fo. 48r.

92. Rieti, Arch. Cap., Lib. proc. civ., third gathering, fo. 3v.

93. Rieti, Arch. Cap., Lib. proc. civ., third gathering, fo. 7v.

94. Rieti, Arch. Cap., Lib. proc. civ., third gathering, between fos. 28 and 29, but of course it is mobile.

95. Rieti, Arch. Cap., Lib. proc. civ., second gathering, fos. 1r–3r.

96. Rieti, Arch. Cap., Lib. proc. civ., third gathering, fo. 48r.

97. Rieti, Arch. Cap., Lib. proc. malef., first gathering, fos. 2r–5r.

98. Rieti, Arch. Cap., Lib. proc. malef., first gathering, fo. 18r.

99. Rieti, Arch. Cap., Lib. proc. malef., first gathering, fo. 20r.

100. Rieti, Arch. Cap., Lib. proc. malef., first gathering, fos. 29r–32r.

101. Rieti, Arch. Cap., Lib. proc. malef., first gathering, fos. 33r–34v.

102. Rieti, Arch. Cap., "1212," fo. vii r (13), the manuscript has an old (roman numeral) foliation and a more modern arabic pagination.

103. Rieti, Arch. Cap., "1212," fo. i r (1).

104. Rieti, Arch. Cap., "1212," fos. v r–vi r (13–15). These activities should probably be seen against, after, the compilation of the Liber Censuum of the church of Rome, two decades before Berardo's work, by Cencius (later Honorius III), which is described in Morris, *The Papal Monarchy*, 214–217, in a way that suggests connection; see, too, 534. For the Porta Cintia holding see 49 of "1212."

105. Rieti, Arch. Cap., Libro VI, fo. 20r.

106. Rieti, Arch. Cap., "Cartolario di Silvestro di don Giovanni" (hereafter Cart. Silv.; the book is called by a much later hand "Liber III," but that is a name repeatedly given to books in the archivio, and it no longer seems to me a helpful designation).

107. Rieti, Arch. Cap., VII.G.12; VI.G.17; VII.D.3.

108. Rieti, Arch. Cap., VII.G.15.

109. Rieti, Arch. Cap., Lib. Int. et Exit., 1382.

110. Rieti, Arch. Cap., IV.C.11; Lib. IV fos. 25–37v; Lib. "6", fos. 5r–6r; Lib. perg. di Matteo Barnabei, particularly from 282 on, specifically 399; Lib. con. et col., I, for example, fos. 82v–83r; VII.G.14 (the 2 December 1348 document, in which the recorded action gives a quick sense of the effect of the Death upon administrative procedure); Cart. Silv., for example, 98–99. Bib. Apos. Vat., Vat. Lat., 4029, fo. 11r.

111. The nature of Ballovino's work, as well as, less thoroughly, Silvestro's, will be made clear in chapters below, which deal with cathedral chapter and prebendaries and with the sort of piety observable in recorded wills and donations.

112. In a paper "Vescovi e vicari generali," 547–567, which I gave to a con-

ference of church historians at Brescia, I tried to explain (and from audience reaction I think pretty clearly failed) my belief in the potential importance of vicars general not only to the development of diocesan government but also to the freeing of bishops to be what they would and could be, not only lazy and greedy absentees, but personal bishops of the sort who had existed before the revolution in bureaucratic government, and even, optimally, to form a new breed of, admittedly rather tame, "holy men." The idea had been particularly thrust upon me by my constant reading of and teaching of *The Book of Margery Kempe*, in which, for me, one of the great surprises is the freedom of bishops and archbishops to speak with Margery and also their serious interest in her religious experience (at least as she describes that interest); by inference, at least, Margery suggested to me that that freedom and interest had been made possible by the presence at the bishops' courts of professional clerks who dealt with the tedious tangles of administration—clerks like Philip Repingdon's functionary in a fur hat, who helped Margery but whom she later failed to recognize.

113. Rieti, Arch. Cap., II.D.9.

114. I have tried to give a quick summary, or at least suggestion, of the Italian development, with some comparative reference to English development, in "Vescovi e vicari generali" and its notes. Historians of English royal government between the reigns of Henry III and Edward III will I think notice an interesting correspondence between the development of specifically designated officials in the great kingdom and this little diocese.

115. It should be remembered, however, that Giovanni di Pietro first appears, in 1265, as episcopal notary for Gottifredo, see above note 59, and that there is, at Mareri-Borgo San Pietro, a reference to the canon Angelo Mathei's acting as the bishop's (Gottifredo's) vicar in 1269; Borgo San Pietro, Archivio di Monastero di Santa Filippa Mareri, no. 31.

116. Both of these bishops are treated at some length, below, in chapter 5. Their careers and connections are examined; and, in fact, Pietro is intended to be one of the chapter's central figures.

117. Rieti, Arch. Cap., II.E.5; III.B.1, fos. 4v–5r.

118. Rieti, Arch. Cap., IV.O.5.

119. Rieti, Arch. Cap., IV.O.5.

120. Rieti, Arch. Cap., Lib. perg. di Matteo Barnabei, 165, 168, 169, 171, 172, 173, 174, 175, 176, 177, 178, 179, 181, 205 (for *vicarii generales*, 173, 174); IV.G.5. (Matteo is back in January and February 1330 [Lib. perg., 378–381]; at this point he is called archpriest of San Sebastiano in Poggio Fidoni.)

121. Rieti, Arch. Cap., Lib. perg. di Matteo Barnabei, 189–305, 306–307 (change in November 1332), 308–348, 391–408, 411 and 413 (change in March/May 1338), 415–446 (see also 472–473); III.B.7; IV.G.8; IV.N.3. In the period between his becoming vicar general on or by 25 June 1325 and 28 September 1334, Matteo Barnabei's last entry recording his presence as vicar general (he went on being present) in this tour of duty, there are well over 50 references to his presence and action in Matteo's book; see too the continuous accounts of Lib. proc. civ. and Lib. proc. malef. for his work for the chapter during the second of the two vacancies.

122. Bib. Apos. Vat., Vat. Lat. 4029, particularly fo. 44r.

123. For Andrea: Rieti, Arch. Cap., Lib. perg. di Matteo Barnabei, 348–377, multiple entries; Matteo's unsure spelling of Andrea's identifying name suggests to me that he was not sure exactly how to spell or pronounce it—unlikely as that may seem.

124. Rieti, Arch. Cap., Lib. con. et col., I, 15v, 33v–34r; he had been in *camera sua* in the house of the heirs of Andrea da Apoleggia.

125. Rieti, Arch. Cap., Lib. perg. di Matteo Barnabei, 6, 8, 22; IV.M.6.

126. Rieti, Arch. Cap., Lib. perg. di Matteo Barnabei, 157; Lib. con. et col., I., fo. 58r (Nicola); Lib. proc. civ., third gathering, fo. 7v, fifth gathering (Pietro). Bib. Apos. Vat., Vat. Lat. 4029, for example, fos. 38r, 44r: in order to ensure publicity and authority for his acts denouncing Reatine resistance the inquisitor acted with and through an impressively substantial group of resident and active archpriests and priests of the diocese of Rieti in the *terra* of Leonessa, fos. 38r–41v. The inquisitorial record establishes the existence of a community of clergy in Reatine Leonessa. There are other interesting examples of, roughly contemporary, geographically divided dioceses and local vicars general and vicars in other parts of Italy: a local vicar at Gualdo Tadino in the diocese of Nocera Umbra in 1326 (Brentano, "Death in Gualdo Tadino," 93); a locally elected vicar at Corneto-Tarquinia within the diocese of Viterbo (Petrucci, "Pievi e parrocchie," 2:947–948).

127. Rieti, Arch. Cap., Lib. perg. di Matteo Barnabei, 446 (Giacomo di don Tommaso, canon); 534–535 (Francesco di Giovanni Bussata: see also Lib. con. et col., I, fos. 75r–76r, an example of his nickname, here, in October 1341, he is a canon of Sant'Eleuterio and a prebendary of the cathedral church; and Lib. proc. civ., second gathering, fos. 3r, 48r; he is archpriest of San Sebastiano of Poggio Fidoni; for the condemnation of his father as a protector of heretics, see Bib. Apos. Vat., Vat. Lat. 4029, fo. 28r); Lib. con. et col., I, fos. 58r, 79r (Nicola), 135v–136r (Francesco Ofagnano), 167r–169v, 172r (Guillelmus). For an extreme case of multiple vicars general, see Sambin, "La 'famiglia' di un vescovo," 241: twenty-one known vicars, three or four or even five at a time.

128. Rieti, Arch. Cap., Lib. perg. di Matteo Barnabei, 189–348. There is a relatively small group of clerks, prebendaries, and one canon continually at work for the church in these years: Giovanni Ratigoni, Petraga Ambrosicti, Gentile de Puntigliano, the canon Corrado de Murro.

129. Rieti, Arch. Cap., Lib. perg. di Matteo Barnabei, 449.

130. Rieti, Arch. Cap., Lib. con. et col., I, 58r–58v.

131. Rieti, Arch. Cap., VII.G.11; II.G.9.

132. For October 1293, see above note 73.

133. Rieti, Arch. Cap., Lib. proc. civ., fourth gathering, fo. 2r.

134. I must apologize to Victoria Morse for the twice repeated use of proto-portolan in talking of Bishop Tommaso the Corrector's verbal map; she will no doubt find it disturbingly inexact. But it is her fascinating discussion of Opecino de Canistris and of portolans in relation to his work that has brought them to my mind, given me what understanding of them I have, and made it impossible for me not to think of them.

135. I have borrowed the phrase from Cornelisen's recent book, *Where It All Began: Italy* 1954, 168: "and our requests for direction as we sidled by, did not

stir any recollection valid for more than a kilometer." The extended passage, it
seems to me, gives an unusually sharp sense of the difficulty of geography without maps particularly in certain sorts of terrain and human settlement. Cornelisen's Abruzzo is not in time, of course, or place that of this book, but it is
relatively close, in place, and helpful through time.

136. The quotation is from Friedman, *Florentine New Towns*, 208. The book
is broader in many ways, including in its discussion of geometry, than its major,
first, title might suggest, and it even touches Cittaducale. Readers of my notes
will know that I have found it very involving. The question of chronology of
change is always a difficult one, and although my first object here has been to
make my reader see my point, against which I will in a way argue later, I do not
want to oversimplify, or to avoid making the reader know that I know that all
historians tend to see the really crucial period of change in almost anything
exactly in the middle of the period on which they are at the time concentrating.
I would suggest as a useful antidote an essay which happens also to be, partly
because I always find its author a particularly powerfully stimulating historian,
one of the things that first made me think, insofar as I have, seriously about
boundary: Sambin, *L'ordinamento parrocchiale di Padova*. Sambin shows a mapping and defining of parish boundary in Padua in the late twelfth and early
thirteenth centuries certainly as exact and sophisticated as Francesco's work in
Poggio Fidoni in 1346. Bowsky's inclusion of and discussion of Talamone and
its 1306 map in *The Finance of the Commune of Siena*, 24–25, 17, and plate 2,
also proved for me very provocative in trying to make myself think about how
thirteenth- and fourteenth-century Reatines viewed the place in which they were
acting. Now, see also Scoppola, "La rocca di Talamone."

Chapter 5

1. The quotation is from Benson, *The Bishop-Elect*, 3. For a recent, very helpful and sensible description of the bishop's position in the Western church, see
Morris, *The Papal Monarchy*, 219–226, 527–535.

2. I would suggest that the reader approach the canon law in connection
with this subject, see what sort of substance it has, through two works which
would seem to come at the actual definition of bishop tangentially: Benson's
Bishop-Elect, and Tierney, *Foundations of the Conciliar Theory*. I myself was introduced to the problem through the unpublished manuscript of Gerard Caspary, "The King and the Two Laws: A Study of the Influence of Roman and
Canon Law on the Development of Ideas on Kingship in Fourteenth-Century
England," which made clear to me as it would to any reader the deep interest
and importance of academic, theoretical discussions by canonists of relations of
bishop, chapter, and clergy to each other and to their dioceses. Caspary's manuscript not only revealed the intense interest of the subject but also at the same
time revealed the kind of mind necessary to make that interest apparent—one
like his, not like mine. The reader of this book will notice immediately that it
deals with practice in the diocese, not with academic or legal thought about the

diocese. This is a statement of fact, but also an apology from a student who, like Benson, Tierney, and Caspary, has had the advantage of the generously shared wisdom and knowledge, the teaching in the best sense, of the dean of American medievalists in our time, Stephan Kuttner. Although I seem to use so little what he has taught me, I trust that he will accept my thanks; I know that he will generously act as if he finds interesting canons and crayfish.

3. In order to make the reader accept and think about the dappled quality of these men, I have drawn on big and seemingly distant guns, besides Issa, Austen, Hopkins, and would here draw on Woolf's Dalloway: one cannot say "that they were this or that." The most remarkable revelation that I know of seeming contradiction in a bishop is Cheney's treatment of Hubert Walter in *From Becket to Langton*, 32–41, of which I have written earlier (*Two Churches*, 220–221 and n. 106). Recent work has been particularly effective in revealing the complexity of fourteenth-century English bishops, see particularly: Haines, *The Church and Politics in Fourteenth-Century England*, especially 199–207; Wright, *The Church and the English Crown*, especially 243–274. Compare my "unturned" Bishop Pietro da Ferentino in *Two Churches*, 183.

4. For Biagio's compromise with the commune: Rieti, A.S., Statuti, I, part III, fos. 125r–125v. For the synodal constitutions see above chapter 4; the pertinent constitution, *Licet ad compescendum*: Paris, B.N. latin 1556, fos. 5v–6r: Martène and Durand, 8, cols. 1505–1506. The vicar general's statement: Rieti, Arch. Cap., Lib. proc. malef., first gathering, fo. 11v. San Benedetto Liber IV, fos. 41v–42r, and see below note 92.

5. See for example Rieti, Arch. Cap., VII.G.15 (14 July 1349: *Dat' et act' Goness' in palatio nostro*); Cart. Silv., 297; a more exact location (*ad siluam planam*) is given in a 10 August 1349 letter copied in Paris, B.N. latin 1556, fo. 33r. VI.M.2 includes a number of Berardo Sprangone documents for Adenolfo's electus/episcopus years, some of which would seem to question this dating (for example, IV.M.2 "1183" and "23 July 1197"), but Berardo's nicely written documents are surprisingly careless of dating, which is sometimes corrected and sometimes (as in the examples cited) offers conflicting incarnation and indiction dates.

6. Rieti, Arch. Cap., II.G.4 (Clement VI letter).

7. Rieti, Arch. Cap., IV.K.10 (March 1188, *electus*); IV.M.2 "1188"; IV.K.9 (1185, Benedetto still bishop).

8. Rieti, Arch. Cap., IV.Q.3 (12 August 1194, *electus*); IV.M.2 "1194" (9 November 1194, *electus*); IV.Q.4 (4 February 1195, no *electus*).

9. Rieti, Arch. Cap., IV.Q.1; IV.M.1; IV.B.2; IV.Q.3; IV.Q.4; IV.M.2; Parchment Book IV for 1212. For San Salvatore Maggiore (IV.P.1) see chapter 3, above, and note 11 below.

10. Rieti, Arch. Cap., IV.P.3, although the testimony in this the San Leopardo case in general argues for the clear distinction between *episcopus* and *electus* and the careful observation of the limited sacramental powers of the elect (particularly here by the archpriest of Corvaro). For a clear and extended discussion of contemporary canonists' opinions of the powers of an *electus*, see Benson, *The Bishop-Elect*.

11. For Abbot Giovanni (Arch. Cap., IV.P.6), see above chapter 3 note 56,

and for family and Rainaldo, notes 56 to 63, and for Tommaso (Arch. Cap., IV.P.1) see chapter 3 note 22 and see *Two Churches*, 109–114. For the Norman barons, see *Catalogus baronum*, 227–230, nos. 1143–1152. For a discussion of the family, see Sacchetti Sassetti, "Rieti e gli Urslingen," 2–3; Ughelli, *Italia sacra*, vol. 1, col. 1201, who had access to some Adenolfo material, some at least at Tre Fontane, called Adenolfo "de Secenariis, nobilis Reatinus," but I have found no evidence that would make this seem a proper identification; an 1188 document within the group of Rieti, Arch. Cap., IV.M.2, calls the elect (in the dative) "Domino Adinulfo de la varite." See Rieti, Arch. Cap., VI.G.9 for the *tenementum* of Lavareta in 1192. A witness, Rainaldo Pinzon', in the San Leopardo case (Arch. Cap., IV.P.3), see above chapters 1 and 3, talks of an *electum de Fortisbrachia*, after Benedetto. For a 1213 dispute between the chapter and Dominus Fortib' see Arch. Cap., IV.Q.8. Fortisbrachia is a name particularly connected with the Brancaleone of Romagnia, a very potent family when it is observable within the diocese, but it is not clear in what way it would be connected with Adenolfo. Rainaldo Pinzon's evidence thus may suggest another *electus* after Benedetto, but before Adenolfo.

12. Ughelli, *Italia sacra*, vol. 1, col. 1201, says "Hic cum Episcopatum abdicasset, factus est Monachus Cisterciensis in monasterium Trium Fontium de Vrbe, ut in monumentis eiusdem Coenobii habetur"; because of Ughelli's own position at Tre Fontane, it seemed to me that he might well be right about this, and in fact his statement is confirmed by a contemporary reference in a Rieti document (Arch. Cap., IV.P.6 (7)), in which a witness in the Santa Croce Lugnano case, the ex-abbot Giovanni by then a brother of San Basilio, speaks of the former bishop of Rieti "iam factus erat monachus apud Sanctum Anastasium." For recent work on Tre Fontane, with excellent pictures of its late thirteenth-century painting, see Mihályi, "I Cistercensi a Roma."

13. Rieti, Arch. Cap., II.D.1; *Innocent IV*, no. 5614. For Tommaso see also Herde, *Beiträge*, 23, 24–25. For a neat recent description of canon law and the theory of provisions, see Wright, *The Church and the English Crown*, particularly 5–14. For the manner of electing bishops and for the sort of bishops who were desired and selected in the early thirteenth century, two works of Cheney are particularly helpful, although he is, of course, primarily concerned with English bishops: *From Becket to Langton* (above, note 1), particularly ch. 2, and within it particularly 20–21; and *Innocent III and England*, particularly ch. 4, 121–178. The best general introduction to episcopal election is probably still Barraclough, "The Making of a Bishop"; Benson's *Bishop-Elect* offers a very full and extended gloss on election and a rich supporting bibliography. For Italy see particularly Giusti, "Le elezioni dei vescovi"; Vasina, "L'elezione degli arcivescovi"; *Two Churches*, 213–218; and particularly Rigon, "Le elezioni vescovili."

14. For Rainaldo da Arezzo's behavior see chapter 1, above.

15. For Nicola see Rieti, Arch. Cap., IV.C.4, in which the witnesses in the bishop's camera at Rieti include the abbot and two monks of San Pastore (on 26 November 1294). Another Nicola document from 24 December 1295 is preserved in the A.S. at Rieti (Fondo San Domenico, no. 8, old 47); it is a letter of indulgence (40 days) "omnibus uere penitentibus et confessis qui deuote accesserint et beneficerint siue pro opere loci ecclesie Sancti Dominici de Reate

siue pro opere hedeficiorum conuentus siue pro necessitatibus quibuscumque fratrum loci eiusdem"; it is a formal open letter formerly sealed, dated on the vigil of Christmas, with incarnation, indiction, and papal year dates; it uses the style *Frater Nicolaus miseratione diuina Reatin' episcopus*, but the initial *F* of Frater was not written, that is, presumably, not completed by the scribe for whom it was reserved (although it may not have been completed because of a scribal error: omission/interlineation; but this explanation would seem to make its retention in San Domenico's archives seem rather strange—and, of course, the retention there of the document without its *F* may suggest that a San Domenico scribe was supposed to write it). Nicola's resignation is mentioned in the letter of translation of his successor Berardo from Ancona, *Boniface VIII*, no. 987. Since the date of translation is 4 February 1296, it is possible that Nicola's letter was not completed because of his resignation; it is conceivable that his resignation was prompted by the sentiments aroused in him by the Christmas season of 1295. In connection with this indulgence, these possible sentiments, and San Domenico, the reader should keep in mind San Domenico's most noted "dugentesca" painting, the Madonna enthroned, with Child, angels, and donors, now kept in the Palazzo Vescovile.

16. Gottifredo: *Clément IV*, no. 139; see too Cascioli, "Nuova serie dei vescovi"; for evidence of Gottifredo within the diocese: Rieti, Arch. Cap., VI.A.3 (October 1265); IV.Q.6 "3" (8 December 1265); IV.K.13 (12 October 1266); Borgo San Pietro, Archivio di Monastero di Santa Filippa, 30 (5 October 1268), 34 (1276). Gottifredo was admonished by the pope not to allow the chapter of Tivoli to proceed to the election of his successor without mandate of the apostolic see, *Clément IV*, no. 189, an act which intensifies the historian's awareness of the significance of this point in time in the changing manner of selecting bishops. Pietro: *Nicholas III*, no. 105 and see below. Andrea: *Honorius IV*, no. 566 and see below. Berardo: *Boniface VIII*, no. 987; in 1281 Berardo had been a papal chamberlain (Battelli, *Latium*, x, 423–424); and see *Honorius IV*, nos. 104, 172, 601, 669; on 19 November 1296, *Berardus miseratione diuina episcopus R* acted in the episcopal palace at Rieti: Rieti, Arch. Cap., VII.F.5; on 24 May 1298, his nephew Berardo, canon of Ancona, was his vicar general at Rieti: IV.O.5; Paravicini Bagliani notes that a Berardo da Poggio Bustone, canon of Rieti, was at Lyons with Ottobono Fieschi, cardinal deacon of Sant'Adriano (and later Pope Hadrian V, 1276) in 1274, and had been his chaplain in 1263: Paravicini Bagliani, *Cardinali di curia*, 1:369; but in spite of the coincidence of names this Berardo continues to be a canon after the episcopal election and even death of Bishop Berardo: Rieti, Arch. Cap., III.B.1, 2; III.C.3, 4. See too Pasztor, "Per la storia dell'amministrazione," 183 (for Berardo as papal chaplain and rector of the Massa Trabaria in 1283; his short rectorship ended in his violent expulsion, the description of which is published by Pasztor); see below chapter 6. Angelo: *Boniface VIII*, no. 4698; of Angelo there are sharply descriptive phrases in Mariano d'Alatri, "Un mastodontico processo," particularly 305. Giovanni: *Boniface VIII*, no. 4836, and see above in chapter 3; on 5 August 1302 Boniface named the Franciscan Matteo bishop of Ìmola to replace Giovanni who had been translated to Rieti to replace the dead Angelo, so in fact the Franciscans did not lose a bishopric in the death and exchange: *Boniface VIII*,

no. 4729; rather they gained a bishopric because Boniface also gave Nepi to a Franciscan, Paolo, on 31 August 1302: *Boniface VIII*, no. 4741 (and see nos. 4334 and 4684). These translations were not regularly translations of bishops from sees with a lower to a higher official value. According to Boyle, *A Survey*, 157, *servitia communia* were "normally reckoned as one-third of the income of any one year" (although these evaluations seem quite formal). In the early fourteenth century the following sees had, in these terms, the following evaluations: Rieti, 900 florins; Tivoli, 300 florins; Ancona, 900 florins; Ìmola, 1,050 florins; Orvieto, 900 florins; Olema, 750 florins; Sora, 300 florins; Nepi, 210 florins; Vicenza, 3,000 florins; Monreale, 6,000 florins; Capua, 4,800 florins; Aquileia, 30,000 florins (and for contrast: Canterbury, 30,000 florins; Lincoln, 15,000 florins; Ravenna, 12,000 florins; Narni, 600 and 900 florins; Sutri, 150 florins; Segni, 120 florins)—figures taken from Hoberg, *Taxae pro communibus servitiis*. To the extent that the figures were thought to represent real income that cannot have been the reason for the translation, for instance, from Ancona to Rieti or Rieti to Orvieto; in both of these cases official convenience seems a likely reason (for an example of Raimond's being active at Orvieto while still *miseratione diuina Episcopus Reatinus*, on 13 August 1344, see Rieti, Arch. Cap., Lib. con. et col., I, fo. 261r). The succession list of these bishops in Eubel's *Hierarchia* is correct and impressive because of his (or its) common-sense correction of the much less reliable Gams (*Series episcoporum ecclesiae catholicae*): Eubel, I. 416 and particularly n.5. Ughelli (*Italia sacra*, vol. 1, cols. 1205–1208) breaks Giovanni's episcopate in two but is otherwise correct in succession; Palmegiani in *La cattedrale* (63–64) also breaks Giovanni in two and makes Berardo Bernardo but is otherwise correct in this part of his succession; Michaeli (*Memorie*, 4:225) has two Giovannis and gives his reader the choice of Berardo or Bernardo.

17. Jacopo: *Boniface VIII*, no. 3183; A.S.V., AA, Arm. I–XVIII, 3895, contains a 4 April 1302 letter from Charles of Valois to Jacopo bishop of Rieti his vicar general; its reference to (genitive) "nobilis uiri Maghinardi Pagani de Susenana" is suggestive: for Mainardo da Susinana, see Waley, *The Papal State*, index references under Susinana and Pagani, and particularly 193–194; would it not make sense for the bishop to have been a Romagnol from near Faenza? For Charles of Valois as rector of four provinces and for his vicars, see Waley, *The Papal State* index under Valois, and particularly 104 and 316.

18. Rieti, Arch. Cap., II.F.1 (collation); see *Clément VI*, no. 147, and nos. 195, 439, 440, 473, 494, 682, 716, 893, 1066. Also Rieti, Arch. Cap., III.B.6 (vacant through translation) and III.B.8, and also II.E.1, II.F.3 (use of vicar general Philip' de Sen') and also Lib. perg. di Matteo Barnabei, 507, present in Rieti, 20 October 1345; see Eubel, *Hierarchia*, Supplementum. For Raimondo and Cola, Anonimo romano, see Porta, ed., *Cronica*, 131, 138. The anonymous author calls the vicar "uno oitramontano, granne decretalista e vescovo de Vitervo" (131) and the editor corrects the Viterbo to Orvieto (n. 268). (For these passages in English translation, see Wright, *The Life of Cola di Rienzo*, 64, 73, 74.) For the climbing of the Campidoglio see Porta, *Cronica*, 113 and Wright, *Cola di Rienzo*, 41. The chronicler's confusion of Viterbo and Orvieto is amusingly echoed by the eminent French editors of *Clément VI* in referring to a letter (no. 3954) in which monies earlier collected by the dead bishop from offerings

at the altars of St. Peter's are being sought for return to the papal camera; the mistake was not made by the compiler of the papal register: Reg. Vat. 142, fo. 52. A nice introduction to Raimond's confusion and/or horror over Cola's behavior is to be found in Cosenza's ed. of Petrarch, *The Revolution of Cola di Rienzo*; see index under Raymond of Chameyrac.

19. Rieti, Arch. Cap., IV.P.1, see above chapter 3. The following are the succession lists of significant modern historians. Ughelli: Adenulphus; Fr. Raynaldus (O.S.B. Sacrae Theologiae Magister); Odo (1227); Raynerius; another Raynerius; Fr. Dominicus; Raynaldus; Thomas. Michaeli (beginning in 1215): Rainaldo I; Rainerio II; Giovanni II; Rainerio III; Rainaldo II; Thomas I. Palmegiani: Adinolfo Secenari; Rainaldo I; Rainerio II; Giovanni II; Rainerio III; Rainaldo II; Tommaso I. Eubel (beginning between 1209 and 1215): Rainaldus O.S.B.; Odo "(sed. 1227?)"; Rainerius; Joannes "(sed. 1236?)"; Rainaldus de Aretio O. Min; Thomas. Eubel's list is very faulty but obviously, unlike the others, presented with considerable hesitation. The presence of all these phantom Rainerios is the result of faulty extension. The two names Rainaldo and Rainerio are, of course, easily confused; and both are frequently and similarly abbreviated. It seems to have been possible for thirteenth- and early fourteenth-century Reatines themselves to have made mistaken extensions (but not of episcopal names); so that the canon Ventura who did not often use his patronymic or surname is sometimes called Ventura Raynaldi and sometimes Ventura Rainerii: Rieti, Arch. Cap., III.B.1; II.B.2; III.D.2; IV.F.4; IV.O.5. That the name of all three bishops Rain' was Rainaldo is perfectly clear in the documents preserved at Rieti and Borgo San Pietro and in *Cronica fratris Salimbene* (never, I believe, is Rainerio used). For Rainaldo de Labro: II.C.1; IV.G.3 (1215, 1230); IV.Q.3 "13" (1215); IV.Q.1 (1220); VI.G.7 (1220); IV.M.4 (1216, 1226); and also Borgo San Pietro, Archivio del Monastero di Santa Filippa, 14 (1231); for 21 February 1234 see IV.P.4 and above chapter 3 note 41; for Rainaldo Bennecelli: Borgo San Pietro, Archivio del Monastero di Santa Filippa, 19. Rainaldo da Arezzo's name is clear in Salimbene. For an example of a gratuitous and misleadingly mistaken extension by the editors of Gregory IX's register, see *Gregory IX*, no. 2927.

20. Rieti, Arch. Cap., IV.M.2; IV.M.3. For Adenolfo at Rieti, see for example: IV.B.2; IV.K.10; IV.M.1; IV.Q.3; IV.Q.4; IV.Q.5; Parchment Book IV, fo. 1.

21. For Gentile de Pretorio at Rieti (besides Tommaso's account in IV.P.1): Rieti, Arch. Cap., IV.M.3 (3 March 1214); Borgo San Pietro, Archivio di Monastero di Santa Filippa, 20. The dorse notation on the IV.M.3 document says 1213, and the papal year date of Innocent III seems to say "xiiij" (1211), but the indiction year is clearly "ij," and, although the year date is not entirely legible, it concludes with four minims. The papal year date must have been written carelessly so that its "v" looks like "ij."

22. Rieti, Arch. Cap., IV.G.3 (for both the 1215 and the 1233 documents—a witness in 1233 is, in the genitive, Alibrandi notarii episcopi); II.C.1; II.C.3; II.C.4; IV.M.4; IV.Q.1; IV.Q.3; VI.G.7; VIII.B.1; VIII.B.3; VIII.B.4; Parchment Book IV, fo. 13; Borgo San Pietro, Archivio del Monastero di Santa Filippa, 14; *Gregory IX*, nos. 2927, 4491.

23. Rieti, Arch. Cap., IV.Q.1; IV.Q.2; IV.O.1; IV.G.8; and Parchment Book IV, fos. 44r–44v.

24. Borgo San Pietro, Archivio del Monastero di Santa Filippa, 19; Rieti, Arch. Cap., IV.O.4, and of course IV.P.1. For reference to death: IV.A.5 and Salimbene, 322.

25. Rieti, Arch. Cap., IV.A.5, II.B.1; also see documents in IV.Q.3 and IV.Q.10.

26. Rieti, Arch. Cap., IV.M.2 (18 September 1198); IV.M.2 (16 December 1206); IV.M.1 "30" (July 1212).

27. Rieti, Arch. Cap., IV.M.1 (20 February 1204).

28. Rieti, Arch. Cap., IV.M.1 "20" (1206, but inconsistency in dating), IV.M.1 (1207) with a witness Sinballo Benetelli (or Benecelli). In the printed version of IV.P.1 (Desanctis, *Notizie storiche*, app. n.2, xv–xix), the bishop is twice given the name *benecelli* without capital and in italics (and it should be noted that in both cases the genitive "Rainaldi" is printed); the manuscript says (1) "Rain' Bnnecell' "; and (2) "R. beneccell," at least as I read it. The names "Senebaldus Bennecellus (or Benetellus)" and "Petrus judex Benectelli" appear in the "1225" survey: Arch. Cap., "1212," fo. xxii r (43).

29. It would seem possible that Rainaldus the bishop is identical with the canon Pbr. Rainaldus, who appears at Rieti between 1200 and 1240 (when he is also called *prepositus*, which, if later usage can be a guide, means *prepositus* of Santa Cecilia, or Sant'Angelo): IV.M.1; IV.G.3; IV.O.1; IV.D.11; IV.P.6; IV.Q.2. But the presence of both Rainaldus Bennecelli and Presbiter Rainaldus Berardi Dodonis in a 1207 document (IV.M.1 "1207") makes identification difficult.

30. Rieti, Arch. Cap., VI.G.8: "in nomine domini, amen. Anno eiusdem mill' cc xxxviii, temporibus domini Gregorii viiii pape anno pontificatus eius xi, indictione xi, mens' martii, die x, in presenctia dompni Johannis Arlocti et Oddonis Alfan' ac aliorum testium (?). Ego quidem dompnus Sinibaldus de Baluiano titulo donationis inter uiuos, pro magno amore quem in te habeo, do, dono, trado atque concedo tibi Johanni Leonis nepoti domini Johannis Episcopi Reatin' irreuocabiliter largiendo id est omnia iura que habeo et mihi competent uel competere possunt quocumque et qualitercumque in ecclesia Sancti Angeli de Arpaniano et te in locum meum eiusdem ecclesie substituo ad honorem et reuerentiam domini episcopi memorati." Gentile's Pretorio may, of course, have been a local place, see Michaeli, *Memorie*, 2:190.

31. *Cronica fratris Salimbene*, 205–207; above chapter 1; see the comprehensive article by Mariano d'Alatri, "Il vescovo nella cronica di Salimbene," particularly 11, 12–16, but also in general both for the article's acute observations and for its bibliography.

32. *Cronica fratris Salimbene*, 322–329, particularly here 322.

33. Sbaralea, *Bullarium franciscanum*, 3:330–331, no. 48 (2 August 1278); the letter is only calendared in *Nicholas III*, no. 105.

34. Because Pietro was a bishop of Sora at the end of the Hohenstaufen period he is fortunate enough to be included in one of the most elegantly scholarly historical works that has been written about medieval Italy in this century, Kamp, *Kirche und Monarchie*, 1:105. In this work Pietro's official career, particularly as it is visible in papal registers, is traced with careful exactness; my de-

scription of that career follows Kamp closely. Another detailed account of the career (in this case because Pietro ended his life as patriarch of Aquileia) is to be found in Paschini, "Il patriarcato di Pietro Gera." For the Spanish mission, see Linehan, *The Spanish Church*, 218–220; *Nicholas III*, nos. 739, 742–743. For Clement IV's collation of his educated chaplain rather than the abbot of Casamari to Sora: *Clément IV*, no. 442: "Petrum Romani seu de Ferentino capellanum nostrum," and see no. 192: "magistrum Petrum dictum Romanum de Ferentino capellanum nostrum"; and nos 268, 934, 1947, 1949, 2014. Carlo F. Polizzi of Padua has discovered and is publishing a document which lists books (more than 25) and other belongings which Patriarch Pietro had deposited with the Dominicans of Venice. The list of books, which Polizzi will explicate fully, includes historical, legal, theological, and liturgical works, and "Seneca" and "Avicenna" as well as Thomas and Bonaventura. I am deeply grateful to Dr. Polizzi for his having told me of the document, shown it to me, and sent me a copy. Although it is difficult to know what books in a prelate's library he knew well or had read, these books suggest an even richer Pietro than was earlier visible, and make seem more serious his title *magister*.

35. Sbaralea, *Bullarium franciscanum*, vol. 3, no. 48.

36. For Giacomo Sarraceno: Rieti, Arch. Cap., IV.Q.2; IV.N.2; VI.G.7; II.C.1 (e, x, y: acts in 1233 as proctor for Bishop Rainaldo de Labro); III.D.2; II.D.3; II.D.4 (absent, *infirmus*, 1253); II.D.5; IV.D.4 (again ill, 1259); III.B.3; III.B.6; IV.H.4; III.B.1; and also Rieti, A.S., San Domenico, 6; see too below chapter 6 and Palmegiani, *Rieti*, 311 (for a remembered bishop Giacomo and S. Lucia, Rieti); sometimes the canon placed first in lists of canons seems quite clearly to be he who is oldest in tenure; Giacomo is so placed, for example, in Rieti, Arch. Cap., III.B.3, 6 (1261); IV.H.4 (4 June 1278); II.C.3 (1280). For Teballo, VI.G.7, and chapter 2 above. For Rainaldo's gift, IV.L.10. It is clearly unlikely that the Giacomo of 1280 is the canon "Jacobbus" of 1181 (IV.Q.2). There clearly seem to have been at least two canons Giacomo, and I have thought that the division between them probably came in the 1220s or 1230s, probably between 1233 and 1238, see "Localism and Longevity," 298. J[erome] P[oulenc] in noticing Sacchetti Sassetti's *Un ospite* (in *Archivum franciscanum historicum*, 59 [1966]: 502) quickly summarized opinions on the connection between the bishop-elect and the early thirteenth-century canons from the family. Poulenc was mistaken, I obviously believe, in his negative reaction to the possibility of a canon's being nearly eighty-five years old, even though I think that it is probable that the Jacobbus of 1220 is not the Jacobus of 1278. Jacobus, who Nicholas III said had voluntarily resigned the see, is not included in a list of canons from 20 March 1286 (IV.H.4), and was probably dead by then.

37. *Cronica fratris Salimbene*, 297; see Mariano d'Alatri, "Il vescovo nella cronica di Salimbene," 9–11 for Salimbene's way of describing and praising men.

38. Linehan, *The Spanish Church*, 255.

39. Palmegiani, *La cattedrale*, 62.

40. Although it is tempting to connect Pietro's *Romanus* with his curial youth or his curial relatives, the curial connection is not at all a sure reason why he was, when he was, called *Romanus* rather than, or as well as, *Egiptius*; the question is sharpened by the association with Pietro of his vicar general at Rieti,

another Petrus Romanus, or Petrus de Roma. The problem of what Pietro was called by his contemporaries and why he was called what he was called is a surprisingly difficult one.

41. For these Egiptius benefices and for the uncle Pietro Egiptius, see Kamp, *Kirche und Monarchie*, 1:104 and nn.63, 64, and 65; *Innocent IV*, nos. 331, 1471, 4453, 7665 and *Urban IV*, nos. 934, 1947, 1949, 2014. As Kamp points out there is a short biographical sketch of Pietro in *Dictionnaire d'histoire et de géographie ecclésiastiques*, vol. 11 (1949), coll. 898–899 (by L. Jadin, under "Capoue," coll. 888–907).

42. Cheney, "Cardinal John of Ferentino"; not only for Giovanni but also for a Pietro and his prebend of North Newbald (and a scathing comment of William Prynne's), see Cheney, *Innocent III and England*, 38–39, 87, 155, 224, 226, 230–231, 296, 94 (and also Clay, ed., *York Minster Fasti*, 57, for the nephew of Cardinal Stefano of Fossanova). For other Ferentino clerks in England, see Sayers, *Papal Judges Delegate*, 136 (Giovanni, Andrea), 328 (Giovanni da Fumone, canon of Sant'Angelo Ferentino) and my *York Metropolitan Jurisdiction*, 126, 132, 186 (Bartolomeo); for Ferentino clerks in Italy, see Waley, *The Papal State*, 104, 316 (Davide, Caetani connection), 236, 241–242 (Riccardo and a nephew), 312, 313, 320 (Orlando, cousin of Alexander IV).

43. *Register of Walter Giffard*, 170 no. 2; Guiraud, Cadier, and Mollat, eds., *Les registres de Grégoire X et de Jean XXI*, no. 81 (Gregory X): concerning a dispute between Cardinal Ancher and William Wickwane, chancellor of York, over a prebend in York minster formerly held by Mgr Pietro "de Egiptii" da Ferentino (by then, 25 October 1272, dead). For "Bartholomeus Giptius" in the circle of Gregorio da Montelongo, patriarch of Aquileia in 1269, Kamp, *Kirche und Monarchie*, 1:104 n. 65, and Marchetti-Longhi, *Gregorio da Montelongo*, 357 and 422.

44. Kemp, *Kirche und Monarchie*, 1:104–105 nn.60–75; *Urban IV*, nos. 192 and 268; *Clément IV*, no. 442; *John XXI* (and *Gregory X*), no. 84; *Martin IV*, nos. 26–28, 87; *Honorius IV*, nos. 560, 592; *Boniface VIII*, nos. 942, 1217, 1569–70, 2541; *Honorius IV*, nos. 818–819, 950–952; *Nicholas IV*, nos. 560–562, 566–567, 570, 698; *Boniface VIII*, nos. 2215, 3131. See Waley, *The Papal State*, 241, where as archbishop of Monreale he is seen active with Riccardo of Ferentino, who has a troublesome nephew (and too conciliatory in the Romagna ? because of bribery), and 318. For the difficulty with Aquileia see for example Paschini, "Il patriarcato di Pietro Gera"; or Traversa, *Quellenkritik*.

45. Not too much should be made of this knightly/baronial distinction: the title knight is applied to extremely elevated central Italian nobles; without a real knowledge of local and extended Egiptius holdings and power it is impossible to gauge the strength of their position in and around Ferentino. The evidence suggests to me, however, a family of some local significance and by the generation after Pietro specifically knightly, but particularly dependent on office, and specifically curial office.

46. Rieti, Arch. Cap., VIII.B.9.

47. Rieti, Arch. Cap., VI.E.1.

48. Rieti, Arch. Cap., II.E.4; "contra generalem libertatem ecclesiasticam" is from VIII.B.9.

49. Rieti, Arch. Cap., III.C.2.

50. Rieti, Arch. Cap., II.E.2. For the copy of a Florentine statute: II.F.1.

51. Rieti, Arch. Cap., II.E.3. Pietro styles himself: "Petrus permissione diuina Episcopus Reatin' in regno Sicilie citra Calabriam super recolligendis decimis et legatis deputatis ad terre sancte subsidium per sedem apostolicam delegatus" and the letter sent from him was described by the notary Andrea da Popleto as having been sealed with a pendant seal of green wax. Although Pietro is here acting as collector, he is securing the archpriest of San Pietro di Popleto to himself and his successors as bishops of Rieti.

52. Mazzoleni, ed., *Le pergamene di Capua*, 2:45–47, no. 145, dated in Capua, notarized, subscribed: "presens scriptum . . . fieri fecimus subscriptione nostra propria subsignatum." There is a brief notice in Ughelli, *Italia sacra*, vol. 6, col. 341.

53. Bianchi, *Documenta historiae forojuliensis*, 245, 249; and for the Cremonese, see Traversa, *Quellenkritik*, 30.

54. Garufi, *Catalogo illustrato*, 61–63, nos. 134, 135 (and one should note that Giacomo has a seal).

55. Rieti, Arch. Cap., III.B.1; II.E.5; IV.M.5; III.B.2. There is a conceivable connection between this Pietro Romano, canon of Ferentillo, and that Pietro Romano, canon of Sant'Angelo Rieti, who made his will in his house on 23 July 1309, chose burial at Sant'Angelo, and made his nephews his heirs (Rieti, A.S., pergamene, comune, 23 July 1309: Bellucci, no. 82); although Giovanni Papazurri's Rieti is noticeably full of Romans (normally called "de Urbe").

56. A.S.V., Fondo Celestini, 19, 20. Pietro uses the style "dei gratia," and Fondo Celestini, 27, 28, 29. Again Pietro, or the second of his Ferentine notaries, uses the style "dei gratia."

57. For the death and burial of Celestine, see Herde, *Cölestin V*, particularly 160. For Tommaso da Ocre's gift, see Paravicini Bagliani, *I testamenti*, 324. For Celestinian monasteries, see Moscati, "I monasteri di Pietro Celestino," and for Sant'Antonio, 114.

58. Marsella, *I vescovi di Sora*, 82. Marsella also called Pietro (81) a "uomo di vasta cultura, cappellano pontificio, esperto conoscitore delle anime." Marsella does not really at all suggest the sort of evidence that led him to arrive at this description, but he does say "era stato anche arcidiacono di York in Inghilterra ed aveva acquistata una meravigliosa pratica della vita pastorale." It would have been marvelous indeed if Pietro had gained experience of the pastoral life from the sort of archidiaconate he had been thought to have held at York, but in fact Kamp (*Kirche und Monarchie*, 1:104 n. 63) has shown that the source in which Ughelli thought he found Pietro's archdeaconry does not contain it. Ruocco, *Storia di Sarno*, 1:207–208, talks of the extent of the diocese of Sarno in the later thirteenth century.

59. This point is made by Kamp, *Kirche und Monarchie*, 1:104 n. 59; and he avoids using the names Gera, Gerra, Guerra by which Pietro has commonly been identified. Although I follow him in this avoidance it does seem to me unlikely that such a long and general usage should have been built on nothing. It is conceivably of some significance that Bishop Pietro's marshal at Rieti on 26 September 1278 was called Guerro (or thus I interpret the oblique Guerro

melescalco of Rieti, Arch. Cap., III.B.1). Given my belief that mistakes like the name Guerra are unlikely to have come out of thin air, it is at least ironic that I have created a mistaken name for Bishop Pietro out of pretty thin air, a name which I hope will deceive no one: in writing of Bishop Pietro in my "Localism and Longevity" I inadvertently typed Vèroli for Ferentino. I did not notice the error in proofreading, and it has generally gone unnoticed. I found it in reading the passage (296) in preparing this chapter. The name Gerra is firmly used by Traversa, for Pietro and his family, who thinks he sees it in the chronicler "Julian": see particularly Traversa, *Quellenkritik*, 33 n. 1 and 47 n. 4, see too 34. I myself have not found the name in "Julian," but "Julian" is a rather difficult source for a historian not from Friuli.

60. *Cronica fratris Salimbene*, 281–282.

61. Scalon, *La biblioteca arcivescovile di Ùdine*, 161–163, no. 92. The codicil, which was written in an interesting manuscript which Scalon describes, is transcribed by Scalon on 162. The 18 line text of the codicil (fo. 58v of MS F.33.III.18, but now called by its Scalon number) is surprisingly difficult to read exactly, and my own transcription differs slightly from Scalon's, but the difference does not affect materially the meaning of the text. (I believe that Scalon has omitted from line 9 of the text the words *quolibet anno in die anniversarii sui* and has replaced them with *quolibet tempore in die depositionis sue*, and we show other minor differences; but, again, the text is in parts very difficult to read.) One should also consult Scalon, *Necrologium aquileiense*, 1:145. For the deposition in Santa Maria, see Dalla Barba Brusin and Lorenzoni, *L'arte del patriarcato*, plate 187. For their help in Ùdine I should particularly like to thank Dottoressa Ivonne Zenarola Pastore, director of the Archivio di stato, Professor Luigi De Biasio, in whose care is the Biblioteca Arcivescovile, Dottor Aldo Rizzi, director of the Museo Civico, and Dottoressa Lelia Sereni, director of the Biblioteca Comunale "Vincenzo Joppi."

62. Tambara, ed., *Juliani canonici*, 31; see the Milan 1738 edition of vol. 14 at cols. 1206–1207. Compare Nicoletti, *Patriarcato d'Aquileia*, 39: "nella chiesa principale fu pomposamente sepolto, avendo con gran gloria governato la sedia un anno sette mesi ventisei giorni" and for Pietro's actual marble tomb, once on the left of the main door, see Paschini, "Il patriarcato di Pietro Gera," 104.

63. F. Jo. Fran. Bernardo Maria de Rubeis, "Dissertationes variae eruditionis": Venice, Biblioteca Marciana, MSS Latin, Clas. XIV, Cod. 133 (Coll. 4284), particularly fo. 308v (a copy of the antiquarian's Venetian manuscript is in the Biblioteca Comunale of Ùdine: Man. Com. 648, see gatherings 328 and 329). See Bianchi, *Documenta historiae forojuliensis*, 10–11. Obviously Pietro was not the first patriarch to include Franciscans in his familia, see Ùdine, A.S., Archivio notarile, Busta 5118, 1296, 1 for a Franciscan chaplain.

64. See above, chapter 2.

65. For the growing number of Franciscan bishops, see Thomson, *Friars in the Cathedral*. It is helpful to recall that Benvenuto's candidacy falls at the midpoint between the death of the first Franciscan bishop of Rieti, Rainaldo, and the translation to Rieti of the second, Angelo. For Benvenuto da Orvieto see Mariano d'Alatri, *L'inquisizione francescana nell'Italia centrale*, 144.

66. *Honorius IV*, nos. 566 (27 July 1286), 592 (20 August 1286).

67. *Nicholas III*, no. 600; see *Innocent IV*, no. 4453 and Kamp, *Kirche und Monarchie*, 1:104.

68. Ughelli, *Italia sacra*, vol. 1, cols. 1205–1207.

69. Cassino, Aula 2, caps. LXXIII, fasc. 1, no. 11: the document is written, in a good hand with fixed margins, in 13 lines on a parchment 20 cm wide and 13.7 cm high; it has a flap, with three holes on flap and body for affixing the seal. I should like to thank Dom Tommaso Leccisotti for admitting me to the archives and allowing me to transcribe the document. For an introduction to Marsi, see Kamp, *Kirche und Monarchie*, 1:28–33; although Kamp stops before the time of Andrea's administration, he includes, as he does for each diocese with which he deals, a concise description of the diocese and a full bibliography for it.

70. For this tenure at Ferentino I follow Eubel, *Hierarchia*. For Cosma e Damiano at Tagliacozzo see Inguanez, "Le pergamene del monastero."

71. Rieti, Arch. Cap., II.E.6 and VII.F.3.

72. Rieti, Arch. Cap., VII.E.2.

73. Rieti, Arch. Cap., IV.D.5; III.B.3; III.B.6; III.D.10; IV.K.13; A.S., San Domenico, 6 (old 99); his real connection with Sant'Eleuterio is suggested by the presence of a Sant'Eleuterio witness on 31 October 1261: III.B.6.

74. Rieti, Arch. Cap., IV.D.5; II.D.10; and IV.O.5.

75. Rieti, Arch. Cap., III.D.10; IV.A.3; *Urban IV*, no. 1186.

76. Rieti, Arch. Cap., III.B.1, 3, 5–6.

77. Rieti, Arch. Cap., IV.O.5 "9."

78. Rieti, Arch. Cap., II.B.2. Lib. perg. di Matteo Barnabei, 7, 15, 16. See too "Vescovi e vicari generali," n. 30: it is extremely strange that a scribe who knew Ventura as well as Matteo Barnabei must have known him would use the wrong patronymic; perhaps he was Ventura Rainaldi Rainerii or Rainerii Rainaldi. See above chapter 4 note 114.

79. Rieti, Arch. Cap., IV.H.4; III.C.2; VII.F.3; IV.O.5 "9"; II.B.2; IV.C.8; IV.F.4; III.B.1, 8, 9, 13–14 (on 8 he objects to a chapter action of transfer on 10 October 1278); Book "6," Lib. perg. di Matteo Barnabei, 2–4, 5, 6, 15–16; in "6" in a reassignment of prebendal holdings in 1307, and in Matteo Barnabei in Bishop Giovanni's synodal acts of 5 February 1315, Ventura's is the second name listed, probably a reference to his seniority. See Brentano, "Who was Bishop Andrea?"

80. Rieti, Arch. Cap., VII.E.8, copy of 23 October; Mazzatinti, in an uncharacteristic mistake, says that Ventura is being provided as bishop: *Gli archivi*, 251.

81. Lib. perg di Matteo Barnabei, 15: 1 March 1315. The reader should be aware of the presence of the canon Ranaldo presbiteri Rinaldi from 1252 to 1260: Rieti, Arch. Cap., II.D.2; II.D.3; IV.D.5; and of the earlier canon the priest Rainaldo from 1200 to 1249: IV.M.2; IV.M.1 "17" and "3"; IV.O.1; IV.P.6 "1," "2," and "7"; IV.G.3; IV.Q.2 (where he is also called, in 1239 and 1240, *prepositus*, that is, probably of a local collegiate chapter like Sant'Angelo).

82. See above chapter 2 and *Two Churches*, 259–260.

83. Gregorovius, *History of the City of Rome*, 6:412; for the exiles see above chapter 4.

84. I mean faintly to echo the joke which Gregorovius repeats (*History of the City of Rome*, 6:476): "It is said that one day he [Gregory XI] asked a prelate, 'Lord Bishop, why do you not go to your see?' To which the bishop answered, 'And you, Holy Father, why do you not go to yours?' " Gregorovius's central Italy in the later fourteenth and early fifteenth centuries is perhaps too disturbed to be credible. See, too, Partner, *The Lands of St. Peter*, particularly 361 for the attack on the "bad shepherds" in the 1370s.

85. These documents have been collected and calendared by Lippens, "Fra Biagio da Leonessa," particularly for the catalog, 6:115–129; Rieti, Arch. Cap., VIII.G.14; IX.F.9; VI.G.15; II.G.6; IV.G.3; VIII.D.11; VII.D.3; VII.G.10; VII.G.17; II.G.7; VII.G.11; VII.G.12; V.D.1; VI.G.17; II.G.9; IV.K.14; and presumably VIII.G.3 and V.B.1 which show Gregory XI responding to episcopal petitions concerning Rieti. See too A.S., Statuti, I, fos. 125r–v.

86. Pastoral examples: Lippens, "Fra Biagio da Leonessa," 6:117, 118, 123, 124, 125, 126, 127, 128, 129; Arch. Cap., VIII.G.14; VI.G.16; VII.G.15; II.G.6; VII.D.3; VII.G.10; VII.G.17; VII.G.11; VII.G.12; VII.G.7; V.D.1; VI.G.17; II.G.9; V.B.1; II.G.10. Papal imposts: Lippens, "Fra Biagio," 6:117–118, 119, 120, 122–123, 126, 128; Arch. Cap., IV.E.4; IV.G.3; II.G.5; IV.G.1; IV.G.2. Albornoz and Naples: Lippens, "Fra Biagio," 6:121, 122, 124–125; Arch. Cap., IV.E.5; VIII.D.10; VIII.D.11; IV.E.6; II.G.7. For Clement VI's commission to Biagio to visit his diocese, and its implications for the definition of episcopal office: Lippens, "Fra Biagio," 6:120; Arch. Cap., I.B.2. For Biagio as one of the conservators of San Silvestro in Capite in Rome, in 1364, see Lippens, "Fra Biagio," 6:125, from *Bullarium franciscanum*, 6:376, no. 911.

87. Michaeli, *Memorie*, 3:86; Ughelli, *Italia sacra*, vol. 1, col. 1208.

88. Rieti, Arch. Cap., II.G.1 (and II.G.2, 3, 4); A.S.V., OS, 22, fo. 34r, Mgr. Neapoleone de Fonterolis da Forlì promises 300 florins, plus 5, on 16 February 1348 (24 cardinals present).

89. Pagliarini, *Croniche di Vicenza*, 105. Modern Vicentine historians have treated Pagliarini's text and sources with cautious doubt. Mantese (below, note 91) uses the Latin text preserved in the Archivio di stato at Vicenza; note that the name is also spelled Paglierini. Pagliarini should now be approached through Grubb's edition of the earliest known Latin edition. Grubb, who establishes very close dating for the core of the *Cronicae* (1497–98), speaks in his introduction of the Biagio passages and of Mantese's reaction to them (xxv). Grubb's *Cronicae* include the Latin texts of the supposed appeals by the civil authorities and people of Vicenza and also by the clergy against Biagio and to Clement VI, upon which texts Pagliarini's own narrative seems to be based. That narrative with "Proh dolore!" in place of "Deh, o dolore!" is also harshly effective in Latin (146–150).

90. Riccardi, *Storia dei vescovi vicentini*, 135.

91. Mantese, *Memorie storiche*, 3:150–158, from which the material in this paragraph is taken; Biagio's relations with the Scaligeri and the Vicentine accusations against him are treated in a fuller political perspective by Mantese on 3:65–70, 74–80. I should like to thank Professor Mantese for his kind advice and help, and also to thank Howard Burns who suggested that I ask Professor Mantese for help.

92. For Biagio's household and officials, see for example Riccardi, *Storia dei vescovi vicentini*, 132–133, including Nicolo da Lionessa, Andrea da Lionessa, Gelucio da Lionessa, and Albert de Clamp', OFM; some of these men were clearly learned in the law and Mantese (*Memorie storiche*, 580) talks of the use by bishops of Vicenza, including Biagio, of vicars general who were canonists; see Mantese (154–158) for additional members of Biagio's *familia*, and for Nicolo and Matteo again (as nephews), but also a monk from Vicenza and a canon of Treviso, for example. Napoleone of Forlì's connection with Biagio and Rieti is complicated by the fact that although he was used by Biagio before Rieti he had other Rieti connections (Raimond: Rieti, Arch. Cap., II.G.4); the connection with the Florentine merchant Andrea Gethi should be noted, and it should be noted that the copied Florentine statute was copied in 1353, see note 50 above. For San Benedetto (Libro IV, fos. 41v–42r) see note 4 above; three of Biagio's *familiares* are present for the action in the cloister (Angeluctio de Cassia, Gualterio Jahanuctii, and Raynallo Jannis de Campania); a notary and scribe of the bishop and chapter redacted the document: Giovanni Nutii Riccardelli da Rieti, notary by imperial authority; the canons are Giovanni de Montegambaro, Ballovino, Lauriano Gilioni, Matteo Maglano, Tommaso Petri, Ludovico Cole, Gianandrea Cecchi, Gianandrea Cole, Nutio Vannis, Therio Lalli, Liberato Berallutii, Pietro Johannutii; the nuns, Donna Nicholasia, Donna Stefanuctia di don Giovanni, Suor Bonarda di Symone, Suor Mariola di don Giovanni, Suor Agostina, Suor Angete di don Oddone, Suor Caterina, Suor Cecilia, Suor Madalena, Suor Benedetta, Suor Ceccharella, Suor Vanna, Suor Paulucia, Suor Lippa, Suor Caritia, Suor Lucia, Suor Jocabutia, Suor Amedeo, Suor Appollonia, Suor Andreuccia, Suor Antonia. Biagio's gift is Libro IV, fo. 49r.

93. See above chapter 3.

94. *Boniface VIII*, no. 4698; and no. 4684 license for loan, no. 4729 Matteo OFM to Ìmola because Giovanni to Rieti, no. 4741 Paolo OFM to Nepi because Angelo (dead) had been translated to Rieti, no. 4836 Giovanni to Rieti because Angelo dead. Angelo had been given Nepi on 1 June 1298, no. 2601. Angelo's services, A.S.V., *OS*, 1, fo. 17v, 300 florins and two; 17 cardinals; promise, dated 15 June 1302, is marked "solut."

95. Mariano D'Alatri, "Un mastodontico processo," 299. See for Angelo also Mariano D'Alatri, *L'inquisizione francescana nell'Italia*, 99–100, 144.

96. Mariano D'Alatri, "Un mastodontico processo," particularly 300–301.

97. Mariano D'Alatri, "Un mastodontico processo," 301, 305.

98. Mariano D'Alatri, "Un mastodontico processo," 305.

99. Mariano D'Alatri, "Un mastodontico processo," 302.

100. Rieti, Arch. Cap., III.D.10; Mariano D'Alatri, *L'inquisizione francescana nell'Italia*, app. 8, 120–121.

101. Rieti, Arch. Cap., IV.M.5.

102. Mariano D'Alatri, "Un mastodontico processo," 305.

103. Rieti, A.S., II.F.1. A.S.V., *OS*, 6, fo. 184r (old 182r), promise of services of 300 florins plus five, 18 cardinals.

104. Lippens, "Fra Biagio da Leonessa," 6:116, n. 4.

105. *Clément VI*, nos. 147, 195, 439, and see through nos. 440, 473, 494, 682, 716, 893, and to 1066 and 1633 (13 April 1348), but no. 1933 (8 February 1349,

another urban vicar and elect of Orvieto): if his anniversary day (see note 109 below), 5 April, is the day of his death, had he died on 5 April 1348 without the curia's being aware of it by 13 April?

106. Rieti, Arch. Cap., Lib. con. et col., II (variously marked: "Sextus Liber Contractuum"; "Liber IV"; "1347"; "Libro Terzo"; "1344–1347") is a paginated paper book with various episcopal and capitular acts which is particularly rich in material from the episcopate of Bishop Raimond. It does not establish the fact that he failed to take his diocesan tasks seriously or that he was never in his diocese, but it does give the names of various vicars general, vicars, and proctors who represented him in Rieti: for example, 22, 13 November 1345, Cicchus Johannis de Bussata, vicarius et procurator generalis (and on 13, 25 October 1344, Cicchus is identified as a prebendary, and on 45–46 in March 1345 as archpriest of San Sebastiano of Poggio Fidoni and on 44 in the same month the church of Rieti grants to him (called here "de Bussata") and his brother Cola right and actions in a piece of land in Torrente). For Ciccho as vicar general see too Lib. perg. di Matteo Barnabei, 534, and see above chapter 4. In the Lib. con. et col., II, 22, on 10 November 1345, Don Francesco da Ofagnano di L'Aquila (de Ofaniano de Aquila) is acting as Raimond's vicar general, he is called a canon, and in fact he was possessed of an expectancy in Rieti on 7 August 1337 when he was a canon of the church of Ofagnano, with benefice, and held a benefice in the church of Santa Maria Ofagnano, L'Aquila and Sulmona dioceses (Vidal, ed., *Benoît XII*, no. 4596): on 28 September 1341 he was listed thirteenth among the canons, was chosen a scrutator for electing, and was a subdeacon (Rieti, Arch. Cap., Lib. con. et col., I, fos. 65r, 65v). On 10 March and 9 July 1345, the vicar general is Filippo "de Senis" (Lib. con. et col., II, 66, 44), who on 21 December 1344 (32–33) could be seen as a prebendary of the church of Rieti involved in the exchange of prebendal benefices. He can be seen acting as vicar general in 1345: Lib. perg. di Matteo Barnabei, 537, 539; and in the acts preserved in II.F.3.

107. Rieti, Arch. Cap., Lib. con. et col., II, 29, 38.

108. Rieti, Arch. Cap., Lib. perg. di Matteo Barnabei, 507.; Lib. con. et col., II, 22.

109. Rieti, Arch. Cap., Lib. con. et col., II, 31. Liber Int. et exit., 1363. Parchment Liber IV, in a section of this book written by the notary by imperial authority, Johannes q. Raynalluctii, Anniversaries, fo. 20r. Ughelli, *Italia sacra*, vol. 1, col. 1208, includes an inscription from old St. Peter's which records the consecration by Raimond, when he was bishop of Rieti and urban vicar, of the altar of Saint Anthony Abbot, which had been built by Nicola degli Astalli, canon of St. Peter's with a conceded indulgence, on 23 March 1344, *Clément VI*, no. 3954 (calendar with mistaken bishopric): A.S.V., Reg. Vat. 142, fo. 52r–v (no. 222) records on 13 September 1348 the effort of the papal camera in Avignon through the treasurer of the Tuscan patrimony to recover monies from offerings at altars of St. Peter's gathered earlier in Raimond's career and not returned to the camera—this memorial to Raimond in papal records makes nice contrast with his memorial at Rieti.

110. Ughelli, *Italia sacra*, vol. 1, col. 1208. Palmegiani (*La cattedrale*, 64) says, "Tommaso II (a. 1339)." A nice example of Tommaso's diplomatic, on

paper, from 1340, is interleaved in Rieti, Arch. Cap., Lib. con. et col., I at present between fos. 64 and 65: It seems to be in the hand of Matteo Barnabei, was sealed, with the seal "nostre curie," is 29 cm wide by 15.5 high, uses the style *dei et apostolice sedis gratia, Episcopus Reatin'*, and enjoins registration. (The use here of the style *apostolice sedis gratia* for a bishop who had been elected by his chapter, should be noted.)

111. A.S.V., Reg. Vat. 175, fo 325r. It is just possible that "Marterio" should be read "Marerio."

112. A.S.V., Reg. Vat. 175, fos. 325r–v.

113. Rieti, Arch. Cap., Lib. perg. di Matteo Barnabei, 415, 454; see above chapter 4 note 46.

114. Rieti, Arch. Cap., Lib. perg. di Matteo Barnabei, 475–476.

115. Rieti, Arch. Cap., Lib. con. et col., I, fo. 65r.

116. Eubel, "Der Registerband," 123–212, nos. 38, 39, 41, 43, 53, 87, 101, 125, 126, 134, 154, 161, 166. For the antipope see Maceroni, *L'antipapa Niccolò V.*

117. Rieti, Arch. Cap., Lib. con. et col., I, fos. 74–75.

118. Rieti, Arch. Cap., Lib. con. et col., II, 17.

119. Rieti, Arch. Cap., Cart. Silv. See above chapter 4 note 103.

120. Rieti, Arch. Cap., Cart. Silv., for example 3, 4, 5, 6, 7, 66, 68, 71–72, 74, 81, 82–84, 85, 88, 91–92, 95.

121. Rieti, Arch. Cap., Cart. Silv., 69.

122. Rieti, Arch. Cap., Cart. Silv., 11–12.

123. Rieti, Arch. Cap., Cart. Silv., 70, 102–103, 90.

124. For Padua, I am, of course, following Rigon, see above note 13.

125. This question has received an extended answer for twelfth-century Auxerre: Bouchard, *Spirituality and Administration.*

126. See above note 34.

127. Rieti, Arch. Cap., IV.O.5.

128. Cavell, "Epistemology and Tragedy," 43.

Chapter 6

1. The chapter's position and attitude during this vacancy is primarily apparent in the three paper Matteo Barnabei books which cover the period: Rieti, Arch. Cap., Lib. con. et col., I; Lib. proc. civ.; Lib. proc. malef.; for all of which see above chapter 4. In his *Papal Monarchy*, 545–549, Morris offers a very sane introduction to the chapter in the thirteenth century.

2. Rieti, Arch. Cap., Lib. con. et col., I, fos. 45r–48r.

3. FOR *cum ex eo*, see Boyle, "The Constitution '*Cum ex eo.*'"

4. Rieti, Arch. Cap., Lib. con. et col., I, fos. 132v–134v, and above chapter 4.

5. Rieti, Arch. Cap., Lib. con. et col., I, fos. 65r–70v: the whole business of the election.

6. For 1307, see Rieti, Arch. Cap., Libr. or Reg. VI, fos. 1r–15r; for August 1347 see Lib. perg. di Matteo Barnabei, 233; for Tommaso's prebend, Lib. con. et col., 114 (and for his anniversary, which suggests the day of his death, 16

February, Lib. IV); for Tommaso Cimini, Arch. Cap., III.B.1; III.B.5; IV.F.4; IV.H.4; IV.I.2; IV.I.3; IV.M.6; VI.D.5; Lib. con. et col., I, fos. 1r, 34r, 39r; Lib. perg. di Matteo Barnabei, 309, 328, 448 (neither this list of citations nor those for other long-lived canons are meant to be exhaustive); for Giacomo di don Tommaso, Arch. Cap., IV.H.4; IV.M.6; IV.N.3 "3"; VI.C.3; VI.C.8; VI.F.6; VI.F.8; Lib. con. et col., I, fo. 21r; Lib. con. et col., II, 31, 47–48, 179; Lib. perg. di Matteo Barnabei, 4, 212–213, 233, 300, 307, 481, 507.

7. For Matteo: Rieti, Arch. Cap., IV.F.4 (1313); III.B.4; III.B.5; IV.H.4; IV.N.3; VI.F.7; Lib. con. et col., II, 31; Lib. perg di Matteo Barnabei, 2–4, 5, 6, 214, 448, 507, 525 (in November 1336, both Matteo and his brother Claudio were canons of Sant'Eleuterio: VI.D.4). For Rainaldo (Rainaldus Matthei Malicoli de Plagis; Jean XXII no. 9987): Arch. Cap.; Lib. con. et col., I, fos. 9v, 34r; Lib. perg. di Matteo Barnabei, 213, 338–339, 363–364, 393, 407, 448, 468, 507, 564. For Giovanni (Jean XXII, no. 13215): Arch. Cap., III.B.6; Lib. con. et col., I, fo. 34r; Lib. con. et col., II, 31; Lib. perg. di Matteo Barnabei, 448.

8. Rieti, Arch. Cap., Lib. IV, fos. 25r–37v. (Giovanni di don Capi or Caputosti's stall and prebend were vacant through his death in 1363: VII.G.11.)

9. Rieti, Arch. Cap., Lib. perg. di Matteo Barnabei, 233; Lib. int. et exit., 1379, fo. 43r (for the months of July, August, and September).

10. Rieti, Arch. Cap., IV.N.3 "6", the will; IV.Q.3 "14", 27 October 1249; II.B.2; II.D.10; III.B.1; III.B.3; III.B.6; III.C.3; III.D.10; IV.D.4; IV.D.5; IV.F.4; IV.K.13; IV.O.4; IV.O.5; VI.A.3; VI.D.2; Lib. perg. di Matteo Barnabei, 2, 4, 5, 6, 22; Lib. int. et exit., 1537, binding; A.S., San Domenico, 6 (olim 99). If the Bartolomeo identified as Bartolomeo domini Tadei, by the notary Ranaldo da Perugia, in 1252 and 1253 (II.D.3, 5) is the Bartolomeo Alfani of 1249, then he is presumably not the Bartolomeo di Oddone Alfani of 1318 (in 1289, in connection with the reception as canon of Bartolomeo de Rocca, VII.F.4, he is identified as Bartolomeo "domini Odonis"); Bartolomeo Alfani is again present in 1259 (IV.D.4). For the canon Oddone Alfani (canon by 1225 until 1253, when he was *infirmus* and represented by Mgr. Nicola on 7 June: III.D.2): II.D.3; II.D.5; IV.G.3; IV.O.4; IV.Q.1; IV.Q.2; IV.Q.3; VI.G.8; for Rainaldo (canon by 1282, dead by 1 December 1313: VII.G.3): II.B.2; III.B.1; III.B.4; IV.C.3; IV.F.4; IV.G.4; IV.H.4; IV.Q.7; VII.F.3; VII.F.4; Lib. int. et exit., 1537, binding. Another Rainaldus Alfani is listed in 1349: Book IV. For Rainallo Alfani see below note 104.

11. The length of Bartolomeo Bontempi's tenure is very securely attested, partly because his distinctive name is normally recorded, although not always in quite the same latinized form. Rieti, Arch. Cap., X.A.4 (Innocent IV to: *Bartholomeo canonico Legionen' nato Bontempi familiaris nostri*, concerning an income from Majorca, 25 July 1254; presumably Bartolomeo brought the papal letter to Rieti; the original with silk and bulla remains there); ? IV.D.5 (in 1260 an unidentified Bartolomeo in addition to Bartolomeo Alfani); II.C.10 (4 February 1261); on 12 April 1324 he is absent from chapter and has given his voice to Corrado de Murro (Lib. perg. di Matteo Barnabei, 182) but he had been present on 23 October 1333 (177); on 11 August 1326 a benefice is spoken of as once his (IV.I.3); his anniversary was celebrated on 5 August (Lib. IV, fo. 19v), he presumably died on 5 August 1324 or 1325, possibly 1326 but a list from 25

June 1325 (Lib. perg. di Matteo Barnabei, 189–190) suggests 5 August 1324; Lib. IV, in the list of books of the cathedral church in 1353, fos. 46r–47v, the book of the sermons he had made, and in Lib. int. et exit., 1392, fo. 19v, land left by him; II.B.2; III.B.1, III.D.10, IV.C.3; IV.C.8; IV.F.4; IV.H.4; IV.I.2; IV.K.13; IV.N.3 "3"; V.E.2; VI.G.12 (where he is canon and co-rector of S. Marone); Lib. perg. di Matteo Barnabei, 2–4.

12. In this list I have in general avoided those long-lived canons of whom I speak in the text, like the priest Paolo, the Sarraceno canons, Tommaso Cimini and the rest, but I have included some, like Sinibaldo Mareri, whose importance to the text is of quite another kind. For purposes of this list I will cite only references which establish the external dates or seem of particular significance: *Sinibaldo Mareri*, 51 years, 1202–1253: IV.M.1, III.D.2; *Tommaso Judicis* (del Giudice), 40 years, 1249–1289: IV.Q.3, VII.F.3; *Matteo Laurentii* (di Lorenzo), 38 years, 1233–1271: IV.G.3, (A.S.) San Domenico, 6; *Bartolomeo di don Rainallo de Rocca*, 30 years, 1289–1319: VII.F.3 (5 August 1289 given kiss of peace and received into his canonry), V.E.2 and Lib. perg. di Matteo Barnabei, 149 (both 7 October 1319)—Bartolomeo had been provided to a canonry at Santa Cecilia, Rieti, by Alexander IV as early as 11 May 1259 (VI.C.1) and is then called a scholar-student and a Reatine—he was patronized by Giacomo Colonna (VII.A.4) and sought and found Cistercian connections (VII.C.6), see below; *Giacomo Pasinelli*, at least 30 years, 1252–1280: II.D.2, 4, 5, III.C.3, and compare IV.Q.7—1242, Giacomo had already been a canon of Sant'Eleuterio, Rieti, for this important family see below; *Rainaldo Beraldi* (Beralli, Veralli), 30 years, 1233–1263: IV.G.3, III.D.10; *Berardo Rainaldi Sinibaldi* (Sinnibaldi, Senebaldi) *Dodonis*, 27 years, 1225–1252: IV.Q.1, 2, II.D.3; *Berardo de Podio* (Poggio Bustone), 25 years, 1278–1303: III.B.1, II.B.2; *Pandulfo Carsidonei* (Carsidonii), 25 years, 1238–1263: IV.D.1, III.D.10; *Berardo Pasinelli*, 23 years, 1230–1253: IV.G.3; *Giovanni Egidii* (di Egidio), 23 years, 1303–1326: II.B.2, Lib. perg. di Matteo Barnabei, 4; *Arecabene* (Arrekabene, Arrekhabene, Arricabeni, Arrecabone, Arrichabene, Arrecabene, Arekabene) *Nicolai* (di Nicola, but normally distinguished by not having a patronymic—but at least once, in 1317, in a document written by Matteo Barnabei, his name is revealingly extended to Arrecabene Nicolai de Ponte: IV.I.8), 23 years, 1303–1326: II.B.2, IV.I.3, Lib. perg. di Matteo Barnabei—Arecabene's name is fifth in the 1326 list, and Giovanni's fourth, in the 1303 list in which both Giovanni and Arecabene are listed as being absent from chapter, Giovanni's name again precedes Arecabene's with Oddone Pasinelli's in between, in 1326 Arecabene's nephew *Rosellus* appears as a witness: Lib. perg. di Matteo Barnabei, 216; *Andrea domini Sinibaldi* (Siniballi), 21 years, 1298–1319: IV.C.3, III.B.5; *Rainaldo Fatuclus* (Fatucli, Fatuculi), 20 years, 1233–1253: IV.G.3, II.D.3, 5 "Mgr", *Innocent IV*, no. 5777, at papal court, 1252. The reader should remember the kinds of sources which reveal this longevity. Occasionally they are really formal and almost necessarily exhaustive lists recorded in formal documents which have to do with joint chapter actions (for example, III.C.3, 1280) or chapter regulation (for example, II.B.2, 1303), or the reapportionment of prebends (for example, III.B.1, 1278–1307), or election, as in that of 30 September 1341. More generally they are lists of witnesses or canons present at an action whose names the notary has chosen to include in his instrument;

and the lists have the potential inadequacies and irregularities that that suggests although repeatedly notaries mention canons who are not present and at times tell the reason for their absence. These lists are also multiple, scattered, and hard to keep together in hand and mind. The positions of canons on lists, particularly those who appear first in the lists, is not entirely random: so, for example, with the names of long-lived canons in mind, one should note the first names in an (again not random) selection: Paolo, 1230: IV.G.3; the priest Rainaldo, 1233, 1239, 1240: IV.G.3, IV.Q.2; Sinibaldo Mareri, 1246, 1249: IV.O.4; Matteo Laurentii, 1260: IV.O.4; Rainaldo Beraldi, 1263: III.D.10; Tommaso Judicis, 1278, 1289: III.B.1, VII.F.3; Giacomo Sarraceno, 1278, 1280: IV.H.4, III.C.3; Andrea domini Sinibaldi, 1324: Lib. perg. di Matteo Barnabei, 181–182; Bartolomeo Bontempi, 1307, 1315, 1317: III.B.1, IV.F.4, Lib. perg. di Matteo Barnabei, 317; Tommaso Cimini, 1338, 1340: Lib. perg. di Matteo Barnabei, 419–420, 448; Giacomo di don Tommaso, 1326, 1346, 1347: III.B.6, Lib. perg. di Matteo Barnabei, 233, 564; Liberato and Deodato, 1364, 1368, 1371, 1379, from Lib. int. et exit. of those years. The senior member does not always head the list, but in this body in which the senior and antiquior seems to have been the assumed designated leader (but see below) it is natural that his name would normally, or at least often, come first and enough so that the placing of Bartolomeo Bontempi's name ahead of Bartolomeo Alfani's makes the observer question the continuity of Bartolomeo Alfani's tenure, and the placing of Angelo (Angeli) Mathei's name first in 1282 and 1286 (III.B.1, IV.H.4) makes one adjust the break in the sequence of figures with that name, who appear in 1242 but in 1246 remember going to Poggio Fidoni with Adenolfo and appear still in 1282 (III.B.1, IV.O.4, 5, IV.Q.2, VI.G.10, and A.S., San Domenico, 6).

13. For the San Leopardo case see above chapter 1, and for the attempted election chapter 5. For the Rainaldus gift, Rieti, Arch. Cap., IV.L.10, and for the appearance in 1181, IV.Q.2; and see: II.C.1, x, y, z; II.D.3, 4, 5, 7, 10; III.B.1, 2, 3, 6; III.C.3; III.D.2, 10; IV.D.1; IV.H.4; IV.M.1; IV.O.4, 5; IV.Q.1; VI.G.7; A.S., San Domenico, 6.

14. Berardo Rainaldi Sinibaldi Dodonis, Sinibaldo Mareri, Berardo Moysi, Jacobus de Ponte, the priest Rainaldo: Rieti, Arch. Cap., IV.D.1; IV.G.3; Berardo Salecti is present in 1220: VI.G.7—and the priest Bartolomeo is almost surely he of the 1222 list: IV.N.2.

15. Rieti, Arch. Cap., IV.O.1; IV.O.5; IV.G.3 (1233).

16. For the Santa Croce case see above chapter 3. Rieti, Arch. Cap., IV.P.6 "1". He is visible as a "canonicus Reatinus" in 1192. In 1215 (IV.G.3) his nephew, Matteo, is present; see IV.M.1; IV.M.2; IV.P.6; IV.Q.11; as well as IV.G.3.

17. Corrado de Murro's intense activity working for the church, both bishop and chapter, is particularly noticeable in the months between July 1326 and March 1327 and in June 1327 there is mention of his house in Rieti: Rieti, Arch. Cap., Lib. perg. di Matteo Barnabei, 207–230, 235–236. Corrado, present from at least 1308 to 1335 (VI.B.4, IV.C.8, IV.G.8, IV.M.6, Lib. perg. di Matteo Barnabei, 4, 363), dead by 5 June 1341 (Lib. perg., 467); "Corradus domini Riccardi de Murro" anniversary 10 August (Lib. IV, fo. 19v; father's anniversary 11 March; mother's 22 July); Corrado's brother Riccardus's bequests to his son Fra Henrico include a house in Castro Morro: Lib. perg. di Matteo Barnabei, 467–468;

see III.B.4, 5; III.C.5; IV.I.3; IV.I.7; IV.N.3 "1"; V.E.2; VI.C.8; Lib. perg., 5, 6, 19, 149–151, 205, 206, 235–236, 305, and chapters 7 and 8 below.

18. Rieti, Arch. Cap., III.C.2.

19. Rieti, Arch. Cap., II.D.4.

20. Rieti, Arch. Cap., IV.O.5 "5"; see III.D.3 for a nice example of an active canon, Matteo Laurentii, acting as yconomo, in 1256.

21. Rieti, Arch. Cap., IV.O.1.

22. Rieti, Arch. Cap., III.B.7.

23. So, for example, in 1233 Bishop Rainaldo de Labro, who used canon proctors, as we know, for a job that would on the surface appear appropriate for one of them, chose dompno Giovanni Arlocco, a clerk of San Giovenale, Rieti, as a proctor in the San Silvestro case: II.C.1 "1." One can observe in 1342 Tommaso Cimini, canon, made camerlengo for a year on 20 June, making Ballovino his substitute: Lib. perg. di Matteo Barnabei, 492–493.

24. Rieti, Arch. Cap., IV.M.2: 1209; also see in other documents recording gifts to Adenolfo, within IV.M.2, the repeatedly used formula "tuisque fratribus"; for "cum concanonicis": IV.G.3, Rainaldo de Labro in 1230, but also an incompletely clear usage of *concanonicus* for Bartolomeo Bontempi in the Giovanni Papazurri document, IV.H.4, discussed immediately below.

25. Rieti, Arch. Cap., IV.H.4.

26. Rieti, Arch. Cap., Lib. perg. di Matteo Barnabei, 209.

27. Rieti, Arch. Cap., Lib. con. et col., fo. 57r.

28. Rieti, Arch. Cap., III.B.1.

29. Rieti, Arch. Cap., III.C.5.

30. Rieti, Arch. Cap., III.C.3. The reader may recall Maitland's playing with singular and plural: "Are we to be angry whenever a noun in the singular governs a verb in the plural?" *Township and Borough*, 13; Maitland was playing with a problem closely related to the chapter's concept of itself.

31. See the canons listed in IV.D.4 and particularly IV.D.5.

32. *Regesta Honorii Papae III*, no. 4897. I discussed this affair at some length in an article "Innocent IV and the Chapter of Rieti," 387–392, at which time I had a clearer but, I think, less correct notion of what was divided and reassembled.

33. *Grégoire IX*, nos. 4261–4262; Rieti, Arch. Cap., IV.D.1; Bishop Giovanni's dispute with his chapter inhibited his rule according to Bishop Tommaso in the historical section of his presentation against San Salvatore Maggiore, see chapters 3 and 5 above.

34. *Grégoire IX*, no. 4431.

35. *Grégoire IX*, no. 4491; Rieti, Arch. Cap., IV.D.2.

36. Rieti, Arch. Cap., IV.D.3. Pietro Capocci, cardinal deacon of San Giorgio in Velabro in dealing with the problem of the income of absent canons at Rieti, in 1249, approved the working arrangement, under Gregory's plan, of the bishop, Rainaldo da Arezzo, with the chapter. IV.D.3 contains both Pietro's letter, maintaining its seal with the figure of San Giorgio, and also Bishop Rainaldo and the chapter's agreeing statement. An absent canon was to get half of his *beneficii*, the other half to be kept in the hands of the cellarer (*cellararius*).

37. Vèroli, Arch. Cap. della Cattedrale, no. 575. The beginning of the doc-

ument is rotted away, but it can be roughly dated by the notary, Leonardo, who was working in Vèroli in the late 1230s (see no. 165), and almost surely a Vèroli historian working in depth with its documents could date it quite closely. The Vèroli archives are described in Scaccia Scarafoni, "L'archivio capitolare della cattedrale di Vèroli." I am grateful to Don Paniccia for having admitted me to the archives and to Richard Mather for having advised me about them and taken me to them.

38. Rieti, Arch. Cap., IV.D.2. The four names are not completely legible.

39. Rieti, Arch. Cap., IV.D.5. The appeals are mentioned in Urban's letter, see note 40.

40. Rieti, Arch. Cap., IV.D.6; for Andrea Rainaldi see above chapter 5; for the palazzo of the canons in 1224, Arch. Cap., IV.N.2 "4."

41. For the specific case of Giacomo de Labro, see Rieti, Arch. Cap., Lib. perg. di Matteo Barnabei, 149 (1319), and below chapter 8.

42. Rieti, Arch. Cap., IV.F.2.

43. Rieti, Arch. Cap., IV.A.4.

44. Rieti, Arch. Cap., IV.F.1.

45. Rieti, Arch. Cap., IV.F.3.

46. Rieti, Arch. Cap., III.D.2; for Bartolomeo's 1254 letter see above note 11.

47. For Magister Salvus: Rieti, Arch. Cap., II.D.2, 3, 5, 10; III.B.3, 6; III.D.2, 5; IV.D.5; IV.I.1; *Innocent IV*, no. 3873; he seems to have been a canon from the late 1240s to the early 1260s, and his is the second name in a 1261 list (III.B.3).

48. Giovanni de Podio is identified as Dompnus in 1280 (III.C.3) when his priesthood is presumably being emphasized; in the early thirteenth century before the conventions of canon lists are formed, priests are regularly identified as *presbiter*, that is *pbr*; for the change in significance of priest canons see below.

49. For these "de Ponte" see for example, Rieti, Arch. Cap., IV.D.1; IV.G.3; IV.Q.2 (which give a range of years for Giacomo de Ponte of at least 1230 to 1242); Jandono (Janni) de Ponte appears in 1315 and 1316: IV.I.7; IV.M.6; Lib. perg. di Matteo Barnabei, 4–6. For Pietro's "de Labro," see II.G.9 (1369). See, too, Jean Coste, "La famiglia *De Ponte* di Roma (sec. XII–XIV)," *Archivio della società romana di storia patria* III (1988): 49–73.

50. Rieti, Arch. Cap., III.D.1, 2, 3; these are among the documents: "Scripturae spectantes ad Communitatem Reatinam" cataloged separately by Mazzatinti (and previously inventoried by Marchetti Tomasi), and kept separately in the armadi of the old tower archives; it is not known how they came to the capitular archives, but this "communal" connection ties the Ponte house documents to Rieti without tying them securely to the chapter: Mazzatinti, *Gli archivi*, 261. For the Ponte houses in Rome, see Brentano, *Rome before Avignon*, 39–40.

51. Rieti, Arch. Cap., Cart. Silv., 206.

52. *Catalogus baronum*, 215, no. 1108.

53. Rieti, Arch. Cap., II.D.7; Rieti, A.S., Fondo comunale, 8.

54. Rieti, A.S., Fondo comunale, 8.

55. Rieti, Arch. Cap., III.C.4; IV.H.4; Lib. perg. di Matteo Barnabei, 2–4.

56. Bib. Apos. Vat., San Pietro in Vaticano, caps. 64, no. 181.

57. A.S.V., Arm. XXXV.14. For the cook, Pietro of Rieti, in 1287, in the

household of Goffredo da Alatri (but not called *magister* as is one of his fellow cooks): Paravicini Bagliani, *Cardinali di curia*, 467 and note 3.

58. Rieti, Arch. Cap., II.D.3.

59. Paravicini Bagliani, *Cardinali di curia*, 268, 256–265.

60. For a later helpful *scriptor*, Magister Pietro di q. Nicola Federici, carrying *tria paria litterarum apostolicarum* for the church, in 1320: Rieti, Arch. Cap., III.D.4.

61. Rieti, Arch. Cap., IV.A.5; the multiple identity, which makes sense, is slightly less sure because, I believe, scribes sometimes did write the proctor's name on the dorse.

62. Rieti, Arch. Cap., II.D.3; II.D.4; III.B.1.

63. Paravicini Bagliani, *Cardinali di curia*, 268.

64. For Risabella see below chapter 8; Rieti, Arch. Cap., III.D.2.

65. Rieti, Arch. Cap., VII.E.2.

66. Rieti, Arch. Cap., III.B.3; III.B.6; III.D.10; IV.D.5; IV.K.13; A.S., San Domenico, 6.

67. Rieti, Arch. Cap., IV.Q.2; II.D.2; a Pasinelli witness is already present in 1157: IV.L.10; and for the priest canon Berardo Pasinelli: IV.G.3; IV.Q.1 (1230–1253).

68. Rieti, Arch. Cap., II.D.2, 4, 5, 10; III.B.1, 3, 6; III.C.3; III.D.2, 10.

69. Rieti, Arch. Cap., III.D.2 (Angelo: IV.D.1).

70. Rieti, Arch. Cap., VII.B.4. The letter (which is dated Orvieto, 6 September 1290) has very much the form and look of contemporary papal letters; it still carries its green cord, inserted and knotted as it would be on a papal letter, and its elegant red wax seal, with no reverse impression, but with an obverse showing two figures (Mary and John) half turned within arched openings in a gothic structure, and, over them in another arch, a crucified Christ; the legend is very damaged but it includes "tris Mat"; the initial *U* is finely and conventionally decorated; the margin and lines of the 14 line text are plumbed.

71. It seems to me that the evidence about Narni gathered by Hagemann, argues a similar localness for that diocese: "Kaiser- und Papsturkunden im Archivio capitolare," 299–304, 296, 302–303, 298, 293–295. The evidence of Giovanni Papazurri's capitular "reform" of 1313, see below note 86, certainly argues for continued episcopal-capitular appointment *proprio motu*.

72. For both Andrea the bishop and Ventura his brother the vicar general see above chapter 5, and also chapter 4, and also particularly Rieti, Arch. Cap., VII.E.8. The canon Berardo da Poggio Bustone, active in Rieti at least from 1261 to 1280 was the chaplain of Ottobuono Fieschi, cardinal deacon of Sant'Adriano, and was in Lyons with him in 1274; Leonardo Arcangeli, at least 1261–1280, was chaplain to Ottone da Tonengo, cardinal bishop of Porto in 1246: Paravicini Bagliani, *Cardinali di curia*, 268, 369, 94; *Innocent IV*, no. 2108, Leonardo's provision.

73. The presence of the Colonna is administrative as well as seignorial: Giovanni Colonna was captain of the city in 1284: Rieti, Arch. Cap., IV.Q.9.

74. The future power, most violently apparent at the end of the fourteenth century, of the Alfani, should shade any thought of the disappearance from power of the old patriciate; it argues a change of locus (if change at all).

75. Rieti, Arch. Cap., VII.E.4; VII.E.5.

76. Rieti, Arch. Cap., III.D.10 (12 pieces). I want to thank Peter Herde, who alerted me to the fact that Mazzatinti had omitted reference to these documents which had been noted by Naudé. From the tables established in Spufford's *Handbook* it is not clear that Sienese and Lucchese values would be different at this date.

77. Pasztor, "Per la storia dell'amministrazione," 182–183; for Mercatello see Leonardi, *Le fondazioni francescane.*

78. See for example *Jean XXII*, nos. 745, 752–754, 758, 765, 767, 769, 779, 815, 842, 1686, 3351, 8046, 8946, 11916, 12545, 13788, 13990, 14612–3, 14640, 15111, 15451, 15687, 15659, 16010, 16411, 17072, 17121. Rieti, Arch. Cap., Lib. perg. di Matteo Barnabei, 328 (1333); Lib. IV, fos. 25r–37v, thirteenth name (1349). See Lippens, "Fra Biagio da Leonessa," 122–123, no. 19 for Matteo Infantis de Reate, in 1359, chaplain of Rainaldo Orsini, cardinal deacon of Sant'Adriano.

79. For Terius Lalli, Rieti, Arch. Cap., IV.I.2; Lib. IV, fos. 25r–37v (1349); Lib. int. et exit., through 1371; or for the prebendary Domenico da Gonessa see Lib. int. et exit., 1363, fo. 53r (still active in 1379), and chapter 8 below; perhaps of more interest, Caterina da Gonessa who carried water for the months of July and August 1363 for 6 soldi: was she connected with the bishop? It may seem, and be, artificial to consider Leonessa foreign and Poggio Bustone or Rocca Sinibalda or Mareri not foreign in the fourteenth century, but this does seem to me the natural contemporary assumption.

80. Rieti, Arch. Cap., VII.F.3. The reception took place in the baptistry church of San Giovanni Battista.

81. Rieti, Arch. Cap., VI.C.1.

82. Rieti, Arch. Cap., III.B.4, 5; and see II.B.2; III.B.1; IV.C.8; IV.F.4; IV.G.8; IV.I.3, 7; V.E.2; VI.B.4; VII.F.3, 4, 5; Lib. perg. di Matteo Barnabei, 2–4, 5, 6, 9, 149, 242, 341–342.

83. Rieti, Arch. Cap., VII.C.6. The seal in brown or white wax remains on the strip.

84. Rieti, Arch. Cap., VII.F.4.

85. Rieti, Arch. Cap., VII.A.4. Red wax seal remains on blue string: gothic structure, Virgin and Child above, cleric in gothic vestments praying beneath.

86. Rieti, Arch. Cap., IV.F.4; for 1307: Reg. (or Libr.) VI, fo. 37r.

87. Rieti, Arch. Cap., Lib. int. et exit., 1371. In 1364 fourteen prebendaries are listed. In the late 1340s, four chaplains act for themselves and eight others: Cart. Silv., 206.

88. Rieti, Arch. Cap., Lib. cont. et col., II, fo. 261r (last written half folio).

89. This prebendal succession is made clear, for example, in Raymond's letter; in the list for July 1379 13 of the 17 prebendaries named are given the "priestly" title *dompnus.* Lib. int. et exit., 1379, fo. 51r. For the provision of a prebendary by Bishop Giovanni Papazurri, through his "executor," Andrea domini Sinibaldi canon and abbot of Sant'Eleuterio in 1332: Rieti, Arch. Cap., Lib. perg. di Matteo Barnabei, 304.

90. Rieti, Arch. Cap., IV.N.3 "1": will; IV.G.4 (2 pieces), Giovanni di Pietro; and see: III.B.1, 4, 5; III.C.4; IV.F.4, 8; IV.G.4; IV.H.4; IV.I.5, 7; IV.M.6; IV.N.3 "3"; V.E.1; Lib. perg. di Matteo Barnabei, 1, 4, 13, 15, 104; binding of

Lib. int. et exit., 1537 (1299); for the family, see II.D.7 (where they form part of the group of retainers with Alfani, Carsidonei, di don Napoleone, and others); IV.O.4 (where there are three brothers "called Capitaneos," in the accusative, in 1261); II.C.3r; VIII.C.4. For Tommaso and wills see chapter 8 below.

91. A December 1345 notarized and sealed (with the bishop's red wax seal) certificate or letter of ordination, written in the name of Tommaso bishop of Terni, states that the bishop, at the instance of Filippo vicar general of R[aimond] bishop of Rieti, has ordained to the priesthood Mando Cicchi, chaplain of the major church of Rieti: Rieti, Arch. Cap., II.E.1; see Bowsky, *A Medieval Italian Commune*, 270, for the rarity of these instruments in the diocese of Siena in the early fourteenth century.

92. Rieti, Arch. Cap., IV.G.4.

93. Rieti, Arch. Cap., Lib. perg. di Matteo Barnabei, 396.

94. Ballovino was a priest at least by 6 October 1341: Lib. con. et col., I, fo. 74r, although Agostino was not then a canon of long tenure. I do not mean to imply that there had been no earlier canon camerlenghi: Berardo Secinari is an obvious example: see too, for example, III.B.7. Some sense of the dimensions, but not the intricacy, of Ballovino's job can be gotten from the amounts he handled; in the accounting year 1364–1365 he dispersed a sum slightly under 500 lire: Lib. Int. et Exit., 1364.

95. Rieti, Arch. Cap., Lib. perg. di Matteo Barnabei, 98–99 (and see the initial listing of canons and prebends in III.B.1/Reg. VI, the list beginning with Dominus Barthomeus [*sic*] Bontempi: eleven holders of prebends [prebendaries?] follow the 21 canons, but they include "Dominus Johannes Magistri Andree," who I think holds this prebend in expectancy of his canonry; the list includes Tommaso Capitaneo, Giacomo di San Liberato, and Petraca Ambrosicti, of whom the first two are called dompno). In a witness list of February 1331 the third and fourth names are "Petrage Ambrosicti, Vannis eius fratris" (genitive): Lib. perg., 282–283; for Accurimbono: III.B.2, IV.N.3, Lib. perg., 4. For an example of an important assignment to Vanni Ambrosicti as proctor of bishop and chapter in 1328: IV.F.5. See IV.F.4 (1313) for notary prebendaries; and Lib. con. et col., I, for example, for Ciccho di Giovanni de Bussata as prebendary.

96. Rieti, Arch. Cap., III.B.1 and Reg. (or Libr.) VI. For a discussion of opposition to prebends in the universal church see Morris, *The Papal Monarchy*, 388–389.

97. Rieti, Arch. Cap., IV.D.3.

98. Rieti, Arch. Cap., III.B.1, fos. 2v–3r (4–5).

99. I have tried to call attention to these sources of income in *Two Churches*, 104–105.

100. In 1332 four canons (Tommaso Secinari, Tommaso Cimini, Andrea di don Sinibaldo, Giacomo di don Tommaso), in the name of the church of Rieti, bought some of this property, houses and attached property in the Porta Romana with public roads on three sides, property which had been that of Stefanello the Spicer (or Spetiari), from another canon of Rieti (Pietro da Posterula), acting as proctor for the owner Don Pietro Orsini of Rome, for 125 florins: Lib. perg. di Matteo Barnabei, 300. In 1364 this property returned 23 lire 15 soldi to the camera; and in 1365, 24 lire 7 soldi 6 denari; the property held at least five

shops by the 1360s. Chapter income and property will be discussed further in chapter 8 below.

101. See above chapter 2.

102. The giunta used for measurement at Rieti may not have been used in the whole diocese. At present at least at Poggio Moiano (over the border in the diocese of Sabina) the conventional measurement is by *coppa*, memorializing a different element of the old plowing and sowing process: at present the *coppa* refers to an area of about 2,000 square meters: I owe this information to Bianca Passeri, whom I would like to thank for it.

103. It should be apparent not only that I find the complex documents III.B.1 and Reg. (or Libr.) VI impressive but also that I find the material within them repeatedly baffling, so that for me to arrive at a definite total conclusion from their use is difficult; it has perhaps seemed more difficult because each of the two has disappeared for a while from the archives, although both have now returned.

104. Rieti, Arch. Cap., Reg. (or Libr.) VI, fos. 1r–17v; for 1349 see instead Libro IV, fos. 25r–37v. (For Rainallo: VI, fos. 7v–8v; IV, fos. 31r–31v.)

105. Rieti, Arch. Cap., Reg. (or Libr.) VI, fos. 16r, 20r.

106. I have borrowed the concept of *inquilini* because of its deliberate non-committal, evocative artificiality from Italo Calvino's *Palomar* in the chapter "La spada del sole."

107. Rieti, Arch. Cap., III.B.4: the rector is Andrea de Felcibus, canon of Santa Maria in Trastevere; see too the chapter assembled on 1 November 1319, III.B.5. The medieval Franciscan calendar preserved in the Arch. Cap. at Rieti lists the feast of Sts. Vitus, Modestus, and Crescentia as 17 Kalends July equals 15 June.

108. Rieti, Arch. Cap., Lib. con. et col., I, fos. 55r–56v.

109. When I used this draft it was between folios 106 and 107 of the book in which the constitutions are recorded (Lib. con. et col., I); it may, of course, not remain there.

110. See for example, Rieti, Arch. Cap., Cart. Silv., 68, 71–72, 90, 91–92; Lib. con. et col., I, fo. 9v.

111. Rieti, Arch. Cap., Lib. con. et col., I, fos. 94v–95v.

112. Rieti, Arch. Cap., Lib. con. et col., I, fos. 64r–64v.

113. Rieti, Arch. Cap., Cart. Silv., 72, 84.

114. Rieti, Arch. Cap., Lib. con. et col., I, fos. 100r–100v.

115. Rieti, Arch. Cap., III.B.3.

116. Rieti, Arch. Cap., Lib. con. et col., II, 227.

117. Rieti, Arch. Cap., Lib. con. et col., I, fos. 57r–57v, 71r–74r, and a loose sheet, paper, Deodato declaration, now between fos. 23 and 24.

118. Rieti, Arch. Cap., Lib. con. et col., I, fos. 137v–138v.

119. Rieti, Arch. Cap., Lib. con. et col., I, fos. 59r–59v.

120. Rieti, Arch. Cap., Cart. Silv., 65.

121. Rieti, Arch. Cap., Lib. con. et col., I, fo. 113r for Camputosto's interest as partial patron in San Giovanni Poggio Bustone and Sant'Angelo Poggio Bustone, and the succession of his sons Tommaso and Buccio to Sant'Angelo; Lib.

con. et col., I, fo. 7v for 19 September 1340; Lib. con. et col., II, 44 for 14 April 1349. Giovanni was dead by 14 September 1363: VII.G.11.

122. Paris, B.N. latin 1556, fo. 10v: Martène and Durand, 8, col. 1516.

123. This is a point I began to argue in "Vescovi e collocazione" (see above, chapter 4 note 11); thinking of what I saw in the diocese of Rieti, admittedly mostly in the 1340s, with the problem of the conference, pieve-parrocchia, in mind, forced me to the conclusion that for Rieti it was the wrong question.

124. For Tommaso the Corrector's list see above chapter 3.

125. See above chapter 1.

126. See above the beginning of chapter 6.

127. Paris, B.N. latin 1556, fo. 10v: Martène and Durand, 8, cols. 1516–1517.

128. Rieti, Arch. Cap., VI.D.4.

129. Rieti, Arch. Cap., VI.D.3; in the Franciscan calendar within the chapter archives at Rieti, the feast of the consecration of the church of "Sancti Heleuterii" has been added on the line for the Ides of August (13 August), but the notation continues onto the line for the next day.

130. Rieti, Arch. Cap., VI.D.5.

131. I am following Mazzatinti's notation of the grant, which he read into the capitular archives: VI.D.1: Mazzatinti, *Gli archivi*, 246. I follow Boschi on the consecration: Boschi, *Notizie storiche sopra la chiesa e il convento di S. Domenico*, and "Di un antico cimitero in Rieti," 22; Boschi talks of 12 canons and an abbot.

132. Rieti, Arch. Cap., VI.C.8. Giacomo de Labro was a canon of Sant'Angelo in 1283: Rome, A.S., "Rieti," 1: Cass. 76, no. 1.

133. Rieti, Arch. Cap., VI.C.5.

134. Paris, B.N. latin 1556, fo. 10v: Martène and Durand, 8, col. 1517.

135. Rieti, Arch. Cap., VI.A.3.

136. A satisfying example comes from April 1349 where one finds together the abbot of Sant'Eleuterio ("Vanni" di don Capo), the provost of Sant'Angelo (Tommaso di Pietro Bonaventure), and the archpriest of San Giovanni "in Statua" (Giovanni Petringoni), all canons: Cart. Silv., 235; but see, for many examples, pergamene in VI.A, D, F, G, and VII.F, G, and a general scattering through all the pergamene and codices surviving from the two centuries.

137. Rieti, Arch. Cap., VI.C.1.

138. Rieti, Arch. Cap., IV.H.4, one of four pieces; see, too, IV.G.7, in which in February 1324 Bishop Giovanni from Collalto writes to "Universis et singulis canonicis et Capitulo Ecclesie Reatin' necnon prepositis, archipresbiteris, prebendariis, et clericis ecclesiarum ciuitatis" condemning them, or some of them, for not having properly proclaimed the excommunication of a clerk of Santa Marina Rieti, who had not paid tithes, and demanding that it be properly proclaimed.

139. Rieti, Arch. Cap., III.B.2.

140. Rigon, *Clero e città*, 34. For Rome, see above, note 107.

141. San Matteo which develops into San Pastore with another retained San Matteo is dealt with at length above in chapter 2; for San Salvatore see chapter 3 above; for San Quirico see above, introduction, and below in this chapter at

note 148; the religious houses dealt with in this chapter, with the exception of San Quirico, will be dealt with less externally in chapter 8.

142. For Tommaso's list see above chapter 3: Paris, B.N. latin 1556, fos. 18r–26r, particularly 24v–25v. It should be noted that Tommaso's list does group the monastic and religious houses, with other (in his, or the composer's, mind) obviously related entities, so that the *loci* of the Franciscans and Augustinians in the city are with their orders not with the city; the exclusion of the male Dominicans in Rieti, see below, could be an oversight.

143. Rieti, Arch. Cap., IV.N.3. The initial attachment to orders of houses of women should be treated with some caution as the case of Borgo San Pietro, below chapter 7, makes clear, although it may be an extreme case within the diocese. A very important essay-article by the Perugia historian Casagrande, "Il fenomeno della reclusione volontaria," particularly at 480–481, in distinguishing among kinds of recluses offers patterns of observation valuable in approaching developing religious communities. In Tommaso's list, the houses of nuns follow the Franciscans and precede Altopascio, fo. 25r; their rubric begins "Moniales habent locum in ciuitate / Santa Lucia" with the notation of one pound of wax owed, then to "Apud Sanctum Petrum de Molito" with the notation of 10 soldi owed each year on the feast of All Saints, then the list proceeds: "Apud Colle Altum ubi sunt fratres / Apud Sanctum Iohannem de Pesculo / Apud Sanctum Iohannem de Machilona / Sanctum Angelum / Apud Lauaretum / Apud Maranam."

144. Paris, B.N. latin 1556, fo. 25r. For the Hospitallers in central Italy see the essay by Luttrell, "Two Templar-Hospitaller Preceptories" in *The Hospitallers.*

145. Paris, B.N. latin 1556, fo. 25r. For Altopascio and its order see McArdle, *Altopascio*, particularly 2–4, with references, but the physical descriptions and plates of 16–23 are of great interest even for historians of an earlier period.

146. Rieti, Arch. Cap., VI.F.5 (1312). For the Reatine presence and interest see Abbazia di Farfa, Archivio, "Regestro de Alardo," "Regesto Abbatis Nicolai" and the discussion of the "tramonto" of Farfa power and its documents in Schuster, *L'imperiale abbazia di Farfa*, 303–346; McClendon, *The Imperial Abbey of Farfa*. I should like to thank Anthony Luttrell and Charles McClendon for having helped me very much with Farfa and, both, for having taken me to its archives and introduced me to its archivists, Dom Massimo Lapponi and Dom Stefano Baiocchi, and to thank them. I should also like to thank Roberta Magnusson for teaching me much of value about early Farfa and having allowed me to read her unpublished paper on Farfa's San Martino, and to thank Mary Ann Rossi for her fascinating discussion of St. Brigid and Farfa delivered in a Rome NEH seminar.

147. Paris, B.N. latin 1556, fo. 25v.

148. For San Quirico see Cheney, "Gervase, Abbot of Prémontré," 25–56; I am indebted to Cheney for having talked to me about and introducing me to the work, Charles Louis Hugo, *Sacrae antiquitatis monumenta* (Étival, 1725) from which my quotations and paraphrases of Gervase come, the first from 1:29. See too Backmund, *Monasticon Praemonstratense*, 1:378–379, who talks of Innocent III's transfer of the monastery in 1215, and the first abbot "Gaufridus."

The monastery is more fully named Santi Quirico e Giulitta. According to legend Giulitta was the mother of Quirico, Clerico, Cyricus, Cyr, and both were martyred at the beginning of the fourth century.

149. Hugo, *Monumenta*, 1:30–33; "Monachos Abruchiae, qui nostrum Ordinem profiteri: sunt etenim Longobardi, astutissimi supra modum, et a diebus antiquis exercitati in adulationibus fraudulentis": 1:31. *Furbi* is my word.

150. Hugo, *Monumenta*, 1:32–33.

151. Hugo, *Monumenta*, 1:32: "ita simplex, ut videatur esse quasi planta vitis infixa terrae, quae virorem suum tantummodo retinens, nec in latum extendit palmites, nec in profundum extendit radices sine fructu et sine propagine, moritura."

152. The canny stillness refers to the complete absence from the record of the dispute with Penne (insofar as I have read it carefully) of any specific reference to order; any emphasis given to the fact that the monastery had become Premonstratensian and so likely to demand Premonstratensian immunities (of the sort that Bishop Tommaso's list tries to deny, and about which Gervase was concerned) might cause additional trouble. The record, which talks of Gerardo "who was abbot and is dead," and is of course composed of memories, does mention Innocent III, the Fourth Lateran Council, and the coronation of Frederick II; but in a list of eight abbots, for example, of which Gerardo is the last, it makes no distinctions. For the record of the dispute see above introduction note 15.

153. Paris, B.N. latin 1556, fos. 24v–25r.

154. For San Francesco see Julian Gardner's appendix to this book. See Sbaralea, *Bullarium franciscanum*, vol. 1, nos. 97, 228. See Mortari, "Rieti," 112; Palmegiani, *La cattedrale*, 91–93: this may be Palmegiani's most interesting and helpful book, but it is difficult to use because of its combination of helpful information and occasional insights and its use of the in-family research of Vincenzo Palmegiani on the one hand, and on the other its carelessness and error (as for example in making Francesco Papazurri a bishop; but this may seem caviling from a historian who can write Vèroli for Ferentino, or Sant'Eustachio for Sant'Eleuterio—and in fact it is very hard to control this sort of detail gathered from many and dispersed record sources, particularly without the help of an editor who also knows the material). Francesco Palmegiani may seem most interesting as part of a family group which includes, besides Vincenzo Palmegiani, Eugenio Duprè Theseider. It has been explained to me by a powerful contemporary Italian historian that a non-Italian is not likely to be able to appreciate Duprè Theseider, and I am an example of that lack of ability. It is surely difficult for an American of my generation to be sympathetic with Francesco Palmegiani's facile fascism and anti-Americanism, so I may constantly fail to appreciate his value or see his depth. Certainly, again, Palmegiani seems to me most sympathetic when he is most local and familial; and in fact the moment in Duprè Theseider which I can most easily appreciate is that in a beautiful letter edited by Vasina and Ghini (in "Ricordo di Eugenio Duprè Theseider," 141–142, no. 5) in which Duprè talks of selling his family house in Rieti; his letters suggest to the outsider the teacher his students must have known. The reader of Palmegiani himself must learn what he can and be wary. (I have tried to put

the Rieti settlement of Franciscans in a wider context in "Early Franciscans and Italian Towns," 28–49.)

155. Rieti, Arch. Cap., VIII.A.2; Sbaralea, *Bullarium franciscanum*, vol. 2, no. 65. For Santa Croce, see Porracciolo and Petroni, "La chiesa di S. Francesco." See *Scripta Leonis*, 142–143, for the friar, a character in a kind of miracle of Francis, alive, who, the friar, *morabatur in loco fratrum de Reate.*

156. Mortari, "Rieti," 130.

157. Rieti, Arch. Cap., III.D.9; A.S., San Domenico, 4 (olim 42), 2; Mortari, "Rieti," 112; Palmegiani, *La cattedrale*, 67–69; Boschi, *Notizie storiche sopra la chiesa*, 8–29. I want to thank Joan Lloyd for pointing out the Dominican distinction to me; for the constitution of the order, see Galbraith, *The Constitution of the Dominican Order.*

158. Rieti, A.S., San Domenico, 7 (olim 103). By 1334 at the latest the contrada was known as "contrada sancti Dominici": Arch. Cap., Lib. perg. di Matteo Barnabei, 332.

159. Written by Guidoni in "L'espansione urbanistica," 156; the phrase *città dei Mendicanti* is his. I know of no independent information about these streets; I depend on Guidoni.

160. For bibliography about this point see "Early Franciscans and Italian Towns" and the discussion of city/country in chapter 8 below; but I would note here a particularly helpful chronology of movement established by Fra Mariano d'Alatri, "I piu antichi insediamenti dei mendicanti," 576, 583 (for Anagni); for an interesting 1256 dispute at Amelia between the Augustinians and the bishop and chapter about building within the old walls, see Rome, Vallicelliana, Capitolino, Archivio Orsini, II.A.I.37 (olim 35). Much recent thought about the friars, and particularly the Franciscans, and their expansion finds its roots in the thought and work of Kaspar Elm.

161. Sbaralea, *Bullarium franciscanum*, vol. 4, no. 168; *Nicholas IV*, no. 502. A list of chapter holdings from the second half of the fourteenth century suggests that the city of Rieti was then thought of as divided into ten parishes: Rieti, Arch. Cap., Libr. IV, fos. 16r–18v.

162. This generalization should not obscure the presence of important local friars like the fourteenth-century Guardiano of the Franciscans, Giacomo Janutii da Rieti, for example, Rieti, Arch. Cap., Cart. Silv., 26, in 1337.

163. *Scripta Leonis*, 150–151, no. 35.

164. Rieti, Arch. Cap., IV.Q.10.

165. Rieti, Arch. Cap., IV.H.4; VI.B.1.

166. Rieti, Arch. Cap., Lib. perg. di Matteo Barnabei, 8; VI.B.1.

167. Rieti, Arch. Cap., VI.E.3. (In a list for 1235, from San Matteo, for example, the list of 28 men includes no place name identifications: IX.A.2.)

168. Rome, A.S., S. Francesco di S. Vittoria in Materano, sec. 13, no. 1.

169. These nuns will be discussed in both chapters 7 and 8; but here I should like to call attention to San Tommaso's being or becoming Cistercian; see Janauschek, *Originum cisterciensium*, lx: San Tommaso fuori Rieti, in 1273, a daughter of Casamari, patronized by the Cistercian cardinal, John of Toledo, bishop of Porto; see too Janauschek, ibid., lxi, for San Benedetto di Fondi. For

San Tommaso see also Canivez, *Statuta capitulorum*, vol. 3, no. 35 and vol. 5, no. 66.

170. Rieti, Arch. Cap., Cart. Silv., 48–50.

Chapter 7

1. Baldelli, *Medioevo volgare*, 236. I hope that the pertinence of the phrase to the chapter will be apparent; but the question of whether, for example, a serious but unconventionally instructed Christian's becoming a "saint" or a "heretic" is decided as if by a throw of the dice should not I think be such an easy question to answer as it has seemed (in both directions) to some of my predecessors.

2. Bib. Apos. Vat., Vat. Lat. 4029, fos. 3r–5v. I do not at all mean to imply that this is an unknown or unpublished document; see principally Luigi Fumi, "Eretici e ribellinell'Umbria," particularly 5:349–420, but see too Fumi's remarkable "Avvertenza," 5:421–422, in which he excuses and explains his publication of offensive documents, *ai dotti* not *al pubblico*, and makes a series of comparisons, including one to rooms in museums in which certain pieces of sculpture are reserved: "si mostrano certe statue che si avrebbe rossore di esporre in piazza a vista di tutti." It will be obvious to the reader that I have actually written the Paolo parts of this chapter from the Vatican manuscript and not from Fumi and that my treatment of the material depends on its relationship to the manuscript in which it was written. That procedure is consistent, I think, with my more general approach to the documents within this book. But I should explain that when I was actually writing I had available to me a photocopy of the manuscript and not of the edition, both of which I had originally read in the Vatican. I was not avoiding Fumi because I believed that my readings would be better than his; quite the opposite is probably true. A reference to Paolo and his document, with some transcription, which most scholars would probably consider more authoritative than Fumi's, is to be found in Ehrle, "Die Spiritualen," particularly 4:8–15, 16–20. But the figure of Paolo has also found its way into, or at least it has been mentioned in, such a relatively general history of heresy as Leff, *Heresy in the Later Middle Ages*, 1:234; Leff's account of the fraticelli in relation to and distinction from other similar movements is lucidly helpful. Paolo's case and the document which contains it have not been, I think, considered before as sources for very local Rieti history, as they are meant to be here, and I hope that may give them a new freshness for anyone who already knows them. They are not meant here to be presented as a contribution to the history of heresy and inquisition.

3. Paolo's first testimony is Vat. Lat. 4029, fos. 6v–7v, but the description of him is from the inquisitor's statement on fos. 6r–6v (Fumi, "Eretici e ribelli," 5: 354–356). One notes, to use a word of Don Giovanni de Canemorto (used in a more serious context), a certain vacillation in the description of the house's location, who lives there when, and (one discovers later) in the fact that at least

once Paolo and Contessa seem to live in different sestieri within the Porta Romana.

4. Bib. Apos. Vat., Vat. Lat. 4029, fos. 3r, 7r, also see a passage left blank on 5r; the name "Piscis" was written in the margin of fo. 7v, with a mark of identification, identical with one placed in the blank space in the text.

5. See Dondaine, "Le Manuel de l'inquisiteur"; Gui, *Manuel*; *Bernard Gui et son monde*; Peters, *Inquisition*, particularly, 59–67; Hamilton, *The Medieval Inquisition*; Wakefield, *Heresy*; Violante, "Eresie urbane"; Wakefield and Evans, *Heresies of the High Middle Ages*; Merlo, *Eretici ed eresie medievali*; Dal Pino, *Il laicato italiano*; Merlo, *Tensioni religiose*.

6. Bib. Apos. Vat., Vat. Lat. 4029, fo. 6r; see Pasztor, "Il processo di Andrea da Gagliano."

7. Taught very convincingly by Lerner in the first chapter of his book *The Heresy of the Free Spirit*; see too Lerner's warning about the use of inquisitorial records, 5. Grundmann's short, lucid explanation of attitudes connected with the "Free Spirit," including sexual attitudes, is still cogent, see, in the Italian translation: *Movimenti religiosi nel medioevo*, especially 332–333.

8. Given, "The Inquisitors of Languedoc." As will surely be obvious I have found this an extremely stimulating introduction to the problems of inquisitorial records; Given's approach to very large and important problems of society and authority through these records brings to themselves a new freshness and attraction; for me the essay was very provocative. For use in Paolo's case see particularly, 343–353.

9. Given, "The Inquisitors," 352.

10. The work of Franciscan inquisitors in central Italy has been studied with particular care and success by Mariano d'Alatri, see especially his *Inquisizione*.

11. Bib. Apos. Vat., Vat. Lat. 4029, fo. 20r; Fumi, "Eretici e ribelli," 5:372.

12. For the miracles, Vat. Lat. 4029, fos. 21r–21v; Fumi, "Eretici e ribelli," 5: 373–374; and below.

13. Vat. Lat. 4029, fos. 6v–7v; Fumi, "Eretici e ribelli," 5:353–354.

14. Vat. Lat. 4029, fos. 8r–8v; Longone and Poggio Bustone are both early Franciscan settlements.

15. Vat. Lat. 4029, fo. 8v; Fumi, "Eretici e ribelli," 5:357.

16. Vat. Lat. 4029, fos. 9r–9v; Fumi, "Eretici e ribelli," 5:357–358.

17. Vat. Lat. 4029, fos. 9v–11v; Fumi, "Eretici e ribelli," 5:358–361.

18. Vat. Lat. 4029, fos. 11v–13v; Fumi, "Eretici e ribelli," 5:361–364; these dates are somewhat suspicious because they precede Contessa's 16 July testimony; they, particularly 25 July, may have been miswritten.

19. Vat. Lat. 4029, fos. 13v–15r; Fumi, "Eretici e ribelli," 5:364–366.

20. Vat. Lat. 4029, fos. 15v–16r; Fumi, "Eretici e ribelli," 5:366–367.

21. Vat. Lat. 4029, fos. 16v–17r; Fumi, "Eretici e ribelli," 5:367–368; the *nobilis et sapiens uir* Don Giovanni de Canemorto did not break his connection with Rieti even after he had acquired a house in Rome and was living there; see Rieti, Arch. Cap., VII.G.9 (1361)—in this example the connection is ensured by ties of patronage, but in August and again in December 1358 Giovanni received a salary of one florin from the church, as Ballovino recorded in his book of accounts (Lib. Int. et Exit.) for 1358. Andrea di don Sinibaldo "de Tortolinis"

de Reate (Lib. IV, fo. 19v) was abbot of Sant'Eleuterio from at least 8 December 1310 to at least 24 November 1336: Arch. Cap., VII.G.3, VI.D.4; by 21 May 1339 Angelo di don Paolo was abbot: VI.D.5. It is interesting to compare Giacomo Leoparducii's talk of torture with the almost exactly contemporary (1327) synodal constitution at Gubbio: "Et licet tortura in multis casibus concedatur iure tamen ut magistra rerum experientia docuit ex ea multa scandala et pericula provenire noscuntur, nec de facili viri ecclesiastici debeant ad tormenta corporum (venire) statuimus": Cenci, "Costituzioni sinodali," 369. The communal statutes of Rieti contain a statute limiting torture, or forbidding it except in certain cases (Rieti, A.S., Statuti, I, fo. 83v), but the cases are numerous enough seriously to limit the effectiveness of the statute: theft, robbery, rape, cutting vines, trees, nuts, mutilation of limb, scarring of face, false instruments or writing, false coining.

22. Vat. Lat. 4029, fos. 16v–17r; Fumi, "Eretici e ribelli," 5:368–369.

23. Vat. Lat. 4025, fo. 17v; Fumi, "Eretici e ribelli," 5:369.

24. Vat. Lat. 4025, fos. 17v–18r; Fumi, "Eretici e ribelli," 5:369–370.

25. Vat. Lat. 4025, fos. 18r–18v.

26. Vat. Lat. 4025, fos. 18v–19v; Fumi, "Eretici e ribelli," 5:371–372.

27. Vat. Lat. 4025, fos. 19v–20r; Fumi, "Eretici e ribelli," 5:372–373.

28. Vat. Lat. 4025, fos. 20r–21v; Fumi, "Eretici e ribelli," 5:373–374 (Fumi reads Fonzianum).

29. Vat. Lat. 4025, fos. 21v–22r; Fumi, "Eretici e ribelli," 5:374–375.

30. Vat. Lat. 4025, fos. 22r–23r: "tetigit membrum ipsius" (fo. 22r)—to whom does *ipsius* refer? Paolo's revealed tastes (or tastes of which he is accused) make it difficult to decide.

31. Vat. Lat. 4025, fos. 23r–23v; Fumi, "Eretici e ribelli," 5:376.

32. Vat. Lat. 4025, fos. 23v–24v; Fumi, "Eretici e ribelli," 5:376–378.

33. Vat. Lat. 4025, fo. 25r; Fumi, "Eretici e ribelli," 5:378.

34. Vat. Lat. 4025, fo. 25v; Fumi, "Eretici e ribelli," 5:379–380.

35. Vat. Lat. 4025, fos. 26r–26v; Fumi, "Eretici e ribelli," 5:379–380.

36. Vat. Lat. 4025, fos. 26v–27v; Fumi, "Eretici e ribelli," 5:380–381.

37. Vat. Lat. 4025, fo. 28r; the entry is incomplete and the text recommences on fo. 33r.

38. Vat. Lat. 4025, fos. 33r–34r; Fumi, "Eretici e ribelli," 5:382–384.

39. Vat. Lat. 4025, fos. 34r–35v; Fumi, "Eretici e ribelli," 5:384–385; I have translated "prope nonam" as "about noon." The whole incident is revealing about the nature and effect of the city's enclosure by wall and river; the information revealed is not straightforward, exactly, but it is understandable.

40. Vat. Lat. 4025, fos. 36r–37v; Fumi, "Eretici e ribelli," 5:386–388.

41. Vat. Lat. 4025, fos. 37v–39r; Fumi, "Eretici e ribelli," 5:388–389.

42. Vat. Lat. 4025, fos. 39r–43r; Fumi, "Eretici e ribelli," 5:390–394. For a threat to a house see the case of the canon Palmerio Leonardi, in chapter 6 note 75 above: Rieti, Arch. Cap., III.D.10.

43. Vat. Lat. 4025, fos. 43r–73v.

44. Vat. Lat. 4025, fos. 45r–45v, 43v–44v: the disorder in chronological arrangement is an obvious clue to the way in which the Vatican manuscript was compiled. Fumi ("Eretici e ribelli," 5:397) reads Bernardo's place of origin as

"de Gonissa" with a (?); I do not find this a possible reading, but of course it could be a correction of a scribal error; I read "Ben" or "Ven" and find Venice more likely. Fumi (395) also reads "de Civitate Sancte Floris de Ibernia" which I cannot identify; the presence of clerical figures from the British isles is worth noting; they must have been, at least by birth, neutral in central Italian oppidal squabbles.

45. Vat. Lat. 4025, fos. 44v–45r; Fumi, "Eretici e ribelli," 5:396. In connection with the phrase "Bona la canapita," as Fumi reads it, which the witness dompno Tommaso testified that someone in Rieti said about the time the inquisitor left Rieti, Fumi has written about *canipa, canapa*: hemp, and its collection, at the time of the inquest: "Anedotti curiosi: La Canapata," in "Eretici e ribelli," 5:445–446.

46. Vat. Lat. 4025, fos. 46v–49r; Fumi, "Eretici e ribelli," 5:397–401. I am unsure which of the two neighboring Monteleone, that in the diocese of Rieti, Monteleone Sabina, or that in the diocese of Spoleto, Monteleone di Spoleto, is intended; in either case the assumed significance of town of origin is exposed.

47. Vat. Lat. 4025, fos. 45v–46v; Fumi, "Eretici e ribelli," 5:397–398.

48. Vat. Lat. 4025, fos. 58r–62v, 50v–52r; the importance of this definition of the *provincia romana* in terms of the boundary of the diocese of Rieti which cut through the territory of Leonessa should be clear to the reader; and it should be thought about in connection with the materials and ideas discussed in chapters 3 and 4 above. For Franciscan provinces and the inquisition see Mariano D'Alatri, *L'inquisizione.*

49. Vat. Lat. 4025, fos. 63r–68r; Fumi, "Eretici e ribelli," 5:406–412. For Viterbo Benedictine houses, see Caraffa, ed., *Monasticon Italiae*, 1:193–196, nos. 290–303—see no. 300 for S. Matteo in Sonza. The reader should note the relative richness of this clerical community.

50. Vat. Lat. 4025, 68r–73r.

51. Vat. Lat. 4025, fos. 75r–76r; Fumi, "Eretici e ribelli," 5:412–413. The chronology of the Vatican manuscript is repeatedly distorted, but this placing of the Tivoli fraticelli inquest after the Rieti-Leonessa-Viterbo inquest is by far the greatest distortion. In spite of its position in the manuscript its reader might immediately guess that the Tivoli inquest did not happen in 1335 because the death of the pope would have intervened (in December 1334) between it and the previous inquests, and that would suggest the necessity of recording new inquisitorial authorization; but there is in fact more exact evidence for the document's referring to events in 1334: on fo. 81r the manuscript dates itself (in March) as in the second indiction; and on fo. 79r it actually offers the date, within a document, 1334 (again in March). Ehrle firmly accepts 1334 ("Die Spiritualen," 4: 8). There is a further problem; the manuscript places, above the first Tivoli action, the date "Indictione secunda, mense Februarii, Die xxviiij"—but neither 1334 or 1335 was a leap year. There was no 29 February in either year. Fumi simply prints "xxviiij" (412); Ehrle quietly emends "XXVIIIa" (8). "29 February" is an odd, unusual error, but not, I think, inconsistent with the recording behavior of the manuscript's scribe.

52. Vat. Lat. 4025, fos. 75r–78r. For the fraticelli see Douie, *The Nature and Effect*, particularly 49–80, and more recently Mariano D'Alatri, "Fraticellismo

e inquisizione" (an essay originally published in *Picenum seraphicum* 10 [1974])—and the references cited in both works. Ronald Musto spent much time talking to me about Angelo Clareno and lent me his beautiful editions of Angelo letters particularly those connected with Gentile of Foligno. I have had the advantages of years' of patient explanation by Charles Till Davis about the problems connected with the writings of Angelo and the other "Spirituals"; I have always come away vastly instructed, and much deepened in my apprecia-tion, and completely convinced that only scholars truly learned in the work of the Spirituals are able to cope with them in any serious way. A reader can get a sense of Davis's learning, lucidity, and complexity in his "Ubertino da Casale." Here, for Angelo, I am particularly dependent on Lydia von Auw's ed. of Angelo Clareno, "Epistole," 1:103. For an outline of Angelo's life see 1:xxii–xxv. For Subiaco see particularly Frugoni, "Subiaco francescano"; but also Egidi, Gio-vannoni, and Hermanin, eds., *I monasteri di Subiaco*, all of the essays, but par-ticularly "Gli affreschi del secolo decimoterzo," 417–485, 439–446, and plate V. For an introduction to Joachim of Fiore whose influence blows around these figures and through these inquisitorial stories see Reeves, *Joachim of Fiore*. In general, too, see Moorman, *A History of the Franciscan Order*, and particularly for Angelo, 312; and for instructions for selected interrogations, see Gui, *Manuel*, 1:158; and for a description of related heresy, again by Gui, translated by Wake-field and Evans, 411–439.

53. Vat. Lat. 4025, fos. 80r–81r.

54. See particularly, *I monasteri di Subiaco*, 1:123–124, for Subiaco's flourishing.

55. Although it is not conclusive in identifying parties or even, for the most part, individuals, the counterpoint between Angelo Clareno's letters and the events recorded in the Vatican manuscript is provocative. The correspondence connects the narrative of the manuscript with a broader and more intellectual world; the local narrative of the manuscript ties the idea and sentiment of the letters to the localness of town and countryside, see "Epistole," 1:xxxviii–xl, liv–lix, 49–52 (no. 11 to Francesco and Giovanni Lotaroni), 253–256 (no. 50 con-cerning the same Citto and Vanne), 256–257 (no. 51 to Andrea da Rieti), 277–279 (no. 58 to Matteo da Rieti and Giovanni Petrignani), and index under "Lo-doroni" and "Petrignani"; for Auw's identification of Giovanni Petrignani, see 10 no. 1, to letter 2, 10–12, addressed to Giovanni Petrignani and "Io., Le. Nicholao, B. et ceteris."

56. Rieti, Arch. Cap., Cart. Silv., 269; Lib. Int. et Exit., 1358. Libro IV, fo. 34v (the prebend—and compare Reg., or Libr. VI, fos. 11r–11v); Cart. Silv., 11 (for Tommaso Secinari's will); Lib. Int. et Exit., 1358, fo. 45r (for Giovanni's singing the Assumption Mass); again Lib. Int. et Exit., 1358 for his receiving commons and his being alive in April 1359, and Lib. Int. et Exit., 1360 for his being dead by the summer of 1360; on the patrician family Petrignani as it de-veloped, right down to the Scipio(ne) Petrignani still alive in 1666, see chapter 1 note 75 for Perotti Cavalli, vii, viii, 97 (and for the Caputosti, whose member Giovanni preceded Giovanni Petrignani as archpriest of San Giovanni Evange-lista, 16).

57. "Epistole," 1:49–52 no. 11, 253–256 no. 50, the quotation from Luke is

on 52; the letter is interwoven with scriptural echoes and citations with which its similar tone and message are reinforced, for example, 51: "Dimittite ergo mortuos sepelire mortuos suos" (Matthew 8:32). The reader should be aware of the presence of other descendants of Eleuterio in the documents (for example, Rieti, Arch. Cap., Lib. perg. di Matteo Barnabei, 554) and of course that there were other Eleuterios at Rieti (for example, III.B.1, 13).

58. For the autobiografia see the text printed in Frugoni, *Celestiniana*, 56–67; Frugoni's transcription can be controlled against the manuscript which Frugoni used as his base: A.S.V., A. A. Arm. I–XVIII, 3327; and for Frugoni's discussion of manuscripts see in *Celestiniana* 25–55, 39–43. Herde has completely revised the bibliography for Celestine V/Peter of Morrone with his *Cölestin V*; and he, Herde, has presented a superb short biography, "Celestino V, papa," in *Dizionario biografico*. I myself have been for some years working on the autobiografia in connections more limited: religion in the Abruzzi, and the development of "intimacy" in medieval biography; I have not published this work as yet but have presented parts of it in lectures, particularly, in "They heard bells everywhere," the third of my Neilson Lectures at Smith College, "Petrified Man: The Pursuit of 'Intimacy' in Late Medieval Biography" (delivered 12 November 1985) and "Peter of Morrone's *Autobiography* as 'a boy in a red sweater,' " a Berkeley faculty research lecture (delivered 10 March 1988).

59. I have discussed Anselm's bread in connection with the dream which encloses it in "Il sogno di Sant'Anselmo." The Anselm bread is of course written by Eadmer but in a version presumably approved by Anselm himself: Eadmer, *The Life of St. Anselm*, ed. Southern, 4–5 no. 2; Bertram Colgrave, ed., *Two Lives of St. Cuthbert* (Cambridge, 1940), 77–79: anonymous, book 1, cap. 7; 174–179, Bede, cap. 7. These stories may be much farther from Cuthbert than Anselm's is from him.

60. Frugoni, *Celestiniana*, particularly 64–65: A.S.V., A. A. Arm. I–XVIII, 3327, fos. 25r–25v. The autobiografia resolves the problem of the nature of the world in which the saint lives and expresses himself, I believe, through increasing emphasis on aerial activity: the sound of bells, the flight of doves, in the realm of the Holy Ghost.

61. Frugoni, *Celestiniana*, 60: Vatican Archive MS, fo. 22v. Recall *Scripta Leonis*, 146–151, no. 34, hail at Greccio, above chapter 2.

62. Chiappini, "Santa Filippa Mareri," 92; Rome, Biblioteca Angelica, vol. X, 10, 30, int. 8, office and appendices printed in Rome in 1545, 187v. I have published two essays about Filippa: "Filippa Mareri, la Santa Baronessa"; and "Santa Filippa Mareri": although here I repeatedly remain verbally close to the earlier essay, my opinions about the sources changed considerably between my writing it and the second essay. Chiappini remains the standard available for the material; and although I have in my own work sometimes adjusted its spelling to that of the Angelica edition, I find it excellent. The essays in the Borgo S. Pietro 1989 volume really replace all earlier secondary work on the saint, I believe, but readers may still find interesting a relatively recent and popular work by Ziliani, *La baronessa santa*, and the more recent Cerafogli, *La baronessa santa*. Bibliography may be found in both of my essays and more fully in the Borgo S. Pietro 1989 volume.

63. See Oliger, "B. Margherita Colonna," 213–214, and my *Rome before Avignon*, 178–179. The study of sanctity and canonization has been significantly changed and advanced by the publication of Vauchez, *La sainteté en occident*, a very richly learned and intelligent book although perhaps a little categorical.

64. This description is based on a tentative use of the *legenda*, Chiappini, "Santa Filippa Mareri," 82–89; and the death is from *lectio* IX, 89.

65. For an unusually strong and sensitive reading of the *legenda*, with conclusions about its reliability very different from my own, in the Borgo S. Pietro 1989 volume: Pasztor, "Filippa Mareri."

66. See *Rome before Avignon*, 175–176 and sources there cited; compare *legenda*, *lectio* VII, Chiappini, "Santa Filippa Mareri," 86–87.

67. Oliger, "B. Margherita Colonna," 206–208, Stephania life, cap. 17.

68. See Bedini, *Bibliotheca sanctorum*, vol. 3, cols. 1179–1181, with painting by Conxolus in col. 1179; and *Acta sanctorum octobris* (Brussels, 1856), 6:362–365; I have discussed the possible connection in "Filippa Mareri, la Santa Baronessa," 294. For the monastery of S. Chelidonia near Subiaco, *Monasticon Italiae*, 1:174 no. 227.

69. There is a fascinating article about the move and the dispute around it in the Borgo S. Pietro 1989 volume: Marinelli, "La valle sommersa."

70. Borgo San Pietro, Archivio di Monastero, nos. 1, 6: Chiappini, "Santa Filippa Mareri," 95, 97.

71. Borgo San Pietro, Archivio di Monastero, nos. 14, 15: Chiappini, "Santa Filippa Mareri," 101.

72. For changes at the convent see, in the Borgo S. Pietro 1989 volume, Maceroni, "Il monastero di Santa Filippa Mareri." For the paintings see, in the same volume, Cantone, "Il ciclo pittorico della capella," and for archives see Terenzoni, "L'archivio storico."

73. Menestò, ed., *Il processo di canonizzazione*, 435 n.160: Fra Giovanni, John, Pulcino, Flea?, de Mevania—Welsh (or perhaps Manx) as well as Franciscan?, and see xxiii–xxiv. This edition is extremely valuable and helpful for the study of hagiography.

74. See Chiappini, "Santa Filippa Mareri," 91–94, 92, 94; 87–88, 85–86, 88–89; readers of hagiography will note the familiarity of this figure.

75. Chiappini, "Santa Filippa Mareri," 83.

76. Chiappini, "Santa Filippa Mareri," 87.

77. Chiappini, "Santa Filippa Mareri," 92.

78. Chiappini, "Santa Filippa Mareri," 93, nos. 11 and 12 (at least I think them the same Gemmas).

79. Chiappini, "Santa Filippa Mareri," 91–92; for the foundations, 75.

80. Chiappini, "Santa Filippa Mareri," 93, no. 21.

81. Chiappini, "Santa Filippa Mareri," 93, no. 19.

82. Chiappini, "Santa Filippa Mareri," 92, no. 7.

83. Chiappini, "Santa Filippa Mareri," 88 (*lectio* VIII), 94; see for example *Scripta Leonis*, 118–119, no. 18.

84. Chiappini, "Santa Filippa Mareri," 94.

85. Chiappini, "Santa Filippa Mareri," 89, from *lectio* IX.

86. The most penetrating discussion which I know, and one which is likely

to change any reader's thought about the possible variety in the formation of female religious groups, is in Casagrande's "Il fenomeno della reclusione volontaria," 480–481. For ideas about city and country, see Violante, "Eresie urbane."

Chapter 8

1. I have taken Petrarch's quotation from Partner, *The Lands of St. Peter*, 327.

2. Rieti, Arch. Cap., IV.N.3 "3."

3. If, as seems likely, the early fourteenth-century palazzo Secinari was that palazzo with the retained and restored gothic window later known as the Palazzo Secinaro, near the upper end of the Via Roma, it was indeed at the city's center. For the observation of Secinaro, including San Quirico, during a Sulmona episcopal visitation in 1356: Celidonio, "Una visita pastorale," 176.

4. The relationship of the various currencies found in this will—and the variety is very noticeable—is most conveniently found in Spufford, *Handbook*, 59–72. In 1309 in Rome, a florin was exchanged at thirty-six soldi of Ravenna (72), and, at the curia, at thirty and thirty-seven soldi provisini of the senate (68). In 1309–15 the florin was at Naples exchanged for thirteen *carlini*, and carlini were reckoned at sixty to the uncia, and two to the *tareno* (62–63) and the *augustale* was the equivalent of seven and one-half tareni (59), so that an uncia was worth slightly less than five florins, the florin was worth slightly over six tareni, and the augustale was worth a little more than a florin. The complexity of currency in the will is in part, but only in part, explained by its dealing with legacies in both the Regno and the papal states.

5. I have accepted this, very desirable, translation of "pro emendatione pomorum" after considerable doubt shared by my Berkeley colleague most practiced in the translation of related documents.

6. For the arrangement of the parts of wills, including legacies and bequests, see Paravicini Bagliani, *I testamenti*, xcvii–cli, which is of course dealing with the much grander exemplars of cardinals' wills. One should see the essays and bibliography in Bartoli Langeli, ed., *Nolens intestatus decedere*, particularly the essay by Rigon, "Orientamenti religiosi." See too references in my "Burial Preference," and now Bertram, "Mittelalterliche Testamente." I do not think it is possible to be sure about the significance of the difference between the use of *locus* and *ecclesia* in Giovanni's will.

7. It is not apparent to me why the notary chooses, or Giovanni chooses, to say twelve denari and not one soldo, but it is apparent that twelve denari becomes the normal sum for gifts to recluses and for some other conventional charitable gifts. The recluses in these wills are frequently grammatically identified as being feminine.

8. I have dealt with the problem of dicing more exhaustively in a paper delivered at Tulane University: "Sin in a Small Italian City: Rieti in the Fourteenth Century." I have sheared the pseudo-Cyprian's phrases slightly, but they are crisp enough: "fugi diabolum persequentem te, fugi aleam inimicam rerum

tuarum": Miodonski, ed., *Anonymus adversus aleatores* (Erlangen, 1889), 110; for Giovanni nude, Rashdall, *The Universities of Europe*, 1:193 n.5; for Zanino di Pietro's panel at Fonte Colombo, see Mortari, "Rieti," 138 and plate 163. In Raymond's penitential, Book II, chs. 11 and 12.

9. Rieti, Arch. Cap., IV.N.3 (one of many documents so identified).

10. See too Rieti, Arch. Cap., IX.C.2.

11. Rieti, Arch. Cap., IV.N.2 (an identification they share with other documents).

12. Rieti, Arch. Cap., IV.N.3 "1320."

13. Rieti, Arch. Cap., IV.M.1 and above chapter 1.

14. Rieti, Arch. Cap., IV.G.3.

15. Rieti, Arch. Cap., VI.G.6 and above chapter 3.

16. Rieti, Arch. Cap., VI.G.5; I have discussed this "tympanum vision" in connection with a Bominaco donation, and changes away from it, toward what has seemed to me more modern notions of wills in the pattern of redemption in my "Death in Gualdo Tadino," 83; I there cited for "Cluniac," Cowdrey, *The Cluniacs*, particularly 121–156.

17. For a number of these relatively mute gifts and bequests for souls' sakes see particularly the documents within Rieti, Arch. Cap. IV.M.1, IV.M.2, and IV.L.10.

18. Rieti, Arch. Cap., IX.B.1. In fact the very short will by the (then ancient) canon Bartolomeo di don Oddone Alfani, healthy in mind and body, made on 20 December 1318 at San Domenico in the presence of seven Dominicans and the canon Giovanni di magistro Andrea, is reticent enough; he left twenty-five florins for his soul to his cathedral church but made no mention of place of burial: Rieti, Arch. Cap., IV.N.3 "6."

19. Rieti, Arch. Cap., IX.B.1.

20. Rieti, Arch. Cap., IV.N.2 "3."

21. Rieti, Arch. Cap., IV.N.3 "1314." It should again be noticed that when the sex of the generalized recluses in these wills is grammatically observable, they are women.

22. Rieti, Arch. Cap., IX.B.1. The most informative extended account, which I know, of the exact nature of related (but much more lavish) funerals is in Sharon Therese Strocchia, "Burials in Renaissance Florence, 1300–1500," Ph.D. dissertation, University of California, Berkeley, 1981.

23. Rieti, Arch. Cap., Cart. Silv., 188–189. For the miracle, *Scripta Leonis*, 186–189. For *lu consolu* in the modern diocese, see Truini Palomba, *La cucina sabina*, 24–25.

24. Rieti, Arch. Cap., IV.N.3.

25. Rieti, Arch. Cap., Cart. Silv., 155.

26. Rieti, Arch. Cap., Cart. Silv., 206–208.

27. Rieti, Arch. Cap., Cart. Silv., 159–162.

28. Rieti, Arch. Cap., Cart. Silv., 163–164. For *miserabiles* see, again, Trexler, "Charity and the Defense of Urban Elites," 74. See too, of course, Tierney, *Medieval Poor Law*, 18, 37, as Trexler suggests.

29. Rieti, Arch. Cap., IX.B.2.

30. Rieti, Arch. Cap., Cart. Silv., 104–106.

31. For the women of the Pescheria, see Brentano, *Rome before Avignon*, 281–284. For the multiplication of Masses see particularly Chiffoleau, "Sur l'usage obsessionnel."

32. Rieti, Arch. Cap., IX.B.1 "1297."

33. Rieti, Arch. Cap., Cart. Silv., 29–31.

34. See for example Rieti, Arch. Cap., IV.N.2 "1222": Famulus will of 1222; IV.N.2 "4": 1224 will of Matteo di don . . . subdiacono.

35. Pagnani, "Frammenti della cronaca del B. Francesco Venimbeni da Fabriano," 165.

36. Rieti, Arch. Cap., IX.B.2.

37. I have discussed this development in "Burial Preferences," 406; I considered a number of these problems of burial and chapter foundation in that paper.

38. Rieti, A.S., Perg. Comm., B. 1309 (will of Pietro Romano, canon of Sant'Angelo).

39. Rieti, Arch. Cap., IX.B.2; see *Die mittelalterlichen Grabmaler*, 1:350, no. lxxxvi, 2, plate 120.

40. Rieti, Arch. Cap., V.E.2; Lib. perg. di Matteo Barnabei, 149–151. For relationships among the lords of Labro, see Arch. Cap., I.C.1; I.D.1; I.D.2; I.E.1; I.E.2.

41. Rieti, Arch. Cap., V.E.1. I assume that *leguminum* means "of beans" here.

42. Rieti, Arch. Cap., Lib. perg. di Matteo Barnabei, 148.

43. See Rossi, "The Devouring Passion," 33: "per li padri"; I should like to thank Louis Rossi for pointing this out to me.

44. Rieti, Arch. Cap., Lib. perg. di Matteo Barnabei, 89, 90, 92, 95–96, 121–122; "Burial Preferences," 408–410; above chapter 1.

45. Rieti, Arch. Cap., Lib. perg. di Matteo Barnabei, 95–96.

46. "Burial Preferences," 410.

47. Rieti, Arch. Cap., IV.N.4 "2": Don Giovanni Andrea di Cola di Venturella de Ciminis di Rieti, canon of Rieti, ill.

48. Rieti, Arch. Cap., Lib. perg. di Matteo Barnabei, 282–284, 341–342, 467; IV.N.3 "1366"; V.E.3; V.E.5 (in the last, in 1367, dompno Ballovino di magistro Giovanni receives three florins from Donna Risabella, widow of Gentile di Amico of Apoleggia for his burial).

49. Celidonio, "Una visita pastorale," 173; Rome, A.S., Santo Spirito, B, 131 and in *Rome before Avignon*, 267.

50. Rieti, Arch. Cap., Cart. Silv., 194–195, 241, and see 216 for another case of the bishop's acting as *patrem pauperum* and designating *pauperes Christi*. The case of the Cimini women seems exactly to illustrate Trexler's point in "Charity and the Defense of Urban Elites" and to unite it with his own work on the bishop's fourth: see particularly his "Bishop's Portion"; but Biagio's own understanding of what he was doing is, of course, hidden.

51. Rieti, Arch. Cap., III.D.2; the foundation and early years of Santa Lucia have been carefully examined recently by Di Nicola in *Il monastero di S. Lucia*, 7–11, and Di Nicola reproduces photographs of Risabella's will and other im-

portant documents and drawings. See too my "Movimento religioso femminile."

52. Chiappini, "Santa Filippa Mareri," nos. 23, 26, 30.

53. Di Nicola, "Le pergamene di Santa Caterina," 22 and no. 14.

54. Rieti, Arch. Cap., VI.G.15.

55. Rieti, Arch. Cap., III.D.1 (originally communal).

56. See above, chapter 6 note 142.

57. Di Nicola, "Le pergamene di Santa Caterina," 20: *carceri "in circuitu dicte ecclesie positis iuxta ecclesiam"* and no. 4.

58. Rieti, Arch. Cap., Libro IV perg. fos. 41v–42r.

59. Di Nicola, "Le pergamene di Santa Caterina," 20, 26 no. 4; for the San Donato sisters see above, introduction note 13.

60. Rieti, Arch. Cap., Cart. Silv., 316.

61. Rieti, Arch. Cap., VI.G.13.

62. Rieti, Arch. Cap., Cart. Silv., 177.

63. Rieti, Arch. Cap., Lib. perg. di Matteo Barnabei, 397. For Sant'Erasmo see Palmegiani, *La cattedrale*, 145–146. For "Ospitalis Capitis Pontis" at Rieti, see Rieti, Arch. Cap., "1212," 4. Fonseca has shown the specific connection between hospitals and bridges, as, for example, briefly, in his "Forme assistenziali e strutture caritative," 286–287. Elisabeth Rothrauff is now working on bridge and hospital in Pisa.

64. Rieti, Arch. Cap., II.G.10. The statutes do not talk of gender. For confraternities now see particularly, I think, with their references: Henderson, "The Flagellant Movement"; Little, *Liberty, Charity, and Fraternity*; and Banker, *Death in the Community*. But for a much longer list see Bowsky, *Piety and Property*, 81 n.203.

65. For Sulmona, Celidonio, "Una visita pastorale," 170.

66. Rieti, Arch. Cap., V.B.7. For San Lazzaro see Pirri, "S. Lazzaro del Valoncello," 86.

67. The reader should be aware of a cluster of dedications to San Vittorino particularly in the area of and across the developing border with L'Aquila.

68. For an introduction to the cult of Barbara, Angeletti, *S. Barbara nella tradizione reatina*; the classical work on the Reatine Barbara, a fascinatingly *finta*-geographical book (with a map of the places of her life, elegantly drawn and reproduced) is Marini, *Memorie di S. Barbara*.

69. For Raimond's style see above chapter 5 note 102; for the Carmelite, Rieti, Arch. Cap., Cart. Silv., 133.

70. Rieti, Arch. Cap., Libro IV, fos. 51r–54v.

71. Rieti, Arch. Cap., V.D.2.

72. Rieti, A.S., Statuti, no. 5.

73. These figures are taken from Rieti, Arch. Cap., Lib. Int. et Exit., for the appropriate years. For civic feasts, in terms of legal recesses, at Rieti at the time of the composition of the statutes see Rieti, A.S., Statuti, I, fo. 76v: Easter days and Sundays, feasts of the Virgin, the twelve apostles and all the evangelists, Sant'Angelo, Nicholas, John the Baptist, Louis, Dominic, Augustine, Francis, Lucy, Mary Magdalen, Catherine, Severio, Elias, All Saints, Epiphany, Pentecost with two days following, Anthony Abbot, Barbara, Eleuterio, Bernardino, Vin-

cent, Palm Sunday to Sunday after Easter, Thursday before Carnival to Quadragesima Thursday.

74. For these relics see Chiappini, "Santa Filippa Mareri," 101, no. XIV. For a particularly important dedication, Rainaldo de Podio's dedication of the church or chapel of Sant'Erasmo in 1306, see Rieti, Arch. Cap., VI.G.10.

75. For the 1220s family: Rieti, Arch. Cap., "1212," 33, fo. 17r; for the tithepayers and their cohorts: III.B.1, on 15 and neighboring pages; for a miscellany of names, III.B.1, 10–13, a miscellany that questions generalization. The Contigliano names come from a Contigliano catasto: Rieti, A.S., Catasto 7; for 1368: Arch. Cap., Lib. Int. et Exit., 1368.

76. For the cross from Posta, see Mortari, "Rieti," plates 155–156, and in the text 136, with its warning about the colors of the restored cross; in this section Mortari refers to earlier work on the cross by Carlo Bertelli, n.65. The preachers for each year are noted on the title page of the camerlengo's account books. These books, it should be noted, cover the chapter's fiscal year which begins, effectively, in July, in the later fourteenth century, as opposed to the nonfiscal year of the Reatine church which, after the style of Rieti, begins on Christmas day (so that what is called in the records 25 December 1318 is what we would call 25 December 1317: see Libr. perg. di Matteo Barnabei, 103, for an actual dating of Christmas itself—obviously rare). For confessions see, for example, Little, "Les techniques de la confession," and the work there cited. For the Franciscans and town swelling see also my "Early Franciscans and Italian Towns."

77. See the appendix on the Rieti cycle below. See too Gardner, "The Cappellone di San Nicola."

78. For dompno Matteo di Lotherio in another guise, as a witness, see Rieti, Arch. Cap., Lib. perg. di Matteo Barnabei, 322; for Giovanni Petrignani's holding Tommaso Cimini's prebend see Reg. (or Libr.) VI, fos. 11v–12r, and Libr. IV, fo. 34v. For the future of the Alfani see Michaeli, *Memorie*, 2:99–106, 169–197.

79. For the Montecassino Passion and Sulmona see, for example, Edward, *The Montecassino Passion*; for Sallust see Fabrizi, "Sallustio nella fantasia," 97. For plates of Canetra, Sambuco, Santa Vittoria, San Domenico, and Sant'Agostino, see *La sabina medievale*, plates 145, 176–177, 89–104, 152–154, 133–137. A sense of the direction in which Reatine Christianity was traveling may be gotten from a prayer added to a breviary in the Archivio Capitolare, formerly called MS 20; it is I think fifteenth-century and carries the superscription: "Whoever says the underwritten prayer each day on bended knee will not be harmed by devil or evil man and thirty days before death will see the mother of our Lord Jesus Christ." The prayer is a meditation on the seven last words.

80. Matthiae, *Pittura medioevale abruzzese*, particularly plates 85–90, 92–94, 96. For the ciborium capital see Mortari, "Rieti," plate 170, and in the text, 138–142 with its reference to the removal of the ciborium in 1803. The best description I know of the actual integration of a religious institution in its society is Osheim, *A Tuscan Monastery*. For the observation of a clear and sharp difference between town and country in the fifteenth-century diocese of Cortona, see Daniel Bornstein's forthcoming "Priests and Villagers in the Diocese of Cortona."

81. Rieti, Arch. Cap., Libro IV perg., fos. 19v–20v. In Ballovino's 1358 accounts see particularly fos. 42r and 45r; for the surplus, the *residuum pecunie* in Agostino's "1379" accounts, fo. 63v.

82. Rieti, Arch. Cap., Cart. Silv., 108–115. For the stunningly spare and modern will of an important spiritual figure who, like his will, offers solutions and problems, helpfully, together, see that from 1318 of Cardinal Giacomo Colonna: Paravicini Bagliani, *I testamenti*, 423–426, no. XXVI.

83. See particularly *Die mittelalterlichen Gräbmaler*, 349, no. LXXXVI, 1, and plate 75, for the Gargano pilgrims at San Francesco.

84. Rieti, A.S., San Domenico, 7.

85. Rieti, Arch. Cap., IX.B.2 "1376." I have not found signs of major change, as in number of Masses, after 1348; but my observed sample was not large enough to produce significant or reliable results. Compare, for change, Cohn, *Death and Property in Siena*.

86. Rieti, Arch. Cap., VII.C.6. For Bartolomeo and Ballovino, see Reg. (or Libr.) VI, fos. 5r–5v and Libr. IV, fos. 29r–29v.

87. The passage is from chapter 7.

Appendix

1. Verani, "Restaurati gli affreschi"; Belting, *Die Oberkirche*, 171 n.52. The fullest published discussion is now Blume, *Wandmalerei*, 42ff., 72ff. Cf. the review by J. Cannon, *Burlington Magazine* 127 (1985): 234–235.

2. Palmegiani, *Rieti*, 303; John R. H. Moorman, *Mediaeval Franciscan Houses*, 408.

3. *Bullarium franciscanum*, 1:381, Doc. XCVII.

4. *Bullarium franciscanum*, 1:516, Doc. CCXXVIII.

5. 20 September 1289 cf. *Bullarium franciscanum*, 4:168ff., Doc. CLXVIII.

6. 10 June 1263, *Bullarium franciscanum*, 2:471, Doc. LXV.

7. Angellotti, *Descrittione*, 23, "l'anno passato"; Palmegiani, *Rieti*, 304 gives the date as 1636.

8. This is particularly noticeable on the south wall of the choir, where the later frescoes are deliberately placed to avoid encroachment on the Liberation of the Heretic.

9. Verani, "Restaurati gli affreschi."

10. In the Upper Church at Assisi the basamento shows a fictive fabric hanging. Cf. White, *The Birth and Rebirth of Pictorial Space*, fig. 8. Blume, *Wandmalerei*, 73 makes the interesting suggestion that the angels emphasize the setting of the Rieti cycle around the high altar.

11. The oblique setting of the base blocks of the framing columns is most effectively observed from just outside the choir itself.

12. Palmegiani, *Rieti*, 304.

13. Tintori and Meiss, *The Painting of the Life*, 160. Borsook, *The Mural Painters* xxv.

14. Tintori and Meiss, *The Painting of the Life*, 144, 184. Borsook, *The Mural Painters*, 10.

15. For example the hexagons framing the angels have an internal dimension of 59 cm equaling one *braccia*.

16. White, *Pictorial Space*, 58.

17. Smart, *The Assisi Problem*, 4. Blume remarks (*Wandmalerei*, 44) that the scenes on the left reflect the founding of the Franciscan order while those on the right wall are posthumous miracles. He suggests an original total of fifteen scenes: even if this were correct, the internal chronology of the narrative sequence would remain difficult to elucidate.

18. The crouching friars in the Vision of the Chariot and Francis and the Knight are closely comparable. Cf. Smart, *The Assisi Problem*, plates 55, 93. The Rieti scenes add some details.

19. The average width of the Assisi scenes is 375 cm; see White, *Pictorial Space*, 54 n.37. At Rieti the width of the scene of the Dream of Innocent III is 178.5 cm or approximately 3 *braccie*.

20. Buchthal, "The *Musterbuch*." The copying process hypothesized by Blume (*Wandmalerei*, 69ff.) derives from suggestions of Kitzinger, *The Mosaics of Monreale*.

21. Thus the painter copies the Freeing of the Heretic normally attributed to the Maestro di Santa Cecilia as well as the Healing of the Knight of Lerida.

22. White, *Pictorial Space*, 40.

23. For Assisi see White, *Pictorial Space*, 46. This organizing device had occurred prominently in the Arena Chapel cycle: cf. Alpatoff, "Giotto's Paduan Frescoes."

24. Toesca, *Pietro Cavallini*, plate XX.

25. For Vescovio cf. Matthiae, "Lavori della soprintendenza"; Gardner, "Pope Nicholas IV," 30. A different chronological sequence is postulated, to my mind unconvincingly, by Tomei, "Il ciclo vetero e neotestamentario di S. Maria di Vescovio."

26. Matthiae, *Pietro Cavallini*, fig. LXXVI.

27. Reflections of the frescoes at Assisi recur in the following of Meo da Siena. Cf. Santi, *Galleria nazionale dell'Umbria*, nos. 30, 31. Scarpellini, "Di alcuni pittori giotteschi." Blume (*Wandmalerei*, 168) dates the Rieti frescoes shortly after 1295, which is very probably too early.

28. For a general discussion of the problem see Gardner, "The Louvre Stigmatization." Blume's contention (*Wandmalerei*, 71, 108ff.) that copying was an official policy of the order lacks any contemporary documentary support. See also note 33 below.

29. Innocent III's vision occurred in Rome: see Gardner, "Päpstliche Traume." The Vision of the Chariot took place in Assisi (*Legenda maior* iv, 4 in *Analecta franciscana*, 10:572), the Vision of the Thrones in "quadam ecclesia deserta" (*Legenda maior* vi, 6 in *Analecta franciscana*, 10:584). The Healing of the Knight took place in Catalonia (*Legenda maior, Miracula* i, 5 in *Analecta franciscana*, 10:629), and the Freeing of the Heretic took place in Rome (*Legenda maior, Miracula* v, 4 in *Analecta franciscana*, 10:639).

30. Chiappelli, "Puccio Capanna." Cf. Blume, *Wandmalerei*, 49ff., 161ff.

31. Blume's book has undoubtedly placed the study of Franciscan cycles on a new footing, but leaves many problems unresolved. Cf. Cannon, review mentioned in note 1 above, 235.

32. Chiapelli, "Puccio Capanna," 212; Blume, *Wandmalerei*, 161.

33. Gardner, "Some Franciscan altars."

Select Bibliography

Primary Sources

Unpublished

This book is not only based, to a large extent, on the documents within the Archivio Capitolare at Rieti (Arch. Cap.); it is also, to a noticeable extent, a book about them. This is apparent in both notes and text. The archive is, and particularly was when I first used it, primarily a collection of individual documents, *pergamene*, which are for purposes of identification divided into *armadi*, and within *armadi*, into *fascicoli*, and within *fascicoli* into *numeri*; the notation II.B.1 means *numero* 1 of *fascicolo* B within *armadio* II. Many of the *numeri* are in fact composite, that is, composed of a number of separate but related items; some of them include small codices.

When I first used these documents they were still stored, much as they must have been when Naudé left them and when Mazzatinti again cataloged them, against the wall of the tower room above the sacristy of the cathedral in thirteen open-faced compartments divided by wooden partitions, one for each *armadio* category including the three additional categories, I, II, III, identified as pertaining to the commune. The *armadi* as a group could be closed by an inclusive two-paneled door. Each *armadio* was identified so that the individual researcher could search for, remove, and replace the documents he or she sought. Among them there was some disorder, in particular some confusion between the similarly numbered capitular and communal collections; some items, moreover, had disappeared, either permanently, or, as it turned out, temporarily.

Besides the *pergamene*, there existed in the archive a number of medieval codices; among these the most physically obvious were the paper "Libri de Introitu et Exitu" (Lib. Int. et Exit.), account books covering the fiscal years

(July to June, bearing the date of the earlier year) from 1355 into modern times, a thick but incomplete series. The account books were deposited within a cupboard, standing up, essentially in chronological order.

Most striking of the other, individual, record codices is the parchment book of Matteo Barnabei (Lib. perg. di Matteo Barnabei), composed of twenty-four paginated gatherings of, originally, twelve folios each, which covers the period from 1315 to 1348 and which is a protagonist of this book. But also important are the "Libri contractuum et collationum, 1340–1347" (Lib. con. et col.), in two volumes; the "Liber processuum causarum ciuilium, sede vacante, 1346–1347" (Lib. proc. civ.); and the "Liber processuum maleficiorum, sede vacante, 1346–1347" (Lib. proc. malef.)—all in paper. The books have various names and numbers written on them and presumably will have a definitive archival name for citation only when the process of reordering the capitular archives has been completed. I have chosen the names that I use now because they seem to me the most sensibly descriptive; and they are the permanent archival names that I would suggest were I asked. To these books should be added the Cartolario di Silvestro di don Giovanni, 1336–1351 (Cart. Silv.), which is of particular value here because of its wills and its materials dealing with the Secinari family and bishop.

The parchment "Libro IV" in the archives includes a list of fourteenth-century anniversaries; and the deceptively numbered codex III.B.1 and "Registro (or Libro) VI" are important in their records of prebendal distribution. The paper document here identified as "Inquest 1225," which records church holdings, was found within the bundle that holds and is identified as being the Liber Introitus et Exitus of 1358. A parchment copy of a fuller version of this inquest, made in 1315, is in the book identified as "1212"; it has now been listed as "Istromenti: 1" by Suor Anna Maria Tassi. A number of codices, including account books, are bound in *pergamene* or leaves of codices, which are themselves significant sources.

The transfer of documents from the old archive room in the sacristy tower to the Archivio Vescovile, within the episcopal palace, where the documents now are, has been attended by some natural difficulties, particularly since it was not possible for the transfer to be supervised by a medievalist. The documents are now, however, in a much safer and cleaner, although not necessarily more accessible, place. They have been and are being carefully placed and cataloged by Suor Anna Maria Tassi. Future searchers should be aware that in the new organization of the documents they may receive new identifications. In any case, as notes within this book will make clear, the codices mentioned here, except for the account books, have acquired over the centuries quite various descriptions and identifications that are written on their bindings and early folios.

The Archivio Vescovile in Rieti (Arch. Vesc.) does not itself contain materials from the thirteenth and fourteenth centuries, but it does have valuable later materials particularly important for topographical identification and description, including the visitations, used here, of Bishops Amulio and Ferretti. Within Rieti city, the Biblioteca Comunale (Bib. Com.) contains a catalog of local works including Romualdo Perotti Cavalli's "Genealogia." The Rieti Archivio di stato (A.S.) has not only *statuti, riformanze,* and *catasti* for neighboring towns for the later middle ages, but also two fonds, San Domenico and Comunale, with *pergamene* from the time of this study. Within the diocese there still exists the valuable archive of the monastery of Santa Filippa Mareri in Borgo San Pietro, with *pergamene* stretching through the entire period covered by this book. (Santa Filippa's early printed *legenda* used here is, however, vol. X, 10, 30, int. 8, in the Biblioteca Angelica, in Rome.)

Two manuscript codices outside of Rieti have been particularly important to this study: Paris, Bibliothèque Nationale (B.N.), latin 1556, which includes both synodal acts and Bishop Tommaso I's list of Reatine churches; Biblioteca Apostolica Vaticana (Bib. Apos. Vat.), Vat. Lat. 4029, the inquisition of Paolo Zoppo. Also in the Vatican library: Vat. Lat. 10372 (for the Hospitallers), and Cod. Barb. Lat. 2406 and 4539, and the fond San Pietro in Vaticano (caps. 64, no. 181). In the Archivio Segreto Vaticano (A.S.V.): A. A. Arm. I–XVIII, 3660 (statutes of the Cicolano), 3895; Arm. XXXV.14; Fondo Celestini; Obligationes et Solutiones; Registra Vaticana: Gregory IX, Gregory X, Benedict XII. In Rome, Archivio di stato: *pergamene,* fondi Rieti, Sant'Agostino di Terni and S. Francesco di S. Vittoria in Materano; Archivio notarile, protocols of Francesco Stephani de Capudgalis. In the Archivio Capitolino (Vallicella), Archivio Orsini (II.A.I.26, 37).

Materials dealing with particular problems and especially episcopal careers came from various archives, although one of the most valuable sets of archives, Ìmola, Archivio Capitolare and Archivio storico comunale, was valuable because a search of them produced no relevant documents. Ùdine, Biblioteca Arcivescovile, MS 92 (F.33.III.18), for Pietro da Ferentino; Venice, Biblioteca Marciana, MSS. Latin, Clas. XIV, Cod. 133 (Coll. 4284), also for Pietro. Cassino, Aula 2, caps. LXXIII, fasc. 1, no. 11, for Bishop Andrea. Vèroli, Archivio Capitolare della Cattedrale, no. 575, for capitular comparison. Sulmona, Archivio della Cattedrale, the manuscripts of the visitation of 1356 and of materials relating to the canonization of Peter of Morrone. Penne, Archivio Arcidiocesano di Penne-Pescara, dispute of 1224.

Published

Analecta franciscana, vol. 10, *Legendae S. Francisci Assisiensis saeculis xiii et xiv conscriptae.* Quaracchi, 1926–41.

Angelo Clareno. "Epistole." In *Angeli Clareni opera,* edited by Lydia von Auw. Vol. 1. Istituto storico italiano per il medioevo: Fonti per la storia d'Italia, 103. Rome, 1980.

Bernard of Clairvaux. "Lettere." In *Patrologia latina,* edited by J. P. Migne. Paris, 1844–55.

Bianchi, Giuseppe. *Documenta historiae forojuliensis saeculi XIII et XIV ab anno 1300 ad 1333.* Vienna, 1864.

Briacca, Giuseppe. *Gli statuti sinodali novaresi di Papiniano della Rovere* (1298). Milan, 1971.

Brooke, Rosalind P., ed. and trans. *Scripta Leonis, Rufini et Angeli sociorum S. Francisci: The Writings of Leo, Rufino and Angelo Companions of St. Francis.* Oxford, 1970.

Canivez, Joseph Maria. *Statuta capitulorum generalium ordinis Cisterciensis ab anno 1116 ad annum 1786.* Vol. 2. Louvain, 1934.

Celidonio, Giuseppe. "Una visita pastorale della Diocesi Valvense fatta nel 1356." *Rassegna abruzzese* 3 (1899): 155–181.

Cenci, D. P. "Costituzioni sinodali della diocesi di Gubbio nei secoli XIII–XV." *Archivio per la storia ecclesiastica dell'Umbria* 1 (1913): 361–372.

Chiappini, Aniceto. "Santa Filippa Mareri e il suo monastero di Borgo S. Pietro de Molito nel Cicolano." *Miscellanea francescana* 22 (1921): 65–119.

Collijn, Isak, ed. *Acta et processus canonizacionis beate Birgitte.* Uppsala, 1924–31.

Davis, Charles Till. Introduction to *Arbor vitae,* by Ubertino. Turin, 1961.

Delaville Le Roulx, J. *Cartulaire général de l'ordre des hospitaliers de St Jean de Jérusalem: 1100–1310.* Paris, 1894–1906.

Di Nicola, Andrea. "Le pergamene di Santa Caterina di Città Ducale." *Il Territorio* 4, no. 2 (1988): 19–50.

Ehrle, Franz. "Die Spiritualen, ihr Verhältniss zum Franciscanerorden und zu den Fraticellen." *Archiv für Litteratur und Kirchengeschichte des Mittelalters* 1 (1885): 509–569; 2 (1886): 106–164, 249–336; 3 (1887): 553–623; 4 (1888): 1–190.

Eubel, Konrad. "Der Registerband des Gegenpapstes Nikolaus V." *Archivalische Zeitschrift,* n.s., 4 (1893): 123–212.

Francis of Assisi. *Writings and Early Biographies: English Omnibus of the Sources for the Life of St. Francis.* Edited by Marion A. Habig. Chicago, 1972.

Frugoni, Arsenio. *Celestiniana.* Istituto storico per il medioevo, studi storici, 6–7. Rome, 1954.

Fumi, Luigi. "Eretici e ribelli nell'Umbria dal 1320 al 1330 studiati su documenti inediti dell'Archivio segreto Vaticano." *Bollettino della deputazione storia patria per l'Umbria* 3 (1897): 257–285, 429–489; 4 (1898): 221–301, 437–486; 5 (1899): 1–46, 205–425.

García y García, Antonio, ed. *Constitutiones concilii quarti Lateranensis una cum commentariis glossatorum.* Monumenta Iuris canonici, series A, Corpus glossatorum, 2. Vatican City, 1981.

Garufi, Carlo Alberto. *Catalogo illustrato del tabulario di Santa Maria Nuova in Monreale.* Documenti per servire la storia di Sicilia, 1st s., 19. Palermo, 1902.

Gui, Bernard. *Manuel de l'inquisiteur.* Edited by G. Mollat. Paris, 1926–27.

Hagemann, Wolfgang. "Kaiser- und Papsturkunden im Archivio capitolare von Narni." *Quellen und Forschungen aus italienischen Archiven und Bibliotheken* 51 (1971): 250–304.

Hoberg, Hermann. *Taxae pro communibus servitiis.* Studi e testi, 133. Vatican City, 1949.

Inguanez, Mauro. "Le pergamene del monastero dei SS. Cosma e Damiano di Tagliacozzo conservate nell'archivio di Montecassino." *Bullettino della deputazione abruzzese di storia patria,* 3d s., 6 (1915): 227–265.

Jaffe, Philip, and L. Loewenfeld, eds. *Regesta pontificum romanorum.* Vol. 2. Leipzig, 1888.

Jamison, Evelyn, ed. *Catalogus baronum.* Istituto storico italiano per il medioevo: Fonti per la storia d'Italia, 101. Rome, 1972.

Kehr, Paul. *Italia pontificia.* Vol. 4. Berlin, 1908.

Lippens, Ugolino. "Fra Biagio da Leonessa vescovo di Vicenza (1335–1347) e di Rieti (1347–1378)." *Le Venezie francescane* 5 (1936): 109–126; 6 (1937): 5–18, 112–132.

Manassei, Paolano. "Alcuni documenti per la storia delle città di Terni e Spoleto." *Archivio storico italiano,* 3d s., 22 (1875), 367–415.

Mariano D'Alatri. "Un mastodontico processo per eresia a Viterbo nello scorcio del duecento." *Collectanea franciscana* 42 (1972): 299–308.

Martène, E., and U. Durand, eds. *Veterum scriptorum et monumentorum historicorum, dogmaticorum, moralium amplissima collectio.* Vol. 8. Paris, 1733.

Mazzoleni, Jole, ed. *Le pergamene di Capua (972–1501).* Vol. 2. Naples, 1957–58.

Menestò, Enrico, ed. *Il processo di canonizzazione di Chiara da Montefalco.* Perugia, 1984.

Oliger, Livario. "B. Margherita Colonna." *Lateranum,* n.s., 1, no. 2 (1935).

Pagliarini, Giovanni Battista. *Croniche di Vicenza.* Vicenza, 1663.

———. *Cronicae.* Edited by James S. Grubb. Padua, 1990.

Pasztor, Edith. "Il processo di Andrea da Gagliano (1337–38)." *Archivum franciscanum historicum* 48 (1955): 252–297.

Petrarch. *The Revolution of Cola di Rienzo.* Edited by Mario Emilio Cosenza. 2d ed., edited by Ronald G. Musto. New York, 1986.

Porta, Giuseppe, ed. *Cronica.* Milan, 1981.

Potthast, August. *Regesta pontificum romanorum inde ab anno post Christum natum MCXCVIII ad annum MCCCIV.* Vol. 1. Berlin, 1874–75.

Powicke, F. M., and Christopher R. Cheney, eds. *A.D. 1205–1313. Councils and Synods, with other Documents relating to the English Church.* Vol. 2. Oxford, 1964.

Pressutti, Pietro, ed. *Regesta Honorii Papae III.* Vols. 1–2. Rome, 1885, 1895.

Register of Walter Giffard, Archbishop of York, 1266–1279. Surtees Society, 109. Durham, 1904.

Les registres d'Alexandre IV. Edited by C. Bourel de la Roncière, J. de Loye, P. de Cenival, and A. Coulon. Bibliothèque des écoles françaises d'Athènes et de Rome. Paris, 1895–1959.

Les registres de Benoît XI. Edited by Ch. Grandjean. Bibliothèque des écoles françaises d'Athènes et de Rome. Paris, 1883–1905.

Les registres de Boniface VIII. Edited by Georges Digard, Maurice Faucon, Antoine Thomas, and Robert Fawtier. Bibliothèque des écoles françaises d'Athènes et de Rome. Paris, 1907–39.

Les registres de Clément IV. Edited by E. Jordan. Bibliothèque des écoles françaises d'Athènes et de Rome. Paris, 1893–1945.

Les registres de Grégoire IX. Edited by Lucien Auvray, S. Clémencet, and L. Carolus-Barre. Bibliothèque des écoles françaises d'Athènes et de Rome. Paris, 1890–1955.

Les registres de Grégoire X et de Jean XXI. Edited by J. Guiraud, E. Cadier, and G. Mollat. Bibliothèque des écoles françaises d'Athènes et de Rome. Paris, 1892–1960.

Les registres d'Honorius IV. Edited by M. Prou. Bibliothèque des écoles françaises d'Athènes et de Rome. Paris, 1886–88.

Les registres d'Innocent IV. Edited by Élie Berger. Bibliothèque des écoles françaises d'Athènes et de Rome. Paris, 1884–1921.

Les registres de Martin IV. Edited by F. Olivier-Martin. Bibliothèque des écoles françaises d'Athènes et de Rome. Paris, 1901–35.

Les registres de Nicholas III. Edited by J. Gay and S. Clémencet. Bibliothèque des écoles françaises d'Athènes et de Rome. Paris, 1898–1938.

Les registres de Nicholas IV. Edited by Ernest Langlois. Bibliothèque des écoles françaises d'Athènes et de Rome. Paris, 1887–93.

Les registres d'Urbain IV. Edited by J. Guiraud and S. Clémencet. Bibliothèque des écoles françaises d'Athènes et de Rome. Paris, 1892–1958.

Regestum Clementis Papae V. Edited by the Benedictines of Monte Cassino. Rome, 1885–92.

Riccardo da San Germano. *Chronicon regni Siciliae.* Edited by Georg Heinrich Pertz. Monumenta Germaniae Historica, Scriptores, 19. Hanover, 1866.

Salimbene of Adam. *Cronica fratris Salimbene de Adam ordinis minorum.* Edited by O. Holder-Egger. M.G.H., SS. Vol. 32. Hanover, 1905–13.

Sansi, Achille. *Documenti storici inediti in sussidio allo studio delle memorie Umbre.* Accademia Spoletina. Foligno, 1879.

Sbaralea, J. H. *Bullarium franciscanum.* 4 vols. Rome, 1759–65.

Sella, Pietro. *Rationes decimarum Italiae nei secoli XIII e XIV: Umbria.* Studi e testi, 161–162. Vatican City, 1952.

———, ed. "Statuti del Cicolano (sec. XIII–XIV)." In *Convegno storico Abruzzese-Molisano,* 1:182–200; 3:863–899. Casalbordino, 1940.

Tables de registres de Clément V publiés par les bénédictins. Edited by Y. Lanhers, C. Vogel, R. Fawtier, and G. Mollat. Bibliothèque des écoles françaises d'Athènes et de Rome. Paris, 1948–57.

Tambara, Giovanni, ed. *Juliani canonici civitatensis chronica (1252–1364).* Muratori Rerum Italicarum Scriptores, 24, pt. 14. Revised edition. Città di Castello, 1906.

Trexler, Richard C. *Synodal Law in Florence and Fiesole: Studi e testi.* Vatican City, 1971.

Ughelli, Ferdinando. *Italia sacra.* Vols. 1, 6. Venice, 1717, 1728.

Vasina, Augusto, and Emanuela Ghini, eds. "Ricordo di Eugenio Duprè Theseider e lettere ad una religiosa già sua allieva." *Rivista di storia della chiesa in Italia* 31 (1977): 128–149.

Vidal, J.-M., ed. *Benoît XII (1334–1342): Lettres communes et curiales.* Paris, 1903–11.

Wright, John, trans. *The Life of Cola di Rienzo.* Toronto, 1975.

Secondary Sources

I have not always thought it necessary to cite again in my notes or bibliography secondary works fully cited in earlier works of my own or, in some cases, of other historians cited here.

Alinari, Arturo. "L'antica chiesa di S. Massimo cattedrale di Forcona." *Bullettino abruzzese*, 4th s., 5 (1935): 67–80.

Alpatoff, M. "The Parallelism of Giotto's Paduan Frescoes." *Art Bulletin* 29 (1947): 149–154.

Amayden, Teodoro. *La storia delle famiglie romane*. Edited by Carlo Augusto Bertini. Vol. 2. Rome [1914].

Angeletti, Colombo. *S. Barbara nella tradizione reatina*. Rome, 1973.

Angellotti, P. *Descrittione della città di Rieti*. Rome, 1635.

Backmund, Norbert. *Monasticon Praemonstratense*. Vol. 1. Straubing, 1949.

Baldelli, Ignazio. *Medioevo volgare da Montecassino all'Umbria*. Bari, 1971.

Baldwin, John W. *Masters, Princes, and Merchants: The Social Views of Peter the Chanter and His Circle*. Princeton, 1970.

Banker, James R. *Death in the Community: Memorialization and Confraternity in an Italian Commune in the Late Middle Ages*. Athens, Ga., 1988.

Barraclough, Geoffrey. "The Making of a Bishop in the Middle Ages." *Catholic Historical Review* 19 (1933–34): 275–319.

Bartoli Langeli, A., ed. *Nolens intestatus decedere: Il testamento come fonte della storia religiosa e sociale*. Archivi dell'Umbria, Inventari e ricerche, 7. Perugia, 1985.

Battelli, Giulio. *Rationes decimarum Italiae nei secoli XIII e XIV: Latium*. Studi e testi, 128. Vatican City, 1946.

Bedini, Balduino. *Bibliotheca sanctorum*. Vol. 2. Rome, 1962.

Belting, H. *Die Oberkirche von San Francesco in Assisi*. Berlin, 1974.

Berlioz, Jacques. "La mémoire du prédicateur: Recherches sur la mémorisation des récits exemplaires (XIIIe–XVe siècles)." In *Temps, tradition, mémoire au moyen âge*, 157–183. Aix-en-Provence, 1983.

Bernard Gui et son monde. Cahiers de Fanjeaux, 16. Fanjeaux, 1981.

Bertram, M. "Mittelalterliche Testamente. Zur Entdeckung einer Quellengattung in Italien." *Quellen und Forschungen aus italienischen Archiven und Bibliotheken* 68 (1988): 509–545.

Blume, D. *Wandmalerei als Ordenspropaganda*. Worms, 1983.

Bornstein, Daniel. "Pittori sconosciuti e pitture perdute nella Cortona tardomedioevale." *Rivista d'arte: Studi documentari per la storia delle arti in Toscana*, 4th s., 42, no. 6 (1990): 227–244.

Borsook, E. *The Mural Painters of Tuscany*. 2d edition. Oxford, 1980.

Boschi, Vincenzo. "Di un antico cimitero in Rieti presso i corpi dei SS Martiri Eleuterio ed Cinzia." *Bollettino della deputazione di storia patria per l'Umbria* 8 (1902): 1–28.

———. *Notizie storiche sopra la chiesa e il convento di S. Domenico Rieti*. Rieti, 1910.

Bouchard, Constance Brittain. *Spirituality and Administration: The Role of the Bishop in Twelfth-Century Auxerre.* Cambridge, Mass., 1979.

Bowsky, William M. *The Finance of the Commune of Siena, 1287–1355.* Oxford, 1970.

———. *Henry VII in Italy: The Conflict of Empire and City-State.* Lincoln, Nebraska, 1960.

———. *A Medieval Italian Commune: Siena under the Nine, 1287–1355.* Berkeley, 1981.

———. *Piety and Property.* Milan, 1990.

Boyd, Catherine E. *Tithes and Parishes in Medieval Italy: The Historical Roots of a Modern Problem.* Ithaca, 1952.

Boyle, Leonard E. "The Constitution '*Cum ex eo*' of Boniface VIII, Education of Parochial Clergy." *Mediaeval Studies* 24 (1962): 261–302.

———. *A Survey of the Vatican Archives and of its Medieval Holdings.* Toronto, 1972.

Brentano, Robert. "Burial Preferences at Rieti around 1300." *Skulptur und Grabmal des Spätmittelalters in Rom und Italien,* 401–411. Österreichischen Akademie der Wissenschaften. Vienna, 1990.

———. "Considerazioni di un lettore di testamenti." *Nolens intestatus decedere: Il testamento come fonte della storia religiosa e sociale.* Archivi dell'Umbria, inventari e ricerche, 5. Perugia, 1985.

———. "Correspondences at Rieti: The Institutional Church and the Face of Christ." *Mélanges de l'École française de Rome: Moyen âge–temps modernes* 93 (1981): 179–188.

———. "Death in Gualdo Tadino and in Rome (1340, 1296)." *Studia gratiana* 19 (1976): 79–100.

———. "Early Franciscans and Italian Towns." In *Monks, Nuns, and Friars,* edited by Edward B. King, Jacqueline T. Schaefer, and William B. Wadley, 29–50. Sewanee, 1989.

———. "Filippa Mareri, la Santa Baronessa, la Santa del Cicolano." In *Saints, Scholars, and Heroes: Studies in Medieval Culture in Honour of Charles W. Jones,* edited by Margot H. King and Wesley M. Stevens, 2:287–297. Collegeville, Minn., 1979.

———. "Innocent IV and the Chapter of Rieti." *Collectanea Stephan Kuttner III: Studia gratiana* 13 (1967): 383–410.

———. "Localism and Longevity: The Example of the Chapter of Rieti in the Thirteenth and Fourteenth Centuries." In *Law, Church and Society: Essays in Honor of Stephan Kuttner,* edited by Kenneth Pennington and Robert Somerville, 293–310. Philadelphia, 1977.

———. "Il movimento religioso femminile a Rieti nei secoli XIII–XIV." In *Il movimento religioso femminile in Umbria nei secoli XIII–XIV.* Regione dell'Umbria, Perugia, 1984, 69–83.

———. "Notarial Cartularies and Religious Personality: Rome, Rieti and Bishop Thomas of Secinaro." In *Sources of Social History: Private Acts of the Late Middle Ages,* edited by Paolo Brezzi and Egmont Lee, 169–183. Pontifical Institute of Mediaeval Studies, Papers in Mediaeval Studies 5. Toronto, 1984.

————. *Rome before Avignon*. New York, 1974.

————. "Santa Filippa Mareri nel movimento religioso femminile del secolo XIII." In *Santa Filippa Mareri e il monastero di Borgo S. Pietro nella storia del Cicolano*. Atti del Convegno di studi di Borgo S. Pietro del 24–26 ottobre 1986. Borgo S. Pietro di Petrella Salto, 1989.

————. "Il sogno di Sant'Anselmo e lo sviluppo della biografia medievale." In *I linguaggi del sogno*, edited by Vittore Branca, Carlo Ossola, and Salomon Resnik, 395–406. Florence, 1984.

————. *Two Churches: England and Italy in the Thirteenth Century*. Berkeley, 1988.

————. "Vescovi e collocazione socio-culturale del clero parrocchiale." In *Italia sacra*, vol. 36, *Pievi e parrocchie in Italia nel basso medioevo (sec. XIII–XV)*, 1:235–256. Rome, 1984.

————. "Vescovi e vicari generali nel basso medioevo." In *Italia sacra*, vol. 43, *Vescovi e diocesi in Italia dal XIV alla metà del XVI secolo*, edited by Giuseppina De Sandre Gasparini, Antonio Rigon, Francesco Trolese, and Gian Maria Varanini, 1:547–567. Rome, 1990.

————. "Who was Bishop Andrea of Rieti (1286–1292)?" *Studi offerti a Cesare Verani: Il territorio* 5 (1989): 85–90.

————. *York Metropolitan Jurisdiction and Papal Judges Delegate*. Berkeley, 1959.

Brooke, C. N. "The Ecclesiastical Geography of Medieval Towns." In *Miscellanea historiae ecclesiasticae*, vol. 5, *La Cartographie et l'histoire socio-religieuse de l'Europe jusqu'à la fin du XVIIe siècle*, 15–31. Bibliothèque de la Revue d'histoire ecclésiastique, 61. Louvain, 1974.

Brooke, Rosalind P. "Recent Work on St. Francis of Assisi." *Analecta Bollandiana* 100 (1982): 653–676.

Brundage, James. "A Twelfth-Century Oxford Disputation Concerning the Privileges of the Knights Hospitallers." *Mediaeval Studies* 24 (1962): 153–160.

Buchthal, H. *The "Musterbuch" of Wolfenbüttel*. Vienna, 1979.

Caiazza, Pietro. "Sinodi pre-tridentini in diocesi di Amalfi." *Rassegna del Centro di cultura e storia amalfitana* 6 (1986): 7–63.

Caraffa, Filippo, ed. *Monasticon Italiae*, vol. l, *Roma e Lazio*. Centro storico Benedettino italiano. Cesena, 1981.

Casagrande, Giovanna. "Il fenomeno della reclusione volontaria nei secoli del basso medioevo." *Benedictina* 35 (1988): 475–507.

Cascioli, Giuseppe. "Nuova serie dei vescovi (cont.): 1210–1318." *Atti e memorie della società tiburtina di storia e d'arte* 4 (1924): 152–208.

Cavell, Stanley. "Epistemology and Tragedy: A Reading of Otello." In *Hypocrisy, Illusion, and Evasion: Daedalus* 108 (1979): 27–43.

Cerafogli, Elia. *La baronessa santa*. Vatican City, 1979.

Cheney, Christopher R. "Cardinal John of Ferentino, papal legate in England in 1206." *English Historical Review* 76 (1961): 654–660.

————. *English Synodalia of the Thirteenth Century*. Oxford, 1968.

————. *From Becket to Langton*. Manchester, 1956.

————. "Gervase, Abbot of Prémontré: a Medieval Letter-Writer." *Bulletin of the John Rylands Library* 33 (1950–51): 25–56.

———. *Innocent III and England.* Päpste und Papsttum, 9. Stuttgart, 1976.

———. *Notaries Public in England in the Thirteenth and Fourteenth Centuries.* Oxford, 1972.

Chiappelli, A. "Puccio Capanna e gli affreschi in San Francesco di Pistoia." *Dedalo* 11 (1929/1930): 199–228.

Chiappini, Aniceto. "Fondazione, distruzione, riedificazione dell'Aquila capitale degli Abruzzi." In *Miscellanei scritti vari in memoria di Alfonso Gallo,* 255–278. Florence, 1956.

———. "Intorno alla fondazione della città dell'Aquila." *Bullettino abruzzese,* 4th s., 6 (1936): 21–31.

Chiffoleau, Jacques. "Sur l'usage obsessionnel de la messe pour les morts à la fin du moyen âge." In *Faire croire,* 236–256. École française de Rome. Rome, 1981.

Clay, C. T., ed. *York Minster fasti.* Yorkshire Archaeological Society, Record Series, 124. Leeds, 1959.

Clementi, Alessandro, and Maria Rita Berardi, eds. *Regesto delle fonti archivistiche degli annali Antinoriani (vol. III–XVII).* Deputazione abruzzese di storia patria: Documenti per la storia d'Abruzzo. L'Aquila, 1980.

Cohn, Samuel K. *Death and Property in Siena, 1205–1800: Strategies for the Afterlife.* Baltimore, 1988.

Colasanti, Giovanni. *Reate: Ricerche di topografia medioevale ed antica.* Perugia, 1910.

Comet, Georges. "Le temps agricole d'après les calendriers illustrés." In *Temps, tradition, mémoire au moyen âge,* 7–18. Aix-en-Provence, 1983.

Cornelisen, Ann. *Where It All Began: Italy 1954.* New York, 1990.

Costantini, Paolo, Silvio Fuso, Sandro Mescola, and Italo Zannier, eds. *L'insistenza dello sguardo: Fotografie italiane* 1839–1989. Florence, 1989.

Coste, J. "I confini occidentale della diocesi di Tivoli nel medioevo." *Atti e memorie della società tiburtina di storia e d'arte* 52 (1979): 104–107.

Cottineau, Henri. *Répertoire topo-bibliographique des abbayes et prieurés.* Vol. 2. Macon, 1935–39.

Cowdrey, H. E. J. *The Cluniacs and the Gregorian Reform.* Oxford, 1970.

Dalla Barba Brusin, Dina, and Giovanni Lorenzoni. *L'arte del patriarcato di Aquileia dal secolo IX al secolo XIII.* Padua, 1968.

Dal Pino, Franco. *Il laicato italiano tra eresia e proposta pauperistico-evangelica nei secoli XII–XIII.* Padua, 1984.

D'Achille, Anna Maria, Antonella Ferri, and Tiziana Iazeolla, eds. *La sabina: Luoghi fortificati, monasteri e abbazie.* Cassa di Risparmio di Rieti, 1985.

D'Agostino, Marco, and Maria Grazia Fiore. "Il monastero di S. Salvatore Maggiore: Nuove problematiche e prospettive di ricerca." *Il Territorio* 3, no. 2 (1987): 5–30.

D'Andreis, Antonio. *Cittareale e la sua valle.* Rome, 1961.

D'Annunzio, G. *Ricerche di storia abruzzese.* Chieti, 1986.

Davis, Charles Till. "Ubertino da Casale and his Conception of 'Altissima Paupertas.' " *Studi medievali,* 3d s., 12, no. 1 (1981).

De Bartholomaeis, Vincenzo. "Federico II e l'Aquila." *Bullettino abruzzese,* 6th s., 3–5 (1953–55, printed in 1961): 100–107.

Delumeau, Jean-Pierre. "La mémoire des gens d'Arezzo et de Sienne à travers des dépositions de témoins (VIIIe–XIIe s.)." In *Temps, tradition, mémoire au moyen âge*, 43–65. Aix-en-Provence, 1983.

De Nino, Antonio. "Nuove congetture sull'origine dell'Aquila." *Bollettino Antinori* 12 (1900): 79–83.

Desanctis, Paolo. *Notizie storiche di San Salvator Maggiore e del seminario di Rieti*. Rieti, 1884.

De Sandre Gasparini, Giuseppina. "Istituzioni ecclesiastiche, religiose e assistenziali nella Verona scaligera tra potere signorile e società." In *Gli Scaligeri (1277–1387)*, edited by Gian Maria Varanini, 393–404. Verona, 1988.

———. "Movimenti evangelici a Verona all'epoca di Francesco d'Assisi." *Le Venezie francescane*, n.s., 1 (1984): 151–162.

De Stefano, Antonino. "Le origini di Aquila e il privilegio di fondazione attribuito a Federico II." *Bullettino della deputazione abruzzese di storia patria*, 3d s., 14 (1923): 7–26.

Di Flavio, Vincenzo. "Le visite pastorali nella diocesi di Rieti dal sec. XVI al XVIII." *Archiva ecclesiae* 22–23 (1979–80): 225–238.

———. "Ombre e luci sul palazzo priorale di Rieti." In *Palazzi municipali del Lazio*, 75–90. Lunario Romano. Rome, 1985.

———. *Sinodo reatino del 1614*. Rieti, 1980.

———, and Andrea Di Nicola. *Il monastero di S. Lucia*. Amministrazione comunale di Rieti: Quaderni di storia urbana e territoriale, 6. Rieti, 1990.

Di Fonzo, Lorenzo. "L'Anonimo Perugino tra le fonti francescane del sec. XIII: Rapporti letterari e testo critico." *Miscellanea francescana* 72 (1972): 117–480.

Di Nicola, Andrea. "Monasteri, laici, ordinari e *Curae animarum* nel Cicolano (sec. IX–XIII). Appunti e spunti per una ricerca." In *San Francesco nella civiltà medioevale con riferimento alla valle reatina al Cicolano e a Corvaro*, edited by Giovanni Maceroni, 213–223. Rieti, 1983.

Dondaine, Antoine. "Le Manuel de l'inquisiteur (1230–1330)." *Archivum fratrum praedicatorum* 17 (1947): 85–194.

Douie, Decima L. *The Nature and Effect of the Heresy of the Fraticelli*. Manchester, 1932.

Duprè Theseider, Eugenio. *Il lago Velino*. Rieti, 1939.

———. *L'abbazia di San Pastore*. Rieti, 1919.

———. "Vescovi e città nell'Italia precomunale." In *Italia sacra*, vol. 5, *Vescovi e diocesi in Italia nel medioevo (sec. IX–XIII)*, 55–109. Atti del II convegno di storia della chiesa in Italia. Padua, 1964.

Edward, Robert. *The Montecassino Passion*. Berkeley, 1977.

Egidi, P., G. Giovannoni, and F. Hermanin, eds. *I monasteri di Subiaco*. Vol. 1. Rome, 1904.

Elze, Reinhard. "Die päpstliche Kapelle im 12. und 13. Jahrhundert." *Zeitschrift der Savigny-Stiftung für Rechtsgeschichte, kanonistische Abteilung* 36 (1950): 145–204.

Eubel, Konrad. *Hierarchia catholica medii et recentioris acvi*. Münster, 1913.

Fabrizi, Filippo. "Sallustio nella fantasia dei popoli Sabini." *Bollettino Antinori* 11 (1899): 95–103.

Ferri, Antonella. "Monteleone. La chiesa di Santa Vittoria." In *La sabina medievale*, edited by Marina Righetti Tosti-Croce, 76–89. Cassa di Risparmio di Rieti. Rieti, 1985.

Fonseca, Cosimo Damiano. "Forme assistenziali e strutture caritative della chiesa nel medioevo." In *Chiesa e società: Appunti per una storia delle diocesi lombarde*, 275–291. Storia religiosa della Lombardia. Brescia, 1986.

Friedman, David. *Florentine New Towns: Urban Design in the Late Middle Ages*. Architectural History Foundation. Cambridge, Mass., 1988.

Frugoni, Arsenio. "Subiaco francescano." *Bullettino dell'Istituto storico italiano per il medioevo e Archivio Muratoriano* 65 (1953): 107–119.

Galbraith, G. R. *The Constitution of the Dominican Order 1216 to 1360*. Manchester, 1926.

Gams, P. B. *Series episcoporum ecclesiae catholicae*. 1873, 1886. Reprint. Leipzig, 1931.

Gardner, Julian. "The Cappellone di San Nicola at Tolentino: Some Functions of a Fourteenth-Century Fresco Cycle." In *Italian Church Decoration of the Middle Ages and Early Renaissance*, edited by William Tronzo, 101–117. Villa Spelman Colloquia 1.

————. "The Louvre Stigmatization and the problem of the narrative altarpiece." *Zeitschrift für Kunstgeschichte* (1982): 217–247.

————. "Päpstliche Traume und Palastmalereien." In *Traume im Mittelalter*, edited by A. Paravicini Bagliani and G. Stabile, 113–124. Stuttgart, 1989.

————. "Pope Nicholas IV and the decoration of Santa Maria Maggiore." *Zeitschrift für Kunstgeschichte* 45 (1973): 1–50.

————. "Some Franciscan altars of the thirteenth and fourteenth centuries." In *The Vanishing Past*, edited by A. Borg and A. Martindale, 29–38. Oxford, 1981.

Garms, Jörg, Roswitha Juffinger, and Bryan Ward-Perkins, eds. *Die mittelalterlichen Grabmäler in Rom und Latium vom 13. bis zum 15. Jahrhundert*, vol. 1, *Die Grabplatten und Tafeln*. Österreichischen Kulturinstituts in Rome. Rome, 1981.

Gentili, Otello. *L'abbazia di S. M. di Chiaravalle di Fiastra*. Rome, 1978.

Giusti, Martino. "Le elezioni dei vescovi di Lucca specialmente nel secolo XIII." *Rivista di storia della chiesa in Italia* 6 (1952): 205–230.

Given, James. "The Inquisitors of Languedoc and the Medieval Technology of Power." *American Historical Review* 94 (1989): 336–359.

Gizzi, Stefano. "La città dell'Aquila: Fondazione e preesistenze." *Storia della città* 28 (1983): 11–42.

Gregorovius, Ferdinand. *History of the City of Rome in the Middle Ages*. Vol. 6. Translated by Mrs. Gustavus W. Hamilton. London, 1898.

Grundmann, Herbert. *Movimenti religiosi nel medioevo*. Bologna, 1974.

Guidoni, Enrico. "L'espansione urbanistica di Rieti nel XIII secolo e le città nuove di fondazione angioina." In *La sabina medievale*, edited by Marina Righetti Tosti-Croce, 156–187. Cassa di Risparmio di Rieti. Rieti, 1985.

Gurevich, Aron. *Medieval Popular Culture: Problems of Belief and Perception*. Cambridge, 1988.

Haines, Roy Martin. *The Church and Politics in Fourteenth-Century England: The Career of Adam of Orleton, ca.* 1275–1345. Cambridge, 1978.

Hamilton, Bernard. *The Medieval Inquisition.* New York, 1981.

Helmholz, R. H. *Marriage Litigation in Medieval England.* Studies in Legal History. Cambridge, 1974.

Henderson, John. "The Flagellant Movement and Flagellant Confraternities in Central Italy, 1260–1400." *Studies in Church History* 15 (1978): 147–160.

Herde, Peter. *Audientia litterarum contradictarum.* Tübingen, 1970.

_____. *Beiträge zum päpstlichen Kanzlei- und Urkundenwesen im 13. Jahrhundert.* 2d edition. Kallmünz, 1967.

_____. "Celestino V, papa." *Dizionario biografico degli italiani,* 23:402–415. Rome, 1979.

_____. *Cölestin V. (1294) (Peter vom Morrone), Der Engelpapst.* Päpste und Papsttum, 16. Stuttgart, 1981.

Hubert, Étienne. *Espace urbain et habitat à Rome à la fin du XIIIe siècle.* Collection de l'école française de Rome, 135. Rome, 1990.

Janauschek, Leopold. *Originum cisterciensium.* Vienna, 1877.

Kamp, Norbert. *Kirche und Monarchie im staufischen Königreich Sizilien,* vol. 1, *Abruzzen und Kampanien.* Munich, 1973.

_____. "Andrea Brancaleone." *Dizionario biografico degli italiani,* 13:809–810. Rome, 1971.

Kitzinger, E. *The Mosaics of Monreale.* Palermo, 1960.

Lambert, M. D. *Franciscan Poverty.* London, 1961.

Lauer, Philippe. *Le palais de Latran.* Paris, 1911.

Lawrence, C. H. *St. Edmund of Abingdon.* Oxford, 1960.

Leff, Gordon. *Heresy in the Later Middle Ages.* Vol. 1. Manchester, 1967.

Leggio, Tersilio. *Le fortificazioni di Rieti dall'alto medioevo al rinascimento (sec. VI–XVI).* Quaderni di storia urbana e territoriale, 4. Rieti, 1989.

Leonardi, Corrado. *Le fondazioni francescane nella terra di Mercatello sul Metauro.* Urbania, 1982.

Linehan, Peter. *The Spanish Church and the Papacy in the Thirteenth Century.* Cambridge, 1971.

Little, Lester K. "Les techniques de la confession et la confession comme technique." In *Faire croire,* 87–99. École française de Rome. Rome, 1981.

_____. *Liberty, Charity and Fraternity: Bergamo in the Times of the Commune.* Northampton, Mass., 1987.

Lombardo, Anna Maria. "Nobili, mercanti e popolo minuto negli atti dei notai romani del XIV e XV secolo." In *Gli atti privati nel tardo medioevo, fonti per la storia sociale: Sources of Social History, Private Acts of the Late Middle Ages,* edited by Paolo Brezzi and Egmont Lee, 291–301. Istituto di studi romani and Pontifical Institute of Mediaeval Studies: Papers in Mediaeval Studies, 5. Rome, 1984.

Ludovisi, Idido. "Corografia storica degli Abruzzi di A. L. Antinori: Amiterno e S. Vittorino." *Bullettino abruzzese,* 3d s., 7 (1917): 185–224; and 9 (1919): 231–243.

_____. "L'organismo del comune aquilano nei secoli XIII, XIV, XV." *Bollet-*

tino della società di storia patria Anton Ludovico Antinori negli Abruzzi 10, no. 19 (1898): 1–41.

———. "Storia dei contadi di Amiterno e Forcona al secolo XIII." *Bollettino della società di storia patria Anton Ludovico Antinori negli Abruzzi* 7, no. 13 (1895): 30–77.

Lugini, Domenico. *Memorie storiche della regione Equicola ora Cicolano.* Rieti, 1907.

Luttrell, Anthony. *The Hospitallers in Cyprus, Rhodes, Greece and the West, 1291–1440: Collected Studies.* London, 1978.

McArdle, Frank. *Altopascio: A Study in Tuscan Rural Society, 1587–1784.* Cambridge, 1978.

McClendon, Charles B. *The Imperial Abbey of Farfa: Architectural Currents of the Early Middle Ages.* New Haven, 1987.

Maceroni, Giovanni. *L'antipapa Niccolo V.* Rieti, 1981.

———. "La diocesi di Rieti nel difficile cammino della civiltà basso-medioevale e S. Francesco nella religiosità del tempo." In *San Francesco nella civiltà medioevale con riferimento alla valle reatina al Cicolano e a Corvaro,* edited by Giovanni Maceroni, 15–83. Rieti, 1983.

———. Il monastero di Santa Filippa Mareri dal Concilio Vaticano I al Concilio Vaticano III." In *Santa Filippa Mareri e il monastero di Borgo S. Pietro nella storia del Cicolano,* 167–190. Atti del Convegno di studi di Borgo S. Pietro del 24–26 ottobre 1986. Borgo S. Pietro di Petrella Salto, 1989.

———, ed. *Il brigantaggio: Genesi e sviluppi delle rivolte postunitarie con particolare riferimento al Cicolano.* Rieti, 1985.

Maceroni, Giovanni, and Anna Maria Tassi. *Società religiosa e civile dall'epoca postridentina alle soglie della rivoluzione francese nella diocesi Rieti.* Rieti, 1985.

Maitland, Frederic William. *Township and Borough.* Cambridge, 1898.

Mantese, Giovanni. *Memorie storiche della chiesa vicentina,* vol. 3, *Il trecento.* Vicenza, 1958.

Marchetti-Longhi, G. *Gregorio da Montelongo primo patriarca italiano di Aquileia, 1251–1269.* Rome, 1965.

Mariano D'Alatri. "Fraticellismo e inquisizione nell'Italia centrale." In *Studi e documenti,* vol. 2, *Eretici e inquisitori in Italia,* 193–217. Rome, 1986–87.

———. "Il vescovo nella cronica di Salimbene da Parma." *Collectanea franciscana* 42 (1972): 5–38.

———. "I più antichi insediamenti dei mendicanti nella provincia civile di Campagna." *Mélanges de l'École française de Rome: Moyen âge–temps modernes* 89 (1977): 575–585.

———. *L'inquisizione francescana nell'Italia centrale nel secolo XIII.* Rome, 1954.

Marinelli, Roberto. *Il Terminillo: Storia di una montagna.* Rieti, 1985.

———. "La valle sommersa e la ricostruzione del monastero di Borgo S. Pietro." In *Santa Filippa Mareri e il monastero di Borgo S. Pietro nella storia del Cicolano,* 327–359. Atti del Convegno di studi di Borgo S. Pietro del 24–26 ottobre 1986. Borgo S. Pietro di Petrella Salto, 1989.

Marini, Saverio. *Memorie di S. Barbara, vergine e martire di Scandriglia*. Foligno, 1788.

Marino, John A. *Pastoral Economics in the Kingdom of Naples*. Baltimore, 1988.

Maroni, Fausto Antonio. *Commentarius de ecclesia et episcopis reatinis in quo Ughelliana series emendatur, continuatur, illustratur*. Rome, 1763.

Marrone, Steven P. *William of Auvergne and Robert Grosseteste: New Ideas of Truth in the Early Thirteenth Century*. Princeton, 1983.

Marsella, Crescenzo. *I vescovi di Sora, monografia storia*. Sora, 1935.

Mascetta Caracci, Lorenzo. "Il latino della chiesa nel dialetto e nel gergo abruzzese." *Rassegna abruzzese di storia ed arte* 1 (1897): 271–276.

Matthiae, Guglielmo. "Lavori della soprintendenza ai monumenti del Lazio: Affreschi in S. M. in Vescovio." *Bollettino d'arte* 28 (1934): 86–96.

_____. *Pittura medioevale abruzzese*. Electa. Milan, n.d.

Mattiocco, Ezio. *Struttura urbana e società della Sulmona medievale*. Sulmona, 1978.

Mazzatinti, Giuseppe. *Gli archivi della storia d'Italia*. Vol. 4. Rocca S. Casciano, 1906.

Merlo, Grado Giovanni. *Eretici ed eresie medievali*. Bologna, 1989.

_____. *Tensioni religiose agli inizi del duecento*. Torre Pellice, 1984.

Michaeli, Michele. *Memorie storiche della città di Rieti e dei paesi circostanti dall'origine all'anno* 1560. Vol. 4. Rieti, 1897–99 (reprinted as Biblioteca istorica della antica e nuova Italia, no. 80, Forni, Bologna).

_____. *Notizie dell'antico monastero detto di S. Pastore nella diocesi reatina*. Rieti, 1860.

Mihályi, Melinda. "I Cistercensi a Roma e la decorazione pittorica dell'ala dei monaci nell'abbazia delle Tre Fontane." *Arte medievale*, 2d s., 2, no. 5 (1991): 155–189.

Mitchell, John. "St. Silvester and Constantine at the SS. Quattro Coronati." In *Federico II e l'arte del duecento italiano*, 2:15–32. Galatina, 1980.

Montagner, Alberto. "Reazione e brigantaggio nel Cicolano (1860–1867)." *Rieti, rivista bimestrale di studi e documentazione* 1 (January–February 1973): 49–88; and 2 (March–April 1973): 89–116.

Montanari, Massimo. *L'alimentazione contadina nell'alto medioevo*. Naples, 1979.

_____. *Porci e porcari nel medioevo*. San Marino di Bentivoglio, 1981.

Moorman, John R. H. *A History of the Franciscan Order from its Origins to the Year* 1517. Oxford, 1968.

_____. *Mediaeval Franciscan Houses*. St. Bonaventure, N.Y., 1983.

_____. *The Sources for the Life of St. Francis of Assisi*. Manchester, 1940.

Morris, Colin. *The Papal Monarchy: The Western Church from 1050 to 1250*. Oxford, 1989.

Mortari, Luisa. *Il tesoro del duomo di Rieti*. Rome, 1974.

_____. "Rieti." In *La sabina medievale*, edited by Marina Righetti Tosti-Croce, 104–155. Cassa di Risparmio di Rieti. Rieti, 1985.

_____. *Museo civico di Rieti*. Rome, 1960.

Moscati, Anna. "I monasteri di Pietro Celestino." *Bollettino dell'Istituto storico italiano per il medioevo e Archivio Muratoriano* 68 (1956): 91–163.

Naudé, Gabriel. *Instauratio tabularii majoris templi reatini*. Rome, 1640.

―――. *Lettres de Gabriel Naudé à Jacques Dupuy (1632–1652)*. Edited by Philip Wolfe. Edmonton, 1982.

Nicoletti, Maria Antonio. *Patriarcato d'Aquileia sotto Pietro Gera*. Ùdine, 1908.

Oliger, Livario. "Due musaici con S. Francesco della Chiesa di Aracoeli in Roma." *Archivum franciscanum historicum* 4 (1911): 213–251.

Osheim, Duane J. *A Tuscan Monastery and Its Social World: San Michele of Guamo (1156–1348)*. Rome, 1989.

Pagnani, Giacinto. "Frammenti della cronaca del B. Francesco Venimbeni da Fabriano († 1332)." *Archivum franciscanum historicum* 52 (1959): 153–177.

Palatini, Leopoldo. "Cenni storici della Badia e prepositura di Sant'Eusanio Forconese." *Bollettino Antinori* 9, no. 18 (1897): 133–160.

―――. "La signoria nell'Aquila degli Abruzzi della seconda metà del secolo XIII al principio del XV." *Bollettino Antinori* 12, no. 24 (1900): 165–257.

Palmegiani, Francesco. *La cattedrale basilica di Rieti con cenni storici sulle altre chiese della città*. Rome, 1926.

―――. *Rieti e la regione sabina*. Latina Gens. Rome, 1932.

Pansa, Giovanni. "Catalogo descrittivo e analitico dei manoscritti riflettenti la storia d'Abruzzo." *Bullettino abruzzese*, 7th s., 1 [years 47–50] (1957–60): 21–197.

Paravicini Bagliani, Agostino. In *Italia sacra*, vols. 18–19, *Cardinali di curia e 'familiae' cardinalizie dal 1227 al 1254*. Padua, 1972.

―――. *I testamenti dei cardinali del duecento*. Miscellanea della società romana di storia patria, 25. Rome, 1980.

―――. "La mobilità della curia romana nel secolo XIII: Riflessi locali." In *Società e istituzioni dell'Italia comunale: L'esempio di Perugia (secoli XII–XIV)*. Perugia, 1988, 155–278.

Partner, Peter. *The Lands of St. Peter*. Berkeley, 1972.

Paschini, Pio. "Il patriarcato di Pietro Gera (1299–1301)." *Memorie storiche forogiuliesi* XXI (1925): 73–107.

Pasztor, Edith. "Filippa Mareri e Chiara d'Assisi, discepole di S. Francesco." In *Santa Filippa Mareri e il monastero di Borgo S. Pietro nella storia del Cicolano*, 55–80. Atti del Convegno di studi di Borgo S. Pietro del 24–26 ottobre 1986. Borgo S. Pietro di Petrella Salto, 1989.

―――. "Per la storia dell'amministrazione dello stato pontificio sotto Martino IV." In *Miscellanea in onore di Monsignor Martino Giusti*, 2:181–194. Collectanea Archivi Vaticani, 6. Vatican City, 1978.

Paul, Jacques. "Expressions et perception du temps d'après l'enquête sur les miracles de Louis d'Anjou." In *Temps, tradition, mémoire au moyen âge*, 19–41. Aix-en-Provence, 1983.

Pellegrini, Luigi. *Abruzzo medioevale*. Studi e ricerche sul Mezzogiorno medievale, 6. Altavilla Silentina, 1988.

Pesce, Giuseppe Lucio. "Aspetti geo-paleontologici nella genesi e successiva evoluzione della conca reatina (Rieti, Lazio)." *Rieti* 2 (March–April 1973): 117–128.

Peters, Edward. *Inquisition*. New York, 1988.

Petrucci, Enzo. "Pievi e parrocchie del Lazio nel basso medioevo. Note e osservazioni." In *Italia sacra*, vol. 36, *Pievi e parrocchie in Italia nel basso medioevo (sec. XIII–XV)*, 2:893–1017. Rome, 1984.

———. "Vescovi e cura d'anime nel Lazio (sec. XIII–XV)." In *Italia sacra*, vol. 43, *Vescovi e diocesi in Italia dal XIV alla metà del XVI secolo*, edited by Giuseppina De Sandre Gasparini, Antonio Rigon, Francesco Trolese, and Gian Maria Varanini, 1:429–546. Rome, 1990.

Pirri, Pietro. "S. Lazzaro del Valoncello: Memorie d'un grande leprosario francescano nell'Umbria." *Archivio per la storia ecclesiastica nell'Umbria* 2 (1915): 37–99.

Porracciolo, Giuseppina, and Donatella Petroni. "La chiesa di S. Francesco e l'oratorio della S. Croce." *Il territorio* 1, no. 2 (1984–85): 195–214.

Pratesi, Fulco, and Franco Tassi, eds. *Guida alla natura del Lazio e dell'Abruzzo*. With the collaboration of the World Wildlife Fund. Mondadori, 1972.

Rashdall, Hastings. *The Universities of Europe in the Middle Ages*, edited by F. M. Powicke and A. B. Emden. Vol. 1. Oxford, 1936.

Reeves, Marjorie. *Joachim of Fiore and the Prophetic Future*. London, 1976.

Reh, Friedrich. *Kardinal Peter Capocci*. Berlin, 1933.

Riccardi, Tommaso. *Storia dei vescovi vicentini*. Vicenza, 1786.

Riccetti, Lucio, ed. *Il duomo di Orvieto*. Bari, 1988.

Ricci, Evandro. *I Peligni Superequani: La Sicinnide e le origini di Secinaro*. Sulmona, 1969.

———. *Elementi di civiltà dei Pelini Superequani*. Sulmona, 1978.

———. *Superaequum e gli antichi Cedici*. Sulmona, 1981.

Righetti Tosti-Croce, Marina, ed. *La sabina medievale*. Cassa di Risparmio di Rieti. Rieti, 1985.

Rigon, Antonio. *Clero e città: "Fratalea cappellanorum," parroci, cura d'anime in Padova dal XII al XV secolo*. Fonti e ricerche di storia ecclesiastica padovana, 22. Istituto per la storia ecclesiastica padovana. Padua, 1988.

———. "Le elezioni vescovili nel processo di sviluppo delle istituzioni ecclesiastiche a Padova tra XII e XIII secolo." *Mélanges de l'École française de Rome: Moyen âge, temps modernes* 89 (1977): 371–409.

———. "Orientamenti religiosi e pratica testamentaria a Padova nei secoli XII–XIV (prime ricerche)." In *Nolens intestatus decedere: Il testamento come fonte della storia religiosa e sociale*, edited by A. Bartoli Langeli. Archivi dell'Umbria: Inventari e ricerche, 7. Perugia, 1985.

Rossi, Louis R. "The Devouring Passion: *Inferno* VI." *Italica* 42, no. 1 (1965): 33.

Rossi Caponeri, Marilena. "Il duomo e l'attività edilizia dei Signori Sette (1295–1313)." In *Il duomo di Orvieto*, edited by Lucio Riccetti, 29–80. Bari, 1988.

Ruocco, Silvio. *Storia di Sarno e dintorni*. Vol. 1. Sarno, 1946–52.

Sabatini, Gaetano. "Saggio bibliografico di mappe e panorami d'Abruzzo." *Bullettino abruzzese*, 7th s., 1 [years 47–50] (1957–60): 199–285.

Sabean, David Warren. *Power in the Blood: Popular culture and village discourse in early modern Germany*. Cambridge, 1987.

Sacchetti Sassetti, Angelo. *Anecdota franciscana reatina*. Potenza, 1926.

————. "Cenni storici." *Guida di Rieti.* 3d edition. Rieti, 1965.

————. "Rieti e gli Urslingen." *Archivio della società romana di storia patria* 3d s., 16–17 (1962–63): 1–24.

————. "Un ospite di S. Francesco a Rieti, Tebaldo Saraceni." *Archivum franciscanum historicum* 59 (1966).

Sahlins, Peter. *Boundaries: The Making of France and Spain in the Pyrenees.* Berkeley, 1989.

Sambin, Paolo. "La 'famiglia' di un vescovo italiano del '300. Ildebrandino Conti 1352." *Rivista di storia della chiesa in Italia* 4 (1950): 237–247.

————. *L'ordinamento parrocchiale di Padova nel medioevo.* Padua, 1941.

Santi, F. *Galleria nazionale dell'Umbria: Dipinti, sculture e oggetti d'arte di età romanica e gotica.* Rome, 1969.

Sayers, Jane E. *Papal Judges Delegate in the Province of Canterbury.* Oxford, 1971.

Scaccia Scarafoni, Camillo. "L'archivio capitolare della cattedrale di Vèroli e la prossima pubblicazione delle pergamene del secolo X–XII." *Archivio della società romana di storia patria*, 3d s., 8 (1954): 91–96.

Scalon, Cesare. *La biblioteca arcivescovile di Ùdine.* Padua, 1979.

————. *Necrologium aquileiense.* Fonti per la storia della chiesa in Friuli, 1. Ùdine, 1982.

Scarpellini, P. "Di alcuni pittori giotteschi nella città e nel territorio di Assisi." In *Giotto e i giotteschi in Assisi*, edited by G. Palumbo, 211–270. Rome, 1969.

Scheiner, Irwin. "The Mindful Peasant: Sketches for a Study of Rebellion." *Journal of Asian Studies* 32 (1973): 579–591.

Schuster, Idelfonso. "Il monastero del Salvatore e gli antichi possedimenti farfensi nella Massa Torana." *Archivio della società romana di storia patria* 41 (1918): 5–58.

————. "Il monastero imperiale del S. Salvatore sul Monte Letenino." *Archivio della società romana di storia patria* 37 (1914): 393–451.

————. *L'imperiale abbazia di Farfa.* Rome, 1921.

Scoppola, Francesco. "La rocca di Talamone." *Storia della città* 28 (1983): 43–58.

Sella, Pietro. *Rationes decimarum Italiae nei secoli XIII e XIV: Aprutium, Molisium: Le decime dei secoli XIII–XIV.* Studi e testi, 69. Vatican City, 1936.

Silvistrelli, G. "Le chiese e feudi dell'ordine dei Templari e dell'ordine di San Giovanni di Gerusalemme nella regione romana." *Rendiconti della Reale Accademia dei Lincei: Classe di scienze morali, storiche, e filologiche* 26 (1917); 27 (1918): 174–176.

Smart, A. *The Assisi Problem and the Art of Giotto.* Oxford, 1971.

Spufford, Peter. *Handbook of Medieval Exchange.* Royal Historical Society Guides and Handbooks, 13. London, 1986.

Storia e tradizioni popolari di Petrella Salto e Cicolano: Atti. Vol. 1. Comune di Petrella Salto. Rieti, 1982.

Terenzoni, Erilde. "L'archivio storico del monastero delle Clarisse di San Pietro de Molito." In *Santa Filippa Mareri e il monastero di Borgo S. Pietro nella storia del Cicolano*, 277–288. Atti del Convegno di studi di Borgo S. Pietro del 24–26 ottobre 1986. Borgo S. Pietro di Petrella Salto, 1989.

Thomson, Williel R. *Friars in the Cathedral: The First Franciscan Bishops, 1226–1261.* Toronto, 1975.

Tierney, Brian. *Foundations of the Conciliar Theory: The Contribution of the Medieval Canonists from Gratian to the Great Schism.* Cambridge, 1955.

———. *Medieval Poor Law.* Berkeley, 1959.

Tintori, L., and M. Meiss. *The Painting of the Life of St. Francis in Assisi.* New York, 1962.

Toesca, P. *Pietro Cavallini.* London, 1960.

Tomassetti, G., and G. Biasiotti. *La diocesi di Sabina.* Rome, 1909.

Tomei, A. "Il ciclo vetero e neotestamentario di S. Maria di Vescovio." In *Roma anno 1300,* edited by A. M. Romanini, 355–376. Atti della IV settimana di studi di storia dell'arte medievale dell'Università di Roma "La Sapienza," (19–24 maggio 1980). Rome, 1983.

Toubert, Pierre. *Les structures du Latium médiéval: Le Latium méridional et la Sabine du IXe siècle à la fin du XIIe siècle.* École française de Rome. Rome, 1973.

Traversa, Eduard. *Quellenkritik zur Geschichte des Patriarchen Peter II Gerra (1299–1301).* Görz, 1936.

Trexler, Richard C. "The Bishop's Portion." *Traditio* 28 (1972): 397–450.

———. "Charity and the Defense of Urban Elites in the Italian Communes." In *The Rich, the Well Born, and the Powerful,* edited by F. Jaher, 64–109. Urbana, 1974.

———. "Diocesan Synods in Late Medieval Italy." In *Italia sacra,* vol. 43, *Vescovi e diocesi in Italia dal XIV alla metà del XVI secolo,* edited by Giuseppina De Sandre Gasparini, Antonio Rigon, Francesco Trolese, and Gian Maria Varanini, 1:295–335. Rome, 1990.

Truini Palomba, Maria Giuseppina. *La cucina sabina.* Padua, 1991.

Van Heteren, Willibrordo. "Due monasteri Benedettini più volte secolari (Rieti)." *Bollettino della deputazione di storia patria per l'Umbria* 12 (1906): 51–80.

Varanini, Gian Maria, ed. *Gli Scaligeri (1277–1387).* Verona, 1988.

———. "La chiesa veronese nella prima età scaligera. Bonincontro arciprete del capitolo (1273–1295) e vescovo (1296–1298)." *Le Venezie francescane,* n.s., 4, no. 2 (1988): 9–72.

Vasina, Augusto. "L'elezione degli arcivescovi ravennati del sec. XIII nei rapporti con la Santa Sede." *Rivista di storia della chiesa in Italia* 10 (1956): 49–89.

Vauchez, André. *La sainteté en occident aux derniers siècles du moyen âge d'après les procès de canonisation et les documents hagiographiques.* Rome, 1981.

Verani, Cesare. *La provincia di Rieti.* Rieti, 1979.

———. "Restaurati gli affreschi nel coro di S. Francesco di Rieti." *Notizie turistico ente provinciale per il turismo, Rieti.* Luglio–agosto 1954, 15–25.

Violante, Cinzio. "Eresie urbane e eresie rurali in Italia dall'XI al XIII secolo." In *Medioevo ereticale,* edited by Ovidio Capitani, 185–212. Bologna, 1977.

———. "Primo contributo a una storia delle istituzioni ecclesiastiche nell'Italia centrosettentrionale durante il medioevo: province, diocesi, sedi vescovili." In *Miscellanea historiae ecclesiasticae*, vol. 5, *La Cartographie et l'histoire socio-religieuse de l'Europe jusqu'à la fin du XVIIe siècle*, 183–204. Bibliothèque de la Revue d'histoire ecclésiastique, 61. Louvain, 1974.

Wakefield, Walter L. *Heresy, Crusade and Inquisition in Southern France, 1100–1250*. London, 1974.

————, and Austin P. Evans. *Heresies of the High Middle Ages*. New York, 1969.

Waley, Daniel. "Constitutions of the Cardinal-legate Peter Capocci, July 1249." *English Historical Review* 75 (1960): 660–664.

————. *The Papal State in the Thirteenth Century*. London, 1961.

White, J. *The Birth and Rebirth of Pictorial Space*. 3d ed. London, 1987.

Wickham, Chris. *Early Medieval Italy: Central Power and Local Society 400–1000*. London, 1981.

————. *The Mountains and the City: The Tuscan Appennines in the Early Middle Ages*. Oxford, 1988.

————. *Studi sulla società degli Appennini nell'alto medioevo: Contadini, signori e insediamento nel territorio di Valva (Sulmona)*. Bologna, 1982.

Wright, J. Robert. *The Church and the English Crown, 1305–1334: A Study based on the Register of Archbishop Walter Reynolds*. Toronto, 1980.

Ziliani, Luigi. *La baronessa santa: Vita e miracoli di S. Filippa Mareri*. Bergamo, 1935.

Index

Paolo, priest, canon of Rieti, 66, 101, 189, 206

Papal court, 5

Papazurri, Francesco, canon of Rieti, 206

Papazurri, Omodeo, 177

Papazurri, Paolo di Nicolucio, of Rome, notary, 214

Papazurri (Pappazuri, Pappazuris), Giovanni, bishop of Rieti, 12, 26, 85, 107–118, 135, 139, 143, 147, 172, 181, 190, 191, 205, 212–213, 214, 219, 223, 261, 296, 298–299, 318

Paper, 16, 31, 126–128

Parchment strip, 67

Parents, 111, 127

Paris, University of, 51

Parishes, 107, 112

Partridges, 37

Pasinelli, Don Filippo, 66

Pasinelli, family, 26–27, 135, 196, 199–200, 231–232

Pasinelli, Francesco, 231–232, 303

Pasinelli, Giacomo, canon of Rieti, 199, 203, 209

Pasinelli, Janni di don Gentile: Buctia, wife of, and daughter of Giacomo de Murro, 197, 288–289

Pasinelli, Matteo di don Filippo, 26–27

Pasinelli, Oddone di nobile Oddone, milite, chaplain of Matteo Orsini, cardinal deacon of Santa Maria in Porticu, canon of Rieti, 199–200

Pasinelli, Senebaldo, 199

Pasinelli, Vanni Nicole, 231–232, 290

Passillum, boundary stake, 73

Passion of Christ, 111

Pastoral care, 107–113; different from alien expectations, 128–129

Pastures, 75

Pater Noster, prayer, 111

Patronage, 100–105, 127–129

Patronymics, 32

Pears, 36

Pendenza, Rainaldo da, canon of Rieti, 44, 69–74

Pendenza, 34, 89, 287–288, 293

Penitus, word used repeatedly by Rainaldo da Arezzo in Salimbene, 48–51, 337–338 n. 100

Penne, 13, 228, 328 n. 15, 397 n. 152

Pens, animal, 68–69, 70–76

Pepper, 68, 316

Peram, 50

Perugia, 25

Pescara, San Clemente di, 226

"Petrabattuta," various spellings. *See* San Silvestro "de Petrabattuta"

Petrella Salto, 34, 37, 38–39, 89

Petrignani, Giovanni, priest of San Giovanni Evangelista, canon of Rieti, 241, 243, 245, 255, 258, 261–263, 274, 312

Petrono Giovanucci, inquisitor's messenger, 249–250

Photograph, photography, 8–9

Piediluco, 86, 130

Pie-safe, 281

Pietrasecca, 81

Pietro, archpriest of San Ruffo, 65

Pietro, Giovanni di. *See* Giovanni di Pietro

Pietro da Ferentino, bishop of Rieti, 21, 64, 84, 98, 135, 137, 143, 147, 151–163, 164, 165, 167–168, 181, 198, 279, 300, 318. *See also* Guerra

Pietro da Roma, vicar general, 98, 137

Piety, popular or lay, 11

Pievi, 38, 40–45, 82, 87, 220

Pigs, 28, 287

Pilgrimage, 290, 318

Pious bequests, 129

Pix, 111

Plagis, Rainaldo de. *See* Rainaldo da Piagge

Plague, 52, 53. *See also* Black Death

Ploughing, 75

Pluralism of benefices, 6. *See also* splintering of churches and livings

Podestà of Rieti, 4, 17, 22, 28, 70, 156–157, 201–202, 248, 252–253; son of, 248

Podio, de, 191, 289, 294

Poggio Bustone, castro and Franciscan hermitage, 26, 28, 219, 239

Poggio Fidoni, San Sebastiano, 221

Poggio Perugino, 88

Polizzi, Carlo, 181

Ponte, Giovanni de, arbiter, 66

Ponticello, Giovanni da, canon of Rieti, 30, 186

Ponticello, Guillemo di Giovanni de, 299

Pontificalia, 50

Poor, 300–301, 304–305; bequests to, 280–305

Poor of Christ, *pauperes Christi,* 52

Thocca. *See* Giovanni de Thocca

Thought, episcopal, about responsibilities, 117

Time. *See* Distance; Memory

Tivoli, city and diocese, 147; inquisitor's court in, 256–259

Todi, bishop of, 198

Toffia, 231

Tolls, 68–76

Tomb miracles of Santa Filippa, 271, 272

Tommaso de Labro, canon of Rieti, 178, 213

Tommaso the Corrector, bishop of Rieti, 22, 65, 85–90, 119, 135, 137, 148–150, 193, 197, 198, 199, 202, 220, 226, 318

Tonsure, 49

Torano, 115

Torino, 48

Tornimparte, 92

Torture, 241–248

Toubert, Pierre, 35

Transarico, abbot of Ferentillo, 41–45

Transhumants. *See* Sheep

Trastevere, Santa Cecilia, 324

Tre Fontane, Rome, house of Cistercian monks, 62, 168

Tribune of cathedral church of Rieti, 54, 117, 120

Trivio San Giovanni, 32

Trozo, Gualterio, 103–104

Tunics, 277–305

Twine, cord, 4

"U," the letter. *See* Letters of the alphabet

Ubaldini, Ottaviano, cardinal, 36

Ubertino da Casale, 61

Ùdine, 154, 161–162, 279

Ùdine, San Francesco, 161–162

Ùdine, Santa Maria di Castello, 161

Urban IV, pope, 54, 193–195

Urban VI, pope, 168, 194

Urso de Piscia, proctor of the clergy of Rieti, 225

Usury, 111

Utility, 50

Vagina of small dog, 237–238

Vallebuono, 81

Valva-Sulmona, diocese. *See* Sulmona

Valviano, 89

Vango, 32

Varro, 23

Vassalli ecclesie Reatine, 43, 105, 156–158, 190

Vassallus, Vassalli, 56, 67

Vasto, 85

Velino river, 20, 34–35, 153, 321

Venimbeni, Francesco, da Fabriano, 293, 408 n. 35

Ventura Rainaldi (Rainerii), canon of Rieti, 13, 128, 157, 167, 191

Verani, Cesare, 328 n. 12

Verardesca. *See* Giovanni di Pietro, wife of

Vergagam, a trap for fish or crayfish, 71

Vernacular, 7, 250–251

Vèroli, 230; chapter of, 193–194

Vescovio, 324

Vestments, 101

Vicars general, vicars, 115, 128–129, 131, 137–140, 141, 158, 167, 171, 174, 185

Vicecomes of church of Rieti, 190

Vicenza, city and diocese, 145, 169–170

Vicovaro, 271

Vienne, 98

Vigliano, Bartolomeo, archpriest of San Tommaso, 98

Vigliano, Luca archpriest of, 94

Vines and vineyards, 18–19, 31–32, 37, 60–61, 209, 212, 246, 276, 279, 296

Vintage, lord's control of, 37

Violence, 73, 74–76

Virgin Mary, 109–110, 174, 306, 307–309

"Vision of the Chariot," 322

"Vision of the Throne," 322

Visitation, 104–106, 114

Vita prima of Thomas of Celano, 78

Viterbo, 25, 26, 171, 230; clergy of neighborhood of, 256

Viterbo, San Francesco, inquisitor's court, 255–256

Vitus, feast of saint, 213

Volta, in or near Rocca Sinibalda, nuns, 302

"Vomit" (Proverbs 26:11), 59–60

Vox publica et fama, defined, 254

Wallet, beggar's, 51

Walls, 9, 18, 22, 31–32, 41–45, 248–256

Walnuts, 28

Water, 8

Wax, 37, 68, 209, 277, 288. *See also* Candles; Seals

Weyer Davis, Caecilia, 4–5

Compositor:	Impressions
Text:	10/13 Galliard
Display:	Galliard
Printer and Binder:	Edwards Bros.